SECOND EDITION

EXPLORING CRIMINAL JUSTICE IN CANADA

RICK RUDDELL

OXFORD

UNIVERSITY PRESS

OXFORD
UNIVERSITY PRESS

Oxford University Press is a department of the University of Oxford.
It furthers the University's objective of excellence in research, scholarship,
and education by publishing worldwide. Oxford is a registered trade mark of
Oxford University Press in the UK and in certain other countries.

Published in Canada by
Oxford University Press
8 Sampson Mews, Suite 204,
Don Mills, Ontario M3C 0H5 Canada

www.oupcanada.com

Library and Archives Canada Cataloguing in Publication

Title: Exploring criminal justice in Canada / Rick Ruddell.
Names: Ruddell, Rick, 1961- author.
Description: Second edition.
Identifiers: Canadiana (print) 20190165367 | Canadiana (ebook) 20190165596 | ISBN 9780199033751
(softcover) | ISBN 9780199039173 (loose leaf) | ISBN 9780199033768 (EPUB)
Subjects: LCSH: Criminal justice, Administration of—Canada—Textbooks. |
LCSH: Criminology—Canada—Textbooks. | LCGFT: Textbooks.
Classification: LCC HV9960.C2 R84 2020 | DDC 364.971—dc23

Cover image: © iStock/ChristopheLedent
Cover design: Sherill Chapman
Interior design: Laurie McGregor

Oxford University Press is committed to our environment.
This book is printed on Forest Stewardship Council® certified paper
and comes from responsible sources.

Printed and bound in Canada

2 3 4 — 24 23 22

Brief Contents

Contents

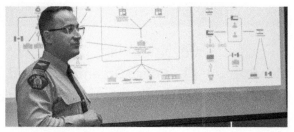

PART III | The Law and The Courts   143

6 Criminal Law   143

7 Criminal Courts and Court Personnel   172

8 Sentencing   200

PART IV | Corrections   228

9 Provincial Corrections: Probation and Short-term Incarceration   228

Contents   ix

ONLINE CHAPTER Victimization

From the Publisher

GUIDE TO THE NEW EDITION OF *EXPLORING CRIMINAL JUSTICE IN CANADA*

A new table of contents better reflects how criminal justice is taught

- To make this edition easier to use in your course, the Criminal Law chapter now appears later in the table of contents, the Youth Justice chapter has moved from online into the book, and part divisions have been added.

▲ "Troopers" in North West Mounted Police (NWMP) dress costume perform at Fort MacLeod Museum in Alberta (on the grounds of Fort MacLeod, which was built in 1874. The NWMP became the RCMP in 1904. Why do you think Canadians (and the RCMP) hold on to these reminders of the RCMP's history? *(Photo credit: source/files/b/bcbse)*

4 | Police Organization and Structure

LEARNING OUTLINE

After reading this chapter, you will be able to

- Describe how Canadian policing evolved from the 1800s to today
- Describe the different urban and rural policing arrangements, and the agencies delivering these services
- Identify some possible reasons for differences in police strength
- Describe the five roles of the police in Canada

**PART V
Youth Justice**

▲ On 5 July 2019, there were only 26 youth held in custody facilities in all of Atlantic Canada (Davie, 2019). Prior to the introduction of the *Youth Criminal Justice Act* in 2003, the number of youth behind bars was much higher; in 2001/2002, the four provinces incarcerated 364 youth (Statistics Canada, 2019a). Why did youth incarceration drop by more than 90 per cent? A change in legislation in 2003 made it more difficult to place non-violent youth in custody, and youth crime rates have been decreasing. The drop in youth incarceration has happened throughout the nation, although in many provinces the unused correctional beds have been filled by adults. *(Photo credit: Canada Free Act 2013)*

11 | Youth Justice in Canada

LEARNING OUTLINE

After reading this chapter, you will be able to

- Describe current trends in youth crime
- Identify the differences between the *Juvenile Delinquents Act*, the *Young Offenders Act*, and the *Youth Criminal Justice Act*
- Provide some reasons why sentences for youth are mitigated
- Describe the differences between open and secure custody
- Identify the pathways to girls' involvement in crime

Provincial and Territorial Corrections Today

Figure 9.4 shows there are about one-quarter million admissions to provincial and territorial correctional facilities in Canada every year, although that number is somewhat deceptive as one person could be admitted more than once in a year. Almost 65,000 individuals were sentenced to terms of incarceration of less than two years in 2016/2017, and that number has increased somewhat from the previous years (Malakieh, 2018). The one constant factor in these places is the constant flow of inmates in and out of these facilities, what some have called the revolving door of corrections (Woo, 2018).

Most people remanded to custody are held for relatively short periods of time. In 2017/2018, half of males (50 per cent) and 59 per cent of females were released within one week, and three-quarters (75 per cent) served one month or less, and only about 5 per cent served more than six months (see Figure 9.5). Again, those are national averages and some adults facing serious charges, such as homicide, can serve years in a provincial facility as their cases work their way through the justice system.

Additionally, the length of stay on remand tends to be higher in northern Canada as there are fewer court dates in some rural locations (see Chapter 7). With respect to inmates sentenced to provincial or territorial custody, the sentences are also very short, and 60 per cent serve less than one month (Malakieh, 2019).

Provincial and territorial correctional centres have a short-term orientation toward inmate care, and this reduces their participation in rehabilitative programs. If the average sentence is one month, there is not much time to assess the inmate's rehabilitative needs and to place them in meaningful programs, even if these inmates wanted to participate in these programs. Providing few amenities other than a bed and meals is often called warehousing.

Inmates are eligible to work toward an early release through their good behaviour, and this earned remission (which was introduced in Chapter 8) further reduces the number of days they will serve in custody. As a result, many correctional centre activities are based on keeping inmates constructively occupied in recreational or work programs such as institutional cleaning, building maintenance, doing laundry, and

warehousing When inmates receive only their basic needs and few or no rehabilitative opportunities.

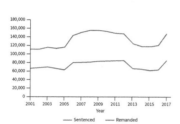

FIGURE 9.4 **Annual Admissions to Provincial and Territorial Corrections, 2000–2018**
Statistics Canada (2019a)

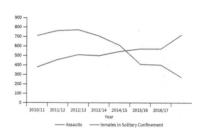

FIGURE 10.2 **The Relationship Between Solitary Confinement and Inmate Assaults, 2010 to 2017**
White (2017)

for violence. Yet, Figure 10.2 also suggests that how prison staff manage prisoners impacts institutional safety. Can you think of factors other than placing prisoners in segregation that might increase or decrease prison violence?

One of the frustrations of working with prisoners who might be a decade or longer away from their release is that staff members have few options other than placing disruptive inmates in segregation—which is like a "prison within a prison." Inmates in segregation might only receive a few hours each day outside their cells, which generally consist of a cement-walled room with a metal bunk that is bolted to the floor and a stainless-steel toilet.

Given the overcrowded, bleak, and sometimes noisy conditions in many facilities, it is not surprising that most inmates will break the institutional rules at some point. Placement in administrative segregation, however, is reserved for prisoners who have engaged in assaults, threatened others, or breached security. In 2015/2016, almost half of all CSC inmates were admitted to segregation at least once; almost three-quarters of male prisoners were returned to the general population within 30 days, while only 6 per cent of women inmates served more than 30 days (Public Safety Canada, 2018, p. 67).

slashing When a prisoner engages in self-harming behaviour by cutting their skin using metal or plastic objects.

As the Eddie Snowshoe case illustrates, there are concerns about the adverse effects of using segregation to manage an offender's behaviour. Long-term confinement in segregation can increase mental health problems such as anxiety and depression (Haney, 2018). Prisoners in segregation sometimes engage in self-harm behaviours such as slashing themselves with sharp objects or hitting their heads against the wall. These incidents tend to happen more often in segregation, treatment centres, and maximum security facilities—places the Office of the Correctional Investigator (2013) has called austere. The Office of the Correctional Investigator statistics show that there are about three self-injuries per day or over 1,100 incidents per year in all the CSC facilities (Zinger, 2017, p. 11). Women tend to be overrepresented in these acts of self-harm, and a relatively small number of inmates who slash are generally responsible for a large proportion of these incidents; these prisoners may be at a higher risk of dying by suicide.

Prisoner Advocacy

In Chapter 9, the role of provincial ombudsmen in advocating for correctional centre inmates was briefly described. Several federal and community-based organizations also advocate on behalf of federal prisoners. The Correctional Investigator of

Chapters 9 and 10 revised to increase student understanding

The new organization of chapters 9 and 10 helps students better differentiate between provincial and federal corrections, and between probation and parole.

▲ Humboldt Broncos assistant coach Chris Beaudry (shown here in a courtroom sketch) gave a victim impact statement following the collision that killed sixteen people. What function do victim impact statements serve in the criminal justice system? (Photo by the Canadian press/Dmitriny Book models)

Online Chapter

Victimization

LEARNING OUTLINE

After reading this chapter, you will be able to

- Describe the Canadian populations most at risk of victimization
- Explain the differences between criminology and victimology
- Describe how the lifestyle exposure model can predict victimization
- Provide a definition of a hate crime

New online chapter on victimization

A new online chapter on victimization provides more extensive coverage and insights on this important topic in criminal justice. The chapter explains victimology as a discipline, describes risks of victimization, and outlines services available to victims of crime in Canada.

Exploring Criminal Justice in Newfoundland and Labrador*

Rick Ruddell, University of Regina, and Hayley Crichton, Memorial University of Newfoundland

This supplement to *Exploring Criminal Justice in Canada* provides additional content about crime and the responses of the police, courts, and corrections that is specific to Newfoundland and Labrador, including issues related to urban and rural crime, as well as crime-related challenges that are distinctive to the province. In addition, there are examples of miscarriages of justice and issues related to the increase in crime between 2014 and 2015. Altogether, these cases, events, and information specific to Newfoundland enable readers to better understand the provincial context that can't be covered in a textbook that focuses on the entire nation.

THE UNIQUE CASE OF NEWFOUNDLAND AND LABRADOR

Newfoundland and Labrador is geographically distinctive in that it encompasses 405,720 square kilometres including the island of Newfoundland. The population, though largely concentrated in St John's, Mount Pearl, and Corner Brook, is spread across both Labrador and Newfoundland. The thinly dispersed population can pose challenges to police and social service agencies that struggle to meet the needs of remote and isolated communities. Indeed, many communities in Labrador are accessible only by air and by coastal boat services operated by the provincial government (boat services are only available between June and November). Additionally, these communities may be further isolated due to the lack of cellular towers and Internet accessibility. Finally, Labrador is home to the first Inuit region in the provinces of Canada to achieve self-governance: Nunatsiavut. As the result of the Labrador Inuit Land Claims Agreement, passed in 2005, the Nunatsiavut Government is a regional government and has authority over central policy areas including health, culture, education, and justice. Communities included in the self-governed region include Nain, Hopedale, Postville, Makkovik, and Rigolet (covering the most northern areas of Labrador). Although Nunatsiavut is self-governed and the rule of law is set out in the Nunatsiavut Constitution, the region is policed in conjunction with the Royal Canadian Mounted Police (RCMP). For these reasons, as well as others related to political and historical arrangements, Newfoundland and Labrador has a distinctive context for exploring criminal justice.

NEWFOUNDLAND AND LABRADOR: CRIME AT A GLANCE

Of the 10 provinces, Newfoundland and Labrador (NL) usually falls close to the national average in terms of the Crime Severity Index (CSI). In 2015 the CSI for NL was 65.6, which was less than the national average (69.7) and about one-half as high as the Saskatchewan CSI (135.8). Like the rest of Canada, rates of crime reported to the police have been dropping since the 1990s, and the rate of violent and property crime offences per 100,000 residents reported to the police in Newfoundland and Labrador is lower today than rates in the 1970s. Information from the General Social Survey (GSS) shows that NL residents reported levels of violent victimization (including physical and sexual assaults and robbery) that were lower than the national rate (55 acts per 1,000 population for NL and 76 for the entire nation) (Perreault, 2015).

While *Exploring Criminal Justice* described the interprovincial differences in the CSI, the following figures show differences in the rates of homicide in the provinces as well as levels of crime in the nine largest cities in Atlantic Canada. Figure 1 shows the homicide rate per 100,000 residents for 2015, and the rate of 0.60 was the lowest in the nation and almost one-third of the national average of 1.68 per 100,000 residents. Of the nine largest cities in Atlantic Canada, Figure 2 shows that there were no homicides at all in Corner Brook and three other cities, and the rate for St John's was 0.97 per 100,000 residents, or about half as many as Cape Breton, Halifax, and Saint John. One has to be fairly careful in interpreting these results, especially in less populated towns and cities because

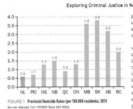

FIGURE 1   Provincial Homicide Rates (per 100,000 residents), 2015
Source: Adapted from CANSIM Table 252-0061.

adding even one homicide offence might make places with a low population appear very dangerous.

The National Inquiry into Missing and Murdered Indigenous Women and Girls initiated in 2016 has brought renewed attention to the issue of violence towards women. According to the Chief Public Health Officer of Canada (2016) more than 200 men and women are victimized every day and most of these individuals are women, and a woman is killed by a family member every four days in Canada. With respect to family violence, risks of victimization increase for women, Indigenous women, people with disabilities, and those who identify as lesbian, gay, bisexual, trans, or questioning (Chief Public Health Officer of Canada, 2016, p. 6). Self-report surveys such as the GSS show that most cases of family violence are never reported to the police. The Canadian Centre for Justice Statistics (2016, p. 3) analyzed the 2014 GSS results and reported that "4 per cent of Canadians in the provinces with a current or former spouse or common-law partner reported having been

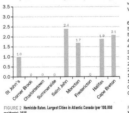

FIGURE 2   Homicide Rates, Largest Cities in Atlantic Canada (per 100,000 residents), 2015
Source: Adapted from CANSIM Table 252-0075.

physically or sexually abused by their spouse during the preceding 5 years." Figure 3 presents the findings from the GSS about self-reported violence and reveals that Newfoundland residents had the lowest rates of victimization in the nation.

Increased attention also is being paid to the issue of sexual violence since the trial and acquittal of Jian Ghomeshi, the CBC broadcaster, in 2016. The Ghomeshi trial further highlighted issues related to reporting sexual assault, such as when reports are made to the police and re-victimization. As noted in *Exploring Criminal Justice*, sexual offences are among the least reported crimes. Perreault (2015, p. 3) analyzed the results of the 2014 GSS and estimated as few as 5 per cent of all sexual offences are actually reported to the police (and only a fraction of those cases result in convictions). Allen (2016, p. 45) reports the rate of sexual assaults reported to the police in Newfoundland is above the national average (69 and 60 offences per 100,000 residents, respectively). Although crime statistics show that NL has rates of sexual violence higher than the national average, we do not know the true number of these offences given the fact that few of these crimes are actually reported to the police.

Figure 4 shows that the total crime rates for the largest cities in Atlantic Canada for 2015, which indicate some variation in the amount of crime occurring in these places, although all were relatively close to the Newfoundland average of 6,356 offences per 100,000 residents (that total includes traffic offences). The crime rates per 100,000 residents in St John's and Corner Brook are higher than those reported for Cape Breton and Halifax. One question that criminologists like to ask is why crime differs so much between these places.

With respect to youth involvement in crime, Allen and Superle (2016, p. 45) found that the number of youth crimes (persons aged 12 to 18 years) reported to the police in Newfoundland and Labrador in 2014 (4,710 offences) was somewhat greater than the national average of 4,322 (see Figure 5). When these researchers examined the types of crimes carried

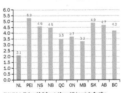

FIGURE 3   Victims of Self-Reported Spousal Violence in the Past Five Years, per cent, 2014
Source: Adapted from Canadian Centre for Justice Statistics (2016).

*The ten provincial summaries follow a common template and although the examples presented in this supplement differ from the other nine, some of the content is very similar or will have identical text.

2

Revised supplementary materials for each of Canada's ten provinces

In addition to the online chapter, the website for *Exploring Criminal Justice* (www.oup.com/he/Ruddell2e) includes invaluable supplemental packets of information for the ten provinces and provides details on key topics—such as police departments, courts, offenders, crimes, and miscarriages of justice—offering useful insights and facts for each.

A Closer Look

Politics and Crime Control: A 2015 Election Promise and Legalizing Marijuana in 2018

Defining the acts that become criminal offences and the ways we control crime are political issues. The legalization of marijuana in 2018 shows how politicians can change laws to adapt to a society's changing beliefs about what is right and wrong. Until the 1960s few were concerned about marijuana use and only two per cent of drug arrests between 1946 and 1961 involved marijuana (Carstairs, 2000, p. 112). As its use became more popular, so did the number of people arrested for various marijuana-related offences, and between 1998 and 2016 there were almost 930,000 arrests for possession (Statistics Canada, 2018a). Despite being illegal its use was widespread. A 2017 poll revealed that over one-third of Canadians (38 per cent) had used marijuana recreationally (Ispos, 2017, pp. 1-2).

Legalizing marijuana was a key promise of the Liberals in the 2015 election. While they promised to quickly introduce new legislation, amending the *Controlled Drugs and Substances Act* (the legislation that made marijuana use illegal) was complicated as changes also had to be made to the *Criminal Code* and 12 other acts, ranging from the *Criminal Records Act* to the *Canadian Victims Bill of Rights*. Changes in criminal justice legislation also impact the operations of provincial and municipal governments, as they are often forced to change their crime prevention and enforcement activities to reflect legislative changes, and sometimes those changes are costly. Prior to introducing the bill to legalize marijuana, the Liberal government formed a task force that received submissions from more than 30,000 individuals and

organizations to capture the public's mood on this issue (Government of Canada, 2018). After considering that feedback the legislation was introduced and the bill passed after readings in Parliament and the Senate, with amendments and review at each point. Figure 1.1 provides a timeline of the legislative steps taken to legalize marijuana.

Although the recreational use of marijuana became legal on October 17, 2018, new laws restricting access to youth, possession, production, and sales were also introduced, and some of those crimes could result in five- to 14-year prison sentences. For example, under the new legislation giving or selling marijuana to a person under 18 years of age could result in a 14-year-prison term. Kirkey (2018) says these sanctions are harsher than current laws regarding intoxicants, such as providing liquor to a minor, which can result in a maximum sanction of only one year's incarceration in Ontario. As a result, people will still be arrested and punished for marijuana-related offences. It will take several years before we have a better understanding of the impact of these new laws and it is likely some marijuana users and sellers may be punished more severely than we imagine.

While recreational marijuana use was legalized there are differences in how the provinces regulate the drug. These provincial regulations define where marijuana can be sold, the minimum age limit for use (18 years old in Alberta and Quebec, 19 years of age in the other provinces), the legality of growing marijuana at home (which Manitoba and Quebec have banned), whether marijuana can be smoked in public or in

a vehicle, and whether landlords and homeowner associations can ban smoking (CTV News, 2018). In addition, many workplaces are also grappling with whether employees will be able to use marijuana on the job or whether marijuana can be smoked on their properties, including on university campuses. Even

before the law came into effect there was disagreement about the constitutionality of the new laws and the fairness of the regulations. As a result, some of the long-term outcomes of the federal law, provincial regulations, and workplace decisions will be heard before Supreme Courts well into the future.

November 2015	Liberals form government
June 2016	Task force to study legalization is formed
November 2016	Results of the Task Force published
April 2017	Bill C-45: Legislation introduced (first reading in the House of Commons)
June 2017	The second reading of C-45 in the House of Commons, followed by the bill being sent to a Committee for review
November 2017	A report is prepared, followed by the third reading and a vote on the amendments based on the report
	First reading of the bill in the Senate
March 2018	Bill C-45 is adopted at its second Senate reading and reffered to a Committee
June 2018	Committee recommendations for amendments are sent to the House of Commons, which accepts the amendments
	Senate passes the amended legislation
	Bill receives royal assent by the Governor General
October 2018	Law takes effect
February 2019	Government waives application fees and removes the waiting period for individuals convicted of marijuana possession and applying for a record suspension (formerly known as pardons)

FIGURE 1.1 Timeline of the Progress of Bill C-45 Through Parliament

including the type of court where the hearing will be held and whether the individual has the right to a jury trial. The maximum sentence that can be imposed on someone found guilty of a summary offence is also limited to a maximum fine of $5,000 and/or six months in jail (although there are ex-

THE STRUCTURE OF THE CRIMINAL JUSTICE SYSTEM

There are three components of the justice system: police, courts, and corrections. The three parts are interrelated but also somewhat independent

see on television, and some of that information is incorrect—for example, it is often based on US examples—or has been simplified, such as a complicated law explained in a 60-second news segment. This section provides a basic foundation of [th]e structure of the criminal justice system that [wi]ll be expanded on in the chapters that follow.

Police

The police are the most visible component of the justice system, and they are the officials we are most likely to encounter. Information from the 2014 General Social Survey (GSS) on Victimization, which is a survey of Canadians conducted

General Social Survey (GSS) An annual survey of Canadians that is conducted by Statistics Canada about a range of social trends, with each annual survey addressing one theme in depth.

Race, Class, and Gender

Missing and Murdered Indigenous Women and Girls (MMIWG)

A May 2014 editorial in *the Globe and Mail* notes the following:

> If a society has the duty to protect its most vulnerable citizens, then Canadians and their governments are completely derelict with regards to Aboriginal women. They represent four per cent of Canada's female population, but nearly a third of the female prison population. They are twice as likely to live in poverty. ("Deadly statistics", 2014, para. 1)

Indigenous women in Canada are at the highest risk of violent victimization of any racial or ethnic group. Boyce (2016, p. 3) reports that Indigenous women are about three times as likely to be victims of violence compared to non-Indigenous women. Research produced by the Canadian Centre for Justice Statistics shows that Indigenous women were almost six times more likely to be murdered than non-Indigenous women in 2017 (Beattie, David, & Roy, 2018, pp. 13-14).

According to the RCMP (2014), between 1980 and 2012, a total of 1,017 Indigenous women were murdered and another 169 were missing (of those missing women, 108 cases were classified as "suspicious" and 61 were thought to be accidental). The RCMP, however, undercounts the true number of these victims, as some of those who were murdered were living in cities not policed by the RCMP.

In June 2019, the National Inquiry into MMIWG (2019) released its report based on the testimony of almost 1,500 people including the family members of victims and people with expertise in the justice system. The report was controversial, as it called the murder of these women *genocide*, which is the deliberate killing of a large group of people (and usually of an ethnic or racial group). The report calls for 231 steps that federal, provincial, and Indigenous governments must take to reduce this violence. Many of these steps are intended to improve the living conditions for all Indigenous women. In addition, there are a number of recommendations specific to the justice system, including toughening punishments for people victimizing Indigenous women, improving the quality

of Indigenous policing, increasing the number of Indigenous people working in the justice system, and providing supports to the victims of crime and their families. In addition, the report calls for improving the access of Indigenous women to the justice system through legal aid, reforming the punishments meted out to Indigenous women, developing better responses to human trafficking (and the sexual exploitation of women), and basing the justice system on traditional Indigenous practices.

The federal government has promised to toughen punishments for victimizing Indigenous women and is looking into the possibilities of reforming the justice system. The stakes for Indigenous women are high, and *the Globe and Mail* editors ("Deadly statistics", 2014) observed that "for an Aboriginal woman living on the margins of society, a caring law enforcement system could mean the difference between life and death."

Individuals can be also victimized by the justice system. In 2015, a 28 year-old Indigenous woman from Alberta—who was the victim of a kidnapping and sexual assault—was incarcerated in Edmonton Remand Centre (pictured here) for five days to ensure she appeared in court as a witness against her attacker (she was experiencing homelessness at the time of the trial). This woman, who was not accused of committing any offence, was transported in the same van as the man who was ultimately convicted of assaulting her. Cryderman (2018, para. 1) notes that while an investigation of this woman's treatment could find no evidence of misconduct on the part of any individual worker, the case is an example of systemic bias.

Thoroughly updated throughout

Rick Ruddell continues his contemporary, solutions-based approach in this new edition, encouraging students to see where and how evidence-based practice is shaping criminal justice in Canada today. Cases, examples, laws, and statistics have been updated throughout the entire book with up-to-the-minute details, including results from the 2016 census released in 2018, Statistics Canada Adult Criminal Court data from 2019, 2019 Missing and Murdered Indigenous Women and Girls report, and more.

A critical, diverse, and practical box program maintained and updated for this new edition

Six different types of boxes in each chapter highlight influential cases, important concepts and events, issues related to diversity, differences in criminal justice practices, myths and commonly held beliefs about the justice system, and various careers in the field.

CASE STUDY

"Case Study" boxes start each chapter with a vignette that outlines a famous or controversial real-world case related to the chapter content and accompanied by critical thinking questions.

A Closer Look

"A Closer Look" boxes provide an in-depth look at important topics, including rural crime, policing, and victimization.

A COMPARATIVE VIEW

"A Comparative View" boxes explore interprovincial and global variation in criminal justice practices and outcomes.

Race, Class, and Gender

"Race, Class, and Gender" boxes discuss how the concepts of race, class, and gender can influence the treatment of individuals in the justice system.

MYTH OR REALITY

"Myth or Reality" boxes address commonly held beliefs about the justice system and explore the evidence to support or refute those beliefs.

Career SNAPSHOT

"Career Snapshot" boxes—written by professionals working in the Canadian criminal justice system—offer students insight into the types of jobs available, different pathways to starting a career, and potential career challenges and opportunities.

 Ancillary Resource Center

EXTENSIVE ONLINE RESOURCES

Exploring Criminal Justice in Canada is part of a comprehensive package of learning and teaching tools that includes resources for both students and instructors. These resources are available at **www.oup.com/he/Ruddell2e**.

For Everyone

In addition to the chapter on Victimization and the provincial briefs listed above, the following online materials are available to further enhance the learning and teaching experiences:

- a list of celebrated cases of crime in Canada that covers the most high-profile and dramatic cases in Canadian history;
- a timeline of milestones in Canadian policing traces moments of historical importance in policing in Canada; and
- a short narrative titled "Surviving a Life Sentence of Imprisonment One Day at a Time," which is based on an interview the author conducted with an individual sentenced to life imprisonment, provides a more personal look at what life is like in the prison system.

For Instructors

The following instructor's resources are available to qualifying adopters. Please contact your OUP sales representative for more information.

- A comprehensive **instructor's manual** provides an extensive set of pedagogical tools and suggestions for every chapter, including overviews, suggested class activities and debates, and links to relevant videos and online teaching aids with discussion questions for each resource.
- Classroom-ready **PowerPoint slides** summarize key points from each chapter and incorporate graphics and tables drawn straight from the textbook.
- An extensive **test generator** enables instructors to sort, edit, import, and distribute hundreds of questions in multiple-choice, true or false, and short-answer formats.
- Invaluable supplemental packets of information are available for each province and provide details on key topics—such as police departments, courts, offenders, crimes, and miscarriages of justice—offering useful insights and facts for use in preparing class lectures and assignments.

For Students

- The **student study guide** includes chapter overviews, learning objectives, key terms, self-grading quizzes, as well as annotated lists of recommended readings and websites to help students enhance their knowledge of the concepts presented in each chapter.

 **www.oup.com/he/Ruddell2e**

Preface

Introductory classes can be difficult for students and instructors because there is so much content that needs to be covered in a relatively short period of time. This challenge is further complicated in criminal justice courses because Canada's justice system is becoming increasingly complex, and the provinces and territories often have somewhat different priorities and approaches to each of their responses to crime presented in the chapters that follow. After teaching many introductory criminal justice courses over the years I found that students often expressed frustration about their textbooks as many of them have become so lengthy that it is almost impossible to cover the content in one semester. There are sometimes so many examples of police, court, and correctional operations that readers can become overwhelmed with details instead of focusing on the key issues. In order to focus on these key issues this book provides a streamlined overview of Canada's justice system using a "back to basics" approach. While some have said that "the devil is in the details," that content can be explored in your upper level courses.

One of the goals in writing this book was to present only the basic information that students need in order to have a working knowledge of Canada's justice system. As a result, a number of factors differentiate this overview of Canada's justice system from other textbooks, including a focus on issues related to Race, Class, and Gender in each chapter and how those factors influence both crime and the search for justice. In addition, each chapter contains a boxed feature titled Myth or Reality, where our ideas about the justice system are challenged and presented in a Canadian context. This is important as many of our ideas about the police, courts, and correctional systems come from our exposure to the US news and entertainment media. This is an ongoing challenge for instructors as Canada's justice system is very different from the US system, and our responses to crime are also distinctively different. As a result, this book focuses on providing a wide variety of Canadian examples, although there are comparative sections in each chapter that contrast Canadian criminal justice practices against those in other nations. Last, each chapter contains a contribution from a criminal justice practitioner who shares information about his or her work experiences, career pathways, and providing practical advice to students considering careers in the justice system.

ACKNOWLEDGEMENTS

Although the author's name is the only name that appears on the cover, it takes dozens of people to transform an idea to the finished book you are reading. The first edition took three years from the time when the book was first proposed until the first copy was printed; the second edition was in development for over a year. During that time, I had the opportunity to work with a great team of professionals starting with Amy Gordon, development editor, who helped me through the process of responding to the reviewer's comments, and making thoughtful revisions to the content so the book was easier to read. I also thank the editorial team at Oxford, including Jess Shulman and Steven Hall. Their hard work made the book more visually appealing, structured, and easier to read, and their attention to detail is very much appreciated.

Six reviewers critiqued the first edition of the book and made a number of recommendations to strengthen the work, including Lorree Bogden (Douglas College), Stephen Dumas (University of Calgary), Tamari Kitossa (Brock University), Lisa Monchalin (Kwantlen Polytechnic University), Kim

Polowek (University of the Fraser Valley), and John Winterdyk (Mount Royal University). Several lawyers helped me with the law and courts chapters in both editions, including Heather Nord (University of Regina), Heather Donkers (Robichaud's Criminal Defence Litigation), and Sarah Burningham (University of Saskatchewan). I also thank the scholars who provided reviews for the second edition, including Annmarie Barnes (Nipissing University), Sheri Fabian (Simon Fraser University), Greg Flynn (McMaster University), Carolyn Gordon (University of Ottawa), Hannele Jantti (Douglas College), Darrell Kean (Langara College), Leslie Anne Keown (Carleton University), Kristen Kramar (University of Calgary), Keiron McConnell (Kwantlen Polytechnic University), Lisa Monchalin (Kwantlen Polytechnic University), Jane Lothian Murray (University of Winnipeg), Ritesh Narayan (Mount Royal Univeristy), William Russell (Seneca College), and Kendra Waugh (Vancouver Island University), as well as those who chose to remain anonymous. One of the challenges in writing the second edition was accepting as many of their suggestions as possible without adding to the page count.

I thank the contributors who graciously commented about their career experiences and provided insight about obtaining jobs in the justice system. My hope is that their comments give readers ideas about potential careers they had not considered.

I offer special thanks to wife Renu who has the patience of a saint, a trait that was frequently tested during the last months of the revisions. Thanks also to my colleagues at the University of Regina, including Sarah Britto, Gloria DeSantis, Hirsch Greenberg, Nick Jones, James Gacek, Muhammad Asadullah, and Heather Nord for their ongoing support and encouragement. I am also grateful for the ongoing support of my friends and family: although the time spent with them is often too short, they are always in my thoughts.

Last, all Canadians owe a special thanks to the workers who respond to antisocial behaviour, crime, and victimization throughout Canada. We do not always appreciate the efforts of these individuals, and they quietly go about their jobs in safeguarding us—often at great personal risk and with little formal acknowledgement.

▲ The interior of the Supreme Court of Canada is adorned by the Canadian coat of arms, which includes symbols of England and France. How does the Canadian criminal justice system reflect the influence of both of these countries? (Photo credit: peterspiro/istockphoto)

An Introduction to Crime and Justice

LEARNING OUTLINE

After reading this chapter, you will be able to

- Describe the different ways of defining and classifying crime
- Describe the three components of the justice system
- Describe the reasons why the number of people in the "criminal justice funnel" decreases before the harshest punishments are imposed
- Describe five main goals of the criminal justice system
- Explain the differences between the crime control model and the due process model
- Explain why wrongful convictions damage the public's confidence in the criminal justice system

Donald Marshall Jr

Donald Marshall Jr., a 17-year-old Indigenous youth from Nova Scotia, was convicted in the 1971 murder of Sandy Seale, a 17-year-old African-Canadian. Marshall served 11 years of a life sentence in prison before his conviction was overturned and he was acquitted by the Nova Scotia Court of Appeal. The *Royal Commission on the Donald Marshall, Jr., Prosecution* (1989) found that one of the factors that led to Marshall's wrongful conviction was that he was of Indigenous ancestry. Other factors that resulted in his conviction included a shoddy investigation completed by the police, witnesses who lied in court, poor representation by his lawyers, and errors made by the judge.

Like many others who served lengthy prison terms after being wrongfully convicted of an offence, Donald Marshall had to overcome the stigma of his conviction and the impact of living 11 years behind bars knowing he was innocent. Given these experiences, his return to the community was difficult. Marshall was unable to hold a permanent job and he was involved in some violent altercations resulting in further court appearances (Armstrong, 2018). Despite those troubles, Marshall was well-regarded for his efforts in educating youth about wrongful convictions and he was also involved in a Supreme Court case that upheld hunting rights for Indigenous people. Donald Marshall suffered from chronic health problems and he died at only 55 years of age.

Critical Questions

1. Marshall received $225,000 in compensation plus interest ($158,000) for the 11 years he served in prison (Ontario Ministry of the Attorney General, 2015) and a lifetime monthly pension from the Nova Scotia government, and all together this compensation totalled more than $1 million. Why should taxpayers be held accountable for compensating the wrongfully convicted?
2. Why would the race or ethnicity of Seale and Marshall influence the outcome of this case?
3. How do our own biases and stereotypes influence the way we interact with others in our personal and professional lives?

INTRODUCTION

Criminal Code of Canada
A federal statute that lists the criminal offences and punishments defined by Parliament, as well as justice system procedures.

There is no shortage of ideas about the causes of crime or how we should respond to criminal acts. Most of our solutions to the problem of crime are pretty simplistic, such as "locking up offenders and throwing away the key." But as we dig deeper into the issues of crime, justice, and punishment, our straightforward solutions often become less certain. For example, should the justice system be used to respond to all crimes defined in the *Criminal Code of Canada* (hereafter referred to as the *Criminal Code*), even when there is not always agreement on whether some acts, such as being married to more than one person, are really crimes? Furthermore, how can we ensure that individuals accused of crimes are treated in a just and fair manner so that we punish the right people and do not wrongly convict innocent individuals? And, if an accused person is found guilty, we must determine how the justice system ought to punish wrongdoers: For example, should youth under 18 years of age be treated differently than young adults or people with mental health problems? If we imprison criminals, who is going to pay for their incarceration, and who decides when prisoners will be returned to the community? These are not new questions and these topics have been asked and debated for centuries by politicians, religious leaders, philosophers, workers in justice systems, and ordinary people. A simple answer to all of those issues is that if easy solutions to controlling crime existed, we would have found them by now.

When considering issues related to crime and justice, many people automatically think of serious offences such as assaults causing bodily harm, robberies, and homicides. Although these acts are relatively rare, they are reported as the lead stories on internet home pages, on television, and on the front pages of newspapers. When asked about serious crime, many Canadians believe that crime rates are increasing, despite the fact that government statistics have repeatedly shown that there are fewer victims of violence today than there were two decades ago. Most of our knowledge about crime and justice has been shaped by the media—and most crime stories reported by the media are about serious offences. In many cases, media reports come from the United States; however, there are considerable differences between the crime rates and the responses to crime in America and in Canada. As a result, we are sometimes confused about the volume and seriousness of crime that occurs in Canada and about how our justice system responds to criminal acts.

With respect to types of crime, Canadians are more likely to encounter antisocial behaviour, which is objectionable conduct such as noisy people loitering in groups or individuals who are drunk, rude, or rowdy in public, and these acts can reduce the quality of our lives. For the most part, these behaviours are infractions of local bylaws or are minor *Criminal Code* offences such as causing a disturbance, and while individuals can be arrested for this conduct, the police often respond to these behaviours with warnings. In terms of *Criminal Code* offences, at some point in our lives most of us have been victims of crime—although most of our experiences have been with relatively minor offences such as property crimes. Although workers in justice systems do not usually consider a minor theft to be a very serious offence, these acts can have a big impact on an individual's life; for example, if someone stole your backpack containing your university textbooks and course notes, it would be costly and time-consuming to replace those items. Even what we consider to be minor violent offences can have a significant impact on a victim, and acts of bullying can have lifelong effects on an individual's loss of confidence. As a result, we have to look beyond the harm of a physical injury and consider the range of emotional and behavioural impacts on an individual. For instance, survivors of assaults may live in fear, and their ability to form positive relationships with others may be affected. In recognition of the impact of crime on individuals, the number of victim services programs—often operated by police services—has greatly increased in the past few decades (Allen, 2014; Department of Justice Canada, 2019).

In the chapters that follow, readers will develop a much broader understanding of the criminal justice system in Canada. In doing so, we will be forced to confront our own ideas about crime, the experiences of victims and offenders, and the roles of justice system workers. In some cases, our ideas about responding to crime might challenge our notions of "common sense"—for instance, we might consider the decision to not place low-risk inmates in correctional treatments or the fact that more lives can be saved through traffic enforcement than through traditional policing. Another goal of this book is to move beyond the task of simply identifying problems (which is relatively easy to do) and examine a number of promising strategies that have been shown to prevent crime, streamline the operations of the justice system, or reduce the likelihood of criminals reoffending.

In order to put these issues into context, this chapter provides a brief description of crime, describes the different components of Canada's criminal justice system, explains how people

antisocial behaviour Conduct that can be disruptive and reduce our quality of life, but might not be considered a criminal act.

accused of crimes flow through the justice system, highlights the goals of the justice system, and examines two ways of looking at our responses to crime using the crime control and due process models. Throughout the following sections, attention will be paid to the role of the media in shaping our ideas about crime and justice, and how our beliefs influence the operations of the justice system.

CRIME AND LAW

Acts that are considered to be crimes in Canada are defined by the *Criminal Code*. Decisions about what acts are defined as crimes are the result of political and legal decisions, and there is not always agreement on what acts should be labelled as crimes. There has been debate for centuries over what are the best responses to control acts defined as crimes. According to the Department of Justice (2015b), laws are rules that forbid some behaviours and are enforced by the courts in order to reduce fear, chaos, and disorder, as well as provide a way to resolve conflicts. Hundreds of years ago when people lived in small communities there was less need for formal ways of regulating behaviour. Most people conformed through informal social control, which refers to the actions and opinions of one's parents, peers, neighbours, and community members—such as their disapproval—that influence our behaviour (e.g., a friend tells you not to drive after drinking). These informal methods, however, broke down when people settled into larger communities and no longer knew their neighbours. Balko (2013, p. xi) points out that "once neighbors stopped speaking the same language and worshipping in the same buildings, shunning and social stigmatization lost their effectiveness."

As the strength of informal social control decreased, more formal approaches to responding to antisocial behaviour and crime evolved. The methods of preventing and responding to crime that emerged were dependent on a nation's history, religious influences, culture, political structures (including the influence of royalty), and

legal systems. These arrangements involved the military, clergy, monarchy, organizations that policed for profit, and different levels of government. Every society has developed its own methods of ensuring that individuals conform to an accepted way of doing things that most people agree with: these standards of acceptable behaviour are called norms. In Canada, the laws that evolved were based on patterns of settlement from different immigrant groups, and the colonists brought with them the laws they were familiar with from their homelands. As a result, there were some differences between Indigenous laws, which differed by Nation and across the continent; early legal systems in what would become Quebec, which was settled by the French; and early legal systems adopted in what would become Atlantic Canada and Ontario, by settlers who were primarily from England.

Prostitution, for example, has been called the world's oldest profession. Although most societies have tried to control whether an individual can sell sex, these efforts have failed because of the number of willing customers and the number of people who will sell sexual services. In December 2013, the Supreme Court of Canada ruled that existing prostitution laws were not constitutional, because they placed sex workers at risk of victimization. In the *Canada (Attorney General) v Bedford* (2013) decision, the chief justice stated that "Parliament has the power to regulate against nuisances, but not at the cost of the health, safety and lives of prostitutes," and "it is not a crime in Canada to sell sex for money."

In striking down Canada's existing prostitution law in 2013, the Supreme Court gave Parliament one year to enact new laws. Although the existing law was considered unconstitutional, it remained "on the books" for one year, meaning that individuals purchasing sex could still be arrested. Most police services did not enforce these laws, because they believed that prosecutors would not bring those cases to court. This example shows how changes in one part of the justice system (the courts) can influence practices in other components (police and corrections). In December 2014,

---

informal social control When people conform to the law and other social norms because of the actions and opinions of other individuals, such as praise or disapproval.

norms Standards of acceptable behaviour that are based on tradition, customs, and values.

new legislation came into effect that made it illegal for individuals ("johns") to purchase sex, expanded police powers to investigate those advertising the sale of sexual services, and enhanced sanctions for pimps and sex traffickers. Selling sex, however, is not illegal.

Smith (2014) reports that any prostitution legislation will be opposed by groups who want the illicit sex trade to continue. Cuciz (2018) says that traffickers "can earn, on average, $300,000 each year, per victim, and often more money the younger the victim." Although the 2014 laws were intended to reduce demand for sexual services, some advocates argue that they have driven prostitution underground and reduced the safety of sex workers (Ivison, 2018). As a result, the constitutionality of the 2014 law was challenged by Hamad Anwar and Tiffany Harvey, operators of Fantasy World Escorts in London, Ontario. In 2015, they were charged with benefiting from someone else's sexual services. Their case was heard in a Kitchener court in June 2019 (Dubinski, 2019), and many legal scholars believe this case will ultimately be heard before the Supreme Court of Canada. Regardless of the eventual outcomes of this case, the balance between the public good and the safety of sex-trade workers will remain controversial.

Public (Criminal) and Private Law

According to the Department of Justice (2015b), there are two types of law: public law and private law.

> Public law sets the rules for the relationship between the individual and society. If someone breaks a criminal law, it is seen as a wrong against society. It includes criminal law, which deals with crimes and their punishments; constitutional law, which defines the relationship between various branches of government … [and] also limits the exercise of governmental power over individuals through the protection of human rights and fundamental freedoms; [and] administrative law, which deals with the actions and operations of government. (Department of Justice, 2015b, p. 2)

By contrast, private law—which includes the *civil law*—refers to the relationships between individuals that often involve contracts, and the courts can become involved when disputes over these arrangements occur; it can also include family law, wills and estates, and real estate transactions. While it is important to understand the distinction between private and public law, most of the descriptions in this book involve criminal, or public law, matters.

The *Criminal Code of Canada*

Canadian law is dynamic, meaning that it evolves along with changes in society, legal decisions (such as the example of prostitution discussed earlier), technology, and notions about the best ways to respond to crime. The *Criminal Code* is a federal statute (an Act of the Parliament of Canada) that was first enacted in 1892. According to Coughlan, Yogis, and Cotter (2013, p. 84), the *Criminal Code* "is amended, usually more than once in each session of Parliament, to take account of necessary changes and innovations in the criminal law." Technology, for instance, has changed the ways that offenders commit crimes, and our responses to those offences (Police Executive Research Forum, 2018). Laws have been rewritten to account for the use of the internet in crimes such as cyberbullying that involve criminal harassment, uttering threats, or intimidation.

The *Criminal Code* is an act that is currently over 1,100 pages (the document is written in both official languages). It is not surprising that the *Criminal Code* addresses all serious offences such as homicide, provides definitions of key terms related to these offences, and outlines the consequences for violating these acts. Yet the *Criminal Code* also includes hundreds of other sections that can result in arrest, prosecution, and sentencing, although many people might not be aware that these laws exist. Canadians who practice witchcraft (section 365), water ski after dark (section 250), or attend an immoral theatrical performance (section 167) are committing crimes and could be arrested, prosecuted, and punished for

public law
A type of law addressing matters that affect society, such as responding to a person who commits a criminal act.

private law
Legal matters that relate to the relationships between individuals or businesses that involve contracts.

Canada.ca/StopHatingOnline

The Government of Canada has had to rewrite laws to account for the use of the internet and other technologies in crimes such as cyberbullying. This screenshot is from a commercial informing the public that actions such as harassment, threat, or intimidation online may be illegal.

engaging in those acts. While individuals charged for those offences are rare, in October 2018 the Halton police charged a 32-year-old woman for "extortion, fraud over $5,000 and witchcraft-fortune telling" (Petrovsky, 2018).

Our ideas about justice can change over time and sometimes result in amendments to the *Criminal Code*. The federal government enacted legislation in 2012 called the *Safe Streets and Communities Act* that was intended to get "tough on crime" by imposing lengthy sentences on people convicted of trafficking drugs or accessing child pornography. Many of these changes in law reflect our ideas about crime and justice. If we believe that people carefully consider the consequences of their actions before engaging in crimes, then tough sentences make sense. But we know from our own experiences that we may have engaged in antisocial or illegal acts without much prior thought, perhaps because we were immature or because we simply did not fully consider the consequences of our actions.

Federal, Provincial, and Municipal Legislation

The federal government, provinces and territories, and municipalities also have the authority to regulate our behaviours through legislation. The powers that different levels of government have to enact laws and manage the criminal justice system were originally laid out in the *Constitution Act, 1867*, where section 91 defines the federal powers and section 92 gives powers to the provincial governments. "The federal government has the exclusive authority to enact legislation regarding criminal law and procedure" and includes the responsibility "for providing a federal police service to enforce federal statutes and to protect national security" (Government of British Columbia, 2017, p. 2). The federal government also has the authority to imprison adult offenders aged 18 years and older serving more than a two-year sentence. Under the *Constitution Act*, the provinces have the **jurisdiction** over the administration of criminal justice, including the operations of the local courts, provincial policing, and the operations of correctional centres.

Federal, provincial, and municipal governments can also enact regulations, although their authority to do so is limited and these regulations cannot infringe on the *Criminal Code*. Although violating these regulations is not a crime, they do regulate many aspects of our lives, can be enforced by the police or other officials working for the government, and can result in fines and sometimes incarceration. The federal government, for example, has established thousands of laws regulating issues ranging from air travel to wastewater treatment. In order to enforce these regulations, the federal government employs thousands of officials, such as the uniformed and armed officials working for the Canada Border Services Agency or federal park wardens, and thousands of them have the power to arrest suspects.

Provinces, territories, and municipalities can also pass laws that relate to their jurisdiction. Provincial issues are often related to health care, education, or transportation. The provinces and territories also have jurisdiction over property rights, which is a broad area that includes the regulation of things that can be owned such as vehicles, real estate, liquor, or animals. As a result, a provincial government can regulate the registration of vehicles and how they are driven on the roadways. Municipalities can also enact bylaws, such as requiring homeowners to clear snow from their sidewalks or giving police the authority to respond to a noisy party, and in Toronto if a homeowner has more than two garage sales a year they can be fined up to $5,000.

One of the challenges for individuals is that there are thousands of federal, provincial, territorial, and municipal laws, regulations, and bylaws, and it is likely that each of us may have broken some of these laws or regulations—often without knowing they exist. The consequences of violating some of these regulations can be severe, including fines that might total tens of thousands of dollars. In order to better understand the severity of different types of offences, legal scholars have developed a number of classifications

for crime, and the following discussion provides some examples.

Classifying Crime

Philosophers and legal scholars have used two categories to classify crimes by their seriousness: *malum in se* (plural *mala in se*) and *malum prohibitum* (plural *mala prohibita*). *Malum in se* refers to an offence that is universally thought of as evil or wrong, such as kidnapping or homicide. *Malum prohibitum*, by contrast, refers to an act that is deemed to be wrong because the government has defined it as unlawful—for example, dangerous driving, a *Criminal Code* offence, is considered *malum prohibitum* "because it has been so designated by statute as a result of a legislative determination that it is dangerous to the community" (Coughlan, Yogis, & Cotter, 2013, p. 202). In most cases, we agree that an act that is *malum in se* is wrong, but sometimes we are confronted by circumstances that are difficult to agree on. For example, should a business owner who fails to fix a delivery truck's brakes be held criminally responsible for a death caused by those faulty brakes? There is even less agreement when it comes to *mala prohibita* offences, such as whether the recreational use of marijuana, prior to October 17, 2018, should have been a criminal act. Only about half of the respondents in national polls conducted before marijuana was legalized believed this was a positive change.

The *Criminal Code* defines acts according to their seriousness: summary offences (also known as summary conviction offences) are considered less serious and carry a lesser penalty than more serious crimes called indictable offences. As Allen (2017, p. 5) observes: "Some offences in the *Criminal Code* can be processed as either summary or indictable offences; these are hybrid offences, and include child pornography, sexual violations against children and some firearms offences," and that decision is made by a Crown prosecutor. These offences are called dual offences or hybrid offences. Whether a person accused of a crime is charged with a summary offence or an indictable offence has a number of consequences for the individual,

jurisdiction
The range of a government's or court's authority (e.g., provinces have jurisdiction over non-criminal traffic matters).

malum in se
An act that is universally considered by the public as being evil or harmful to society, such as homicide.

malum prohibitum
An act that is defined as illegal or wrong by a government, but is not considered wrong in itself, such as speeding on a highway.

summary offences
Crimes that carry a less serious punishment in which judges can impose a jail sentence of up to six months and/ or a maximum fine of $5,000.

indictable offences
Serious offences, such as homicide, where the defendants must appear in court and cases are heard before federally appointed judges.

dual offences
Offences that can be prosecuted as either summary offences or indictable offences.

A Closer Look

Politics and Crime Control: A 2015 Election Promise and Legalizing Marijuana in 2018

Defining the acts that become criminal offences and the ways we control crime are political issues. The legalization of marijuana in 2018 shows how politicians can change laws to adapt to a society's changing beliefs about what is right and wrong. Until the 1960s few were concerned about marijuana use and only two per cent of drug arrests between 1946 and 1961 involved marijuana (Carstairs, 2000, p. 112). As its use became more popular, so did the number of people arrested for various marijuana-related offences, and between 1998 and 2016 there were almost 930,000 arrests for possession (Statistics Canada, 2018a). Despite being illegal its use was widespread. A 2017 poll revealed that over one-third of Canadians (38 per cent) had used marijuana recreationally (Ispos, 2017, pp. 1–2).

Legalizing marijuana was a key promise of the Liberals in the 2015 election. While they promised to quickly introduce new legislation, amending the *Controlled Drugs and Substances Act* (the legislation that made marijuana use illegal) was complicated as changes also had to be made to the *Criminal Code* and 12 other acts, ranging from the *Criminal Records Act* to the *Canadian Victims Bill of Rights*. Changes in criminal justice legislation also impact the operations of provincial and municipal governments, as they are often forced to change their crime prevention and enforcement activities to reflect legislative changes, and sometimes those changes are costly. Prior to introducing the bill to legalize marijuana, the Liberal government formed a task force that received submissions from more than 30,000 individuals and

organizations to capture the public's mood on this issue (Government of Canada, 2018). After considering that feedback the legislation was introduced and the bill passed after readings in Parliament and the Senate, with amendments and review at each point. Figure 1.1 provides a timeline of the legislative steps taken to legalize marijuana.

Although the recreational use of marijuana became legal on October 17, 2018, new laws restricting access to youth, possession, production, and sales were also introduced, and some of those crimes could result in five- to 14-year prison sentences. For example, under the new legislation giving or selling marijuana to a person under 18 years of age could result in a 14-year-prison term. Kirkey (2018) says these sanctions are harsher than current laws regarding intoxicants, such as providing liquor to a minor, which can result in a maximum sanction of only one year's incarceration in Ontario. As a result, people will still be arrested and punished for marijuana-related offences. It will take several years before we have a better understanding of the impact of these new laws and it is likely some marijuana users and sellers may be punished more severely than we imagine.

While recreational marijuana use was legalized there are differences in how the provinces regulate the drug. These provincial regulations define where marijuana can be sold, the minimum age limit for use (18 years old in Alberta and Quebec, 19 years of age in the other provinces), the legality of growing marijuana at home (which Manitoba and Quebec have banned), whether marijuana can be smoked in public or in

including the type of court where the hearing will be held and whether the individual has the right to a jury trial. The maximum sentence that can be imposed on someone found guilty of a summary offence is also limited to a maximum fine of $5,000 and/or six months in jail (although there are exceptions for some sexual offences). These issues are described in more depth in Chapter 7.

THE STRUCTURE OF THE CRIMINAL JUSTICE SYSTEM

There are three components of the justice system: police, courts, and corrections. The three parts are interrelated but also somewhat independent of each other. For the most part, our knowledge of the Canadian justice system is based on what we

a vehicle, and whether landlords and homeowner associations can ban smoking (CTV News, 2018). In addition, many workplaces are also grappling with whether employees will be able to use marijuana on the job or whether marijuana can be smoked on their properties, including on university campuses. Even

before the law came into effect there was disagreement about the constitutionality of the new laws and the fairness of the regulations. As a result, some of the long-term outcomes of the federal law, provincial regulations, and workplace decisions will be heard before Supreme Courts well into the future.

November 2015	Liberals form government
June 2016	Task force to study legalization is formed
November 2016	Results of the Task Force published
April 2017	Bill C-45: Legislation introduced (first reading in the House of Commons)
June 2017	The second reading of C-45 in the House of Commons, followed by the bill being sent to a Committee for review
November 2017	A report is prepared, followed by the third reading and a vote on the amendments based on the report
	First reading of the bill in the Senate
March 2018	Bill C-45 is adopted at its second Senate reading and reffered to a Committee
June 2018	Committee recommendations for amendments are sent to the House of Commons, which accepts the amendments
	Senate passes the amended legislation
	Bill receives royal assent by the Governor General
October 2018	Law takes effect
February 2019	Government waives application fees and removes the waiting period for individuals convicted of marijuana possession and applying for a record suspension (formerly known as pardons)

FIGURE 1.1 Timeline of the Progress of Bill C-45 Through Parliament

see on television, and some of that information is incorrect—for example, it is often based on US examples—or has been simplified, such as a complicated law explained in a 60-second news segment. This section provides a basic foundation of the structure of the criminal justice system that will be expanded on in the chapters that follow.

Police

The police are the most visible component of the justice system, and they are the officials we are most likely to encounter. Information from the 2014 General Social Survey (GSS) on Victimization, which is a survey of Canadians conducted

General Social Survey (GSS) An annual survey of Canadians that is conducted by Statistics Canada about a range of social trends, with each annual survey addressing one theme in depth.

every five years, shows that about one-third of respondents came into contact with the police in the previous year, whereas only one-fifth came into contact with the courts (Cotter, 2015). The results of the 2012 Canadian Community Health Survey reveal that about one in 10 of these interactions are for traffic violations, while other contacts are as victims (3.9 per cent) or as witnesses (3.4 per cent); the rest of these encounters are for non-criminal matters (Boyce, Rotenberg, & Karam, 2015, p. 23).

On May 15, 2018, there were about 69,000 police officers employed in Canada, which works out to about two officers for every 1,000 residents; this includes over 39,000 officers employed by municipal police agencies and 11,411 employed by the three provincial police services of Ontario, Quebec, and Newfoundland and Labrador (Conor, Robson, & Marcellus, 2019) (see Figure 1.2). The Royal Canadian Mounted Police (RCMP) employed over 18,000 officers in different roles—most were contracted by the municipalities or provinces to provide police services, and the remainder were engaged in federal policing. When it comes to federal policing, the RCMP are responsible for enforcing over 200 statutes such as drug offences, customs regulations, economic crimes, and immigration offences.

Policing is a provincial responsibility, and eight provinces and about 150 towns or cities contract with the RCMP to provide policing services. Prior to the 1930s, all of the provinces had their own provincial police services, but most were disbanded in favour of RCMP contract policing. Today, most Canadian cities are policed by municipal police services, whereas most rural communities and small towns are served by provincial police services or the RCMP. The Ontario Provincial Police (OPP) provides provincial and rural policing in Ontario, while the Sûreté du Québec (SQ) provides policing services in Quebec. Newfoundland and Labrador are policed by the Royal Newfoundland Constabulary (RNC), which provides municipal services and also polices the countryside surrounding North East Avalon, Corner Brook, and Labrador West; the RCMP, covers the remaining areas of the province. With the exception of Ontario and Quebec, the remaining provinces have entered into renewable 20-year policing agreements with the RCMP, and these agreements will be the provincial policing model for the foreseeable future. All of the policing in the Northwest Territories, Nunavut, and Yukon is carried out by the RCMP. In addition to the federal or provincial police, there are a number of regional services such as the Durham Regional Police Service in Ontario. As of January 1, 2019, there were also 36 self-administered Indigenous police services. Those self-administered police agencies are much like municipal departments, although they are operated by First Nations rather than local governments.

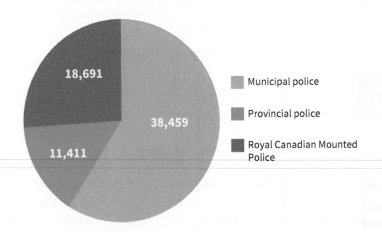

FIGURE 1.2 Number of Canadian Officers Employed by Police Services
Adapted from Conor, Robson, and Marcellus (2019)

Since policing is a provincial responsibility, each province spells out the roles and responsibilities for the police services. Section 4 of the Province of Ontario's *Police Services Act* describes the five core roles for police agencies in that province: (a) crime prevention, (b) law enforcement, (c) maintaining the public peace, (d) emergency response, and (e) assistance to victims of crime (along with one additional role called "any other prescribed policing functions"). Although the Ontario example of these core services is relatively consistent across the country, there will be some differences in the way that the police are deployed from province to province. Priorities for policing are based on political decisions and negotiations between political leaders and police officials. There are a limited number of officers, so their activities have to be prioritized in part based on input from the public. For instance, parents may be concerned about impaired drivers in their neighbourhoods and they may raise this issue with their municipal government leaders. These civic leaders, in turn, will request that the police increase enforcement efforts in these locations.

One of the things that most people find surprising about police work is that officers spend a relatively small portion of their time in law enforcement or "crime fighting" and that most of their activities are related to maintaining order. Most calls to the police are not about criminal matters and are instead related to barking or loose dogs, noisy neighbours, vehicles speeding through neighbourhoods, or drunken behaviour. Other calls have little to do with policing at all—they are related to civil matters, such as two neighbours squabbling over who should fix a broken fence shared between their two yards. Robertson (2012, p. 351) describes the police as a social service agency that "responds to a variety of emergencies and all manner of personal crises,

By permission of the Royal Newfoundland Constabulary

The police are the most visible component of the criminal justice system, and they are the officials we are most likely to encounter in our day-to-day lives. The Royal Newfoundland Constabulary is one of Canada's oldest police services and dates back to 1729. Although mounted police can play an important role in crowd control, they are also very popular with the public.

including crimes in progress, domestic disputes, disturbances, motor vehicle collisions, injuries from accidents, sudden deaths (including suicides), psychotic episodes of mental illness, and locating lost children and vulnerable adults."

Courts

Canadian courts are based on English common-law systems and are adversarial, meaning that there are two parties who have opposing positions and their cases are heard before an impartial judge. In criminal matters, people accused of crimes are represented by lawyers who are called defence counsel. The state or Crown, by contrast, is represented by lawyers who are called Crown attorneys, counsel, or prosecutors. The judge hears evidence about the case and reserves judgment until all the evidence is heard, and in the process determines whether the Crown has proven its case beyond a reasonable doubt.

There are hundreds of local courts in Canada, and they employ thousands of court staff who process hundreds of thousands of criminal matters. In 2016–2017, almost 360,000 cases were heard in adult courts across the nation (involving about 1.2 million *Criminal Code* offences), and there were an additional 29,000 youth cases that accounted for almost 115,000 offences (Miladinovic, 2019, p. 3).

There are four levels of courts in Canada, and they are shown in Figure 1.3.

> First there are provincial/territorial courts, which handle the great majority of cases that come into the system. Second are the provincial/territorial superior courts. These courts deal with more serious crimes and also take appeals from provincial/territorial court judgments.... At the next level are the provincial/territorial courts of appeal ... while the highest level is occupied by the Supreme Court of Canada. (Department of Justice, 2005, p. 2)

Most cases related to criminal justice—as well as violations of provincial traffic regulations, municipal legislation, or provincial and federal

inferior courts
Provincial and territorial courts that have limited jurisdiction and deal with less serious adult and youth criminal matters, as well as civil, family, traffic, and municipal bylaw cases.

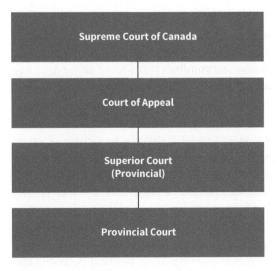

FIGURE 1.3 Criminal Courts of Canada
Department of Justice (2015b).

regulations—are heard in provincial or territorial courts. These courts—known as inferior courts—also hear matters relating to youth aged 12 to 17 years charged with *Criminal Code* offences. Larger cities sometimes have specialized courts such as drug, mental health, or domestic violence courts to manage specific types of offenders. Specialized courts enable the judges, prosecutors, and defence counsel to develop an expertise in dealing with these cases. These courts have a treatment orientation, and research has shown that they are usually effective in responding to these special-needs offenders (Mays & Ruddell, 2019). Inferior courts also process minor disputes between individuals, such as small claims, and may also hear family law cases and traffic matters.

More serious criminal matters, such as criminal prosecutions for indictable offences, are heard in superior courts operated by provincial or territorial governments. These courts are known by different names throughout the country (Court of Queen's Bench in Alberta, Saskatchewan, Manitoba, and New Brunswick; Supreme Court in British Columbia, Newfoundland and Labrador, Northwest Territories, Nova Scotia, Prince Edward Island, and Yukon; and Superior Court in Ontario and Quebec). Practices are somewhat different in Nunavut as that territory has one unified court, the Court of Justice. The Department of Justice (2015) observes that although the provinces are responsible for these superior courts, the judges working within them are appointed by and have their salaries paid by the federal government.

Every province has courts that hear appeals of decisions made by the lower courts. These appellate courts review decisions and can overturn or uphold decisions and sentences. For example, both the individual who was sentenced and the prosecutors can appeal the severity of a sentence imposed by a provincial or superior court judge. Appellate courts are usually composed of a panel of three judges who rule on the appeals brought before them. The military courts also have the Court Martial Appeal Court of Canada. The ability to review lower court decisions is important in order to correct errors and ensure that accused people or those convicted of an offence have case outcomes that are just and fair.

Parties who do not agree with the decisions of the appellate courts take these matters to the Supreme Court of Canada, which is the final court of appeal. According to the Department of Justice (2015a, p. 10), the Supreme Court "has jurisdiction over disputes in all areas of the law. These include constitutional law, administrative law, criminal law, and civil law." The Supreme Court is distinctive in that it can choose to hear a case or let the decisions of the provincial or territorial courts of appeal stand. As noted in the case of prostitution discussed earlier, the Supreme Court has the ability to overturn laws that are unconstitutional. In addition, the Supreme Court can make changes in the law that place increased demands on the justice system. One of the most significant examples of this was a 1991 decision that required prosecutors to disclose information about their investigations to defence lawyers, even if that information might lead to a not-guilty verdict (*R v Stinchcombe*, 1991). This one decision has been costly for police and prosecutors because of the increased administrative burdens on these agencies to collect and report this information, but this requirement was important to ensure the fair treatment of people accused of committing crimes (Bowal & Brierton, 2018)

Corrections

On any given day, there are about 40,000 adults and about 800 youths (people under 18 years of age, although that total does not include youth in Quebec facilities) incarcerated in federal and provincial/territorial correctional facilities (Malakieh, 2019). Malakieh (2019) also reports there are about another 104,000 adults and 7,000 youth supervised in the community (that total does not include youth from Nova Scotia, New Brunswick, or Quebec).

There are two adult correctional systems in Canada. Adults who are arrested, awaiting a court date, sentenced to under two years of incarceration, or awaiting a transfer to federal corrections are held in facilities operated by provincial governments. These facilities go by different names and in most provinces they are known as provincial correctional centres. In Ontario, by contrast, they are known by different labels. Nine are called jails, which are older facilities that were originally built and run by city governments but are now operated by the province (Ontario Ministry of Community Safety and Correctional Services, 2018). These facilities tend to be small, of antiquated design, and primarily hold local residents awaiting a court date. Detention centres also hold people arrested and awaiting court dates, and these larger facilities often serve several counties. Detention centres can also hold inmates sentenced to short terms (under 60 days) of incarceration. Last, correctional centres in Ontario hold inmates sentenced to terms of incarceration of two years or less. Arrangements for adult corrections vary somewhat throughout the nation, and the names of these facilities also differ, but they fulfill two key functions: to hold individuals awaiting their court dates and to hold inmates serving sentences of less than two years.

Many provincial governments also operate treatment centres to help individuals who have specialized needs. In Saskatchewan, for example, impaired drivers convicted of a second drinking

Supreme Court of Canada The highest court in Canada; it only hears cases that are being appealed out of a lower court.

jails Facilities where individuals are held awaiting their court appearances (called provincial correctional centres in most provinces, but jails in Ontario).

detention centres Facilities where individuals are held awaiting their court dates or serving short periods of incarceration (called provincial correctional centres in some provinces).

correctional centres Facilities that hold inmates sentenced to terms of incarceration of two years or less.

Bernard Weil/Toronto Star via Getty Images

Detention centres in Ontario hold people arrested and awaiting court dates, and these larger facilities are intended to serve several counties. Detention centres can also hold individuals sentenced to short terms (under 60 days) of incarceration.

specialized facilities include eight Aboriginal healing lodges that are operated or funded by the CSC and "use Aboriginal values, traditions and beliefs to design services and programs for offenders," including "Aboriginal concepts of justice and reconciliation" (Correctional Service of Canada, 2016).

In order to reintegrate ex-prisoners to the community, the CSC also has 15 community correctional centres that allow inmates to enter the community in a structured and gradual manner. In communities that are not served by these centres, the CSC contracts with non-government organizations, such as the Salvation Army, to house these individuals. Parolees living in these placements, which are sometimes called halfway houses, are on day parole, which enables them to attend school, treatment, or work during the day and return to the community correctional centre in the evening.

There are about three adult probationers or parolees serving a sentence in the community for every inmate in custody, and most of them are serving a probationary sentence. As shown in Figure 1.4, most probationers live in the community and they are expected to abide by a number of conditions on their probation orders that were imposed by a judge. Every probation order will have the following conditions: (a) keep the peace and be of good behaviour; (b) appear in court when ordered by the court; and (c) advise the court or probation officer about any change of name, address, or employment. Individuals with specific treatment needs, such as being convicted of family violence, are often required to attend specialized treatment. Probation officers, who are provincial employees, monitor the progress of these individuals and often require low-risk probationers (e.g., those with no history of involvement in violent crimes) to report monthly and advise them of any major life changes. Higher-risk probationers are often required to report to their probation officers more frequently and attend specialized treatment programs such as anger management for people convicted of violent offences.

Prisoners released from a federal penitentiary prior to the end of their sentence are on either

special handling units High-security units within a maximum-security penitentiary where the movement of prisoners is very controlled.

day parole A type of release for federal prisoners who live in a community-based facility and usually work, attend school, or participate in treatment during the day.

probation officers Provincial officials who prepare reports for the courts about sentencing options for individuals convicted of crimes and monitor their activities if serving community-based sentences.

and driving offence are placed in short-term treatment as part of their sentence. Various other treatment facilities exist throughout the nation, including those designated for people with mental illnesses, as they are overrepresented in Canada's criminal justice system (Department of Justice, 2018b).

Those convicted of the most serious offences in Canada, and sentenced to two years or longer, are held in facilities operated by the Correctional Service of Canada (CSC). In 2016/2017, the federal prison system held over 14,000 prisoners in penitentiaries across Canada. These institutions vary in size and include small treatment centres such as the Shepody Healing Centre in Dorchester, New Brunswick, with a capacity of 50 inmates—although most federal penitentiaries are much larger. Security in these facilities ranges from minimum (some may have only a fence around the perimeter) to maximum, where movement of the prisoners is strictly controlled. Several facilities also have special handling units that hold the most difficult-to-manage or dangerous prisoners in very strict conditions (e.g., inmates are locked in their cells for 23 hours a day and have little or no interaction with other prisoners). Other

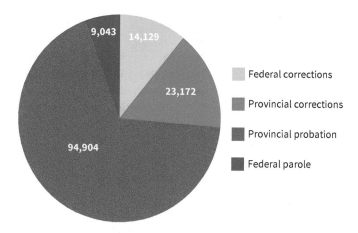

FIGURE 1.4 Individuals Under Correctional Supervision
Malakieh (2019)

parole or statutory release, and their stay in the community is monitored by parole officers. Over 9,000 federal parolees were supervised in the community in 2017/2018 and the time they will serve on parole varies greatly. Some will serve a period of months until their prison sentences expire while those convicted of homicide offences will be under correctional supervision for the remainder of their lives. As the sentence has already been imposed by a judge, any release on parole must first be approved by the Parole Board of Canada, which reviews each case and bases the decision to release the individual back to the community on comprehensive reports and assessments conducted by CSC staff members. Some prisoners receive a statutory release, which is a release granted after an inmate serves two-thirds of their sentence that is mandated by law, rather than a reward for their good behaviour.

In terms of youth offenders, there were about 800 youths held in facilities operated by the provincial or territorial governments in 2017/2018 (that total does not include youth in Quebec). Much like adult prisons, secure custody facilities (also known as closed custody facilities) for youth have a high-security environment, although rehabilitative programs such as education, mental health treatment, or job training are tailored to the individual needs of the youth. Most youth remanded in custody prior to their court appearances are placed in these higher-security facilities to ensure that they will not escape. Open custody facilities, by contrast, are community-based operations that tend to be fairly small and often have fewer than 20 residents. Like day parole programs for adults, most of the youth in these facilities attend school or work during the day and return to the facility in the evenings.

COMMON ELEMENTS IN THE CRIMINAL JUSTICE SYSTEM

Cole, Smith, and DeJong (2018) identify a number of common elements in the criminal justice system, including discretion and filtering. Employees of a justice system can exercise a lot of discretion when they come across someone engaged in criminal behaviour. This discretion is present in all components of the criminal justice system. A police officer who confronts a shoplifter has a number of options: the officer can choose to caution or warn the individual and then release him or her, or the officer can arrest the suspect and take him or her into custody. A prosecutor then decides whether to proceed with the charge and take the matter to court or whether to drop the matter. Correctional officials—whether they work in community corrections such as probation or parole or in a correctional centre or prison—also wield a considerable amount of power over the

parole A form of conditional release from a federal correctional facility to the community, where the ex-prisoner is supervised by a parole officer.

statutory release A form of supervised release that is automatically granted after federal prisoners with determinate sentences of three years or longer have served two-thirds of their sentences (does not apply to dangerous offenders or lifers serving indeterminate sentences).

secure custody facilities High-security youth custody facilities that are usually large and often look similar to adult correctional centres. Also known as *closed custody facilities*.

open custody facilities Low-security youth custody facilities that are generally small and are sometimes located in residential neighbourhoods.

individuals they supervise. Probationers who have violated the conditions of their probation order (conditions imposed by the judge at sentencing) can have their probation revoked after a probation officer notifies the prosecutor they have breached their probation and the case is reviewed by a judge.

Discretion

The ability to use discretion enables workers in the criminal justice system to operate in a more effective and efficient manner. There is no shortage of crimes, and the police could not possibly arrest every wrongdoer. So, officers establish some priorities—typically, they will act more formally in cases of serious incidents, and they will ignore or deal with less serious offences in an informal manner such as by giving the individual a warning. Like many other issues presented in this chapter, there is not always agreement on what offences should be handled informally. Many of us do not believe that arresting a young person for doing something that many of us did as youngsters—such as stealing a chocolate bar from a store—is a smart practice. In addition to the seriousness of the crime, discretion could also relate to an officer's priorities and

beliefs. An individual's demeanour might also influence an officer's decision to make an arrest, and the outcome for a cooperative and respectful individual may be different than for a rude and confrontational suspect. Last, each police service in consultation with community leaders establishes priorities for enforcing the laws, so in some jurisdictions, apprehending street racers, for example, might be a more important priority than arresting homeless people engaging in minor theft.

Filtering

The concept of a funnel has been used to describe the movement of people through the criminal justice system. Figure 1.5 shows that only a small percentage of people charged with committing a crime are ever sentenced to prison. According to Public Safety Canada (2018, p. 13) there were about 2.1 million incidents reported to police in 2016. Of that total, almost a quarter million adults were found guilty and about 70,000 of these offenders were sentenced to provincial or federal corrections. At every point in the system, individuals are filtered out. In some cases, the police are aware of an offence, but they use their discretion

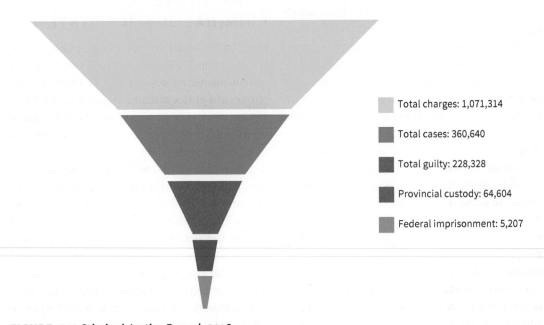

Total charges: 1,071,314

Total cases: 360,640

Total guilty: 228,328

Provincial custody: 64,604

Federal imprisonment: 5,207

FIGURE 1.5 Criminal Justice Funnel, 2016
Public Safety Canada (2018)

Tannis Toohey/Toronto Star via Getty Images

Individuals in alternative measures programs are often required to make restitution for their offences, such as by making a payment to a crime victim to cover the losses from an offence, apologizing to the victim(s), participating in victim–offender mediation, completing community service work, or participating in some form of treatment such as a substance abuse program.

to deal with the situation in an informal manner (e.g., by warning the individual). Prosecutors might not pursue a case if there is insufficient evidence to secure a conviction. Of all the people charged in 2016, 228,328 resulted in a guilty plea or the individual being found guilty. Only about a third of individuals found guilty were incarcerated, and most of them served their sentences in provincial correctional facilities.

One aspect of filtering is sequencing, which means that the handling of people suspected of wrongdoing follows a set pattern. Canada's system of justice is based on the principle that an accused person is innocent until found guilty beyond a reasonable doubt. As a result, the justice system does not punish individuals before they are convicted. Instead, the police investigate a possible offence and may arrest a suspect. Unless the individual is accused of a serious offence or is considered to

pose a risk to the community or to the witnesses, most of them are released with a promise to appear in court. The information about the case is then sent to a prosecutor who reviews the case and determines whether prosecution is in the interests of justice and whether prosecution will be successful—as a result, some cases do not proceed to court.

Some first-time and minor offenders (both youth and adults) avoid the justice system by participating in alternative measures programs, which are called extrajudicial sanctions for youth. Individuals in these programs are often required to make restitution for their offences such as making a payment to a crime victim to cover the losses from an offence, apologizing to the victim(s), participating in victim–offender mediation, completing community service work, or participating in some form of treatment such

sequencing
The treatment of people involved in the justice system follows a set pattern that is dictated by law and policy.

alternative measures programs
Programs that divert individuals involved in minor crimes, such as property offences, from the formal justice system and usually require the individual to participate in community service work, make restitution to victims, attend counselling, or make an apology to victims.

extrajudicial sanctions
Alternative measures programs for youth.

restitution
When an individual makes a payment to the victim for the losses that were experienced by the victim, such as property damage or loss.

as a substance abuse program. These alternative measures programs are funded by provincial or territorial governments.

Individuals accused of crimes who do not participate in alternative measures will appear in court, and again our perceptions about these processes are often shaped by television and films. While most of us believe that trials are common, a review of court statistics from British Columbia shows that only about six per cent of cases proceeded to a full trial (British Columbia Courts, 2018a, 2018b). Instead, most individuals plead guilty to sentences that have been arranged—in **plea agreements**—by the accused's defence counsel and the prosecutor. These agreements usually involve the accused making a plea of guilty in return for a lesser punishment (e.g., charges are dropped or the punishments recommended by the prosecutor are reduced). Plea agreements benefit both parties because the accused receives a lesser punishment and the prosecutor does not have to prepare a case or go to court. Crime victims, however, are sometimes angry when offenders are not harshly punished; this issue is addressed in Chapter 7.

Most criminal matters end in a community sentence, and as described earlier, about 150,000 people are placed on some form of community supervision every year (Malakieh, 2019, p. 19). In 2017/2018, almost 250,000 adults were admitted to provincial or territorial correctional centres, although most of them were released within a few days after their court appearances (Malakieh, 2019). About 5,000 adults are admitted each year to federal corrections and they are all sentenced to at least two years. This shows that only a very small percentage of all individuals charged with a crime are harshly punished.

plea agreement An agreement arranged by a defendant's counsel and a prosecutor that usually involves the accused pleading guilty in return for a less serious punishment.

GOALS OF THE CRIMINAL JUSTICE SYSTEM

Ensuring public safety is a cornerstone of a civil society, as peace and order provide a foundation from which we can carry out our daily activities without fear. According to the Government of British Columbia (2018), there are five main goals of the criminal justice system:

- preventing crime;
- protecting the public;
- supporting victims of crime, their families, and witnesses;
- holding people responsible for crimes they have committed; and
- helping offenders return to the community and become law-abiding members of the community.

Like so many other issues presented in this book, many of these goals can be looked at from a number of perspectives. Although most of us would agree that these five broad goals are important, there is less consensus when it comes to how we will achieve those goals or which of them should be the first priority.

Preventing Crime

Everybody agrees that it is better to prevent a crime than to respond to offences that have already occurred. There is less agreement, however, on the best way to prevent crime. Traditional crime prevention programs are intended to deter potential wrongdoers by detecting crimes and then arresting and punishing wrongdoers. Many scholars believe that if the justice system is perceived as efficient, fair, and legitimate, the public will be less likely to commit crimes (Tyler & Trinkner, 2017). There is, however, growing interest in crime prevention activities that come from outside the traditional criminal and youth justice systems, as many scholars contend that crime is a predictable outcome of poverty, addictions, and breakdowns in the health, educational, and social service programs. In an influential statement, Irvin Waller (2014), a prominent Canadian criminologist, for instance, argues that we need to act smarter by lowering the costs of the justice system and using those savings in developing interventions that focus on preventing crime.

Protecting the Public

One of the most important roles of the justice system is to protect the public. Some of the efforts of the police, courts, and correctional systems are intended to identify offenders who pose the most risk to society and to respond to their crimes. Of the three components of the justice system, the police have the most visible role. Yet, prosecutors also protect the public by focusing their efforts on individuals who represent the biggest threat to public safety: organized crime offenders, gang members, violent criminals, and those with lengthy criminal histories. Once received by the federal correctional system, they undergo risk and needs assessments in order to identify those who pose the biggest risk, and correctional programs are tailored to respond to their risks and unmet needs. Individuals sentenced to provincial custody, by contrast, are likely to receive fewer opportunities for rehabilitation.

It is important to acknowledge that a growing number of interventions intended to protect the public and prevent crime are also conducted by individuals who are not employed in justice systems. For example, there has been an increase in the number of security personnel who supplement the activities of the police. A review of Statistics Canada (2018b) labour data shows there were over 120,000 security officers in 2017, or almost two of these officials for every police officer. As policing costs increase, there may be more interest in expanding these alternatives to the police (Kiedrowski, Ruddell, & Petrunik, 2019). This may result in some crime prevention, enforcement, investigative, and service-related activities shifting from public policing to private security (Montgomery & Griffiths, 2015). In addition to having implications for the justice system, these changes may also impact employment prospects for those studying criminal justice.

Supporting the Victims of Crime, Their Families, and Witnesses

An Angus Reid Institute (2018, p. 1) survey reports that "roughly one-in-eight Canadians (13 per cent) say they have personally been the victim of a crime that involved the police in the last two years." In the past, victims of crime often received shoddy treatment by justice system officials, and after a police officer took their statements, the victims were often dismissed or forgotten. Since the 1980s, there has been an increased awareness of the short- and long-term losses that victims of crimes experience, including harms inflicted by the operations of the justice system. The rights of crime victims were formally recognized after the introduction of the *Canadian Victims Bill of Rights* that came into effect on July 23, 2015. The legislation is intended to give victims a greater voice and provide them with more access to information about investigations and offenders, as well as compensation. Wemmers (2017) says that victims have the right to report crimes, protect themselves or their property (in certain circumstances), request restitution, submit victim impact statements, and request a publication ban

THE CANADIAN PRESS/Chad Hipolito

Many women on college and university campuses are psychologically, physically, and sexually victimized and few of those acts are ever reported to the police. Survivors of abuse from Canadian universities were interviewed for a *Maclean's* report on violence on campus; the reporters found that university personnel often acted with little compassion toward victims, and programs for victims failed to live up to their expectations (Schwartz, 2018). This photo shows a sign created by students at the University of Victoria that contained messages of support and information following an assault of a student on campus in 2015.

dangerous
offenders
Individuals
who the court
has deemed to
be a threat to
the life, safety,
or physical or
mental well-
being of the
public.

that limits the information the media can report about a case. While victims are able to make these requests, there is no guarantee they will be granted, a topic addressed in the online chapter on victimization.

Holding Offenders Responsible

Canadians often express mixed feelings when it comes to holding individuals accountable. We are often willing to give a break to young people and first-timers or those involved in non-violent offences, but we also want violent criminals punished harshly. As indicated on pages 17 and 18, there were 228,328 people convicted of offences in 2016 but just over 5,000 were sentenced to terms of imprisonment longer than two years. This raises the question of whether our justice system is holding wrongdoers fully accountable. In a 2018 survey on Canadians' perceptions of the court systems, only 41 per cent of Canadians reported they had complete or a lot of confidence in their provincial courts, although this was up from 19 per cent in 2012 (Angus Reid Global, 2014; Angus Reid Institute, 2018). Results from the 2014 GSS show that only about 20 per cent of Canadians have a great deal of confidence in the justice system and courts, while another 37 per cent have some confidence (Cotter, 2015). These findings suggest that most Canadians are not satisfied with the way that justice is administered—although only a very small proportion of us have much knowledge about what actually happens in courts or the actual sentences offenders receive (Roberts, 2016).

A review of custody sentences conducted by Public Safety Canada (2018, p. 11) shows that "over half (58 per cent) of all custodial sentences imposed by adult criminal courts are one month or less." Even for those who were sentenced to a federal penitentiary in 2016/2017, "almost half (49.7 per cent) of the total offender population was serving a sentence of less than five years with 23.4 per cent serving a sentence of between two years and less than three years" (Public Safety Canada, 2018, p. 41). Few prisoners will serve their entire sentence behind bars and most will receive some sort of early release; the exceptions are federal

prisoners who are designated as dangerous offenders or those sentenced to life imprisonment.

Despite those relatively short sentences, rates of some forms of reported crime, such as homicide, are at their lowest levels since the 1960s (Beattie et al., 2018), suggesting that some things must be on the right track when it comes to crime control. Although policy-makers generally want to use sanctions such as imprisonment sparingly, the public thinks otherwise. Although the fact that the murder rate today is lower than it was when the death penalty was last used in 1962, an Abacus poll conducted in 2016 found that almost 58 per cent of Canadians said the death penalty was morally right (Anderson & Coletto, 2016), and Angus Reid Global (2013) reports that 63 per cent of their survey participants wanted capital punishment reinstated. Supporters felt that capital punishment deterred potential offenders, that the death penalty was more cost effective than imprisoning a murderer for life, and that the punishment fit the crime (Angus Reid, 2013).

Helping Prisoners Return to the Community

As shown in Figure 1.5, almost 65,000 offenders were admitted to provincial custody in 2016 to serve a sentence (Public Safety Canada, 2018), and none will serve a sentence of two years; over one-half will serve one month or less (Miladinovic, 2019). In 2016/2017, almost one-half of federal prisoners were imprisoned for less than five years (Public Safety Canada, 2018, p. 41), and most non-violent federal prisoners are returned to the community on day parole within a year or two. One of the challenges in attempting to reduce re-offending is that many ex-prisoners return to the same conditions from which they came: impoverished neighbourhoods with high rates of substance abuse, a lack of positive role models, few job opportunities, or high numbers of gang members. A second barrier to their re-entry is that short incarceration sentences make it difficult to provide meaningful rehabilitative opportunities for these people. For example, if one-half of provincial sentences are less than a month in length, how do we rehabilitate an individual during that time? Last,

Race, Class, and Gender

Missing and Murdered Indigenous Women and Girls (MMIWG)

A May 2014 editorial in *the Globe and Mail* notes the following:

> If a society has the duty to protect its most vulnerable citizens, then Canadians and their governments are completely derelict with regards to Aboriginal women. They represent four per cent of Canada's female population, but nearly a third of the female prison population. They are twice as likely to live in poverty. ("Deadly statistics", 2014, para. 1)

Indigenous women in Canada are at the highest risk of violent victimization of any racial or ethnic group. Boyce (2016, p. 3) reports that Indigenous women are about three times as likely to be victims of violence compared to non-Indigenous women. Research produced by the Canadian Centre for Justice Statistics shows that Indigenous women were almost six times more likely to be murdered than non-Indigenous women in 2017 (Beattie, David, & Roy, 2018, pp. 13–14).

According to the RCMP (2014), between 1980 and 2012, a total of 1,017 Indigenous women were murdered and another 169 were missing (of those missing women, 108 cases were classified as "suspicious" and 61 were thought to be accidental). The RCMP, however, undercounts the true number of these victims, as some of those who were murdered were living in cities not policed by the RCMP.

In June 2019, the National Inquiry into MMIWG (2019) released its report based on the testimony of almost 1,500 people including the family members of victims and people with expertise in the justice system. The report was controversial, as it called the murder of these women *genocide*, which is the deliberate killing of a large group of people (and usually of an ethnic or racial group). The report calls for 231 steps that federal, provincial, and Indigenous governments must take to reduce this violence. Many of these steps are intended to improve the living conditions for all Indigenous women. In addition, there are a number of recommendations specific to the justice system, including toughening punishments for people victimizing Indigenous women, improving the quality of Indigenous policing, increasing the number of Indigenous people working in the justice system, and providing supports to the victims of crime and their families. In addition, the report calls for improving the access of Indigenous women to the justice system through legal aid, reforming the punishments meted out to Indigenous women, developing better responses to human trafficking (and the sexual exploitation of women), and basing the justice system on traditional Indigenous practices.

The federal government has promised to toughen punishments for victimizing Indigenous women and is looking into the possibilities of reforming the justice system. The stakes for Indigenous women are high, and *the Globe and Mail* editors ("Deadly statistics", 2014) observed that "for an Aboriginal woman living on the margins of society, a caring law enforcement system could mean the difference between life and death."

flickr/Jason Woodhead

Individuals can be also victimized by the justice system. In 2015, a 28 year-old Indigenous woman from Alberta—who was the victim of a kidnapping and sexual assault—was incarcerated in Edmonton Remand Centre (pictured here) for five days to ensure she appeared in court as a witness against her attacker (she was experiencing homelessness at the time of the trial). This woman, who was not accused of committing any offence, was transported in the same van as the man who was ultimately convicted of assaulting her. Cryderman (2018, para. 1) notes that while an investigation of this woman's treatment could find no evidence of misconduct on the part of any individual worker, the case is an example of systemic bias.

rehabilitative programs add to the expense of corrections, and taxpayers are not always willing to pay those increased costs. As a result, the return to the community for these ex-inmates is often less successful than we hope.

CRIME CONTROL AND DUE PROCESS MODELS

Crime Control Model

There are a number of different ways of understanding our responses to the operations of the justice system. One of the most straightforward explanations was first described by Herbert Packer (1968), who believed that two models could be used to make sense of our formal responses to crime. The first approach he identified is the crime control model, which is based on the notion that protecting society is more important than protecting the rights of any individual. In order to ensure public safety, this model says that the police and prosecution should aggressively pursue, investigate, arrest, and prosecute wrongdoers—and once they are found guilty, they should be punished swiftly and severely. Supporters of the crime control model believe that the people working within the justice system will act in a professional and lawful manner to carry out those goals.

Supporters of the crime control model believe that it is important that the justice system be seen as acting in an efficient manner to deter potential offenders. In order to achieve this goal, the justice system is thought to work best if it is informal and if it treats everybody in a uniform manner. As a result, cases that are alike will have similar outcomes. Packer introduced the idea of assembly-line justice, which is the rapid and routine processing of cases with the lowest use of resources, much like the assembly line in a factory. While Canada's justice system is based on the notion of innocence until proven guilty, the supporters of the crime control model presume that most defendants are in fact guilty. Cases would be dropped from the assembly line if the accused was found to be innocent or if there were problems with the case against the accused.

Due Process Model

While advocates of the crime control model visualize an ideal system, other scholars and practitioners recognize that some people accused of crimes are innocent and that police and prosecutors make mistakes that result in injustices such as wrongful convictions. As a result, they believe that acting swiftly to determine guilt is not as important as finding the truth and eliminating errors. Supporters of this position are advocates for the due process model; they believe that the innocent need to be protected and that even wrongdoers need protection to ensure their rights are not violated. In contrast to the view of the justice system as an assembly line, supporters of the due process model favour a system similar to an obstacle course where the obstacles are safeguards for those accused of crimes. Whereas supporters of the crime control model believe the police and prosecutors carry out the most important work, most of the protections advocated by supporters of the due process model take place in courts.

In describing the due process model's emphasis on the presumption of innocence approaches, Mays and Ruddell (2019) observe the following:

> Saying defendants are presumed innocent does not mean that they likely are innocent or that it is possible they will be found innocent. It means that guilt is not to be assumed. Therefore, guilt can exist only when the state has proven the defendant guilty beyond a reasonable doubt and the jury has returned a verdict of guilty. (p. 22)

Supporters of the due process model will sometimes make statements such as, "it is better to let ten guilty people go free than convict an innocent person," a sentiment first expressed by Sir William Blackstone, an English jurist in the 1760s (Volokh, 1997). Although those ideas might not be popular today, they have existed for hundreds of years because many people believe that a legal

---

crime control model
An approach to justice that is based on the philosophy that it is more important to protect society than the rights of any individual.

assembly-line justice
An approach to justice where a priority is placed on quickly processing minor matters in criminal courts with the assumption that most defendants are guilty.

due process model
An approach to justice that is based on the philosophy that the justice system needs to protect the rights of a defendant.

system based on due process protects individuals against the power of the state.

Many believe that it is important to achieve a balance between the due process and crime control approaches to justice. Roberts (2016, p. 5) observes that "the ultimate arbiter of conflicts between the two models of criminal justice is the Supreme Court of Canada." Justice systems that place too much emphasis on the crime control approach could end up wrongfully convicting innocent people, whereas a system that prioritizes the due process protections of the accused could result in guilty people evading punishment. These are significant problems for justice systems, as the "Comparative View" box on wrongful convictions describes.

After reading the descriptions of Packer's two models, most of us will recognize that we fall into one category or the other. Most supporters of the crime control approach are politically conservative, whereas advocates of the due process model often consider themselves liberals or civil libertarians. Yet, it is important to recognize that these two models do not exist in a pure form, and they are not intended to represent the right or wrong way of looking at justice. Instead, they provide us with two viewpoints to interpret the ways that justice systems respond to crime and the way criminal cases are processed.

In the chapters that follow, there will be numerous examples of justice policies that are based on these two approaches. For example, after the Harper government's win in the 2006 federal election, there was a movement to get tough on crime and criminals—policies that are related to the crime control model. One example of tough on crime legislation is the 2012 *Safe Streets and Communities Act*, which toughened punishments and made prison mandatory for some drug production and trafficking offences. However, after the 2015 election of the Liberal government, Prime Minister Justin Trudeau repealed some of those laws and, in addition to legalizing marijuana, the Liberal government introduced legislation in 2018 to reform the justice system, including cracking down on intimate-partner violence and reforming the jury system (Canadian Press, 2018).

Pgiam//iStock Photo

It is important to achieve a balance between the due process and crime control models. Roberts (2016, p. 5) says that "the ultimate arbiter of conflicts between the two models of criminal justice is the Supreme Court of Canada."

An example of a due process protection is that Canadians without the money to pay for a lawyer can apply for legal aid services. It was long ago recognized that poor defendants were at a significant disadvantage in court given that the state has almost limitless resources to prosecute them. In 2017/2018, almost half a million applicants received services from legal aid, and half (50 per cent) of these services were for criminal matters while the remainder were for civil matters such as immigration and refugee claims or family law cases (Department of Justice, 2019).

SUMMARY

One point that emerges in any discussion of the Canadian justice system is that there is a lack of agreement on the best way to respond to offences, and this debate is complicated by the fact that we do not always agree on what acts should be crimes. These disagreements about the best way of responding to crime and achieving justice have been debated for centuries and will not be resolved in the near future. Fortunately, there are a number of things that we can agree on: the main goals of

A COMPARATIVE VIEW

Wrongful Convictions

When it comes to wrongful convictions, we do not know the full extent of these miscarriages of justice, although the work of Innocence Canada led to the release of 21 wrongfully convicted Canadians between 1993 and 2018 (and they also assisted in other cases). In 2019, Innocence Canada was reviewing 81 cases where prisoners claimed innocence, and most of those convictions were for murder or manslaughter offences. Figure 1.6 shows that there is some interprovincial variation, as there are more claims of wrongful convictions in Manitoba, New Brunswick, and Nova Scotia (there was only one case for Nunavut

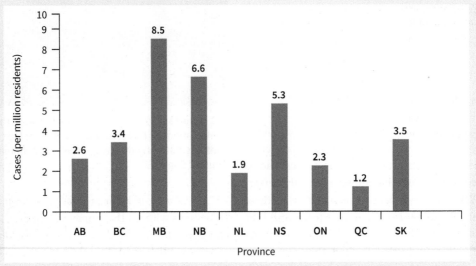

FIGURE 1.6 **Cases Under Wrongful Conviction Review per Million Provincial Residents, 2018**
Adapted from Innocence Canada (2019)

the criminal justice system, the three components that make up the justice system, and Packer's (1968) classification of justice systems. These will serve as a foundation for the remainder of our exploration of criminal justice.

Although we may all agree on the five goals of the justice system, each one of us will place a different value on issues such as crime prevention, holding individuals who have committed crimes accountable, and the best way to protect the public. Policy-makers, politicians, other stakeholders with an interest in the system, and the general public often disagree on these issues, and they also often disagree on which level of government should pay for these initiatives. For example,

many Canadians support putting more police officers on the streets but are reluctant to pay higher taxes to achieve that goal.

A basic description of the three components of the justice system was presented in this chapter, and this discussion serves as a foundation for more in-depth analyses in the chapters that follow. An important point to consider is that formal justice systems are a relatively new development in history, and even a century ago the police, courts, and corrections played a much smaller role in our lives. It is also likely that conformity was higher a century ago, when most people abided by the expectations of the community because they did not want to disappoint their friends and family.

and none for the Northwest Territories, Yukon, or Prince Edward Island). Based on this variation, supporters of the due process approach might suggest there is a rush to judgment in some provinces.

There are three remedies for people maintaining they have been wrongfully convicted: (a) conviction review, (b) commissions of inquiry, and (c) compensation. According to Campbell and Denov (2016, p. 235), conviction reviews are authorized in the *Criminal Code* and enable people claiming their innocence to "ask the federal Minister of Justice to review the circumstances of their case in order to ascertain whether a miscarriage of justice 'likely' occurred." These reviews are carried out by the Department of Justice, although requests for reviews are rare. In the five years between 2013 and 2017 only 12 applications per year were made to the Minister, but that number increased to 18 completed applications in 2018 (Department of Justice, 2018a). If a claim of innocence is supported, it is reviewed by the Minister of Justice, who can order a new trial or appeal, or refer the matter to the provincial court of appeal—although the process often takes years. Commissions of inquiry, by contrast, investigate the factors that led to wrongful convictions and are intended to prevent further wrongful convictions. Most people proven to have been wrongfully convicted receive some sort of monetary compensation, and a review of Canadian cases reveals that these amounts have varied between $105,000 and $10 million (Campbell & Denov, 2016, p. 238).

Tony Bock/Toronto Star via Getty Images

Roméo Phillion of Ontario served almost 32 years in prison before his murder conviction was overturned.

Even today in some remote Canadian settlements the police might pass through town only once or twice a month—suggesting that informal social control can regulate most wrongdoing in these places. One of the limitations in our knowledge, however, is that we simply do not know how these communities "self-regulate" and whether it is because of consensus, fear of letting down one's friends and family in a close-knit community, or some individuals in these communities ruling through fear and intimidation. These informal approaches, however, do not work very well in cities, where citizens tend to be anonymous and might not be very concerned about what others think of them.

Last, two methods of understanding the operations of justice systems were introduced: the due process and crime control approaches. After reviewing that section, most readers will find that they identify with one of these models. Understanding these competing perspectives gives us a framework to make sense of criminal justice. Throughout the chapters that follow, readers will be exposed to a number of ideas that might challenge their viewpoints about justice, being tough on crime ("lock criminals up and throw away the key"), and the limits to due process protections ("it is better to let ten guilty individuals walk free than to imprison an innocent person").

MYTH OR REALITY

Crime, Justice, and Offenders: Myths and the Media

Most of our ideas about crime, criminals, and the operations of the criminal justice system come from watching television or films, or from the websites we browse. The news accounts we see on television are often based on violent crimes such as murder, which rarely occur. Few of us are interested in the types of crimes that occur most often such as shoplifting and other minor thefts or when somebody fails to show up for their court date, which comprises about one-fifth of all criminal charges. In analyzing the television news industry, Kerbel (2018) observes that "if it bleeds, it leads" because the public is fascinated by murder, bloodshed, and mayhem. The trouble with the overrepresentation of violent crime is that watching news reports makes the public believe that violent crime is widespread and that we have a high risk of being victimized.

There are some other shortcomings about the content of the news accounts we receive. One that often frustrates criminologists is that these reports are often very short and seldom tell the audience the entire account of what occurred, which can mislead viewers. Crime is a complex social problem with multiple causes, and responses to crime are often complex and difficult to understand, especially when most news accounts are only a minute or so long. Thus, the messages we receive can over-simplify these complex problems. This problem can be compounded on internet blog sites when only one position is presented.

After 2017, Donald Trump and other US politicians raised the issue of "fake news," by which they mean news accounts that are biased or inaccurate. In Canada, publishing false news that results in harm is against the law; section 181 of the *Criminal Code* states that "Every one who willfully publishes a statement, tale or news that he knows is false and that causes or is likely to cause injury or mischief to a public interest is guilty of an indictable offence and liable to imprisonment for a term not exceeding two years."

The entertainment media is also guilty of misleading the public about crime and justice to make their programs more interesting. Britto, Ruddell, and Jones (2019) analyzed the content of two popular Canadian television police dramas, *19-2*, a series set in Montreal that ran from 2014 to 2017, and *Rookie Blue*, a series depicting the duties and lives of Toronto police officers,

which ran from 2010 to 2015. As in most crime dramas, violent crimes such as murder, sexual assault, robbery, and assault were highly overrepresented compared to their actual rates in these cities. Officers in these programs seldom responded to the social service challenges that represent most of police work. These shows also reinforced the dangers of police work, and in a single season the actors would draw their firearms more than a typical Montreal or Toronto officer would in their entire career. A more serious issue is that police officers in these programs regularly committed violations of suspects' *Charter* rights, which could lead viewers to think that these violations are acceptable and normal police conduct (Britto et al., 2019).

The public is also fascinated by true crime stories. An entire television network—Investigation Discovery, which has been called "the murder network"—was founded in 2008 and produces about 500 new true crime programs every year. Fallon (2018, para. 7), who studies the media, reports that "Investigation Discovery has consistently been the most-watched cable network among women aged 25 to 54. Not Lifetime, not the Hallmark Channel, not HGTV."

Actress Missy Peregrym starred in the Canadian police drama *Rookie Blue*, which ran 2010–2015. Surette (2015, p. 59) observes that "in every subject category—crimes, criminals, crime fighters, attorneys, correctional officers, and inmates; the investigation of crimes and making of arrests; the processing and disposition of cases; and the experience of incarceration—the media construct and present a crime-and-justice world that is opposite the real world."

Canwest/Entertainment One/Shaw Media/Thump/Kobal/Shutterstock

Career SNAPSHOT

Victim Advocacy

When we think about working in the justice system, our first thoughts are often about careers as police or correctional officers. There are, however, a diverse number of career opportunities that support the activities of the criminal and youth justice systems. These jobs often operate in the background and few of us will interact with these officials. Crime victims in the past often received poor or dismissive treatment by the police, courts, and corrections. The treatment of victims has improved, thanks in part to support from individuals working within victim services agencies. Although these careers can be fulfilling, they can also be emotionally taxing. These jobs typically require a bachelor's degree in the social sciences or in social work.

Profile

Name: Heidi Illingworth
Job title: Federal Ombudsman for Victims of Crime
Employed in current job since: October 2018
Present location: Ottawa, Ontario
Education: BA (Honours) Law with a concentration in criminology and criminal justice, Carleton University

Background

I have extensive experience in community-based victim services, advocacy, and academia. Prior to my appointment as Ombudsman, I spent 20 years in front-line service delivery for victims of serious crime and interpersonal violence. I served as the executive director of the Canadian Resource Centre for Victims of Crime for more than 11 years, where I developed a number of resources to support victim-service providers, as well as individual victims of crime and their families. I was also very fortunate to develop curriculum and serve as a part-time professor in the Victimology graduate certificate program at Algonquin College for seven years.

Work Experience

Office of the Federal Ombudsman for Victims of Crime
I was honoured to be appointed to serve as Federal Ombudsman for Victims of Crime in October of 2018. Together with my team, we provide direct service to victims, such as information and referrals to services offered by other levels of government, we investigate complaints against federal agencies, and we make recommendations to the federal government that bring positive change for victims in the criminal justice system. Our vision is to see every victim across Canada treated with compassion and respect and provided with the information, support, and services they need to help restore their health and well-being.

In 2007, the Government of Canada created the Office of the Federal Ombudsman for Victims of Crime to serve as an independent resource for victims in Canada. The ombudsman's role is to ensure the federal government meets its commitments to promote access to existing government programs and services, and to identify and explore systemic and emerging victim issues. The office operates at arm's length from the federal departments responsible for victim issues, namely the Department of Justice and the Department of Public Safety.

Canadian Resource Centre for Victims of Crime (CRCVC)
I started working at CRCVC after my third year in university, and became its executive director in 2007. Each day working for a tiny, charitable organization dedicated to survivors of violence was very meaningful and profound. I was able to support survivors in the aftermath of traumatic experiences like intimate-partner violence, sexual violence, and homicide. As a result, I learned that too many women in Canada live in fear of current or ex-partners, and escaping violence is not easy, especially where children are involved.

For me, the best part about working in victim services as an advocate was being able to effect positive change. I worked to support people who faced incredible personal hardship, but I also advocated for systemic changes to services, policy, and programs that operated too bureaucratically or without sensitivity to the lived experiences of victims. Finding gaps in various systems and proposing solutions is work that requires patience but is also very fulfilling.

One of my powerful career experiences at CRCVC was accompanying the mother of a murdered child to meet the killer face-to-face in prison. It was an incredible honour to be present as a support person and to witness the dialogue between these parties. The victim's mother was able to express how deeply the crime affected her family, as well as her determination to hold him personally accountable, to ensure that he will never harm anyone else. She did not forgive the offender, but this restorative justice encounter

Continued

allowed her to let go of some of the anger she held on to for many years. Such emotional experiences take a toll and, as a young person starting out in the field, I did not anticipate this level of impact, nor did my schooling properly prepare me for it. I have learned how to cope with the trauma my work exposes me to through training and professional development opportunities, and I remain healthy enough to continue in this field.

Advice to Students

I recommend that students interested in working with people affected by crime and violence, whether in policy work or direct victim services, seek out one of the academic programs offering specialized graduate studies in victimology. Many of these programs require an undergraduate degree in social work and/or criminology as a prerequisite for admission.

In addition to academic preparation to work in this field, you should also consider ensuring that you are adequately prepared mentally and emotionally to withstand the demands such work entails. This means developing coping mechanisms and a support network to help deal with stress.

It is also very important to have volunteer experience. Try volunteering with a local victim services program, as they offer intensive training to volunteers that will prepare you for what to expect and how to assist victims of crime. As with other jobs in the criminal justice system, many victim-service agencies are police-based and require applicants to have clean background checks in order to be involved.

REVIEW QUESTIONS

1. What are the differences between summary offences and indictable offences? How do these classifications differ from *malum in se* and *malum prohibitum*?
2. Describe the main goals of the justice system.
3. What are the three components of the criminal justice system? How are they related to each other?
4. How do the concepts of discretion, filtering, and sequencing help us to explain how the number of people in the "criminal justice funnel" decreases?
5. What is the main difference between informal and formal social control?

DISCUSSION QUESTIONS

1. Compare and contrast the due process and crime control models. Which model do you think has the most public support?
2. What factors might explain the provincial differences in cases of alleged wrongful convictions?
3. Of the goals of the justice system, which one do you feel is the most important? Why?
4. Why is it important that the government regulate *mala prohibita* acts?
5. Of the three components of the justice system, which is the most important in ensuring that everybody is treated in a just and fair manner?

INTERNET SITE

Juristat publications are produced by the Canadian Centre for Justice Statistics, a division of Statistics Canada. The articles provide the most up-to-date information on crime in Canada and on the operations of Canada's adult and youth justice systems.
https://www150.statcan.gc.ca/n1/en/catalogue/85-002-X

CASES CITED

Canada (Attorney General) v Bedford, 2013 SCC 72, [2013] 3 SCR 1101

R v Stinchcombe, [1991] 3 SCR 326

▲ RCMP Sgt. François-Olivier Myette explains the dismantling of an international money laundering network during a 2019 news conference in Montreal. How do you think Canada's levels of crime compare to the rest of the world? What might account for the differences between countries? (Photo credit: the canadian press/Ryan Remiorz)

Crime in Canada

LEARNING OUTLINE

After reading this chapter, you will be able to

- Describe the five major types of crime
- Explain the differences between "crimes in the streets" and "crimes in the suites"
- Describe the three measures of crime commonly used in Canada
- Describe why traffic enforcement is important for saving lives
- Explain how urban crime and rural crime differ

Do White-Collar Criminals Deserve Harsher Sentences?

Our ideas about crime and victimization often focus on "crimes in the streets," including criminal activities where victims have lost property or experienced violence in public places. These street crimes are often carried out by individuals who have addictions or mental health problems and come from marginalized populations. By contrast, there has generally been less interest in crimes such as fraud and theft committed by people who are widely trusted, such as the managers of retirement funds, and who tend to be well-off and educated. We call these white-collar offenders: individuals who are self-employed or work for governments or corporations and engage in financially motivated crimes. Once convicted, they are seldom treated very harshly by the justice system.

In some cases the justice system or government departments that regulate investments do not seem very serious about collecting the fines or restitution imposed on white-collar offenders. One example is the case of Michael Lathigee and Earle Pasquill, who defrauded 700 investors for $21.7 million, and were expected to return the stolen money to investors and each pay a $15 million fine. Although the crimes occurred in 2008, it took until 2015 for the fines to be levied by the British Columbia Securities Commission

(BCSC), and by January 2018, they had not made any payments to the Commission. This lack of payment was not unusual: A review of BCSC files showed they collected only two per cent of $510 million in fines between 2008 and 2017 (Hoekstra, 2018). Are things any different in the rest of the country? Robertson and Cardoso (2018) carried out an investigation for the *Globe and Mail* newspaper on the Canadian securities industry and found that over $1.1 billion in fines had not been collected. They also found that one of every nine people convicted of white-collar crime went on to commit additional frauds.

Most white-collar criminals are highly educated first-time offenders with no criminal histories who represent little risk of violence. As a result, their crimes are often punished with fines, which are routinely ignored by these offenders. Writing for *The Lawyer's Daily*, Burns (2018) says that the low fine-collection rate is not due to a lack of enforcement, but rather is because most of them lack the money to pay their debts. We might ask what happens when someone on probation for vehicle theft (as one example) is unable or unwilling to pay their fine, and whether white-collar criminals and those found guilty of vehicle theft should receive the same treatment.

white-collar offenders People who engage in financially motivated, non-violent crimes.

Critical Questions

1. What message is sent to the public when the theft of $21.7 million can be settled by imposing a fine that is never collected?

2. Does imposing a relatively minor punishment for white-collar criminals deter others from committing similar crimes?

3. It has been said that "the rich get richer and the poor get prison." Based on the results of the investigations reported above, do you agree with that statement?

INTRODUCTION

Before we explore how justice systems respond to crime, we first have to understand the different types of crime and examine the amount of crime that actually occurs. This can be accomplished by reviewing current crime statistics that provide a snapshot of what is happening today as well as by looking at long-term trends to see whether crime rates are increasing or decreasing. Understanding the nature of crime is important for developing effective crime-reduction strategies. It is also useful to look at the issue of crime severity and how the volume and seriousness of crimes differ across the country. One of the challenges of describing crime in a nation as large as Canada is that there are places with very high levels of crime as well as communities where serious offences rarely occur. The workload and activities of the police, courts, and corrections will be shaped by the number and severity of offences that occur.

There are various sources of information on crime rates, public perceptions of crime, and the operations of the justice system. The most up-to-date and comprehensive source on Canadian crime topics is the series of profiles published each year by the Canadian Centre for Justice Statistics (CCJS), which is renowned for its data quality, relevance, and accuracy (Statistics Canada, 2018b).

CCJS researchers report on the number of offences and the total severity of all crimes reported to the police in Canada. In a report for the CCJS, Perreault (2015, p. 40) examined the 2014 General Social Survey (GSS) results and found that only about one-third of crimes are ever reported to the police. Few minor offences, such as the theft of inexpensive items, are reported because of the modest loss and the belief that the police cannot solve those crimes, but even some victims of serious offences do not involve the police.

In addition to describing the nature of crime, this chapter also provides a brief overview of how crime impacts our lives. Not only are victims harmed by crimes, but the fear of encountering crime influences our activities, such as whether we decide to walk alone after dark or stop at a convenience store if there is a group of noisy people loitering outside. In addition to reducing our quality of life, the threat of crime can lower property values and also the decisions of businesses. The Canadian Broadcasting Corporation (2011), for example, reported that Air Canada would no longer place its employees in downtown Winnipeg hotels because of concerns over its employees' safety and risk of being victimized. Altogether, the total cost of all crime in Canada, including pain and suffering, is estimated to be over $80 billion annually (Easton, Furness, & Brantingham, 2014, p. 96).

Canadian Centre for Justice Statistics (CCJS) An organization operated by Statistics Canada that produces reports on crime, offenders, victims, and the operations of the justice system.

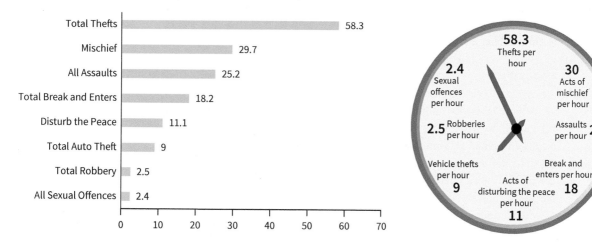

FIGURE 2.1   Offences Reported to the Police, Number per Hour, Canada, 2016

Source: Adapted from Statistics Canada (2018). Evaluation of the Canadian Centre for Justice Statistics Program (2011-2012 to 2015/2016). Ottawa, ON.

Although serious crimes capture most of the attention of the media and politicians, they are relatively rare: In 2017, for example, there were 660 homicides in Canada, or slightly less than two per day (Beattie, David, & Roy, 2018). Less serious offences occur more frequently, and Figure 2.1 shows the total number of offences reported to the police per hour in Canada in 2016. Theft is the most common offence reported to the police, followed by acts of mischief (such as vandalism), minor assaults, and break and enters. Serious offences such as robbery and sex crimes occur less often.

FIVE TYPES OF CRIME

Although hundreds of offences are defined in the *Criminal Code*, most researchers focus on a limited number of crimes that pose the highest risks to public safety or that reduce our quality of life the most. Crimes can be categorized into five broad groups: (a) crimes against the person, (b) property crimes, (c) crimes of the powerful, (d) organized crime and gangs, and (e) antisocial behaviour.

Crimes Against the Person

Crimes against the person, also referred to as violent crimes, contribute to fear and reduce our quality of life, as the possibility of being victimized sometimes prevents us from engaging in activities that we would otherwise do, such as taking a walk after dark. In this section, we define the four main types of violent crime: homicide, sexual assault, robbery, and assault.

Homicide

According to section 222 of the *Criminal Code*, "A person commits homicide when, directly or indirectly, by any means, he causes the death of a human being." Although this definition seems fairly straightforward, the act of homicide can be considered not culpable or culpable. Non-culpable homicides are not considered offences, such as when a doctor or nurse medically assists a terminally ill patient in ending their life, the guidelines for which are defined in section 241 of the *Criminal Code*. Culpable homicide, by contrast,

is considered an offence and includes murder, manslaughter, and infanticide. Murder refers to acts meant to cause death or bodily harm likely to cause death, and the *Criminal Code* further distinguishes between first-degree murder—a planned and deliberate act—and second-degree murder, which is a deliberate act that was unplanned.

Section 234 of the *Criminal Code* defines manslaughter as culpable homicide that is not murder or infanticide. Manslaughter is considered to be either an unlawful act (an illegal act) that was not intended to cause death, such as a driver involved in a street race that results in a fatal crash, or criminal negligence, which is an act that "shows wanton or reckless disregard for the lives or safety of other persons" (section 219). One example of manslaughter is a case where a contractor operating a poorly maintained backhoe with nonfunctional brakes collided with an employee, resulting in a fatality (*R v Scrocca*, 2010).

Sexual Assault

Although homicide is one of the most accurately reported offences, sexual assault is among the least reported given the reluctance of many victims, both female and male, to report their victimization to the police. Additionally, police are more likely to label sexual assault cases as 'unfounded' than other violent crimes, which, until the changes to reporting unfounded cases in 2016, meant fewer reported cases were recorded in police statistics. Allen and McCarthy (2018, p. 6) define sexual assault acts as:

- Sexual assault level 1: involves minor physical injuries or no injuries to the victim.
- Sexual assault level 2: includes sexual assault with a weapon, threats, or causing bodily harm.
- Aggravated sexual assault level 3: this results in wounding, maiming, disfiguring, or endangering the life of the victim.

Some people are at higher risk of victimization. While the total number of police-recorded level 1 through 3 sexual offences decreased somewhat between 2012 and 2016, the number of sexual assaults

---

homicide
When someone causes the death of another person.

first-degree murder
A planned and deliberate act that results in death.

second-degree murder
A deliberate but unplanned act that results in death.

unlawful act
An act that is not authorized or justified by law.

criminal negligence
An act that shows reckless disregard for the lives or safety of other people.

sexual assault
An assault of a sexual nature, including assaults committed by individuals of the same sex or assaults committed against one's spouse.

Race, Class, and Gender

Infanticide: Do Laws Established in 1948 Reflect Justice Today?

Although it rarely occurs, the crime of infanticide—the murder, by a female person, of her newly born infant—can challenge our ideas of justice. On the one hand, we realize that the women involved in these crimes throughout history have often been socially isolated and struggled with mental illness. On the other hand, the sentences imposed on them can often seem minimal, such as the probationary sentence imposed on a Montreal woman convicted of a 2017 infanticide (Feith & Quan, 2018). The *Criminal Code* mitigates punishments for women convicted of infanticide "if at the time of the act or omission she is not fully recovered from the effects of giving birth to the child" (section 233), and "every female person who commits infanticide is guilty of an indictable offence and liable to imprisonment for a term not exceeding five years" (section 237). Some have questioned whether the punishments reflect the seriousness of these crimes, especially when there is more than one victim, and Kay (2014) said the minor punishments imposed in these cases amounted to "an open season on unwanted infants." Advocacy organizations, on the other hand, say that removing the infanticide offence from the *Criminal Code* would subject women to harsh punishments that are inappropriate given the challenges they face (Women's Legal Education and Action Fund, 2014).

So what are the facts today? These crimes rarely occur; only 26 such offences were recorded by Statistics Canada (2018c) between 1998 and 2017, and there was only one between 2010 and 2016, although most publicized cases involved more than one victim.

Prior to 1948, these acts were classified as murder and women convicted of this crime could face the death penalty. Back then, women had fewer options and supports than they do today, as birth control was less reliable, abortion was illegal, and the stigma of out-of-wedlock births was greater (many women committing these crimes were young and unmarried). As a result, juries were often unwilling to convict women for this offence, as the punishment generally didn't fit the circumstances surrounding these crimes. So the infanticide offence was introduced with the mitigated sentence.

Things have changed in the past 70 years, and some argue that a mitigated punishment no longer makes sense, as women today have many more services as supports available to them. Still, Kramer (2006, p. 2) observes that "sometimes the women kill their newly born babies because they have been raped or otherwise coerced into sex by male employers, relatives, co-workers, or boyfriends. The women usually conceal and/or deny their pregnancies, give birth alone, and then dispose of the body of the baby." The Women's Legal Education and Action Fund (2014) points out that "young, socially isolated and otherwise marginalized women, who commit the offence often in desperate and tragic circumstances, should have access to the reduced culpability offence."

So, how can we manage these rare cases and see that justice is served? It might depend on how you define justice. Appellate courts in Ontario (*R v LB*, 2011) and Alberta (*R v Borowiec*, 2015) ruled that women who killed their infants were not guilty of first- or second-degree murder. The Supreme Court, in the *R v Borowiec* (2016) case, upheld the existing 1948 infanticide law, and this decision will stand for the foreseeable future.

against children increased by 74 per cent during the same time, and increased another 8 per cent in 2017 (Allen, 2018). Keighley (2017) notes that some of this increase may be due to changes in the way that these offences are defined and counted (which is a common problem when comparing any type of information over a number of years). Keighley notes, however, that crimes against children, like other sexual offences, are undercounted and some are reported years after they occur. Most often it is the people we trust who victimize children; for example, the Canadian Centre for Child Protection

MYTH OR REALITY

Stranger Danger

Most of the public's knowledge about the justice system comes from watching television and films, and many of the messages that we receive from the media are misguided or wrong. One commonly held view is that most violent crimes are carried out by strangers. But is that view correct? Homicide is considered the most serious crime, so it is well-reported to police, and the CCJS produces an annual report of homicides in Canada.

Figure 2.2 shows the accused–victim relationship for the 443 homicides in Canada in 2017 where the relationship was known. The figure shows the likelihood of being murdered by an acquaintance (32.4 per cent), a family member (31.1 per cent), a partner from a criminal relationship (13.4 per cent), or an intimate partner (5.7 per cent), compared to the risk of being harmed by a stranger (17.5 per cent). Do these findings change your perception of "stranger danger"?

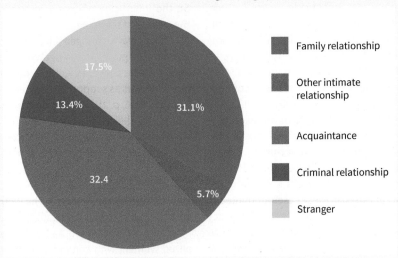

FIGURE 2.2 Homicides by Accused–Victim Relationship, Canada, 2017
Source: Adapted from Beattie, David, and Roy (2018)

robbery
An act of theft that also involves violence or the threat of violence.

assault
A crime of violence that can range from a relatively minor act (level 1, also called common assaults) to a serious crime resulting in severe bodily harm (level 3).

(2018, p. 9) found that school personnel committed sexual offences against almost 1,300 students between 1997 and 2017. Moreover, the CBC reports that at least 222 coaches involved in amateur sports had been convicted of sexual offences in the last 20 years (Campigotto, 2019, para. 1).

Robbery

Robbery is considered a crime against the person because it involves a threat or the use of violence to carry out a theft—even if the victim is not physically harmed. Sentences for robbery can be severe, including life imprisonment. Robbery is primarily an urban crime and is eight times more likely to occur in an urban area than in the countryside (Francisco & Chenier, 2007). Justice system personnel are generally very concerned about robberies because neighbourhoods and cities with high robbery rates tend to have higher murder rates (United Nations, 2014)

Assault

Assault is the most commonly reported violent crime, and over 230,000 of these offences were reported to the police in 2017. Similar to the classification of sexual offences, assaults are classified into three types, with level 3 (aggravated assaults) being the most serious. Statistics Canada (2018c)

These findings about victim–offender relationships vary somewhat by age. Burczycka and Conroy (2018, p. 70) report that 59 per cent of child and youth victims of family violence were victimized by a parent, but that as children age, they are more likely to be victimized by acquaintances, peers, and strangers. Some of our fears about victimization do not match reality. Older Canadians, for example, are often fearful of crime, but their age group is least likely to be victimized (Hayman, 2011; Perrault, 2015; also see Figure 2.3), and of those who are, one-third are victimized by a family member such as a child, spouse, or sibling (Burczycka & Conroy, 2018, p. 82).

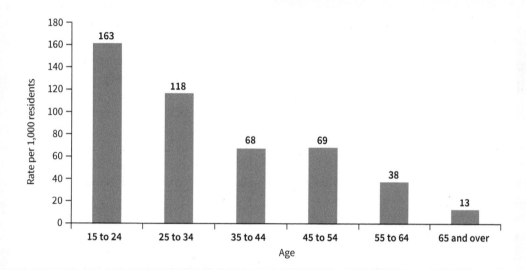

FIGURE 2.3 Violent Victimization Rate per 1,000 Residents by Age Group, 2014

Source: Adapted from Perreault (2015)

reports that about 70 per cent of these reported assaults were level 1 offences, followed by level 2 (22 per cent) and level 3 (1.5 per cent) crimes. About five per cent of all assaults were committed on peace officers, and there were about 2,000 "other" assaults, such as criminal negligence causing bodily harm, in 2017 (Statistics Canada, 2018c).

Property Crimes

While violent crimes receive most of the public's attention, it is far more likely for us to be victims of property offences. The three types of property offences commonly reported to the police are break and enter, theft of a motor vehicle, and theft not involving a motor vehicle (commonly reported as being either over or under $5,000). The crime clock in Figure 2.1 shows there is about one break and enter every three minutes and a vehicle theft every seven minutes. Although minor thefts are common, few are reported due to the modest losses, whereas break-and-enter offences and vehicle theft are more likely to be reported since the damages involved are often much greater. In addition, offences involving a greater loss must be reported to the police in order for the victims to receive insurance payouts. The following discussion provides working definitions of the three major types of property crimes.

adriaticfoto/Shutterstock

Robbery is considered a crime against the person because it involves a threat or the use of violence to carry out a theft—even if the victim is not physically harmed. There were almost 23,000 robberies in 2017 (Allen, 2018).

Break and Enter

break and enter When an individual breaks into a residence or business, usually with the intent to steal items.

Although a common public perception is that most break-and-enter offences involve breaking into homes, Coughlan, Yogis, and Cotter (2013) observe that these offences can involve other structures such as businesses. Even though these acts are considered to be a property crime, they can have a devastating psychological effect on some victims, who may experience feelings of violation after someone intrudes in their home and goes through their belongings.

Motor Vehicle Theft

motor vehicle theft The theft or attempted theft of a land-based motorized vehicle.

Motor vehicle theft refers to the theft or attempted theft of a land-based motorized vehicle and does not include boats or aircraft. In 2017 there were about 85,000 motor vehicle thefts in Canada (Allen, 2018). Altogether, automobile theft accounted for about $1 billion in property losses, which increases the cost of insurance for all motorists.

theft Taking another person's possessions without his or her consent.

Theft

identity theft When an individual obtains another person's information in order to commit offences such as fraud or forgery.

Theft is taking another person's possessions without his or her consent, and thefts under $5,000 are the most commonly reported crimes. Technology has changed the impacts of theft—particularly when it comes to identity theft, which involves "acquiring another person's signature, bank account number, Social Insurance Number, passport number, or other personal information for the purpose of committing one or more offences, such as fraud or forgery" (Coughlan, Yogis, & Cotter, 2013, p. 158). Identity theft has become commonplace as offenders realize that it can be profitable and that they are at little risk of being arrested (Goodman, 2015; Police Executive Research Forum, 2018). The Canadian Anti-Fraud Centre (2018) reports that there were almost 5,000 complaints about fraud per month between 2016 and 2018. Many of these offences were internet-based, and Statistics Canada (2018c) reports the number of cybercrimes reported to police increased by more than half (58 per cent) between 2014 and 2016. While there is a direct financial loss to identity theft, it can take years for some victims to restore their credit and when asked about the impact of identity theft on their credit, three-quarters said it was severely distressing (Identity Theft Resource Center, 2017).

Crimes of the Powerful

Much of the public's attention is focused on street crimes such as violent and property offences. Less consideration has been paid to the crimes of the powerful, which Kauzlarich and Rothe (2014) define as occupational and organizational crimes; Reiman and Leighton (2017) call these offences "crimes in the suites." Occupational crimes are committed by workers for their own benefit in the course of their employment. These offences are called white-collar crimes because these individuals tend to be well-educated or hold professional positions. Most occupational crimes involve offenders defrauding their own company or customers, such as accountants who steal from their employers, or employees who lie on their expense accounts. Individuals in professions may also engage in unethical conduct or crimes, such as doctors who carry out unnecessary surgeries or accountants who mismanage their clients' funds for their own gain. Most governments, at some point in their histories, have also engaged in state

A Closer Look

Auto Theft

There are some differences in the types of vehicles stolen across Canada. The Insurance Bureau of Canada (2019) reports that of the top five vehicles stolen in Alberta, all were trucks, whereas there were only two trucks on Ontario's top-five list in 2018 (see Table 2.1). These comparisons remind us that even though the number of offences might be similar, there can be significant differences across the country within specific types of crime. The motives for property crimes such as auto theft also vary. Tremblay and Sauvetre (2013, p. 169) studied young car thieves in Montreal and classified them into two groups: jockeys (who stole vehicles to sell them for profit) and joyriders, who took cars for fun. While joyriding sometimes results in collisions or police chases, the jockeys who steal vehicles for profit have a greater impact on the total number of thefts in a city as they treat their efforts as a business rather than a thrill-seeking act.

Hodgkinson, Andresen, and Farrell (2016, p. 50) researched vehicle thefts in Vancouver and found that while the number of stolen autos decreased by 84 per cent between 2003 and 2013 for the entire city, there were several **hot spots** where these offences were more likely to happen. In 2003 the highest number of thefts occurred in the richest neighbourhoods, but by 2013, the hot spots had moved to the Downtown Eastside, an area with high rates of poverty and crime. These researchers speculated that one reason for this change was that the downtown area had a higher proportion of older vehicles that lacked the chips in keys that make newer cars more difficult to steal. Linning, Andresen, Ghaseminejad, and Brantingham (2017) also found there was an element of seasonality in British Columbia's vehicle thefts—they tended to increase when temperatures were very low or high. This finding is no surprise to police in prairie cities where thefts increase in very cold weather when drivers leave their cars unattended to warm up. The problem was so bad in Calgary that police initiated Operation Cold Start, a public education campaign to reduce the number of stolen vehicles (Schmidt, 2018).

TABLE 2.1   Top Five Vehicle Thefts, Alberta and Ontario, 2018

Alberta Vehicle Thefts	Ontario Vehicle Thefts
1. 2006 Ford F250 (Truck)	2004 Chevrolet/GMC Tahoe/Yukon (SUV)
2. 2006 Ford F350 (Truck)	2006 Chevrolet/GMC Silverado/Sierra (Truck)
3. 2007 Ford F350 (Truck)	2003 Chevrolet/GMC Tahoe/Yukon (SUV)
4. 2004 Ford F350 (Truck)	2007 Ford F350 (Truck)
5. 2005 Ford F250 (Truck)	2003 Chevrolet/GMC Suburban/Yukon XL (SUV)

Source: Adapted from Insurance Bureau of Canada (2019)

street crimes Violent, property, and public order offences that are contrasted against crimes of the powerful (such as white-collar crimes).

occupational crimes Offences that are committed by individuals for their own benefit in the course of their employment.

white-collar crimes Non-violent crimes that are committed for monetary gain and include acts of corruption.

hot spots Areas where a high volume of crimes occur (e.g., near rowdy bars).

or political crimes, especially during the settlement of new colonies, and particularly related to the treatment of Indigenous peoples in those lands.

Occupational crimes result in high financial losses for organizations. Price Waterhouse Coopers (2018) surveyed Canadian businesses and found that 55 per cent of them reported losses due to theft, fraud (a form of deception that causes injury to another person), and cybercrimes in the previous two years. The number of businesses reporting these losses is increasing and these crimes can have significant costs. Why does this matter? These crimes affect everybody, because higher costs are passed along to customers. These offences also have a direct impact on these firms by reducing employee morale, harming business relations, and negatively affecting the companies' reputation.

Organizational crimes are offences committed by businesses or employees to increase profits to benefit their organization. Examples of organizational crimes include bribery (e.g., paying government officials who award a contract

organizational crimes Offences committed by employees of legitimate businesses that are intended to increase profits or otherwise benefit the organization.

sirtravelalot/Shutterstock

price-fixing
When business owners engage in a conspiracy to reduce competition or to keep prices of a product or service artificially high.

Occupational crimes are committed by workers for their own benefit in the course of their employment. These offences are called white-collar crimes because most of these offenders are well-educated or hold professional positions.

to a business), corporate fraud, price-fixing, the sale of faulty or unsafe products, tax evasion, and environmental crimes. SNC-Lavalin, one of Canada's largest engineering firms, has been accused of fraud and corruption in contracts with Libya in 2015, although the case was still before the courts in 2019, which shows how slowly these cases move through the justice system (Connolly, 2019).

With respect to environmental crimes, Volkswagen issued cash settlements to about 20,000 owners of Volkswagen, Audi, and Porsche vehicles and paid a $2.5 million civil penalty for cheating on emissions tests on diesel vehicles sold in Canada (Layson, 2018). The American justice system, by contrast, treated company officials more harshly for their roles in the emissions scandal, and imprisoned one Volkswagen executive for seven

years (CBC, 2017). These offences are widespread; Price Waterhouse Coopers (2018, p. 12) found that one-quarter of the companies surveyed had been asked to pay a bribe and that some Canadian firms lost opportunities because their competitors paid bribes to officials. Because of these crimes, consumers and taxpayers pay higher costs while unethical corporations increase their profits.

Corporate crimes have direct and indirect costs. Most of these offences have a direct cost to consumers, such as overcharging the public for goods or services. Some business leaders have engaged in conspiracies to avoid competition, which is called price-fixing and occurs when prices are kept artificially high. In these cases, consumers are unaware that a crime has been committed because the losses to any one customer are usually fairly small, though these losses can add up over a period of years or over numerous organizations. For corporations, price-fixing is very profitable when millions of consumers pay higher prices over a long period of time.

Price-fixing offences are difficult to investigate and prosecutions are rare. One extreme price-fixing scandal occurred when several Canadian supermarket chains colluded with bread producers to keep the cost of bread high between 2001 and 2015. Markusoff (2018) calculated that a family buying one loaf of bread per week paid $400 more than they should have over that period of time. One supermarket chain has offered consumers a $25 gift card to compensate them for their losses, although that's a small cost of doing business, especially when few victims will ever apply for the gift card. Several law firms have launched class action lawsuits to obtain settlements on behalf of all Canadian residents, although this case is unlikely to be heard by any court for years.

The public also experiences indirect losses from corporate crimes. When corporations evade taxes, for example, all taxpayers pay more to fund government services. Corporations can also engage in environmental crimes such as illegally dumping toxic materials in the countryside. Once these sites are discovered, taxpayers are also responsible for the cleanup costs. Pierson and Bucy (2018) observe that trade fraud, where importers inaccurately label shipments of goods coming into the country,

The Canadian Press/Justin Tang

Marie Henein (right, shown here with her client Vice-Admiral Mark Norman, who was accused of breach of trust, but was later cleared) is one of Canada's most prominent criminal defence lawyers. When asked about the need for defending white-collar criminals, she said, "I don't think [white-collar crime enforcement is] a growing market for criminal lawyers at all. And that is because white-collar crime requires resources to investigate and prosecute and, though there have been attempts to improve that, it's not done with really the same force that you have in the United States. So, our large white-collar crime prosecutions are few and far between." (Cited by Macnab, 2018, para. 3). Henein's comments raise the question of why officials in Canada's justice system fail to investigate and prosecute white-collar criminals.

results in the loss of billions of tax monies. They observe that "Realistically, there is little chance these modern-day smugglers will be caught. Countries' borders are too vast, the volume of imports too great, global customs inspections too porous, and law enforcement resources too few for effective monitoring or deterrence of trade fraud" (Pierson & Bucy, 2018, p. 4). Reducing the number of these crimes is important because every dollar lost to this fraud is added to the taxes each of us pays.

Unsafe worksites can also result in employee injuries and deaths, and again the costs are borne by taxpayers as the cost of health care and compensating injured workers increases. Bittle (2016,

p. 333) observes that workplace injuries and deaths due to unsafe working conditions have historically been considered "accidents," but he argues that these acts should instead be considered "serious matters deserving of criminal justice attention." How serious is the problem? In 2017, 920 workers were killed on the job, which is about 40 per cent more than the number of homicides (Association of Workers' Compensation Boards of Canada, 2018, p. 240).

Other indirect costs to society include harms from the sale of counterfeit, defective, or unsafe products. General Motors, for example, continued to sell certain models of cars it knew had faulty ignition switches, and it is estimated that the defective vehicles resulted in 124 deaths and hundreds of injuries (Gardner, 2018).

Counterfeit items also threaten public safety, one example being when a British Columbia woman died after taking counterfeit medications (CTV News, 2017). Even food is routinely misrepresented, by diluting it with cheaper alternatives (such as putting corn syrup in honey, or mixing vegetable oil into olive oil). Dangerfield (2018) reports that the six most commonly faked foods in Canada are things we commonly consume: olive oil, parmesan cheese, seafood, honey, coffee, and saffron (a spice). A study led by a University of British Columbia researcher found that about one-quarter of seafood products sold in Vancouver stores and restaurants were mislabelled and were actually products of lesser value or quality,

genocide
The systematic killing of a population, such as an ethnic, racial, religious, or national group.

crimes against humanity
Violent acts and persecution of a civilian population that are committed as part of a systematic attack.

with 91 per cent of the fish labelled as snapper (the fish most likely to be mislabelled) actually being something else (Hu, Huang, Hanner, Levin, & Lu, 2018). While few of these acts result in serious harm they do cheat the public and over time many of us are victimized by these offences.

While very few Canadian corporate criminals are ever prosecuted or imprisoned, in September 2018 the federal government introduced legislation so that corporations could enter into deferred prosecution agreements with prosecutors that "require the accused to cooperate with law enforcement, acknowledge their wrongdoing, give up any profits gained from the wrongful act, and pay a monetary fee; in exchange, the accused no longer faces the prospect of conviction" (Dentons Canada LLP, 2018). Phrased another way, by entering into these agreements, corporations can pay a fine to avoid prosecution. While the government believes that this approach will increase compliance with the law, it further reduces the risk of incarceration for white-collar criminals. In February 2019, Jody Wilson-Raybould, the former Minister of Justice and Attorney General, revealed that she had been pressured by officials in the Prime Minister's Office to change the decision of federal prosecutors to prosecute SNC-Lavalin rather than entering into one of these agreements.

Some of the most destructive crimes of the powerful are state or political crimes such as genocide, which is the systematic killing of a population, such as a racial, ethnic, religious, or national group. Genocide includes the Second World War holocaust where millions of Jews, Roma, Jehovah's Witnesses, members of the LGBTQ community, and people with disabilities were killed as part of the Nazi government's attempt to reduce the number of people they considered racially or genetically undesirable. Crimes against humanity include genocide, and Coughlan, Yogis, and Cotter (2013, p. 84) define these crimes as "any of a number of acts (including murder, enslavement, torture, rape, apartheid, or persecution of an identifiable group) when committed as part of a widespread or systematic attack directed against any civilian population." One of the controversial interpretations of

The Canadian Press/Adrian Wyld

The issue of enforcing corporate crime became a political crisis for the federal government in 2019 after Jody Wilson-Raybould, the former Minister of Justice and Attorney General of Canada, alleged that she was unsuccessfully pressured to overturn the public prosecutor's decision to prosecute SNC-Lavalin, a large engineering firm, and instead pay a fine in a deferred prosecution agreement. The political independence of prosecutors in making decisions about prosecuting crimes is an important issue underlying the rule of law, which is a cornerstone of Canada's legal system (see Chapter 6).

the findings from the National Inquiry into Missing and Murdered Indigenous Women and Girls (2019) report was that the deaths of Indigenous women amounts to genocide. Given the definition presented by Coughlan, Yogis, and Cotter (2013), do you agree these murders were a genocide?

Critical criminologists argue that crimes are defined by the rich and powerful and that the police are used to control the poor and the middle class in order to protect the interests of the upper class. Critical criminologists contend that not enough attention has been placed on the crimes of the powerful and that these offences are not taken seriously (Reiman & Leighton, 2017). Mays and Ruddell (2019) observe that the 2008 financial crisis led to hardships experienced by hundreds of millions of people throughout the globe—including job losses, bankruptcies, the taxpayers' bailout of banks, and the loss of individuals' homes—and that no high-profile officials were ever punished for their involvement in the financial meltdown. As Will, Handelman, and Brotherton (2013, p. xiii) ask, "How did the movers and shakers of a world financial and economic system make the decisions they did, creating untold social harm to millions, and yet fail to be held accountable by our various governments?" Pontell, Black, and Geis (2014, p. 1) summed up the situation when they observed that the financial institutions were too big to fail, and their employees were too powerful to jail. Enforcement agencies, they contend, have often turned a blind eye to fraud.

critical criminologists Scholars who argue that justice systems are designed to maintain class relationships.

Organized Crime and Gangs

The general public typically does not spend much time thinking about the harms caused by members of organized crime. Few of us realize that

Kristoffer Tripplaar/Alamy Stock Photo

General Motors CEO Mary Barra testified before a Senate subcommittee on the failure of General Motors to recall vehicles that were known to have defective ignition switches that resulted in accidents and fatalities. In order to avoid criminal charges, General Motors was ordered to pay a fine of $900 million to the US government, and has paid out about $2.5 billion in personal-injury and wrongful-death claims to more than 400 individuals and families (Gardner, 2018). If corporate executives are not held criminally responsible for actions that result in deaths and injuries, would this deter them or other executives from criminal behaviour in the future?

a relatively small number of the individuals involved in criminal enterprises engage in a significant amount of crime. The Criminal Intelligence Service Canada (2014) estimates that there were 672 of these criminal organizations in Canada in 2013. Not only are organized crime groups commonplace, but they are also enduring: Schneider (2018) notes that organized crime in Canada dates back at least 400 years. Many traditional criminal organizations such as the mafia were established generations ago and have defied law enforcement interventions since their founding.

Organized crime offenders tend to be generalists, meaning that they engage in a broad range of criminal activities, including selling weapons, counterfeit items, antiquities or cultural artifacts, drugs (both illicit drugs and counterfeit prescription medications), endangered species,

gemstones, alcohol, cigarettes, firearms, illegally harvested timber, or even people who are forced to work in the sex trade. They may also participate in illegal sports wagering, environmental crimes (including the illegal disposal of electronic and radioactive waste), and financial crimes. Munch and Silver (2017, p. 14) found that over one-third of first-degree murders and over half of drug-related violations in Canada were related to organized crimes.

Many outlaw motorcycle gangs and street gangs fit the *Criminal Code* definition of a criminal organization, which is a group of three or more people who come together to commit one or more serious offences that are intended to result in a material benefit. In February 2014, the Hells Angels Motorcycle Club was designated as a criminal organization in Manitoba, and Bolan (2018)

Outlaw motorcycle gangs, such as the Hells Angels, have engaged in a considerable amount of crime. The Criminal Intelligence Service Canada (2014) reports that "organized crime poses a serious long-term threat to Canada's institutions, society, economy, and to individual quality of life."

reports that judges in Alberta, Ontario, and Quebec have made similar rulings. This label makes it easier for police to conduct investigations on these groups, and prosecutors are no longer required to prove they are members of an organized crime group each time they prosecute them. Although it is well-known that organized crime offenders and gang members are responsible for a considerable amount of crime, the "RCMP has sidelined more than 300 investigations, mostly into organized crime, as it redirected more than $100 million to its national security squads" after the murder of two soldiers in Ontario and Quebec in 2014 (Freeze, 2017, para. 1). This example again shows how political priorities can influence the operations of justice systems.

Antisocial Behaviour

For the most part, the four types of crime that have been described present the greatest risk to personal safety or result in the most direct or indirect personal loss. While most antisocial behaviours—which we defined in Chapter 1 as objectionable conduct, such as being rude, rowdy, or drunk in public—do not pose much of a risk to the public, they make many people feel uncomfortable and reduce our quality of life: think about the last time you had an early morning class and you were kept awake by your neighbours having a loud party. Responding to these problems often takes a considerable amount of police time and resources, and the individuals engaging in these acts are usually well-known to the police.

The South Kesteven District Council (2018) in the United Kingdom identifies three categories of antisocial behaviour, and they are as applicable to Canada as they are to England. The first category is defined as personal and relates to a specific individual or group behaviour including aggressive, rowdy, and vulgar actions; intimidating groups taking over public spaces; public drinking or drug use; prostitution; panhandling; and street racing or aggressive driving. The second category is nuisance neighbours, including those who are noisy, intimidating, harassing, rowdy, engaged in vandalism, or not caring for their pets (e.g., letting

dogs run loose). The third type of antisocial behaviour is related to environmental conditions, such as graffiti, littering or illegal dumping (e.g., garbage on the street), vandalism, and arson. Although some of these acts are defined as offences in the *Criminal Code* or are violations of municipal bylaws, they are often handled informally by the police using warnings. The police in some cities, such as New York, have aggressively responded to this antisocial behaviour in the belief that if minor incivilities are addressed, serious crimes are reduced, but this strategy has fallen out of favour in most places.

MEASURING CRIME

Crime is difficult to measure accurately because most offences do not come to the attention of the police (e.g., an individual who drives a vehicle while intoxicated but arrives safely home). Even when there is an obvious victim—such as a student whose textbooks are stolen—few people report minor offences, because they know it is unlikely the thief will be caught. In order to determine the most precise indicator of crime in Canada, the CCJS uses three different measures: (a) the rates of reported crime per 100,000 residents, (b) the Crime Severity Index, and (c) surveys of Canadians to determine how many people have been victimized. Knowing how crime is measured and reported is important in our exploration of criminal justice, as we first have to know the nature and seriousness of the problem before we can develop crime-reduction strategies. The most important factor to consider is that the rates of crime and the Crime Severity Index are based on offences reported to the police and published in the Uniform Crime Reporting (UCR) Survey. The third measure, an indicator of victimization, is collected through the General Social Survey on Victimization, which is conducted every five years. The last survey was conducted in 2019, but there is a two-year lag before the results are published. The strengths and limitations of these measures are briefly described in this section.

Crime Rates from the Uniform Crime Reporting Survey

The traditional method of measuring crime is based on the rate of crime per 100,000 residents in the population. We use rates every day, such as when determining how many kilometres your vehicle can travel per litre of fuel or how many calories you can burn from walking on a treadmill for an hour. Rates enable us to make comparisons, and without that information, it would be very difficult to know the seriousness of a crime problem or how it differs between places or changes over time.

When we make comparisons of crimes, we often start with homicide because of the seriousness of the crime and because it is the most accurately reported offence. But, if we just report on the number of offences, we still don't know the extent of the crime problem. For example, in 2017 there were 46 homicides in Montreal and eight homicides in Halifax, but unless we take each city's population into account, we do not know which city is a more dangerous place. Figure 2.4 shows the homicide rates in selected Canadian cities and reveals that even though there were fewer murders in Halifax, it was a more dangerous place to live than Montreal based on the reported crimes

per 100,000 residents. So, how do these cities compare to the rest of the nation? In 2017 Canada's national homicide rate was 1.80 per 100,000 residents, which was similar to rates in the 1960s (Allen, 2018; David, 2017). Because we are using rates to describe the volume of murders, we can also compare with other cities across the globe, and the 2017 rates for London and New York were 1.2 and 3.4, respectively, which are both far below the rate in the city of Los Cabos, Mexico, which had a homicide rate of 113.3 people per 100,000 residents (Stow & Akbar, 2018).

There are some limitations to using crime rates, especially when the rates of similar offences are added together to make a single measure, such as the violent crime rate (which includes homicides, sexual assaults, robberies, and assaults). According to Wallace, Turner, Matarazzo, and Babyak (2009, p. 8), "The traditional crime rate is heavily influenced by fluctuations in high-volume, less serious offences. This is because each offence reported by police, regardless of its seriousness, carries exactly the same weight in calculating the crime rate." In other words, a common assault that results in minor injury counts the same as a murder if we're including them both in the violent crime rate.

Crime rates also fail to give us a very accurate picture of crimes occurring in small jurisdictions.

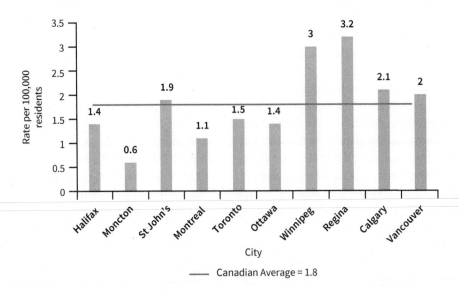

FIGURE 2.4 Homicide Rates per 100,000 Residents, Selected Cities in Canada, 2017

Source: Allen (2018)

A Closer Look

How to Calculate a Crime Rate per 100,000 Residents

Crime rates are calculated by multiplying the total number of crimes by 100,000 and then dividing that total by the population. Rates can be calculated for a city, a province, or an entire country. For example, the following formula and calculations were used to determine the homicide rates in Halifax and Montreal in 2017:

Formula: $\dfrac{\text{number of offences x 100,000}}{\text{population}}$

Halifax: $\dfrac{8 \text{ homicide victims x 100,000}}{431,721 \text{ (2017 population)}} = 1.4$

Montreal: $\dfrac{46 \text{ homicide victims x 100,000}}{4,148,023 \text{ (2017 population)}} = 1.1$

In a town of 500 residents, for example, if there was one murder in a year, the homicide rate would be 200 murders per 100,000 residents, or over 100 times the national average. Despite those limitations, crime rates are still used, especially for serious crimes such as robbery and homicide, enabling us to make comparisons between cities, provinces, and nations. The search for a method to more accurately depict the volume and seriousness of crime led to the introduction of the Crime Severity Index, which is a measure unique to Canada.

Canada's Crime Severity Index

In 2009, the CCJS introduced the Crime Severity Index (CSI), which measures the volume of crime reported to the police and applies a weight to

different types of crime so that the impact of more serious offences is better reflected. The weight assigned to each type of crime is calculated based on the average sentence imposed for the crime. Keighley (2017, p. 7) reports, "The more severe the average sentence, the higher the weight assigned to the offence, meaning that the more serious offences have a greater impact on the index. Unlike the traditional crime rate, all offences, including *Criminal Code* traffic violations and other federal statutes such as drug offences, are included in the CSI." Figure 2.5 shows the CSI for the same set of cities as reported in Figure 2.4, and Figure 2.6 shows the CSI by Canadian province. When it comes to the CSI, cities with the highest CSI also tend to have high homicide rates.

Crime Severity Index (CSI) A measure of the volume and seriousness of crime based on all *Criminal Code* and federal statute offences reported to the police.

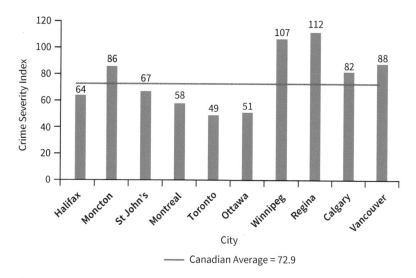

FIGURE 2.5 Crime Severity Index, Selected Cities in Canada, 2017
Source: Allen (2018)

violent Crime Severity Index
A measure of the volume and seriousness of all violent offences that includes homicide, all three levels of assault, robbery, sexual assault, uttering threats, forcible confinement/kidnapping, attempted murder, and criminal harassment.

non-violent Crime Severity Index
A measure that considers all crimes that are not included in the violent CSI category.

youth Crime Severity Index
A measure of the volume and seriousness of all crimes committed by youth between 12 and 17 years of age.

A COMPARATIVE VIEW

Interprovincial Variation in the Crime Severity Index

In 2017, the CSI for Canada was 72.9, and as shown in Figure 2.6, the western provinces were all above the national average. Allen (2018) reports how the CSI in the territories was also higher than the national average: Yukon = 189.3; Northwest Territories = 303.8, and Nunavut = 297.6. In addition to the overall CSI, the CCJS also reports a violent Crime Severity Index and a non-violent Crime Severity Index. These indices allow us to better understand the nature of crime in different jurisdictions. While Saskatchewan had the highest overall CSI, Manitoba led the nation in terms of violent CSI. A youth Crime Severity Index is also calculated to account for crimes committed by people between 12 and 17 years of age (see Chapter 11 on youth justice).

Both the crime rate and the CSI show a decrease in the number of offences reported to the police since the rates of crime peaked in the early 1990s—a pattern similar to what has occurred in the United States. Figure 2.7 shows that from 2002 to 2017, the total CSI decreased by almost one-third and the violent CSI dropped

by 16 per cent. According to these statistics, Canadians are now safer than they were years ago, at least when it comes to crimes reported to the police. There has been, however, an uptick in crime since 2014; some of the violent crime increase has been linked to gang activities (Beattie et al., 2018). When it comes to national statistics, most annual changes tend to be minor, although slight decreases or increases in the crime rate can add up over several years.

About 6 per cent of the Canadian population lives in the northern areas of the provinces or in one of the three territories (Allen & Perreault, 2015). Despite the relatively sparse population in northern Canada, the crime rates in these regions can be high. Allen and Perreault (2015, p. 8) state that "among the 50 police services that reported the highest Crime Severity Indexes (CSIs) in 2013, 32 were located in the Provincial North, 8 in the Territories, and 10 in the South." Although most of the crimes in the northern provincial regions and the territories are relatively minor (mischief, disturbing the peace, and theft account for almost 43 per cent of all offences in those locations), the homicide rate in 2013 was 1.3 per 100,000 residents in southern Canada, but 3.1 per 100,000 residents in the northern provincial regions, and 5.2 per 100,000 residents in the territories (Allen & Perreault, 2015).

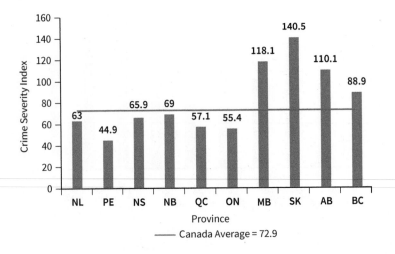

FIGURE 2.6 Crime Severity Index, Canada and the Provinces, 2017

Source: Allen (2018)

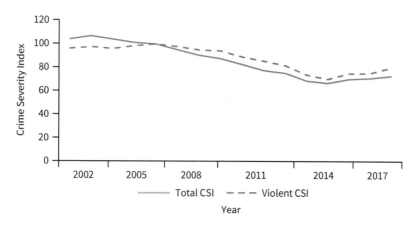

FIGURE 2.7 Total and Violent Crime Severity Index, Canada, 2002–2017
Source: Allen (2018)

In closing our description of crime severity, it is important to recognize that the activities of the police, courts, and corrections are driven primarily by minor offences that occur frequently. Figure 2.8 shows the percentages of the top 10 types of offences—in terms of volume—that were processed by adult courts in 2015/2016. The most common offences include theft (which includes motor vehicle theft), impaired driving, assaults, and crimes related to the administration of justice such as not complying with a court order or breaching the terms of one's probation. Altogether these 10 offences accounted for almost 70 per cent of all criminal matters. The most serious crimes are rare; robberies account for less than 1 per cent of all offences, and homicide offences account for about 0.1 per cent of all cases before the courts. These offences tend to be fairly stable over time and Miladinovic (2019) found that the top 5 crimes in 2017 were identical to the 2015/2016 offences.

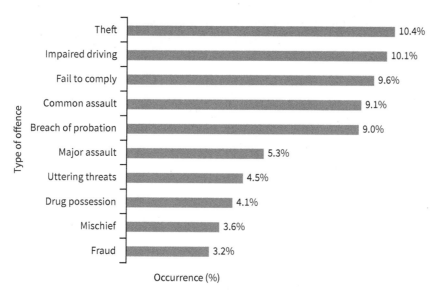

FIGURE 2.8 Top 10 Adult Court Offences, Canada, 2015–2016
Source: Maxwell (2017)

Jacob Lund/Shutterstock

Researchers report that minor offences, such as personal property thefts, rarely come to the attention of the police.

Victimization Surveys

Only a fraction of offences ever come to the attention of the police, so researchers developed a third way of estimating the number of offences that occur: by asking people whether they have been victimized in the previous year and if those crimes were ever reported to the police. Whether these studies were conducted in Canada or in other nations, levels of unreported crime are always higher than the levels of crime reported to the police. In Canada, this information on victimization is collected in the GSS every five years (the GSS on victimization was last conducted in 2019).

Some researchers refer to the difference between the amount of unreported and reported offences as the dark figure of crime. Perreault (2015) found that in 2014 about one-fifth of Canadians were estimated to have been victims of crime in the previous 12 months, which had decreased by about a quarter since 2004. Figure 2.9 shows that even serious offences, such as robberies and assaults, are reported less than half the time. Sexual assaults are the least reported offence, and Conroy and Cotter (2017, p.17) estimate that as few as 5 per cent of sexual assaults ever come to the attention of the police.

Scott (2015, p. 97) observes that "it is critical for anyone studying victims of crime to recognize that without the victim's courage to report a

dark figure of crime The difference between the amount of crime that occurs and the amount of crime that is reported to the police.

criminal act, very few criminals would ever be apprehended." Some victims are reluctant to contact the police because they fear retaliation or because the perpetrator is a family member or loved one whom the victims do not want arrested. Other victims believe their behaviours might have contributed to the offence, or they are embarrassed to go to the police, such as when a customer is robbed by a sex worker. Figure 2.10 shows the top seven reasons why people did not report their victimization. The reasons vary somewhat depending on the type of offence; a greater percentage of victims of a violent offence reported that fear of revenge prevented them from reporting a crime (18 per cent of violent crime victims compared to 5 per cent of property crime victims).

Limitations of Victimization Data

One of the strengths of the GSS victimization data is that it is based on a survey of 33,000 individuals (Perreault, 2015, p. 7). Although victimization data is a valuable source of information about crime, it also suffers from some limitations. For example, the survey is conducted every five years, which limits our knowledge, although patterns of victimization do not tend to change much over the short term at the provincial, territorial, or national levels.

Another limitation of Canadian victimization surveys is that only people aged 15 years and older are asked whether they were crime victims, while a review of CCJS data shows that children and youth are at high risk of violence. Ogrodnik (2010, p. 8) reports that the police-reported victimization rate for 12- to 14-year-olds was much higher than the adult victimization rate. Cotter and Beaupre (2014, p. 10) also found that people under the age of 15 have the highest rates of police-reported sexual victimization. In their analysis of victimization data Burczycka and Conroy (2017, p. 27) reported that one-third of Canadian adults had experienced physical or sexual abuse or had witnessed family violence as children. Those researchers also found that respondents of Indigenous ancestry and those who were gay, lesbian, and bisexual had higher overall rates of victimization.

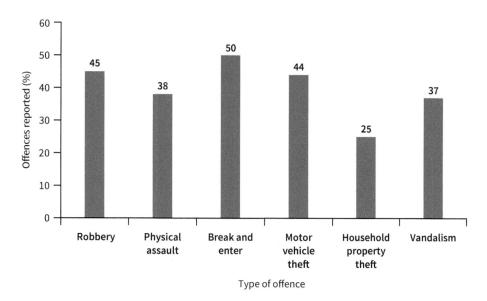

FIGURE 2.9 Percentage of Offences Reported to the Police, 2014
Source: Perreault (2015)

One crime that overwhelmingly affects young people and seldom comes to the attention of the police is cyberbullying. Holfeld and Leadbeater (2015) found that about one-fifth of grade 5 and 6 students across Canada had received text messages that were upsetting, and 12.1 per cent felt uncomfortable about content someone had posted on their online page or wall in the previous year. Riddell, Pepler, and Craig (2018) summarized the Canadian research on cyberbullying, and the most recent studies show that girls were more likely to be victimized than boys, youth aged 14 to 16 years were more vulnerable to victimization, and between 25 and 33 per cent of young Canadians have been victims of these acts.

Limitations of Police-Reported Crime Statistics

All of the measures of crime suffer from limitations that reduce their accuracy. The previous sections highlighted the fact that only a fraction of crimes are actually reported to the police. Yet, even when the police are notified of a crime, the offence might not be officially counted. Newark (2013, p. i) observes of the CSI that "in a case involving drug dealing, weapons, assault and flight from police by an offender on bail and probation, only what was deemed to be the 'most serious' offence would be reported." In addition, some police service policies make it difficult to report minor crimes (Moulton, 2013). For example, requiring a victim to come to police headquarters to file a theft report on an item with little value discourages many victims from reporting the offence.

Self-Reported Crime

Although records of police-reported crime and surveys of victims provide us with a picture of the crime problem, our knowledge is incomplete. An individual might, for example, carry a concealed handgun every day for a year and never come to the attention of the police. In order to gain a more complete understanding of crime, social scientists since the 1930s have asked members of the public whether they have engaged in crimes or other antisocial behaviours. The results of these self-report surveys increase our understanding about how much crime actually occurs. The information collected from these surveys also enables us to determine when individuals start committing offences, what types of offences they commit, and whether crime differs based on gender, race,

self-report surveys A type of survey where respondents answer questions about their attitudes, beliefs, or experiences, including being an offender or crime victim.

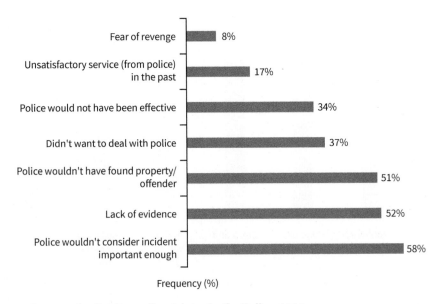

Fear of revenge — 8%

Unsatisfactory service (from police) in the past — 17%

Police would not have been effective — 34%

Didn't want to deal with police — 37%

Police wouldn't have found property/offender — 51%

Lack of evidence — 52%

Police wouldn't consider incident important enough — 58%

Frequency (%)

FIGURE 2.10 Reasons for Not Reporting Crimes to the Police, 2014

Source: Perreault (2015)

and age. The most comprehensive Canadian self-report studies have been conducted with surveys of students, including the National Longitudinal Survey of Children and Youth (NLSCY); the International Self-Report Delinquency Study (ISRD); and the Canadian Student Tobacco, Alcohol, and Drugs Survey (CSTADS). The CSTADS asks respondents about substance use (including illegal drug use), while the other surveys ask respondents about their involvement in crime.

The results of self-report studies generally find that many young people engage in crime: Fitzgerald and Carrington's (2011) analysis of the NLSCY found that about one-fifth of the 12- to 17-year-old respondents had committed a violent crime, about twice as many (37.8 per cent) had committed a property crime, and about one-fifth had used illegal drugs in the year prior to the survey. The CSTADS, by contrast, reports that in 2016/2017 over one-third (34.5 per cent) of grade 12 students across Canada had used marijuana in the previous 12 months and that older youth were more likely to have used amphetamines, cocaine, or prescription medications to "get high" in the previous year (Government of Canada, 2018). In one unusual self-report study Statistics Canada (2018a) used an online survey to ask Canadians

what they paid for marijuana prior to its legalization; the provincial and territorial differences are reported in Figure 2.11.

Self-report surveys increase our understanding of the hidden world of crime, delinquency, and drug use. Most of these surveys ask participants about their province of residency so that interprovincial comparisons can be made. One important factor to remember when looking at national or provincial results is that there is often a lot of variation within the provinces and territories and that averages always mask trouble spots (places with very high rates of crime, delinquency, or drug use) and more peaceful places.

REGULATING TRAFFIC: SHOULD BAD DRIVING BE A CRIME?

Most of us believe we are pretty good drivers and that other motorists are the real problem. While certain driving-related acts, such as impaired and dangerous driving, are considered *Criminal Code* offences, most people breaking traffic regulations, such as speeders, are violating a provincial statute, which is not a crime, and, if caught, they are given a citation that can be paid without a court

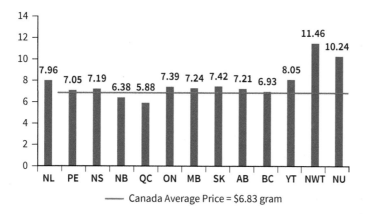

FIGURE 2.11 Self-Reported Price per Gram of Cannabis in the Provinces and Territories in February 2018.

Prior to the legalization of marijuana, Statistics Canada (2018a) asked Canadians what they paid for the illegal drug and over 17,000 people responded to the online survey: these individuals reported the average price for the nation was $6.83 per gram, although that price decreased somewhat to $6.51 (from a non-legal seller) after the drug was legalized (Statistics Canada, 2019). The legal price of marijuana is set at about $10 per gram in most provinces and taxes push that amount over $11. Do you think Canadians will buy the more expensive legal marijuana from a store or continue to buy it illegally from dealers at lower prices?

Source: Statistics Canada (2018a)

appearance. How serious is the problem of traffic safety? According to Transport Canada (2019) 1,841 people died in traffic crashes in Canada in 2017, which was 2.7 times the number of homicide victims. Not only are traffic crashes responsible for needless deaths, but for every fatal crash in 2017, there were about five collisions resulting in injuries requiring hospitalization and over 80 crashes where the driver or passenger was injured (Transport Canada, 2019). Traffic fatality rates are higher in Canada compared to other developed nations. A review of World Health Organization (2015) data shows that traffic fatalities in Canada are almost twice as high as in the United Kingdom and higher than in many European nations. Like many national averages, traffic fatality rates vary across the country, and the rate in Saskatchewan was more than two times higher than it was in Ontario in 2016. Figure 2.12 shows the differences in traffic fatalities across Canada.

So how can we reduce traffic fatalities? The main causes of traffic fatalities are impaired driving, speeding, not wearing seat belts, violating traffic rules at high-risk intersections (e.g., not coming to a complete stop before entering a highway), and distracted driving, such as talking on a cell phone or texting while driving. One question asked throughout this book is whether the justice

system is the best avenue for reducing these risky behaviours. With respect to prevention, public education campaigns, safer roads, driver training, and graduated driver licensing programs for new drivers have been successful in reducing traffic fatalities by 30 per cent between 2007 and 2016 in Australia (Department of Infrastructure and Regional Development, 2017, p. 54; Road Safety Education, 2015). A speed bump might be more likely to deter a driver from speeding than a police car parked on the side of the road.

Research shows that traffic enforcement saves lives. DeAngelo and Hansen (2014) analyzed what happened when 35 per cent of Oregon's highway troopers were laid off in 2003 due to a budget cut. In the years that followed, highway fatalities increased by 17 per cent and injury-causing collisions increased by 12 per cent. When these researchers compared collisions and fatalities in the surrounding states, there was no similar increase. DeAngelo (2018) also studied the impact of adding traffic enforcement units in Saskatchewan, and he found these efforts reduced fatalities and collisions.

Drinking and driving also contributes to fatalities, and over 36,000 criminal cases related to impaired driving were heard in adult courts in 2016/2017, making it one of the most common

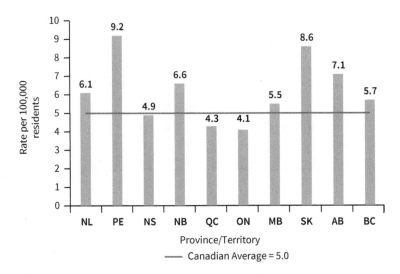

FIGURE 2.12 Traffic Fatalities per 100,000 Residents, 2017

Source: Adapted from Statistics Canada (2018)

offences (Miladinovic, 2019). While the number of these offences has been decreasing, this might be due to the introduction of new enforcement strategies. In British Columbia, for example, most suspected impaired drivers are managed through provincial traffic sanctions rather than *Criminal Code* violations. BC drivers failing a roadside breath test can have their driving privileges immediately revoked by the police, their vehicles impounded, and severe fines imposed. As these sanctions fall under a provincial regulation the standard of proof is lower than for a violation of the *Criminal Code*, and anybody punished using these provincial regulations does not receive a criminal record.

Mothers Against Drunk Driving (2018) estimate that alcohol or drugs were involved in over half of the people (55.4 per cent) killed in crashes in 2014. If their estimate is correct, more than twice as many people are killed each year due to the impaired operation of motor vehicles than from homicides. Again, there is some variation across the country. Perreault (2017) found that the average rates of impaired driving were higher in the countryside than in urban areas. One explanation for this is a lack of public transportation and taxi options, as well as the fact that drivers in rural areas are on the road for greater distances, which might increase their likelihood of getting into a collision.

There may also be a link between personality traits such as aggression and involvement in dangerous driving. In other words, people who are

Research shows that traffic enforcement saves lives. Although nobody is happy getting a ticket, traffic enforcement seems to be one of the best ways to get drivers to abide by traffic regulations. Some drivers, however, don't pay their fines. As one example, in November 2017 the Royal Newfoundland Constabulary caught a suspended driver who owed $158,000 in unpaid fines, although only a portion of those fines were related to driving (Canadian Press, 2017).

aggressive and violent toward others might also drive aggressively and their road rage can contribute to collisions (Waller, 2014). Willett (1964/2001) found a relationship between drivers who had been convicted of property and violent crimes and their later involvement in dangerous driving offences. A study carried out in Europe found that traffic fatalities are higher in nations where the residents are more aggressive and that an individual's criminal history may be a good predictor of involvement in fatal collisions (Castillo-Manzano, Castro-Nuno, & Fageda, 2015). A review of crash statistics from Australia conducted by Fleiter, Watson, Watson, and Siskind (2015) also showed that drivers with criminal records were more likely to get into crashes compared with those with no criminal history. Altogether, these findings suggest that people with criminal histories may be more dangerous on the roads than drivers without criminal records.

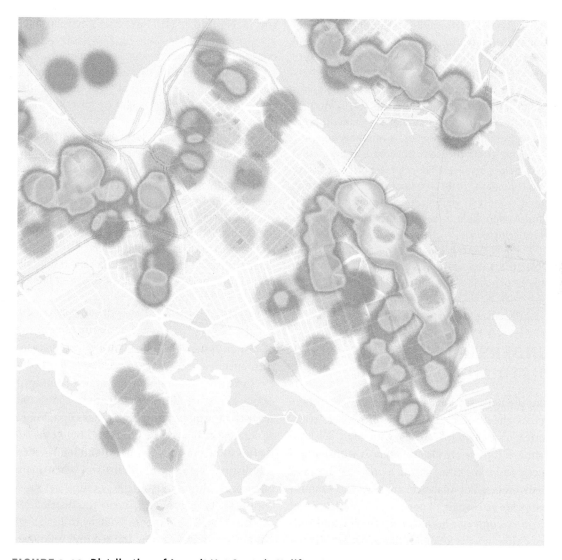

FIGURE 2.13 Distribution of Assault Hot Spots in Halifax, January to June, 2018

This map shows 859 assault offences reported to the Halifax Regional Police in the first six months of 2018. Places on a map with a high concentration of offences are called hot spots. Crime maps like this one show that crimes are not distributed randomly throughout a city, and are often concentrated in specific locations; not surprisingly, for example, many assaults occur near bars and taverns.

Source: David Hamp-Gonsalves; used with permission

A Closer Look

Rural Crime

Over 80 per cent of Canadians live in cities, and city dwellers today have fewer connections to the six million people living in rural areas than they did decades ago. Although a common perception is that rural life is quiet and peaceful, rates of crime in some rural places are higher than in the largest cities. The issue of rural crime was widely reported in the media in the Prairie provinces starting in 2016 after a series of high-profile violent offences. In response to the fear of crime both the Alberta and Saskatchewan governments announced funding to deploy more officers in rural areas. An Alberta politician said that "crime in rural Alberta is at epidemic proportions" (as cited by Corbella, 2018). According to the CBC, rural Saskatchewan residents were feeling frustrated and helpless given their isolation, a growing crime problem, and the lengthy time it takes before a police officer can respond to calls for help (Hamilton, 2018). A lack of recent information about crime and victimization, however, makes it almost impossible to say whether rural crime has actually increased.

Crime is overrepresented in rural Canada. Allen (2018, p.11) reports that although accounting for only 17 per cent of the national population, "police in rural areas reported 25 per cent of violent crime, 18 per cent of property crime and 24 per cent of other *Criminal Code* offences," and the "crime rate in rural areas was 30 per cent higher than in urban areas." With respect to the Prairie provinces, crime is 42 per cent higher in rural Manitoba than in the province's urban areas, 38 per cent higher in rural Alberta, and 36 per cent higher in rural Saskatchewan (Allen, 2018, p. 11). These interprovincial differences are reported in Table 2.2. This data raises the question of *why* rural crime rates are higher, and is it being committed by local residents, or are outsiders committing crimes in rural areas because they think their risks of being caught are lower?

Some types of crime rarely occur in urban areas. Agricultural crimes such as rustling (stealing cattle), wildlife-related offences, crimes against the environment (such as illegally dumping toxic waste), large-scale marijuana grow operations, and crimes committed in the name of the environment (e.g., environmentalists attacking oil pipelines) rarely occur in the city. Some rural crimes are identical to those taking place in cities, except the items targeted may differ, such as the theft of agricultural chemicals, machinery, fuel, or livestock in rural areas. In addition to

UNDERSTANDING CRIME DISTRIBUTION

The previous sections show that the CSI differs across the country: there are provinces, territories, and cities in Canada with high levels of crime. But there are also differences within provinces, and some cities within a province are safer than others. For instance, in 2017 the Ontario homicide rate was 1.38 per 100,000 residents; but there was only one homicide for Guelph and Sudbury although the homicide rate of 5.8 per 100,000 residents in Thunder Bay was over four times the provincial rate. One key question to ask is, why do these differences exist? Answering this and other important questions helps to direct the activities of justice system personnel in order to increase their effectiveness.

To further complicate our understanding of crime, there are differences in the volume and severity of crime even within cities. By taking a closer look at how crime is distributed, we realize that most crime does not occur randomly: there are distinct patterns in where and when many offences occur. To illustrate how crime can differ within a city, Figure 2.13 shows the distribution of assaults in Halifax from January to June 2018 (Hamp-Gonsalves, 2019). The red and yellow areas on the map show the highest concentrations of crime. A review of this map shows that even though there were places with high rates of crime, safe neighbourhoods are the norm.

TABLE 2.2 **Urban and Rural Crime Rates, 2017**

Province	Total Crime Rate per 100,000 Residents		Total Violent Crime Rate per 100,000 Residents	
	Urban	Rural	Urban	Rural
Newfoundland	5,185	5,765	1,386	1,228
Prince Edward Island	4,348	3,549	904	869
Nova Scotia	5,211	4,696	1,281	1,194
New Brunswick	5,618	4,373	1,299	1,203
Quebec	3,357	3,377	979	1,314
Ontario	3,810	3,703	824	987
Manitoba	7,964	11,309	1,521	2,933
Saskatchewan	10,138	13,829	1,445	3,118
Alberta	7,920	10,964	1,158	1,870
British Columbia	7,546	6,418	1,070	1,367
All provinces	5,051	6,210	990	1,532

Source: Statistics Canada (2018)

lacking information about the extent of rural crime, we have little knowledge about who commits these offences. While some property and violent rural crimes are committed by local residents, individuals from the cities also commit crimes in the countryside (Alberta MP Rural Crime Task Force, 2018).

SUMMARY

After reading this chapter, you will likely have gained a greater appreciation for the complexity of understanding crime. Although it is relatively easy to describe how crime differs across the country, explaining why this variation occurs is a more complicated matter. Generally, we know that crime is associated with a number of social problems, including unemployment, poverty, and substance abuse, and that it involves a high proportion of young males in the population. Often the highest levels of crime occur in places with the highest levels of concentrated poverty and marginalized populations. Knowing why crime varies by location is an important first step in developing crime prevention interventions. If, for instance, we find that crime is a result of poverty and marginalization, then tackling those conditions might be the best method of crime prevention. Most of the crime control strategies described in this book, however, are based on the efforts of the police, courts, and correctional personnel, who respond to crime after the act occurs.

Although there are limitations in our attempts to describe the true amount of crime, violent crime rates have generally dropped over the past two decades. Perhaps the best indicator of this is the homicide rate, which in 2014 was at its lowest level since the 1960s, although it has increased somewhat after 2015 (see Allen, 2018).

In fact, Canadians are almost twice as likely to be killed in an impaired driving crash than become a murder victim, and far more likely to die from a work-related injury than from an assault. Some forms of crime, such as identity thefts and other cybercrimes, however, are increasing (Identity Theft Resource Center, 2017).

While most of this book focuses on Canadian responses to antisocial behaviour and street crime, many critical criminologists argue that we are overlooking the crimes of the powerful, such as officials who commit crimes on behalf of corporations—the "crimes in the suites." We have all been victimized by paying higher prices for our goods and services, and if your family ate two loaves of bread a week from 2002 to 2014, they were swindled out of over $800 due to price-fixing (Markusoff, 2018). In addition, we all pay higher taxes due to the indirect costs of corporate crime, such as paying to clean up toxic dump sites or to cover the health care costs for those injured in workplace accidents or injured from unsafe products. While these crimes affect all of us, seldom are white-collar criminals prosecuted or imprisoned. When it comes to corporate criminals like the ones described in the case study that introduced this chapter, Reiman and Leighton (2017) observe that "the rich get richer and the poor get prison." After reading the chapter, do you agree with them?

Career SNAPSHOT

Crime Analysis

Many students are fascinated by issues of crime and justice, although they have less interest in working directly with the public or with offenders. Careers in crime analysis, research, education, and program evaluation may be good alternatives for those students. Often the individuals working in these careers are employed by police services, as well as by provincial or territorial governments or the federal government. Their duties are often related to the collection and analysis of crime data and mapping these results. Some duties of crime analysts may be related to examining law enforcement practices and evaluating their effectiveness. These jobs typically require at least a bachelor's degree and additional graduate training in crime analysis, geographic information systems (for crime mapping), and statistics.

Profile

Name: Amy Balfour
Job title: Manager, Strategic Services, Regina Police Service
Employed in current job since: 2009
Present location: Regina, Saskatchewan
Education: MA, Justice Studies, University of Regina; Graduate Certificate, Tactical Criminal Analysis, Justice Institute of British Columbia (JIBC)

Background

As a child and young adult, I was always asking "why?" Although most children grow out of this stage, I did not. Asking questions about human behaviour propelled me to also ask tough and sometimes uncomfortable questions. As a student, I was intrigued by what drives people to do certain things and even more fascinated about why some people make bad decisions. In my personal life, I was always drawn to helping people and lending an ear. I began working with youth in a correctional facility and became overwhelmed by the callousness that some of the youth expressed. After learning about their life histories, I became even more dedicated to helping children. I spent several years working with children and youth with abusive, traumatic, and violent histories.

I learned from working with youth that hope is always possible and extraordinary things can happen when people commit to change. So, I did just that. While working as a server and bartender at a local restaurant, I focused on bettering my education and people skills. I learned that I could keep asking the question "why?" to find solutions to problems. My niche in analytical work came as I built upon relationships I gained through practicum placements in my field of study. Relationships with police officers, parole officers, and youth workers landed me some of my first jobs, and I am forever in debt to many of them who are leaders and innovative thinkers today.

Work Experience

Born and raised in Regina, I have dedicated my time working to reducing victimization and harm to people at risk. I graduated from the University of Regina in 2005 with a Bachelor of Arts degree in Human Justice and a Master of Arts degree in 2008; my graduate work focused on youth involved in the sex trade. More recently, I have completed a graduate certificate in Tactical Criminal Analysis from JIBC to further understand the role intelligence plays in my daily work.

I have been employed at the Regina Police Service since 2009. As a certified law enforcement planner and as a member of the International Association of Law Enforcement Planners, the International Association of Crime Analysts, the Canadian Criminal Justice Association, and the International Association of Law Enforcement Intelligence Analysts, I continue to be dedicated to improving police practice through evidence-based research and analysis.

As the supervisor of administrative, strategic, and tactical crime analysis, as well as policy development, I have learned the challenges associated with effective and actionable crime analysis. Social media, technology, and increases in access to data have become so much a part of our daily lives that it is easy to get caught up in an overload of information. Technological advances emerge every year, but our training on how to navigate those tools can quickly fall behind. The best part about being an analyst is being able to turn vast amounts of information into intelligence to help investigators in deployment and conviction. One of the benefits of being an analyst is the ability to work with front-line members like patrol as well as investigative units like Major Crimes on critical and sensitive cases, while making a difference by applying sound analytical skills to operational initiatives.

Advice to Students

Obtaining work as a crime analyst can be challenging. Some people tell me that they are interested in the work but cannot pass the background checks or a polygraph ("lie detector"). Avoiding negative peers and criminal activity will improve your ability to pass background checks and progress through the hiring processes. Education in criminal justice, police studies, psychology, and sociology will provide you with the basics to understanding the role of law enforcement and justice in society. Also, taking some specialized courses on statistics, crime mapping, and critical thinking will make you a more competitive job candidate.

REVIEW QUESTIONS

1. What are three different ways of reporting crime in Canada?
2. Describe how organizational crimes differ from street crimes.
3. What are the five different forms or classifications of crime?
4. What are some key differences between urban and rural crime?
5. What are some of the limitations of the three different measures of crime?

DISCUSSION QUESTIONS

1. The *Criminal Code* section on infanticide was introduced in 1948 when conditions for women were much different than they are today: Should the mitigated sentence (a five-year maximum) apply to women who kill their children today, or can these rare events be better managed outside the criminal justice system, such as mental health treatment? Why or why not?
2. Despite the substantial costs to society, why has there been so little priority placed on investigating, prosecuting, and punishing those involved in occupational or organizational crimes?
3. Should impaired driving, which results in about twice as many deaths as murders in Canada, be prosecuted more harshly, or are there other ways to reduce these crimes?

4. What are the strengths of using reports of victimization rather than offences reported to the police to understand the full extent of crime?

5. What are some possible explanations for the differences in levels of crime between cities and provinces highlighted in this chapter?

INTERNET SITE

Those who are interested in learning more about corporate crime and who question whether the poor are at a disadvantage in the justice systems of developed nations will enjoy reading Reiman and Leighton's (2017) work, which is summarized on the following website.

http://www.paulsjusticepage.com/reiman.htm

CASES CITED

R v Borowiec, 2015 ABCA 232
R v Borowiec, 2016 SCC 11, [2016] 1 SCR 80

R v LB, 2011 ONCA 153
R v Scrocca, 2010 QCCQ 8218

3 Controlling Crime

LEARNING OUTLINE

After reading this chapter, you will be able to

- Describe the six main crime control philosophies
- Identify the social and political reasons for the differential use of incarceration
- Describe various factors that shape our ideas about crime and justice
- Explain how crime control philosophies shape our notions of justice and the operations of justice systems

Vigilante Justice, Drunk Driving, and the Long Road to the Supreme Court of Canada

Richard Suter was charged with impaired driving causing death after a May 2013 incident in which he crashed his sport utility vehicle into an Edmonton restaurant's patio, killing two-year-old Geo Mounsef, who was eating with his family. Suter refused to give a breath sample based on the instructions of his legal aid lawyer, although it turns out this was poor advice. Suter was granted bail and pled guilty in June 2015 to refusing to provide a breath sample, a crime that is punishable by life imprisonment when a crash leads to a death.

While awaiting sentencing Suter was abducted from his home by three men impersonating police officers and he was blindfolded, driven across town, beaten, and had his thumb cut off. According to the Canadian Broadcasting Corporation (2015), Geo Mounsef's mother, Sage Morin, "pleaded with supporters to let the courts deal with Suter," and said, "justice for Geo will not come in the form of violence."

In June 2015, Edmonton Police charged Steven Vollrath with kidnapping, aggravated assault, possession of a weapon, and impersonating a police officer for his role in the vigilante attack on Suter. In November 2016 Vollrath received a 12-year prison term for what the judge described as "kidnapping for a heinous reason—to extract vengeance by inflicting serious harm" (Johnson, 2016, para. 10). Suter maintains that he had no prior relationship with Vollrath,

and the two co-accused kidnappers have never been identified or charged.

What became of Richard Suter? He was sentenced in December 2015 to four months in jail, and given a five-year driving prohibition for refusing to provide a breath sample to police after the crash. One week after the sentencing, the Crown appealed the sentence, saying that it was "demonstrably unfit" and "not proportional to the gravity of the offence" (Blais, 2015). Suter served his four-month custody sentence, but the Alberta Court of Appeal agreed with the prosecutors and extended Suter's sentence to 26 months, and he was returned to custody.

Suter's lawyer appealed his sentence extension to the Supreme Court of Canada, saying that the Alberta Court of Appeal made errors interpreting the law. The Supreme Court heard Suter's case in October 2017, and in June 2018 they reduced his sentence to time served (about 10 months) and upheld the 30-month driving prohibition. The Supreme Court said that getting bad advice from a lawyer and being the victim of vigilante justice should mitigate an individual's punishment. The man convicted of kidnapping and assaulting Suter will serve a much longer prison sentence (12 years) than the 10 months Suter served behind bars. The Supreme Court hearing on the *R v Suter* case can be viewed at: http://www.cpac.ca/en/programs/supreme-court-hearings/episodes/53464557.

vigilante justice
The unlawful practice of a person or group of people who take the law into their own hands without legal authority to do so.

Critical Questions

1. What are some of the reasons why acts of vigilantism—or vigilante justice—may occur?

2. Should a person's sentence be adjusted because they acted on bad legal advice? Why or why not?

3. Why should victims of vigilante justice be given shorter sentences?

INTRODUCTION

The responses of the police, courts, and correctional systems are not uniform throughout Canada. Instead, there are differences in the ways that suspects, wrongdoers, victims, and members of the public are treated. These differences are expected given that Canada is a very diverse country in terms of its multicultural population, its two official languages, the prosperity of different regions, and the varied histories of justice systems. Even factors such as whether a victim or person accused of committing a crime lives in a rural or urban area can influence how they are treated by the personnel working in the justice system.

In Chapter 1, crime control strategies were described as being the result of political decisions, and there is not always agreement on the best way to approach the crime problem. Few of our ideas for addressing crime are new, and the debate over the best ways to control crime and punish wrongdoers has gone on for centuries. As these debates change, so do our definitions of crimes, priorities for crime control, and methods for investigating and punishing wrongdoers. There are six main crime control philosophies, and being able to describe them is important because they shape the operations of the police, courts, correctional systems, and ultimately how the public and offenders are treated by justice systems. For example, a police service that believes in deterring impaired drivers may invest heavily in late-night roadside checks and develop call-in programs where citizens can report impaired drivers. Provinces that have a more rehabilitative orientation, by contrast, may place more convicted impaired drivers in treatment-oriented programs rather than in correctional centres and may invest in public education campaigns. All jurisdictions blend a number of these approaches in response to the crime problem, and most political leaders consider the public's opinions about priorities for reducing crime.

In the following sections, we'll look at six crime control philosophies, and identify a number of factors that influence our ideas about crime. Although most of these philosophies of crime can be traced back hundreds or even thousands of years, they are still fiercely debated and each is important to understand, because they all shape the way that we treat individuals involved in the justice system today.

CRIME CONTROL PHILOSOPHIES

Packer's (1968) crime control and due process models provide us with a framework to organize the six philosophies that have influenced our responses to crime. The first three philosophies described in this section—retribution, deterrence, and incapacitation—are related to the crime control model and focus on the offence. By contrast, the concepts of restitution, rehabilitation, and restorative justice are more closely aligned with the due process model and a focus on the individual who committed the crime. These six crime control philosophies can be identified in section 718 of the *Criminal Code*, which describes the following goals of sentencing:

(a) to denounce unlawful conduct;
(b) to deter the offender and other people from committing offences;
(c) to separate offenders from society, where necessary;
(d) to assist in rehabilitating offenders;
(e) to provide reparations for harm done to victims or to the community; and
(f) to promote a sense of responsibility in offenders, and acknowledgement of the harm done to victims or to the community.

It is important to acknowledge that none of these six approaches exists in a pure form and that they are blended to reflect the characteristics of the community and the circumstances of the case, including proportionality, which is identified in the *Criminal Code* as a fundamental principle of sentencing. The issue of sentencing is addressed in depth in Chapter 8.

"Tough on Crime" Practices: Retribution, Deterrence, and Incapacitation

Getting tough on crime is not a new approach to justice. In the early colonial settlements of pre-Confederation Canada, corporal punishments were common, and the Correctional Service of Canada (2014a) reports the following:

> People who broke the law suffered harsh consequences, often in public. They could be whipped (called "flogging") or branded (marked on the skin with burning hot metal); they could be put in pillories (wooden frames with holes for a person's head and arms) or stocks (wooden frames with holes for the individual's arms and legs) and made to stand for hours or days on display out in the open. Other times, convicts were simply sent away, transported or banished to other countries and left to fend for themselves.

Wrongdoers were also put to death. The first executions in the colony that would eventually become Canada occurred more than four centuries ago, and prior to contact with the English and European explorers, Indigenous peoples also used a range of punishments including the execution of wrongdoers or their banishment, which would, in effect, be a death sentence given the importance of community in the members' mutual survival. From the 1500s to 1800s there were few due process protections for people suspected of crimes, and punishments were swift and severe. This reliance on physical punishment was consistent with European practices imported by colonists. The use of incarceration is a relatively new way of responding to crime: It was not until 1835 that the first Canadian penitentiary opened in Kingston, Ontario.

Retribution

Retribution is one of the most straightforward crime control philosophies and is based on the notion of taking revenge on wrongdoers. Also referred to as retributive justice, it has been a leading crime control philosophy throughout history, and it can be traced back almost four thousand years to the Code of Hammurabi. These early laws stressed vengeance, and the principle of retribution is often expressed by the notion of *lex talionis*, or the biblical principle of "an eye for an eye, a tooth for a tooth." Lengthy prison terms or corporal and capital punishment are often associated with retribution.

The expression *just deserts* is also used to describe retribution by suggesting that wrongdoers will get "what's coming to them" and that the punishment should reflect the seriousness of the crime. The retributive approach leads to questions about how much punishment an individual deserves, and this is the issue of proportionality, which suggests "that penalties be proportionate in their severity to the gravity of the defendant's criminal conduct" (von Hirsch, 1994). The question of whether the punishment fits the crime is posed in the Moussa Sidime case highlighted in the "A Closer Look" box later in this chapter. Retribution may underlie some of our punishments, but today it is seldom used to justify a sentence.

Deterrence

Many of the activities of the police, courts, and correctional systems are based on the principle of deterrence, which is the belief that criminal behaviours can be discouraged and prevented by punishing offenders. Deterrence can be broken into specific deterrence (also known as individual deterrence) and general deterrence. Specific deterrence is based on the notion that the pain or consequences of being punished will deter an offender from committing further crimes. General deterrence, by contrast, is the belief that after witnessing or learning about another person's punishment, the general population will be less likely to violate the law. Both of these ideas are popular, but most research has not found a clear relationship between deterrence efforts and crime reduction.

Although the idea of deterring crimes through the activities of the police, courts, and corrections is attractive in theory, it is difficult to apply

---

retribution
A crime control philosophy that involves taking revenge on the offender often through harsh punishments, as expressed by the biblical principle of "an eye for an eye, a tooth for a tooth."

just deserts
An expression used to suggest that a punishment reflects the seriousness of an offender's crimes ("they got what they deserved").

deterrence
The use of punishment to discourage wrongful behaviour.

Library and Archives Canada, Acc. No. 1989-466-61

This drawing is from a public hanging in Montreal in 1837, when the death penalty was commonly used. There were few due process protections for people suspected of crimes, and punishments were swift and severe.

this approach in today's complex world. Some scholars propose that deterrence is more likely to work when punishments are applied with swiftness (also called celerity), certainty, and severity (Nagin, 2013). There are a number of barriers to those three requirements. First, potential offenders must know that their behaviours are actually crimes. However, because so many laws and regulations exist, we do not always know whether our actions are crimes, especially when it comes to *mala prohibita* acts (see Chapter 1). Second, few individuals think they will be caught as they believe they are better at avoiding detection than others (Collins & Loughran, 2017). Third, the structure of the Canadian justice system works against swift punishments because the system is founded on the principle of providing due process protections to people accused of committing crimes. As a result, it may be years before a criminal case is resolved and the individual is sentenced, and appeals can add years to that process. One way to examine this issue is to look at the **case processing time** (also called the charge-processing time), which is the time between the arrest and the resolution of the case. Miladinovic (2019) found that the median case processing time was about four months, and Maxwell (2017) notes that the length increased substantially for multiple and serious offences, and only half of homicide offences were resolved within 471 days (p. 37). The Richard Suter case that started this chapter took over five years from the day the offence happened until the Supreme Court decision was published, which shows that our justice system can move very slowly.

Another limitation of the deterrence approach is that punishments for most crimes are not very severe, especially for first-time and non-violent offenders. Miladinovic (2019, p. 8) found that 44 per cent of Canadian adults found guilty of a crime were sentenced to probation, and whereas over

case processing time The time between an individual's arrest and when the case is resolved, such as when a sentence is imposed or the case is stayed. Also called charge-processing time.

one-third were incarcerated, the median sentence for these individuals was only 30 days (that total does not count time served on remand). Only about 3 per cent of people found guilty are sentenced to prison for two years or longer, and the sentences of many provincial or federal inmates are reduced if they earn an early release or are granted parole.

Altogether, these examples show that the criminal justice system is not set up to do a very good job of deterring the public from becoming involved in crime. There is not much certainty of being punished, as only a portion of crimes reported to the police result in an arrest, and less than two-thirds of the accused are found guilty (see Miladinovic, 2019). In addition, the system's ability to process a case does not lead to swiftness, and few offenders receive severe sentences. Given these facts, deterrence is unlikely to work very effectively, although some provinces still rely on this approach to confront specific crimes. In order to deter drunk driving, for example, Prince Edward Island courts sentence over 90 per cent of persons convicted of their first drunk driving offence to short custody sentences. Writing about PEI's deterrence-based approach, Anthony Doob, a highly regarded University of Toronto criminologist, notes that "people—whether they are considering stealing something, hitting someone, or drinking and driving—are not generally put off by potential penalties. They are more concerned with getting caught" (as cited in Yarr, 2018).

Incapacitation

This approach to crime control is based on the notion that if offenders are held apart from society (incapacitated), they are not able to commit any further crimes in the community. On the face of it, incapacitation seems to make sense, but there are some limitations to this approach. We have long known that a relatively small number of prolific or high-volume criminals are responsible for a large number of offences (Greenwood & Abrahamse, 1982; Wolfgang & Tracy, 1982). Commenting on the arrest of a Kelowna suspect, Leslie Smith (2018), an RCMP spokesperson, says that "In any given community prolific offenders account for 80 per cent

of all crime committed." A cross-national study found that active or "high-frequency" adolescent offenders were present in all 30 developed nations they examined (Rocque, Posick, Haen Marshall, & Piquero, 2015). These cases are common to Canada as well, and Revell (2018) described how the Alberta RCMP laid 25 *Criminal Code* and two *Highway Traffic Act* charges against a 34-year-old man who already had six outstanding arrest warrants for 72 criminal charges. These cases are not uncommon, yet even when we apprehend individuals with multiple convictions, the punishments they receive are not very harsh: for example, a Regina offender with nearly 100 convictions for break-and-enter offences was sentenced to three years in custody on a break-and-enter charge (Polischuk, 2015).

Supporters of the crime control model argue that by imprisoning these very active criminals—called serial or chronic offenders, career criminals, or habitual offenders—our crime rates would plummet. This is the idea behind selective incapacitation, which refers to locking up the individuals who pose the highest risks. Selective incapacitation was the basis for introducing "three strikes" laws in the United States in the 1990s that imposed lengthy prison sentences for people with multiple convictions (based on baseball's "three strikes and you're out!"). Many states today, however, are slowly dismantling their three-strikes programs because they found that holding non-violent prisoners for decades was costly and did not have the crime control results they had hoped for (Mays & Ruddell, 2019).

In order to get tough on repeat homicide offenders, the *Protecting Canadians by Ending Sentence Discounts for Multiple Murders Act* was enacted in 2011. This change to the *Criminal Code* enabled judges to sentence individuals who were involved in multiple murders to serve their life sentences consecutively, where the second sentence would start after the first 25-year sentence ended. Prior to that change, offenders would serve their life sentences concurrently, which means they could apply for parole after serving 25 years no matter how many people they killed. For example, Alexandre Bissonnette, the shooter who killed six men

incapacitation A crime-reduction strategy based on the idea that removing offenders from society reduces reoffending.

selective incapacitation A concept based on the notion that incapacitating the highest-risk offenders will reduce crime (e.g., "three strikes" policies in the United States are based on this idea).

in a Quebec City mosque in 2017, was sentenced in February 2019 to life imprisonment, without the possibility of parole for 40 years, although prosecutors appealed that sentence, as they had sought a 150-year sentence (*Montreal Gazette*, 2019).

Judges have always had the ability to harshly punish repeat offenders, who were previously called "habitual offenders" and violent repeat offenders; some are known today as dangerous offenders. Section 753 of the *Criminal Code* enables judges to designate individuals as dangerous if they are considered to be a threat to public safety. Prisoners with this designation are imprisoned based on an indeterminate sentence, which means that they can only be released after they demonstrate to the Parole Board of Canada that they can be safely reintegrated into the community. Public Safety Canada (2018, p. 59) reports that the Correctional Service of Canada was supervising almost 620 of them in 2017, and about another 20 are added to that total each year. Of those dangerous offenders, almost all are behind bars and less than 5 per cent are being supervised in the community (Public Safety Canada, 2018, p. 60).

In order to ensure that serious offenders do not "fall through the cracks" of the justice system, individuals convicted of serious crimes can be flagged for enhanced prosecution if they reoffend. This information is recorded in the National Flagging System, which is reported in the Canadian Police Information Centre (CPIC) database. CPIC is operated by the RCMP and can be accessed by the police and other law enforcement personnel, such as officials from the Canada Border Services Agency, to obtain information about the criminal histories of Canadians. According to Public Safety Canada (2017, p. 1), a flagging system is important, as high-risk individuals are a mobile population and some relocate across the country because they are well-known to the personnel in the justice system in their hometowns. An evaluation carried out by Public Safety Canada (2017, p. 11) suggests about 10,000 high-risk offenders are tracked throughout the country. According to the Nova Scotia Public Prosecution Service (2013, p. 2), the criteria for being flagged include convictions for sexual offences

Tara Bradbury/The Telegram. © The Telegram/A SaltWire Network Publication

In July 2017 a Newfoundland and Labrador judge ordered Gordie Bishop, a man with a 27-page criminal record, to leave the province for at least one year. Both the Crown prosecutor and Bishop's lawyer put forward this unusual sentence in a joint submission, and the judge agreed with their plan (Bradbury, 2017). Bishop told the court that he planned on moving to Fort McMurray, where his mother lives. How would you classify this modern use of banishment: as a method of deterrence, incapacitation, or retribution?

against children, having committed particularly violent sexual offences or acts of brutal violence, involvement in arson, psychiatric assessments that show the individual is dangerous, escalating involvement in violence, or having committed violent offences while on probation or parole.

Reforming Offenders: Restitution, Rehabilitation, and Restorative Justice

Crime control philosophies that support retribution, deterrence, or incapacitation focus on the offence. Another set of philosophies shifts the focus to offenders and their capacity to make changes in their lives to reduce their future involvement in crime. The three approaches to this philosophy are restitution, rehabilitation, and restorative justice. Restitution involves the offender repaying the victims or the community for the damages experienced from the crime. By contrast, rehabilitation is when an

National Flagging System A system that tracks people who have been convicted of serious violent crimes to ensure that their prior criminal histories are considered by prosecutors if they reoffend.

Canadian Police Information Centre (CPIC) A database that can be accessed by law enforcement personnel that reports the criminal histories of Canadians.

CP PHOTO/Edmonton Journal – Ian Scott

Dangerous offenders can be imprisoned indefinitely. Lisa Neve was classified as a dangerous offender, but that classification was overturned prior to her release in 1999 (when this photo was taken). She testified to the Senate Committee on Human Rights in 2018 about the effect the designation has on the prisoner. Do you think dangerous offenders should be released into community supervision?

rehabilitation
The process of helping offenders develop the skills, knowledge, and attitudes they require in order to reduce their likelihood of recidivism.

recidivism
Occurs when a person who has been previously convicted of an offence reoffends by committing another crime.

example, community leaders in northern Europe forced wrongdoers to make reparations (called *wergild*) to the families of murder victims. The Canadian Council of Academies (2019) observes that restitution made to victims or their survivors was also used by Indigenous peoples prior to contact with the European and English explorers. Making restitution was important for the survival of a victim's family because there were no social services to support survivors. These payments were also important in reducing the prospect of retaliation from a victim's family. Restitution is used today primarily for property offences, and it is often a condition of an individual's probation. If probationers do not pay their court-ordered restitution, they are in violation of their probation order and may be returned to court and punished more harshly for breaching the conditions of their probation.

Compensating crime victims was authorized in the 1892 amendments to the *Criminal Code*. Despite the fact that restitution has a common-sense appeal, a review of the 2014–2015 adult court statistics shows that there were less than 5,000 cases where restitution was the only sentence, although restitution is often combined with other probationary sentences (Maxwell, 2017). So, is restitution an effective crime control strategy? McDonald (2010) studied Saskatchewan crime victims who were owed restitution and found that most restitution orders were for mischief, theft, and fraud offences. Restitution payments were often made to the courts, who in turn issued the funds to the victims. In cases where restitution has not been made, victims can take steps to ensure that it is provided, but McDonald (2010) notes that this often requires victims to have knowledge of the justice system and requires efforts on their own part.

In July 2015 the *Canadian Victims Bill of Rights* came into effect and this federal legislation gave crime victims the right to seek restitution. According to section 16, "every victim has the right to have the court consider making a restitution order against the offender" (p. 5), and section 17 says that "every victim in whose favour a restitution order is made has the right, if they are not paid,

offender makes positive changes in their attitudes or behaviours so they can live crime-free. Restoration or restorative justice extends the concept of restitution to include structured and supervised contact between the offender and the victim, and it provides an opportunity for the victim to safely confront the person who has caused them harm. The ultimate goal of these approaches is to protect society by reducing **recidivism** (reoffending).

Restitution

One of the oldest approaches focused on reforming offenders is restitution, which involves compensating victims, their families, or the community for the losses they experienced due to a crime. Restitution dates back centuries—for

A Closer Look

Does the Punishment Fit the Crime?

Moussa Sidime, a 74-year-old retired architect from Quebec who killed his 13-year-old daughter with two slaps to the face, was sentenced to 60 days in a provincial correctional centre on May 21, 2014. Noutene Sidime was struck by her father because she did not complete her chores and had been disrespectful toward him. The Canadian Press (2014) notes that the pathologist who examined the young woman did not find bruising from the slaps but determined that "the slaps caused her head to move in such a violent motion an artery in her head ruptured and oxygen was cut off to her brain. She died in hospital two days later." Family members testifying in support of Moussa Sidime said the death was a freak accident and that he was a gentle man who was remorseful for causing his daughter's death.

Sidime pled guilty to the manslaughter offence. Although the Crown prosecutor recommended that a prison term be imposed, the judge sentenced Sidime to a 60-day sentence to be served intermittently (he served two days a week for 30 weeks), followed by a two-year probationary sentence that was served in the community. Perreault (2014) explains that "an intermittent sentence allows an offender to serve a sentence in segments, generally on weekends, while having to adhere to conditions when not in custody." Among other things, intermittent sentences allow people to serve sentences of 90 days or less without having to be away from their work or studies. Under Canadian law, manslaughter does not specify a minimum sentence unless it involves a firearm, so the sentence imposed was within the guidelines available for the judge.

Short sentences for manslaughter offences are controversial because many people feel that justice has not been served and that the punishment does not fit the seriousness of the crime. On the other hand, the evidence in this case suggests that the elderly parent did not intend on causing such harm, and the assault was out of character for him. Given that Moussa Sidime, who had no previous criminal convictions, represents a low risk to the community, we have to ask whether a lengthy prison term—at a cost of $120,571 per year in 2017/2018 (Malakieh, 2019)—is an appropriate punishment. Yet, many would argue that the lenient sentence imposed on Sidime would not deter others from committing similar violent crimes. Regardless of whether we think that justice has been done, Noutene Sidime lost her life, and that is the real tragedy.

intermittent sentence Sentences of 90 days or less that are served in segments of time rather than all at once; can be imposed on inmates who would be unduly harmed by full-time incarceration, such as losing their job or interrupting their studies.

---

to have the order entered as a civil court judgment that is enforceable against the offender" (p. 5).

Like other approaches that address the offender, there are positive and negative aspects of making restitution. For example, repaying a homeowner for the damages and losses that occur in a residential break and enter will cover the victim's economic losses. But it is hard to put a price tag on the psychological effects of victimization, and homeowners may experience feelings of violation and fear in their own home for years after the break-in. How does one place a monetary value on feelings of fear and violation? Even when the individual pays restitution, the victims might not receive their funds. McDonald (2010) found that sometimes the payments were mishandled and victims were not informed that restitution orders had been made. Moreover, researchers have found that in some provinces only a small proportion of payments are actually made to victims (Rhodes, 2013).

Rehabilitation

The history of rehabilitation is much shorter than that of compensating crime victims, as most rehabilitative efforts take place in the community when the individuals are serving probationary sentences or fulfilling parole requirements, although rehabilitation also occurs in correctional facilities. Prior to the Kingston Penitentiary opening in 1835, there were no facilities in Canada where long-term prisoners could be held, and formal probation operated by provincial authorities was only introduced in the early 1900s. Even after the first penitentiaries were constructed, there were few rehabilitative interventions other than making prisoners work within the facility and participate in religious programs. Even though inmates participated in work programs, they were forbidden to speak to each other, and these early prisons were described by the Correctional Service of Canada (2014b) as "cruel and unhealthy places."

Although reformation or rehabilitation of inmates was a stated goal of penitentiaries in the early 1900s, more sophisticated programs that addressed prisoners' unmet needs—such as addressing their limited educational histories or problems with substance abuse—did not become widely implemented until the 1950s. Even though well-intentioned, many of these programs were operated by staff with little training, and knowledge of a prisoner's risks and needs was undeveloped. As a result, most of the interventions that were introduced were ineffective. There was also growing recognition that special-needs populations required a different approach to correctional rehabilitation, including people with mental illnesses, young offenders (until the introduction of the *Young Offenders Act* in 1984, 16- and 17-year-olds were regularly placed in penitentiaries), and Indigenous and women offenders. As a result, correctional systems today rely on a more individualized approach to treatment than in the past.

There is also recognition that preparing prisoners for community re-entry is of key importance given that most prisoners will return to the community following their release. In fact, the iron law of imprisonment maintains that with the exception of a small number of prisoners who die behind bars, they all come back to society. As a result, it is in the public's best interest that these ex-prisoners are released to the community with fewer psychological, physical, and health-related problems than when they were admitted.

In order to make a gradual transition from prison to the community, halfway houses were established throughout the nation and the practice of day parole was introduced. Day parole allowed prisoners to reside in a community placement while remaining under correctional supervision. Despite these approaches, many ex-prisoners have difficult adjustments and some will reoffend within the first few years of their release. These failures are not surprising, as making a significant change in one's life is not an easy undertaking: think about your attempts to lose weight, quit smoking, or stick with a budget. Prisoners returning to the community wanting to make changes must also overcome problems such as addictions, limited work histories, and a lack of support

iron law of imprisonment The concept that most prisoners will return to the community, so it is in the public's best interest to help those individuals succeed in their re-entry.

Kingston Penitentiary. Library and Archives Canada, e011001298 / MIKAN 4349142, 4348645

Kingston Penitentiary was the first penitentiary in Canada. This ledger from 1913 shows one of its inmates at the time. The prisoner was 15 years old, and he was sentenced to prison for three years for "shopbreaking."

systems. Moreover, many of them do not have things that many of us take for granted, such as a safe place to live, a bank account, transportation, or the support of their families. Despite the obstacles to re-entering the community, Public Safety Canada (2018, p. 94) reports that 93 per cent of federal day parolees successfully complete their sentences, and almost 90 per cent of individuals on full parole are successful.

Restorative Justice

Restorative justice (RJ) approaches challenge the traditional operations of Canada's justice system. Supporters of RJ argue that the focus of an adversarial justice system on the offence and assigning blame has been unsuccessful in reforming individuals involved in crime (Zehr, 2014). The Canadian Council of Academies (2019, p. 21) described RJ approaches of Indigenous peoples prior to contact with the European and English explorers and they observed that addressing wrongdoing was based on "teasing, shaming, ostracism, reparation and requiring compensation," and that "periods of shaming or ostracism could be followed up by ceremonies

to reintegrate an offending individual into the community" with the goal of restoring balance. Some of these RJ concepts have been integrated into today's justice systems. One of the main goals of restorative justice is to repair the harm experienced by the victim and the community as a result of the crime. Although victim impact statements (reports from victims about the losses they experienced) are considered prior to sentencing, traditional justice systems have an impersonal approach to dispensing justice that often leaves victims and their families dissatisfied. Western approaches to justice are often abstract (e.g., offences are prosecuted in the name of the Queen), and offenders do not always appreciate the harms caused by their actions. As a result, RJ is intended to move away from our traditional and abstract notions of law and justice and toward concepts that are more easily understood by offenders and victims alike, such as "making things right." Table 3.1 shows the differences between the traditional retributive and restorative justice approaches.

Restorative justice interventions often focus on the harms that occurred when a crime was

restorative justice An alternative approach to conventional practices of justice that focuses on interventions intended to repair the harm that was experienced by the victim and the community when the offence occurred.

TABLE 3.1 Comparison of Retributive and Restorative Justice Approaches

Retributive Justice (Current System)	Restorative Justice
Focus on establishing blame and guilt	Focus on problem solving, liabilities and obligations, and the future
Stigma of crime permanent	Stigma of crime removable
No encouragement for repentance and forgiveness	Possibilities for repentance and forgiveness
Process depends on professionals	Direct involvement by participants
Victim ignored—offender passive	Victim and offenders involved, victim's needs and rights recognized, offender encouraged to accept responsibility for their actions
Offender is held accountable by the punishments they receive	Offender accountability based on learning about the impact of their actions and helping decide how to make things right
"Debt" owed to state and society	Debts/liability to victim recognized
Response focused on the offender's past behaviour	Response focused on harmful consequences of the criminal act
Imposition of pain to punish and deter/prevent	Restitution as a means of restoring both parties, reconciliation/restoration as a goal

Adapted from Canadian Resource Centre for Victims of Crime (2011)

committed and the steps offenders must take to repair the damage to the victim and the community. The nature of these interventions differs somewhat across the country and most RJ interventions today are based on victim–offender mediation, where the victim and the offender voluntarily meet with a facilitator and the group discusses the offence and its impact on the victim. The facilitator or mediator uses that information to develop a solution to repair the harm, and most of these interventions result in the offender making restitution. In some cases the individual might agree to carry out some form of community service—especially if the victim is a public agency—and some people agree to do some personal service for the victim, such as shovelling their sidewalks during the winter. Other examples of restorative justice include youth justice conferences and circle sentencing.

According to the Department of Justice (2015, p. 1), "a youth justice conference is a group of people who are asked by a decision-maker, such as a judge, to come together to give advice on the case of a young person who is involved in the youth criminal justice system." These groups are brought together in a structured setting to provide the decision maker with advice about appropriate sentences and the "ways in which the young person can repair the harm done to the victim" (Department of Justice, 2015, p.1). In addition to victims, their supporters (such as family members), the offender, and representatives from the community (including the police) have also participated in these interventions.

While judges could facilitate a youth justice conference, most are run by trained mediators. Circle sentencing, by contrast, was developed for Indigenous offenders in the early 1990s, and the consequences or sanctions for the offender are developed by a judge after consultation with members of the circle. This approach was based on healing circles in Indigenous traditions. As Lightstone (2018, para. 14) observes, "sentencing circles can be a valuable way of getting input and advice from the community to help the judge set an appropriate and effective sentence"; and "often

the circle will suggest a restorative community sentence involving some form of restitution to the victim and other measures the judge may decide to accept, or not."

So how many sentencing circles are occurring? Adam (2014, p. A1) reports that they have fallen out of favour, and in Saskatchewan the number of circles decreased from a high of 39 in 1997 to only 6 in 2012, and an estimated 3 in 2017 (Saskatchewan Ministry of Justice, 2018). Adam could not pinpoint a specific reason for the decreased number but suggested that reasons may include challenges with initiating and organizing the circles, as the process can be very labour intensive and time-consuming. These low numbers do not seem distinctive to Saskatchewan and a search of the annual reports of the English-speaking provincial courts in 2018 did not reveal any mention of sentencing circles, although anecdotal accounts suggest they are occurring in some provinces, such as Nova Scotia. There is a similar lack of information about youth justice conferences and anecdotal information suggests they are being replaced by victim–offender mediation. Fagan (2017), however, notes that an increasing number of provinces have introduced specialized courts (also known as *Gladue* courts) to work with Indigenous people accused of crimes, and some sentencing circles are carried out in these courts (see Chapter 7).

Restorative justice interventions have traditionally targeted young people who have committed non-violent first-time offences, although this approach has also shown success with Canadians who committed serious crimes (Rugge & Cormier, 2013). Kennedy, Tuliao, Flower, Tibbs, and McChargue (2018) also found that RJ interventions reduced recidivism. The Washington State Institute for Public Policy (2018) reports that the community receives a two-dollar crime-reduction benefit for every dollar spent on restorative justice conferencing.

Restorative justice practices underlie many current justice practices and the approach is well integrated into Nova Scotia's justice system. Furthermore, Manitoba introduced the *Restorative*

---

youth justice conference
A group of community members, sometimes including a judge, who come together to develop a sanction for a young person who has committed an offence.

circle sentencing
A justice practice intended for Indigenous offenders, where sanctions for criminal conduct are developed by members of a circle, including a judge, the offender, victims (and their supporters), the police, and other community members. In some jurisdictions these practices are called healing or peacemaking circles.

Justice Act in 2014 to promote restorative justice in their justice system, though its long-term effects have to be determined (Courtemanche, 2015). Braithwaite (2018), a long-term advocate for restorative justice, believes that restorative justice interventions such as cautions (warnings) should be a first response to lawbreakers with a gradual increase in the use of more formal methods, including using incapacitation as a last resort. Despite the fact that restorative justice has a popular appeal and research shows that it is an effective crime-reduction strategy, formal interventions based on these approaches, such as circle sentencing, are used less frequently today, although most jurisdictions do use alternative measures or victim–offender mediation, which are based on a restorative justice philosophy.

Conflict Perspective

A popular perspective among critical criminologists is that the police, courts, and correctional systems are used by powerful social groups to maintain their privileged status. It is no secret that a very small percentage of the population controls a large amount of the wealth, and they are reluctant to give up their economic or political power. Huey (2015, p. 196) defines the conflict approach as having a "focus on the unequal distribution of power in society—for example, due to class, race, or gender. Conflicts between classes or groups are driven to a large extent by this unequal power and unequal access to resources." Some critical criminologists argue that as workers, the poor, students, women, or visible minorities challenge the status quo for more political and economic clout, powerful social groups feel threatened and have used the justice system to reduce these threats or silence social protests (see Beare & Des Rosiers, 2015).

Reiman and Leighton (2017) argue that the real purpose of the criminal justice system is to maintain economic and political inequality. During times of economic and political insecurity, such as periods of high unemployment and economic downturns, marginalized groups may be policed more aggressively. Even during periods of economic stability, some groups can be singled out for harsh treatment. People experiencing homelessness, for example, are a visible population who may be targeted by the justice system. Although not having a home is not a crime, many of the aspects of living outside are subject to municipal bylaws. The Alberta Civil Liberties Research Centre (2015) observes the following:

> Bans on sitting or sleeping on sidewalks, erecting nighttime shelters, public urination, spitting, swearing, or panhandling may appear neutral on their face, but they are often directly targeted at criminalizing the homeless. When we criminalize behaviors that homeless persons cannot reasonably avoid (for example, sleeping outside) we are effectively denying their ability to legally exist in any space.

Violating these bylaws often results in court appearances and fines, which are unlikely to be paid by people living on the street and have limited resources. Bellemare (2018, para. 8) reports that many residents of a Montreal homeless shelter owe thousands of dollars in fines for "minor offences from jaywalking, to smoking too close to bus shelters, to carrying open liquor." These fines can add up; for example, one 50-year-old Montreal man who had been living in the subway racked up $110,000 in fines (Canadian Broadcasting Corporation, 2016). As a result of not paying these fines, these individuals might then be in violation of a court order and subject to stricter punishments such as incarceration. One question that emerges from these cases is why the police would issue so many tickets to people they know can never pay their fines.

Wealthy people also engage in crime, although Reiman and Leighton (2017) argue that many crimes of the powerful are not defined as crimes even though they may result in injury or death. In Chapter 2, we gave the example of the failure of executives working for General Motors to fix faulty ignition switches that led to over a hundred deaths. The company executives knew that the switches were faulty, and they chose to keep producing unsafe cars rather than fix the problem. Given those facts, were these deaths really accidents? A similar question is posed regarding the Westray Mine disaster, discussed below: Was this an accident or a mass murder?

An Example of Critical Criminology: The Westray Mine Disaster

On May 9, 1992, an explosion in a coal mine near the town of Plymouth, Nova Scotia, killed all 26 miners who were working underground. A week after the disaster, an inquiry was ordered. A final report was delivered five years later. Justice K. Peter Richard, who carried out the investigation, reported that the disaster "is a story of incompetence, of mismanagement, of bureaucratic bungling, of deceit, of ruthlessness, of cover-up, of apathy, of expediency, and of cynical indifference" (Province of Nova Scotia, 1997).

Critical criminologists point out that the legal system does a poor job of deterring corporate leaders from engaging in practices that could harm their employees, the public, or customers. The Westray Mine disaster is an example of corporate misconduct that some consider an accident, while Desjarlais (2001) called this act "the worst case of corporate mass murder in Canada." As we learned in Chapters 1 and 2, individuals and corporations can be held accountable for negligence that results in harm, but in this case nobody ever went to jail despite the fact that shortcuts in safety measures taken by the owners and operators of the mine led to this tragedy.

The five-year inquiry into the disaster found that the explosion resulted from the failure of the company's management and government inspectors to act on safety concerns. The Canadian Broadcasting Corporation (2012) reports that the company operating the mine "was charged with 52 non-criminal counts of operating an unsafe mine," and that "charges of criminal negligence and manslaughter had been laid against mine managers . . . , but these came to nothing when the Crown stayed proceeding, saying there was not enough evidence to ensure a conviction." Twenty-five years after the disaster the families of the victims are still angry. One union official said: "Not enough CEOs go to jail yet, and we don't want a whole bunch of them in jail—just one or two would be good. That would send a message to companies that it's not OK to take lives or injure people for the cost of doing business," (MacDonald, 2017, para. 26).

In response to the failure of the justice system to hold corporate owners or managers accountable for negligence that results in injury or death, the so-called "Westray Bill" (Bill C-45) was enacted in 2004 to make officials responsible for worker and public safety more criminally accountable by amending section 217.1 of the *Criminal Code*. So what has changed? The Association of Workers' Compensation Boards of Canada (2018) reports that in 2016 there were almost a quarter million workplace injuries that resulted in lost time, and 904 workers lost their lives in job-related accidents; by contrast, 611 Canadians were murdered that year (Beattie, David, & Roy, 2018). Given these findings, we might question the effectiveness of the legislation intended to make workers safer.

Bittle (2012, p. 2) observes that since the Westray Bill was enacted, "only a handful of charges have been laid," and instead of holding corporate criminals accountable, the legislation created an industry where "lawyers and consultants offer for-fee courses that potential offenders can take to learn about the new law and the steps they must follow to avoid criminal responsibility." Miedema (2015) reports that ten years after the legislation was introduced, only ten cases had been prosecuted under section 217.1 of the *Criminal Code*. All but one of those cases involved fatalities, and of those prosecutions, only five individuals were convicted and only two of them were incarcerated. As a result, while it is now easier to prosecute corporate executives for endangering lives, these offences seldom result in criminal convictions. Given that these prosecutions are very rare—about one a year—and unlikely to result in a custodial sentence, will our current enforcement practices deter potential corporate criminals?

A COMPARATIVE VIEW

Rates of Imprisonment

Rates of violent and property crime are generally quite similar in most wealthy nations, although punishments for these offences can vary greatly. Figure 3.1 shows the rates of imprisonment per 100,000 residents in the G7 nations for males and females. The United States is a world leader in the use of imprisonment, with a rate that is over six times greater than Canada's. In addition to custodial punishments, of the G7 nations only Japan and the United States impose the death penalty. Executions, however, are rare and in 2017 there were four executions in Japan and 23 in the United States. The number of executions in the United States has dropped from a high of 98 in 1999, and this punishment seems to be falling out of favour (Death Penalty Information Center, 2019). As noted earlier, despite the fact that the murder rate in Canada in 2017 was about the same as when the last executions were carried out in 1962, surveys consistently find that about two-thirds of Canadians support the death penalty.

One important question that arises after looking at the incarceration rates in Figure 3.1 is: why do nations with similar rates of crime have such different punishments? Differing cultural, religious, historical, legal, and political traditions influence the types of sanctions that nations use. In a study of imprisonment in 81 developed nations, Jones, Ruddell and Winterdyk (2017) found that countries with higher homicide rates, common-law systems (found in nations colonized by the English), the death penalty, and less economic stability had higher imprisonment rates. These findings suggest that factors other than crime influence the way that countries punish their wrongdoers.

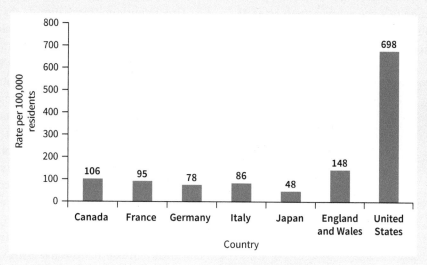

FIGURE 3.1 **Imprisonment Rates per 100,000 Residents, G7 Nations**
Adapted from Walmsley (2016)

PUBLIC OPINION, THE MEDIA, AND PUNISHMENT

The general public has expressed mixed feelings about punishing people who have committed crimes. On one hand, we want to hold repeat and violent offenders accountable for their crimes and acknowledge the harms done to victims and the community. On the other hand, we are reluctant to punish youth or first-time and minor offenders too severely, as many people have engaged in minor crimes at some point in their lives, and we realize that a criminal conviction can have life-long consequences in terms of reduced opportunities for work and travel. But how do we form our ideas about crime, and why do some people support harsh punishments while others support offender rehabilitation? Roberts (2016) observes the following:

> There is a relationship between public opinion and the political willingness to punish offenders although it is difficult to determine which comes first—much like the chicken and the egg. When crime rates are high, we tend to have more negative feelings toward offenders and are supportive of severe punishments for offenders. Politicians, in turn, get their cues about issues from the public and may be more supportive of tough punishments for criminals in response to public opinion. Although some might argue that the opposite is true and that the public actually gets its ideas about crime and justice from politicians. (p. 13)

evidence-based practices Strategies that research has demonstrated to be effective and have positive impacts.

The criminal justice system is linked to the political system, and that relationship has both positive and negative effects. Most of us would agree that public policies should be shaped by the will of the people. To some extent the public is able to influence the operations of Canadian justice policies if they participate in the political process by emailing their member of parliament and voting, join public interest groups (such as Mothers Against Drunk Driving or other victim advocacy groups), and engage in advocacy efforts through their unions, which is common for employees of justice systems. In democracies, crime control strategies should be introduced after being debated, and all stakeholders should have the opportunity to present their positions. It is also important that decisions about the best strategies to reduce crime be based on what the research demonstrates are effective methods of crime control—which is the basis of evidence-based practices (Savignac & Dunbar, 2015).

One important observation is that some Canadian political parties support "tough on crime" policies, as offenders are generally an unsympathetic group with voters and there is little political risk in this position. This tough on crime and criminals approach is called penal populism, and is rooted in developing policies based on "common sense" rather than scientific evidence. Penal populism focuses on victims, and supporters of this approach are often reluctant to involve academic or government experts on crime in decision-making. Kelly and Puddister (2017, p. 395) say that "penal populism can be largely about appearing to be tough on crime through the introduction of a steady stream of criminal justice policy bills by a party to satisfy its core supporters, with little concern about effect or implementation." The hazard of basing policies on penal populism is that ineffective or harmful laws or practices can be introduced, and once laws are enacted there is often resistance to changing them. One important difference between Canada and the United States is that issues related to crime control are less political in Canada largely because prosecutors and judges in most US jurisdictions are elected, most

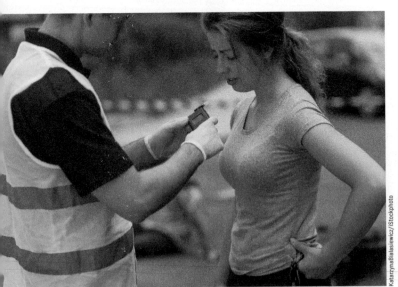

Public interest groups, such as Mothers Against Drunk Driving, have played an important role in changing justice policies in Canada, including the introduction of new impaired driving laws in 2018, which, among other changes, allow officers to administer a breathalyzer test on any driver pulled over.

run their political campaigns based on being tough on crime, and many prosecutors use their positions to seek higher political offices.

Many scholars have argued that the news and entertainment media shape our ideas about crime and justice (Douai & Perry, 2018). In terms of the influence of the media, Gamson, Croteau, Hoynes, and Sasson (1992, p. 373) point out that "we walk around with media-generated images of the world, using them to construct meaning about political and social issues." As noted in Chapter 1, most news accounts focus on relatively rare events such as homicide. But we know from our review of serious crime in the previous chapter that homicide is a relatively rare offence and murder rates are lower today than they were 40 years ago. The entertainment industry also provides us with a constant stream of films and television programs that feature serious and violent crimes, and these images also shape our ideas about crime and justice.

People who watch more hours of television news and crime dramas may also be more fearful of crime. Serani (2008, p. 249) observes that individuals "exposed to the media are more likely than others to:

- feel that their neighbourhoods and communities are unsafe;
- believe that crime rates are rising;
- overestimate their odds of becoming a victim; and
- consider the world to be a dangerous place."

The priorities of television news reporters may also contribute to stereotypes about who is committing crimes. Kappeler and Potter (2018) summarized the media research and report that visible minorities are overrepresented in US television news accounts of crime as offenders while White people are overrepresented as victims. They argue that inaccurate portrayals of race and crime contribute to our stereotypes about different racial groups and might increase the public's fears of minority groups.

Britto (2015) summarized the findings of various media scholars on the attitudes of frequent viewers of crime-related programs and noted that frequent viewers generally have less accurate knowledge of the justice system but have greater fear of crime, support for the police, and punitive attitudes, as well as unrealistic expectations of the criminal justice system (this is called the *CSI* effect; see Figure 3.2 and "A Closer Look" box).

The likelihood of victimization is also inaccurately portrayed on television. Parrott and Titcomb Parrott (2015) observe the following in their analysis of gender and racial stereotypes in fictional crime dramas:

> White female television characters stood [a] greater chance of being victims of crime than White male, Black female, and Black male television characters. White female television characters stood the greatest chance of being victims who suffer serious harm or death. White women stood a greater chance of being rape or sexual assault victims, being victims of serious harm at the hands of an assailant, and being attacked by a stranger. (p. 70)

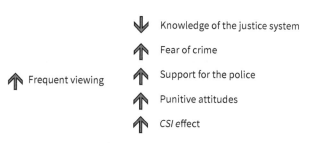

FIGURE 3.2   The Effect of Frequent Viewing of Crime-Related Programs on Various Attitudes
Adapted from Britto (2015)

A Closer Look

The *CSI* Effect

Television programs that highlight forensic investigation are popular with viewers, but these programs can create unrealistic expectations of the justice system—this is known as the *CSI* effect. *CSI: Crime Scene Investigation* was introduced in 2000 and ran for 15 seasons; other series highlighting the use of science to fight crime remain popular. While the settings and characters in these television series differ, they often feature the use of cutting-edge scientific methods to quickly solve cases. Like other fictional programming, what is portrayed on television does not always reflect reality. Huey (2010) interviewed Canadian police officers, who said that these programs have changed the public's expectations about scientific evidence, the speed at which investigations are completed, and how often biological evidence—such as DNA—is actually collected and used.

Inconsistent with what we see on television or films, usable biological evidence is not present at most crime scenes. It is more likely to be collected at the scene of violent crimes such as sexual assaults or homicides and is rarely collected in property crimes or robberies (Peterson, Sommers, Baskin, & Johnson, 2010). Even when such evidence is collected, the technology and techniques we see on television do not always exist, and it sometimes takes months to obtain test results. The average

CSI effect Unrealistic expectations about the use of scientific evidence in criminal investigations that are based on inaccurate information portrayed on television.

wait times reported by the RCMP (2017a), for example, from the day a sample is received at their crime labs to the completion of the results, are shown in Figure 3.3. The average time to analyze ranges from a low of 44 days to a high of 234 days, although these are based on routine requests, and police services can make an urgent request if needed. Urgent requests typically take about one-third the time, although less than 2 per cent of all requests are priorities. (Firearm evidence refers to examining bullets, spent cartridge cases, or the actual gun. Trace evidence, on the other hand, refers to non-biological evidence such as fibres located at a crime scene or paint recovered after a motor vehicle hit and run. Toxicology refers to testing for the presence of drugs, poisons, or alcohol and most often is requested in cases of violent crimes. Crime labs also examine documents such as passports, banknotes, and payment cards such as credit cards to determine whether they are genuine.)

There is also a dark side to the popularity of forensic investigation programs, as offenders are now using the information presented in these programs to avoid detection (Cole & Dioso-Villa, 2011). Police investigators call this *forensic awareness*, which Simon Fraser University researchers Reale, Beauregard, and Martineau (2017, p. 6) define as "the taking of additional steps and adapting the modus operandi used in a crime to hide evidence to ultimately avoid apprehension." Even if forensic evidence is collected, it might not be linked to an individual and it may take years before a sample

In reality, however, males are more likely to be crime victims, and in 2017 African-Americans in the United States, who make up about 15 per cent of the population, accounted for 60 per cent of murder victims (where race of the victim was known; see Federal Bureau of Investigation, 2018 – Expanded homicide data Table 1). In Canada, Indigenous people are overrepresented as victims of crime. Beattie, David, and Roy (2018, p. 13) report that the murder rate for Indigenous peoples was six times higher than the non-Indigenous population.

Since many of our crime-related programs are from the United States, some Canadian viewers may not distinguish between events in the two nations. As a result, watching a media report about an act of police brutality occurring in Florida may influence a New Brunswick resident's perceptions about Canadian policing as they might believe that the use of force in the two nations, such as police shootings of suspects, is identical, but there are sharp contrasts in the two countries (see Chapter 6). Furthermore,

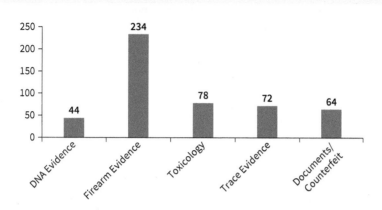

FIGURE 3.3 Average Wait Times (Days) to Analyze Forensic Evidence, 2016–2017
RCMP (2017)

can be matched to an offender whose information is entered into Canada's National DNA Data Bank after their involvement in a crime. In addition, in the United States, human errors and misconduct have resulted in scandals and wrongful convictions due to shoddy investigations. Mays and Ruddell (2019) contend these miscarriages of justice are more likely to happen when crime labs are operated by municipal police departments rather than independent crime labs that have no stake in the outcomes of the analyses.

In Canada, forensic services such as crime labs are independent of local police services and are run by the RCMP (for provinces receiving contract policing) and by the provinces of Ontario and Quebec. The RCMP (2017b, p. 15) produces an annual report of its activities; the following describes an average day in the operations of the National DNA Data Bank:

- 100 crime-scene DNA samples are submitted
- 100 DNA profiles of convicted offenders are submitted
- Staff make 32 matches (where evidence is linked to a suspect or a person whose DNA was previously submitted to the data bank)

In addition to identifying people responsible for committing crimes, the DNA evidence that is analyzed also excludes or eliminates suspects.

some viewers may confuse the operations of Canadian and American justice systems, which have significant differences especially in terms of crime rates (the United States has a higher homicide rate), policing arrangements, court systems (the US system is more adversarial and politically charged), and often harsher punishments. So, while there are similarities between the two systems, watching US programs can distort our understanding of the way Canadian justice systems operate.

CRIMINAL JUSTICE AND THE INDIGENOUS PEOPLES OF CANADA

One of the key goals of Canada's criminal justice system is to ensure that victims, suspects, and people accused of crimes are treated in a just and fair manner. Every chapter in this book highlights examples of race, class, and gender in relation to criminal justice and describes how members of different ethnocultural groups are sometimes disadvantaged when they interact with justice system personnel. While we can clearly see that certain ethnocultural groups are overrepresented in the criminal justice system, it is a more complicated task to explain why these disparities occur. In this section, we take a closer look at the overrepresentation of Indigenous people in the Canadian criminal justice system, and describe how officials have worked to reduce this overrepresentation.

Canada is a diverse nation. Statistics Canada (2018) reports that about one in four Canadians were born in another country and that visible minorities account for over 20 per cent of the national population. Although Indigenous people (a term that includes Métis, Inuit, and First Nations people) represent about 5 per cent of the national population (Statistics Canada, 2018), they are overrepresented at each point in the criminal justice system. With respect to corrections, in 2017/2018 Indigenous adults comprised 30 per cent of admissions to provincial sentenced custody, 29 per cent of admissions to federal custody, and almost half of youths admitted to custody (43 per cent) were Indigenous (Malakieh, 2019). A review of correctional statistics shows the problem is getting worse. Between 2007/2008 and 2017/2018 the proportion of the Indigenous population admitted to both adult and youth corrections increased, while the number of non-Indigenous inmates decreased (Malakieh, 2019).

There are a number of reasons for the overrepresentation of Indigenous people in the Canadian justice system, including their marginalization, history of discrimination and forced assimilation, involvement in street crime, police practices, and the possibility of biased treatment within the justice system. In terms of involvement in crime, Brzozowski, Taylor-Butts, and Johnson (2006, p. 1) report that crime rates on reserves were about three times greater than crime rates in the rest of Canada. Lithopoulos (2013) also found that in 2012, incidents of crime on reserves were 3.7 times higher than the Canadian average. With respect to homicide, Indigenous people were 11 times more likely than non-Indigenous people to be accused of these crimes.

Rates of victimization are also high for Indigenous people. Boyce (2016) notes that Indigenous women were almost three times more likely than non-Indigenous women to report being victims of violence. Rates of sexual victimization are also high, and Perreault (2015, p. 17) reports that Indigenous women "recorded a sexual assault rate of 115 incidents per 1,000 population, much higher than the rate of 35 per 1,000 recorded by their non-Indigenous counterparts." Indigenous women are at much higher risk than non-Indigenous women of being murdered. In 2017, for example, Beattie et al. (2018, p. 14) report the homicide rate for Indigenous women was 4.4 per 100,000 residents—which is more than twice the national murder rate—but this represents a decrease from a high of 7.6 per 100,000 residents in 1996 (Royal Canadian Mounted Police, 2015, p. 10).

The overrepresentation of Indigenous people within the justice system as suspects, offenders, and victims has negative outcomes for all Canadians. High rates of victimization reduce the participation of Indigenous people in society. In addition, high crime rates have harmful psychological effects on victims and on community residents that may contribute to higher levels of substance abuse, feelings of hopelessness, low self-esteem, post-traumatic stress disorders, and negative attitudes toward authority figures (Lithopoulos & Ruddell, 2016). Perreault (2015, p. 20) identifies a number of reactions linked to being victimized, including anger, frustration, fear, shock, annoyance, depression, and sleeping problems.

The overrepresentation of Indigenous peoples in the justice system has been the subject of various government reports since the 1960s and 1970s. According to the Royal Commission on Aboriginal Peoples (1996), the overrepresentation of Indigenous people in the criminal justice system can be attributed to the effects of the discriminatory government policies that were intended to assimilate Indigenous people into the general population. Most of these practices were a result of the colonization of Canada by European and English settlers. Colonization had long-term harmful effects on Indigenous peoples, which in turn

Indigenous women are almost three times more likely than non-Indigenous women to report being victims of violence. Indigenous women are also at higher risk of being victimized and sexually assaulted, and six times more likely to be murdered than non-Indigenous women. A Strawberry Ceremony to remember missing and murdered Indigenous women and girls has been held annually on February 14 since 2005 (pictured here).

affected their traditional way of life and resulted in changes to their social, economic, religious, and political structures. The effects of these experiences contributed to the poverty, unemployment, substance abuse, and crime found in many Indigenous communities today. The final report of the Truth and Reconciliation Commission (2015) described the Government of Canada's attempts to assimilate Indigenous people into broader Canadian society as cultural genocide. The placement of Indigenous children in residential schools was the foundation for the government's strategy of assimilation. Although the public's perception is that these events took place long ago, the last residential school in Canada closed in 1996, and there are about 41,000 survivors of residential schools still living on First Nations (First Nations Information Governance Centre, 2018, p. 140), while an unknown number are living off-reserve.

Throughout the 1980s and 1990s, over a dozen provincial and federal commissions and inquiries identified strategies to reduce the risks of victimization and the overrepresentation of Indigenous people in the justice system. In response to those endeavours, a series of federal and provincial initiatives were created to respond to the needs of Indigenous people. In 1991, the federal government introduced the Aboriginal Justice Strategy, and the key goals were to develop alternatives to the mainstream justice system for Indigenous peoples and to make justice systems more responsive to their distinct needs and values. One important component of this strategy was the introduction of the First Nations Policing Program, which enabled Indigenous communities to take more control over how they were policed (and who would provide those services—see Chapter 5). In addition, the number of Indigenous people working in the justice system has increased.

First Nations Policing Program
A federal government policing strategy that gives Indigenous communities the choice between operating their own police services or contracting with other police organizations to police their communities.

Race, Class, and Gender

Treatment of Women: What Are the Effects of Chivalry and Paternalism in the Criminal Justice System?

Our beliefs about the punishment of wrongdoers are shaped by many influences including our ideas about the roles of women. We know that in 2017 women were involved in one of every four incidents reported to the police (25 per cent), and most of these defendants were accused of property crimes (shoplifting is the most common), followed by administration of justice offences, such as breaching their probation (Savage, 2019). Males were more likely than women to be found guilty of violent crimes (52 and 40 per cent, respectively) and property crimes (65 and 49 per cent, respectively) (Savage, 2019). When it comes to sanctions, Savage (2019) found a greater percentage of males were sentenced to custody for violent crimes (39 per cent compared with 22 per cent for women offenders). Public Safety Canada (2018, p. 39) reports that the number of women being admitted to prison increased by over one-fifth between 2006/2007 and 2016/2017. In 2016/2017, 402 women were admitted to federal prisons, although there were less than 700 women prisoners in all federal facilities.

It has been suggested that women are held to a different standard than men by the criminal justice system and that police are more reluctant to arrest them. This differential or more lenient treatment, if it truly exists today, has been called **chivalry**.

chivalry The lenient treatment of girls and women by employees within justice systems.

evil woman hypothesis Women who commit violent offences may be treated more harshly by the justice system.

paternalism The unfair treatment of girls and young women based on the rationale that their treatment was in their best interests.

Mays and Ruddell (2019) suggest there may be exceptions to chivalry, and when females commit distinctly male-like crimes, such as violent offences, the criminal justice system may respond harshly in what Romain and Freiburger (2016, p. 195) call the **evil woman hypothesis**. Members of sexual minorities, such as lesbians or bisexuals, may also be treated more severely. Some US scholars have also observed that middle-class and White women are treated less severely, as are those who display contrition, vulnerability, deference, and sobriety (Gartner, 2011). By contrast, Wane (2013, p. 119) observes that African-Canadian women may be punished more harshly because they may be stereotyped with labels such as single mothers, welfare abusers, drug addicts, or immigrants. Indigenous girls and women, as noted above, are highly overrepresented in corrections (Malakieh, 2019).

The past treatment of girls in youth justice systems has been called **paternalistic**, and young females were sometimes treated more harshly than males. Prior to the introduction of the *Young Offenders Act* in 1984, some young women—most often those from low-income families—were placed in custody facilities for experimenting with their sexuality. Bala (1997, p. 6) notes that "female adolescents were often sent to training school for the vaguely worded status offence of 'sexual immorality,' which in practice was used almost exclusively against girls, typically those from socially disadvantaged backgrounds." The *Young Offenders Act* and the *Youth Criminal Justice Act* ended this practice of putting youth not accused or convicted of a *Criminal Code* offence in custody.

There was also a philosophical shift in the treatment of Indigenous peoples, including a movement away from interventions based on deterrence and incapacitation, and a greater emphasis on restorative justice. While initiatives such as family group conferencing and sentencing circles seem to have fallen out of favour, restorative justice principles underlie many interventions throughout the justice system. In addition, Maurutto and Hannah-Moffat (2016) describe how there are a growing number of specialty courts for Indigenous peoples (see Chapter 7). The personnel working within justice systems also receive training about Indigenous issues so they have a better appreciation of Indigenous culture, histories, and traditions, and how these factors

Are young women treated more harshly by the justice system today? A review of youth and adult court statistics shows that slightly more girls appeared in youth courts than women in adult courts in 2014/2015 (23 per cent compared with 20 per cent of adult women) (Maxwell, 2017; Miladinovic, 2016). Like their adult counterparts, most young women appearing in youth courts were accused of relatively minor offences such as theft, common assault, and administration of justice offences such as failure to appear in court or breach of probation. When it comes to placement in custody, Statistics Canada's (2019c) youth court statistics for 2017/2018 show that girls represented about a quarter (23 per cent) of youth serving a custodial or community sentence, and about 52 per cent of all female youth behind bars or on probation were of Indigenous ancestry.

A review of correctional statistics shows that the number of youth behind bars has decreased by over 80 per cent since 1998 (Statistics Canada, 2019b), and youth crime has not increased. Despite this positive outcome, we sometimes fail to consider the harmful impacts of incarcerating young people, and Cesaroni and Pelvin (2016) remind us that:

> For many young inmates, incarceration is the first significant period that they have spent away from their family, friends, and home community. A custodial sentence increases disengagement from family, pro-social peers, and familial/social values at a critical stage of the young offender's development. In addition custody removes youths from local schools and therefore may affect young people who already have little commitment to their school. (p. 279)

These impacts may be more severe for Indigenous youth if they are removed from supports such as elders, or if youth facility staff do a poor job of connecting them with traditional activities, cultural practices, or teachings (Cesaroni, Grol, & Fredericks, 2018). Although young people continue to be incarcerated, Bala and Carrington (2016) note that the introduction of the *Youth Criminal Justice Act* in 2003 (which replaced the *Young Offenders Act*) has reduced the overall number of youth entering custody (see Chapter 11).

It is almost impossible to look at a statistic such as the number of people in custody and determine if bias toward girls and women exists in the justice system or where it exists. We have to remember that incarceration statistics reflect the discretion exercised by officials throughout the system: a police officer's decision to arrest, a prosecutor's decision to bring the matter to court, the ability of the accused to access legal aid, the decision to grant or refuse bail (and if the accused served pretrial detention), a probation officer's sentencing recommendation on a pre-sentencing report, and ultimately the judge's sentence. Discriminatory treatment could exist at any one of these points, and bias can be extremely difficult to identify. Sometimes information about the race and ethnicity of offenders and victims is not collected. Wane (2013) is critical that the Canadian Centre for Justice Statistics does not report the ethnocultural characteristics of visible minority populations in the criminal justice system, as we cannot make any definitive statements about representation in the system (e.g., whether things are getting better or worse). These are serious challenges for researchers examining issues related to the overrepresentation of different ethnocultural groups in justice systems (Meng, 2018).

influence how Indigenous peoples perceive the world. Last, the police, courts, and correctional agencies operated by municipal, provincial, and federal governments are attempting to deploy a more representative workforce by hiring a greater number of Indigenous staff members.

In addition to changing the operations of the justice system, legislation was enacted in 1987 to modify the *Corrections and Conditional Release Act* to provide correctional programming to address the unmet needs of Indigenous federal inmates. Section 718 of the *Criminal Code* (which pertains to sentencing) was also amended in 1995 so that sanctions other than incarceration would be considered at sentencing. Last, the landmark *R v Gladue* decision of the Supreme Court of Canada in 1999 directed judges to recognize the distinctive circumstances of Indigenous people convicted of an offence at sentencing (see Chapter 8). Despite these initiatives, the number of Indigenous people involved in the justice system has been increasing and Macdonald (2018) says that Canada's justice system is biased and works against Indigenous people at every point in their involvement.

Since the 1990s a number of strategies have been introduced to reduce the high rates of Indigenous offending and victimization. For the most part these approaches have been well-intentioned and have increased the employment of Indigenous peoples in the justice system. Corrado, Kuehn, and Margaritescu (2014) observe that some of these initiatives have been successful—especially in terms of reducing the incarceration of Indigenous youth. Despite these efforts, however, levels of crime in some Indigenous communities remain high and the number of Indigenous people in provincial and federal corrections has been increasing. As a result, some stakeholders have stated that making changes to the existing justice system merely reinforces the status quo and does not adequately address the root causes of Indigenous crime and victimization. The search for more effective approaches to crime control will continue. Given the failure of traditional approaches, the best crime prevention solutions might lie outside the justice system and may require new ways of looking at justice.

SUMMARY

The operations of the Canadian justice system are shaped by six different crime control philosophies that have been the source of debate for centuries about the proper treatment for wrongdoers. These debates will not be resolved in the near future. Keeping with Packer's (1968) framework, the concepts of retribution, deterrence, and incapacitation are aligned with the crime control approach, while restitution, rehabilitation, and restorative justice are more closely related with the due process perspective. By now, you should have a good understanding of what perspective best aligns with your beliefs. One question that flows from that observation is, what attracts us to those beliefs? Moreover, how are our beliefs about crime and offenders formed? Are they the result of our upbringing (e.g., the values and beliefs expressed by family members and people important to us), or do the types of television programs we watch—and the internet sites we visit—influence our beliefs? Or are our ideas about crime and justice influenced by messages from political leaders or advocacy groups such as Mothers Against Drunk Driving?

It is also important to acknowledge that our ideas about what acts are defined as crimes and our ideas about how we should treat people we call offenders are also shaped by our upbringing in a nation that was founded as a colony of England and France. As noted in Chapter 1, our legal traditions and ways of carrying out formal social control are rooted in those traditions, and it is sometimes difficult for us to consider methods of working toward justice that do not include "fixing" or changing a person who committed a crime. Canada's justice system is based on the notion that people involved in crime need to change in order to live crime-free. In most respects, it is easier to base a justice system on "fixing" individuals than on addressing long-term entrenched social problems such as poverty and economic inequality, inadequate housing, and homelessness. It is also difficult for some of us to confront our prejudice and stigma toward the poor and marginalized, and our stereotypes of people who are "different" from us.

There is no shortage of ideas about the best ways of reducing crime. Lilly, Cullen, and Ball (2019) observe that "ideas have consequences," which means that our ideas about crime and offenders shape the crime control solutions that we develop, and they observed the following:

If offenders are viewed as genetically deranged and untrainable—much like wild animals—then caging them would seem to be the only option available. But if

MYTH OR REALITY

Do Tough Punishments Deter Crime?

Deterrence is a popular approach to crime reduction, as "tough on crime" sanctions should reduce wrongdoing. If a person chooses to commit a crime, then they should "do the time," and that notion has a common-sense appeal. Despite the popularity of this approach, deterring crime has never worked very well. A commonly used example of the failure of deterrence is Anderson's (2002) observation of pickpocketing:

In the late eighteenth and early nineteenth centuries, picking pockets was among 220 capital crimes in England. Thousands were executed before the attending masses. Undeterred by the fate of their colleagues, pickpockets routinely worked the crowds at public hangings. (p. 295)

One wonders why thieves continued to pick pockets while others were being hanged for the same offence. Did they believe they would not be caught, or if caught, did they believe they would not be punished? Or are there other factors that push a person

toward engaging in crime unrelated to the fear of punishment?

As noted in Chapter 2, rates of violent crime in Canada and the United States dropped around the same time and have generally been lower over the past two decades. One popular explanation for the US crime decline is that locking up more offenders and keeping them in prison longer deters others from committing violent crimes. In order to take a closer look at this relationship, the use of imprisonment and homicide in Canada and the United States from 1980 to 2016 is compared. Although homicide rates in both nations peaked in the early 1990s and then decreased, the US rate was higher than the Canadian rate. In the United States, the homicide rate dropped by 47 per cent between 1980 and 2016. By contrast, the Canadian rate dropped by about one-third during the same years. One question that criminologists and policy-makers like to ask is whether the use of incarceration had an impact on the homicide drop in the two nations.

Table 3.2 shows the changes in the imprisonment rates per 100,000 Canadian and US residents for the same years as the homicide rates (1980–2016). The US incarceration rate (that includes both jail and prison populations) grew more than threefold (from 222 to 669 per 100,000 residents), while in Canada the federal and provincial incarceration rate increased only slightly (9 per cent). These results suggest that a slight increase in the use of incarceration in Canada had almost the same impact as tripling the US jail and prison population. If an increased likelihood of being imprisoned deterred people from murdering others, we have to question why the decrease in the homicide rate was about the same in the two countries while there was almost no change in the Canadian incarceration rate.

TABLE 3.2 Change in Homicide and Incarceration Rates, Canada and the United States, 1980–2016

	Canada (%)	United States (%)
Homicide Rate	⬇ 30	⬇ 47
Incarceration Rate	⬆ 9	⬆ 201

Adapted from Beattie, David, and Roy (2018); Bureau of Justice Statistics (2019); Federal Bureau of Investigation (2018); Statistics Canada (2019a).

mass imprisonment
The overuse of imprisonment as a crime control strategy.

offenders are thought to be mentally ill, then the solution to the problem would be to treat them with psychotherapy. Or if one believes that people are moved to crime by the strains of economic deprivation, then providing job training and access to employment opportunities would seem to hold the promise of diminishing their waywardness. (p. 5)

One factor that sets Canadian justice systems apart from our American counterparts is that Canadian approaches tend to be less politicized and more likely to be run by professional bureaucrats who have expert knowledge of the crime problem. As a result, Canada has managed to largely avoid the destructive wars on drugs and the

three-strikes policies that have resulted in mass imprisonment in the United States. Many states are currently dismantling these programs because they cannot afford the high costs of imprisoning low-risk offenders.

As you read through the chapters that follow, you are encouraged to think about Canada's criminal justice policies and their effects on offenders, victims, and justice-system stakeholders. Not only are misguided justice practices costly, but they also result in lost opportunities as the funds spent on ineffective policies could instead be used for other crime-reduction strategies. Writing about Canadian justice policies, Tonry (2013, p. 474) observed that "the best way to fashion a humane and effective sentencing system is to take small steps cautiously. Doing nothing may be the best policy."

REUTERS/Lucy Nicholson

Canada has managed to avoid the destructive wars on drugs and the three-strikes policies that have resulted in mass imprisonment in the United States. Many states are currently dismantling these programs because they cannot afford the high costs of incarcerating low-risk prisoners. In this photo, inmates walk around a gymnasium where they are housed due to overcrowding at the California Institution for Men, a state prison in Chino, California.

Career SNAPSHOT

Regional Communications Officer

There are tens of thousands of jobs within the justice system that support the activities of the police, courts, and corrections. Most of us are unaware these jobs exist or of the important role the individuals in these positions have in the smooth operations of the justice system. Many of them do not have direct contact with offenders. The personnel working for the Parole Board of Canada (PBC) play a key role in the safe transition of federal prisoners returning to the community, and their employees work in a number of diverse roles, including working with victims. One of the challenges for crime victims is that they are often unaware of the operations of the justice system or their rights as victims since the introduction of the *Canadian Victims Bill of Rights* in 2015 (see the online chapter on Victimization).

Profile

Name: Kerry Gatien
Job Title: Regional Communications Officer, Parole Board of Canada
Employed in current job since: 2011
Present location: Kingston, Ontario
Education: MSSC (Criminology), University of Ottawa

Background

Growing up, I had a variety of life experiences that influenced me in choosing a career in the criminal justice system (CJS). In my youth, there were times when my family lived in less desirable areas, which exposed me to different forms of crime and violence. As an active student and community member, though, these circumstances also enabled me to meet police officers, and I took the opportunity to interact with them and learned about their jobs and the issues facing our community. These experiences kick-started my interest in the CJS and I began focusing my education and volunteering initiatives towards law, policing, and victims.

Following high school, I enrolled in the criminology program at the University of Ottawa. Throughout the program, I ensured that my student placements were within the CJS, which included working for an organization that helped first-time young offenders learn to make better choices. After earning an Honours degree in Criminology, I applied for work as an officer at various police departments. While waiting for their responses, I completed one semester of a master's degree in Criminology at the University of Ottawa before being hired by a municipal police service.

Work Experience

After my graduation from university I worked as a police officer for 12 years, both on patrol and as a school resource officer. It was while working in the school system that I began giving presentations to students, and discovered the importance of information sharing and dialogue.

I finished my master's degree while working as a patrol officer, often attending classes before and after my shifts. I had always aspired to become an investigative detective; however, my family situation changed, resulting in a need for a more consistent schedule. I then found work as a policy analyst in the federal government, which I enjoyed, but my heart remained in the CJS. After working as an analyst for 2 years, I applied to the Parole Board of Canada as a Regional Communications Officer (RCO) in Kingston, Ontario, and was successful in getting the job!

My role as an RCO is to help victims of federal offenders navigate and participate in the parole process, ensuring that their rights under the *Canadian Victims Bill of Rights* are respected. My primary responsibilities include providing victims with information about the offender that harmed them, advising them of their rights and responsibilities, and facilitating and attending hearings with them.

The biggest challenges I face as an RCO relate to the misconceptions people have about the CJS. Despite our best efforts, there is a knowledge disconnect regarding the Board's jurisdiction and role in the CJS, particularly as it relates to the Board's decision-making process and the services we provide. I have come to realize that my approach in working with victims must balance compassion and empathy along with education and understanding around the purpose of parole, which focuses on rehabilitation and community reintegration—and this can be very challenging.

It is very rewarding for me to know that I have helped make a positive and proactive difference in the lives of others. When a victim thanks me for helping them participate in an offender's conditional release process, I know that I have helped make an undeniably difficult process just a little bit easier.

Advice to Students

Choose work that is meaningful to you. Decide what your values, passions, and goals are, and do what moves you closer to them. Reflect on your personal interests and strengths, assess how they could translate into professional

Continued

skill-sets, and consider what and where the relevant work opportunities may be. When you find work you like—own the role—as good work is easy to spot and tends to be rewarded in kind.

For students interested in pursuing work in the CJS, I recommend researching the various roles, attending career fairs and conferences, and seeking volunteer and/or part-time job opportunities in the CJS field. Talk to as many people as you can about their work, absorb as much information as possible and maintain professional connections. If considering working in victim services, a sense of compassion, perspective, and empathy are essential traits, along with facilitation skills and the ability to multi-task and prioritize.

Perhaps most important, though, are interpersonal and communications skills. This includes knowing and being able to adapt to the needs of your audience, conveying difficult information with clarity, and keeping calm in the face of challenging, often emotional, situations. Lastly, making life choices that keep you out of conflict with the law is also necessary, as this kind of work requires being able to obtain a security clearance.

REVIEW QUESTIONS

1. What is the difference between chivalry and paternalism in relation to the treatment of girls and women in the justice system?
2. How do the crime control philosophies of retribution, deterrence, and incapacitation differ from restitution, rehabilitation, and restorative justice?
3. How do politicians, the news, and other entertainment industries shape public opinion about crime and punishment?
4. What does the statement "ideas have consequences" mean when it comes to influencing crime control strategies?
5. Why do "tough on crime" punishments fail to deter offenders?

DISCUSSION QUESTIONS

1. Why is there a reluctance to collect data on the racial and ethnocultural characteristics of individuals in Canada's criminal justice system?
2. Does paying $1,000 in restitution have the same punitive impact on a middle-class offender as it does on a low-income individual? Would making offenders complete community service work have a better deterrent effect than paying financial restitution?
3. Restorative justice approaches have been criticized for being "soft on crime." Does it matter if an intervention is soft on crime if it works?
4. Why is it so difficult to reform offenders?
5. What factors formed your opinions about the ways that offenders should be treated?

INTERNET SITE

Although the last Canadian executions occurred in 1962 and capital punishment was abolished in 1976, the majority of Canadians support the reintroduction of the death penalty. The Death Penalty Information Center (a US group that opposes the death penalty) provides information about the use of the death penalty in the United States and in other countries, and the site may be helpful to those interested in studying this issue.

www.deathpenaltyinfo.org

CASE CITED

R v Gladue, [1999] 1 SCR 688

▲ "Troopers" in North West Mounted Police (NWMP) dress costume perform at Fort MacLeod Museum in Alberta (on the grounds of Fort MacLeod, which was built in 1874. The NWMP became the RCMP in 1904. Why do you think Canadians (and the RCMP) hold on to these reminders of the RCMP's history? (Photo credit: wwing/iStockphoto)

4 Police Organization and Structure

LEARNING OUTLINE

After reading this chapter, you will be able to

- Describe how Canadian policing evolved from the 1800s to today
- Describe the different urban and rural policing arrangements, and the agencies delivering these services
- Identify some possible reasons for differences in police strength
- Describe the five roles of the police in Canada

Investigating Crimes

The murder of 15-year-old Tina Fontaine drew international attention to the issue of missing and murdered Indigenous girls and women. On August 17, 2014, Tina's body—which had been wrapped in a duvet weighed down with rocks—was found in the Red River near Winnipeg. Barghout (2018, para. 3) says that Tina, originally from Northern Manitoba, had travelled to Winnipeg to visit her birth mother, and in her six weeks in the city she had come to the attention of "police officers and security officers, hospital staff and Child and Family Services." She was declared a missing person by her hometown RCMP on July 10, 2014. Child and Family Services (CFS) placed her in a hotel, but she left shortly thereafter (the staff were not allowed to physically stop her from leaving), and she was reported missing four more times in the next few weeks. Tina was hospitalized after being found unconscious on the street on August 8, 2014, and returned to the CFS placement. On August 9 she again left the hotel and was not seen afterward. Family members contend that the vulnerable teenager fell through the cracks in the systems that were supposed to protect her. A report from the Manitoba Advocate for Children and Youth (2019) highlighted how the police, health officials, and care workers failed to act in the days before her murder despite her involvement in risky behaviours and the fact that she was being sexually exploited; the report also found that she required better care and support prior to her 2014 trip to Winnipeg.

On December 8, 2015, Winnipeg police charged 53-year-old Raymond Cormier, a man with 92 previous criminal convictions, with Fontaine's murder. Cormier had allegedly been giving the teenager drugs (Barghout, 2018), and police recordings played in court suggest he had sex with her (Nicholson, 2018). Despite having circumstantial evidence suggesting his guilt, Cormier was found not guilty of Fontaine's murder in February 2018. Indigenous groups were outraged that this young woman's murder had gone unpunished. Critical scholars such as de Finney (2017, p. 11) observe that Tina Fontaine's murder shows how Indigenous girls are "dehumanized, exploited, and portrayed as dispensable damaged goods."

So why couldn't the criminal justice system produce justice for Tina Fontaine? Unlike what we see depicted in television and films, there was almost no evidence linking the suspect to the murder, and a pathologist could not even conclusively say she had been murdered even after an autopsy that lasted two days (Canadian Press, 2018; May, 2018). Broadbeck (2018, para. 4) says the prosecution had a weak case and "there was no confirmed cause of death, no crime scene and very little to glean forensically from Tina's body. There were no witnesses who saw Tina's killer. And there was no forensic evidence linking Cormier to her." With respect to the investigation, Broadbeck (2018) reports that the police engaged in a six-month undercover operation they hoped would produce a confession. Prosecutors also used the testimony of Cormier's associates about comments he made about Fontaine, but he calls their testimony in court highly suspect.

In order for a person to be found guilty of a crime in Canada the jury must find they are guilty beyond a reasonable doubt, a topic addressed in Chapter 7. As Broadbeck (2018, para. 10, 11) says: "Tina Fontaine did not get justice, but it wasn't through lack of effort or diligence by police. They threw a ton of resources at this case but they simply couldn't gather the evidence required to get a guilty verdict. The jury had no choice but to acquit. They did their job. And the justice system, including Justice Glenn Joyal who presided over the case, did its job."

The Manitoba Advocate for Children and Youth (2019) prepared a comprehensive report that provides an overview of Fontaine's case, which can be accessed at https://manitobaadvocate.ca/wp-content/uploads/MACY-Special-Report-March-2019-Tina-Fontaine-FINAL1.pdf.

Critical Questions

1. The police officers involved in this case spent thousands of hours in the investigation, but were unable to obtain enough evidence to secure a conviction. How does this match with our understanding of crime and police work from television?
2. Macdonald (2017) says that "criminal trials may change the world—but it is never their goal.... The only issue is proving guilt beyond a reasonable

doubt." Should juries in criminal trials consider the political outcomes of their decisions? Why or why not?
3. What has the greater harm to society: a wrongful conviction of an innocent person or an injustice because a guilty person is not found guilty? Would your answer change if the victim was a member of your family?

INTRODUCTION

There are about two police officers for every thousand Canadians, and as noted in Chapter 1, about two-thirds of them are employed by municipalities. Most of us automatically think of the police in their role of controlling and responding to crime, although crime-fighting accounts for only about one-quarter of their duties. The remainder of their time is spent in social service tasks: looking for lost children, investigating sudden deaths (and notifying family members), responding to complaints such as noisy parties or barking dogs, and engaging in community policing activities such as providing crime-prevention information to citizens or consulting with police advisory boards on local policing priorities (Robertson, 2012). Traffic enforcement also accounts for a significant proportion of officer time, including issuing tickets and responding to collisions. We seldom consider that officers are also required to appear in court to testify and to attend training, and that these activities take them "off the streets."

With respect to their crime-fighting role, the police in a democratic society must achieve a balance between enforcing the law and respecting the rights of the individuals they encounter, whether they are suspects, victims, witnesses, or members of the public. In particular, dealing with suspects is not always an easy undertaking as the public generally supports a "tough on crime" agenda but can become hostile to police officers who overstep legal or ethical boundaries. In complex and difficult-to-manage scenarios, such as responding to

people with mental illness, officers may feel they are in a "lose–lose" situation, as no matter what they do, their actions are criticized. Many of the situations the police encounter are due to shortcomings in the health, education, or social service sectors—what people call the social safety net. In some places the police have become the "lead agency that deals with homeless, mental illness, school discipline, youth unemployment, immigration, youth violence, sex work and drugs" (Heyer, 2018). This is an example of mission creep, where organizations assume additional duties that were never envisioned by the founders of these agencies. As you read through this chapter ask

mission creep Occurs when organizations take on more duties than were originally envisioned by the founders of those agencies.

Police recognize the importance of being involved in communities. Above, two police officers pose with children during Canada Day celebrations in Vancouver, BC.

dbimages/Alamy Stock Photo

yourself whether the police are the right agency to tackle these social problems. Meares (2017, p. 1365) says that "it is unfair to expect police to solve what is fundamentally a social safety net problem with the crude tools of crime-fighting simply because they are available twenty-four hours a day, seven days a week, and 365 days a year."

Provinces have jurisdiction over policing, and they all have established sets of legal guidelines that police services must follow. In Ontario, for example, a declaration of principles is outlined in the *Police Services Act*. The guiding principle is that the police are responsible for ensuring the safety and security of all people and property in the province while abiding by the fundamental rights guaranteed by the *Charter*. The need for cooperation between police services and the communities they serve is also highlighted. Other principles include the importance of being attentive to the needs of crime victims. Respecting the multiracial and multicultural nature of Ontario's populations is also recognized, including First Nation, Inuit, and Métis populations. The declaration ends with an acknowledgement that police services need to be representative of the populations they serve, and that all peoples must receive equitable levels of policing. Underlying all of these principles is the goal of a healthy and mutually beneficial relationship between the public and the police—something that is easy to describe, but difficult to achieve.

Police provide an important service to the public in terms of law enforcement, but as noted earlier, this aspect represents only a fraction of their work, and we often tend to overlook their other duties. Moreover, in recent years there has been growing agreement that the police "cannot go it alone," and they rely on the public's support in order to carry out their duties. In dozens of Saskatchewan and Ontario jurisdictions, for example, the police have introduced proactive crime control strategies that are intended to respond to the unmet needs of at-risk individuals and families, such as young people who are experimenting with alcohol and drugs, before they get into more serious trouble (Nilson, 2018). Altogether, we find that policing is slowly moving from reactive to proactive crime-reduction strategies that are more likely to involve the community and focus on crime prevention.

In order to illustrate what is happening with police organizations today, this chapter first presents a brief description of the evolution of policing, followed by a review of the structure of Canadian policing. There is a diverse range of police services in Canada—from small agencies employing fewer than 10 officers to large provincial police services and the RCMP. The size of the agency, the professionalism of organizational leaders, and the training that officers receive shapes their interactions with the public and contributes to the success of front-line officers (also called rank-and-file officers) in crime prevention and control.

THE EVOLUTION OF CANADIAN POLICING

Policing has greatly transformed over the years as Canada has developed from a rural country that depended on agriculture to an industrialized urban nation with a diverse multicultural population. Cities have increased in population size largely due to rural residents moving from the countryside to cities and immigration from other nations. These demographic shifts led to changes in the way that policing was carried out. For most of Canadian history, policing was undertaken by officers working in small-town agencies with fewer than 10 officers. These small agencies evolved into larger, well-funded police services, and the officers working within them are now more representative of the communities they serve as well as better trained and more professional. The big city police department or large regional, provincial, and federal service is now the norm, and there are fewer than 50 police services with less than 50 officers and the number of these small departments is dropping every year.

Policing has passed through a number of evolutionary stages, and this chapter briefly highlights how these early influences set the stage for modern policing in Canada. This approach is useful for understanding the transition of policing from relatively small stand-alone police services (agencies that are not part of a larger organization) to today's larger services.

front-line officers Officers who occupy front-line policing positions (e.g., up to the rank of sergeant) and do not have executive authority.

stand-alone police services Police services that are typically small and are not part of a larger police organization.

The four stages discussed in this chapter are the pre-modern era (prior to 1820), the political era (1820 to 1940), the professional era (1940 to 1980), and the community policing era (1980 to the present). By taking a closer look at how policing arrangements evolved in Canada, we will be better able to understand today's policing arrangements. The following sections provide a brief overview of these four stages and explore how they led to modern policing.

Pre-Modern Era (Prior to 1820)

Prior to their contact with the first English and European settlers, Indigenous people had developed customary justice systems to resolve disputes and respond to wrongdoing. These justice systems were similar to the practices of Indigenous people across the globe, where most disputes were resolved informally by tribal leaders, although some First Nations also had individuals who played a role in order maintenance. It is important to note that there was no one way that Indigenous peoples confronted wrongdoers, as concepts of reconciliation, healing, and harmony differed across the nation (Canadian Council of Academies, 2019, p. 20). Jones, Ruddell, Nestor, Quinn, and Phillips (2014, p. 22) report that these justice systems often had a restorative approach, and behaviours were "controlled and regulated through shaming, ostracism and compensation for a victim's loss." Some wrongdoers, however, were physically punished or executed, while others were banished from the community, which may have been an actual death sentence. These systems were in place before the lands that would become Canada were colonized by the English and European settlers.

The military was responsible for maintaining order in the first settlements prior to Confederation in 1867. The British navy, for instance, policed

First Nations
A term used to describe the Indigenous people of Canada, not including the Inuit or Métis; the term can also refer to the lands set aside for Indigenous peoples.

Courtesy of Operation Lifesaver

Railway police officers have the same powers of arrest as municipal police officers and receive the same training, but they work for corporations. Most of their duties are related to crime and accident prevention, although they also investigate crimes that occur on railway property. The railway police are one example of how policing arrangements established in the 1800s have persisted over time.

the Newfoundland coastal outports, and British troops responded to crimes occurring on the island. As immigration increased throughout the 1700s and 1800s, people brought with them ideas of controlling crime that they had experienced in their homelands. Several Canadian municipalities claim to have had the first formal police service. The Royal Newfoundland Constabulary, founded in 1729, claims to be the oldest police service in Canada, although the town of York (which later became Toronto) is also credited as being one of the first Canadian police departments that deployed uniformed officers who were paid a salary (rather than receiving fees for arrests).

Political Era (1820 to 1940)

By the early 1800s, local politicians were instrumental in establishing police services and many of them used the police to further their interests, whether they were legal or not. One characteristic that was consistent across these small-town and city police services is that they were often controlled by local political leaders composed of mayors and council members (or aldermen). In some places, the crimes of the rich and politically powerful were overlooked, and the poor and members of minority groups were over-policed (Thomson & Clairmont, 2013).

In this era, police chiefs served at the will of mayors and council members, and they were sometimes directed by these political leaders to ignore certain types of offences or suspects (e.g., being asked to overlook the impaired driving of the mayor's supporters). If chiefs enforced the law against the wishes of their employers, they could be replaced by new chiefs who would carry out the wishes of their political masters (Thomson, 2003). Police officers were also treated unfairly and some were fired for enforcing the law, even when their actions were fair, lawful, and appropriate. As a result of this political interference, many officers working in small-town police departments suffered from low morale and rapid turnover (that is, officers would not stay in these jobs for a long period of time).

Although political leaders play a role in identifying crime problems and in prioritizing issues for

In 1855, the city of Charlottetown hired six police officers to serve a population of about 6,500 residents. This picture depicts a group of officers in the early 1900s. Few of these officers received any formal training prior to being hired, and many police services expected their officers to provide all of their own equipment, including uniforms and sidearms.

the police based on public concerns, the police have to be independent of inappropriate political interference in order to have the trust and confidence of the public. How have the police done at avoiding inappropriate political interference? In the following paragraphs, the evolution of Canadian policing from a political to a professional model is briefly described. Although the first settlers imported ideas about policing from their homelands, the policing arrangements that eventually developed in this country were distinctively Canadian.

North American police services were modelled after large municipal services that were first established in England and France in the 1820s and 1830s. The French deployed uniformed officers (the Sûreté) in Paris by 1829 (Gillis, 1989). At about the same time, Sir Robert Peel founded London's Metropolitan Police Service with 1,000 full-time uniformed officers. The evolution of the London police from an initial idea to a functioning agency took almost a decade due to public opposition to the police, as they were thought to be a threat to liberty. In order to convince the public that the police were not an occupying army, constables patrolling the streets were unarmed—a

Royal Newfoundland Constabulary Established in 1729, this police force claims to be Canada's oldest police service and still provides services throughout Newfoundland and Labrador.

over-policed Refers to when members of a social group or neighbourhood are treated suspiciously, watched, stopped, searched, questioned, or otherwise paid attention to by the police by virtue of being members of that group.

political interference The inappropriate use of political authority to influence police operations.

tradition that still exists (although there are armed response teams today). Peel is considered to be the father of the modern police service, and he introduced "centralized command, the beat system, crime prevention and the uniform" (Marquis, 2016, p. 12). Peel's principles are widely cited today (see the boxed feature "A Closer Look: Robert Peel's Nine Principles of Policing" in this chapter).

Policing was also occurring in the countryside. A rural police force, modelled on the Royal Irish Constabulary (RIC), patrolled the Quebec countryside from 1839 to 1842, and a frontier police force was established in Ontario by 1864—although there is little information about that service. The RIC influenced police organizations throughout Canada, as many former RIC officers held leadership positions in municipal and provincial police services as well as with the North-West Mounted Police (NWMP). The need for formal social control on the Prairies became apparent after the 1869–1870 Red River Rebellion (where Métis people in Manitoba engaged in an uprising against the government; some call this the Red River Resistance), and following the Cypress Hills Massacre in 1873 when American hunters and whisky traders participated in the massacre of 20 or more Indigenous people in southern Saskatchewan. Although the NWMP was initially intended to be a temporary police force, it eventually became the Royal Canadian Mounted Police (RCMP) in 1920.

Because Canada was a rural nation, most policing prior to the 1940s occurred in small towns and the countryside. Rural and small-town policing emerged in a patchwork fashion, meaning that there was very little consistency across the nation.

Royal Irish Constabulary (RIC) A police force that emphasized mounted patrols and was a model for early rural Canadian police services.

North-West Mounted Police (NWMP) A police force established in 1873 in response to lawlessness in the North-West Territories (in what is now Alberta and Saskatchewan) and to reinforce Canadian sovereignty in that region. The organization became the Royal North-West Mounted Police in 1904 and the Royal Canadian Mounted Police in 1920.

WS Collection/Alamy Stock Photo

The Canadian North was policed by the North-West Mounted Police (NWMP), which became the Royal North-West Mounted Police in 1904 and the Royal Canadian Mounted Police in 1920. Writing about the NWMP, Fanning (2012, p. 519) observes that it "was a consciously rural institution. As much as possible, the force sought to avoid intruding in urban affairs, as both its mandate and duties were concerned primarily with rural, isolated, and vulnerable settlements."

The Police Association of Ontario (2014) notes that "the quality of policing depended very much on the political and financial priorities of the local municipal council." Few small municipalities could afford professional police services, and they experimented with different types of policing—such as hiring a town constable for a year or two, or relying on part-time officers—but few written records exist to tell us the complete story of these early police organizations, in Canada or elsewhere (see Anderson, 2011). We do know, however, that for the most part, officers working for municipal police services were recruited locally and were poorly trained; they were overworked (six-day work weeks were common); and they lacked job security, workers' compensation, or pensions. While these officers worked long hours with few benefits, arrests were rare and most of their work was in response to relatively minor offences such as public drunkenness, disorderly behaviour, and vagrancy (Marquis, 2016, p. 41).

During the political era, provincial police services were also established throughout the country to serve the rural areas and small towns, and the lifespan of these agencies is shown in Table 4.1. While each of the provinces has had one provincial police service, the Canadian North was policed by the NWMP, which became the Royal North-West Mounted Police (RNWMP) in 1904 and the RCMP in 1920. Even when the mounted police were posted in the Arctic in the early 1900s, their primary role was to ensure sovereignty (which is a nation's claim on its territory) rather than maintaining order or fighting crime.

While most of this discussion about the political era has centred around the inappropriate influences of local politicians on the police, provincial and federal politicians were also responsible for deploying the police in response to various threats. One example that ended in injuries and death is worthy of mention: the 1935 On-to-Ottawa Trek that started in Vancouver and ended in Regina.

The On-to-Ottawa Trek occurred during the Great Depression that started in 1929. In 1935, a group of unemployed men, many from federal relief camps, decided to travel by freight train from British Columbia to Ottawa to protest joblessness and poor working conditions with the hope that the federal government would find them work. The movement increased in size as they travelled east, until Prime Minister Bennett ordered that the trains be stopped in Regina, and the protesters set up camp there. Although a small group of individuals were permitted to meet with Bennett in Ottawa, talks quickly broke down and the men returned to Regina. On July 1, 1935, the strikers and

Royal North-West Mounted Police (RNWMP) The policing authority of the Canadian North from 1904 to 1919; it became the RCMP in 1920.

sovereignty A nation's claim on its territory.

TABLE 4.1 Provincial Police Services

Province	Provincial Police Service	
	Established	Disbanded
Newfoundland and Labrador*	1729	Active
Prince Edward Island	1930	1932
Nova Scotia	1928	1932
New Brunswick	1927	1932
Quebec	1870	Active
Ontario	1909	Active
Manitoba	1870	1932
Saskatchewan	1917	1928
Alberta	1917	1932
British Columbia	1871	1950

*The Royal Newfoundland Constabulary provides provincial policing services to the rural areas surrounding North East Avalon, Corner Brook, and Labrador West, and the RCMP serves the rest of the province.

A Closer Look

Robert Peel's Nine Principles of Policing

There are references to Robert Peel's nine principles in almost every policing book. In a review of these principles, Loader (2016, pp. 429–430) speculates that the principles were written at least a century after Peel died and that they were taken from newspaper accounts and Peel's speeches or writing. Peel's nine principles of policing are as follows:

1. To prevent crime and disorder, as an alternative to their repression by military force and severity of legal punishment.

2. To recognize always that the power of the police to fulfill their functions and duties is dependent on public approval of their existence, actions, and behaviour, and on their ability to secure and maintain public respect.

3. To recognize always that to secure and maintain the respect and approval of the public means also securing the willing cooperation of the public in the task of securing observance of the law.

4. To recognize always that the extent to which the cooperation of the public can be secured diminishes, proportionately, the necessity of the use of physical force and compulsion for achieving police objectives.

5. To seek and preserve public favour, not by pandering to public opinion, but by constantly demonstrating absolutely impartial service to law, in complete independence of policy, and without regard to the justice or injustice of the substance of individual laws, by ready offering of individual service and friendship to all members of the public without regard to their wealth or social standing; by ready exercise of courtesy and good humour; and by ready offering of individual sacrifice in protecting and preserving life.

6. To use physical force only when the exercise of persuasion, advice, and warning is found to be insufficient to obtain public cooperation to an extent necessary to secure observance of law or restore order; and to use only the minimum degree of physical force that is necessary on any particular occasion for achieving a police objective.

7. To maintain at all times a relationship with the public that gives reality to the historic tradition that the police are the public and that the public are the police; the police being only members of the public who are paid to give full-time attention to duties which are incumbent on every citizen in the interests of community welfare and existence.

8. To recognize always the need for strict adherence to police executive functions, and to refrain from even seeming to usurp the power of the judiciary of avenging individuals or the state, and authoritatively judging guilt and punishing the guilty.

9. To recognize always that the test of police efficiency is the absence of crime and disorder and not the visible evidence of police action in dealing with them (Loader, 2016, pp. 429–430).

Despite the fact that these principles originated almost 200 years ago, they are still used to define today's ideal police–community relationships.

---

protesters had congregated in downtown Regina when they were confronted by armed RCMP and Regina police officers. When the dust from the riot cleared, one Regina police officer and a protester had been killed, 45 protesters and bystanders were injured, and 130 rioters were arrested. In his analysis of the Regina confrontation, Anastakis (2015, p. 148) observes that "despite claiming to fight the Great Depression on behalf of ordinary Canadians, the state remained squarely on the side of the employers, often with deadly consequences."

Professional Era (1940 to 1980)

The professional model of policing—also called the traditional model of policing—gradually replaced the political model that was seen as ineffective, corrupt, and brutal (Dobrin, 2006, p. 19).

professional model of policing A model that emphasizes a "top down" style of police management with an emphasis on random patrols and rapid response, where citizens play a passive role in crime control.

Advocates of the professional model praised its objectivity, reliance on science, and freedom from political interference. In his analysis of Canadian policing, Robertson (2012) notes the following:

> The professional model sought to apply the benefits of new technology, especially in communications, to police a more mobile society. The professional model incorporated a centralized approach, applying command and control techniques. This allowed for the introduction of random patrols with rapid response to calls for service. Standardization and training were emphasised to produce consistent service and results, limited individual initiative and local variation. (p. 352)

Civil service rules were also introduced by political and police leaders to reduce cronyism and nepotism (i.e., when friends and family members of police leaders were hired instead of the most qualified people for the job). This step increased the quality of officers, as did the introduction of formalized training at police academies. These ideas were revolutionary, as police officers were historically recruited from local towns and received little (or no) training prior to starting their jobs.

Prior to the establishment of provincial policing standards, officers were often poorly equipped because uniforms or sidearms were not always supplied—even up until the 1970s in Nova Scotia (Thomson, 2003). In some small towns, the only uniform that officers received was an armband designating them as police officers, and they were also expected to use their personal vehicles as their departments did not own any. Most of the crimes confronted by small-town officers were relatively minor, and antisocial behaviour and public order offences such as public drunkenness, disorderly conduct ("rowdyism"), and property crimes were the norm (McGahan & Thomson, 2003). Most of these offences were handled informally and few arrests were made. Police were typically hired on the basis of their physical size, and some suspects were beaten rather than arrested. According to a

former officer, "The physical part of the job was more important than the brains. . . . You had to beat heads first, then they [the public] respected you" (McGahan & Thomson, 2003, p. 28). Street justice, where suspected wrongdoers were beaten by the police and then released, was commonly applied, and while the individuals never received a criminal record for breaking the law, they never received any due process protections either.

Throughout the 1970s, political leaders increased the quality of policing by introducing provincial police standards, such as Manitoba's *Police Services Act*. These standards specified the hours of training required for new officers, the requirements for ongoing annual training for all officers (e.g., first aid and firearms re-qualification), the types of equipment officers required, and the practices for detaining prisoners. Many small towns found it costly to comply with these requirements, and so they contracted with the OPP, RCMP, or SQ to provide policing services. A growing number of officers were also being represented by professional associations and police unions. The Police Association of Ontario, for instance, was established in 1933 to represent the interests of Ontario's officers. Similar organizations advocated on behalf of police officers throughout the country, and these efforts resulted in better working conditions and enabled collective bargaining. Although most Canadian officers are now represented by unions, officers and civilian members of the RCMP were not permitted to bargain collectively until January 2015, when the Supreme Court found the federal government's ban on their unionization was unconstitutional (see *Mounted Police Association of Ontario v Canada*, 2015).

Community Policing Era (1980 to the Present)

By the 1980s, there was a growing awareness that the police needed to establish more productive relationships with communities and their stakeholders if they wanted to reduce crime. Police services started involving the public in their decision-making, and those consultations

cronyism
Occurs when friends of people in authority are appointed to jobs without regard to their qualifications.

nepotism
Preferential hiring carried out by people in powerful positions of their family members.

street justice
Occurs when a suspected offender is forced to submit to an unauthorized punishment by a police officer, such as doing push-ups in return for not getting a speeding ticket.

revealed that issues of concern were sometimes unrelated to crime, such as reducing visible signs of disorder (e.g., removing abandoned vehicles and graffiti) or confronting antisocial behaviour. In addition, the public wanted to play a larger role in the oversight of the police by providing formal guidance to police services, and police advisory boards were being established throughout Canada. Today, most provinces require that police activities be overseen by these advisory boards (also called police-management boards).

Civilian involvement in police activities is a key part of community-oriented policing, although this is a catch-all term that refers to a number of strategies intended to bring the police and the public together, which was one of Peel's principles. The methods that police services have used to involve communities varies greatly, although most services have incorporated what van Steden, Miltenburg, and Boutellier (2014, p. 144) call the three pillars of community policing:

- citizen involvement: The police consult the public about identifying and prioritizing community problems (including crime and disorder).
- problem-solving/problem-oriented approach: The police analyze crime information and draw on the insight of community members to develop strategies to prevent crime- and disorder-related problems.
- decentralization: Decision-making moves closer to the front lines, such as to patrol officers rather than police administrators. Community centres are sometimes established in troubled neighbourhoods. Officers are removed from motorized patrols and instead patrol on foot or bicycles.

All together, these three steps are intended to create better working relationships between the police and the people they police—ideas that were first proposed by Peel nearly two centuries ago.

The idea of community-oriented policing may be more popular with politicians, police leaders, and researchers than with front-line officers who typically still favour the traditional model of policing with its reliance on motorized patrol and rapid response. Moreover, despite the fact that their role in enforcing the laws accounts for less than a third of their activities, most police officers identify with their crime-fighting role. Robertson (2012, p. 352) questions "whether a community policing model truly reaches out to all members of the community or is simply paid lip service"— suggesting that we spend more time talking about community policing than actually implementing the approach. Writing about the community policing movement, Marquis (2016, p. 195) observes that "within the police studies literature there is little agreement as to what this movement actually was, why it appeared or what it has accomplished, yet after almost four decades most police forces continue to insist that they are following its principles, and many academics report on it as a genuine innovation."

Acceptance of community-oriented policing has varied, and some police services have been reluctant to surrender much control to the public. In addition, one of the challenges of community policing is that these initiatives sometimes work best in healthy communities that are well organized and have low levels of crime. Troubled neighbourhoods, by contrast, often have to overcome their mistrust of the police before wanting to participate in community policing. According to the International Association of Chiefs of Police (2014, n.p.), "In order for communities and law enforcement to build solid relationships, there must be an element of trust, fairness, and even respect. However, all of those coveted attributes must be earned through actions, not just words; and that takes time." There is some debate about the success of community policing and whether it will play a very important role in the future of policing. Leighton (2016, pp. 137–139) says that interest in community policing in Canada peaked in the 1980s, and the future of policing will have to be responsive to vulnerable people (such as the elderly), the increasingly multicultural nature of Canadian society, the changing nature of crime due to technology, and confronting an ongoing fiscal crisis where policing costs are

community-oriented policing An approach to policing that relies on community involvement to take a proactive approach to reducing antisocial behaviour and crime.

lip service When more time is spent talking about something than actually implementing the approach.

continuously increasing. James Sheptycki (2017) a prominent police scholar from York University, observes that debates about the nature of policing should start with asking what matters in policing, or in other words, what is good policing? All of us will have different definitions about what constitutes good policing, but good police–community relationships are a foundation for any successful crime control strategy.

POLICE STRUCTURE IN CANADA

As of May 15, 2018, there were about 69,000 officers in Canada working in four basic types of police organizations (Conor, Robson, & Marcellus, 2019). The RCMP, with over 18,000 officers (who are also called members), is the largest police service in Canada. The RCMP is responsible for federal policing and also contracts with eight provinces and hundreds of municipalities to provide police services across the country. The Ontario Provincial Police and Sûreté du Québec patrol the highways and the countryside as well as serve small towns in those provinces. There are also a number of regional services, such as the Durham Regional Police in Ontario, that provide police services both in cities and in the surrounding countryside. Most Canadian officers, however, work for local municipalities— these range in size from agencies with fewer than 10 officers to large police forces such as the Montreal Police Service, which employed over 4,500 officers in 2018 (Conor et al., 2019).

One of the cornerstones of community-oriented policing is that the police should reflect the characteristics of the community. Historically, the police could best be described as "pale and male," but this is changing. Corsianos (2009) reports that police matrons (who worked with female arrestees and juveniles who were detained) were employed by the Toronto Police Service in 1887. The first policewomen in Canada, Lurancy Harris and Minnie Miller, were hired by the Vancouver Police in 1912, and a number of municipal services hired women officers over the next decade (Corsianos, 2009). However, it was not until 1974 when the largest Canadian police services, the OPP and the

RCMP, trained their first women officers, and the proportion of women officers has been increasing ever since then. Table 4.2 shows the increase in women officers from 1986 to 2017. Over one-fifth (22 per cent) of officers were women in 2018 and a growing number of them hold leadership positions (Conor et al., 2019). So, does having more women officers make a difference in a police service? Carmichael and Kent (2015a) found that Canadian police services with a greater number of women officers killed fewer suspects. These researchers speculated that having a greater proportion of women officers changed the department culture and their influence reduced the use of force.

With respect to the reporting number of Indigenous and visible minority officers, it is difficult to show changes over time in the number of these officers as much of the data about race and ethnicity is based on self-reported information, which is not consistently collected and is incomplete. Conor et al. (2019) however, report that while about one-fifth (22.3 per cent) of Canadians are visible minorities, they only accounted for 8 per cent of all police officers in 2018. In terms of officers of Indigenous ancestry, they accounted for 4 per cent of all police officers, which was slightly above their representation in the national population (5 per cent of Canadians reported being of Indigenous ancestry). When looking at the national averages, we should remember that there are some police services with much higher proportions of Indigenous officers, including many First Nations police services, and 30 per cent of the Prince Albert Police Service officers are of Indigenous ancestry. The growth in the proportion of visible minority and Indigenous officers is also shown in Table 4.2 (note that the changes in women's policing are shown for over 30 years, while the statistics for the visible minority and Indigenous officers only represent five years).

Police Consolidation

In addition to an increased focus on community involvement, there was a move to consolidate police services during the 1980s. This shift was sometimes the result of regionalization, and it involved joining together several smaller police agencies to form a single organization that served

TABLE 4.2 Percentage change in Women, Indigenous, and Visible Minority Police Officers in Canada

Change in Women Officers, 1987 to 2017	Increase 386%
Change in Visible Minority Officers, 2011 to 2016	Increase 2.4%
Change in Indigenous Officers, 2011 to 2016	Increase 15%

Conor (2018)

Policing: An Expensive Proposition

Taxpayers across Canada are concerned about the rising costs of policing (Berman, 2018). Conor (2018, p. 25) reports that the per capita cost of policing in 2016/2017 was $405, which was an increase of about half since 2004/2005. Because municipalities use property taxes to fund police services, wealthier communities typically have more money for policing. Large cities have some advantages when it comes to paying for police services. The cost of policing in small cities such as Saskatoon or Regina accounts for 20–25 per cent of municipal budgets, while larger cities pay a smaller proportion. In Toronto, for instance, the total budget for 2018 was $11.2 billion and policing costs accounted for over $1.1 billion, which accounts for 10.5 per cent of the city's total budget (City of Toronto, 2018). Police services in larger cities are often able to their contain costs because they can operate more efficiently.

Many smaller communities, on the other hand, are struggling to pay for police services. For example, the average per capita cost of policing in Canada was $405 in 2016/2017, but for the 22,000 residents of Amherstburg, Ontario, the cost was $658 a year (Baxter, 2018). In order to save costs, smaller towns and cities have laid off officers and disbanded their local police services, and many are now contracting with larger policing forces.

a number of cities or an urban–rural region. An example is the Halton Regional Police Service, which was founded in 1974 when the municipal police services from five Ontario cities (Burlington, Oakville, Milton, Georgetown, and Acton) and several townships merged into a single agency. Some municipalities replaced their local police departments after contracting with the OPP, RCMP, or SQ. Lithopoulos (2014) reports that in 1988 there were 406 Canadian municipal police services, but this had decreased to 142 by 2012, a decrease of almost two-thirds. Table 4.3 shows the decrease in municipal police services in Canada from 1988 to 2012. While all provinces experienced a reduction in the number of municipal police services, the drop was greatest in Quebec, as the province lost 82 per cent of its municipal police departments.

TABLE 4.3 Decrease in Municipal Police Services in Canada, 1988–2012

Province	Number of Municipal Police Services		
	1988	2012	Reduction (%)
Prince Edward Island	4	3	25
Nova Scotia	25	11	56
New Brunswick	26	9	65
Quebec	164	30	82
Ontario	138	54	61
Manitoba	10	7	30
Saskatchewan	17	10	41
Alberta	10	7	30
British Columbia	12	11	8
Total	406	142	65

Adapted from Lithopoulos (2014). Statistics Canada, CANSIM tables 254-004 and 254-006;

contract policing
A form of policing where a police service, such as the RCMP or OPP, provides policing to a municipality under a contract.

There is a long history of contract policing in Canada, as small towns find it very expensive to operate a police department with only a few officers. In April 2018 the town council of Espanola, Ontario, voted to disband its 20-officer police service and contract with the OPP (White, 2018). While towns disbanding their police services can reduce policing spending, the larger police service might not provide the same level of service, especially if no officers from the larger agency actually live in the community—thus reducing positive police–community relationships.

Police Strength

police strength
The ratio of police to civilians; the Canadian average is about two officers for every 1,000 residents.

Like any other human service agency, police services spend the greatest proportion of expenditures on staff salaries. The number of officers per 1,000 residents is called police strength, and this rate varies throughout the nation. Figure 4.1 shows the number of police officers in various Canadian cities in 2017. Montreal and Halifax had the highest number of officers per 1,000 residents (2.3 and 2.2 officers, respectively), while Kingston, Ontario, and Abbotsford, British Columbia, had fewer officers (1.5 and 1.4 officers per 1,000 residents). Ruddell and Thomas (2015) found that crime explains some of the differences in how many police are deployed in Canada's largest cities but that

other factors also influence how many officers are "on the streets." Wealthier cities tend to have greater police strength, and communities that have their own municipal police service employ more officers than cities contracting with the RCMP. As a result, economic factors seem to play an important role in how the police are deployed. One possible reason for this finding is that politicians in wealthier communities may win votes by expanding the size of their police service, as hiring more officers is usually considered good politics.

Rural Policing

Most police research is conducted on large municipal police services, which is understandable given that only one-fifth of Canadians live in rural areas. Given the vast spaces that must be policed, there are over 10,000 officers working in provincial policing, rural areas, small towns, and Indigenous communities (Ruddell, 2017). Although we often think of the countryside as having a slow pace of life, homicide rates are higher in rural areas than in cities, and as noted in Chapter 2, overall rates of crime severity also tend to be higher in rural Canada (Allen, 2018). A number of high-profile rural crimes in 2016 and 2017 have led to an increased frustration of rural residents who feel unsafe as police response times are often very lengthy. For example, the Ottawa

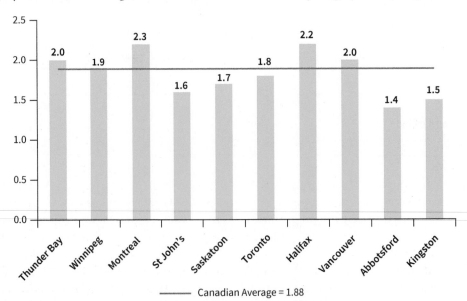

FIGURE 4.1 Officers per 1,000 Residents, Select Canadian Cities, 2017
Conor (2018)

A COMPARATIVE VIEW

Police Strength: Canada's Place in the World

Most developed nations have about two officers per 1,000 residents in the population, although many southern European nations have several times that number. Figure 4.2 shows that Greece, Belgium, Spain, and Cyprus have over 3.4 officers per 1,000 residents. When confronted with that statistic, scholars are curious about the reasons for this difference. In order to better understand this issue, Ruddell and Thomas (2009) conducted a cross-national study of police strength and found that countries that have more violent crime had more officers on the payroll. In the first several chapters of this book, a number of cross-national comparisons were made, and these comparisons can be tricky to evaluate due to the use of different definitions of crime and justice system personnel. The European statistics, for example, count border security guards as police officers, although Canada Border Services Agency officers are not classified as police in

Canada. The total number of police in Canada would be somewhat higher if these officials were counted.

Given the findings from comparative studies, an interesting research question would be to look just at the differences in police strength in Canada. Carmichael and Kent (2015b) examined police strength in 40 Canadian cities between 1996 and 2006, and they report that police strength increased with the size of a city's minority population, income, and poverty rate. These findings support a conflict perspective where scholars argue that the police are used to reinforce existing social relationships based on inequality by controlling the poor and minority populations. Carmichael and Kent (2015b, p. 275) observe that "conflict theorists assume that the legal code not only reflects the interests of the powerful but that the entire criminal justice system is a vehicle through which the dominant members of society enforce their views and regulate minority populations."

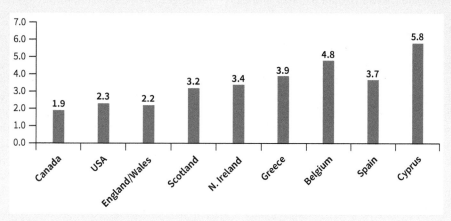

FIGURE 4.2 Police Officers per 1,000 Residents, 2015

Adapted from Eurostat (2019)

Police Service (2018, p. 46) reports that in 95 per cent of the priority-one calls (where there was an imminent danger to life) an officer was on-scene within 15 minutes. In a rural area, by contrast, the response time might be an hour or more, depending on where a crime occurs, the road and weather conditions, and the number of officers on patrol; it might also be difficult for officers to find a farmhouse or other rural location if it is located off the main roads.

Rural policing is carried out by the provincial police in Ontario and Quebec, and some municipal or regional police agencies such as the Peel Regional Police in Ontario patrol both urban and rural areas. With those exceptions, the remainder of the nation's rural areas are served by the RCMP, which has contracted with eight provinces to provide policing until the 2030s—although the parties can opt out of these agreements with two years' notice.

Race, Class, and Gender

Policing Indigenous Communities: Were First Nations Police Services Set Up to Fail?

In 1992, Canada became the only country that had developed a comprehensive national policing strategy for Indigenous people, known as the First Nations Policing Program (FNPP). The FNPP involves three levels of government (federal, provincial/territorial, and the First Nations), and police services operating under the umbrella of the FNPP served over 450 Indigenous communities. About one-third (154) of those communities were policed by 36 self-administered Indigenous police services, while the remaining communities received police services from larger police forces, such as the RCMP, OPP, and SQ (Mugford, 2018). Self-administered Indigenous police services are very much like municipal police services, although the management and oversight of these agencies is undertaken by the chief and band council rather than a mayor and city councillors.

Whether Indigenous communities are policed by a self-administered or contract police organization, Clairmont (2013) notes that policing Indigenous communities is challenging given the lasting effects of colonialism and the lack of economic opportunities in many First Nations. Police officers also report that social problems in some of these communities are severe, ranging from substance abuse to family violence (Ruddell & Jones, 2018). Most Indigenous communities are located in rural areas, and policing costs increase while community well-being (such as employment and health) decreases with the distance from urban areas (Ruddell, Lithopoulos, & Jones, 2015). In addition, rates of crime and victimization on First Nations are several times higher than the national average (Lithopoulos, 2013). With respect

self-determination Occurs when Indigenous communities are able to exert more control over their economic, social, and cultural development, including taking ownership over policing.

to homicide, for example, Indigenous people represented almost a quarter of homicide victims in 2017, although they account for about 5 per cent of the national population. In addition, "the rate of Aboriginal persons accused of homicide in 2017 was 12 times higher compared to non-Aboriginal accused persons" (Beattie, David, & Roy, 2018, p. 14). Given those challenges, one might assume that First Nations police services would require more funding than municipal police services.

Many self-administered police agencies have struggled. The Auditor General of Canada (2014) reports that these agencies are chronically underfunded and expected to do their work under adverse conditions, such as not having enough officers to provide proper backup or provide timely responses to calls for service. These are not new challenges, and Wes Luloff, former president of the First Nations Chiefs of Police Association, reported that these agencies were "set up to fail" due to a lack of support and funding (cited in Barnsley, 2002). Kiedrowski, Jones, and Ruddell (2017, p. 595) examined this issue and found these police services had been neglected by federal and provincial governments. These governments believed "that by doing nothing or ignoring the problem, the challenges confronting Indigenous policing would somehow manage or resolve themselves," [and this practice] "is in keeping with a long history of promising much, but delivering little to Indigenous people."

Given those challenges, one might ask why an Indigenous community would want to establish its own police service instead of leaving it to the RCMP, OPP, or SQ. One important concept underlying the FNPP is that it allows a community to take a step toward **self-determination**, which means that they can take control over some aspects of the justice system that had previously been denied to them due to the paternalism of government policies going back over a century.

ROLE OF THE POLICE IN CANADA

So far, this review of Canadian policing has focused on the four different policing arrangements—federal, provincial, regional, and municipal—and we've learned that most police officers are employed by municipal governments. Although officers may have different employers, there are a number of common elements in terms of the duties that officers carry out. A starting point in understanding the priorities of a police service is to review the agency's mission statement, which is a statement summarizing the agency's goals. For example, the Royal Newfoundland Constabulary (2018, p. 11) provides the following mission statement:

> We are committed to providing a fully integrated police service that fosters community partnerships to build safe and healthy communities.

Most Canadian police services express a similar set of values in their mission statements, including the protection of the public and an emphasis on forming partnerships with communities. Although the content of mission statements may differ, the values outlined in these statements are important for the staff working in police agencies. Maguire and Dyke (2012) analyzed responses from over 10,000 Canadian police officers in a survey about professionalism, and they found that over 80 per cent of officers reported being very familiar with the values of their employers. Furthermore, about two-thirds of these officers identified with the values of their organizations, and most officers believed that the mission statements were consistent with their beliefs about policing.

Mission statements also clarify the broad priorities of police agencies, although more specific roles or guidelines for police services are defined in provincial legislation. For example, section 11(1) of Ontario's *Police Services Act* spells out the six main functions for police agencies in that province:

1.   crime prevention
2.   law enforcement
3.   maintaining the public peace
4.   emergency response
5.   assistance to victims of crime
6.   any other prescribed policing functions

While these roles are similar for police services across the nation, there is probably less agreement on which roles should be prioritized. For example, politicians and members of the public might disagree on whether crime prevention or law enforcement ought to be the most important priority.

If law enforcement, or what some call fighting crime, occupies only a fraction of an officer's time, what other activities make up an officer's day? The key functions of the police, as highlighted in Ontario's *Police Services Act*, are described in the following pages. The final category—any other prescribed policing functions—is a "catch-all" statement to account for future changes, as policing acts are rarely changed: Ontario's *Police Services Act* was in place from 1990 until a new act was introduced in 2018, and it only came into effect in 2019.

Crime Prevention

All of us would agree that it is more desirable to prevent a crime than to respond to an offence that has occurred. While increased attention has been paid to crime prevention, deterring potential offenders is difficult given the limited number of officers we can put on the streets. The National Academies of Sciences (2018, p. 1) describe preventative or proactive policing as placing a priority on "prevention, mobilizing resources based on police initiative, and targeting the broader underlying forces at work that may be driving crime and disorder" instead of waiting to respond to crimes that have actually occurred. The National Academies of Sciences (2018, p. 2) identified four proactive approaches: (a) focusing officer attention on high-crime areas (hot spots); (b) identifying crime-related problems, and developing solutions to those problems (which is a problem-oriented approach); (c) targeting the small number of individuals who are responsible for committing a large number of offences (such as some gang members); and (d) using the strengths of a community to identify and control crime.

Ever since police vehicles were introduced, random preventative patrol (where officers patrol areas randomly throughout a community) was thought to deter potential wrongdoing and prevent crime. But with the exception of urban neighbourhoods with the highest levels of crime, police patrols are rare. In the suburbs, a patrol car might pass through a neighbourhood only once a day, and this minimal police presence would not deter anybody motivated to commit an offence. Rural communities might receive even fewer patrols, and officers have reported that some remote villages in northern Canada might receive only one or two visits from the police each month.

As police patrols are unlikely to have much of a deterrent effect on motivated offenders, other crime prevention approaches have been used. The police have been involving citizens in neighbourhood watch programs for decades. Similar programs also exist throughout rural Canada and are known as "farm watch" in rural areas or as "cottage watch" in lakeside communities. These programs encourage community members to report suspicious activities, behaviours, and people—the community members become the "eyes and ears" of the police. Although these programs have been around for a long time, we do not know how many of these groups are actually active nor how many volunteers are involved in them. Kang (2015) found that few people actually participated in these organizations. Studies of neighbourhood watch programs generally find that participation is highest "with wealthier, long-term residents who own their own homes" (Brunton-Smith & Bullock, 2018, p. 15).

So, are these programs effective? Finegan (2013, p. 105) examined US neighbourhood watch associations and observed that some of these programs suffer from "a lack of training, poor organization, tendencies to target certain demographic groups, and overzealous interactions with suspects." Even if neighbourhood watch programs are effective in deterring potential offenders, those individuals might just commit an offence in a place that has fewer people actively monitoring the neighbourhood (i.e., the issue of displacement, which was addressed in Chapter 2). As a result, these programs

might not reduce overall levels of crime, but instead they might push offenders into less organized communities. Despite these limitations, neighbourhood watch programs are low cost and enable the police and public to engage in partnerships, so it is likely that they will be around for a long time, and especially as they evolve using social media. There are a growing number of online groups where members post photos of unusual activities occurring or people acting suspiciously in their neighbourhoods, but there are also dangers associated with these efforts. Writing about online groups based in Winnipeg, Marchand (2017) describes how some posts misinform readers or suggest that innocent people are wrongdoers, and some contributors have posted pictures or made comments that could violate somebody's privacy. Despite those challenges it is likely the number of people participating in these forums will increase.

Law Enforcement

Although the crime prevention activities of civilians can deter some offences, responding to crimes and conducting investigations are the two key roles carried out by the police. Their training and the manner in which the police are deployed and equipped enables them to respond to serious incidents or to investigate violent crimes.

There is no shortage of laws to enforce, and because the police are spread relatively thin—with fewer than two officers for every 1,000 residents in all of Canada—political and police leaders establish enforcement priorities for their police services. Preventing and responding to crimes of violence are key priorities, but when it comes to property, traffic, and public order offences, there is less agreement on what should be prioritized. With respect to preventing harm and saving lives, for example, some researchers have found that increasing traffic enforcement in Canada can provide a good return on policing dollars in terms of fewer deaths and collisions (DeAngelo, 2018). Yet, aggressive traffic enforcement can also lead to tension between the police and the public.

When it comes to policing, one controversial practice is when people on the street are stopped and questioned. These activities go by a number of different names including stop, question, and frisk in the United States; carding and street checks in Canada; and stop and search in the United Kingdom. All of these practices involve collecting information from the individuals who are stopped—but who are not under arrest—and the information about the individual is recorded in police databases. With respect to Canada, Tulloch (2018) says there is a difference between carding and street checks:

- Carding happens when an officer "randomly asks an individual to provide identifying information when the individual is not suspected of any crime, nor is there any reason to believe that the individual has information about any crime" (p. 4).
- Street checks occur when "information is obtained by a police officer concerning an individual, outside of a police station, that is not part of an investigation. This is a very broad category of police information gathering, and much of it is legitimate intelligence gathering of potentially useful information."

Very few of us would say that stopping people randomly walking down the street is a good practice, but there are two views on street checks. Some believe it is good police work that enables officers to collect information on individuals in suspicious situations, such as officers stopping a person with a backpack at a time and place when many property crimes occur (Griffiths, Montgomery, & Murphy, 2018, p. 7). The information obtained in these interactions can be used "in investigating crimes, locating missing persons, solving crimes, and crime analysis" (Griffiths et al., 2018, p. 8). Others believe these practices are discriminatory and that individuals are subject to these interactions based on their race, ethnicity, or sexual preferences.

Canadian studies have generally found that members of visible minority groups and Indigenous peoples are disproportionately likely to be carded. Warnica (2015) reports that some young

men in Ontario have been stopped dozens of times by the police (see also Meng, 2017). Similar studies in western Canada found a similar overrepresentation of Indigenous peoples in street checks (Dhillon, 2018; Mohamed & Waters, 2017). Most criminologists would say that carding and street checks have increased tensions between the police and minority communities. As a result, several provincial governments placed restrictions on the way these checks can be carried out.

While the number of street checks has declined, one problem is that violence in the largest Canadian cities has increased, and a number of police spokespeople say the two factors are related (Doucette, 2018). The police in the United Kingdom also say that decreasing the number of stop and searches led to significant increases in violent crimes involving knives, including murders (Shaw, 2019), although research does not show a clear link between these stops and crime reduction (Bradford & Taratelli, 2019). In New York City, by contrast, the violent crime rate dropped at the same time as the practice of stop, question, and frisk ended (Smith, 2018). The problem with these observations is that they are not backed up with research, so we have no clear understanding of the impact of reduced street checks: in some places there appears to be no rise in violence, while in other cities, violent crimes increased. As a result, the increase in violent crime could be caused by other factors, such as a higher involvement in gang activities.

Although political and police leaders establish priorities for policing, individual officers also have their own interests. Some officers will prioritize arresting impaired drivers, while others are more interested in intervening in incidents of family violence. Officers are generally free to use their discretion in their duties, which is a cornerstone of modern policing. Schulenberg (2014, p. 299) observes that "discretion is the use of judgment in a given situation to take action or not in the form of a verbal warning, formal caution, traffic ticket, or an arrest and charges being laid." As noted in Chapter 1, one problem with discretion is that Canadians do not always agree on the types of offences that ought to be enforced. Most of us

carding
A controversial police practice where information is collected about people who are stopped at random and questioned.

street checks
A practice where individuals engaged in suspicious activities are questioned by the police.

discretion
Refers to when judgment is used to determine which of several options to pursue; in the case of policing, this includes whether to take no action, provide a warning, make a formal caution, issue a ticket, or arrest a suspect.

Police services throughout the country have engaged in practices called carding and street checks for decades, where individuals are stopped by the police and asked to provide personal information. In a June 2018 press conference Jennifer Evans, then Chief of the Peel Regional Police, said that restrictions limiting the use of carding introduced in Ontario in 2017 reduced police effectiveness and may have contributed to an increase in violent crime (Hayes & Gray, 2018).

agree, however, that violent crimes should be investigated and the people involved in these crimes be brought before the courts.

In addition to the seriousness of a crime, there are a number of other factors that an officer must consider before arresting a suspect. Some of these factors include the age of the suspect, whether the suspect was a leader or a follower in the offence, and the relationship between the offender and the victim. Dawson and Hotton (2014, p. 671) examined the likelihood of arrest in incidents of intimate-partner violence in Canada and found that recommendations that charges be laid increased when there were injuries, multiple victims, and incidents involving more serious offences, such as serious assaults (level 2 or 3) or kidnapping. These researchers also found that charges were recommended more often in incidents with

female rather than male victims and those in intimate relationships rather than couples who were separated. A police officer's discretion also determines how sexual offences are investigated and how these cases are managed. In a study carried out by the *Globe and Mail*, Doolittle (2017) found that police determined that about one-fifth of sexual assault claims across the country were unfounded, or in other words, no crime had occurred. One striking statistic in Doolittle's report was that the percentage of unfounded claims ranged from 2 per cent in Winnipeg to 51 per cent in St. John. That finding suggests that some police services are more likely to believe individuals who say they have been sexually assaulted.

While we realize that police officers use their discretion in order to prioritize their activities, they are sometimes criticized because their decisions may be shaped by bias or stereotypes about offenders and victims, whether that bias is conscious or not. As a result, officer attitudes toward race, gender, ethnicity, age, or sexual preference may play a role when it comes to issuing a traffic ticket, arresting a suspect, or using force. Ngo, Neote, Cala, Antonio, and Hickey (2018) describe the racial profiling of minority groups in Calgary by the police, and a number of Canadian scholars have argued that over-policing of Indigenous and visible minority groups occurs (Comack, 2012; Tanovich, 2006)

Maintaining the Public Peace

Many calls for service received by the police are related to acts that reduce our quality of life, even though these acts might not be criminal. Although definitions differ, order maintenance or maintaining order generally refers to taking action to ensure a sense of safety and comfort in public spaces. Order maintenance activities include responding to antisocial behaviour such as aggressive, rowdy, vulgar, and unruly activity. These acts range from verbally harassing people on the street, panhandling, noisy parties, public urination, prostitution, and groups of people taking over public spaces. Other such acts are directed at property and include littering and vandalism, posting graffiti, and illegally dumping garbage (see South Kesteven District Council, 2019). The police often become involved when informal controls have broken down and people are reluctant to confront those who are engaging in such behaviours. The police typically attempt to resolve order maintenance issues in an informal manner, often by warning individuals rather than issuing citations or making arrests.

Some aggressive order maintenance strategies have been introduced and in 2000 the Ontario *Safe Streets Act* (*SSA*) came into effect. This legislation made it easier for police to crack down on acts that reduce the quality of life in public spaces, such as panhandling, squeegee cleaning, or the reckless disposal of used needles or condoms. O'Grady, Gaetz, and Buccieri (2013, p. 545) found that officers from the Toronto Police Service increased

the number of tickets issued for these acts by 1,500 per cent between 2000 and 2010. These researchers said that increasing the number of tickets was intended to control disorderly people as well as controlling the homeless. O'Grady and colleagues (2013) could not attribute the increased number of tickets to complaints from business owners or members of the public, changes in crime (which decreased), or the number of homeless people in Toronto, which also decreased during the same time. Because this law has been seen as criminalizing the behaviours of the poor and the homeless, the Fair Change Community Legal Clinic (2018) launched a *Charter* challenge to repeal the *SSA*.

order maintenance Involves managing minor offences, antisocial behaviour, and other conduct that disturbs the public, such as loud parties.

A police officer confronts an unidentified man sitting in the street in Ottawa, Ontario. Although the police issue thousands of tickets to people experiencing homelessness for crimes such as loitering, few of them will ever pay their fines. Mathieu (2018) describes how one Toronto man accumulated $65,000 in fines, mostly from loitering, littering, drinking in public, panhandling, and trespassing charges.

**public order
policing**
The use of police
during mass
demonstrations
(such as protests)
to maintain the
balance between
the rights and
interests of
government,
society, and
individuals.

Order maintenance also involves formal responses to protests and demonstrations, an issue that has drawn considerable attention in recent years. De Lint (2004, p. 2) defines public order policing as "the use of police authority and capacity to establish a legitimate equilibrium between government and societal, collective and individual rights and interests in a mass demonstration of grievance." Public protests are a long-standing Canadian tradition, and many of us are sympathetic to the issues and groups involved in these protests. We are, however, less tolerant of protests that infringe on our movement or our quality of life—such as when a protest group blocks a highway or railroad, or restricts our access to a business or a medical, educational, or social service agency. The police are sometimes reluctant to intervene in these protests; these situations are seen as "lose–lose" propositions, as no matter what happens in a confrontation, their actions will be criticized. Molnar, Whelan, and Boyle (2019, p. 5), for example, contend that the response of the Toronto police to the G20 meetings in 2010 was "one of the most significant contraventions of civil liberties in Canadian history."

Emergency Response

The police are also expected to coordinate responses to emergencies or natural disasters where public safety or lives are threatened. Emergencies include transportation-related incidents involving aircraft, boats, or trains. Many of these incidents are relatively minor and responses are easily coordinated by a few officers. Some of these emergencies, by contrast, threaten the health and safety of large numbers of people, including the release of hazardous chemicals after the crash of a commercial truck or a train derailment. Natural disasters include ice storms, forest fires, floods, and tornados. While many of these originate in rural areas, they can have a significant impact on city dwellers, such as the wildfires that struck Fort McMurray, Alberta, in 2016, and destroyed about 2,400 homes and buildings.

The police are often first responders to disasters, and they are tasked with managing these

first responders
Professionals
who respond to
emergencies,
such as police
officers,
paramedics,
and firefighters
(both paid and
volunteer).

emergencies until further help arrives, which may take hours or days depending on the location of the community and the nature of the disaster. Officials from human or social service agencies also respond to emergencies and natural disasters. In addition to the police, responders include local fire departments and provincial and federal agencies such as the military or coast guard. In addition, private organizations such as the Canadian Red Cross often respond to disasters. All provincial and territorial governments have agencies that are tasked with preparing for disasters (e.g., establishing plans and delivering public education) and help coordinate responses to major or long-term disasters, and the recovery afterward. These agencies go by different names; one example is New Brunswick's Emergency Measures Organization.

Assistance to Victims of Crime

As noted in the online chapter, police services are playing a larger role in providing assistance to crime victims. Allen (2014, p. 3) reports that over one-third (36 per cent) of victim services were offered by police agencies and that the police served almost 460,000 victims in 2011/2012. Although Canada has made progress in the treatment of victims of crime in terms of the variety of services delivered to victims, Waller (2014) argues that there is still a lack of attention paid to victims and especially to female survivors of sexual and family violence.

When it comes to the actual services that police agencies deliver, Allen (2014, p. 5) found that the most common types of interventions were: (a) protection services, including safety training and learning how to assess the risk of victimization; (b) participation-related services, such as accompanying victims to court, supporting victims when they are attending court, and helping with the preparation of victim impact statements; (c) crisis-related services, which include responding to crises that victims are undergoing or debriefing these individuals after they have experienced traumatic incidents; (d) information services, such as what to expect from the justice system and how to access services; and (e) medical-related

A Closer Look

Police Responses to the Lac-Mégantic Train Disaster

The police can become involved in all aspects of a disaster—from being the first responders on the scene to investigating the aftermath. The Lac-Mégantic train derailment that occurred in the Quebec town of 5,900 residents on July 6, 2013, provides an example of the roles of the police in a disaster. Forty-seven townspeople died and 40 buildings in the downtown area were destroyed in the fire and explosions that followed the train derailment and spillage of six million litres of crude oil. Immediately after the train crash and the explosions that followed, the police responded to the emergency and coordinated a response that included local community residents and volunteer firefighters. Dolski (2013) reports that over 200 firefighters responded to the disaster, including some from neighbouring US towns.

Once the immediate risks were contained and the fires extinguished, the Sûreté du Québec (SQ) played a key role in securing the scene, assisting in the evacuation of over 2,000 residents, and recovering the remains of the people killed in this tragedy. The police also carried out a year-long investigation into the causes of the disaster. Ultimately, prosecutors determined that several company managers and executives as well as the train's engineer were responsible for the tragedy. Three individuals were charged with 47 counts of criminal negligence causing death, which could have resulted in life sentences. Others were charged with lesser offences that placed them

in jeopardy of fines and a maximum six-month custody sentence (Press & Blatchford, 2015). Similar to other serious and complex criminal cases, it took years to resolve the issue. The trial of the three former railway workers started on October 2, 2017, and a jury found them not guilty on January 19, 2018, after deliberating the case for nine days.

Shortly before the fifth anniversary of the disaster in 2018, the Crown decided that it would not pursue a prosecution of the Montreal, Maine, and Atlantic (MMA) railway as there was little chance of a conviction. The bankrupt railway was, however, fined $1 million for violating the *Fisheries Act* (as the waters surrounding the accident scene were contaminated). Five former MMA workers were ordered to pay $50,000 in fines, and one worker received a six-month probationary sentence. In addition to the employees who were punished, Irving Oil was ordered to pay $4 million for violating safety requirements under the *Transportation of Dangerous Goods Act*. Similar to the Westray Mine disaster discussed in Chapter 2, nobody was ever imprisoned for their roles in this disaster. Did the inability to hold people accountable in this case affect future wrongdoing? Page (2018, para. 1) observes that "rail safety advocates say that five years after the Lac-Megantic train derailment, not enough has been done to prevent similar tragedies," and that the number of runaway trains has actually increased by 10 per cent.

services, such as escorting an assault victim to a hospital. Altogether, these services are intended to support victims in terms of psychological and physical healing and to help them make sense of the justice system.

SUMMARY

While Canadian policing has been evolving into its current state for the past 200 years, the most sweeping changes occurred over the past five decades. Provincial standards, experienced leaders, and unionized police services have helped

to increase the professionalism of officers. In addition, officers have been given more extensive training and better equipment, including improved technology (such as computers), to increase their effectiveness. Since the 1980s, the number of small-town police agencies has decreased, and the smallest police services continue to disband. There are both positive and negative consequences of that change. Local politicians can contract with regional, provincial, or federal police services to provide services more cheaply than maintaining their own police organizations. Larger agencies can be operated more cost-effectively, but more

MYTH OR REALITY

Most Police Duties Are Related to Fighting Crime

The television programs and films we watch often focus on the investigation of serious crimes. While detectives or plainclothes officers may focus on these offences they represent only 10–15 per cent of all officers. We have to remember that law enforcement accounts for only a fraction of police work. In order to illustrate the non-enforcement duties of the police, Figure 4.3 shows that RCMP officers in Saskatchewan responded to over one-quarter million calls in 2017 (RCMP, 2018). Most of these originated in the countryside or in small municipalities. About two-fifths (39.2 per cent) were related to traffic, one-quarter were non-criminal matters (such as missing individuals), and less than one-third (30.7 per cent) were related to *Criminal Code* matters, while the remainder of the cases were related to violations of federal drug laws or provincial statutes. The focus of rural and urban police services differs somewhat; rural officers may devote more time to highway patrol, while officers in cities might respond to a greater number of calls related to antisocial behaviours and other non-criminal matters.

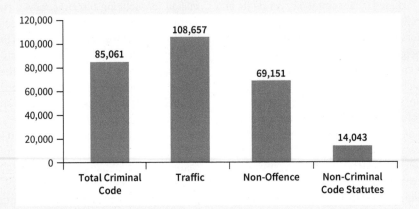

FIGURE 4.3 **RCMP Occurrences in Saskatchewan, 2017**

Royal Canadian Mounted Police (2018)

importantly, those agencies can often be more selective when hiring, and they can provide more extensive training, opportunities for career growth, and more capable supervision. On the other hand, many small-town residents feel that their relationships with the police became more formal once they lost officers who lived and worked in their communities.

Although we tend to think of the police in their crime-fighting role, responding to crimes and carrying out investigations accounts for only about one-quarter to one-third of their activities. While these activities are the most important roles for the police, officers are also responsible for maintaining the peace, engaging in crime prevention, responding to emergencies, and providing services to victims. Police officers in a democratic society are given a unique set of powers—to detain or use force on citizens—so we expect that they be well-trained and will act in a professional manner. Some scholars have argued that more effective police services can be provided if the demographic characteristics of those being policed are similar to the police. In Canada, the proportion of women officers has increased and the number of women in higher ranking positions doubled between 2005 and 2017 (Conor, 2018). Conor (2018) finds that the proportion of Indigenous and visible minority officers is also increasing, although at a slower rate than for women. There are about two officers for every 1,000 Canadians, which is less than

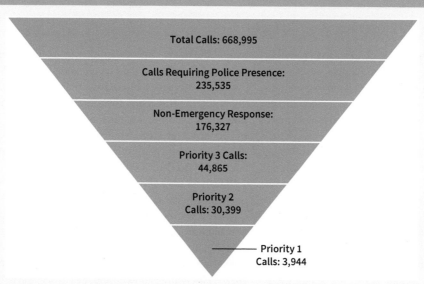

FIGURE 4.4 Calls for Service, Ottawa Police Service, 2017

Although 911 lines are intended for emergencies, only about one in 170 calls require an urgent response due to the immediate threat to a life (Priority 1); there is a threat to life, the presence of serious injuries, or weapons (Priority 2) in about one of 20 calls. Priority 3 calls are ones in which no threat is imminent but a delay in response could place people or evidence at risk.

Adapted from Ottawa Police Service (2018)

In addition to law enforcement representing less than one-third of all calls to the police, only a small proportion of all 911 calls are related to life-threatening emergencies. Many Canadian police services classify calls for service (e.g., to 911) on the basis of priority. In Ottawa, calls that represent an immediate threat to life are classified as P1, and the level of priority declines to P7, which are calls related to picking up property, such as confiscated or stolen items. Figure 4.4 shows the number of calls for service received by the Ottawa Police Service in 2017. Unlike what we see on television, the number of emergency calls where there is an immediate threat accounts for about one in 170.

many southern European nations. Yet there is also some variation in the number of officers deployed throughout Canada, and some cities have higher levels of police strength. Researchers examining this issue generally find that wealthier communities tend to deploy more officers, even if they have less crime than their poorer counterparts (Ruddell & Thomas, 2015). Other jurisdictions want to keep their property taxes low and deploy fewer officers. McClearn, Freeze, and Dhillon (2018, para. 2) point out that Vancouver residents pay $420 per capita for their municipal police, but the North Vancouver city government contracts with the RCMP and pays only $230 per capita. The main difference between the two cities is that in North Vancouver the officers have much higher caseloads and response times may be longer.

Having described the roles and responsibilities of the police, and the different arrangements across the nation, the next chapter offers a closer look at the more controversial aspects of policing, including the recruitment of new officers, the existence of a police subculture, and police mistakes and misconduct. The structures that we have developed to make the police more accountable are also described. The one common factor is that all of these issues can be controversial, as most of us have strong views about the police, how they should carry out their duties, and how to hold them accountable.

Career SNAPSHOT

Search and Rescue Preparedness Officer

It is not unusual for police officers to switch careers as their interests and family responsibilities change. In the first edition of *Exploring Criminal Justice in Canada*, Marina Carbonell's role as a police officer with the Royal Newfoundland Constabulary was featured, but she has since moved on to the Canadian Coast Guard, where she serves as a Search and Rescue Preparedness Officer off the coast of Newfoundland and Labrador. She attributes her ability to switch careers on her continuing education throughout her career and her willingness to learn new duties as a police officer.

Profile

Name: Marina Carbonell
Job title: Search and Rescue Preparedness Officer, Inshore Rescue Boat Coordinator, Atlantic North (Canadian Coast Guard)
Employed in current job since: 2018
Present location: St. John's, Newfoundland and Labrador
Education: BSc, Biology (Dalhousie, 2012), BA, Police Studies (Memorial, 2013), MA, Sociology (Memorial, 2018)

Background

My initial career intentions were to work within the sciences, and I had a specific interest in laboratory work and research. This interest led me to the pursuit of a bachelor's degree in biology, but a summer work term in a laboratory helped me realize that it was not the right fit for me. A conversation with a close friend who had just become a police officer led me to apply to the Royal Newfoundland Constabulary; I completed their training program in 2007 and served with them until 2018. After having my first child in 2012, I went back to university and finished the Bachelor of Science program at Dalhousie University; I completed the Bachelor of Arts in Police Studies at Memorial University the following year. I finished my Master of Arts degree in 2018. In 2018, I was offered an amazing opportunity with the Canadian Coast Guard, working in Search and Rescue. I moved over to the federal public service as a Search and Rescue Preparedness Officer, Inshore Rescue Boat Coordinator for Atlantic North.

Work Experience

As with policing, technology is ever-changing in the marine world and with Search and Rescue. Huge strides have been made in technology in terms of locating people during critical incidents, but difficulties in using technology or maintaining communication can be disastrous. When people are in emergency situations, communications is usually the first thing to fail and that can be difficult to overcome. Ongoing training to upgrade our skills, training with the community and other agencies, and ongoing Search and Rescue exercises help us develop those skills and improve our critical teamwork skills.

The best part of my job is helping people. When someone needs help on the water and we respond, it can be incredibly rewarding. In addition, as the Inshore Rescue Boat Coordinator, I screen, hire, train, and supervise summer students who work as Search and Rescue Officers at multiple stations. Working with the students and seeing them grow as individuals and employees is also very rewarding. The Inshore Rescue Boat positions are student positions that offer post-secondary students operational real-life experience working on the water and helping mariners in distress from May to September. For students looking to explore an operational job, it is an amazing experience!

The most surprising thing about my career, which I hadn't considered at the onset, was how much I could change over time and the importance of education. When I became a police officer, I thought I would spend a full career in that profession. I was goal-oriented, wanted to work in specific sections, and had planned out my career to retirement. After having a family, my priorities changed. My education, training, and experience allowed me more choices and helped me work toward a career that provides a better work-life balance than policing. I was raised to believe that I could be anything I wanted to be and have everything I wanted, but it is very difficult to "have it all" when it comes to working a demanding career and raising a family. What has made the difference for my career is the freedom of choice, and that freedom has been a direct result of the education I have worked hard to complete.

Advice to Students

There are many volunteer opportunities and work-related activities that are assets to any operational-type position. Work experience or volunteer experience working with children, people with disabilities, and people with mental health needs can make a huge difference in a person's abilities on the job. Extracurricular activities helped me build my resume and make me more marketable. It is difficult to develop a great resume in the beginning of your career, both academically and professionally, but extracurricular activities can set you apart and help get your foot in the door. A lot of front-line employees have worked with youth in care, have volunteered with youth in activities such as organized sports, Beavers/Scouts/Girl Guides, or have volunteered with organizations like Big Brothers or Big Sisters. Depending on your location, it can be rewarding to volunteer with organizations helping new Canadians get situated after immigrating to Canada, or volunteering with Special Olympics. In addition, the Canadian Red Cross and many local hospitals are often looking for reliable volunteers.

Whether students are looking to work in policing or with the federal government, they should avoid any criminal behaviour; but apart from that, students need to be conscious of their online presence and how they represent themselves. As public servants, we must demonstrate a non-biased, open-minded outlook, while maintaining a professional deportment in our community. Fighting with strangers on the internet or posting inappropriate photos does not present the image of a community leader.

REVIEW QUESTIONS

1. Describe how Canadian policing evolved.
2. Why are Robert Peel's principles of policing still relevant today?
3. What are some of the challenges associated with Indigenous policing?
4. What were some of the advantages of the consolidation of many small police agencies into larger police services?
5. What are the five core roles of police services?

DISCUSSION QUESTIONS

1. In England, most police officers do not carry firearms. Should Canadian police officers carry firearms, or might this actually escalate police use of force?
2. After many small-town police services disbanded in Canada, residents benefited from more professional policing, but they also lost officers who lived in their communities and might have been able to resolve problems more informally. Do you think this was a good trade-off, or is this a bad deal for small-town residents, and why?
3. In the introduction we question whether the police are the most appropriate social agency to deal with failures in the social safety net (such as a shortage of addiction services or mental health treatment). After reading this chapter, did you change your mind about the role of the police?
4. How would being stopped and searched by the police five times in one year change your perceptions about the police or the justice system?
5. Would doubling the number of officers in a community result in double the level of safety? Why or why not?

INTERNET SITES

The RCMP *Gazette* magazine has been published four times a year since 1939 and provides a review of current issues in policing and police research.
www.rcmp-grc.gc.ca/gazette/index-eng.htm

The Centre for Public Safety and Criminal Justice Research has a database called the Public Safety Search Database that can be searched to find information on criminal justice and public safety issues.
http://cjr.ufv.ca/search-widget/

CASE CITED

Mounted Police Association of Ontario v Canada (Attorney General), 2015 SCC 1, [2015] 1 SCR 3

▲ The Toronto Police Marine Unit patrols the shores of Toronto Harbour. How much of a police officer's time, would you guess, is spent solving crimes, and how much is spent attempting to prevent future crimes? (Photo credit: Elijah-Lovkoff/iStockphoto)

Police Activities, Operations, and Challenges

LEARNING OUTLINE

After reading this chapter, you will be able to

- Describe the different operational activities of the police
- Describe the three different policing styles
- Identify some of the key challenges in recruiting new officers
- Identify the major challenges confronting the policing industry
- Outline the methods used to hold the police accountable
- Describe the negative aspects of a police subculture

A Family's 10-Year Struggle to Understand their Daughter's Murder

We expect a lot from the police, but like members of every other occupation, officers make errors in judgment. Unlike in most careers, however, the consequences of police mistakes can be permanent. Waby (2016, p. 42) observes that "officers frequently discover that lessons are learned the hard way, often under harsh public scrutiny." For instance, in September 2008 police were called to investigate reports of shots fired at a rural home near Mission, British Columbia. A constable responded to the 911 call but he didn't get out of his vehicle to further investigate the incident, nor did he talk to the neighbour who made the call. A tape played at the coroner's inquest over nine years later revealed that the officer had joked with the dispatcher about the call because he didn't find it credible (CBC, 2018b, para. 7). Four days later, a neighbour visited the home and found Guthrie McKay dead, and although Lisa Dudley was alive (she had been shot in the head and neck), she died on the way to the hospital. After this incident the officer involved was reprimanded and lost pay (but was later promoted).

Investigations later revealed that the Dudley and McKay murders were related to a dispute over a drug debt, and involved threats, an extramarital affair, and a hit-man (CTV News Vancouver, 2017, para.

4). All together, four individuals were involved in the murders; the gunman, who received $25,000 for the killings, the two associates who aided him, and the man who hired them. The man who shot Dudley and McKay pled guilty to first-degree murder and was sentenced to life imprisonment, while his associates were convicted of manslaughter and received seven- and eight-year sentences. Tom Holden, the man who hired the three killers, received a ten-year prison sentence after pleading guilty to conspiracy to commit murder. After entering his plea, Holden was out on bail until his sentencing, and the victim's father said, "I'm mystified how a man who admits to murder can walk out of a courtroom" (as cited by Woodward, 2016, para. 9).

A coroner's inquest was held on June 11, 2018, and the jury made nine recommendations, including making changes in the way that 911 calls were handled by dispatchers and officers responding to potential cases of serious bodily harm. Dudley's family also launched an unsuccessful lawsuit to seek damages from the province. In February 2019, Dudley's family was again in the news as they attempted to obtain their daughter's personal belongings, which had been seized during the investigation and were still being stored by the police—those belongings were finally returned in June 2019 (Mills, 2019).

Critical Questions

1. How many mistakes do you make in your job every day? How does your situation compare with the events faced by the officer in this case? Why do we hold police officers to a higher standard than other professions?
2. University professors have the luxury of sitting in a comfortable chair while thinking of better ways that controversial problems, such as the use of force, could have been solved, whereas workers

in justice systems who interact with unpredictable people may have only a few seconds to come up with solutions in frightening and stressful situations. What implications does this observation have for your views of policing?
3. It took nine years between the murders and when the last person was sentenced for the crime, over nine years for a coroner's jury to hear about the circumstances of Dudley's death, and almost

11 years for her belongings to be returned to the family. Do you agree with the statement that justice delayed is justice denied? Or do you believe that the justice system should move slowly and deliberately in order to reduce errors and miscarriages of justice? Why or why not?

INTRODUCTION

In the previous chapter, we explored the evolution of Canadian policing and the core police roles. There are differences across the country in how the police are deployed and in the priorities placed on their daily activities. Regardless of how the police are deployed, however, they are a controversial force in society, as almost everybody has a strong opinion about their roles. Our feelings toward the police are often polarizing, and although some people express a great deal of support for the police, others feel that their activities should be tightly controlled. For the most part, we are generally less trusting and forgiving of public employees, including the police, than we once were. National studies show, however, that about three-quarters of Canadians have a great deal or some confidence in the police, which is the highest of all public institutions (Cotter, 2015, p. 4), and Canadians rank their police services more favourably than people in most other nations (Clark, Davidson, Hanrahan, & Taylor, 2017)

In this chapter, a number of contemporary issues and challenges of the police are explored. One significant topic is how the police are deployed in various roles. In his analysis of Canadian policing, Robertson (2012) identifies two broad issues about the police that need to be considered: (a) the context in which the police operate and (b) police activities. Some of these issues are controversial, such as the use of force and police militarization (which can occur when the police are given military training and equipment). This chapter ends with a discussion of police subculture—the informal rules and expectations that shape officer attitudes and behaviours. Because of their role as law enforcers, the police often feel isolated and separate from the public, and this can lead to a strong occupational culture. Although the police subculture contributes to high levels of mutual support and promotes positive values such as honesty and integrity, the culture has also been criticized as it can lead to a resistance to change and can support different forms of misconduct, such as covering up the misdeeds of other officers, which is an issue that police leaders have attempted to change for generations.

POLICE ALLOCATION

Approximately one-third of Canadian adults report coming into contact with the police each year, and for the most part, these interactions are with patrol officers, who account for about two-thirds of all police positions. Although most officers work in patrol, the police are also deployed in a number of diverse work roles. According to Cordner (2019), there are three main operational police roles:

1. **Operations:** Includes officers involved in patrol, traffic enforcement, and criminal investigation, as well as specialized duties such as crime prevention (e.g., crime watch), school resource officers, and community policing.

2. **Administration:** Includes officers who manage the day-to-day operations of the agency and oversee units such as human resources, budgeting, and professional standards (e.g., investigating public complaints).

3. **Auxiliary services:** Include personnel involved in communications (e.g., taking calls for service from the public and directing officer activities), preserving evidence, keeping records, and detention (e.g., receiving arrestees and ensuring that they attend their court appearances and are transferred to provincial or federal facilities).

police militarization Occurs when police services use military equipment, tactics, and training as regular methods to police civilians.

police subculture A set of informal rules and expectations that shape police attitudes, values, and behaviours.

The Canadian Press/Andrew Vaughan

Roziere and Walby (2017) argue that the Canadian police are becoming increasingly militarized and that there is an overuse of military equipment and methods when dealing with routine situations such as responding to domestic disputes rather than high-risk situations. While some say the use of military equipment might contribute to a mindset that the police are at war with citizens, a New Brunswick Provincial Court judge ruled that the RCMP violated the Labour Code by *not* issuing officers with high-powered rifles that would increase their safety (*R v The Royal Canadian Mounted Police*, 2017).

How the police are allocated is an important decision, and political leaders and the community members they represent have a voice in these arrangements. Some questions concerning police allocation include the following: What types of offences should receive more attention from the police? What neighbourhoods require more patrols? Should more civilian employees be hired so that officers engaged in administrative work can return to the street? Although all of these operational questions are political, they are also related to agency funding, and all North American police services are attempting to cut costs without sacrificing services (Huey, Cyr, & Ricciardelli, 2016).

POLICE CHAIN OF COMMAND AND POLICE OFFICER RANKS

Police services are sometimes called paramilitary organizations, as they are organized along military lines and have a chain of command where lines of authority are clearly defined by the organization. Police organizations have a top-down orientation and, similar to the military, the chain of command is based on rank. Most Canadian front-line officers are called constables or officers—although the RCMP uses the term *members* for sworn officers—who are in turn supervised by corporals, sergeants, inspectors, superintendents, and chiefs; the job titles can vary somewhat by

paramilitary organizations Services organized along military lines, which have a chain of command where lines of authority are clearly defined by the organization.

chain of command The lines of authority in a police organization, which are clearly defined and range from a constable (on the bottom of the pyramid) to the chief or commissioner (at the top).

sworn officers Police officers with the legal authority to arrest and use force (as opposed to peace officers, who have less legal authority).

police service. The following list shows the titles of various police ranks (starting at the entry-level position of special constable, which is typically a uniformed official with limited police powers).

- Police Chief/Commissioner
- Deputy Chief/Deputy Commissioner
- Superintendent
- Inspector
- Sergeant/Staff Sergeant
- Corporal
- Detective/Investigator
- Constable/Officer
- Special Constable (also called Cadet, Peace Officer, or Community Service Officer)

As constables are promoted to higher ranks, they supervise more subordinates and their responsibilities increase. Officers in some Canadian police services receive their first promotions relatively early in their careers: sometimes within the first five years, which is much shorter than in the past (Hogan, Bennell, & Taylor, 2011). Although this is a positive step for these new supervisors, some critics argue that these officers have spent relatively little time on the job and do not have the depth of experience needed to make the best decisions.

OPERATIONAL ACTIVITIES

Cordner (2019) discusses a number of operational activities carried out by the police, which are described in this section.

Patrol

Patrol is considered the backbone of policing, and about two-thirds of officers are engaged in this work. Most patrol activities are the result of calls for service from the public, such as 911 calls. In some busy cities, responding to calls can occupy an entire shift, leaving officers with little time to engage in preventative patrol or to fully investigate incidents. In addition to responding to calls, patrol officers often provide backup to other officers or to professionals from other organizations who may be in dangerous or confrontational situations, such as probation officers or child protection workers.

Traffic

Research in Canada shows that traffic officers save lives and reduce the number of serious collisions through their enforcement activities (DeAngelo, 2018). Traffic officers issue tickets to violators, ensure the orderly flow of traffic around collisions or construction zones, and arrest dangerous and impaired drivers. In addition to their enforcement duties, some traffic officers work in specialized roles, such as accident reconstruction. Their activities are also supported by non-police officers, such as Transportation Enforcement Officers in Ontario; these personnel have fewer enforcement powers and generally focus their efforts on commercial vehicles such as semi-trailers. Traffic enforcement is especially important in the countryside, given that over one-half of all fatalities occur on rural roads (Transport Canada, 2019).

Criminal Investigation

Although patrol officers are responsible for solving a high proportion of crimes (as they are the first to talk to victims), all large police services employ detectives—also called plainclothes officers—to investigate serious crimes, such as sexual assault, child exploitation, and homicide. Police personnel in these investigative roles account for between 10 and 15 per cent of all officers in many municipal departments. By contrast, officers working in smaller agencies can call on experts from larger police services when confronted with complex investigations that are beyond their ability to investigate properly. The Sûreté du Québec, for example, will lead the investigation of serious crimes in smaller Quebec municipalities, even though those towns may have their own stand-alone police departments.

Drug Suppression

Despite the fact that the recreational use of marijuana was legalized in October 2018, there are still a number of offences associated with marijuana sales or trafficking. It is too soon, however, to determine the impacts of this change in the law and how many people will be prosecuted for trafficking. One of the hazards of making any substance or act illegal is that it can attract the attention of organized crime. An example is the spread of opioids, which has been linked to a massive increase in overdose deaths. While opioids are widely used, the demand for this drug is fulfilled by trafficking, and this leads to other crime-related problems, including the spread of organized crime offenders (Hayes, 2017). As a result of the potential harm these drugs pose to the public, most large police services deploy officers in drug-suppression activities. As part of their federal policing responsibilities, the RCMP has a number of units tasked with it—and especially crimes involving gangs and organized crime. Some police officers involved in drug suppression act in undercover roles, where they infiltrate organizations to gather evidence about drug crimes.

Drug enforcement can be a controversial issue; some scholars maintain that Canadians have waged a low-level war on drugs. Khenti (2014) argues that this war has been waged against the poor and the marginalized, and that Blacks have been disproportionately affected by these practices. Khenti contends that the over-policing of Black men has resulted in a growing number of them receiving criminal records for the possession of drugs and being placed in custody. A further consequence of over-policing (or the perception that one's community is being over-policed) is that it reduces trust and confidence in the police, and this makes it more difficult for the police to get a community's participation in investigations (Tyler, 2006).

Organized Crime and Gangs

The Criminal Intelligence Service Canada (2014, para. 8) estimates that there are over 670 organized crime groups active in the nation and that they pose a "serious long-term threat to Canada's institutions, society, economy, and to individual quality of life." These organizations have persisted in Canada for over 300 years (Schneider, 2018). Members of these organizations become involved in any illicit activity where they can make a profit, including drug production and distribution, cybercrime, smuggling cigarettes and firearms from the United States, and human trafficking.

Police services throughout the nation respond to organized crime by participating in task forces where officers from federal, provincial, and municipal agencies share information and carry out combined investigations. Most large municipal police services also have officers who respond to gang crimes, investigate gang activities, and share information with justice system partners such as correctional officials and prosecutors. One of the challenges of responding to organized crime is that it is increasingly international. As a result, officers in Canadian police services are partnering with officials from other nations, and most of these initiatives rely on the exchange of intelligence with partner organizations (Criminal Intelligence Service Canada, 2014). So how serious is the problem? Upon his retirement as Commissioner of the RCMP, Bob Paulson said that "organized crime is the biggest threat facing Canadians" (Stone, 2017, para. 1).

Specialized Operations

The police in Canada's largest cities encounter a greater number of complex and dangerous situations than do officers working in small towns. As a result, all urban police services have emergency response units known as special weapons and tactics (SWAT) teams or emergency response teams. Officers in these units have access to military-style equipment, such as automatic firearms and armoured vehicles. This equipment was intended to be used in high-risk situations, such as responding to suspects who are barricaded in homes, as well as during confrontations with armed suspects, large-scale protests, or hostage situations. Depending on the size of the jurisdiction, the officers in these units might be employed on a part- or full-time basis (e.g., a certain number of SWAT-trained officers might

undercover roles Officers carry out investigations in a covert manner that can involve immersing themselves into criminal worlds.

special weapons and tactics (SWAT) teams or emergency response teams A group of officers who receive specialized training and have access to military-style weapons to confront armed and/or dangerous suspects.

canine (K9) officers
Officers who are partnered with dogs to engage in patrol activities, detect drugs or explosives, and track suspects or escaped prisoners.

aviation units
Officers who use fixed-wing aircraft and helicopters for traffic enforcement (including vehicle pursuits), transporting prisoners, and providing information to officers on the ground.

marine units Officers who are deployed in boats to patrol waterfront areas and harbours, including conducting search and rescue activities, promoting water safety, and engaging in crime prevention.

executive protection
Protection provided by police officers to the Prime Minister, the Governor General of Canada, provincial premiers, mayors of large cities, and visiting dignitaries.

be engaged in patrol duties and then assemble as a team when needed). Roziere and Walby (2018, p. 1) have expressed concern that these units are being used in low-risk situations such as "warrant work, traffic enforcement, community policing, and even responding to mental health crises and domestic disturbances." On the other hand, many believe that the ambush murders of four RCMP officers in Mayerthorpe, Alberta, in 2005, and three RCMP officers in Moncton, New Brunswick, in 2014 might have been prevented if the officers had had access to better body armour and more sophisticated firearms (Dion, 2017). The RCMP was found negligent in the Moncton shootings because the officers did not have the proper equipment or training (Canadian Broadcasting Corporation, 2017).

Officers are also employed in a variety of other specialized units, including bomb disposal squads ("bomb squads"), who respond to incidents of unexploded bombs. Most large municipalities also employ canine (K9) officers, who are partnered with dogs to search for drugs, suspects, evidence, and explosives, and are also used to apprehend suspects. Most mid-sized police services (e.g., Calgary, Edmonton, and Winnipeg) and all of the largest police services have aviation units, where fixed-wing aircraft or helicopters are used to enforce traffic regulations, assist patrol officers in their responses to emergency situations such as vehicle pursuits, and give officers a "bird's-eye view" of an incident. Last, in some waterfront cities, police services such as the Cape Breton Regional Police Service, Halifax Regional Police, and Vancouver Police Department have marine units (also called lake patrol or marine squads), where officers patrol the waterfront to control crime and engage in search and rescue operations.

Federal and provincial police services also deploy specialized units. Public buildings and national historic sites, such as the grounds surrounding the Parliament Buildings in Ottawa, are protected by the RCMP. Provincial legislatures also receive protection from various enforcement agencies, such as the Alberta Sheriffs. In addition, the Prime Minister, dignitaries, and some provincial premiers receive protection from police officers—this is called executive protection or protective policing. All large police services also have some personnel engaged in anti-terrorist activities, measures that have taken on a greater importance since the October 2014 murder of Corporal Nathan Cirillo, who was shot while guarding the Tomb of the Unknown Soldier in Ottawa, and the subsequent attack on Parliament (National Post, 2014). The Parliamentary Protective Service was founded in 2015, and its armed officials work with the RCMP to enhance security on Parliament Hill.

Crime Prevention

Despite a growing interest in crime prevention, a relatively small percentage of all officers carry out these duties. Some officers work with neighbourhood watch programs (or farm watch or cottage watch in the countryside), while others deliver public education campaigns, and developing strategies with community members to reduce their risk of victimization.

Youth Services

Young males are overrepresented in their involvement in crime. As a result, most large municipal police services assign officers to work with youth who have been convicted of serious offences or are persistent offenders. Some officers work specifically with youth gang members and their families. In addition, almost all urban agencies place constables in schools, and these school resource officers are expected to form positive relationships with students and deliver anti-crime or anti-drug programs to students. Although there is a long history of placing officers in schools, these programs can be controversial. In 2017, for example, the Toronto District School Board removed officers from their schools as they believed some students were intimidated by the police (Nasser, 2018). A study by Carleton University professors Linda Duxbury and Craig Bennell (2018), however, found that students in five Peel Region high schools felt safer when officers were present; they reported being less stressed-out, and missed fewer days of school. While the findings in the Duxbury and Bennell study have been criticized, using research to take a closer look at these issues is the only way we will increase our understanding about these practices.

Community Policing

As noted in Chapter 4, community policing initiatives take a number of different approaches, as municipalities often have differing notions of community policing. In some cities, neighbourhood police stations are placed in high-crime areas in order to give the police a more visible presence. Perhaps more importantly, most large police services—especially those responsible for policing diverse populations—have units that were formed to reach out to specific ethnocultural groups. The Toronto Police Service (2016), for instance, established an Aboriginal Peacekeeping Unit in 1992 in order to build stronger relationships between the police and an estimated 85,000 Indigenous people living in that city.

Similar community policing programs have been developed throughout the country to build relationships with different ethnocultural populations. These initiatives are increasingly important given that almost three out of 10 Canadians are members of visible minority groups or of Indigenous ancestry (22.3 and 4.9 per cent respectively) (Statistics Canada, 2018c, 2018a). In addition, many members of ethnocultural groups who emigrated from other countries have had negative interactions with the police in their homelands and have a mistrust of the police. Community policing initiatives are intended to build bridges between these groups and the police.

POLICING STYLES: LEGALISTIC, WATCHMAN, AND SERVICE

So far, this review of policing has described the importance of the relationships between the public and the police, something Robert Peel felt was important two centuries ago. As noted in Chapter 4, most police organizations have a formal mission statement that describes the way in which the agency's staff members are expected to interact with the public (e.g., with professionalism and through partnerships). Every organization develops its own culture and way of conducting operations, and researchers have identified a number of distinct policing styles. Much of this work has been based on Wilson's (1968) research finding that police departments balanced three functions: law enforcement (the legalistic style), order maintenance (the watchman style), and providing needed services (the service style). According to Wilson (1968), what made police services different was which of these three activities was most valued, and especially the priority they placed on an enforcement or crime-fighting role. These organizational priorities, in turn, shaped the relationships that officers established with the public.

In their analysis of Wilson's work, Zhao and Hassell (2005, pp. 413–415) examined these three policing styles, which are summarized as follows:

- **Legalistic style:** This policing model emphasizes professionalism and formal relationships with the public in bureaucratic (top-down) agencies where officers are noted for their strict enforcement of the law. Officers have a high number of contacts with the public, and their productivity is demonstrated by high arrest rates and/or by issuing many traffic tickets. Officers working in these agencies tend to use less discretion when dealing with the public, and even minor conflicts can end in an arrest.
- **Watchman style:** Officers in agencies with a watchman approach focus on order maintenance, such as reducing antisocial behaviour. Agencies with this orientation tend to be more involved with their community than their legalistic counterparts and are more concerned about the effects of wrongdoing—rather than focusing on the wrongdoer. As a result, their approach is often less formal and officers use their discretion to maintain the peace rather than strictly enforce the law. Because most

school resource officers Officers placed on a part- or full-time basis in schools to provide security, teach classes, act as positive role models, and build positive relationships with students.

disputes are handled informally, there are few arrests for minor offences or antisocial behaviour.

- **Service style:** Police services that embrace a service style place a priority on public satisfaction and being responsive to community needs. As a result, this model may be closer to the ideal of community policing as there are frequent contacts between officers and civilians, and many disputes are handled informally. Although every complaint about crime or order maintenance is taken seriously, the investigation of serious crimes is prioritized. This approach might be more common in small towns or in wealthy city suburbs.

None of these approaches is likely to exist in a pure form, as police services establish different priorities that balance these different styles. In addition, there are also differences within a police service, or even within different times and locations that officers are working. Officers working in high-crime patrol zones or working night shifts might have a more legalistic orientation. Last, some officers may have a different style than their agency: an officer with a preference for informally handling disputes might be employed by a police service with a legalistic orientation.

Although Wilson's (1968) study has been widely cited, his observations about the police are from the 1960s and his research was based on observations of only eight US cities. Since that time, much has changed in the police industry, including employing a more professional and diverse workforce, the establishment of standards, an increased growth in civilian oversight, and a growing transparency in police operations (Chrismas, 2013). Despite those changes, Wilson's work is still widely regarded, and researchers still find that police organizations have different styles of policing.

Wilson (1968) attributed some of the differences in policing styles to the local political culture. As noted earlier, politics have always played a role in how police activities are prioritized. In carrying out his research, Wilson found that local politicians influenced how the police operated,

patrol zone
A defined area within a community that officers are assigned to patrol.

including the number of officers employed and their priorities, such as policing the city centre rather than the suburbs. These priorities are often a result of citizen input (e.g., complaints about speeders in school zones) and consultation with police leaders about the most effective ways to deploy officers. As a result, where, when, and how the police are deployed will influence the relationships between the public and the police.

CURRENT CHALLENGES IN POLICING: THE CONTEXT FOR POLICING

Robertson (2012) provides an overview of Canadian policing and highlights the key issues and challenges confronting police services. In the sections that follow, Robertson's (2012) overview is presented—in somewhat modified form—using two key themes: (a) the context for policing and (b) police operations. The context for policing can be traced back to Peel's principles (see Chapter 4) and the preferred relationships between the police and the public, as well as factors that strengthen those relationships: the appropriate use of force, police oversight and accountability, and the political independence of the police. These issues are addressed in the following section.

Police Use of Force

Policing is the only occupation in a democratic society whose members are authorized to use force to protect property and the public. Peel was concerned that the police used force sparingly to reduce the perception they were an oppressive force. More recently, questions about the appropriate use of force were raised after a series of highly publicized police shootings in the United States in 2015 and 2016. Even though shootings of Canadian civilians by the police are rare, the use of lethal force still occurs. Robertson (2012) observes that most officers are reluctant to use force—and it is used as a last resort.

Guidelines for the police use of force are defined by section 25 of the *Criminal Code*, and each police service has a use-of-force guideline (often called a continuum) that depicts how much force should be used in a given situation. Officers are expected to use only as much force as necessary to control a situation, and this can include officers raising their voice, placing their hands on a suspect, and striking a suspect, as well as using less-than-lethal weapons such as a conducted energy device (e.g., a taser) or a baton to strike a suspect. If these non-lethal methods cannot stop the threat posed by a suspect, lethal methods such as shooting an individual can be used—depending on the seriousness of the threat.

In order to reduce the possibility that Canadian officers will use excessive force, more Canadian police services are providing their officers with training focusing on de-escalating volatile situations and using a range of interventions with non-compliant or threatening suspects. Three Canadian studies shed light on the use of force and all reveal these incidents represent a very small proportion of all interactions with the public:

Hall, Votova, and Wood (2013) examined use of force in seven police services between 2006 and 2013, and they found that of 3.5 million interactions between the police and public, there were fewer than 5,000 use-of-force incidents (less than 0.01 per cent), although six suspects died of gunshot wounds.

Boivin and Obartel (2017) examined the police use of force in a Quebec city of 1.5 million residents—employing more than 2,000 officers—and they found that there were 1,451 use-of-force incidents between 2008 and 2011.

Wittmann (2018) reports that the Calgary police had 2.7 million interactions with the public between 2012 and 2017, and found that force was used in only 3,254 cases. When it came to using deadly force, the Calgary police killed eight suspects during those five years, or about one suspect for every 350,000 interactions with the public. These results are presented in Figure 5.1.

When it comes to suspects injured by the police, Hall et al. (2013) found that most were males

under 30 years of age who were under the influence of alcohol (60.8 per cent) or drugs (25.4 per cent) or were suffering from distress or a mental illness (21.4 per cent). Not surprisingly, the Quebec study reveals that most use-of-force incidents happened in places with low levels of informal social controls and high levels of crime (Boivin & Obartel, 2017).

Police Oversight and Accountability

Writing about Canadian policing, Chrismas (2013, p. 63) observes that officers are under quadruple jeopardy as they answer to the public, their direct chain of police command, the courts, and oversight bodies such as community advisory boards or police commissions. There are also complaints commissions and watchdog agencies that examine the use of force in police-civilian interactions. In other words, police activities are more closely scrutinized today than in the past. Moreover, in recent years,

less-than-lethal weapons Alternatives to firearms that are intended to temporarily incapacitate or confuse an individual.

conducted energy devices Less-lethal devices, such as tasers, that send an electrical charge that temporarily incapacitates an individual.

The Canadian Press/Jonathan Hayward

Officers are expected to use only as much force as necessary to control a situation, and this can include using less-than-lethal weapons such as tasers. Tasers can have lethal effects, however, and Reuters (2019) reports that almost 1,100 Americans were killed by the police use of these weapons between 1983 and December 31, 2018. The death of Robert Dziekański during his arrest at the Vancouver Airport in 2007 illustrates the potential danger of these weapons (Oriola, Rollwagen, Neverson, & Adeyanju, 2016).

A Closer Look

Becoming a Police Officer in Canada

Police services throughout the country are actively looking for qualified candidates for vacant officer positions. An important first step in thinking about a policing career is learning what an officer's job involves. The Police Sector Council (2013, p. 34) observes that a constable must "protect the public, detect and prevent crime and perform other activities directed at maintaining law and order. Constables respond to emergency situations, participate in planned enforcement operations and conduct investigations." The Police Sector Council (2018) observes that a constable should be able to master nine main competencies:

1. Adaptability: Adjusts their behaviours and approaches in light of new information and changing situations.
2. Ethical Accountability and Responsibility: Takes responsibility for actions and makes decisions that are consistent with high ethical policing standards.
3. Interactive Communication. Uses communication strategies in an effort to achieve common goals, influence, and gain others' support.
4. Organizational Awareness. Understands and uses organizational awareness to deliver optimal services (can identify issues important to stakeholders).
5. Problem Solving: Identifies problems, implements solutions, and evaluates the outcomes of their actions.
6. Risk Management: Manages situations and calls to mitigate risk and maintain a safe environment for self and others.
7. Stress Tolerance: Remains focused on results in the face of ambiguity, change, or strenuous demands.
8. Teamwork: Works cooperatively with members of the work team and contributes to an environment that leads to achievement of established goals.
9. Written Skills: Communicates ideas and information in writing to ensure that information and messages are understood and have the desired impact.

ride-along When members of the public accompany a police officer on patrol to learn about policing.

Police recruiters are interested in candidates who can master these tasks. These competencies are often difficult to demonstrate, and it takes a long time to assess whether a job applicant has the ability to develop those competencies. As a result, being hired as an officer is a lengthy process, and it often takes over a year between the time individuals submit their application and the time they start training.

Prior to Recruitment

Learning the steps of becoming an officer is important for those interested in policing careers. Students can speak with officers at recruiting seminars or university career days about policing jobs to increase their understanding of the hiring process. Many larger municipal police services also offer citizen academies—classes that are usually offered in the evenings and delivered over several months, through which participants are exposed to the inner world of police operations. Some participants who were interested in policing careers choose not to apply after attending those academies, but those who remain interested proceed with a greater awareness of the job expectations. Students interested in policing can sometimes participate in a ride-along (when members of the public accompany an officer on their duties for a shift) or complete a practicum (internship) with a police agency in order to learn more about police roles and operations.

Police services are interested in hiring individuals with a high degree of personal integrity, reliability, psychological stability, honesty, problem-solving and communication skills. Although the application process will vary somewhat throughout the country, it will primarily focus on candidates demonstrating their skills and positive character. Applicants with criminal records and histories of illegal or unethical behaviours (both detected and self-reported) will often be excluded or deferred (most police services require a three-year period free of any criminal behaviour). While applicants cannot do much to change their past wrongdoing, those interested in police careers must steer clear of trouble, including staying away from friends or associates involved in criminal activities. In addition, a high level of physical fitness is important to successfully complete academy training, and potential recruits must pass a number of physical and medical tests (including hearing and vision tests) during the selection process.

Potential applicants today have a number of advantages over previous generations of officers. First, most pre-employment physical testing is described and/or shown on police service websites or is available on YouTube, enabling a prospective applicant to prepare for these tests. Second, there are a number of guides that help prepare potential applicants for written policing exams. Third, online forums (such as www.Blueline.ca) allow individuals interested in Canadian law enforcement careers (including non-policing jobs) to interact with recruiters and officers who will answer questions about police careers and the application process. Fourth, almost all large police services have websites that clearly show the application requirements and provide hints on preparing for the selection process.

Police Recruit Training

Once selected for a police officer position, candidates must attend and complete basic police recruit training, which typically lasts 20 to 24 weeks—although there is no national standard. The training requirements for officers differ somewhat across the nation, but most police services provide between 650 and 800 hours of instruction. The Saskatchewan Police College reports its hours of training, and they are shown in Table 5.1. Although the training takes a total of 695 hours, the Saskatchewan Police Commission (2018, pp. 7–8) reports that "most police services also provide one to two weeks of selective training pertinent to their agencies when the recruits graduate from the College."

Before training academy graduates are made permanent employees, they must complete a period of supervised instruction by field training officers; these are experienced officers who provide instruction and coaching to new officers. The length of these field training programs varies, but most police services require a six-month period before constables are considered ready to work independently. All together, the time between sending the first application in the mail and becoming a permanent police service employee can be years.

field training officers Experienced police officers who train and mentor new police officers during their first months on the job.

TABLE 5.1 **Saskatchewan Police College Training Areas**

Topic	Hours
Criminal law	103
Wellness	22
Orientation to recruit training	7.5
Introduction to policing and daily detailing	62
Criminal law (e.g., *Criminal Code*, federal and provincial statutes)	95.5
Wellness	22
Diversity awareness	9.5
Communication skills and de-escalation	23.5
Professionalism, ethics, and integrity	12
Traffic control and enforcement	17.5
Introduction to investigations	38
Mental health	24
Interpersonal violence and abuse	22
High risk investigations	40
Defensive tactics	96.5
Emergency vehicle operation	38
Firearms	77
Conducted Energy Weapons (e.g., tasers)	11
Public and officer safety training	60
Drill (includes graduation)	46.5
Total	695

Saskatchewan Police Commission (2018, pp. 7–8)

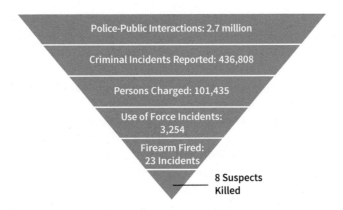

FIGURE 5.1   Police use of Force in Calgary, Alberta, 2012–2017

Interactions with the public rarely result in the use of force, and in five years the Calgary Police Service had 2.7 million interactions, of which eight resulted in a suspect being killed or about one in every 340,000 interactions (five of those fatal shootings happened in 2016).

Adapted from Wittmann (2018)

citizens have proven to be watchdogs of police activities, as anybody with a smart phone can record police–citizen interactions—effectively placing the police under public surveillance. Citizens, using their cameras, have recorded incidents of police misconduct and have posted these videos online.

In terms of formal civilian oversight of the police, guidelines are usually laid out in the *Police Services Act* in each province. Ferdik, Rojek, and Alpert (2013, p. 104) observed that these formal methods of civilian oversight emerged to "compensate for governmental failures to combat police deviance and equalize the balance of power between public officials and citizens." In Saskatchewan, for example, all communities larger than 5,000 residents must have a board of police commissioners. These boards are responsible for providing general direction to the police as well as specific guidance on policies and priorities, developing budgets and long-term plans, negotiating agreements with police associations, and hiring and disciplining police chiefs. In Ontario, by contrast, three agencies provide oversight to the police in addition to civilian boards: the Special Investigative Unit (SIU), the Office of the Independent Police Review Director, and the Ontario Civilian Police Commission (OCPC). Amendments to Ontario's *Police Services Act* in 2018 were intended to give these oversight agencies more

authority in terms of the types of incidents they can investigate, although in 2019, the Ontario government announced plans to eliminate the OCPC and introduce a Law Enforcement Complaints Agency (CBC, 2019).

Any public service will generate complaints from the public when mistakes or misconduct occur. The process by which a citizen can raise a complaint about the police varies somewhat across the nation. The RCMP, for instance, has a Civilian Review and Complaints Commission, which is an agency created by Parliament to investigate citizen complaints. Individuals can also make a complaint with any RCMP detachment or with the province's or territory's police commission.

Most large municipal police services have their own investigatory bodies that respond to public complaints or carry out internal investigations of police mistakes or misconduct—often these units are called professional standards sections—although in smaller agencies, complaints might be investigated by a supervisory officer or the chief. For the most part, the topics of these investigations range from relatively minor incidents such as an officer accused of being rude to allegations of false arrest, excessive use of force, or *Charter* violations. In 2016/2017, for instance, the RCMP's Civilian Review and Complaints Commission (2018, p. 5) received 2,644 complaints, and the top five allegations (their definitions are summarized) were:

1. *Neglect of duty*: When officer(s) failed to carry out a duty, such as improperly caring for a prisoner or performing their work below RCMP standards.

2. *Improper attitude*: Where an officer was rude, disrespectful, or lacked empathy.

3. *Improper use of force*: Where the force used was unnecessary, applied too harshly, or inappropriate to the situation.

4. *Irregularity in procedure*: When an officer violated privacy rules or inappropriately accessed information, such as using a police database to access information about a friend or family member.

5. *Improper arrest*: When officer(s) failed to promptly inform a suspect why they were being arrested, or failed to advise the individual about their rights, such as access to counsel.

Responding to Police Misconduct

Although every police service in Canada has mechanisms in place so that civilians can report police misconduct, there are a number of barriers to making public complaints. For example, many people who feel they were mistreated by the police may lack confidence that their claims will be taken seriously. Their confidence in being heard is also decreased when complaints have to be made directly with the police or with mixed (police/independent) systems (Prenzler, Mihinjac, & Porter, 2013, p. 155). Prenzler, Mihinjac, and Porter (2013) also found that complainants become more skeptical when the matters are more serious, such as with the inappropriate use of force. It is therefore likely that a "dark figure of police misconduct" exists: misconduct that occurs but is never reported or counted (Reiner, 2010, p. 211).

So how much police misconduct actually occurs? Like crime, many minor incidents of misconduct go unreported. More serious incidents, however, are likely to be formally reported and investigated by an independent body. Less serious allegations, by contrast, are normally investigated by the police service. In Ontario, for example, from April 1, 2017, to March 31, 2018, the Office of the Independent Police Review Director (2018, p. 33) reported that a total of 3,399 officers (of 23,830 sworn officers in the province) had had complaints made against them for the entire province. Figure 5.3 shows the complaint process, and like the criminal justice funnel presented in Chapter 1, the number of officers actually punished for misconduct is a very small proportion of all cases: in the end fewer than 100 of the claims were substantiated. For claims of misconduct that are substantiated, the consequences for officers can be severe, including losing their jobs. In some cases officers will resign their positions prior to any hearing.

Professional standards units also investigate complaints made directly to a police service. As these matters are managed internally there is seldom a public record of the officers involved, the nature of the incident, or the punishments imposed on any officer. Davis (2018, para. 6) reports that the "Toronto Police Service handed out penalties in over 600 internal discipline cases between 2014 and May 3, 2017," and these cases involved both civilian and police personnel. While some may be critical of the hidden nature of how the police manage these cases, few employers, whether government or private companies, will disclose personnel matters, given the employees' right to privacy.

In cases where the objectivity of a police service might be questioned, such as after the police shooting of a civilian suspect, investigators from civilian agencies or other police services typically conduct the investigations. Procedures, however, vary throughout the country. Over half of the provinces (Alberta, British Columbia, Manitoba, Nova Scotia, Ontario, and Quebec) have independent civilian agencies that investigate incidents where individuals are killed or seriously wounded by the police. In Atlantic Canada, Nova Scotia's Serious Incident Response Team has investigated cases in Newfoundland and Labrador, and Prince Edward Island (Berman, 2018). Tutton (2017) observes that officials in Atlantic Canada have proposed establishing a single agency to investigate serious incidents in all four provinces. If that partnership happens, Saskatchewan will be the only province

A COMPARATIVE VIEW

Use of Lethal Force in Canada and the United States

The use of firearms by the police is rare and few police officers will fire their weapons at a suspect in their entire career. An estimate of the number of fatal police shootings in the United States and Canada in 2017, shown in Figure 5.2, was developed using information from the *Washington Post* (2018) and Macroux and Nicholson (2018). These figures show that Canadian officers are about one-quarter as likely to kill a suspect using their firearms as are American officers. This comparison only shows people fatally shot by the police, although other suspects die in police custody from other causes, such as after being wounded by a conducted energy device or a vehicle crash. Those incidents are not reported because this information is inconsistently reported in both nations.

Why do these differences exist? One stark difference between Canada and the United States is the number of guns on the streets. Gun ownership in Canada is much less prevalent than in the United States—Karp (2018, p. 4) reports there were 120.5 civilian-owned guns for every 100 Americans compared with 34.7 guns for every 100 Canadians at the end of 2017. Furthermore, Americans often carry those guns in public places; Lott (2017) reports that over 16 million Americans have permits to carry concealed firearms. One outcome of having a greater number of guns on the streets is a homicide rate that is almost three times the Canadian rate. About 70 per cent of US murders are committed with guns, whereas firearms are used in about one-third of murders in Canada, although that proportion has been rising (Beattie, David, & Roy, 2018). Last, American police officers are about 45 per cent more likely to die from an assault than their Canadian counterparts. Thus, not only do US police officers encounter more guns on the streets, but individuals are more likely to use them on each other and the police.

When confronted with a suspect armed with a deadly weapon such as a knife or firearm, the police

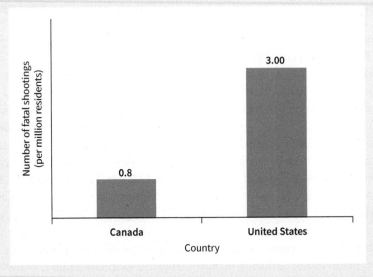

FIGURE 5.2 **Number of Fatal Police Shootings per Million Residents, Canada and the United States, 2017**
Based on CBC (2018); Washington Post (2018)

are taught to shoot until there is no longer a threat. As a result, Canadian officers are trained to shoot at the centre mass, which is an individual's upper midsection (the largest part of the body); they are not trained to wound a suspect, such as by shooting at their arm. Although hits in the centre mass can result in fatal wounds, only a fraction of suspects shot by the police are killed. Between 1992 and 2017, Ontario police officers shot 402 people, and about one in three (37 per cent) died from their wounds (Special Investigations Unit, 2018). One of the challenges of commenting on officer-involved shootings in a thoughtful manner is the lack of accurate national statistics collected by government bodies in either Canada or the United States on fatal and non-fatal police-involved shootings. Instead, we have to rely on newspaper investigations about the lethal use of force. A CBC study of suspects killed by police shootings between 2000 and 2017, for instance, reveals that Indigenous and Black people were overrepresented compared with their presence in the population, while Whites were under-represented (Marcoux & Nicholson, 2018).

One problematic type of officer-involved shooting is when suicidal individuals deliberately provoke a confrontation with the police in order to be killed, which is called suicide by cop (SBC) or police-assisted suicide. Often an individual will point an unloaded or replica gun at the police and then be shot. In some cases, they have a suicide note in their pocket or have told friends or family members that they intended to commit suicide. While it is difficult to accurately classify these events (as we do not always know the individual's true motivation), some researchers have found that anywhere from one-quarter to one-third of police shootings in the United States and Canada were SBC (Lord, 2014; Mohandie, Meloy, & Collins, 2009). Some find it hard to believe that a person would want to be killed by the police, but an example was captured on video after the April 2018 van attack on Yonge Street in Toronto, which killed ten people and injured another 13. After exiting his vehicle, the driver of the van pointed an object at the lone officer who stopped him; the suspect yelled "kill me" and "I have a gun in my pocket." The officer realized the object was not a firearm, holstered his sidearm, and instead used a baton to restrain the subject (CBC, 2018a).

officer-involved shootings Occur when police officers discharge their firearm, including accidental and intentional discharges.

suicide by cop Occurs when individuals deliberately provoke the police into shooting them, such as by pointing an unloaded firearm at an officer.

An example of an attempted suicide by cop incident occurred when 25-year-old Alek Minassian pointed an object at a Toronto Police Constable Ken Lam and yelled, "Kill me." The incident was captured on video; a screenshot of this video appeared on the next day's cover of the New York Post (left). The full video can be seen at: https://www.cbc.ca/news/canada/toronto/officer-praised-taking-van-attack-suspect-custody-peaceful-1.4632661

FIGURE 5.3 Public Complaints of Police, Ontario, 2017–2018
Source: Adapted from the Office of the Independent Police Review Director (2018, p. 33)

without an independent police watchdog agency. Despite the fact that external bodies are responsible for investigating serious offences, there is still public criticism that when the police are investigating the police, there is a lack of objectivity.

Litigation

One difference in achieving police accountability in Canada and the United States is the number of lawsuits launched in both nations. Although lawsuits for improper police conduct are regularly filed in US courts, there is less litigation in Canada. Lawsuits have an impact on officers and their organizations. Because matters are before the courts, officers accused of wrongdoing or of making a mistake cannot comment to the media—or even their friends and family members—about the events that led to the lawsuit. As these cases can drag on for years, officers must often endure the negative perceptions of community members, family, and friends before the matter is resolved (Chrismas, 2013). Lawsuits are also costly to police organizations in terms of the amount of time and expenses involved in responding to allegations about their officers.

While we tend to think of civilians launching a lawsuit to seek damages for an inappropriate use of force or arrest, a series of class action lawsuits have been initiated since 2010 by employees of police services who allege they were mistreated by other employees in these agencies (class action lawsuits are brought by a group of people who allege the defendant harmed them). A series of class action lawsuits were launched in 2012 by female officers of the RCMP alleging discrimination, intimidating behaviour, and harassment, and civilian employees of the RCMP have made similar allegations (Houlihan & Seglins, 2018a). Two veteran male officers have also claimed they were bullied and harassed while working for the RCMP, and in June 2018 they launched a $1.1-billion class action lawsuit on behalf of officers, civilian staff, and volunteers (Houlihan & Seglins, 2018b). The RCMP is not the only police service where employees have alleged mistreatment: female officers from the Waterloo Regional Police have also initiated class action lawsuits, claiming "unwanted sexual advances, career sabotage and personal attacks" (Germano, 2018, para. 4).

Body-Worn Cameras (BWCs)

In addition to their actions being captured by citizens with smartphones, the police are also under scrutiny from cameras placed on the dashboards of police vehicles, and closed-circuit television (CCTV) cameras are installed in most police stations. While video recordings of incidents do not always tell us the complete story of what occurred, they can provide an unbiased record of incidents. Body-worn cameras (BWCs) show what happens in interactions between the police and the public, but the evidence is mixed as to whether these cameras reduce complaints. Braga, Sousa, Coldren, and Rodriguez (2018, p. 512) found that officers using BWCs "generate fewer complaints and use of force reports" [and] "made more arrests and issued more citations" than officers without BWCs. In his analysis of BWC in Canada, Bud (2016) points out that factors such as privacy rights, the costs of using these cameras (including storage costs for the data collected), and a lack of legislation governing their use need to be considered before a police service uses these tools.

Public Support for the Police

The police require the public's cooperation in reporting crimes, in helping with investigations, and in appearing in court as witnesses. Tyler (2006) also found that when the police are seen as more legitimate by the public, people are more willing to abide by the law. As a result, the police are increasingly interested in how the public perceives them. Generally speaking, national polls of Canadians show our trust and confidence in the police has been mixed over the past few decades:

- Trust in the police dropped from 69 to 57 per cent between 2007 and 2012 (Ipsos Reid, 2012).
- In the 2014 General Social Survey, trust in the police was higher than trust in Canada's school system, banks, the justice system or courts, the media, federal Parliament, and major corporations (Cotter, 2015).
- Three-quarters (76 per cent) of Canadians had a somewhat or very positive opinion on policing in polls conducted in 2016 and 2017 (Insight West, 2016; 2017).
- Over three-quarters (79 per cent) of respondents said RCMP officers demonstrated professionalism in their work, and 75 per cent said their officers provided a quality service to the public in 2017 (RCMP, 2018a).

Trust and confidence in the police varies throughout the nation, and Cotter (2015) reports that respondents in Newfoundland and Labrador express the highest confidence while British Columbia respondents reported the lowest.

Confidence in the police also differs by gender, ethnic group, and age. The results of Canada's General Social Survey show that women, older respondents, and non-visible minorities have greater confidence in the police (Cotter, 2015). Members of visible minority groups or Indigenous people (First Nations, Métis, or Inuit) expressed less confidence in the police (Cotter, 2015), and these results are consistent with the findings of previous Canadian studies (e.g., Cao, 2011, 2014; Sprott & Doob, 2014). University of Windsor researchers contend that contact with the police may play a more important role in shaping a person's perceptions about officers than an individual's race or ethnicity (Alberton & Gorey, 2018). Cotter (2015) found that people who had contact with the police in the previous 12 months and crime victims

Some police services have reported reductions in citizen complaints when officers wear body-worn cameras (BWC). Many believe that BWCs will reduce police misconduct and citizen complaints. Very few large police services, however, have adopted this technology. Montreal and Halifax, for instance, will not adopt BWCs because of their expense and the challenges of storing data the data collected by these cameras (Valiante, 2019).

rated the police lower than people with no contact and non-victims. Police activity is often concentrated in neighbourhoods with a high proportion of members of minority groups. As a result, young males living in those places may have more contact with the police than their counterparts in the suburbs, and thus have less trust and confidence in the police.

Police Independence

The political independence of the police is important in order for them to carry out their duties in a professional and non-biased manner. As noted in Chapter 4, inappropriate political influence defined policing until the 1940s and long afterward in small municipal police services. Because of this inappropriate influence, municipal policing was seldom a long-term career as chiefs and officers were often fired without cause and had little recourse to challenge those decisions. The introduction of professional standards, police

unionization, and the public's rejection of inappropriate political influence led to police professionalization. Robertson (2012, p. 348) observes that "government direction of police is deliberately circumscribed to limit inappropriate political influence and operational interference.... At the same time, policing is a highly regulated area of public service, subject to legislated standards, directives, guidelines and procedures."

Despite those safeguards, the police are operated by governments, and it is difficult to be fully independent of municipal, provincial, and federal politicians, especially when they control the agency's budget and when mayors, premiers, or the Prime Minister can fire police chiefs who won't embrace the leader's philosophy. As a result, the police are seldom fully independent of political influence, but any influence that does exist must be appropriate. The question of how much influence is appropriate created a crisis for the federal government in 2019, when Jody Wilson-Raybould, the former Attorney General and Minister of Justice, testified that she was the target of inappropriate pressure from the Prime Minister's Office after her office would not stop the prosecution of SNC-Lavalin, a large engineering company. It is important to acknowledge that politicians do have a role in establishing police priorities (such as which crimes to focus on) and operational strategies such as where police are deployed within a community. Ideally, these decisions should be directed from the public to their political representatives, should be based on a problem-solving approach, and should involve community stakeholders.

CONTEMPORARY CHALLENGES IN POLICE OPERATIONS

Increasing Legal Complexity

Our expectations of the police are high: we count on officers to follow the rule of law, to be professional, and to work long hours with individuals who are often living on the margins of society,

When Brenda Lucki was appointed as Commissioner of the RCMP in May 2018 she received a mandate letter from Prime Minister Trudeau reinforcing the importance of maintaining the political independence of the RCMP. In it, he said that "I want to be clear that the Government of Canada recognizes and respects that police independence underpins the rule of law and ministerial direction cannot infringe on the RCMP in the exercise of police powers in police investigations" (RCMP, 2018b, para. 2).

The Canadian Press/Justin Tang

who are openly hostile to the police, or who pose a risk to officers. The nature of police work is also growing more complex. A series of Supreme Court decisions since the 1990s, for instance, have increased the expectations of the police to ensure that the due process protections of suspects are upheld. What sort of impacts have these changes had? Public Safety Canada (2012) calculated that the processing time for an impaired driving offence has increased over 300 per cent in the past three decades, and it now takes over five hours of an officer's time to process a single offence, and that does not account for court appearances if the accused pleads not guilty. There are also more protections for suspects under police surveillance. Chrismas (2013) writes that warrant applications for electronic surveillance—which used to be 25 to 35 pages long—have grown to 350-page documents. The hazard for officers taking shortcuts that violate a suspect's constitutional rights is that the case might not proceed to court.

Technology Is Changing the Nature of Crime

Technological changes have led to new ways of carrying out crimes, such as internet-based fraud, and the nature of crime has also been changing. As noted in Chapter 2, there are an increasing number of victims of internet-based offences and many of these crimes are committed by criminals from other nations. Gang members and other organized crime offenders are also becoming involved in cybercrimes, and the Police Executive Research Forum (2018, p. 5) asks:

> Why rob a convenience store if you can get on a computer... and rip off major US banks or credit card companies? It's a much "cleaner" way of profiting from crime, with no potentially dangerous face-to-face encounters with victims. The risk is lower and the payoff higher, with criminal penalties in some cases being essentially non-existent.

In other words, as the rewards of cybercrimes increase and there continue to be few risks of being punished, more offenders will be drawn to these crimes, and more of us will be victimized. As a result there will be a growing need for investigators with cyber-related investigative skills. As they may never leave the police headquarters, it is unlikely that sworn officers would be needed to conduct these investigations. Thus, civilian personnel may play a greater role in crime control in the future.

Technology is Changing the Way Police Carry Out Investigations

There are a growing number of technology-related resources that police can draw upon when investigating crimes. The Police Executive Research Forum (2018, p. 6) points out that information can now be retrieved from social media accounts (of victims and suspects), records of cell phone usage, security cameras, automated licence plate readers, and traffic enforcement cameras. Police can also obtain information from a victim or suspect's Fitbit, GPS devices, or dashboard or in-house surveillance cameras (Police Executive Research Forum, 2018). As a result, the officers involved in complex investigations may be examining information from dozens of devices. Some technological changes intended to improve police effectiveness include the use of big data and predictive software; these practices are discussed in Chapter 12. These tools enable officers to forecast where and when crimes might occur and who might commit them. The use of these tools evokes strong reactions from civil libertarians concerned about our due process protections and our privacy. Fasman (2018) observes that our privacy laws were developed during an era of postal services and landline phones and have not caught up with new technologies.

Civilianization

The employment of civilian personnel in police organizations is referred to as civilianization. The number of civilians employed by police services has been growing at a faster rate than the number of officers. Between 1962 and 2017, the rate of civilian personnel working for police

civilianization The employment of civilian personnel in police organizations.

TABLE 5.2 Growth in Sworn Officers and Non-Sworn Police Personnel per 100,000 residents in Canada, 1962 to 2017

Sworn Officers: Change between 1962 and 2017	34%	⬆
Civilian Personnel: Change between 1962 and 2017	155%	⬆

Conor (2018)

TABLE 5.3 Annual Salaries of Winnipeg's Auxiliary Cadets and Officers

Role	Annual Salary
Auxiliary cadet	$34,631
Fourth-class constable (starting salary)	$55,964
First-class constable	$101,753

Winnipeg Police Service (2019)

forces in Canada per 100,000 residents more than doubled, and almost 30,000 are currently employed, whereas the number of police grew by about one-third this is shown in Table 5.2 (Conor, 2018, p. 20). All of these employees work in roles that are intended to support the activities of sworn officers by freeing them to engage in their core enforcement duties such as responding to and investigating crimes.

There are two types of civilian personnel: administrative support staff and uniformed officials without full police powers. With respect to the first category, management, professional, and clerical support workers now account for one-fifth of all police service personnel (Conor, 2018, p.10). As the size of the agency increases, more specialized workers are required, including dispatchers (who take calls from the public and direct officer activities), crime analysts, and administrators in specialized roles such as finance or human resources.

The second category of civilian personnel are uniformed civilians who have less enforcement powers than sworn officers. These officials go by different titles, including cadets, special constables, security officers, and bylaw enforcement officers (Conor, 2018, p. 10). These officials direct traffic around collisions, collect information about minor crimes, guard crime scenes, provide security at public events, and enforce municipal bylaws such as laws restricting public drinking. The annual salaries of Winnipeg's auxiliary cadets and sworn officers are shown in Table 5.3. The difference between a first- and fourth-class constable is the time spent on the job, and first-class constables generally have at least five years of experience. Police officer salaries tend to be fairly similar across the country and Conor (2018, p. 15)

reports that "the average annual salary for police personnel in Canada in 2016/2017, including both police officers and civilians, was $97,004."

Because cadets or special constables are paid less than police officers, police services hire them to free officers for more enforcement-related duties and to increase police visibility (Kiedrowski, Ruddell, & Petrunik, 2017). Police services can hire five of these non-police officials for the same cost as two senior constables, making them a cost-effective alternative. There are also an increasing number of these uniformed officials working on First Nations, where they are called band constables, community safety officers, or peacekeepers. In addition to supporting the police, these officials can act as a bridge between the police and the community. Many officials work in these positions to gain experience for employment as sworn officers, and McGuckin (2018) reports that of the 2018 class of Winnipeg police officer trainees, 45 per cent had worked as cadets.

Representative Workforce

One of Peel's principles, outlined in Chapter 4, was that the police are the public, and the public are the police. This means that the police should reflect the populations they serve—but that has not always been the case. The police have been criticized for being too "pale and male." The first women constables for the RCMP and OPP entered their training academies in 1974—although some municipal police services had employed women officers in the early 1900s (Corsianos, 2009). Today, policing is a more diverse profession, and Conor (2018) reports that slightly more than one in five Canadian officers are women (21 per cent), which is less than the proportions employed in England and Wales or by the Australian Federal Police, with 29 and 36 per cent respectively (Allen & Jackson, 2018; Australian Federal Police, 2018), but almost twice as many as the United States (12.1 per cent) (Federal Bureau of Investigation, 2017).

Although women have made significant inroads in policing, a number of scholars have drawn our attention to their efforts to overcome the masculine nature of police work—what some call the boys, club. Interviews with women officers from Ontario reveal they've had to overcome discrimination, harassment, stereotypes, and being treated as tokens (Bikos, 2016). Bikos says that these discriminatory attitudes are rooted in the male-oriented police culture. Langan, Sanders, and Gouweloos (2018) interviewed 52 women officers from Canada and they found that a normal event in a woman's life, such as becoming pregnant, can have negative social and career impacts. This finding confirms research done by Cordner and Cordner (2011), who say that women officers have to overcome a number of employer policies unfriendly to both their recruitment and their job retention.

The underrepresentation of minority officers in Canadian police services is a long-standing issue. Jain (1987, p. 791) found that of the 14 police services he examined in his research the proportion of visible minority officers ranged from zero to three per cent. In a follow-up study, Jain, Singh, and Agocs (2000) said that Canadian police services had created policies and practices that inhibited the recruitment of Indigenous and visible minority officers. Have we increased the proportion of officers from different ethnic and racial groups? Conor (2018, pp. 7–8) reported that the number of Indigenous and visible minority officers was growing and accounted for 5.4 and 8.4 per cent, respectively, of all officers in 2016. One gap in our knowledge, however, is that some police services do not collect or provide information about the ethnocultural status of officers, nor do all officers self-disclose their ethnicity.

We tend to think of diversity only in terms of gender, race, and ethnicity, but other factors are also related to workplace diversity. Until the

Francis Vachon

The Winnipeg Police Service has invested in auxiliary cadets, uniformed officials who support the activities of police officers and increase police visibility.

JayLazarin/iStock Photo

Although the police were once criticized as being too "pale and male," the profession is more diverse today, and more than one in five Canadian officers are women. Still, police services have not achieved representative parity with Canadian society. What are some of the things policing departments can do to encourage diverse recruits? Should diversity be an ongoing goal?

1980s, for example, police services routinely hired new police officers who were in their early twenties, and few had more than a high school education. Today, by contrast, many newly hired officers

Race, Class, and Gender

Women Police Leaders

Women are being promoted into a growing number of police leadership positions. Gwen Boniface, for instance, was appointed as OPP Commissioner in 1998; Beverley Busson was appointed as RCMP Commissioner in 2006, and Brenda Lucki became the RCMP's second female commissioner in 2018. Women have also held chief positions and led large municipal police services for over 20 years. Christine Silverberg became chief of the Calgary Police Service in 1995, and she was the first woman to hold that rank in a major city. These women often had to overcome discrimination from their male colleagues. Chief Silverberg, for instance, tolerated sexist comments as she moved up the ranks working in three Ontario police services, and the day after her appointment as chief in Calgary, someone painted a pink outline of a body on the steps of the police headquarters (Underwood, 2018). Conor (2018, p. 7) reports that 15 per cent of senior officers in Canada are women.

Policing is a physically and psychologically demanding career, and adding leadership responsibilities adds additional stress. A survey of Canadian police officers conducted by Duxbury and Higgins (2012) revealed some interesting findings in terms of the workplace and non-work demands on women command officers (those holding positions of higher rank than sergeant). According to Duxbury and Higgins (2012), women of all ranks were less likely than their male counterparts to have children (p. 21), and when it came to women command staff, over one-half (51 per cent) had no children, compared to only 7 per cent of male command staff (p. 23). Women command staff were also less likely to have been married than their male counterparts. Despite the fact that women in command positions had made those sacrifices for their careers, only 82 per cent reported earning more than $100,000 per year, compared with 98 per cent of males in leadership positions (Duxbury & Higgins, 2012, p. 22), although those salaries are much higher today.

have college diplomas or university degrees and various surveys suggest that about one-third of all Canadian police officers have a post-secondary education (Ruddell & Eaton, 2015). In addition to having more years of post-secondary education, many new police officers have worked in other occupations, and this also builds the capacity of police services to look at old problems in new ways.

The Expansion of Private Policing

Although the focus of this chapter has been on the publicly funded police, there are a growing number of private security officers and private investigators in Canada, and many of them carry out duties that were formerly done by the police—this is known as private policing. Bayley and Nixon (2010) note that Canada and the United States have the highest per capita employment of security personnel in the developed world. Statistics Canada (2018e) reports that the country had 122,310 security personnel in 2017, and the actual total is probably greater due to the challenges in defining these workers' jobs (for example, is a bouncer in a bar considered a security officer?). The number of private security officials grew by 50 per cent between 1991 and 2017 whereas the public police have only increased by about one-fifth during the same time (Statistics Canada, 2018e).

The roles of private security and the police are often complementary, as employees of both sectors work toward preventing and responding to anti-social behaviour and crime. Police services are increasingly using employees of private security firms to support their operations in non-crime-fighting roles (Montgomery & Griffiths, 2015). For example, in several provinces, members of the Canadian Corps of Commissionaires operate laser radar in traffic enforcement roles (they have no direct contact with vehicle operators). The Commissionaires have a long history of providing services to the

private policing Involves the social control efforts of individuals who are not government employees, but instead are hired to provide security or policing services.

police, including guarding crime scenes, supervising prisoners, or providing the front desk security in police stations. Police services employ these personnel as their support allows officers to focus on their core roles of fighting and investigating crime. Not all stakeholders, however, support the use of private security to carry out tasks formerly done by the police. The Police Association of Ontario (2018, p. 1) opposes the outsourcing of police duties to private firms; they say that the 2018 changes in Ontario's *Police Act* allow for "the privatization of core policing duties critical for public safety, like prisoner transport," and they express concerns that police privatization in the United Kingdom led to investigatory errors and increased crime. Some are critical that a two-tier policing arrangement exists, where the richest Canadians are able to purchase additional private services, raising the question of whether the rich should be safer because they are able to afford private security. On the other hand, some would argue that a reduced need for the police to patrol wealthy neighbourhoods frees them to spend more time in higher crime areas.

Police Officer Subculture

An occupational culture is a set of attitudes, beliefs, and values associated with a profession, and the police have a distinctive culture that can contribute to a number of negative outcomes including how peers and members of the public are treated (Iacobucci, 2014). What differentiates the police from other occupational cultures is that their job is inherently dangerous and officers depend on each other for their safety. Some officers can develop an "us versus them" mindset and become inherently suspicious of the public given how often officers are misled. This suspicion, in turn, leads to social isolation, whereby the police tend to spend most of their on- and off-duty time associating with other officers—further reinforcing the "us versus them" culture. Campeau (2015) interviewed officers in a mid-sized Ontario city and found that some traits of the police culture have withstood change for decades, including isolation, solidarity, machismo, conservatism, and mission-action, when officers seek excitement.

Hall (2002) observes that some Canadian officers believe they must protect each other whatever the cost and that loyalty to the organization and profession counts more than anything. What emerges from that belief is called the "blue wall of silence," whereby some officers obstruct investigations into police mistakes or misconduct. As this code is intended as a way for officers to protect each other, it can also lead to further misconduct as officers claim ignorance of the unethical or illegal actions of their co-workers. Because the police depend on their peers for their safety, officers are sometimes reluctant to confront the misconduct of other officers.

In addition to contributing to misconduct, there are several other negative aspects of the police subculture. As most officers identify with the crime-fighting role, they tend to resist reforms that would shift their job duties toward more proactive or social service–focused responsibilities, or what Ontario officers called social work (Iacobucci, 2014). Duxbury, Bennell, Halinski,

A growing number of women officers are assuming leadership positions in Canadian police services. In 2017, Brenda Butterworth-Carr, an Indigenous woman originally from Yukon, was appointed deputy commissioner and officer in charge of the RCMP "E" Division (British Columbia), the largest division in the nation. In 2019 she left her position with the RCMP to became the Director of Police Services for the province of British Columbia.

and Murphy (2018) interviewed 103 Canadian policing experts and found that the police culture was a powerful force in resisting change. Resistance to change, however, may be a survival skill, as some police services undergo almost continual reform and officers are never quite sure what reforms are fads (sometimes called the "flavour of the month") and which will persist. As a result Mays and Ruddell (2019, p. 79) say that most officers will take a wait-and-see approach when reforms are initiated. This reluctance to change is one reason why most police reforms have failed (Schafer & Varano, 2017).

In their study of the RCMP, Murphy and McKenna (2007, p. 6) observe that the following factors have led to the formation of a police subculture:

- **solidarity:** Loyalty to other police officers above all others.
- **authoritarianism:** Belief in, and willingness to exercise, coercive power over others.
- **suspicion:** A mistrust of others that is formed by negative contacts with non-officers.
- **conservative outlook:** Caused by the moralistic and negative nature of police work.
- **prejudicial attitudes:** A tendency to prejudge others using stereotypes based on an officer's values and work experiences.

The police subculture is also a product of an organization's values, mission, leadership, and how members are rewarded (e.g., are officers punished or rewarded for their community involvement?). As a result of the relationship between organizational factors and leadership, there is no single police subculture, and it varies according to where an officer is employed (Cordner, 2017). In addition, occupational cultures are dynamic, meaning that they change over time, and some negative aspects of the police subculture—such as the acceptance of women, minority, and non-heterosexual officers—have changed. Campeau's (2015) study of Canadian officers also identifies the changing nature of the police subculture in an environment where external accountability and oversight have increased.

SUMMARY

Despite the transformation from a blue-collar occupation to a well-paid profession where officers better reflect the demographic characteristics of the communities they serve, policing remains a controversial profession. Advocates of the crime control model support hiring more officers and expanding their powers, believing that justice is denied when police operations are "handcuffed" by budget cutbacks or court decisions that make police work more difficult. Supporters of the due process position, by contrast, argue that police activities should be closely scrutinized by professional standards units, civilian oversight boards, the media, and the courts. Moreover, they express concern about how unrestrained use of new technologies threatens our privacy (Canadian Civil Liberties Association, 2016). The public tends to identify with either of these positions, and given those feelings, it is unlikely that many controversies surrounding the police—including questions about the appropriate or excessive use of force—will ever be resolved.

If we are to judge the progress of Canadian policing against Peel's principles, we find that the police more closely reflect the populations they serve (in terms of gender and race), that force is used as a last resort in most cases, and that police activities and operations are increasingly transparent. Issues that breed mistrust of the police, such as their criminal behaviours (on- or off-duty) and misconduct, are addressed by the professional standards units of police services and the courts. In the 1980s and 1990s, for instance, it was rare that an off-duty officer's wrongdoing, such as driving while impaired, would end in an arrest, but arrests for criminal acts are more likely to happen today. The downside to holding the police more accountable and publicizing their failures is that our mistrust of them may increase, despite the fact that in the past misconduct and illegal behaviour was more widespread and hidden. Perhaps the most powerful oversight of police activities today is the eagerness of the public to capture interactions between the police and the public on

MYTH OR REALITY

Dangers of Police Work

Policing is a dangerous job and officers are at risk of violence simply by wearing a uniform. In an average year, three or four Canadian police officers are killed on the job. About half of them die in accidents, and between 2014 and 2018 nine officers were murdered. How does this compare with the likelihood of being murdered for an average Canadian? Table 5.4 shows that the homicide rate for police officers is higher than the general population over 18 years of age, but we have to interpret that statistic carefully, as one police homicide can drastically impact the homicide rate because their numbers are so low compared to the general population. Despite the fact that police are at greater risk of being murdered than other Canadians, their profession is not among the most dangerous; the Association of Workers' Compensation Boards of Canada (2019, Table 36) reports that the highest risk occupations were construction, manufacturing, and transportation. Workers in other occupations, however, are seldom intentionally killed.

While the discussion so far has been about fatalities, officers are also at very high risk of being assaulted. Every year between 2012 and 2017 there were about 10,000 reported assaults on peace officers in Canada (Statistics Canada, 2018d). Considering there are about 69,000 officers in Canada, this suggests that officers have about a one in seven chance of being assaulted in a given year. That likelihood is higher for officers working directly with the public, such as patrol officers, than for those working in administrative jobs.

In addition to accidents and assaults we are now recognizing that a large percentage of officers suffer from psychological injuries such as post-traumatic stress disorder (PTSD), which occurs after exposure to traumatic events. Carleton et al. (2018a) received surveys from almost 6,000 Canadian public safety personnel about their reactions to job-related stressors. These researchers found that over one-third (36.7 per cent) of municipal or provincial police officers and one-half of RCMP officers (50.2 per cent) reported having one or more symptoms of mental health disorders such as anxiety, depression, alcohol abuse, or PTSD. Sawa, Ivany, and Kelley (2019) report that police organizations with a negative workplace culture, including agencies that tolerate bullying and harassment, make it difficult for these officers to seek help.

These disorders can have a significant impact on these officers. Carleton et al. (2018b) found that about 10 per cent of their sample of public safety personnel had thought about suicide in the prior year and about 4 per cent of the sample had developed a plan to kill themselves; 18 of their respondents had actually attempted suicide. There are no agencies that collect information about the number of police officers who commit suicide for the entire country, but Bueckert (2019) says that nine Ontario officers killed themselves in 2018, which shows the seriousness of the problem. If those figures are similar throughout the entire country, it suggests the likelihood of a police officer dying from suicide is much higher than their risk of being murdered or accidentally killed on the job.

TABLE 5.4 **Policing and the General Population: Homicide Rates per 100,000 Residents, Canada, 2014–2018**

	Police Officers	All Canadians Over 18 Years Old
Average homicides per 100,000 residents	2.6	2.1

Adapted from: Conor, Robson, and Marcellus (2019); Statistics Canada (2018)

their mobile phones and share these occurrences (whether positive or negative) over social media.

Some of what ails the police industry is due to the negative aspects of an occupational culture that resists reform and has difficulty moving away from the traditional crime-fighter identity, even though that role represents only a fraction of formal police duties. As a result, some initiatives that are inconsistent with the traditional policing model, such as community-oriented policing, have not been fully adopted in some places. Despite a resistance to change, there is growing recognition of the social service roles that officers play and belief that the police should be involved in these roles (Meares, 2017). Millie (2013) argues that while the police currently carry out these social service duties, other organizations, professions, and volunteers may be more effective at tackling these tasks, freeing the police to focus on their crime-fighting and investigative expertise.

A number of police leaders, researchers, and politicians have argued that the police need to be "reinvented" or "reimagined" in light of their changing roles (Lum & Nagin, 2017; Tonry, 2017). Although the policing industry has been undergoing reform for over a century, there is little agreement about what changes (if any) should occur. Bayley and Nixon (2010) observe that the public police are slowly losing their traditional monopoly on policing. As highlighted in this chapter, duties formerly carried out by sworn officers are now undertaken by civilian employees, volunteers, and private security agencies. This is part of a global trend. For the most part, these changes in Canada have been gradual, and it is unlikely that there will be significant changes in policing in the next few decades.

Career SNAPSHOT

Police Officer

There are numerous opportunities during a policing career to become involved in a diverse range of job experiences, from working in an aviation unit to carrying out criminal investigations in other nations. While municipal police officers generally spend most of their careers in a single location, provincial police or RCMP members may be transferred every few years to different places, although in some of these cases the officer has applied for a transfer to a more desirable location or to earn a promotion. In addition to working in Canada, some RCMP officers work in other nations. There is also a growing number of Canadian police officers who have participated in year-long international assignments sponsored though the United Nations.

Closer to home, Sergeant Rick Abbott describes his experiences with the Edmonton Police Service.

Profile

Name: Rick Abbott
Job title: Sergeant, Edmonton Police Service
Employed in current job since: 1996
Present location: Edmonton, Alberta
Education: BA, Sociology, University of Saskatchewan

Background

Growing up, I had numerous family and friend connections to the policing world. As a result, one of my earliest recollections, in terms of careers, is that I wanted to be a police officer. I grew up in a rural Saskatchewan city, and parallel to my interest in policing was a passion for hunting and the shooting sports. Although these pastimes are only lightly related to police work, the shooting skills that I developed would eventually play a large part in my career with the Edmonton Police Service.

Work Experience

Prior to starting my policing career, I worked my way through university as a nurse's aide in a mental health treatment centre and as a social service worker in a secure custody youth facility. Both of these jobs prepared me for police work. Working with people with mental illnesses, many of whom had previous conflicts with the law, helped me better understand their behaviours. In addition, many of the youth I worked with in secure custody were Aboriginal youth from northern Saskatchewan, and I learned about their needs; I got to know them from the "other side" prior to wearing the police cap.

Much of my career with the Edmonton Police Service (EPS) has been in specialized roles. During my first five years in downtown Edmonton, I worked as a constable in their patrol services and beats program (foot and bicycle). After that assignment, I worked for eight years in the tactical section as a sniper. My experiences hunting and shooting were pivotal in my effectiveness as a sniper dealing with high-risk situations and offenders. After leaving the tactical section, I went on to teach with the firearms training unit where I led their carbine program for three years teaching the use and deployment of our patrol rifle to over 200 members of the EPS.

Most recently, I was promoted out of the firearms training unit and am back on the beat as a sergeant in the downtown core, supervising a crew of beat officers. My career has been quite specialized. Nonetheless, one of my primary attractions to policing has been the variety of paths one may choose in a singular profession. The variety is fascinating. One could work in two very separate roles such as sniping in a tactical unit and working with the Child at Risk Response Team (CARRT), where officers are paired with a social worker who helps kids in bad situations. Both are very important tasks in today's world, yet dissimilar in every sense of the word. One aspect of policing that I didn't expect would play such a large part in the work is writing. A degree in the liberal arts helped me prepare for the massive amount of writing that is required in everyday policing tasks. Articulation of our actions is the only way to prevent professional, legal, and political problems from arising from the often controversial duties of our work.

Advice to Students

It is important to have a "plan B" as there is no certainty that one will be hired for a job in policing. Police agencies are looking for adults with life experience. Officers today come from a diverse range of educational and work experiences that can be completely unrelated to law enforcement. These experiences benefit not only the individual, but also the police service and the entire community. Some of my most successful colleagues have backgrounds with no obvious connection to policing. I have friends who were nurses, carpenters, lawyers, butchers, or electricians, and all of them went on to contribute in very meaningful ways with the EPS.

Police agencies are looking for mature people with a variety of experiences, but I believe we lose many good candidates who may have lived a little too much. I was hired at 26 years of age and clearly remember around the age of 20 thinking that I had to make good choices to avoid ruining my chances of being hired as a police officer. Not to mince words, but it's important that alcohol be used responsibly and drugs be avoided in our youth so as to not avert a chance at a very rewarding career in policing.

REVIEW QUESTIONS

1. Describe why the number of operational roles increases with agency size.
2. What are some of the challenges in recruiting new police officers?
3. What mechanisms are in place to ensure that the police are accountable to the public?
4. Why can occupational culture be a destructive force in policing?
5. What factors differentiate the three different policing styles?

DISCUSSION QUESTIONS

1. Why is patrol considered by many to be the most important role in policing?
2. What is the police service style in your community?
3. Describe some strategies to change the culture of a police service.
4. Describe the four methods of holding the police accountable. What do you think is the most effective method?
5. What is the most significant challenge confronting the police today?

INTERNET SITE

The Federal Bureau of Investigation (FBI) is considered one of the leading law enforcement agencies in the world. Their *Law Enforcement Bulletin*, which has a magazine format, is published monthly and provides an overview of current issues in law enforcement. **https://leb.fbi.gov/archives**

CASE CITED

R v The Royal Canadian Mounted Police, 2017 NBPC06

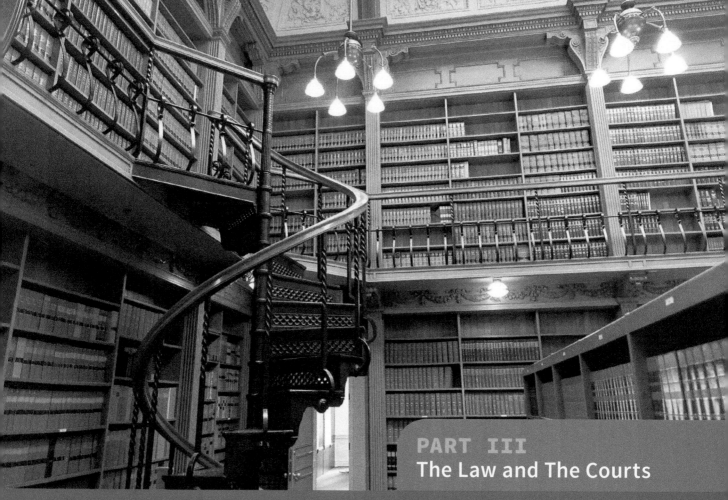

▲ The Great Library of the Law Society of Ontario, in Osgoode Hall, Toronto, houses a renowned collection of historic legal materials. Do you think historical precedent is important in Canadian law?   (Photo credit: Archive PL/Alamy Stock Photo)

6   Criminal Law

LEARNING OUTLINE

After reading this chapter, you will be able to

- Provide reasons why the criminal law is dynamic
- Identify two main elements of a crime
- Explain the differences between procedural law and substantive law
- Describe various justification and excuse defences for committing a crime
- Describe how court operations differ in Canada and the United States

Representing Oneself in Court: The Case of Dellen Millard

There is an old saying that "a man who is his own lawyer has a fool for his client" because of the disadvantages a person has representing themselves in a criminal trial. Without legal training, a defendant will have a very difficult time trying to obtain a not guilty decision in a trial. People accused of crimes are not eligible for legal aid services if they earn more than $14,453 per year in Ontario, which makes someone working half-time at a minimum wage job ineligible for legal aid (Ruby & Enenajor, 2017, para. 10). But hiring a lawyer is expensive and in 2018 a simple one-day trial on a summary offence such as theft can cost from $2,500 to $6,000 (Bruineman, 2018, p. 22). Lacking the funds to hire a lawyer, a growing number of defendants are representing themselves in court (see the "Myth or Reality" box in this chapter). Legal scholars have pointed out that self-represented defendants pose several challenges for the court; one of the foremost is that they are incredibly disadvantaged when their opponent is a skilled Crown prosecutor.

Ruby and Enenajor (2017, para. 15) observe that "the right of a person to defend himself is deeply entrenched in our judicial system." Most self-represented defendants simply want their day in court, although there are a number of cases where the defendant has subjected victims or the family members of a deceased victim to difficult questioning on the stand, and the nature of their questions has further victimized them. Ruby and Enenajor (2017) say, however, that "checks and balances exist in our system to ensure that the right to cross-examine is not abused," and a key role of the judge in these cases is to ensure that abusive questioning does not occur. But if defendants are representing themselves in court, where does the judge draw the line between legitimate questions intended to get to the truth and questions that are intended to make crime victims and their families uncomfortable?

The December 2017 trial of Dellen Millard, who was accused of murdering his ex-girlfriend, Laura Babcock, is an example of how a defendant can re-victimize the friends and family of a murder victim. Millard had been convicted of the murder of Tim Bosma in 2016 and sentenced to life imprisonment. At his trial for Babcock's murder he questioned her father, her ex-boyfriend, and the former girlfriend of his co-accused. Acting as his own lawyer, Millard asked Babcock's father if he had ever hit or abused her, and questioned him about "her personal life, her drug use and work as an escort" (Dunn, 2017, para. 13). The fact that Millard was representing himself was unusual; most defendants who act as their own lawyer do so because they can't afford counsel, but Millard was wealthy, having inherited his father's estate.

Did these victims need to be questioned by Millard? Prior to the trial, Crown prosecutors argued that a lawyer be appointed by the court to question those three witnesses, which is allowed under section 486.3 of the *Criminal Code*. The judge presiding at the trial, however, denied this request. And as for Millard? He and his co-accused were convicted of the Babcock murder. Both are serving consecutive life sentences, which means that they cannot apply for parole until 2063. In September 2018, Millard was found guilty of killing his father and was sentenced to another 25 years in December 2018, so he will not be eligible for parole until he is 102 years old.

Critical Questions

1. An Ontario resident who has an income greater than $14,453 is ineligible for legal aid assistance, while the annual minimum wage salary for that province is $29,120 (at $14 an hour). Is this an appropriate limit for legal aid assistance or should it be increased or lowered? Why or why not?

2. Describe some risks of having defendants with no formal legal training defending themselves in court on serious charges.

3. Judges can use section 486.3 of the *Criminal Code* to prevent a self-represented defendant from questioning vulnerable people (such as the victims of their alleged crimes). When should a judge allow or disallow such questioning?

INTRODUCTION

Formal written laws are dynamic, meaning that they are evolving in response to changes in the broader social, technological, and political environments. In the past, people living in small communities would often conform through informal methods of social control. But as people moved from the countryside to cities, they became more anonymous and their behaviours were less likely to be influenced by the approval or disapproval of others. The number of new immigrants also increased around the 1830s, and many of these individuals were poor and may have been perceived as a threat to the social order (Baehre, 1981). Because of these social changes, it became more important to enact laws to respond to antisocial behaviour and crime, and to establish police agencies, courts, and prison systems to enforce these laws. Critical criminologists often point out that most responses to acts defined as crimes protect the interests of the rich while punishing acts committed by the poor, such as being homeless.

In addition to the limitations of informal social control to regulate our behaviours, our lives have become increasingly complex, and laws have had to adapt to changing technology. Therefore, the number of laws "on the books" has increased. Offences unknown a decade ago—such as **sexting** (transmitting sexually explicit images online or via text) of minors—had to be formally defined as crimes, and punishments for these offences had to be specified in the *Criminal Code*. In August 2016 six Nova Scotia boys were charged with possessing and distributing child pornography after texting images of some 20 teenage girls, which was the first test of section 162(1) of the *Criminal Code* (Bresge & Tutton, 2016). When sentenced in September 2017 all six youth received conditional discharges and as part of their sentences they were required to attend counselling and complete community service work. The number of sexting incidents is increasing. When section 162(1) was introduced in 2015 there were 340 occurrences, but this number grew to almost 1,500 in 2017 (Statistics Canada, 2018a).

Changes in our attitudes and values have also resulted in changes to laws, and Canadian society has generally become more permissive over time. **Adultery**, when a married person has a sexual relationship with a person to whom they are not married, was once a crime in Canada if committed "in the home of a child." As times changed, however, people became more accepting of these acts, and the law changed in 1985 to reflect these attitudes. Although this change in law was not very controversial, it shows the dynamic nature of criminal laws in modern societies. In some nations, however, adultery is a crime that is still punishable by death.

One of the cornerstones of Canadian law is that all individuals are considered equal and no one is above the law, including politicians, police officers, and representatives of the Crown such as lieutenant-governors and the governor general. According to Coughlan, Yogis, and Cotter (2013, p. 300), the **rule of law** is "a foundational principle of the Canadian constitution, dictating that the law is supreme over any body of government or individual." Forsey (1980/2012, p. 31) observed that "if anyone were above the law, none of our liberties would be safe," and he noted that an independent judiciary (the courts) safeguards the rule of law by defining "the limits of federal and provincial powers." Many people are skeptical about whether the

sexting
Transmitting sexually explicit images online or via text message.

adultery
When a married person has a sexual relationship with a person to whom they are not married.

rule of law
The principle that the law is supreme over any individual or body of government.

A Closer Look

Understanding Legal Citation

Throughout this book, court cases are described in a form of shorthand—known as legal citation—and this section will help us figure out what these citations really mean. For example, the *Sipos* decision of the Supreme Court of Canada in 2014 addressed the issue of the conditions under which an individual could be labelled as a dangerous offender (which imposes an indeterminate prison sentence on the individual, making it very difficult for them to be released to the community). That case can be written in the form of a neutral legal citation as follows:

R v Sipos, 2014 SCC 47

In this case, "*R*" refers to *Regina*, which is the Latin term for *queen* (criminal offences are prosecuted in the name of the monarch), and "*v*" is an abbreviation for *versus*—so in this example, the Crown was prosecuting an individual named Sipos. The number 2014 refers to the year of the decision, while SCC means that the decision was made by the Supreme Court of Canada. Last, the number 47 in the citation refers to the fact that the *Sipos* case was the forty-seventh judgment issued by the Supreme Court of Canada in 2014.

Traditional legal citations are reported somewhat differently as they include the source where the decision was published (in what are called "case reporters"), which may help an individual find that case. Supreme Court cases, for example, use the letters SCR to show that the decision was published in the *Supreme Court Reports*. Using the traditional citation format, the *Sipos* case is written as follows:

R v Sipos, [2014] 2 SCR 423

In this example, the square brackets around the year 2014 refer to the decision being reported in the *Supreme Court Reports* volume for that year, the "2" refers to the second volume in 2014, and "423" is the page on which the case is found. Thus, the key difference between neutral and traditional citations is that the traditional format provides additional publication information.

Provincial appellate courts also issue judgments, and while fewer of these cases are reported in this book, a case from Ontario serves as an example. In the case reported below, Smickle appealed the constitutionality of a mandatory minimum sentence for illegally possessing a prohibited firearm. The citation is written as follows:

R v Smickle, 2013 ONCA 677

This citation is like those used by the Supreme Court of Canada, although a key difference is that the decision was rendered by the Court of Appeal for Ontario, which is abbreviated as ONCA. The last number in the citation, 677, means that it was the 677th decision made by the Court of Appeal for Ontario in 2013. All provincial courts of appeal use a two-letter abbreviation (e.g., Prince Edward Island is PE), followed by the abbreviation CA to designate that the decision was made by a court of appeal (e.g., PECA). An online guide to legal citations is available at http://citations.duhaime.org/Country/Canada.aspx.

rich and powerful are really held to the same standards as the general public. The allegations that staff members from Prime Minister Justin Trudeau's office applied undue pressure on Jody Wilson-Raybould, the former Attorney General and Minister of Justice, to change her decision to prosecute SNC-Lavalin, raised the issue of whether officials in the Prime Minister's Office were above the law (Harris, 2019).

EVOLUTION OF CANADIAN CRIMINAL LAW

Beverley McLachlin (2013), the former Chief Justice of Canada, observes that "Parliament makes laws setting out crimes. If people violate those laws, they are prosecuted by Crown attorneys, and tried by the courts." The criminal laws enacted by Parliament are a work in progress, and we can directly trace changes in the law going back almost 1,000 years. In Canada, criminal laws are rooted in the English common-law system that dates back over 800 years, although the English borrowed ideas about the law from the Romans, Greeks, Assyrians, and Egyptians (Plucknett, 2010).

England's King Henry II is credited with establishing a more uniform or common approach to justice shortly after being crowned in 1154. Henry created legal tribunals in order to resolve disputes between individuals. The term common law refers to an approach to the law that sought uniformity and was based on precedent (as judges would attempt to follow each other's decisions), which in turn created a common set of legal principles. In 1215 the Magna Carta was first written in part by the Archbishop of Canterbury and was recognized by King John of England: this document established that everybody, even the king, was subject to the law and that all free men (a very small portion of the population) had the right to justice and fair trials (Breay & Harrison, 2015). The common law continued to evolve throughout the reign of Edward I (1239–1307), and there was increasing recognition of the protection of individual rights (Plucknett, 2010).

The criminal law that we have today replaced informal methods of seeking justice based on local traditions or practices of resolving disputes, which is called customary law. Whereas the law had once been applied in an unpredictable manner, decisions were now becoming more consistent and uniform across the United Kingdom, and the colonists imported these practices when they settled in Canada.

Although the focus of this chapter is on criminal law, the common law is also the basis of resolving other disputes, including problems arising from businesses, marriage breakdowns, and property rights. The common law has been called "judge-made" law because decisions made by the courts are also sources of law upon which we rely to interpret all statutes, including statutes related to criminal law, and it guides the courts and lawyers in sentencing in criminal matters. The common law is based on the notion of *stare decisis*, which is a legal principle whereby courts are bound by their prior decisions and the decisions of higher courts.

Although all Canadians are governed by the common law in respect to criminal matters, Quebec's approach to civil law differs somewhat and can be traced back to the French Napoleonic Code that originated in 1804. According to the Government of Quebec, "the Civil Code of Quebec is a general law that contains all of the basic provisions that govern life in society, namely the relationships among citizens and the relationships between people and property" (Friesen, 2012, p. 125). Consequently, this approach defines the limits to civil rights, such as leasing items or property, sales contracts, and family matters.

Common-law legal systems are present in most English-speaking nations colonized by the British, including Australia, New Zealand, India, the United States, and some African and Caribbean nations. Although there will be some differences in the procedures used in these nations, they have a number of common features. These include topics that we are familiar with from television, such as the adversarial nature of the system (where both parties present their cases to a judge, who acts as an impartial arbitrator); the presumption of a defendant's innocence; and the reliance on case law where judges make decisions about current cases based on the outcomes of prior judgments, which is called precedent. Underlying all of these common features is the principle that the rights of the individual are balanced against the interests of society.

In addition to the presumption of innocence, there are two other key elements of the Canadian justice system. The first is the burden of proof, which requires that Crown prosecutors must prove that the accused person is guilty prior to a conviction (or accept a plea of guilt). The standard of proof for a criminal conviction is "beyond a reasonable doubt." If guilt cannot be proven, Canadian judges or juries must acquit a defendant even if they think that he or she is probably guilty. As a result, the priority of the defence counsel is not to prove innocence but instead to

common law
An approach to law that is based on tradition, where judges follow decisions or precedents made by other courts.

stare decisis
A legal principle whereby courts are bound by their prior decisions and the decisions of higher courts.

precedent
The practice of judges basing decisions about current cases on the outcomes of prior judgments.

was $948 million, and that of the almost half a million applicants who were approved for services, about 50 per cent obtained help for criminal matters.

There is a growing concern that many Canadians are losing access to legal aid services; news reports since 2018 reveal that many provincial legal aid organizations are underfunded and some provinces are cutting services (see Zakreski, 2018). While in tough economic times the public is not sympathetic to people accused of crimes, the consequences of underfunding these services can be costly. The Canadian Bar Association (2015), for example, reports that inadequately funded legal aid systems result in: (a) slower court processes; (b) job losses when suspects are unnecessarily incarcerated; and (c) further marginalization of people who cannot fully participate in society.

The Canadian Press/Doug Ives

To increase fairness and access to justice, most impoverished Canadians accused of committing crimes are eligible for legal aid services that are subsidized by the federal and provincial governments. Pictured above is Jennifer Chan in her legal aid office in 2017.

CANADIAN CHARTER OF RIGHTS AND FREEDOMS

Until 1982, the limits to authority that could be carried out by different levels of government in Canada were defined by the *Constitution Act, 1867* (also called the *British North America Act, 1867*). The *Canadian Charter of Rights and Freedoms* (hereafter the *Charter*) is the first part of the *Constitution Act, 1982*, which defines the relationships Canadians have with the government, including guarantees of basic rights and freedoms, democratic rights, legal rights, the ability of citizens to move freely throughout the nation, the protection of equality under the law, the recognition of two official languages, the acknowledgement of Indigenous rights, and the ways the *Charter* can be applied by Parliament and provincial legislatures.

Of special interest to this review of the criminal law are the legal rights defined in sections 7 through 14 of the *Charter*. According to the Government of Canada (2017), these sections "set out rights that protect us in our dealings with the justice system. They ensure that individuals who are involved in legal proceedings are treated fairly,

substantive law
Consists of the written rules that define crimes and punishments, and the rights and obligations of citizens and criminal justice personnel.

procedural law
Focuses on the rules that determine the enforcement of rights or due process.

Canadian Charter of Rights and Freedoms
The part of the Constitution that defines the rights and freedoms of Canadians, including those accused of committing crimes.

raise enough doubt that a conviction cannot be made. It is important to remember that if an accused person is found "not guilty" by a judge or jury, it does not necessarily mean the accused is innocent, but rather there was doubt that the accused committed the crime. It is possible that the accused did not commit the crime, but all we know for certain is that the Crown prosecutor failed to prove their guilt.

This chapter is organized around two types of criminal law: substantive law and procedural law. Substantive law refers to the rules that define rights and obligations. Procedural law, by contrast, focuses on the rules that determine the enforcement of rights, or what is called due process. In order to increase fairness and access to justice, most impoverished Canadians accused of committing crimes are eligible for legal aid services subsidized by the federal and provincial governments. The costs of ensuring criminal defendants have access to state-funded counsel are high: the Department of Justice Canada (2019) reports that the entire expenditure in 2016/2017

especially those charged with a criminal offence." A closer look at these principles reveals they are fairly broad and are intended to define the authority of the state and limit the conduct of overzealous government officials. Sections 7 to 14 of the *Charter* outline the following legal rights:

Life, liberty and security of person

7. Everyone has the right to life, liberty and security of the person and the right not to be deprived thereof except in accordance with the principles of fundamental justice.

Search or seizure

8. Everyone has the right to be secure against unreasonable search or seizure.

Detention or imprisonment

9. Everyone has the right not to be arbitrarily detained or imprisoned.

Arrest or detention

10. Everyone has the right on arrest or detention
    (a) to be informed promptly of the reasons therefor;
    (b) to retain and instruct counsel without delay and to be informed of that right; and
    (c) to have the validity of the detention determined by way of *habeas corpus* and to be released if the detention is not lawful.

Proceedings in criminal and penal matters

11. Any person charged with an offence has the right
    (a) to be informed without unreasonable delay of the specific offence;
    (b) to be tried within a reasonable time;
    (c) not to be compelled to be a witness in proceedings against that person in respect of the offence;
    (d) to be presumed innocent until proven guilty according to law in a fair and public hearing by an independent and impartial tribunal;
    (e) not to be denied reasonable bail without just cause;
    (f) except in the case of an offence under military law tried before a military tribunal, to the benefit of trial by jury where the maximum punishment for the offence is imprisonment for five years or a more severe punishment;
    (g) not to be found guilty on account of any act or omission unless, at the time of the act or omission, it constituted an offence under Canadian or international law or was criminal according to the general principles of law recognized by the community of nations;
    (h) if finally acquitted of the offence, not to be tried for it again and, if finally found guilty and punished for the offence, not to be tried or punished for it again; and
    (i) if found guilty of the offence and if the punishment for the offence has been varied between the time of commission and the time of sentencing, to the benefit of the lesser punishment.

Treatment or punishment

12. Everyone has the right not to be subjected to any cruel and unusual treatment or punishment.

Self-crimination

13. A witness who testifies in any proceedings has the right not to have any incriminating evidence so given used to incriminate that witness in any other proceedings,

except in a prosecution for perjury or for the giving of contradictory evidence.

Interpreter

14. A party or witness in any proceedings who does not understand or speak the language in which the proceedings are conducted or who is deaf has the right to the assistance of an interpreter.

Several other sections of the *Charter* are also applicable to criminal matters. Section 15, for example addresses the issue of equal protection for all people, and states that discrimination cannot be made on the basis of race, national or ethnic origin, colour, religion, sex, age, or mental or physical disability. Last, section 24 enables individuals to seek remedies in a court in the event that their *Charter* rights have been violated.

Some of the terms used in the *Charter* are not commonly encountered, nor are the meanings clearly described within the *Charter*; defining these terms can be a complex task. For instance, the term **fundamental justice** has been used to describe the principle that people who act reasonably may not be punished or sent to prison "unless there is some proof that they did something wrong" (Government of Canada, 2017). Yet, the topic of fundamental justice is so broad and complex that entire books have been written to explain the concept (e.g., Stewart, 2012). On the other hand, the term *habeas corpus* may be more familiar to readers as it refers to the ability to question an individual's detention by the state, and "in the criminal law context, it is used to bring the petitioner before the court to inquire into the legality of his or her confinement" (Coughlan, Yogis, & Cotter, 2013, p. 152).

But even when terms used in the *Charter* seem straightforward, they can be interpreted from a number of perspectives. What, for example, constitutes a "reasonable time" to bring a case to trial, as highlighted in section 11? Terms such as *reasonable* and *unreasonable* are not clearly defined in the *Charter*, so it is likely that some of these matters will end up before the Supreme Court for clarification.

fundamental justice
A principle of Canadian justice that states that people who acted reasonably may not be punished unless there is proof that they did something wrong.

habeas corpus
The right of a person who is being detained to challenge the legality of his or her detention before a court.

The Supreme Court determined that less serious matters, for instance, must be resolved in a time period of 18 months from the time the individual is charged with a crime to the conclusion of their trial, whereas more serious cases—often heard in superior courts—must be completed within 30 months from the time the individual is charged until the conclusion of the trial (see *R v Jordan*, 2016).

Other terms and descriptions in the *Charter* are also vague, such as the section 12 prohibition of cruel and unusual punishments. Several Supreme Court cases have considered what constitutes a harsh punishment, and this pitted the Supreme Court against the former Harper government's "tough on crime" agenda. In order to deter potential offenders from committing crimes, the federal government introduced a number of mandatory minimum sentences for certain drug and firearm offences and people found guilty of these offences were required to serve a mandatory minimum prison sentence. Some organizations and scholars are critical of mandatory sentences as they remove the judge's discretion to consider factors such as the individual's role in the offence (e.g., whether the accused was a leader or a follower) or prior criminal history, or to consider other factors that might reduce or mitigate responsibility (Chaster, 2018).

Judges are also critical of mandatory sentences as they feel their hands are tied at sentencing. This influenced the 2015 Supreme Court decision that found that mandatory minimum sentences for weapons offences were cruel and unusual punishments.

Because the sections related to criminal law in the *Charter* were written in a manner that is open to interpretation, additional challenges will be launched by defence lawyers and prosecutors as new laws are introduced. It is not unusual to challenge or reconsider existing laws, as the criminal law must adapt to changing political, economic, social, and legal circumstances.

Technology is also shaping the boundaries of the criminal law. Some self-driving or driverless cars currently being tested do not have a steering wheel, brake or accelerator pedals, or controls for turning signals. As the person in the vehicle has no control over its operation, does that mean that if they were impaired, he or she could not be charged with a crime? Alternatively, could blind, elderly, or preteen passengers legally operate these self-driving cars? Laws will also have to account for vehicles that malfunction and lead to injury or death. Such questions will most likely be addressed in courts and by legislatures in the future, but these issues illustrate why the criminal law will continue to evolve.

ELEMENTS OF A CRIME

The previous chapters identified the differences between summary and indictable offences and described how laws emerged to respond to crime. One interesting question that we need to address is, "what is a crime?" This is an important issue because an individual cannot be prosecuted for an act that is not defined as an offence in the *Criminal Code*. Individuals can be charged with a **crime of omission**—an act that they did not commit, such as a teacher who fails to report a case of abuse to child welfare authorities or to the police—or with a crime of commission, which is a criminal act that was actually carried out. Individuals, however, cannot be charged with an offence if the act was not defined in the *Criminal Code* when the crime occurred. There are two main elements of a crime that have to occur together:

- *actus reus*, and
- *mens rea*

The Criminal Act (*Actus Reus*)

While all of us have our own ideas of what should (and should not) be a crime, a criminal act—known as *actus reus*—has to be considered wrong by society (e.g., morally wrong) and either cause harm to an individual or cause general harm to society by affecting all Canadians. The harm must also be considered serious, and the remedy must be made through the justice system. Most of us would agree that an individual who assaults a stranger on the street or vandalizes a neighbour's property is guilty of a crime, but what about offences that are not seen as harmful? If a person

is gambling at an unlicensed casino—which is called a gaming house in the *Criminal Code*—are they committing a harmful act?

Some scholars might argue that illegal gaming threatens the social order despite there being no direct victim—these acts are sometimes called **victimless crimes**. Because there is less agreement on whether these acts involve any wrongdoing, there is usually more opposition to laws against them. Yet, advocates for the criminal punishment of illegal gaming argue that these operations are a $14-billion business (Warren, 2018), and since nobody pays taxes on these revenues to governments, it places a burden on all taxpayers. Furthermore, illegal gaming contributes to the expansion of organized crime, and there is a link between these operations and serious offences. Those outcomes, some argue, are costly to taxpayers, and all of us are burdened with the costs of responding to the consequences of these acts—even though they appear to have no direct victim.

crime of omission An act where the accused has failed to take some action, such as a school social worker failing to report child abuse to child welfare authorities.

actus reus The criminal action or conduct of a person committing an offence.

victimless crimes Acts that are legally defined as crimes even though there is no direct victim (e.g., illegal gambling).

While we think of illegal gambling as a victimless crime, in June 2017 an unlicensed gaming club in a Woodbridge, Ontario strip mall exploded and York Regional Police arrested two men for their role in the arson (Edwards, 2017). There are hundreds of unlicensed gambling houses in Ontario, and some are tied to organized crime: in July 2019, the York Regional Police arrested 15 individuals allegedly involved in an international criminal organization that promoted illicit gambling in these clubs (Herault, 2019). Is the criminalization of "victimless" crimes worth the regulation of people's behaviour for society as a whole?

A Closer Look

Landmark Supreme Court Cases: Top 10 Criminal Law Cases in Canada

One of the most difficult aspects of establishing a "Top 10" list of criminal law cases is that there is not always agreement on which cases are the most important. The 10 Supreme Court cases briefly described below are widely cited, and they have all either set an important precedent, established a significant legal principle, or otherwise changed the interpretation or practice of the law.

R v Askov, [1990] 2 SCR 1199

Issue: Trial within a reasonable time
Summary: Several men were charged with conspiracy to commit extortion in November 1983, and a trial date was set for October 1985. The case, however, could not proceed on that date and was rescheduled to September 1986. The defendants made a motion to stay the proceedings because of an unreasonable delay, which was granted by the judge. The Court of Appeal for Ontario directed that the trial proceed, but the Supreme Court agreed with the trial judge, and a stay of proceedings was granted because of the excessive time it took to get the matter to trial.

R v Ewanchuk, [1999] 1 SCR 330

Issue: There is no defence for implied sexual consent
Summary: A woman protested a man's sexual advances but eventually stopped saying "no," which the accused interpreted as implied consent for intercourse. The Supreme Court held that there was no defence for implied consent and that "no means no."

R v Feeney, [1997] 2 SCR 13

Issue: Unreasonable search and seizure
Summary: Police investigating a murder entered the home of a suspect after they knocked on the door but did not receive a response. The man was found in bed and was asked to go outside, where the officers noticed that his clothes were covered in blood, and whereupon he was read his rights and arrested. The accused was ultimately convicted of second-degree murder, and his appeal that the search and seizure was not reasonable was rejected by the British Columbia Court of Appeal. The Supreme Court overturned that decision, and ruled that the police should not enter someone's home without a search warrant.

R v Gladue, [1999] 1 SCR 688

Issue: The constitutionality of a provision in the *Criminal Code* to allow for less punitive sanctions based on the historical overrepresentation of Indigenous people in the justice system
Summary: Nineteen-year-old Jamie Gladue stabbed her common-law husband during an argument, and she was convicted of manslaughter and sentenced to three years in prison. The British Columbia Court of Appeal upheld her sentence, finding that section 718.2(e) that allows courts to mitigate the sentences of Indigenous people did not apply because she lived off-reserve. The Supreme Court held that Indigenous people do not have to reside on a reserve in order to benefit from the provisions of section 718.2(e), nor should their lifestyle be considered. While her three-year sentence was not reduced, she was paroled.

R v Mann, [2004] 3 SCR 59

Issue: Police powers when detaining a person as part of an investigation
Summary: Two Winnipeg police officers stopped an individual suspected of being involved in a break and enter. A search revealed that the suspect possessed marijuana, and he was arrested and charged with trafficking. The trial judge ruled that the search was unreasonable because it went beyond a pat-down search conducted to ensure officer safety, and the defendant was acquitted. The trial court's decision was overturned by the Court of Appeal for Manitoba, which found that the search was reasonable and ordered a new trial. The Supreme Court overturned the Court of Appeal's decision, finding that the original acquittal was correct and that the police did not have the right to search beyond a pat-down

to ensure the individual did not have a concealed weapon.

R v Martineau, [1990] 2 SCR 633

Issue: *Mens rea* requirement for murder
Summary: An adult and a 15-year-old young offender carried out a robbery at a trailer that resulted in a double murder: the adult shot both victims (and was convicted of murder) and the youth was charged with second-degree murder. The youth maintained that he did not know a violent crime was planned, yet he was also convicted. His conviction was overturned as the Supreme Court ruled that he did not have the intent to kill or the knowledge that a murder would occur.

R v Morin, [1992] 1 SCR 771

Issue: Trial within a reasonable time
Summary: A woman was charged with impaired driving in January 1988, and the trial did not occur until March 1989. Her lawyer claimed that the delay was unreasonable given the *Askov* (1990) decision, and a stay of proceedings was requested, which was rejected by the judge. The defendant was convicted and the Court of Appeal for Ontario stayed the conviction as the accused was not tried within a reasonable time. The Supreme Court dismissed that appeal and clarified what constituted a reasonable delay. In the 2016 *R v Jordan* decision, the Supreme Court specified actual timelines for courts from the time the individual is charged to the end of a trial.

R v Seaboyer, [1991] 2 SCR 577

Issue: Evidence relating to the sexual reputation of a complainant of sexual assault
Summary: Seaboyer was accused of the sexual assault of a woman he had been drinking with in a bar. At trial, the judge did not allow the accused to cross-examine the complainant with respect to her prior sexual conduct, and Seaboyer was ultimately convicted. The Court of Appeal held that the judge

had not allowed the appellant to make a full defence. The Supreme Court clarified the law and ruled that the Court of Appeal's decision be dismissed and that Seaboyer's conviction would remain. (Note: The case of *R v Gayme*, which had a similar argument, was decided at the same time.)

R v Stinchcombe, [1991] 3 SCR 326

Issue: Crown duty to disclose evidence to the defence
Summary: A lawyer was being tried on charges of theft and fraud. His defence attorney requested access to information collected by the Crown. This request was refused and the defendant was later convicted. The Alberta Court of Appeal affirmed the conviction, but the Supreme Court disagreed and ordered that a new trial be conducted. The Supreme Court ruled that the Crown has a duty to disclose all relevant information to the defence, even if that information could lead to an acquittal.

R v Stone, [1999] 2 SCR 290

Issue: Determining the proper test for automatism (a state of impaired consciousness)
Summary: Stone killed his wife and claimed the offence was involuntary due to psychological factors including insane automatism and non-insane automatism. The judge allowed for a defence of insane automatism, and Stone was convicted of manslaughter and sentenced to seven years. The Crown appealed this sentence, saying that the non-insane automatism defence should have been left to the jury to decide (which might have resulted in a harsher sentence), but the original verdict was upheld by the British Columbia Court of Appeal. The Crown appealed the decision to the Supreme Court, which found that the conviction was appropriate and used this case to establish guidelines for defendants using the insane and non-insane automatism defence.
Acknowledgement: Heather Donkers of Robichaud Criminal Defence Litigation aided in the development of this "top 10 list" of landmark cases.

The Guilty Mind (*Mens Rea*)

mens rea
The state of mind of a person committing a criminal act.

intent
The criminal intention (guilty mind) in *mens rea*.

negligence
An act that shows disregard for the well-being of others.

reckless behaviours
Occur when people act in a manner that they know is dangerous or risky.

wilful blindness
Occurs when an accused is aware that a crime was likely being committed but chose to ignore the facts.

alibis Witnesses or other forms of evidence that show that the defendant could not have committed the offence.

justification defences
Used when the accused admits to committing an offence but the act was justified under the circumstances.

excuse defences
Based on the argument that one's criminal conduct can be excused because the accused could not form the intent to commit a crime.

Determining whether an individual committed a crime or *actus reus* is relatively easy for a prosecutor to establish in some cases. Obtaining a conviction, however, also relies on showing that the individual intended on committing the act—or *mens rea*, which is a Latin term for the "guilty mind." Coughlan et al. (2013, pp. 208–209) refer to *mens rea* as the "mental element or intent required for the commission of a criminal act" and may include individuals with differing levels of "intention, knowledge, recklessness, [or] wilful blindness." In other words, the prosecutor must establish that the accused did something that he or she knew was wrong and that the accused intended to commit the crime.

After taking a closer look at these requirements, we can see that it might sometimes be difficult to prove that the accused had *mens rea*. First, with respect to intent, people can be convicted of an offence if they meant to commit harm, did not care about the outcomes of their actions, or could foresee that their actions might be harmful. Individuals can also be arrested for failing to take steps that a reasonable person would take to limit harm, which is called criminal negligence. Negligence can be the result of an act of commission or omission that shows disregard for the well-being of others. An example is leaving an infant unsupervised for several hours, something that a reasonable person would not do because this act places a helpless child in a vulnerable situation. We can also be convicted for engaging in reckless behaviours—acting in a manner that we know is dangerous or risky—such as driving twice the speed limit in a busy downtown neighbourhood at lunchtime.

Last is the issue of wilful blindness, which occurs when a person is aware that the law is being violated but chooses not to be fully aware of the offence. For example, if you were offered $1,000 by a known drug dealer to transport a sealed package across town, you might suspect that it contained illegal drugs, but by not asking the question "What is in the package?" some individuals may

believe they are not legally responsible. Prior Canadian cases, however, have established that this is seldom a successful defence.

Mens rea is a complicated subject as it forces us to interpret an individual's state of mind based on their actions and statements, and this may also require us to understand what happened during an offence. That is a significant challenge because many arrestees are under the influence of alcohol or drugs at the time of an offence (Pernanen, Cousineau, Brochu, & Sun, 2002), and we have known for over a century that eyewitness testimony is not very reliable (Innocence Project, 2019). In fact, faulty eyewitness testimony was responsible for almost three-quarters of proven wrongful convictions in the United States (Innocence Project, 2019).

DEFENCES

An accused person has a number of possible defences against a criminal charge, and his or her counsel can use various strategies to raise reasonable doubt. The three main strategies are alibis, justification defences, and excuse defences. Although we are familiar with alibi defences from watching television, their use in Canadian courtrooms has some guidelines, which are briefly described below. A broader discussion of justification and excuse defences follows.

Alibi Defences

We are all familiar with the alibi defence, where the accused claims that he or she was elsewhere at the time and scene of a crime, so it is impossible they were directly involved in the offence. Some alibis are of more value than others. Being filmed in the company of a dozen police officers a hundred kilometres from the scene of a crime is of more value than having one's mother say that they were at home when the crime occurred. Although there are some challenges with alibi evidence, such as whether the jury believes the mother of the accused, an alibi is a rather straightforward defence—you either have a solid alibi or your alibi lacks credibility. Of course, an individual can hire another person to commit a crime, such as in the case study that started Chapter 5, in which Tom Holden hired three men to kill a Mission, British Columbia couple with whom he was involved in a dispute.

There are some guidelines around the use of an alibi at trial. The Supreme Court decided in *R v Cleghorn* (1995) that alibi evidence must be adequate and timely. The Defence Group (2018, para. 2) defines an adequate alibi as "one that contains sufficient detail to allow the police to verify its validity," whereas a timely alibi is "one that is revealed to authorities well before trial," which provides the police with enough time to conduct a proper investigation. Prior appellate court decisions have ruled that an alibi that has been fabricated (made up) by the defendant can be used against them when the judge or jury is deliberating their guilt. If the defendant does not testify and the alibi is subject to cross-examination, the alibi will also have less credibility in deliberations.

Justification Defences

In a justification defence, an individual admits to committing an act that is being prosecuted as a crime, but argues that the act was justified due to particular circumstances, such as if committing the act was considered the less serious option available. Justifications for committing crimes include consent, duress, entrapment, necessity, provocation, and self-defence (or defence of others).

Consent

Consent has been used as a justification for various types of assault, and consent to borrow property has been used as a defence against theft. In assault cases, the accused does not dispute that an assault occurred but argues that the conduct was permitted. One example is fighting in a hockey game, as players can expect some degree of physical contact in that sport. Consent has also been

consent A defence that is almost always used by defendants accused of assault, where they contend that the victim was a willing party in the offence, such as when a hockey player injures another player.

Some alibis are of more value than others, but in general, an alibi is a rather straightforward defence—you either have a solid alibi or you lack one. Would someone's presence at the gathering depicted above (a small group of friends and family playing cards at home) likely be a strong alibi or a weak alibi?

used as a justification for fights and for domestic or sexual assaults, but cannot be used for murder. Consent defences are seldom used and are unlikely to be successful in cases where there were serious injuries, where the assault was accompanied by threats or where the accused was in a position of authority.

Duress

duress
A defence where the accused people claim that their actions were not voluntary but that they acted in response to being threatened by another person.

A person accused of a crime can use the justification of **duress**, which means the individual does not act voluntarily but acts in response to threats from another person. Coughlan et al. (2013, p. 85) observe that "because of some (external) trigger, the accused responds by committing an offence." Section 17 of the *Criminal Code* defines the conditions that must be met in order for this defence to be successful: (a) the accused was under threat of serious injury or death; (b) the accused had no reasonable means

to avoid committing the crime; and (c) the harm caused by the offence was proportional to the harm avoided. In other words, was the act reasonable?

Since the *R v Lavallee* decision of the Supreme Court in 1990, women in abusive relationships can use this justification if they have injured or killed their abusers. According to *Duhaime's Law Dictionary* (2018) battered woman syndrome (also called the battered spouse syndrome) refers to cases where "expert evidence is led to demonstrate that a female defendant in an abusive relationship comes to believe that to save herself she must kill her husband first." Sheehy, Stubbs, and Tolmie (2017; p. 13) point out that courts have placed some limits on this defence and have rejected some duress claims if it is clear that a "safe avenue of escape was available, that the woman's behavior was inconsistent with duress, or that the man's overt violence had tapered off before the crime was committed."

Peter Kirillov/Shutterstock.com

Consent has been used as a justification for various types of assault. In such cases, the accused does not dispute that an assault occurred but argues that the conduct was permitted by the victim, such as fighting in a hockey game.

Entrapment

Entrapment occurs when police or government officials persuade or lure an individual into carrying out an offence that he or she would not otherwise have committed. Unlike other defences, this justification can be made only after the accused is found guilty, and the burden is on the defence counsel to prove that entrapment occurred. In the case of *R v Mack* (1988), the appellant testified that "he had persistently refused the approaches of a police informer over the course of six months, and that he was only persuaded to sell him drugs because of the informer's persistence, his use of threats, and the inducement of a large amount of money." In the *Mack* (1988) case, the Supreme Court found that this type of behaviour "violates our notions of 'fair play' and 'decency'" and in 2014, the Supreme Court placed further limits on police investigations.

So when it comes to entrapment, what constitutes fair play and decency? In June 2015, John Nuttall and Amanda Korody, a couple described as recovering from drug addictions and as being poor and socially isolated, were found guilty of plotting to attack the British Columbia legislature. Their counsel claimed, however, that an "undercover officer feigned friendship, injected meaning into their otherwise isolated lives, as well as money, nice clothes, spiritual guidance and attention" (Canadian Broadcasting Corporation, 2015). Altogether, the investigation lasted five months and involved more than 200 police officers who earned over $900,000 in overtime payments in addition to their regular salaries (Azpiri & Daya, 2017). In July 2016 a BC Supreme Court judge stayed the conviction, saying that the plot wouldn't have occurred if the RCMP hadn't organized it. In January 2018 the Crown appealed the actions of the provincial court and requested a new trial, but the BC Court of Appeal upheld the stay of prosecution, calling the RCMP's conduct a "travesty of justice" and finding that the couple was "manipulated by police to conduct the terror operation" (Canadian Press, 2018, para. 1).

Necessity

Another justification defence is necessity, where an illegal act was carried out to prevent a more serious harm, a situation where the individual had "no choice" but to break the law. While Canadian law allows for the necessity defence, it is rarely used and only occasionally successful. In 2013, a Saskatchewan woman charged with impaired driving successfully used a necessity defence. The woman was at a house party where one of the hosts—her brother-in-law—became violent, and the woman and her two friends used a vehicle to escape. In their attempt to escape, the brother-in-law rammed their vehicle with his truck. Although the case was prosecuted, the judge found that the woman acted reasonably as she feared for her safety (Mok, 2013). According to Mok (2013), "Whether an illegal action is deemed a necessity is based on three requirements: the harm being done must be less than the harm that is being avoided; there must be a direct threat of immediate peril; and there must be no legal alternative."

Provocation

Defendants can use a defence based on the claim that they were provoked into committing a crime, although this excuse can only be used for murder, and successful defences can only reduce the charge to manslaughter. The guidelines for using a provocation defence are outlined in the *Criminal Code*. Supreme Court decisions have placed strict limits on the use of a provocation defence. Nowlin (2018, p. 74) observes that after 2015 the act triggering a homicide must be an indictable offence, and that in changing the law, "Parliament put hot-tempered Canadians on notice that homicidal responses to the slings and arrows of insults and unrequited love can no longer result in manslaughter convictions. Neither can short-tempered honour killings."

Self-Defence

The notion behind a self-defence justification is that an individual has inflicted harm on another person in order to ensure his or her own safety or

necessity
A type of defence claiming that an illegal act was committed in order to prevent a more serious harm, such as speeding to get to a hospital for emergency treatment.

provocation
A defence based on an accused claiming that he or she was provoked into committing a crime, although this defence can only be used to argue that an act of murder be reduced to manslaughter.

self-defence
A defence arguing that the harm that was inflicted on another person was carried out to ensure the defendant's safety or the safety of others.

the safety of others. In 2013, the federal government introduced legislation that made it easier for ordinary people to take reasonable steps to defend themselves and/or to carry out a citizen's arrest without fear of legal consequences.

In order to make a determination surrounding guilt, the court considers a number of factors, including the nature of the use of force, the roles of the individuals in the incident, the presence or use of a weapon, the characteristics of the parties in the incident (e.g., whether one individual is younger or physically larger), and the relationships between the participants, such as whether they are strangers or family members.

When it comes to self-defence, some of our misunderstanding about what is appropriate or legal may come from television programs, news accounts, and films that are from the United States. It is important to realize the differences in the manner that self-defence is considered in the Canadian justice system. Some US states, for instance, have introduced stand your ground laws (also known as the castle doctrine), which gives people the right to protect their lives and property by using force that would be considered excessive in Canada.

Excuse Defences

People accused of crime can also claim that their illegal behaviour can be excused based on the defence that they could not form the intent to commit an offence, based on age, automatism, mental disorder, or a mistake.

Age

The age defence recognizes that children younger than 12 years of age cannot be held criminally responsible for an offence, although 12- to 17-year-olds are accountable for their actions under the *Youth Criminal Justice Act* (YCJA). Sanctions for youth sentenced under the YCJA are generally mitigated to a fraction of what adults convicted of similar offences could receive. For example, the maximum sentence for 16- or 17-year-olds convicted of first-degree murder in Canada is life imprisonment, and they are required to serve

10 years in an adult penitentiary before being eligible to apply for parole—this contrasts with the mandatory 25 years that adults who committed a similar offence are required to serve. Once individuals turn 18 years of age, they are considered adults, but judges often mitigate the severity of punishments for young adults.

Automatism

Defendants can claim that they acted in a state of automatism if they committed a criminal offence when they were in a state of impaired consciousness. This offence is "premised on the principle that a person should not be held criminally responsible for actions over which she or he had no physical control" (Sheehy, Stubbs, & Tolmie, 2017, p. 5). This defence is rarely used, and in the 1999 case of *R v Stone* (one of the "Top 10" list of criminal law cases discussed earlier), the Supreme Court of Canada recognized that automatism may be classified as either a mental disorder (insanity) caused by a disease of the mind or a non-mental disorder (non-insanity). The former would result in a finding of not criminally responsible due to a mental disorder. Non-insane automatism, by contrast, refers to cases where the individual had no control over his or her actions and the cause could be traced back to an injury (e.g., a physical blow), a medical condition such as diabetes or a stroke, or some severe psychological occurrence, such as seeing their child killed (Myrah, 2012, p. 26).

Mental Disorder

One of the most troublesome issues in the Canadian criminal justice system is the challenge of responding to and managing people with mental health problems (P/MHP). Research conducted by the Canadian Centre for Justice Statistics shows in 2012 there were about one million contacts between P/MHP and the police (Boyce, Rotenberg, & Karam, 2015). Cotton and Coleman (2010) found that in Canada, P/MHP were three times more likely to encounter the police than were members of the general population, and McCann (2013, p. 2) reports that up to one-quarter of all

stand your ground laws Laws that give some US residents the right to use force to protect their lives and property in a way that would be considered excessive and illegal in Canada. Also known as the *castle doctrine.*

age defence A defence that considers immaturity and recognizes that youth under 12 years of age cannot be held criminally responsible; sanctions might also be mitigated for young defendants.

automatism An involuntary act where an individual is in a state of impaired consciousness and lacks the intent to commit a crime.

police calls for service in Vancouver are related to P/MHP. When people with a mental illness commit a criminal act, they may lack the *mens rea* to be held fully responsible for the act, but this defence is rarely used unless the defendant is accused of a serious crime. First, it must be proven that the accused was suffering from a mental illness to use the mental disorder defence. When cases of P/MHP come before the courts, judges rely on the expert opinions of psychiatrists and psychologists to determine whether the accused was suffering from a serious mental illness.

Some P/MHP convicted of crimes are found "not criminally responsible on account of mental disorder" (NCRMD). In a Canadian Centre for Justice Statistics report, Miladinovic and Lukassen (2014) note that in 2011/2012 there were 268 NCRMD cases in the entire country, which was about the same number of cases per year as in the previous six years (or less than 0.1 per cent of all adult criminal court cases). Those researchers reported that of a total of 1,908 NCRMD cases between 2005 and 2012, less than two-thirds (63 per cent) of cases were violent offences (usually assaults) and 13 of the cases were homicides, which averages to about two murders per year (Miladinovic & Lukassen, 2014). This relationship is shown in Figure 6.1. Although some very high-profile NCRMD homicides have been carried out by people with mental illnesses, these cases are very rare.

While minor crimes committed by people with mental illnesses are common, it is the rare

mental disorder defence An excuse defence based on the argument that people suffering from serious mental disorders are incapable of forming *mens rea* to be held fully accountable.

One emerging area for NCRMD is that of elderly people suffering from dementia who commit violent acts, generally on other nursing home residents. Palmer (2019), a psychiatric nurse, says that most of these acts are minor assaults that are seldom reported to the police. Some lawyers have argued that people suffering from dementia cannot form the criminal intent necessary for their acts to be considered crimes, but these defences have not generally been successful. As a result, these individuals can end up in the criminal justice system and Campbell (2018, para. 6) observes that "they are often left languishing in forensic hospitals and prisons, institutions that are generally ill-suited for someone with the disease."

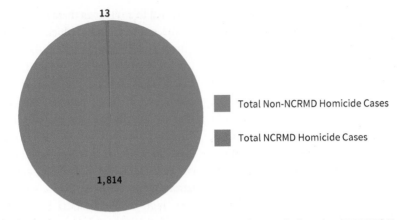

FIGURE 6.1 Total Not Criminally Responsible on Account of Mental Disorder (NCRMD) Homicide Cases, Canada, 2006–2012

Adapted from Miladinovic and Lukassen (2014)

mistake defence
A defence where accused people claim they were unaware of the law and therefore unaware that they'd committed a crime, or that they were aware of the law but honestly believed they were not breaking it.

but serious cases of violence that can reduce our confidence in the justice system, especially after the mental health of the person who committed

While incidents of serious violence involving people with mental illness are often discussed, as with the case of Vince Li, there are only about two cases a year in Canada of homicide where the defendant is found not criminally responsible on account of mental disorder. According to Chris Summerville of the Schizophrenia Society of Canada, "of the 300,000 people in Canada who live with some form of schizophrenia, the vast majority lead quiet, law-abiding lives hoping for some quality of life" (see CBC, 2012).

the offence is restored. While cases such as Vince Li, the man who beheaded a passenger on a Greyhound bus in 2008, are well-reported, these occurrences are rare. In fact, people suffering from mental illnesses may be at high risk of being victimized, and Burczycka (2018) found that people suffering from a mental-health related disability were four times more likely to be victimized than those without a disability.

Mistake Defences

Two types of mistake defences have been used. The first is a mistake of law and refers to when the accused person claims they did not realize they had committed an illegal act. There is an old saying that "ignorance of the law is no excuse." While most people know that violent or property crimes are offences, there are some obscure acts that are defined as offences in the *Criminal Code*. For example, many people might be surprised to learn that it's a criminal offence to assist a deserter from the Canadian Forces, as defined in section 54.

A mistake of fact, by contrast, occurs when the accused person was aware of the law but honestly believed that the act they committed did not break it. One of the leading Canadian cases addressing mistake by fact is *R v Park* (1995), where a man claimed that he had a woman's consent before having sex with her. Both parties agreed that a sexual act occurred. While the accused claimed

Race, Class, and Gender

Hate Crimes

hate crimes
Offences intended to intimidate or harm a person or the group to which they belong based on race, ethnicity, gender, sexual orientation, national origin, disability, or other similar factors.

Some offenders are motivated by bias or hatred. There has been increased attention to **hate crimes** (also called bias-motivated crimes) since the mid-1990s, and this greater awareness reflects Canada's growing diversity—as almost one in every four Canadians is a member of a visible minority group or an Indigenous person. Yet, hate crimes go beyond our racial or ethnic identity, and Perry (2011, p. 367) notes that offenders have also targeted individuals based on their "religion, sexual orientation, disability, class, nationality, age, gender, gender identity, or political affiliation." In a study of hate crimes reported to the police carried out by the Canadian Centre for Justice Statistics, Armstrong (2019, p. 3) found that 2,073 of these crimes were reported in 2017 and the number of these offences has been increasing since 2013. Forty-three per cent of these crimes were motivated by race or ethnicity, 41 per cent by religion, and the remainder were based on sexual orientation (10 per cent) or factors such as mental or physical disabilities, occupation, language, or political beliefs (6 per cent).

There were about 1.9 million total offences reported to the police in 2016 (Allen, 2018 p. 3), so the fact that only 2,073 were hate crimes suggests these offences are rare. On the other hand, it is also likely that hate crimes are under-reported, and that a much larger number of people are victimized each year with bias never established as a motivating factor. As many survivors of hate crimes are members of ethnocultural groups that lack trust and confidence in the police (Cotter, 2015) or fear the police, they may be reluctant to report their victimization, suggesting that the number of criminal offences that are reported is lower than their true number. The victimization statistics reported in the 2014 General Social Survey and shown in Figure 6.2 indicate that some groups of people are at a higher risk than others of being a victim of a violent crime. Although the average violent victimization rate in Canada is 76 incidents per 1,000 people aged 15 years and older, some groups of people, including members of sexual minorities, people

with a disability, and women, have higher rates of victimization.

Armstrong's (2019, p. 3) study showed that nearly two-thirds (62 per cent) of hate crimes were non-violent and almost half of them were mischief offences. Most of the violent crimes committed were relatively minor offences, such as assaults (10 per cent), uttering threats (14 per cent), and harassment (5 per cent), while assault with a weapon and aggravated assault accounted for about 5 per cent of all hate crimes (about 100 offences in 2017) (Armstrong, 2019). Yet, even though these crimes are defined as minor offences, one act might have a harmful impact on an individual or an entire population. When a mosque in Ottawa was covered in posters containing white supremacist messages in January 2018, this act would be defined by the *Criminal Code* as mischief. Yet these offences might also inspire fear throughout an entire community.

Figure 6.3 shows the motivations for hate crimes that were reported to the police in Canada in 2017. The highest proportion of police-reported hate crimes was for acts directed at racial or ethnic groups. Of those, the largest number of these offences was directed toward Black populations, followed by Arab/West Asian, South Asian, East and

One hate crime that unsettled the entire nation occurred when a 27-year-old man killed six worshippers and wounded five others at a Quebec City mosque in January 2017. Prime Minister Trudeau said, "These people died of bullet wounds, but also of ignorance and hatred." (CBC News, 2018). Pictured above are some of the thousands who attended the vigil following the attack.

Continued

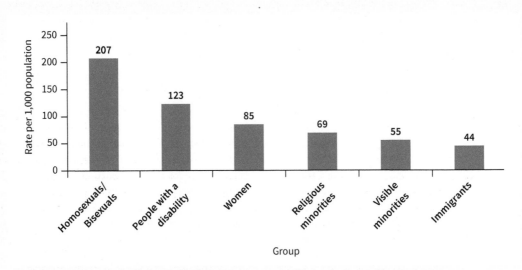

FIGURE 6.2 Violent Victimization Rate per 1,000 Canadian Residents Aged 15 Years and Older by Selected Groups, Canada, 2014

Adapted from Perreault (2015)

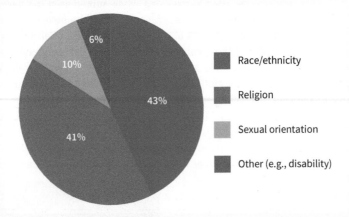

FIGURE 6.3 Police-Reported Hate Crimes by Motivation, Canada, 2017

Adapted from Armstrong (2019)

Southeast Asian, Whites, and Indigenous peoples. With respect to religion, the group that was victimized the most was the Jewish population, followed by Muslims and Catholics. The "other" classification included people with physical or mental disabilities and people who spoke different languages, and it also included crimes based on factors such as occupation or political beliefs.

Hate crimes have been defined in the *Criminal Code* since 1970, but section 718.2 was only amended in 1996 to allow for harsher sentences for hate or bias-related offences. Even though hate crimes reported to the police are rare and most

are relatively minor, these acts are likely greatly under-reported. Moreover, unlike other crimes, hate crimes may have a devastating effect on victims as most of these crimes are unprovoked attacks on individuals based on who they are rather than anything specific they have done. Some hate-motivated assaults have resulted in serious injuries and deaths. The murders of six worshippers at a Quebec City mosque in January 2017 led to vigils across Canada on the anniversary of these killings (CBC, 2018). The killer was sentenced to a 40-year prison term in 2019, but the Crown has appealed that decision and is seeking a 50-year prison term.

he had consent, the victim maintained she had not consented to the activity. This case was heard before the Supreme Court in December 1994, and in June 1995 the Supreme Court upheld an earlier conviction from the province of Alberta, rejecting the claim of a mistake in fact.

THE CRIMINAL JUSTICE WEDDING CAKE MODEL

There are several different ways of understanding the operations and priorities of justice systems. In Chapter 1, the due process and crime control models were introduced as a way of understanding the operations of justice systems.

Walker (2015) developed another way of describing how the criminal justice system works and the priorities of the system. He presented the idea of a four-layered cake, shown in Figure 6.4, where the least attention is paid to criminal cases in the base or lowest layer (which is composed of minor summary offences such as property crimes, simple assaults, and public order crimes), while the cases that tend to be the most widely reported are in the top layer—what Walker calls "celebrated cases." Walker (2015) argues that although there

are differences in the way that system officials treat cases from layer to layer, cases within each layer are generally handled fairly similarly. Thus, the officials devote more time, energy, and resources to serious and publicized cases, and that attention decreases with the more common and less serious offences that represent much of the work of the justice system. In terms of crimes, most media attention is paid to violent crimes where there is some factor that sets these crimes apart from other offences, such as multiple or vulnerable victims (e.g., children or the elderly), extreme cruelty, or a celebrity victim or offender.

Few indictable offences receive much media attention, and the second and third layers of Walker's (2015) cake are composed of serious and lesser indictable offences such as "regular" murders (with no distinguishing circumstances), manslaughter offences, sexual assaults, and robberies. For similar reasons, individuals who are in the first and second layers of the "cake" receive more attention from the justice system than those in the third or fourth layer, and those found guilty in those first two layers are apt to receive harsh punishments.

The third layer of the cake is generally composed of cases of less serious indictable offences,

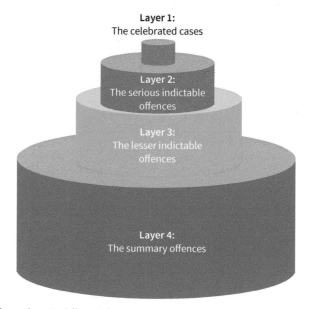

FIGURE 6.4 Criminal Justice Wedding Cake

Adapted from Walker (2015)

A COMPARATIVE VIEW

Canadian and US Court Operations

Most of our exposure to issues of crime and justice comes from watching US television programs and films, and there are significant differences between the American and Canadian approaches to justice, especially the activities and organization of court systems. Although there are similar elements between the two nations, as both countries have legal systems based on the common law, Table 6.1 shows the key differences between the two nations in terms of court systems. In some respects, the Canadian criminal law is easier to understand because the system is unified, which means that all Canadians are subject to the same law (the *Criminal Code of Canada*), whereas in the United States, there are 50 state criminal codes and one federal criminal code, resulting in considerable differences in how people convicted of crimes are treated. In 31 US states, for example, offenders convicted of first-degree murder can be executed, whereas in the remaining 19 states (and the District of Columbia) the most severe sentence is life imprisonment (Death Penalty Information Center, 2019).

One factor in US justice systems that contributes to harsh sentences is that most judges and chief prosecutors (called district attorneys) are elected, and some of these officials pander to the media and support harsh sanctions on offenders because they do not want to be seen as being "soft on crime." Having elected officials may also reduce the independence of the judiciary and prosecutors, as some align with political parties. Judges and prosecutors may solicit election contributions from donors—which may create the appearance of favouritism. On the other hand, because they are elected, US justice officials may be more sensitive to public opinion and more willing to impose or support severe sentences on serious and repeat offenders, which is what the American public desires (Pfaff, 2017). One question that we should ask is whether the activities of justice systems should be driven by public opinion or expert knowledge.

There are also procedural differences in the two nations, including the ways that everyday matters and trials are carried out. In Canada, for example, court proceedings are typically low-key events, and the Provincial Court of British Columbia (2018a) says they are more respectful, dignified, and formal than those in the United States. For example, in Canada, the prosecution and defence counsel are expected to remain behind their tables, whereas in

TABLE 6.1 Differences Between Canadian and US Court Systems

Canada	United States
• All courts are part of the same unified system, where the ultimate authority rests with the Supreme Court of Canada.	• There are state and federal courts, and appellate courts exist for both systems; the Supreme Court of the United States is the ultimate court.
• Judges are appointed by the government and are politically independent. • As judges are not elected, there are few external pressures to be "tough on crime."	• Vacancies for judges are filled by the state's governor, and the judge must be re-elected. • Judges may impose harsh sentences because they do not want to be seen as being "soft on crime," and they do not want to lose public confidence and future elections.
• One criminal law—the *Criminal Code of Canada*—applies in all provinces and territories.	• There are 50 state criminal codes and one federal criminal code.
• The costs of operating local courts, the salaries of judges and prosecutors, and legal aid services are funded by the provinces or territories.	• Local courts and legal aid services are funded by the municipality or county. • Funding these operations is often a challenge for small and rural counties—which may put some low-income defendants at a disadvantage—as legal aid services are sometimes limited.

Canada	United States
• Prosecutors are civil service appointees who represent the Crown in the prosecution of people accused of crimes. • The prosecution of offenders tends to be a low-visibility role for most Canadian prosecutors.	• Chief prosecutors (also called district attorneys) are elected in most jurisdictions. • Prosecutors often use their experiences as a stepping stone to higher political office—making it politically dangerous for them to be perceived as "soft on crime."
• About 5 per cent of criminal cases result in a jury trial, and some criminal cases are heard by a judge alone (which is a choice of the accused).	• Of all criminal cases, less than 5 per cent go to a jury or bench trial (trial by judge alone).
• Cameras in courtrooms are very rare (in jurisdictions where cameras are authorized, the use of cameras must be approved by the prosecution, defence, and judge—which rarely occurs). • Proceedings in the Supreme Court of Canada are broadcast on television.	• Cameras in courtrooms are authorized in 38 states, and this makes the justice system more transparent and easily accessible to the public. • The Supreme Court of the United States does not allow cameras.
• Jurors who serve in criminal trials are forbidden from speaking about deliberations or about what went on in the jury room.	• Jurors are free to speak about their deliberations and it is common for them to appear before the media to describe their deliberations.
• Civil cases (such as lawsuits) are rare in Canada, and losers can be ordered to pay the other side's legal costs. • Civil cases with a jury are less common in Canada and in some cases the litigants may not be able to ask for a jury trial. • Awards to litigants tend to be limited, and damages in civil cases are not as high as in US cases.	• Lawsuits are common, and losers are rarely liable for the costs of a failed lawsuit. • Punitive damages can be very high for pain and suffering.
• Canadian courts will sometimes use examples of court decisions from other common-law nations to answer Canadian legal questions if no precedent exists.	• US courts are reluctant to make reference to legal decisions from other nations.
• Canadians are entitled to a trial in either English or French.	• All trials are in English.
• Most judges and counsel wear formal black robes and white collars (in superior and appellate courts and before the federal courts). • Court procedures are formal and emphasize restraint and good manners.	• Most judges wear robes, but defence counsel and prosecutors wear business attire. • Attorneys have more leeway in their courtroom behaviour than in Canada, and some courts tolerate some theatrics at trial.

the United States they may approach the judge and the witnesses being questioned. Cameras are also allowed in US courtrooms, which may also lead to "grandstanding" on the part of the judge or counsel. Furthermore, in Canadian courtrooms there are no gavels or sidebars (informal meetings between the judge and the counsel), and comments cannot be stricken from the record (Ellwood Evidence Inc., 2014). Instead of informal "sidebars" heard before the courts, motions with respect to substantive or procedural matters are heard in hearings held in judges' chambers. In both civil and criminal cases, counsel often are required to meet with judges in scheduled pretrial conferences to work out procedural issues

Continued

and logistics such as the evidence of expert witnesses or the number of witnesses to be called.

Altogether, while there are similarities between the court operations in Canada and the United States, as proceedings in both countries are adversarial and based on the rule of law, there are significant differences in the manner that courts are funded and operated. It is important to be aware of these differences so that we might better appreciate the strengths and weaknesses of the Canadian justice system.

In Canadian courtrooms, there are no gavels or sidebars (informal meetings between the judge and the counsel), and comments cannot be stricken from the record.

such as assaults, break and enters, or drug trafficking. These cases tend to be processed fairly quickly and most are resolved through plea bargains. In terms of punishments, most result in very short custodial sentences in a provincial correctional centre, although some offenders will serve probationary sentences.

Unlike what we see on television crime programs, most of the work carried out by workers within the justice system involves managing a large volume of relatively minor offences: petty thefts, simple assaults, impaired driving, and acts of mischief. These offences are often committed by youth and young men who were under the influence of alcohol or drugs at the time of the offence. These cases are usually resolved very quickly, and they receive little formal attention by the media or the justice system. Incarceration for these cases is rare (with the exception of short sentences for someone's second conviction for impaired driving), and many people who plead guilty are fined or placed on probation. Packer's (1968) example of an assembly-line approach to justice applies to these relatively minor matters, as most prosecutors want these cases resolved quickly.

Walker's (2015) model provides us with another way of looking at the operations of justice systems and the attention given to different types of cases. Because celebrated cases attract so much of our attention, we begin to think that those cases are normal. Yet we know that serious and violent crimes are relatively rare and are typically carried out by individuals who are involved in conflicts with people they know. In most of these cases, the police make a quick arrest and the cases are resolved through a plea bargain. As a result, jury trials are relatively rare, and account for about 6 per cent of all cases in British Columbia every year. Moreover, most criminal defendants are not represented by a dream team of lawyers, but instead by a lawyer working for legal aid, and an increasing number are representing themselves in court as they are ineligible for legal aid.

SUMMARY

Although at times all of us are skeptical about whether justice systems are fair and unbiased, people accused of committing crimes can benefit from a number of procedural protections enshrined in the *Canadian Charter of Rights and Freedoms*. In addition to ensured access to justice through government-funded legal aid services for low-income defendants, there are also a number of advocacy organizations that work toward justice for both victims and offenders, such as the Canadian Bar Association, the Canadian Civil Liberties Association, the Women's Legal Education and Action Fund (LEAF), and provincial law societies.

Despite the fact that there are services in place to support people accused of crimes, achieving justice is not a simple proposition. Laws are dynamic, and both the written law as well as the informal operations of justice systems change according to shifting social values, technological changes, and the priorities of different political parties and public opinion (e.g., being "tough on crime"). Regardless of these changes, there are a number of common elements of crimes that have remained stable over time, including the need for a prosecutor to prove beyond a reasonable doubt that the accused committed a guilty act (*actus reus*), that the accused intended on committing the crime (*mens rea*), and that the act and intent occurred at the same time. Individuals charged with a criminal offence can use a number of justifications or excuses for their criminal conduct, although many of these defences are difficult to prove.

All of us have an interest in ensuring that justice systems are fair and unbiased, and there is broad public support that people accused of committing crimes should receive protection from the state. A survey carried out for the British Columbia Legal Services Society reports that 82 per cent of respondents believed that "everyone should have the right to access the justice system, even if the government has to spend more money on it" (Sentis, 2015, p. 6). This is a complex and expensive undertaking, although prior research has shown that when people see the law as legitimate, they have more trust in the system and believe that they will be treated fairly. As a result, people are more likely to follow the law, and even offenders will be more law abiding (Tyler, 2006). In fact, Tyler (2006) argues that belief in the legitimacy of the system is more important in regulating behaviour than is the fear of being punished. Perhaps that is the strongest argument for the rule of law and the notion that all of us stand equal before the courts.

MYTH OR REALITY

Equality Before the Law

This chapter started by describing some of the issues about defendants representing themselves in criminal courts. The Canadian justice system is guided by the rule of law, which is the principle that we are all equal before the law. Although that is an admirable goal, is it realistic when it comes to the way the world really operates? In other words, does a homeless person from a marginalized social group have the same access to justice as a rich and politically powerful defendant? Beverley McLachlin, the former Chief Justice of Canada, in discussing issues surrounding access to justice in Canada, said that "we have a wonderful justice system. But the problem is that it's often inaccessible for one reason or another to ordinary men and women, ordinary Canadians" (cited in CBC, 2017). The poorest Canadians can access legal aid services if they are at risk of incarceration, while the rich can afford to hire private counsel to represent them. But what about the working poor or middle-class defendants who do not qualify for legal aid? How expensive is it to have a lawyer represent you in court? Table 6.2 shows the national and regional costs.

These amounts are based on averages, and a defendant might pay less if they hire a lawyer with fewer years of experience or who works for a larger firm. Alternatively, a famous criminal defence lawyer might cost many times the national average for representation. After CBC broadcaster Jian Ghomeshi was found not guilty of sexual assault charges in 2016, it was estimated that the legal fees for his trial were at least $200,000 to $300,000 and could have been as much as $500,000 (Boudreau, 2016).

A Department of Justice Canada study carried out by Hann, Nuffield, Meredith, and Svoboda (2002) examined self-representation at nine provincial court sites and found that some courts had over 36 per cent of first-appearance defendants representing themselves in court, although by sentencing only about one-quarter were self-represented. Like many other issues related to the criminal justice system, there is a lack of recent information about self-represented defendants for the entire nation. The Provincial Courts of British Columbia (2018b), however, report that between 2012/2013 and 2016/2017 about one-fifth of all defendants in those courts were self-represented. Figure 6.5 shows that there has been a slight decrease in the number of these defendants in British Columbia, although in most other provinces the numbers seem to be increasing (CBC, 2018).

The problem for defendants representing themselves is that their unfamiliarity with the "ins and outs" of the justice system places them at a significant disadvantage when their opponent is a Crown counsel with legal training and courtroom

TABLE 6.2 Costs of Hiring a Criminal Defence Lawyer

Type of Representation	National Averages (Firm with 1–4 Lawyers)	Western Provinces	Atlantic Canada	Province of Ontario
Summary criminal offence (one-day trial; e.g., impaired driving)	$5,501 to $6,000	Less expensive	Less expensive	More expensive
Bail hearing	$1,000 to $1,500			
Criminal offence (one-day trial)	$5,001 to $6,000			
Simple plea of guilt	$1,001 to $2,000			
Trial longer than seven days	$20,001 to $26,000			
Appeal to provincial court of appeal (e.g., challenge of the severity of one's sentence)	$10,000 to $20,000			

Adapted from Bruineman (2018, pp. 22–23)

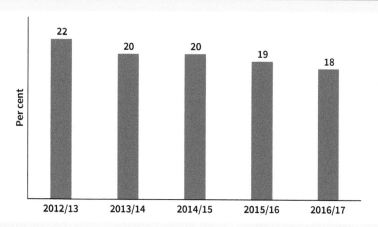

FIGURE 6.5 Self-Represented Defendants in British Columbia Provincial Courts, 2012/2013 to 2016/2017

Provincial Court of British Columbia (2018b)

experience. Many defendants representing themselves may be further disadvantaged given that offenders tend to have poor literacy skills, suffer from addictions or mental illnesses, or come from marginalized groups that already mistrust the justice system. Because of those limitations, the Canadian Judicial Council (2006, p. 2) published a statement on self-represented people, which states that:

> Judges, the courts and other participants in the justice system have a responsibility to promote opportunities for all persons to understand and meaningfully present their case, regardless of representation.

In 2017, the Supreme Court of Canada, in the *Pintea v Johns* case, decided that courts should recognize the Judicial Council's guideline on unrepresented defendants. In order to support self-represented defendants, the provincial courts now provide individuals with online resources to educate them about court procedures, and in Quebec and some other provinces, self-represented defendants can access lawyers who will not appear in court but will give advice.

So, is equality before the law a myth or a reality? There is no doubt that prior to the introduction of legal aid services in the 1970s, low-income defendants had little legal representation and therefore less access to justice. The promise of legal aid was that economically disadvantaged people could benefit from receiving counsel that was provided by the state, and they *can* benefit, but only if they are eligible. In the 1997 *R v Bernardo* case, the Court of Appeal for Ontario held that "the costs associated with the appointment of counsel must be accepted as the price of the proper administration of justice."

kittirat roekburi/Shutterstock

Sometimes things end badly for self-represented litigants. On June 3, 2015, a British Columbia mother who was representing herself in a family matter was sentenced to a 30-day incarceration term (15 days were suspended) and a 90-day term of probation for overzealous advocacy. The judge held her in contempt because she had defied several court orders, but a blogger asks, "If a lawyer stridently opposed an order that they believed to be unfair and unjustified, wouldn't they just be doing their job?" (National Self-Represented Litigants Project, 2015).

Career SNAPSHOT

Criminal Defence Lawyer

There are numerous careers in the justice system for lawyers, including defence counsel, prosecutor, and judge, and these jobs are profiled in Chapter 7. To become a lawyer in Canada, one has to first obtain a bachelor's degree and then be accepted into a law school; the latter includes three years of classes and a year in an articling position that is like a paid internship. Altogether, the pathway to becoming a lawyer in Canada is lengthy, demanding, and expensive, but it can be very rewarding.

In terms of defence counsel, many lawyers work for legal aid, and some—like Jordana Goldlist, who is profiled below—have their own law firms, requiring them to be a lawyer and a business person. Careers in the law can pay very well, but these jobs are also stressful as a client's freedom rests upon the knowledge and skills of their counsel.

Profile

Name: Jordana H. Goldlist
Job title: Owner: JHG Criminal Law (Criminal Defence Lawyer)
Employed in current job since: 2008 (as a lawyer); owner of JHG Criminal Law since 2015
Present location: Toronto, Ontario (takes cases from all of Southern Ontario)
Education: BA (Philosophy), York University; LLB/J.D., Osgoode Hall Law School

Background

I wanted to be a criminal lawyer since I was a child, when I watched a family member go through the justice system. I wanted the power that the lawyer had, both in the courtroom and with our family. But then I went through hard times during my teens, including group homes, homelessness, and street life. When I came out of it, at 19 years old, I thought my experiences would preclude me from being a lawyer. I knew I needed an education so went back to high school, graduating when I was 21 years old. I was on the Dean's Honour Roll by the end of my undergrad studies at York University, and when I was 25 I started at Osgoode Hall Law School.

Fifteen years after starting law school, I'm living my childhood dream. Now I can be selective with the cases I take, making sure the case and the client are worth the time it takes to defend them (which is, on average, 2–3 years, depending on the charges). Controlling my schedule leaves me time for volunteer work and public speaking. I encourage youth to find transferable skills in their adverse experiences. Struggle can be an asset in the business world and not an obstacle if you learn to use it to your advantage. And I am trying to teach the rest of the world to avoid judging people by their titles until knowing their character. We write people off as "criminals" but if we gave people real opportunity to do different, some would excel. Our society needs to do a better job of offering people the chance to change.

Work Experience

I started my career in civil litigation, but my passion was always for criminal cases. I made the switch two years into my career and never looked back. I spent five years working at a large firm focused on street crime, learning how to be a lawyer and building a client base. I always had an entrepreneurial spirit, and I followed it in February 2015 by founding JHG Criminal Law. I currently employ two lawyers on contract and a full-time associate. I now focus my time on people charged with murder, drug, and firearms offences. The stakes are high so it's essential that I am always prepared, armed with an understanding of the law as it applies to each case and a strategy to win. The best part of my job is fighting for people who want to fight, no matter the odds, and the most rewarding cases are those correcting an injustice in the system.

Advice to Students

My advice to students is to always follow your passion. That means taking the classes that interest you, volunteering with the organizations that move you, and taking the jobs that excite you. Also, make connections. Take classes, jobs, and opportunities that will help connect you to people in your field and build those contacts by keeping in touch. In addition, always treat the people you meet with respect; you never know when you will cross paths later. Finally, don't focus on the money. If you plan right and follow your heart, the money will come. It may take longer and you may have to work harder but if you enjoy what you do it doesn't even feel like work.

Watch Jordana Goldlist's TEDx talk entitled "Who Judges the Judge?" where she explains why we should judge people based on their character rather than on the labels, such as "criminal," that we attach to them. Her talk can be accessed at https://www.youtube.com/watch?v=G4GvfOHV2Tc.

REVIEW QUESTIONS

1. Describe how laws are dynamic, and explain some reasons why the *Criminal Code* will change over time.
2. Identify the elements of a crime.
3. Explain the differences between procedural law and substantive law.
4. What are some commonly used excuses for committing a crime?
5. Contrast the differences between Canadian and US court operations. Why should we learn about those differences?

DISCUSSION QUESTIONS

1. Wealthy defendants can afford a more sophisticated legal defence (e.g., by hiring teams of defence counsel and experts to help with their case) compared to economically disadvantaged defendants who must rely on legal aid services, which might be limited by high caseloads. How can we ensure that people with limited finances receive an adequate defence, or should we care?
2. Why should we care that as many as one-quarter of defendants in some courts are representing themselves in criminal cases?
3. Of *mens rea* and *actus reus*, which do you think is the most difficult for the prosecutor to prove?
4. Walker (2015) developed a method of understanding the attention that criminal cases receive. Provide an example of a celebrated case and discuss how these matters shape or change our ideas about crime and justice.
5. Judges and chief prosecutors in many US jurisdictions are elected, whereas in Canada these officials are appointed by governments. What implications does this have for the officials' independence? In addition, which approach—electing or appointing—makes these officials more responsive to the public?

INTERNET SITE

Canadian court cases can be accessed through the CanLII (Canadian Legal Information Institute) website, which provides full text records of court cases. This is a great resource for students examining leading cases.
https://www.canlii.org/en/

CASES CITED

Pintea v Johns, 2017 SCC 23, [2017] 1 SCR 470
R v Askov, [1990] 2 SCR 1199
R v Bernardo (1997), 105 OAC 244
R v Cleghorn, [1995] 3 SCR 175
R v Ewanchuk, [1999] 1 SCR 330
R v Feeney, [1997] 2 SCR 13
R v Gayme, [1991] 2 SCR 577
R v Gladue, [1999] 1 SCR 688
R v Jordan, 2016 SCC 27, [2016] 1 SCR 631
R v Mack, [1988] 2 SCR 903
R v Mann, 2004 SCC 52, [2004] 3 SCR 59
R v Martineau, [1990] 2 SCR 633
R v Morin, [1992] 1 SCR 771
R v Park, [1995] 2 SCR 836
R v Seaboyer, [1991] 2 SCR 577
R v Sipos, 2014 SCC 47, [2014] 2 SCR 423
R v Smickle, 2013 ONCA 678
R v Stinchcombe, [1991] 3 SCR 326
R v Stone, [1999] 2 SCR 290

▲ Justice Edith Campbell (left), shown here at her swearing-in June 2018, was the first resident woman justice (and first person bilingual in English and French) to serve on the Yukon Supreme Court. In February 2019, Justice Suzanne Duncan became the second woman to serve. How important is representation at all levels of the criminal justice system? (Photo credit:Mike Thomas/Yukon News)

Criminal Courts and Court Personnel

LEARNING OUTLINE

After reading this chapter, you will be able to

- Describe the main roles of provincial and federal courts
- Describe the roles of provincial appellate courts and the Supreme Court of Canada in ensuring justice
- Explain the steps in a criminal investigation and trial
- Describe the roles of members of the courtroom work group (including judges, Crown prosecutors, and defence counsel)
- Discuss the changing role of victims in Canadian courts
- Explain why specialized courts have been established to respond to specific types of offenders or offences

Open Courts, Publication Bans, and Privacy: The Rehtaeh Parsons Case

It is important that the actions of the justice system be transparent and that the public be able to witness court operations. In addition, the media's freedom to publicize court proceedings, which is called the open court principle, has been called one of the hallmarks of a democratic society (Scassa, 2018). One challenge that courts have to confront is balancing the public's right to be informed with the need to protect the identity and privacy of crime victims and witnesses. Publication bans were introduced to protect the identity of crime victims and witnesses, and the conditions on which they can be used are outlined in section 486 of the *Criminal Code*. While testimony is still heard in an open court, judges may ban publication about some aspects of these proceedings (such as a victim's identity), although these bans are rare. Exceptions include cases involving child victims and survivors of sexual assault; judges will issue a publication ban for victims of sexual offences who are under 18 years of age.

A high-profile case where a publication ban was ordered took place after the 2013 death of Rehtaeh Parsons, a 17-year-old Nova Scotia student. Parsons died after attempting suicide 17 months after being sexually assaulted; a picture of the offence taken by one of the participants was texted to classmates, resulting in cyberbullying, victim blaming, and harassment. After Parsons' death, the judge imposed a ban on reporting her name as well as the names of the individuals accused of the sexual assault (as they were young offenders at the time of the offence, their identities were protected by law). Once a publication ban has been ordered, the victims and witnesses are forbidden to discuss the case with the media unless they apply to have the ban terminated and can explain to the judge why the need for a ban has changed (Alberta Justice and Solicitor General, 2013). The CBC describes a case where the survivor of sexual abuse wanted the ban on using her name lifted so she could tell her story to other potential victims, but as the CBC (2018, para. 2) observes, "according to the *Criminal Code*, her identity is not hers to share."

What was unusual about the Parsons case was that the Halifax newspaper *The Chronicle Herald* violated the publication ban, as did members of the "hacktivist" group Anonymous, who both revealed Parsons' identity. The young woman's parents also opposed

The "hactivist" group Anonymous was actively involved in the publication of Rehtaeh Parsons' name, as part of an effort to increase public awareness of cyberbullying. While Anonymous was prominent between 2008 and 2016, its influence has faded (Bernard, 2018).

open court principle Gives the media the freedom to publicize court proceedings, although some information, such as the identity of a child victim of sexual abuse, may be subject to a publication ban.

publication bans Made by courts in order to protect the identity of some victims or specific information about cases.

the publication ban, as they believed that reporting the case would increase awareness about cyberbullying and sexual violence. Parsons' father has said that if Anonymous had not been involved in the case, it is possible that no prosecutions would have taken place (Omand, 2015). Civil libertarians, however, have been critical that the activities of this advocacy group are akin to vigilantism. The publication ban was ultimately lifted, but individuals will be prosecuted if Parsons' name is used in a derogatory manner.

Although Parsons died in 2013, her case continues to impact the operations of Nova Scotia's justice system. Like other high-profile criminal justice cases, the Parsons tragedy led to a number of inquiries about how the justice and school systems, and the mental health and addictions services in Halifax, responded to this case. Altogether, the inquiries highlighted deficiencies in the manner in which the system handled this case. In addition to changing agency practices, Nova Scotia also enacted a tough anti-cyberbullying law, but that legislation was struck down in December 2015 by the province's Supreme Court because it infringed on *Charter* rights (Canadian Press, 2018). In July 2018 the Nova Scotia government introduced the *Intimate Images and Cyber-protection Act*, which would give victims of online harassment the ability to seek damages from their abusers in civil courts, but it is too soon to gauge the impact of this legislation. Parsons' case shows us the dynamic nature of the criminal law and brings attention to offences that were unknown a decade ago but are significant problems today.

Critical Questions

1. The CBC describes a case where the survivor of sexual abuse wanted the ban on using her name lifted so she could tell her story to other potential victims, but as the CBC (2018a, para. 2) observes, "according to the *Criminal Code*, her identity is not hers to share." What does this tell us about the justice system?

2. What effect does the involvement of activist groups such as Anonymous have on the administration of justice by threatening to publicize—or actually publicizing—the names of people whose identities are protected by courts through publication bans?

3. Publication bans may be less effective today given that bloggers from other nations can post information about Canadian cases with little fear of prosecution. What implications might this have for getting victims and witnesses to testify?

INTRODUCTION

Most Canadians have a greater understanding of what happens in the criminal courts than they do of the daily operations of the police or corrections. Courts are open to the public, and while there are few cameras in Canadian courtrooms—the exception is the Supreme Court of Canada—reporters have access to both adult and youth courts and can freely report on cases, although publication bans do occur. Moch (2018, p. 3) observes that "the open court principle is vital to the administration of justice, as it ensures transparency, accountability, and integrity of the courts," while also acknowledging that judges have the discretion to limit some public access.

Although we have an ability to witness what occurs in Canadian courts, our trust and confidence in those institutions has changed over time. A survey conducted by the Angus Reid Institute (2018) reported that only 41 per cent of respondents had complete confidence or a lot of confidence in the leadership and operations of the provincial criminal courts (that proportion increased to 51 per cent for confidence in the Supreme Court of Canada). Cotter's (2015, p. 4) study of public confidence in institutions for Statistics Canada found that 57 per cent of Canadians expressed a great deal or some confidence in the justice system. Like other national averages, there are some differences between the provinces. Respondents from New Brunswick and Ontario had the highest confidence, whereas respondents from British Columbia, Manitoba, and Quebec had the lowest confidence in the courts and justice system. What explains this lack of confidence in the operations of the courts?

With the exception of being stopped by the police for violating traffic regulations, few of us have much contact with the justice system. As a result, our opinions about the system come from other sources. Anthony Doob (2014), a prominent University of Toronto criminologist, observes that our understanding of the courts and justice system are a result of: highly publicized cases; our experiences with the police, courts, and corrections; and the views of people we trust (including politicians and justice system officials). One of the challenges is that a high-profile case—such as one involving a judge's misconduct—could be from the United States, and this could shape Canadians' opinions even though the conditions in Canada may be completely different. By contrast, the messages that we receive about a court—such as a blog post about a Supreme Court of Canada decision—could present inaccurate information and may be based on a flawed analysis. Last, our ideas about fair treatment by the courts could be formed based on specific experiences—such as a dispute over paying a traffic ticket with an overworked court clerk. Rarely are our ideas about crime and justice, and especially the courts, based on research.

So, why is the public's knowledge about crime and justice important? Roberts (2016, p. 13) argues that "only when the public has a realistic understanding of crime and justice can an informed debate over crime control policies take place." This chapter focuses on the organization and operations of Canadian courts, followed by a description of the 12 steps in a criminal trial—from investigation to the possibility of appeal. The chapter ends with a description of specialized courts and their effectiveness in responding to individuals with special needs.

COURT ORGANIZATION

The intent of the courts is to "help people resolve disputes fairly—whether they are between individuals, or between individuals and the state.

This photograph shows a Manitoba provincial courtroom. Although the layout of provincial courts may vary across the country, typically judges sit on a raised platform and the defence counsel and Crown prosecutors sit at tables facing the judge. The accused may sit in a dock (or prisoner's box), which is often placed in the left-hand side of the courtroom, close to the defence table.

Studio Shai Gil Inc.

Superior courts differ from provincial courts in that they are designed to hold trials and have formal seating arrangements for witnesses and jury members. Pictured is a courtroom from the Thunder Bay Consolidated Courthouse in Ontario.

At the same time, courts interpret and pronounce law, set standards, and decide questions that affect all aspects of Canadian society" (Department of Justice, 2016, p. 1). Each province and territory has its own court system, and each jurisdiction pays for the personnel and resources needed to carry out its courts' operations.

The Four Levels of Criminal Court

There are four levels of court in Canada that address criminal matters. This section describes the characteristics of these courts:

1. **Provincial and territorial courts.** Most of the criminal court work is done by the provincial and territorial courts, which are also called inferior courts. All

offenders make their first appearance in these courts, and most cases are resolved here. According to the Department of Justice (2016, pp. 3–4), provincial and territorial courts handle:

- most criminal offences (both summary and indictable offences);
- family law matters (e.g., child support and protection, adoption);
- youth justice (e.g., administering the *Youth Criminal Justice Act* for 12- to 17-year-olds who have violated the *Criminal Code*);
- traffic and bylaw violations;
- provincial and territorial regulatory offences;
- claims involving money;

- small claims, which are civil cases of disputes involving relatively small amounts of money; and
- all preliminary hearings and inquiries, which are held to determine whether there is enough evidence to warrant an entire trial.

Nunavut has a distinctive court arrangement as its territorial and superior courts are combined so that a single court can hear any criminal matter. This approach is well-suited to Nunavut given that there are only 25 communities in the territory.

2. **Provincial and territorial superior courts.** These courts hear serious criminal matters and family law cases including divorces. The superior courts are known by different names across the country, including the Court of Queen's Bench (Alberta, Saskatchewan, Manitoba, and New Brunswick), Supreme Court (Newfoundland and Labrador, Prince Edward Island, Nova Scotia, British Columbia, Northwest Territories, and Yukon), and Superior Court (Ontario and Quebec).

3. **Provincial and territorial courts of appeal.** Appellate courts hear criminal

Executive Office of the Nova Scotia Judiciary

This photograph shows a courtroom from the Nova Scotia Court of Appeal. Provincial and territorial courts of appeal differ from regular courtrooms, as three judges rule on cases in appellate courts. Appellate court justices may ask questions at any point in the proceeding, and they may make a decision on the appeal immediately or inform the parties of their decision at some point in the future.

The Supreme Court of Canada has jurisdiction over disputes in all four areas of the law—administrative, civil, constitutional, and criminal—and they hear about 60 cases a year. The Supreme Court consists of a chief justice and eight associate judges. To be appointed to the Supreme Court, one must have been a superior court judge or have at least 10 years' experience as a lawyer. According to the *Supreme Court Act*, three of these judges must be from Quebec, and the government has traditionally appointed three judges from Ontario, two from the western provinces, and one from Atlantic Canada.

cases from the provincial and territorial courts or the superior courts. According to the Department of Justice (2016, p. 7), courts of appeal can hear "commercial disputes, property disputes, negligence claims, family disputes, bankruptcies, and corporate reorganizations." The Ontario Ministry of the Attorney General (2015) observes that there are a number of decisions that an appellate court can make, including dismissing the appeal (after the court finds that there were no serious errors at trial) or ordering a new trial if the court finds that there *were* serious errors.

Sentences imposed by lower courts can also be increased or lowered by appellate courts.

4. **Supreme Court of Canada.** The Supreme Court has jurisdiction over disputes in all four areas of the law: administrative, civil, constitutional, and criminal. Between 2007 and 2017 the Court received an average of 460 applications per year (which are called a "leave to appeal") and heard an average of 56 cases a year (Supreme Court of Canada, 2018). The Supreme Court justices will only hear cases they consider important and that have a national interest, although some offenders have the automatic right to appeal.

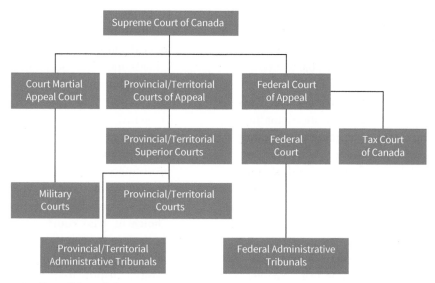

FIGURE 7.1 Outline of Canada's Court System
Department of Justice (2016)

Other Canadian Courts

The description of the four levels of court provided in the previous section presents a somewhat simplified version of Canada's courts. Figure 7.1 presents an outline of Canada's court system and shows that there are also federal courts that deal with military, tax, and federal matters. Federal courts hear disputes related to issues such as claims against the federal government, interprovincial disputes, matters related to immigration and refugees, and cases involving Crown corporations (Department of Justice, 2016, p. 8). Similar to criminal courts, the federal courts also give individuals the right to appeal decisions, and most federal legal matters may be heard by the Federal Court of Appeal. Last, there are two specialized courts: the Tax Court of Canada and military courts. The Tax Court of Canada is a superior court that hears cases between taxpayers and the federal government. Military courts (or courts martial) hear cases related to wrongdoing committed by members of the military or civilian employees.

STEPS IN A CRIMINAL INVESTIGATION AND TRIAL

In Chapter 1, the justice system was described as operating in a sequential manner, which means that all criminal cases occur in a similar order, which is outlined by the *Charter* and entrenched in the *Criminal Code*. As a result, the Canadian justice system prevents us from punishing suspects and defendants before their guilt has been established. Manitoba Justice (2018) describes the 12 steps that occur after a crime has been committed, from the investigation of an offence to its resolution, including the possibility of an appeal. The 12 steps are summarized as follows:

1. **Investigation.** An investigation is carried out by the police after a crime is reported or the officers witness an offence. In some cases, investigations might be conducted by other officials, such as a private investigator or civilian worker carrying out a fraud investigation, and their results given to the police. Some investigations occur fairly quickly, while others can take years, particularly if the crime is unusually complex.

2. **Laying a charge.** If the police believe that a person has committed a crime, they may lay a charge, although the police have considerable discretion. The decision to proceed with a charge may rest on the quality of the information, the willingness of the witnesses to appear in court, and the harm

that was done when the crime occurred. If the police proceed with laying a charge, they deliver a package of information to the Crown prosecutor that contains all of the materials relevant to the case.

3. **Deciding whether to prosecute.** Crown attorneys also use their discretion in deciding whether to proceed with a prosecution, asking two key questions: (a) "Is there a reasonable likelihood of conviction?" and (b) "Is it in the public interest to proceed?" If the answer to both questions is "yes," the prosecutor will proceed but will use his or her judgment—called prosecutorial discretion—to decide the severity of the charge (e.g., whether an offence is an aggravated assault or an attempted murder) and the number of offences to be prosecuted.

4. **Requiring the accused to attend court, entering a plea, and bail.** Most individuals charged with a minor crime are given a document by the police, such as a notice to appear, which advises them of the date and time to appear in court. Section 515 of the *Criminal Code* enables accused people to be detained until their court date if the Crown prosecutor can successfully argue that the individual represents a risk to public safety.

People who have been arrested and detained must be brought before a justice of the peace or a judge for a bail hearing within 24 hours to determine whether they can be released. Although the term *bail* is commonly used, the formal language is judicial interim release. Individuals can be released on their promise to appear, or by providing reasonable bail—which must be within the reach of the individuals or their surety (see the "A Closer Look" box in this chapter for more on bail).

Bail decisions are somewhat controversial among members of the public. We want the legal system to detain dangerous people to ensure public safety, yet we also recognize that accused people have not been convicted of a crime and that detaining them is a restriction on their liberty. Renaud (2016, p. 158) explains that "in Canada, individual liberty is at the heart of a free and democratic society . . . [and] the importance of this fundamental freedom is embodied in the presumption of innocence and more specifically in the notion of bail."

5. **Decision about type of offence.** Crown prosecutors determine whether they will proceed with a summary or indictable (more serious) offence.

6. **Choice of trial court and election by the accused.** Matters involving individuals charged with summary offences are resolved in provincial courts. For those accused of committing an indictable offence—as long as the crime is not within the jurisdiction of the provincial court—the accused may choose to be tried by a provincial court judge without a jury and without a preliminary inquiry, by a justice from a superior court (such as Queen's Bench Court) without a jury, or by a superior court justice and jury.

7. **Preliminary inquiry.** A preliminary inquiry or hearing is sometimes held to determine whether there is enough evidence to go to trial. During these hearings, the Crown prosecutor and defence counsel can call and cross-examine witnesses. If the court determines that there is sufficient evidence to go to trial, a court date is set. If there is not enough evidence to proceed, the case is closed. In 2018 the federal government announced that it would introduce legislation to restrict preliminary hearings to crimes that carry a life sentence.

8. **Plea negotiation.** There are relatively few criminal trials in Canada, as most cases are resolved through plea agreements. The idea behind a plea agreement is that the accused agrees to plead guilty to lesser (or fewer) offences or to a less severe sentence on the original charge, in exchange for having no trial. When it comes to

---

prosecutorial discretion
Refers to the prosecutor's authority to decide whether to proceed with a case, withdraw a charge, enter into a plea agreement with defence counsel, or prosecute an offence as a summary or indictable offence.

justice of the peace
A person who is appointed to carry out judicial functions such as authorizing searches, reviewing the legality of a suspect's detention, and determining whether there are sufficient grounds for a criminal case to proceed to court.

judicial interim release
A form of pretrial release where defendants can be released on their promise to appear in court or by providing bail.

surety
A responsible person, such as an employer or family member, who ensures that the accused will appear in court.

sentencing, the Crown prosecutors and defence counsel often make a joint submission where they both recommend the same punishment. Judges, however, are not obliged to accept these submissions and can impose a lesser or more severe punishment. Verdun-Jones (2016) reminds us that while judges are often criticized for the sentences they impose, most of these sentences are the result of plea agreements.

Negotiating a plea also has several advantages for the justice system. Trials are expensive, and even if a prosecutor has a solid case, there is no guarantee that the accused will be found guilty beyond a reasonable doubt. This is especially true in cases where the facts are confusing, such as with the prosecution of Senator Mike Duffy on 31 charges of fraud, breach of trust, and bribery, in which he was found not guilty on all those charges after a 62-day trial (Canadian Press, 2016). Even if the prosecutor does have a solid case, juries may be reluctant to convict some defendants. Other factors might influence the Crown prosecutor to accept a plea agreement, such as a reluctance to force a witness or victim to testify.

While plea bargaining can both benefit the accused and save prosecutors from taking a case to trial, it does mean that some innocent defendants plead guilty to crimes they did not commit. Carling (2018) describes the case of a man who pleaded guilty to the charge of being unlawfully in a dwelling house, despite having been incarcerated in a city 200 kilometres away from where the crime occurred when the offence happened. The defendant felt that the judge's sentence in a plea bargain would be shorter than the months he would spend on remand awaiting a trial. The sentence was ultimately overturned.

9. **Trial.** Anyone accused of a crime for which the punishment is five years or longer has the constitutional right to a trial by jury, and the accused can choose between a trial by judge or judge and jury—although trials by jury are mandatory for serious crimes such as murder. Canadian juries are composed of 12 people who must be 18 years of age. Judges might appoint 13 or 14 jurors for a lengthy trial (so there are replacements if a juror becomes ill or otherwise no longer able to participate), but only 12 jurors can deliberate in the case.

Trials involve the presentation of evidence by the Crown prosecutor and defence counsel. The accused person is assumed to be innocent until they are found guilty beyond a reasonable doubt, and the judge (or judge and jury) decides whether the Crown has successfully made its case. Trials begin with the presentation of the Crown's case that includes evidence and testimony that supports the charges. The Crown asks questions of the witnesses in a direct examination, and once they are finished, the defence counsel can cross-examine the prosecutor's witness.

Once the prosecution has presented all of their evidence, the defence counsel presents their case and may question witnesses, who can also be cross-examined by the Crown prosecutor. After the defence is finished presenting their case, both sides summarize their cases and their reasons for recommending conviction or acquittal.

10. **The verdict.** After the defence and Crown counsel have summarized their cases, the court decides whether the Crown has met the standard of guilt beyond a reasonable doubt and will either convict or acquit the accused. In a jury trial, the judge instructs the jury on the law that applies to the case, and the jury decides on the guilt of the accused. Three results are possible: guilty, not guilty, or a hung jury. A hung jury occurs when the jury is not able to reach a unanimous decision and they believe that a decision cannot be reached. If this

happens, the judge may order a new trial (with or without a jury). If the accused is found not guilty, they are free to go and cannot be tried again on the same charge, unless the Crown prosecutor appeals the verdict and the appellate court orders a new trial.

11. **Sentencing.** The judge is responsible for the sentence, and it is common for them to order a pre-sentence investigation report. These reports are compiled by probation officers and address the offender's strengths and weaknesses, including their potential for rehabilitation and risk to the public. In cases of plea bargaining, the Crown and defence counsel will make joint sentencing recommendations, but the judge is not required to accept those recommendations when meting out the individual's sentence.

12. **Appealing the verdict or sentence.** Appeals are requests for a higher court (such as the provincial courts of appeal) to change a lower court's decision. Unlike in the United States, the severity of a sentence in Canada can be appealed to a higher court. Crown prosecutors can also appeal non-guilty verdicts. Although appeals of sentences are rare compared to the volume of criminal cases, they are more likely to occur when it is thought that the trial judge made an error on a point of law.

Although the 12 steps identified look relatively straightforward, many of the case studies that start each chapter of this book show it can take years before complicated cases are resolved. At each of those 12 points, decisions are made about the matter and whether (and how) it should proceed. In a complicated case, dozens of participants might be involved, including the police officers investigating the offence(s), civilian workers who analyze the evidence collected from a crime scene, the prosecutor and defence counsel (and their colleagues), the court personnel, and correctional

courtroom work group Composed of the judges, Crown prosecutors, defence counsel, and court clerks from a local court.

staff, including probation officers who might write pre-sentence reports for the courts. Moreover, although these stages were briefly described in this section, entire books have been written about each of these 12 elements, and there are countless subtle rules, guidelines, and laws that defy easy explanation. Last, while the formal operations of justice systems are shown in these 12 steps, there are also a set of informal and unwritten practices at each point in the process, and these minor variations in carrying out the work of the criminal justice system can have a significant impact on an individual's case.

ASSEMBLY-LINE JUSTICE

Sitting in any provincial or territorial courtroom for a few hours would help any of us understand the term *assembly-line justice*. As noted in Chapters 2 and 3, most criminal matters processed by provincial and territorial courts are relatively minor offences. For instance, impaired driving, theft, common assault, failure to comply with a judge's order, and breach of probation accounted for nearly half of all adult court cases in 2016/2017 (Miladinovic, 2019). These minor cases seldom receive any publicity and they are dealt with relatively quickly. Few of them ever result in any form of incarceration, either; as noted in Chapter 3, about two-thirds of adult criminal court cases (63 per cent) result in a finding of guilt, and probation is the most common sentence (Miladinovic, 2019, p. 3).

In Chapter 6, we looked at the adversarial nature of Canada's court system along with the fact that defendants have a right to a vigorous defence. Given that right, one might ask, why are most cases processed so quickly? In response to that question, we introduce two concepts. The first is the presence of a group of court professionals who have been called the courtroom work group. This concept, originally identified in the United States, defines these groups as being composed of judges, Crown prosecutors, and defence counsel, although they may also include probation officers and court personnel such as clerks. In most courts, these officials know each other and work together for years. As a result, they have a stake in getting along by ensuring that most minor cases move quickly through the system.

One way that the courtroom work group can maximize their efficiency is to put aside adversarial behaviour—at least for minor criminal cases—and instead make decisions about sentences based on a shared understanding of punishments for various crimes. As a result, if you watched court proceedings for a month, you would have a pretty good understanding of the average sentences for a given type of crime—this average has been called the going rate. Casper and Brereton (1984, p. 131) define the going rate as "shared beliefs about appropriate sentence levels for defendants charged with given crimes who possess similar records." Once these going rates or sentencing norms are adopted by the group, there may be resistance to change. As a result, some offenders believe that legal aid counsel are not very effective, but it is important for the work group to get along as they often work together for many years, and participation in the work group may be more important to the members than providing a vigorous defence for a one-time client. Grech (2017) carried out a study of bail hearings in Ontario courts and she observed that some of the outcomes of these hearings were the result of the informal culture in the courts of "getting along."

So, does the presence of a courtroom work group mean that a defendant cannot receive a vigorous defence? Addario (2015) commented on defence counsel who engage in overzealous lawyering and observed that, unlike what we see on television, "lawyers who fling wild accusations lose credibility. They also lose their cases. The profession shuns such lawyers, giving the worst a short shelf life in the private bar." Of course, these observations pertain to minor criminal matters; as the potential punishments increase, there is a similar increase in adversarial lawyering.

Sylvestre, Damon, Blomley, and Bellot (2015) conducted a study of bail and sentencing conditions, which included observing what occurs in courts. Their description of a Vancouver court is similar to the assembly-line justice that occurs throughout the country:

> The atmosphere is a curious mix of theatre and the mundane. The majesty of the Crown and the colorful red sash of "Your honor" combine with a highly bureaucratic and routinized process. The cases are dealt with quickly, often taking only a few minutes to process. The assembly line of the criminal justice system rolls forward, with only the occasional moment of confusion and hesitancy.
>
> The only variation is that of the alleged offenders who are brought, one by one, before the court, some in person, and others via video feed from a suburban remand centre. Most of them are charged with petty offences (stealing $159 worth of meat and cheese from a Safeway store, assaulting a common-law partner, using a fake ID, failing to report to a bail supervisor, and so on), with contextual and extenuating circumstances noted quickly by the defence lawyer (grew up in Nova Scotia, a history of abuse, a heroin addiction, a background of mental illness). Standing in a glassed-in prisoners' box, they wear bright red, loose fitting tracksuits and trainers. All are reserved and respectful. Some look worried, others simply confused, perhaps going through withdrawal. They say little, if anything, but appear as bit players in a much larger performance. The judge periodically addresses the accused person, not unkindly, explaining the process, making sure they understand the orders. (Sylvestre, Damon, Blomley, & Bellot, 2015, p. 1347)

The assembly-line approach to dispensing justice, where minor cases are quickly processed, is a defining feature of the justice system. The fact that cases are quickly processed is not a serious limitation, but as described in the previous chapter, a growing number of Canadians are appearing in court unrepresented by counsel. In addition, legal

going rate
The average sanction or punishment for a criminal offence in a local court, which can vary between different courts.

aid services are often stretched thin, which increases the likelihood of errors occurring during the legal process. Writing about justice in the United States, Bellin (2015) argues that when defendants have "tireless attorneys fighting for justice," the criminal justice system "works as it is supposed to—making the government earn every day of prison time it inflicts. But in most cases, the system is just an assembly line . . . [that] often produces a rough equivalent of justice, but just as often . . . it inflicts only pain—unnecessary suffering for defendants, victims and everyone else unfortunate enough to come into contact with the overburdened criminal courts."

Although rare in Canada, jury nullification occurs when a jury refuses to convict an obviously guilty person because the jury believes that the conviction and punishment may be worse than the crime. Murchison (2013) reports that Canadian juries have attempted to nullify the law in only three high-profile cases. It is likely that other juries have failed to convict people who were obviously guilty on less serious matters. Some minor crimes may lend themselves to nullification—for instance, obtaining a conviction for the possession of a small amount of "magic mushrooms" (psilocybin) would be difficult in a city where the university population is high—and prosecutors might be reluctant to pursue those types of cases.

jury nullification Occurs when a jury refuses to convict an individual who is obviously guilty, as the jury believes that the conviction and punishment are worse than the crime that was committed.

COURTROOM WORK GROUP

Judges

As noted earlier in this chapter, there are a number of key players in courts. Judges have the highest visibility, and the pathways to "the bench" are not easily achieved. First, potential candidates must have graduated from a law school and have practised law for at least five years, although most people appointed to the bench have more experience than that. All Canadian judges are screened by officials from the provincial or federal government, and successful judges are then appointed by a province's lieutenant-governor (for provincial court judges) or by the Governor General of Canada (for federal appointees).

With respect to provincial court judges, lawyers can apply to become a judge or they can be nominated by peers in the legal profession. Their application is reviewed by a committee that makes recommendations to the provincial or territorial minister of justice or attorney general. These recommendations are based on a review of the individual's character and include screening for disciplinary action as a lawyer, involvement in criminal or civil matters, substance abuse, and financial problems such as bankruptcies (Canadian Broadcasting Corporation, 2010a).

The process of appointing federal judges who will sit in the appeal, superior, Supreme, and Queen's Bench courts in the provinces is similar in that applications and nominations for the bench are carefully screened by members of Judicial Advisory Committees (JACs) for each province that include four representatives from the legal community (e.g., the Canadian Bar Association, the provincial law society, and nominees from the province's chief justice and attorney general), three members of the public, and one non-voting member representing Judicial Affairs. Fine (2017) says that the diversity of these JACs increased after changes were introduced in 2016, and the government has placed a priority on appointing more judges who reflect the gender and visible minority representation in Canada's population. The stakes are high for potential candidates, as the annual salary for federally appointed judges is over $300,000 per year for those serving in appeal, superior, Supreme, or Queen's Bench courts, and is higher for chief and associate chief justice positions and for judges serving in federal courts and the Supreme Court (Office of the Commissioner for Federal Judicial Affairs Canada, 2019).

The Office of the Commissioner for Federal Judicial Affairs Canada (2019) reports that as of March 2019 there were almost 1,200 federal judges sitting on the provincial or territorial superior courts (e.g., Court of Queen's Bench or Superior Court), family courts, and appellate courts. Although they are hearing cases in the provincial Supreme or Queen's Bench courts, they are called federal judges because they are appointed (and their salaries are paid) by the federal government.

Judges sitting on the Supreme Court of Canada, the Federal Court of Appeal, the Federal Court, and the Tax Court of Canada are fairly uncommon, as there are fewer than 100 of these judges in the entire country. Of the federally appointed judges, 41 per cent were women, and that proportion has been slowly increasing (Office of the Commissioner for Federal Judicial Affairs Canada, 2019).

The pathways to the Supreme Court bench are different across the globe. Canadian judges apply to a committee, and, if successful in their applications, they are appointed by the Governor General of Canada based on recommendations from the Minister of Justice; they do not have to be confirmed by politicians as they do in the United States. In many European nations, by contrast, potential judges are prepared for the bench with specialized university training, and their appointments are a bureaucratic rather than political process. Once judges are appointed to the bench, the demands on them are high. The decisions they make have a significant impact on the lives of people accused of crimes, victims, and the other members of the courtroom work group. And despite the high-profile role of judges in the courtroom, many of their duties are invisible to the observer. Cole (2016, p. 75) explains that judges "also supervise pretrial conferences, meet with lawyers, see police officers about search and other kinds of warrants, write judgments (quite lengthy at times), and stay current with a large number of areas of the law."

Crown Prosecutors

Crown prosecutors go by a number of names, including Crown counsel or Crown attorneys. Prosecutors are seen as acting independently of government, and the British Columbia Ministry of Justice (2016) observes that "they do not represent the government, the police or the victim of an offence. . . . [T]hey perform their function on behalf of the community." In that role, prosecutors are expected to be independent and to make decisions on charging individuals based on what is in the public interest without political interference. Crown counsel do, however, provide support and information to different branches of government and the police about criminal matters.

Like judges, Crown prosecutors are lawyers, although many prosecutors have less formal experience as lawyers when initially appointed to these positions. As a result, Crown prosecutors start their careers handling minor cases with some supervision and then prosecute more serious offences once they are more experienced. What is distinctive about the role of prosecutors is their ability to exercise discretion and act in the public interest.

The British Columbia Ministry of Justice (2016, p. 1) notes that Crown prosecutors' "duty is not to obtain a conviction at any cost, but to ensure that the trial process is fair to all, that evidence is presented thoroughly and accurately, and the integrity of the justice process is maintained." This approach is unlike what occurs in the United States, where chief prosecutors (or district attorneys) are elected. Pfaff (2017) argues that this electoral pressure contributes to miscarriages of justice and an over-reliance on incarceration as prosecutors must not appear weak to the electorate by being "soft on crime."

Even though there is less pressure on Canadian prosecutors to win at all costs, some of them have engaged in misconduct, and their conduct has resulted in lawsuits. In March 2018, a Supreme Court of British Columbia judge awarded a Victoria couple $1.7 million for malicious prosecution by the Canada Revenue Agency (CRA). In his written decision, Justice Punnett explained that the conduct of the CRA was "high-handed, reprehensible and malicious" and that "a government agency maliciously used the criminal justice system to pursue the plaintiffs" (*Samaroo v Canada Revenue Agency*, para. 325 and 330).

Not all prosecutions are carried out by government-paid Crown prosecutors employed by provincial or federal governments. In cases where the public might perceive that prosecutors could be biased—such as an investigation of the wrongdoing of other prosecutors—the province can appoint special prosecutors, who are experienced lawyers paid by the province to look into specific cases. Most of the issues addressed by these special prosecutors are high-visibility offences. The prosecution

special prosecutors Experienced lawyers who are appointed by a province or territory to investigate offences where government prosecutors might be perceived as biased, such as the investigation of an alleged case of prosecutorial misconduct.

THE CANADIAN PRESS/Jonathan Hayward

Although prosecutors had evidence that Ivan Henry had not committed a series of sex crimes in the 1980s, they proceeded with his prosecution, which resulted in his wrongful conviction and imprisonment for 27 years; he was released in 2010. In 2015 the Supreme Court of Canada ruled that he could sue Crown prosecutors for withholding evidence favourable to the defendant (Mulgrew, 2016). This was an important decision as it lowered the threshold for suing prosecutors for wrongful convictions. Henry received an $8-million settlement for his wrongful conviction, but he has since been sued by five women claiming he sexually assaulted them in the 1980s (Fraser, 2018).

provincial prosecutors
Officials (including police officers in some courts) who prosecute minor criminal cases (e.g., summary matters), traffic cases, and infractions of local bylaws.

paralegals
Licensed paralegals have some legal training and perform legal work for law firms and lawyers.

of minor criminal cases is also sometimes carried out by professionals other than Crown prosecutors: In rural communities throughout Canada, summary cases, traffic cases, and local bylaw matters are sometimes prosecuted by police officers rather than by Crown prosecutors, and in this role these officers are called **provincial prosecutors**.

Defence Counsel

Individuals who have been accused of committing a crime and have been detained by the police have a *Charter* right to be represented by a lawyer or counsel. Guaranteeing the right to counsel is intended to reduce injustices by increasing our due process protections. Although that right exists in

reality, in practice most suspects do not speak with their counsel until their first court appearance.

Like judges and Crown prosecutors, defence counsel are trained lawyers, although they may be supported by other professionals such as **paralegals** (licensed paralegals have basic legal training and may represent their clients in traffic courts and carry out legal research—although their roles vary between the provinces). According to the Alberta Ministry of Justice and Solicitor General (2018), defence counsel's responsibilities are to ensure:

- that full disclosure is provided by the Crown;
- that all evidence bearing on the accused's case is disclosed or produced;
- that all legal issues bearing on the accused's case are fully explored and properly adjudicated [e.g., that all evidence was collected according to constitutional standards];
- that all evidence supporting the accused's case is tendered at trial;
- that Crown witnesses are cross-examined and weaknesses in the Crown case are explored;
- that an accused is convicted only when the Crown has satisfied its constitutional burden of proving guilt beyond a reasonable doubt;
- that, where an accused is convicted, the penalty is proportionate to the gravity of the offence and to the degree of culpability of the accused;
- that all options are explored for rehabilitation and reintegration of the accused, consistent with community safety; and
- that apparent errors made in trials are properly reviewed on appeal.

The justice system expects a lot from defence counsel and there are a number of factors that make their jobs difficult. Many accused people receive services from legal aid counsel. Legal aid lawyers, however, are cutting services to some groups (e.g., refugee claimants in British Columbia), and placing restrictions on services, such as no longer funding non–legal aid lawyers for murder trials in Newfoundland and Labrador.

Support Personnel

Although judges, prosecutors, and defence counsel are considered to be the main players in the courtroom, they are supported by a number of other professionals. Court clerks, for instance, are responsible for putting together the docket (the cases scheduled for court that day) and ensuring that the cases flow through the court. Their duties might include "calling cases, reading charges, administering oaths to witnesses and interpreters, recording and maintaining exhibits, monitoring court audio recordings, recording decisions and completing court records" (British Columbia Ministry of Justice, 2018, para. 7). These clerks are supervised by court administrators. In major centres like Toronto, Montreal, or Vancouver, court administrators may be responsible for overseeing the operations of dozens of courtrooms.

The Department of Justice (2017) also provides funding for Indigenous courtwork services in the three territories and seven provinces (the exceptions are New Brunswick, Newfoundland and Labrador, and Prince Edward Island). Indigenous courtworkers play an important role in providing services to any Indigenous person accused of an offence and to their family members who are seeking help. In addition to advocating on behalf of their clients, courtworkers offer support for these individuals, provide information about the rights of people accused of crimes and what they can expect in court, provide translation services, and help their clients navigate their way through the justice system.

The arrangements for ensuring security in courtrooms vary across the nation. Sheriffs in most provinces are responsible for escorting and transporting detainees and prisoners serving sentences. The roles and responsibilities of these uniformed officials vary—in Alberta and Saskatchewan, for example, sheriffs are armed, whereas in Nova Scotia they are not. In rural and small-town courts, police officers may provide all of the court security, and in some places, the provincial police or RCMP are primarily responsible for transporting prisoners and providing courtroom security.

court clerks Responsible for ensuring that a court's paperwork and records are maintained, creating the court's docket, and sometimes administering oaths to witnesses.

docket The list of cases scheduled for court for the day.

Indigenous courtworkers Provide services to Indigenous people accused of an offence and to their family members, including advocating on the accused's behalf, providing information about the accused's rights and what to expect in court, and offering translation services.

sheriffs In many provinces, sheriffs provide court security and transport prisoners from the court to correctional facilities.

A Closer Look

Rural Courts and Access to Justice

Courts in Canada's largest cities are formal, permanent structures staffed with dozens of professionals who manage hundreds of cases. There is, however, a shortage of both lawyers and courthouses in rural areas and these two factors reduce access to justice for rural peoples. The Canadian Bar Association (2013, p. 16) says that the number of lawyers in rural areas has been decreasing as younger lawyers are reluctant to work in the countryside and their older counterparts are retiring. Baxter and Yoon's (2014) survey of rural Ontario lawyers reveals that less than 15 per cent of them specialized in criminal matters. Moreover, these researchers found that sparsely populated areas serve as an "advice desert" where lawyers are not easily available for consultation; this might have a greater impact on Indigenous peoples than their non-Indigenous counterparts. Although technology may help rural people communicate with their counsel this may be a poor substitute for face-to-face contact with them.

In addition to fewer criminal defence lawyers in the countryside, there is a declining number of rural courts. Court proceedings in small towns throughout rural Canada are often conducted only once or twice a month and are carried out in makeshift facilities that were never intended to be courts, such as First Nations band offices, Royal Canadian Legion halls, school gyms, social service boardrooms, and church buildings. A Postmedia News (2017) story about court held in a northern Saskatchewan curling rink describes the informal nature of these arrangements, as shown by the foosball tables that are pushed aside to make room

Continued

Postmedia

The community of Blaine Lake, Saskatchewan, uses the lounge above their curling rink as a courtroom once a month. Make-do facilities such as this one create several challenges for the courtroom work group, detainees, victims, witnesses, people accused of crimes, and sentenced prisoners. These facilities do not provide holding cells, meeting rooms, or prisoner's docks, reducing privacy and increasing the risk of escapes and disturbances.

for the Crown and defence counsel's tables, and the menu board hanging above the proceedings, advertising eggs for sale. These make-do facilities create a number of challenges for the courtroom work group, detainees, victims, witnesses, people accused of crimes, and sentenced prisoners. One of the foremost challenges is that most of these places lack holding cells, meeting rooms, or prisoner's docks, reducing privacy and increasing the risk of escapes or of individuals causing disturbances (although these acts are rare). Incarcerated suspects often meet with their lawyers in kitchens in community halls or unsecured offices. Defence counsel in a makeshift northern Quebec courtroom even met with their clients in bathroom stalls because there were no private meeting spaces (Fennario, 2015).

Depending on where a rural community is located, the entire courtroom work group sometimes travels together. There are, for example, 15 fly-in communities in northern Saskatchewan where court is held, and even getting from the airport (or dock if a float plane is used) to the courtroom may be an hour's drive. As a result, the work groups sometimes rely on the RCMP for transportation. In a report prepared for the Saskatchewan Provincial Court Judges Association (2011, pp. 59–60), Judge Sid Robinson observes the following:

The court party's arrival at court in an RCMP truck creates a huge optics issue. First, having the Crown, defence lawyers and judge arrive as a group can lead local citizens to believe that matters have been discussed and decided before court even starts. Secondly, arriving in a police truck can suggest that the court party is little more than an arm of the RCMP. . . . I do what I can to let people know that I do not make deals before court and that I do not work for the RCMP.

Griffiths, Murphy, and Tatz (2015, p. 7) point out that the police in remote communities may be the only permanent representatives of the justice system.

Arranging court dates in rural or remote locations requires court staff to make flight arrangements, securing accommodations for the judge and court workers and a secure place for the prisoners with the police, as not all communities have cells to hold them overnight. Despite the fact these temporary courts offer less than ideal arrangements, they are important for providing rural people with access to the justice system. Travelling to urban courts is expensive and a lack of public transportation increases the possibility of missing a court date, which could result in failure to appear charges.

Despite the advantages of rural courts, provincial governments in New Brunswick, Newfoundland and Labrador, Nova Scotia, Ontario, and Saskatchewan have closed rural satellite courts or courthouses between 2015 and 2017. These cuts are part of a long-term reduction of rural services. Although all governments must spend taxpayer dollars carefully, decreasing access to the justice system may be a significant barrier to justice for rural people.

A Closer Look

Bail: The Decision to Detain or Release

Many minor crimes are dealt with a promise of the accused person to appear in court; they are only temporarily detained and then released. When a person is arrested, a police officer gives them an appearance notice, requiring them to appear in court on a specified date. An appearance notice is given to a person before they have been formally charged with an offence. Once a person is charged, a summons can be sent to the accused by mail or delivered in person. Either the appearance notice or a summons can require the individual to appear at the police station to have their fingerprints and pictures taken prior to their court appearance. If they fail to appear at the police station to have their fingerprints taken or do not appear in court to answer to the charges against them, a warrant for their arrest can be issued.

But what about people accused of more serious offences? On any given day there are about 15,000 inmates held on remand and most of them have not been convicted of a crime (a small proportion of them have been found guilty and are awaiting sentencing). One important question is: why they are held in custody? First, if a police officer wants to detain an arrestee, they must appear before a judge or justice of the peace within 24 hours for a hearing and the Crown must justify the reasons for keeping the accused in custody. According to the British Columbia Prosecution Service (2017, p. 2) the three grounds for detaining an individual are set out in the *Criminal Code*:

- To ensure the accused person attends court;
- To ensure the safety or protection of the public, including any victims or witnesses; or,
- To maintain confidence in the administration of justice.

In cases where someone is accused of committing a relatively minor crime, bail hearings tend to be relatively short proceedings, although if the matter is adjourned because the judge requires more information, they will remain in custody until that information is provided, which could be several days or longer. For serious or multiple offences, a bail hearing could last several days; very serious or complicated cases can take longer. In her study of an Ontario court, Grech (2017, p. 145) found that the Crown challenged the release of the accused in about one-quarter of the hearings.

The individual's guilt is not assessed in bail hearings; the only decision considered is whether

Continued

the accused can be released from custody. Allowing them to reside in the community is important, as detaining them could have adverse impacts on their employment, education, and family relationships, especially when a trial date is set months or even years into the future. In the *R v Antic* (2017, para. 2) case the Supreme Court of Canada observes that:

> The right not to be denied reasonable bail without just cause is an essential element of an enlightened criminal justice system. It entrenches the effect of the presumption of innocence at the pre-trial stage of the criminal trial process and safeguards the liberty of accused persons.

In deciding whether to release the accused until their trial, the judge has to weigh the risks to the public against their freedoms. If they are detained, they will be placed on remand in a provincial correctional centre. Conditions in remand units are generally harsh, and the individual may have no access to rehabilitative programs while in custody (as they have not been convicted of an offence). As a result, some people will plead guilty to avoid a lengthy stay in remand prior to a trial (Canadian Civil Liberties Association, 2014).

Before an accused person is released into the community, the judge might require them to show the court a bail plan, where the Crown's concerns, such as a substance abuse problem or a lack of community supports, are addressed. Some accused will be required to pay an amount of money called bail to guarantee they will appear in court. The Canadian Civil Liberties Association (2014, p. 102) reports that the average amount of bail in five provinces and Yukon was about $2,700, although the accused is only required to pay if they fail to appear in court. The judge may also require that the accused have a surety, who is a person willing to supervise them and report to the police or court if the accused is not abiding by conditions of their release.

Although there are no national statistics that describe bail conditions, Malakieh (2018, p. 10) reports that the average person on bail in Alberta had eight bail conditions, while those on bail in British Columbia had an average of seven conditions. The most common bail conditions were to report to one's supervisor, reside at a place approved by the court, and keep the peace and be of good behaviour (Malakieh, 2018). In her Ontario study of bail conditions, Grech (2017, p. 156) was told by a defence counsel that the accused would agree to almost any conditions to be released from custody. Does this set the individual up to fail? If the accused violates their bail conditions, they are returned to court, their bail may be revoked, and they may be remanded into custody until their trial.

SPECIALIZED COURTS

specialized courts Courts that specialize in working with distinctive groups of offenders, including people with mental illnesses or individuals convicted of specific offences such as domestic violence. Also called *problem-solving courts* or *therapeutic courts*.

Traditional provincial courts have a generalist orientation, which means that they handle a wide range of cases from wilful damage to murder. Most of these cases are processed efficiently, but sometimes the offenders who pass through these courts commit further crimes. Throughout this book, we have talked about the fact that a large number of individuals in the criminal justice system have some type of special need, such as substance abuse problems or mental illnesses, or have been convicted of crimes (such as domestic violence) where a specialized type of intervention might be beneficial and might hold them more accountable. Some

offenders, and particularly those with mental illnesses, are caught in a revolving door between the criminal justice system, community mental health services, and social services (Michalski, 2017). People with mental health problems, for example, are routinely arrested for very minor offences, brought before the courts, and then released back to the community—and some appear before the local courts dozens of times.

In response to these special-needs offenders, a growing number of specialized courts—also called problem-solving courts or therapeutic courts—are being established across Canada. Drug treatment courts, for example, were first introduced in Toronto in the 1990s, and Nova Scotia has even introduced a specialized court in Dartmouth to manage the challenges of offenders with opioid addictions (Irish, 2017).

Specialized courts enable the members of the courtroom work group to develop an expertise in dealing with offenders, making their interactions with these individuals more effective. Often the prosecutors and defence counsel work with probation officers and other team members who have specialized training—such as addictions counsellors, mental health specialists, and other helping professionals. The individuals before these courts are often on probation; Hannah-Moffat and Maurutto (2012) note that "participation in these programmes gives offenders the opportunity to avoid jail" (p. 214), and in "less serious cases, defendants are told that if they successfully complete the programme, the charges may be withdrawn, or they will get an absolute or conditional discharge" (p. 205).

Specialized courts for adults originated in the 1980s in the United States, and today there are thousands of problem-solving courts in America (National Institute of Justice, 2017; Strong, Rantala, & Kyckelhahn, 2016). By developing an expertise in either offenders or distinctive offences (such as domestic violence), it is thought that the courts can provide a more effective service. The National Institute of Justice (2017) identifies the following advantages of specialized courts:

- offender screening and assessment of risks, needs, and responsivity;
- offender monitoring—such as drug testing—and supervision;
- graduated sanctions and incentives; and
- treatment and rehabilitative services.

Altogether, specialized courts have a strong rehabilitative outlook, but they are also supported by the coercive power of the justice system. As noted by the National Institute of Justice (2017), offenders' risks and needs are identified, and treatment plans are developed to address their unmet needs. Offenders may be brought before the court on a regular basis, such as every month, so the judge can monitor their progress. In specialized courts,

Julia Manoukian

Nova Scotia's Mental Health Court. Canadian court officials overwhelmingly reported that problem-solving courts enhanced the quality of life for participants, aided in their mental health or addiction recoveries, and reduced their criminal justice contacts after they finished the program.

the members of the courtroom work group act in a non-adversarial manner while acknowledging a number of shared goals. These interventions, however, can only work if they are supported by community-based services, which can be expensive but are a fraction of the $120,571 it cost to hold a federal prisoner in 2017/2018 (Malakieh, 2019).

We know that people with mental health or addiction problems will occasionally relapse (or reoffend), and specialized courts respond with a series of graduated sanctions, which means that sanctions or punishments start with the least restrictive response and then get more severe if the offender continues to engage in unacceptable behaviour. What makes a specialized court system different than referring an offender to an external treatment program (which is the norm for probationers) is that the specialized court is in a better position to use coercive power to ensure the individual is complying with their treatment. Some people are uncomfortable with using coercion to force offenders to comply with treatment. Lutze (2014, p. xi),

graduated sanctions Punishments that start with the least restrictive response and then become more severe if the individual continues to reoffend.

A COMPARATIVE VIEW

Cross-National Differences in the Rule of Law

The rule of law goes beyond what judges and lawyers do in their work. The World Justice Project (2019, p. 4) identifies four principles underlying the rule of law:

1. The government and its officials and agents as well as individuals and private entities are accountable under the law.
2. The laws are clear, publicized, stable, and just; are applied evenly; and protect fundamental rights.
3. The process by which the laws are enacted, administered, and enforced is accessible, fair, and efficient.
4. Justice is delivered . . . by competent, ethical, and independent representatives and neutrals who are of sufficient number, have adequate resources, and reflect the makeup of the communities they serve.

We could shorten all of these statements into one simple question: Can an ordinary person receive decent, fair, and respectful treatment from government officials without fear or the use of bribery?

All cross-national comparisons can be tricky to make, as richer, developed nations have more options to provide health, educational, social service, or criminal justice interventions than do poorer nations. The World Justice Project (2019) developed an index that classifies the rule of law based on nine different themes. These indices can be useful as they give us a type of "report card" that enables government officials to identify and overcome weaknesses while building on strengths. Figure 7.2 shows that Germany has the highest level of rule of law among the G7 nations, but Canada is tied for the second-highest value (higher values are associated with more effective and less corrupt systems). So, is there room for improvement? The highest values for criminal justice go to the Nordic countries—Denmark, Norway, Sweden, and Finland received the top four global rankings and all had values of 0.85 or higher. As a result, while Canada's index (0.81) is consistent with the other G7 nations, there is still a need for improvement before Canada can be the highest-ranked criminal justice system.

writing about probation and parole officers, observes that "community corrections is a unique profession that possesses the coercive power of the criminal justice system to manage offenders' risk and garners the power of the helping professions to address offenders' needs."

Most specialized courts in Canada are related to domestic violence or mental health issues, although other types exist or are being developed. A Saskatchewan mental health court, for instance, is developing separate arrangements for offenders afflicted with fetal alcohol spectrum disorder (FASD). FASD is caused by exposure of the fetus to alcohol during the mother's pregnancy, and people suffering from FASD have problems with their memory, learning, attention, and interpersonal communication, as well as physical ailments. Medwick and Chudley (2018, p. vii) estimate that about 1 per cent of the Canadian population is affected by FASD and that these people have problems with "homelessness, substance abuse, interactions with the law, unemployment, mental illness, school drop-out, and breakdown of the family unit." Although some individuals with FASD have appeared before mental health courts, their needs are quite distinctive, and in some places with a high prevalence of these people, specialized court-based interventions may be required.

In the United States, specialized courts are more prevalent. Some cities have introduced courts to tackle the problems of gun violence (gun courts), driving while intoxicated, and prostitution. In addition, a number of specialized offender groups have also been targeted by specialized courts, including gamblers, people experiencing homelessness, and most recently, military veterans. In large cities such as Toronto, Montreal, and Vancouver, there may be enough offenders to warrant these specialized courts, but in smaller cities and towns the number of these cases is so low that these strategies might not be worthwhile. This may be another example of how rural and

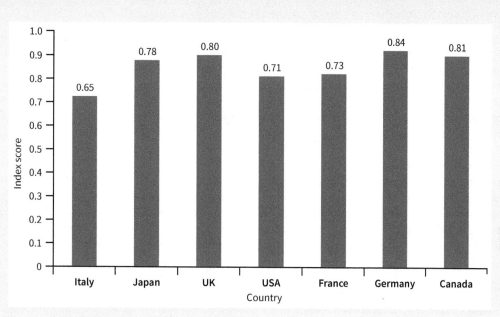

FIGURE 7.2 Rule of Law Index, 2019, G7 Nations
Adapted from the World Justice Project (2019)

small-town residents cannot benefit from services taken for granted by their urban counterparts.

Some of the strongest evaluations of specialized courts have been published by the Washington State Institute for Public Policy (2018), which found that every dollar spent on drug courts provided a $2.83 benefit to participants and taxpayers (including reduced crime). There was an even stronger benefit when individuals appeared in mental health courts, with a $5.62 benefit to taxpayers for every dollar spent on these courts.

In order to receive the best return on our investments in these courts, however, the specialized services must match the needs of the clients, and an evaluation of a Toronto youth mental health court suggests this does not always occur (Davis, Peterson-Badali, Weagant, & Skilling, 2015). Moreover, in their study of a Vancouver drug treatment court, Somers, Rezansoff, and Moniruzzaman (2014) found that the interventions of the court were more successful with women and Indigenous peoples.

Despite those limitations, these courts appear to offer very promising benefits in terms of cost savings. There is still a need to carry out long-term evaluations to determine the most effective treatment approaches and the types of offenders who are most likely to benefit from these interventions.

Specialized courts attempt to balance the coercive powers of the justice system with rehabilitation and treatment opportunities that match the needs of offenders. The challenge of balancing those goals is that it is easy to hold offenders accountable and impose punishments on those who fail to abide by their probation conditions, but in some cases there are not enough community resources to support the individual's rehabilitation. Writing about courts in Nunavut, Ferrazzi and Krupa (2016) point out that it may be difficult to balance treatment and criminal justice and that there may be some concerns around a lack of due process protections. Hannah-Moffat and Maurutto (2012) suggest that Ontario prosecutors pressured

Race, Class, and Gender

Representative Juries, Justice, and the Colten Boushie Case

On May 21, 2015, the Supreme Court decided in *R v Kokopenace* that the manslaughter conviction of an Indigenous man from Ontario should stand, even though there was a lack of Indigenous people on the jury. Like other issues related to the outcomes of marginalized people in the justice system, there are no easy answers to the issue of **representativeness**. On the one hand, individuals have a *Charter* right to a representative jury. On the other hand, some people have been critical of the way that Ontario prepares its **jury rolls** (lists from which potential jurors are drawn), and they maintain that the province does not do enough to ensure representative juries. So, what is a representative jury? According to the Supreme Court, "what is required is a representative cross-section of society, honestly and fairly chosen," and in terms of the jury roll, "representativeness focuses on the process used to compile it, not its ultimate composition" (*R v Kokopenace*, 2015).

The Supreme Court observed that "requiring a jury roll to proportionately represent the different religions,

representativeness A concept related to the composition of juries and whether they reflect the demographic characteristics of a community.

jury rolls The lists from which a jury is drawn; in Ontario, lists of potential jurors are compiled using the most recent voters' lists and the band lists from First Nations.

races, cultures, or individual characteristics of eligible jurors would create a number of insurmountable problems. There are an infinite number of characteristics that one might consider should be represented, and even if a perfect source list were used, it would be impossible to create a jury roll that fully represents them" (*R v Kokopenace*, 2015).

The issue of representative juries was again raised with the case of Gerald Stanley, who was acquitted of the second-degree murder of Colten Boushie, a 22-year-old Indigenous man from Saskatchewan. One of the issues raised after Stanley's acquittal was that no Indigenous people served on this jury. Kent Roach (2018, para. 8), a prominent University of Toronto law professor, said that the jury selection showed the "alienation and exclusion of Indigenous people from the justice system." In order to remedy this shortcoming, Roach recommended that the *Criminal Code* be amended to make jury panels more representative, enabling those who have served more than a year in prison to serve on juries (they are currently excluded) and abolishing peremptory challenges—where lawyers can exclude some potential jurors. The federal government has introduced legislation "changing the jury selection process to foster more representative juries" (Senate of Canada, 2019, para. 2).

some defendants into pleas of guilt even when the Crown had weak cases that might never have gone to trial. Furthermore, in their analysis of six Canadian specialty courts, Quirouette, Hannah-Moffat, and Maurutto (2015) found that some specialized courts required homeless offenders to maintain residence in shelters, but failing to abide by the rules of those shelters sometimes resulted in these individuals breaching the conditions of probation, which put them at risk of incurring more criminal charges. As a result, supporters of the due process perspective may approach the issue of specialized courts with both optimism and skepticism. These

examples again show that our interventions can have unanticipated or unintended results.

Critics argue that specialized courts coerce offenders into treatment, and they question whether such programs have the same impact as voluntary treatment. Supporters of the crime control approach, by contrast, do not share the same concerns about coerced treatment, citing the many people who engage in addictive behaviours who might not participate in treatment if they were not afraid of being incarcerated. The promise of a discharge is a further motivation to comply with the expectations of the court.

MYTH OR REALITY

The Independence of Prosecutorial Discretion and the Robert Latimer Case

Crown attorneys use their discretion to decide whether they will prosecute a person accused of a crime. They are likely to proceed if there is a reasonable likelihood of conviction and if bringing the matter before a court is in the public's interest (Manitoba Justice, 2018). They also have discretion about the charges that can be filed, and as noted in Chapter 2, a homicide can be prosecuted as an act of manslaughter, first-degree murder, or second-degree murder. The Department of Justice and Public Safety of Newfoundland and Labrador (2007, p. 5-1) observes that "considerable care must be taken in each case to ensure that the right decision is made. A wrong decision to prosecute and, conversely, a wrong decision not to prosecute, both tend to undermine the confidence of the community in the criminal justice system." Are prosecutors truly independent, or is the decision to prosecute—and the decision about which offence to pursue in court—guided by public and political opinions?

In most cases, the decisions to prosecute serious crimes are non-controversial, but the Robert Latimer case was controversial as it involved an otherwise loving father who murdered his profoundly disabled 12-year-old daughter, Tracy, in 1993, because he wanted to end her suffering. Tracy suffered from brain damage that occurred at birth: she was a quadriplegic who had undergone a number of painful surgeries (Canadian Broadcasting Corporation, 2010b). Latimer claimed that "surgery performed on Tracy a year before she died had turned her from 'a happy little girl' into a victim of constant agony. Tracy could not walk, talk or feed herself. At her death she weighed less than 40 pounds," and Tracy was scheduled to undergo additional surgeries "to stabilize metal rods they had inserted into her back to help her stay upright" (DePalma, 1997). Latimer killed his daughter by running a hose from the exhaust pipe to the cab of his vehicle, and she died of carbon monoxide poisoning while the other family members were at church. Tracy's murder was seen by many as an act of mercy or love, and not an act of malice, and a 1999 Ipsos Reid poll found that about three-quarters of Canadian adults believed that Latimer killed his daughter out of compassion.

But advocates for the disabled thought otherwise, and DePalma (1997) notes that "handicapped people and the organizations representing them say that anything less than a stiff sentence would send a message that the lives of severely disabled people are worth less than the lives of everyone else." Despite the fact that public opinion was overwhelmingly supportive of Latimer, he was charged with first-degree murder and was ultimately convicted of second-degree murder, although that conviction was overturned by the Supreme Court of Canada because the prosecutor had engaged in misconduct. A second trial also resulted in a conviction of second-degree murder. The jury asked that Latimer's sentence be mitigated, and a two-year sentence was imposed (one year behind bars with the remainder served in community supervision) rather than the 10-year mandatory minimum sentence. The Saskatchewan Court of Appeal reinstated the mandatory sentence. Latimer appealed that decision and the Supreme Court of Canada upheld the 10-year sentence.

The homicide occurred in 1993, and Latimer started serving his prison sentence in 2001. He was only granted day parole in 2008 and full parole in 2010. Some people believe that Latimer was slow to be released because he did not express a proper amount of remorse for his actions, and some considered him to be a threat to public safety. In a 2017 interview, Latimer said that "what I did was right, and the government and the authorities can't understand that. Or the fact that what they've done is wrong—they can't understand that" (MacPherson, 2017).

It is said that "hard cases make bad laws," or in other words, crimes that rarely occur and are the result of very unusual circumstances do not always fit neatly in the *Criminal Code* when it comes to questions of what punishments should be imposed. While we should not design laws around these rare acts, our criminal laws should also allow the exercise of discretion. Writing about the Latimer case, Roach (2017, p. 25) observes that "the criminal law will lose legitimacy if there are too many cases where there is a wide divergence from the public's verdict and those produced by state law." By reviewing the Latimer case, we can see problems with the definitions of crime, punishment for an act considered by most of us to be an act of mercy, and the struggles of one person against the power of the justice system for doing something he considered the "right thing to do." On the other hand, we also understand the position of people with disabilities who consider Latimer to be an unrepentant killer.

Serving on a jury is an important civic duty and any adult can be called to serve on one, although individuals with some criminal records are generally excluded, as are police officers. In addition to the demands on their time, there is a growing recognition that jurors can be exposed to disturbing evidence, such as pictures of victims, that can be traumatizing. Jurors on the Paul Bernardo trial in the 1990s, for example, were traumatized after viewing videos of his victims being tortured (Previl, 2019).

SUMMARY

Most of our knowledge about what occurs in Canadian courts comes from the entertainment media, as few of us spend time in courtrooms. This is both a good thing and a bad thing. First, an hour's exposure to a provincial or territorial court would reveal that most crime is minor and that most cases are handled in a relatively low-key manner. The facts are reported, sentences are imposed, and there is very little of the drama portrayed in US television programs. It is important to remember that there were almost 360,000 adult court cases in Canada in 2016/2017, and nearly half were for impaired driving, theft, common assault, failure to comply with an order, or breach of probation (and a case could involve more than one criminal charge) (Miladinovic, 2019). These are hardly the types of crimes that would rate an episode of *Law & Order*. McKnight (2016, p. 28) has written about media misrepresentations of crime in Canada and observes that "the picture of crime painted by the media is . . . distorted."

This chapter shows that the personnel employed within Canada's court systems attempt to balance the goals of due process and crime control approaches. It is possible that the crime control model, with its focus on swift resolution of minor cases (the assembly line), may be the norm for minor offences in provincial and territorial courts, but as the potential punishments for the accused become more severe, there is an increased need to ensure that due process protections are respected, and proceedings become more adversarial.

The description of court organization and personnel presented in this chapter suggests that there are subtle differences in the way that Canada's justice system is administered across the country. There are, for example, hundreds of provincial courts throughout the nation, and although their actions are guided by the *Charter* and the *Criminal Code*, there is some variation in how they operate. These differences may originate in the courtroom work groups, the culture of each court, and to some extent where the court is located. Spending an afternoon in a downtown Toronto court will be a totally different experience than spending a few hours in the Wunnumin Lake court, which is held in a school gym in the Northern Ontario First Nation. One question that comes from acknowledging those differences is whether some Canadians accused or convicted of crimes are at a disadvantage because of where they appeared in court.

One way we can increase the effectiveness of court systems is to provide specialized services for difficult-to-manage groups of offenders or for those who commit crimes that may require a more sophisticated response than those offered by regular courts. As a result, there is growing interest in establishing specialized courts for offenders convicted of crimes such as domestic violence or for individuals who have specialized needs such as people with mental illnesses. These strategies are in response to a "revolving door" situation where some offenders are arrested, required to appear in court, punished, and then released only to reoffend again. Evaluations have shown that tackling the underlying problems or providing resources to respond to such offenders' unmet needs in specialized courts are cost-effective approaches (Washington State Institute for Public Policy, 2018). While these efforts are commendable and a step in the right direction, we have to be mindful that people living in the countryside might not be able to access these services, and Canadian researchers have been critical that these courts may have unanticipated consequences such as increasing the punishment for some participants (Quirouette, Hannah-Moffat, & Maurutto, 2015). Like so many other issues raised in this book, there are no easy answers.

Career SNAPSHOT

Crown Prosecutor

Prosecutors play a vitally important role in the justice system, and one significant difference between Canadian and US systems is the non-political role of the prosecutor in Canada. The emphasis of the justice system in Canada is to seek the truth and not a conviction at all costs, and that creates a justice system less likely to result in wrongful convictions as a result of misconduct (Campbell & Denov, 2016). Like other professions within the justice system, there is tremendous diversity in the roles that prosecutors can play, including working for the federal or provincial governments, prosecuting relatively minor cases in a general caseload, or specializing in the prosecution of serious violent offenders.

Profile

Name: Omar Siddiqui
Job Title: Crown Counsel, Manitoba Justice
Employed in current job since: 2004 (as a lawyer); 2013 (as provincial prosecutor)
Present Location: Winnipeg, Manitoba

Continued

Education: BA (Honours), University of Winnipeg; MA, McGill University; LLB, Osgoode Hall Law School

Background

I decided to pursue a career as a lawyer following the advice given to me from an elder scholar from my community. He impressed upon me that if I was interested in making a change in the underlying structures of society, law was the discipline I should consider. From that moment, I was guided by that advice. I ended up in law school and ultimately prosecuting on behalf of both the federal and provincial Crown.

Work Experience

I articled in family law at Legal Aid Manitoba and then did some policy work before joining the federal Department of Justice as a civil lawyer in the area of refugee and immigration law. After two years, I moved to the criminal section of the Department of Justice (now the Public Prosecution Service of Canada) and prosecuted drug offences under the *Controlled Drug and Substances Act* (crimes ranging from simple possession to major drug trafficking) for approximately seven years, before starting with Manitoba Justice prosecuting general *Criminal Code* offences from robberies to sex assaults and murders. I have found there is no other area of law that so directly and frequently engages *Charter* rights and requires practitioners to engage in analysis, articulation, and ultimately in-depth interpretation of some of our most cherished rights such as the right to silence and the right not to arbitrarily be detained or imprisoned. Criminal law is often the forum through which we directly engage in conversations related to our commitment to liberty and our willingness to allow the state to intrude on that freedom.

There are a number of challenges in working as a federal or provincial prosecutor. In addition to the usual issues of large caseloads, work-related stress, and pressure, I am finding that my role as a Crown prosecutor is increasingly critical in addressing the accessibility of the legal system particularly to victims. It is critical for Crowns to be trauma-informed, culturally competent, and broadly aware of how our decisions impact real people and real communities, how important it is to involve and keep victims and families informed in the process, and how crucial it is to work toward the creation of a safe environment for victims within the justice system.

With respect to career experiences that stand out in my mind, I recall walking back from court in my robes and being asked by a member of the public from an identifiably and historically socially disadvantaged community, "Are you on their side or our side?" That impressed upon me how many bridges people working within the justice system need to build with the citizenry.

I also recall my first jury trial on a particularly gruesome set of facts involving death and dismemberment. It started with a man who was looking through dumpsters and found a pair of human arms—the hands were fingerprinted, which led to an address, which led to a man opening the door to the police with the words, "I got into a fight with my roommate." We argued for a conviction on second-degree murder, challenging the accused on his version of events and the gruesome way the victim's body was treated. He stuck to his story that the death was not intended, and ultimately a jury of 12 citizens believed him and found him not guilty of murder but guilty of manslaughter. It is admirable (though some might disagree) how much faith we put in the adversarial process: that two sides arguing it out will present two versions that ordinary citizens must decide upon, and what they decide will be the "truth" that forever impacts people's lives.

In terms of my most rewarding experience, I realize after over a decade of practice that I am uniquely positioned to assist the public (through teaching, speaking, engaging, or just conversing) and, in particular, to help historically disadvantaged communities, some of which are overrepresented in the justice system. The Constitution and our legal principles, if applied progressively, can be an instrument through which we can realize a better and more just world. There was a time when this was not the case and the highest offices in our land justified cultural genocide and mass confiscation of liberty. The law need not be used anymore to reinforce the patterns of our past history; rather, it should be a mechanism for reconciliation and justice.

Advice to Students

Law school is increasingly competitive, so I recommend that students take whatever undergraduate courses they excel at to ensure top marks. If you get admitted into law school and it takes a toll on your mind and soul like it did mine, know that that is normal, that it may not be an easy place to be or to think outside the box, but that ultimately you will meet students and teachers who are committed, progressive, and supportive and who will form part of your network as you push toward your graduation. After law school, it is often hard to obtain a job, but there are support networks available. If you befriend a lawyer whom you respect and admire, and whose reputation in the Bar is sound, know that those personal connections are important in this profession. But every jurisdiction has its unique characteristics, and every legal association has its own culture.

REVIEW QUESTIONS

1. Explain why the term *assembly line* could be used to describe the work of the provincial courts. Is that approach more consistent with the crime control or due process model?
2. Describe why it is in the best interests of the courtroom work group to establish a going rate for minor offences.
3. Why is it important that the poor have access to state-funded counsel such as legal aid?
4. What are some advantages of developing specialized courts?
5. Describe how a case flows through the justice system, prior to trial and afterward, and explain the importance of the accused proceeding through the system in a sequential manner.

DISCUSSION QUESTIONS

1. Some judges seem to resist imposing severe sanctions on serious wrongdoers, which is inconsistent with the desires of ordinary Canadians. Do you think that the judiciary is out of touch with the public?
2. Rural suspects and offenders may be disadvantaged for a number of reasons, including that prosecutions might be carried out by police officers (who might lack the objectivity of full-time prosecutors), legal aid services might be provided by travelling lawyers, and few rehabilitative services might be available in the countryside. How can governments overcome those barriers to justice?
3. Discuss the pros and cons of using coercion in specialized courts to ensure that offenders fully participate in rehabilitative programs.
4. Define the rule of law and provide a few reasons why some nations would prioritize this principle.
5. What are the advantages and disadvantages of having representative juries? Should the additional costs of making juries more representative be considered when thinking about just and fair outcomes for accused people at trial?

INTERNET SITE

"Why I Went to Law School" is a campaign that features 100 stories from Ontario lawyers about why they decided to go to law school. Their accounts provide examples of individuals fighting injustice and racism, and advocating for victims of crime.

www.oba.org/News-Media/News/2014/June2014/Why-I-Went-to-Law-School-campaign-update-First-100

CASES CITED

R v Antic, 2017 SCC 27, [2017] 1 SCR 509
R v Kokopenace, 2015 SCC 28, [2015] 2 SCR 398

Samaroo v Canada Revenue Agency, 2018 BCSC 324

▲ Dellen Millard, illustrated at left in this sketch showing his sentencing hearing, was sentenced to three counts of first-degree murder for the killings of Laura Babcock, Tim Bosma, and his father, Wayne Millard, and he will not be eligible to apply for parole for 75 years (Faris, 2019). Unlike in the United States, consecutive life sentences have only been used in Canada since 2011. Do you think harsher sentences discourage potential criminals? (Photo Credit: The Canadian Press/Alexandra Newbould)

8 Sentencing

LEARNING OUTLINE

After reading this chapter, you will be able to

- Describe different types of sentencing options for "getting tough" on offenders, including indeterminate sentences, truth in sentencing, and mandatory minimum sentences
- Describe different community-based and custodial sentencing options
- Provide some possible reasons for the interprovincial variation in sentencing
- Explain why aggravating and mitigating factors are considered at sentencing
- Explain why pre-sentence reports are completed, and discuss the importance of *Gladue* reports for Indigenous offenders

What is the Correct Punishment for Bad Driving Causing Serious Injuries or Death?

In June 2017, 20-year-old Felix Laframboise fell asleep driving on Ontario's Highway 401 and he rear-ended a van. The van crashed; the driver, Kristine Cadieux, was killed and her husband Robert "suffered a fractured vertebra, a concussion, whiplash and broken ribs. The injuries from the crash have left him unable to work" (Burgess, 2018, para. 24). Three children were left without a mother and the business the husband and wife operated has struggled since the crash.

The police investigation revealed that Laframboise was not intoxicated, nor was he texting or committing any other crime. As a result, he was charged with careless driving, which is not a criminal offence; punishments for violations of this regulation are spelled out by Ontario's *Highway Traffic Act*. On January 9, 2018, Laframboise appeared in court and pleaded guilty, accepting responsibility for falling asleep and expressing his apologies to the family for their loss. As this was not a criminal matter, the case was prosecuted by an articling law student instead of a regular Crown prosecutor, and her ability to prosecute the case was hampered as the proceedings were conducted in French and she could not speak the language, nor did she have an interpreter. The justice of the peace presiding over the court sentenced Laframboise to a $2,000 fine (the maximum amount for careless driving), and the matter was closed.

Cadieux's family was upset with the outcome of the case; they had not been aware that Laframboise would be sentenced on January 9, 2018, so they were not in court, nor did they have the opportunity to submit a victim impact statement to the court. There were also criticisms that a student was prosecuting the case without the proper supervision of a Crown prosecutor, and that the student and a paralegal who was helping her did not have the file with them when the case was before the court (Egan, 2018a). The Crown appealed the sentence, and on March 27, 2018, Laframboise received an 18-month licence suspension. As Cadieux's family was present at this hearing, they were able to present their victim impact statement and Laframboise was able to apologize and express his remorse directly to the family. Egan (2018b) reports that Robert Cadieux was upset with the police investigation and how the case seemed to have fallen through the cracks in the criminal justice system.

CRITICAL QUESTIONS

1. After this incident, Ontario introduced laws to enhance punishments for careless driving causing death or bodily harm and the maximum penalties increased to two years of incarceration, $50,000 in fines, a five-year licence suspension, and six demerit points. Do you think this would deter careless or fatigued driving? Why or why not?

2. What is the correct punishment for a driver who falls asleep and unintentionally causes the death of another individual? Should all drivers who cause an accident resulting in death be charged with dangerous driving? Would your answer change if your family member was harmed in such an accident, or if it was you who was driving?

3. Canada has two official languages and dozens of other languages are spoken, but how can the criminal justice system ensure that everybody understands what is happening in court proceedings? Whose responsibility should it be?

INTRODUCTION

Few of us spend much time in courtrooms, so our ideas about sentencing are often shaped by what happens on television programs or in films: judges impose a sentence on an individual and the matter might take only a minute or two. When it comes to what happens in real courtrooms, however, the process is more involved and time-consuming. As the seriousness of the offence increases, so does the time it takes to consider an appropriate sentence. In the case of violent offences, a number of reports and assessments may be ordered, which may take several months to complete. The long wait until a sentence is imposed can be tough on everybody involved in the process—victims want the case resolved so they can get on with their lives, and an individual accused of committing a crime could be remanded in custody for months

Justice Denise Bellamy in her office. There is a lot at stake when an individual is sentenced; the judge must carefully consider the risks to the public as well as the individual's likelihood of rehabilitation when considering options such as imprisonment.

until their case is decided and, if they are found guilty, a sentence is imposed.

Like other legal issues described in the previous chapters, sentencing is a complex process that is guided by the *Charter* and the *Criminal Code*, and it involves a large number of justice system personnel as well as the victim(s) and the offender. Why should the act of sentencing be so complicated? Perhaps the best answer to that question is that all of us have a stake in ensuring that sentences for wrongdoing are appropriate and that they protect public safety, maintain confidence in the justice system, and provide fair outcomes for the victims and the offenders. With so many stakeholders, however, it is rare that everybody will walk away happy after a sentence is imposed.

Judges impose sentences, and although over 90 per cent of criminal cases are resolved through plea bargaining, their workloads are demanding. In 2015/2016, provincial court judges in British Columbia were given an average of 961 new cases a year (Provincial Court of British Columbia, 2018, p. 32). Over one-half (56 per cent) of these new cases were for criminal matters (both adult and youth) while the remainder involved small claims, child protection, and family matters. The Provincial Court of British Columbia (2018) reports that the number of adult criminal cases is increasing by 2 to 3 per cent per year and that judges were dealing with increasingly complex and serious criminal matters. While judicial workloads have eased somewhat in recent years, an average adult defendant still has to wait over six months for a two-day trial, and nine months for a trial lasting five or more days (Provincial Court of British Columbia, 2018, p. 45).

In addition to being busy, judges are responsible for work that is stressful and carried out in public. A judge remarked that "it is the only job where everything you do is public. The hearings are public, the judgment is public [and] the judges are publishing their errors" (Wilson, 2012). Cole (2016, p. 87) describes the court as "usually intense, sometimes tragic, always human, and endlessly fascinating." The *Criminal Code* provides judges with considerable discretion at sentencing, and even commonplace offences, such as the break and enter of a residence, can result in a sentence of life imprisonment—although sentences imposed for this crime are seldom very severe. Maxwell (2017, p. 20) reports that of the almost 6,000 adults who pleaded guilty to break-and-enter offences in 2014/2015, only 60 per cent were sentenced to custody, and the median sentence length was 120 days.

In this chapter, we take a closer look at sentencing and the various options that judges might consider. The section on tough sentences describes both the pros and cons of getting tough on crime. In addition, we will examine different factors that are considered at sentencing, and we will examine the interprovincial variation in custody sentences and the fact that some provinces do punish more harshly.

SENTENCING OPTIONS

Canadian judges have a number of sentencing options. In analyzing adults convicted in Canada in 2016/2017, Miladinovic (2019) found that sentences were resolved in a variety of ways, which are listed in Table 8.1. The most common adult sentences are probation, custody, and fines, as well as "other" sentencing options, which are described later in this section.

Probation

Probation is the most commonly imposed sentence in Canada, and it refers to the release of the individual to the community under the supervision of

TABLE 8.1 Types of Sentences in Adult Criminal Courts, Canada, 2016/2017

Sentence	Cases (%)
Probation	44.0
Custody	38.0
Fine	31.0
Conditional sentence	3.5
Restitution	2.5
Other	73.0

Note: The total adds to more than 100 per cent, as judges often impose a number of conditions (such as fines and/or restitution) on a probationary order.

Statistics Canada (2019a)

a probation officer. There are three standard conditions in probation orders: keeping the peace and being on good behaviour, reporting to the court when required, and advising the court or probation officer of any changes in address or job. Judges may also impose additional conditions of probation that are specific to the individual's offence, such as requiring an individual who is struggling with a substance abuse problem to participate in addictions treatment. Some probationary conditions are strict, requiring adult offenders to abide by curfews and/or residency clauses (where the probation officer must approve the individual's living arrangements), abstain from using drugs and/or alcohol, restrict their travel outside the province, or limit contact with certain individuals such as the offender's co-accused (Lincoln County Law Association, 2015). Last, judges can also impose restitution orders, fines, or requirements for community service work (where the probationer must work in the community in jobs such as picking up litter alongside highways, or working in a library or community centre) as part of the probation order. Although judges have a great deal of discretion in terms of the conditions they can impose, probationary terms cannot exceed three years, and the median probationary term in 2014/2015 was 365 days (Maxwell, 2017, p. 4).

Fines are imposed in less than one-third of all adult court cases (31 per cent), and restitution (where payments are made to a victim for the losses from the crime) accounts for another 2.5 per cent of cases (Statistics Canada, 2019a). Both fines and restitution are often conditions of probation, so probationers must pay these costs or risk being returned to court on a breach of probation offence.

Many probationers find it difficult to abide by their conditions of probation. Failure to comply with a probation order, however, can result in additional charges and further punishments. This is relatively common, and in 2016/2017, over 22,000 probationers pleaded guilty to failure to comply (Statistics Canada, 2019a). Courts interpret failure to comply with a probation order as showing a lack of respect for the justice system, and being convicted of this crime may make it difficult for

community service work A condition of a probation order that requires an offender to participate in unpaid work programs that benefit the community, such as working at a library or a community centre.

breach of probation A violation of an offender's condition of probation, such as using drugs or alcohol when it is forbidden, or violating a curfew.

failure to comply Violating the conditions of a probation order is a criminal offence that can result in additional charges and further punishments.

administration of justice offences
Offences that occur because an individual disobeys a pretrial condition or an imposed sentence, such as failing to attend court or failing to comply with a probation order. Also known as *system-generated offences*.

conditional sentences
Custodial sentences of up to two years that are served in the community. Individuals who do not meet the conditions of their release can be returned to court and ordered to serve the remainder of their sentence in a correctional centre.

concurrent sentence
Multiple sentences that are served at the same time (e.g., a person sentenced to two 11-month sentences to be served concurrently would be released after 11 months).

consecutive sentence
Multiple sentences that are served one after the other (e.g., a person sentenced to two 11-month sentences to be served consecutively would be released after 22 months).

them to receive a community-based sentence in the future. However, judges can be very forgiving before they impose a custodial sentence on probationers for breaching the conditions of their orders. Offences such as failure to appear in court or breach of probation are reported as administration of justice offences, but they are commonly called system-generated offences (see Burczycka & Munch, 2015, for a review).

Conditional Sentences

Conditional sentences allow individuals to serve their custody sentences in the community if they follow strict conditions. The British Columbia Branch of the Canadian Bar Association (2015) reports that "judges will use a conditional sentence only if they are satisfied that you won't be a danger to the community and you don't have a history of failing to obey court orders. . . . A conditional sentence usually has strict conditions, including a curfew." Conditional sentences were introduced in 1995 to reduce the use of incarceration, offering an individual a last chance to avoid a correctional centre or prison sentence. These alternatives to custody are seldom used and account for about 5 per cent of all adult court cases.

Custodial Sentences

Offenders sentenced to a term of incarceration of less than two years serve their sentences in provincial or territorial correctional centres. Most provincial sentences are relatively short, and in 2016/2017, the median sentence length was about one month (Miladinovic, 2019, p. 8). While all individuals sent to federal prisons serve two years or longer, about half are sentenced to fewer than five years and most are released to the community prior to the end of their sentences (Public Safety Canada, 2018).

Individuals sentenced to custody for more than one offence can be ordered to serve their sentences concurrently or consecutively. For example, say an individual is found guilty of four counts of break and enter, and the judge sentences her to nine months on each count. If the judge orders her to serve the four counts as

a concurrent sentence, all the sentences run at the same time (concurrently), and she will be released in nine months. If, however, the judge orders her to serve the four counts consecutively (a consecutive sentence), then she will be incarcerated for 36 months.

In order to reduce the harms of imposing a custodial sentence, judges can order that a sentence be served intermittently as opposed to continuously. Intermittent sentences allow the inmate to serve several days a week (typically on weekends) on sentences less than 90 days long. During the days when they are not incarcerated, the individual is expected to follow the conditions of a probation order. In most jurisdictions, intermittent sentences are managed in low-security community-based correctional facilities where residents "come and go" on the honour system, their movements only counted a few times a day, although they can also serve their time in provincial or territorial correctional centres. By serving their sentences on weekends, they are able to keep their jobs, continue meeting their family commitments, and/or maintain their education. Although well-liked by many receiving this type of sentence, this can lead to overcrowding and security problems in correctional facilities (Doucette, 2018).

Other Options

Table 8.1 also includes an "other" category, and this classification can include an absolute discharge, conditional discharge, suspended sentence, community service order, and prohibition order. According to Coughlan, Yogis, and Cotter (2013), an absolute discharge involves finding guilt without registering a conviction:

> An absolute discharge is only available in situations where (1) there is no minimum penalty for the offence; (2) the offence is not punishable by imprisonment for fourteen years or life; (3) the Court considers an absolute discharge to be in the best interests of the accused and not contrary to the public interest. (p. 3)

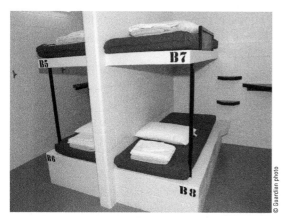

© Guardian photo

Prince Edward Island sends more than two times as many individuals to correctional facilities than do other Maritime provinces, but PEI also has the lowest average sentence length in the country.

Judges are more likely to consider absolute discharges for first-time and younger adult offenders who have committed relatively minor offences. Bowal, Callbeck, and Lines (2014) observe that an absolute discharge is essentially a pardon and is appropriate "if the offence is minor in nature or consequence but the individual would lose much with criminal conviction and sentence."

A conditional discharge is similar to an absolute discharge, except that some conditions are attached to the discharge, such as making restitution to a victim. Although both absolute and conditional discharges will appear on an individual's criminal record, the absolute discharge remains for only one year while the conditional discharge remains for three years. If the offender fails to abide by the conditions of their discharge (e.g., they fail to make the restitution ordered by the court), the judge might revoke the discharge, in which case the original conviction remains on their criminal history. Individuals who successfully fulfill all of the court's conditions and wait the one- or three-year period must request in writing that they want the discharge removed.

INTERPROVINCIAL SENTENCING DIFFERENCES

There is some interprovincial variation in the proportion of adults sentenced to custody, and these differences are shown in Figure 8.1. In 2016/2017, slightly more than one-third (38 per cent) of all Canadians found guilty were incarcerated. However, Miladinovic (2019, p.8) reports that Prince Edward Island courts sentence the highest proportion of guilty offenders to custody of any province (67 per cent), which is about two-thirds more than the national average. Miladinovic (2019, p. 8) points out that one explanation for this is PEI's high rate of incarceration for impaired driving cases (89 per cent compared to 8 per cent for the rest of the nation), although judges there also send more individuals to custody for sexual assault,

absolute discharge The least severe sanction that can be imposed, resulting in a finding of guilt but with no conviction registered.

conditional discharge Requires the individual to comply with a number of conditions, and after they fulfill those conditions, the discharge becomes absolute.

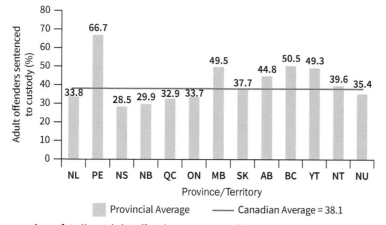

FIGURE 8.1 Proportion of Guilty Adult Offenders Sentenced to Custody, 2016/2017
Statistics Canada (2019a)

major assault, being unlawfully at large, and some drug offences than other provinces. There are two other factors that are distinctive about adult criminal cases on the Island. First, although PEI uses incarceration at a higher rate than other provinces or territories, its sentences tend to be short. Statistics Canada (2019b) reports that the average custody sentence for the entire nation is 108 days, while the average sentence length in PEI is 69 days, which is the second lowest in the country: Figure 8.2 shows the average sentence length in days for all the provinces. Second, the median charge-processing time (the time from an individual's first appearance until they are sentenced) in

PEI adult courts is 36 days, which is about one-third of the national average of 124 days (Miladinovic, 2019).

The interprovincial variation in custody sentences receives relatively little attention. Figure 8.2 reveals that the average sentence for the entire nation is 108 days, but it ranges from 59 days in British Columbia to 155 in New Brunswick. The differences between provinces become even more apparent when we look at the total incarceration rate per 100,000 provincial residents, as shown in Figure 8.3 for 2016/2017. The incarceration rates in the three territories (not shown) were even higher, in part due to the smaller populations.

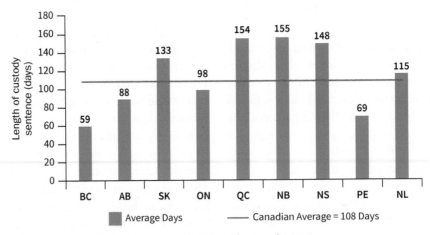

FIGURE 8.2 Average Custody Sentence Length in Days by Province, 2017

Note: Data are not available for Manitoba

Statistics Canada (2019b)

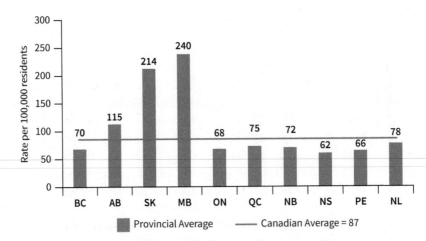

FIGURE 8.3 Provincial Incarceration Rates per 100,000 Residents, 2016/2017

Adapted from Malakieh (2018)

A COMPARATIVE VIEW

Prison Waiting Lists

Although crime is present in every nation, the methods that different countries use when incarcerating offenders are sometimes surprising. Mohsin (2014) observed that Norway does not have enough prison beds for offenders sentenced to incarceration. As a result, there were a large number of people who had been convicted of a crime but were living in the community awaiting a bed to become available before starting their sentences. This is not a new problem: Norwegian prison officials have used waiting lists since the 1990s. These lists are typically reserved for non-violent offenders who sometimes have to wait a year or longer before their prison admission. Drelsinger (2018) observes that not only are prisons in Norway more comfortable than ones in North America, but the country's approach to incarcerating people is more humane, which reduces prison misconduct and recidivism. While Norwegians generally support practices such as waiting lists, since September 2015 Norway has been paying the Netherlands to hold several hundred of its prisoners in order to reduce the number of individuals on the waiting list; lower numbers of incoming prisoners might eliminate the need to send prisoners to the Netherlands after 2019 (Berglund, 2017).

While the idea of waiting to be admitted to prison might seem unusual, Canadians receiving a custodial sentence can be ordered by a judge to report to a provincial correctional centre or federal prison at a future date. These postponed admissions are often granted for some compelling reason, such as finishing an employment contract or a semester at school. As in Norway, these types of creative sentences are often reserved for people convicted of non-violent offences who have complied with the conditions of their bail or other community release.

The reasons for the differences in the use of custody are often complex, but the factor that should drive the use of incarceration is levels of crime. We would expect provinces with the highest rates of police-reported crime, such as Manitoba and Saskatchewan, to also have the highest use of custodial sentences. Yet Sprott and Doob (1998) analyzed the use of custody and found a weak relationship between the amount of police-reported crime or people charged and the use of custody. Instead, the differences in the number of admissions and the length of sentences across the provinces and territories may be the result of factors such as public support for offender rehabilitation or punishment. Neil and Carmichael (2015) examined the provincial use of incarceration and found that as the size of the Indigenous and visible minority populations increased, so did the use of custody—which supports the conflict perspective described in Chapter 3, where populations that are seen as threatening are harshly controlled by the justice system.

In Chapter 3, we looked at the crime control philosophy of deterrence, which is based on the idea that punishments are more likely to work when they are swift, certain, and severe. A number of prominent Canadian scholars have challenged that notion by arguing that the severity of punishment is not as important as its certainty and swiftness (Doob, Webster, & Gartner, 2014). It is possible that Prince Edward Island's justice system officials are following the latter approach, as punishment is more certain and swift there than in other provinces, but it is also less severe. The PEI model may be working, as the province's overall crime severity index is the lowest in Canada (44.9 compared with the national average of 72.9), and the violent crime severity index is the also the lowest in the country (38.9) and less than one-half the national average (80.3) (Allen, 2018). Although factors other than certainty, swiftness, and severity of punishment could influence crime rates, this is a subject that warrants a closer look.

There are also differences in the degree of punishment imposed *within* provinces. Many of us have heard that some judges or courts are stricter than others, and this issue was addressed in Chapter 7 when we looked at differences in the going rate. One issue that has received comparatively little attention in Canadian studies is the issue of justice by geography, where differences in case outcomes are the result of court location. US researchers examining this issue have generally focused on case outcomes in urban and rural juvenile courts: Menart (2018) reports that harsh punishments for juveniles (prosecuting them as adults) occurred in some California counties, which was the same finding as an earlier study reported by Feld and Schaefer (2010). There is a lack of Canadian research examining whether geography is a factor in case outcomes in either adult or youth courts. Issues such as justice by geography are called extralegal factors—conditions that are not related to the offence but that may affect an offender's sentencing. Most studies of these extralegal factors have focused on issues of how a person's status as a woman, membership in a marginalized group, or financial situation affects one's sentence—and research suggests that these issues are worthy of further attention.

THE PRINCIPLES OF SENTENCING

There are several principles of sentencing, including proportionality, aggravating and mitigating factors, totality, and crimes motivated by bias or hatred. There are also some special considerations when sentencing youth, people with mental illnesses, or Indigenous people convicted of a crime.

Proportionality

The most important principle of sentencing is proportionality, as sentences must reflect the seriousness of the crime and the individual's responsibility in committing the crime. We can ask more simply, "Does the punishment fit the crime?" We do not treat all people the same at sentencing, as

a number of individual factors about the offender, the nature of the crime, and their role in the offence (e.g., as a follower or leader) are considered by judges. As a result, there is some variation in the severity of sentences, and there are positive and negative aspects of those differences. Most of us, for example, would want our good qualities to be considered by a judge prior to sentencing, such as the volunteer work we do or our good conduct at school or at work. Yet whenever there are differences in the severity of punishment for a offence, it might also suggest that bias has occurred. To shed some light on these differences, we take a closer look at sentences for homicide.

Homicide includes manslaughter, first-degree murder, and second-degree murder offences. The number of these offences has been rising since 2014, and in 2017 there were 660 homicides (Allen, 2018). Cotter (2014) reports that about three-quarters of these crimes are cleared (solved) by an arrest; clearances also include cases when suspects die from suicide or other causes prior to an arrest. Figure 8.4 shows the outcomes of the 328 homicide cases heard in adult courts in Canada in 2016/2017; less than half of these cases result in someone being convicted (142 cases were stayed, nine defendants were acquitted, and there were 38 "other" decisions, a category that includes individuals whose cases were waived out of the province or who were found unfit to stand trial). When it came to sentence length, the average sentence was 3,517 days, while the median sentence was 2,190 days (Statistics Canada, 2019b).

The considerable difference in the severity of punishments for homicide offenders raises questions: why is one convicted murderer placed on probation while another serves the remainder of his or her life under correctional supervision? Most of those sentencing differences are related to the circumstances of the offence. The type of crime that individuals are ultimately convicted of determines how much time they will spend behind bars, especially for first- and second-degree murder. As a result, prosecutors play a key role in case outcomes. Manslaughter, as you will recall from Chapter 2, involves no intention to cause death, whereas first-degree murder is a planned

---

justice by geography The differences in case outcomes that are a result of where a court is located (e.g., some rural courts may be more punitive than urban courts).

extralegal factors Conditions that affect sentencing but are not related to the offence, such as the location of a sentencing court.

proportionality The principle that the sentence imposed on offenders is proportionate to the seriousness of their offence and their degree of responsibility.

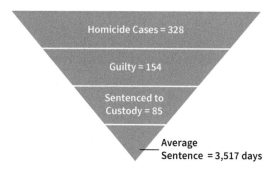

FIGURE 8.4 Homicide Cases in Canadian Adult Courts, 2016/2017

Statistics Canada (2019c)

and deliberate offence (or part of another crime), and second-degree murder is a deliberate act that was unplanned.

As there is no minimum sentence for manslaughter, some people convicted of it are sentenced to probation. Community-based sentences for manslaughter are relatively rare, and usually there is some defence that leads to these lesser charges (see the "Closer Look" box in this chapter

for one example). The sentences for first- and second-degree murder, however, are prescribed in the *Criminal Code*. Every adult convicted of second-degree murder must serve a minimum of 10 years before being eligible for parole, while first-degree murderers must serve a minimum of 25 years prior to parole eligibility, and some offenders, such as Dellen Millard, will serve consecutive life sentences; Millard will not be eligible to apply for parole until he has been in prison for 75 years. We also have to remember there are no guarantees that inmates will ever be paroled, as they have to demonstrate to the Parole Board of Canada that they represent a low risk to the community; public safety is the board's main concern (see Chapter 10).

Aggravating and Mitigating Factors

Differences in sentencing can also relate to the distinctive characteristics of the offence or offender. Section 718.2 of the *Criminal Code* allows judges to consider aggravating or mitigating

TABLE 8.2 **Mitigating and Aggravating Circumstances Considered at Sentencing**

Mitigating Circumstances	Aggravating Circumstances
First offender	Prior jail sentence for related or like offence (within past five years)
Youthful offender	On bail, probation, or parole for related or like offence
Low risk to reoffend	Significant physical injury to victim
Isolated incident (out of character)	Lengthy record, with escalation in seriousness of offences
Spontaneous offence (e.g., no planning)	Planned, deliberate, or sophisticated
Guilty plea	Abused position of trust or authority
Remorse (accepts responsibility)	Vulnerable victims (child, elderly, or disabled)
Follower, not leader (in the offence)	Significant value of property involved (e.g., loss or damage over $50,000)
Cooperation with authorities	Leader (in offence)
Employed or in school	Multiple charges
Sole provider or caregiver for dependents	Prior outstanding charges
Participation in rehabilitation (e.g., treatment or counselling)	History of breaching court orders
Community or family support	Motivated by greed or profit
Unfortunate background	Motivated by hate, prejudice, or bias
Dated, minor, or unrelated criminal record	Numerous victims
	Damage to victims (e.g., financial loss)

Adapted from Legal Aid Ontario (2019)

A Closer Look

Battered Woman Syndrome in Homicide Cases: Unanticipated Outcomes

Family violence is a serious social problem. In 2016 for all of Canada there were almost 55,000 child and youth victims of family violence (Conroy, 2018), over 4,000 cases where family members assaulted a senior (Savage, 2018), and over 93,000 incidents of intimate-partner violence reported to the police (Burczyka, 2018). Intimate-partner violence refers to crimes committed by current and former spouses, common-law partners, dating partners, or any other **intimate partners**. Prior research shows that about 79 per cent of family-violence victims are women (Burczycka & Conroy, 2017). While those are the actual numbers of cases coming to the attention of the police, about 70 per cent of domestic violence victims never report the crime (Canadian Centre for Justice Statistics, 2016). Sometimes family violence is lethal. According to Beattie, David, and Roy (2018, p. 33), of the 443 murders in 2017 where the perpetrator was identified, more than one-third of them (162) were family members or were involved in an inmate relationship.

Some women suffering abuse have used a **battered woman defence** after killing their abuser. Canadian defendants have used this defence with varying degrees of success since the 1911 case of Angelina Napolitano, a 28-year-old from Sault Ste. Marie, Ontario, who killed her sleeping husband with an axe. Napolitano, who had suffered physical attacks and had been stabbed by her husband, was initially sentenced to death for the homicide, but her sentence was later commuted to life imprisonment;

> **intimate partners** Current and former spouses, dating partners, or other intimate relationships.
>
> **battered woman defence** A defence that has been used by some victims of domestic violence who argued they had no way of escaping their victimization and had no other choice but to attack their abuser.

she served 11 years behind bars before her release. In 1990 the defence was formally recognized by the Supreme Court in the *R v Lavallee* decision (MacLean, Verrelli, & Chambers, 2017).

Although the battered woman defence has been used in Canada for several decades, Sheehy (2014) reports that defendants have had varying results. Sheehy, Stubbs, and Tolmie's (2012, p. 390) examination of Canadian murder records found there were "36 cases resolved during the period 2000–2010 involving battered women defendants who had killed their violent partners and were charged with homicide." Of those 36 cases, two women were convicted of or pleaded guilty to murder, 21 were convicted of manslaughter, and the rest either were acquitted or their cases did not proceed to trial (Sheehy et al., 2012, p. 394). The decisions to prosecute battered women who kill their spouses are made by prosecutors who may hold strong opinions about these cases, and Sheehy (2018, p. 112) says that "the Ottawa Crown office has stood out for its vigorous, no holds barred efforts to prosecute battered women who kill." In other words, battered women in Ottawa may be more likely to be prosecuted than women in other communities. Sheehy's comment reinforces the observation made throughout this book that justice is administered differently throughout the country and the outcomes of an individual accused or convicted of committing a crime might depend on where the act occurred.

The number of intimate-partner homicides has been decreasing since the 1990s. Between 1996 and 2017 the number of men killed by intimate partners decreased by over one-third (38 per cent), whereas the number of women victims dropped by about one-sixth (16 per cent) (Burczycka, 2018; Cotter, 2014); this is shown in Table 8.3. The decreased number of murders has been attributed to providing

> **aggravating factors** Facts that might lead to a more severe sentence, including if the offence involved a particularly vulnerable victim, such as a child, or if the crime was related to bias, prejudice, or hate.
>
> **mitigating factors** Facts related to the individual that might encourage a judge to impose a less severe sentence, such as if the individual is a youth, a young adult, or a first-time offender.

factors at sentencing. Aggravating factors are circumstances that a judge might take into account when considering a severe sentence. Mitigating factors, by contrast, help to explain the individual's role in the offence or recognize the positive

characteristics of the individual that might warrant a less severe sentence.

Legal Aid Ontario (2019) summarizes the aggravating and mitigating circumstances judges might consider when sentencing an individual;

TABLE 8.3 Intimate-Partner Homicide Victims, Canada: Variation, 1996 to 2017

Female Victims	Male Victims
16% ⬇	38% ⬇

Based on Burczycka (2018); Cotter (2014)

better access to community-based resources such as domestic violence shelters, giving victims alternatives to violence.

Efforts to expand the number of domestic violence shelters, provide additional services to women victims, and increase police training about family violence are intended to save women from being harmed by their male partners. One unanticipated outcome of these policies, however, is that more men have actually been saved than women. A similar trend has been seen in the United States (Reckdenwald & Parker, 2011). The introduction of better victim-service programs has reduced the number of women killing men as they are now able to escape abusive or intolerable situations without resorting to violence, although this was not the intention of the advocates who introduced these services and supports for women.

Steve Russell/Toronto Star via Getty Images

Efforts to expand the number of domestic violence shelters, provide additional services to women victims, and increase police training about family violence are intended to save women from being harmed by their male partners, but these changes have also had the unintended effect of saving their violent male partners.

these are presented in Table 8.2. One factor that will not result in a lighter punishment is cultural values that conflict with the *Criminal Code*. In 2015, the Ontario Court of Appeal said that "cultural norms that condone or tolerate conduct contrary to Canadian criminal law must not be considered a mitigating factor on sentencing" (Perkel, 2015). All together, aggravating factors tend to focus on the offence, whereas mitigating factors tend to address the positive aspects of the individual's character including his or her potential for rehabilitation.

Totality

As noted earlier in this chapter, when an individual is found guilty of committing more than one offence, a judge can sentence them to custodial terms to be served concurrently or consecutively. There are some limits to the severity of the punishment that can be meted out using consecutive sentences, and those limits are guided by the principle of totality. Totality is described in section 718.2(c) of the *Criminal Code*, which states that "where consecutive sentences are imposed, the combined sentence should not be unduly long or harsh." The Supreme Court in *R v Johnson* (2012) explained the importance of totality: "If sentences are unduly harsh and excessive, confidence in the fairness and rationality of the sentencing process is lost. . . . [T]he overall length of incarceration may work against the attainment of the various goals of sentencing" (as cited in Manson, 2013, p. 488).

One issue in considering totality, however, is that people do not always agree on what constitutes a harsh or excessive sentence. Judges also disagree on how severe a sentence should be when an individual has committed multiple offences. In February 2018, for example, the Court of Appeal of Newfoundland and Labrador reduced to 30 months the 60-month sentence of a 74-year-old who had sexually molested four girls. The Court of Appeals said the judge erred by not considering the totality principle and that the sentence of 60 months was "unduly long and harsh" (*R v O'Keefe*, 2018, at para. 39). When reducing his sentence by half, the Court of Appeal said that his advanced age was only of minimal consideration. This example shows the complexity of sentencing decisions and the factors judges consider when making those decisions.

Sentencing in Canada is intended to be just and fair, and section 718.2(b) of the *Criminal Code* states that "a sentence should be similar to sentences imposed on similar offenders for similar offences committed in similar circumstances." This brings us back to the issue of the going rate, which was introduced in Chapter 7. Experienced court observers can often accurately predict an individual's sentence based on their past criminal history and the seriousness of the current offence. This does not mean, however, that custodial sentences need to be imposed, and section 718.2(d) of the *Criminal Code* states that "an offender should not be deprived of liberty, if less restrictive sanctions may be appropriate in the circumstances."

totality
A sentencing principle that considers the overall length of a sentence and requires that a single global sentence be imposed to avoid an unjustly long sentence.

"Tough on Crime" was one of the pillars of the Conservative Party of Canada's federal platform running up to the 2019 election. Tough-on-crime policies are often considered a politically safe issue, as criminals are seldom seen as a very sympathetic group by the public and few politicians want to be seen as being "soft on crime." While getting tough is often politically popular, simplistic solutions to complex problems such as crime are seldom effective. Political party changes at the federal level often result in legislative changes, reminding us that the law can change.

Section 718.2(e) extends that guideline by directing judges to consider the special circumstances of Indigenous offenders when considering custodial sentences (see the "Race, Class, and Gender" box in this chapter on the challenges of sentencing Indigenous people).

GETTING TOUGH ON OFFENDERS

Roberts, Stalans, Indermaur, and Hough (2003) explain that simplistic criminal justice practices such as getting tough on crime are popular with the public. Some politicians who want to attract voters promise to put more police officers on the streets and to take offenders off the streets by imposing longer prison sentences. Issues of crime control can attract voters because criminals are generally an unsympathetic group and most Canadians want lengthy prison sentences imposed on serious and violent offenders. A study of English-speaking common-law nations reveals that Canadians are just as punitive as the public in Australia, New Zealand, the United Kingdom, or the United States when it comes to support for harsh punishments for young offenders and support for the death penalty (Kornhauser, 2015).

As noted in Chapter 3, this political advocacy for punitive criminal justice practices, whether they are effective or not, is called penal populism. One of the problems with penal populism is that studies have repeatedly shown that getting tough on everybody who has committed a crime is a poor criminal justice practice. Doob, Webster, and Gartner (2014, p. A-3), prominent Canadian scholars, examined studies of crime control policies and observed that "no reputable criminologist who has looked carefully at the overall body of research literature . . . believes that crime rates will be reduced, through deterrence, by raising the severity of sentences handed down in criminal courts." The "tough on crime" approach taken by the former Conservative federal government from 2006 to 2015 has been criticized because it rejected evidence-based practices that were demonstrated to reduce crime in favour of politically popular strategies that were less effective or might have even contributed to more crime (see Kelly & Puddister, 2017).

Additional problems with getting tough on crime include the fact that imprisoning people is an expensive proposition and that incarceration can be harmful to both the prisoner and their families due to the disruption it has on their household income, future employment prospects, and reputation in their communities. In terms of the Canadian costs of imprisonment, in 2017 the average unattached individual or family paid $11,439 in direct taxes (Palacios & Lammam, 2018). As Figure 8.5 shows, it would take seven taxpayers to pay for the imprisonment of a provincial inmate for one year ($84,915) and ten taxpayers to pay for the imprisonment of a federal inmate ($120,571; see Malakieh, 2019, p. 6). As a result, if there are less-restrictive and more cost-effective options for offenders, such as supervision in the community, we can reserve the harshest sanctions for the most serious and violent offenders.

Rates of crime in Canada have been dropping since they peaked in the late 1970s, and the 2017 homicide rate, shown in Figure 8.6, was the same as the 1968 rate, although rates have been increasing somewhat since 2014 (Allen, 2018). One question emerges from that finding: If Canada's crime control strategies are not on the right track, then why have serious and violent crime rates dropped so much? Supporters of "tough on crime" policies point out that many US jurisdictions have "three strikes" sentencing laws that enable judges to impose prison terms in the 25-year range for offenders who have committed their third felony offence. Harsh sentences for repeat Canadian offenders have been authorized for decades, and Public Safety Canada (2014) notes the following:

> Canada introduced its first high-risk offender laws in 1947, when Parliament amended the *Criminal Code* to give the courts the authority to designate certain repeat offenders as "habitual offenders." Under those provisions, individuals who had been convicted of three or more

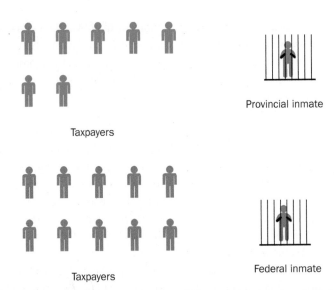

Taxpayers

Provincial inmate

Taxpayers

Federal inmate

FIGURE 8.5 **Number of Taxpayers Required to Financially Support One Provincial or Federal Inmate in 2017**
Adapted from Malakieh (2019)

separate indictable offences and who were "persistently leading a criminal life" could be found to be habitual offenders and sentenced to indeterminate imprisonment.

Even though judges could designate repeat criminals as habitual offenders, there was dissatisfaction with the practice, as it was not applied in a similar manner across the nation. The alternative, introduced in 1977, was to give judges the authority to designate repeat violent individuals as dangerous offenders, a topic covered in the paragraphs that follow.

While those interested in punishing offenders more severely often desire American crime control practices, it is important to note that most states are becoming less punitive. Kaeble and Cowhig (2018) report that US jail and prison populations have decreased for nine consecutive years, although the population in 2016 was only 6.5 per cent less than the 2008 peak. A further example of the softening of US criminal justice policies was the enactment of the First Step Act, which allows for the compassionate release of sick and elderly prisoners as well as decreased sentences for some

truth in sentencing Limits the amount of a sentence that can be granted as "time served" when an individual has been remanded prior to sentencing.

drug offenders (Johnson, 2019). Furthermore, the number of executions carried out in 2018 was 25, which was down from the peak of 98 in 2000, and the number of people sentenced to death in 2018 was half the number sentenced to death in 2011 (Death Penalty Information Center, 2019). The US federal government has also restricted the use of mandatory minimum sentences for people convicted of drug offences, and some states are making it more difficult to sentence offenders to decades-long prison terms. The Pew Charitable Trusts (2018) observes that 35 states have either reduced their tough-on-crime sentencing schemes, made it easier to release prisoners, or improved community corrections to keep more offenders in the community.

Supporters of the crime control model maintain that violent and repeat offenders should be incapacitated. They argue that mandatory minimum sentences, truth in sentencing, designating violent criminals as dangerous offenders, and harshly punishing murderers are good practices. Some supporters of the due process approach agree that we need the option to incapacitate some dangerous criminals, but they also believe that these sanctions should rarely be used. Moreover, supporters of the due process perspective argue that sentencing practices should be rational and guided by research (e.g., asking whether these approaches are effective in reducing crime), and sentencing should be based on the circumstances of the individual and the crime they committed. The problem, as highlighted in Chapter 3, is that it is very difficult to predict who will be dangerous in the future. The following sections highlight some of these approaches to getting tough on crime.

Mandatory Minimum Penalties

There are a number of sentencing options that are intended to "get tough" on certain types of offenders or offences. Mandatory minimum penalties (MMPs) remove the discretion from the judge as anybody found guilty of the offence receives the minimum sentence regardless of any mitigating factors (although judges can impose sentences that are longer than the minimum). The logic behind MMPs is that all individuals are treated the same by the judge. As a result, this type of sentencing shifts the power in the court to the Crown prosecutors who determine the charge.

Mandatory minimum penalties in Canada date back to the 1890s (Caylor & Beaulne, 2014), and mandatory sentences for impaired driving and firearms-related offences were introduced throughout the 1900s. Allen (2017, p. 3) observes that a series of laws starting in 2005 "laid out new or more severe minimum penalties for drug offences, impaired driving, firearms offences, and sexual offences involving children as well as child pornography." These mandatory penalties can be imposed for a single offence, such as specific types of sex crimes committed against children, or for repeat offences, such as the mandatory incarceration for repeat drunk driving convictions.

The number of MMPs was expanded after the federal government enacted the *Safe Streets and Communities Act* in 2012. MMPs were mandated for offences related to the possession, distribution, and manufacturing of some illicit drugs; for offences involving the sexual exploitation of

© (2007) Her Majesty the Queen in Right of Canada as represented by the Royal Canadian Mounted Police

The individual who killed Alberta RCMP constable David Wynn (pictured above) and wounded auxiliary constable Derek Bond in January 2015 had 98 prior convictions and outstanding charges that he accumulated between 1999 and 2015, and he had been admitted to correctional facilities 16 times. Many of those offences were related to violence and the unlawful possession of restricted or prohibited firearms. Despite his long criminal history and inability to abide by conditions of prior releases, he was released from custody after paying $4,500 in bail. He failed to appear for his court dates, and his freedom ultimately led to the shooting of the officers.

children; and for some violent and firearms offences. There has been broad opposition to these policies, especially from civil libertarians who believe that mandatory sentences threaten individualized justice, which enables judges to consider mitigating factors as well as the distinctive characteristics of an offence when imposing a sentence.

In 2013, the Ontario Court of Appeal sided with a judge who found that a three-year mandatory sentence for possessing a loaded prohibited

individualized justice Enables judges to consider aggravating and mitigating factors as well as the individual's strengths and limitations when imposing a sentence; it is the opposite of mandatory sentences.

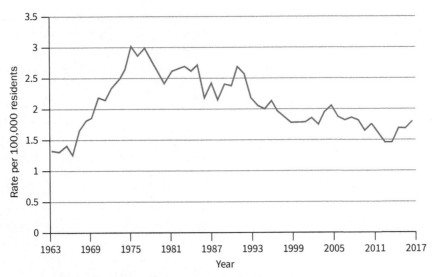

FIGURE 8.6 Homicides in Canada, Rate per 100,000 Residents, 1963–2017

Adapted from Boyce (2015) and Allen (2018)

firearm was cruel and unusual, and it was therefore considered an unconstitutional punishment. This case was heard by the Supreme Court in 2015, which agreed with the Ontario court and struck down the mandatory minimum sentence (see *R v Nur*). The British Columbia Court of Appeal struck down a one-year mandatory sentence for drug trafficking in 2014 by calling that sentence cruel and unusual, and its decision was upheld by the Supreme Court in April 2016 (*R v Lloyd*). Fine (2018, para. 20) says that these decisions led to a "steady unravelling of mandatory minimum cases" and observes that appellate courts have stuck down more than a dozen different minimum sentences.

MMPs are an example of a criminal justice policy that "looks good on paper" but is difficult to implement in a fair and consistent manner. While the intent of these policies is to deter people from committing crimes and to treat wrongdoers consistently, there are barriers to those goals. First, some people may not be aware of the law, which thereby reduces its deterrent effect. Second, as prosecutors lay charges, they ultimately decide whether the individuals are vulnerable to MMPs, and they can use that power

to force a defendant into a guilty plea. As a result, if we have two people who commit the same crime (e.g., illegally carrying a loaded prohibited firearm), one person could receive the mandatory sentence while the other might avoid the punishment by pleading guilty to an offence that does not carry a mandatory sentence. Because of those inconsistencies, the current Liberal government has pledged to reduce the number of these sentencing schemes (Fine, 2018).

Truth in Sentencing

The number of arrestees and defendants remanded to custody has been increasing since the 1990s, and since 2004/2005 the remand population has exceeded the sentenced provincial and territorial population (Malakieh, 2019). One popular explanation for the increase was that inmates on remand deliberately delayed their court dates for trials and sentencing in order to receive a larger "time served" credit when they were eventually sentenced. Because conditions for remanded inmates in provincial correctional centres are harsher than for sentenced inmates (e.g., they reside in crowded, austere, and high-security living units that offer little or no rehabilitative programming), judges typically gave a "two-for-one" credit if the individual was ultimately sentenced to a term of incarceration. Thus, if an inmate served one year on remand and was sentenced to three years in custody, the judge would subtract two years from their sentence as time served.

Bill C-25, the *Truth in Sentencing Act*, was passed in October 2009, and that amendment to the *Criminal Code* limits the credits that judges could allow for time defendants spent on remand. According to Porter and Calverley (2011, p. 17), judges could no longer grant credit in excess of one day for every day spent on remand without having a justification, and even with justification, they could give only 1.5 days of credit for every day served on remand. Judges are not, however, obliged to extend any credit for time served on remand. Despite that change, however, the number of adults remanded to custody has increased, suggesting that other factors are responsible for the high number of people awaiting their days in court.

Increasing the Severity of Life and Indeterminate Sentencing

A number of legislative changes made it harder for prisoners serving a life sentence to be granted parole, and made it possible to delay the parole eligibility for offenders convicted of multiple murders. Every prisoner sentenced to a determinate sentence is advised of their release date, which is also known as their warrant expiry date, although most inmates receive some type of early release for good behaviour or as part of a planned release to the community on parole (see Chapter 10).

There is, however, no formal release date for prisoners serving a sentence of life imprisonment—also known as lifers (their preferred term)—or for dangerous offenders serving indeterminate sentences. What is distinctive about lifers or dangerous offenders is they will remain under correctional supervision, whether they are living in an institution or the community, for the rest of their lives.

About 175 people are sentenced to indeterminate sentences and admitted to federal prisons every year (Public Safety Canada, 2018, p. 58). Since they are under correctional supervision until their deaths, these numbers keep growing. As of April 2017, there were almost 5,500 lifers, or slightly less than one-quarter of the total CSC population (Public Safety Canada, 2018, p. 59). Included in that total are several dozen prisoners who were originally sentenced to death, but whose sentences were commuted to life imprisonment after capital punishment was abolished in 1976. When compared with prison systems in other developed nations, Canada's prison system has a much higher proportion of prisoners with life or indeterminate sentences (Penal Reform International, 2018, p. 3).

Life imprisonment sentences are mandatory for individuals convicted of first- or second-degree murder. First-degree murderers are not eligible to apply for parole until they have served 25 years in prison, while people convicted of second-degree murder must serve 10 years before they can apply for parole. An amendment to the *Criminal Code* in March 2011, known as the *Protecting Canadians by Ending Sentence Discounts for Multiple Murders Act,* made it possible for parole eligibility to run consecutively. As an example, the killer of three Moncton RCMP officers in 2014 must serve three consecutive 25-year terms—a total of 75 years—before he is eligible to apply for parole. There does appear, however, to be a lack of consistency in how these sentences are imposed. In three high-profile multiple-murder homicide cases in 2018/2019, there was a significant difference in the amount of time these offenders would have to serve before they were eligible to apply for parole. Faris (2019) points out that Dellen Millard was sentenced to three counts of first-degree murder and won't be eligible to apply for parole until he serves 75 years. Alexandre Bissonnette, by contrast, will not be eligible to apply for parole until he serves 40 years for killing six worshippers in a Quebec City mosque, while Bruce McArthur will not be eligible to apply for parole for 25 years for killing eight Toronto men (Faris, 2019).

determinate sentences Sentences that have a warrant expiry date on which the inmate will be released from a correctional centre or federal prison.

warrant expiry date An inmate's release date from custody.

indeterminate sentences Sentences imposed on dangerous and life-sentenced offenders who do not have a formal release date and remain under correctional supervision for the rest of their lives, whether in an institution or in a community.

A Closer Look

Sentence Calculation in Provincial and Territorial Correctional Centres

Sentence calculation is carried out by correctional officers after an individual is admitted to a custody facility. Calculating the length of an inmate's sentence seems like a relatively straightforward task, but it can be a complex undertaking. For example, the release dates of two inmates might differ if one is sentenced to a 30-day term while the second receives a one-month sentence in a 31-day month (leap years must also be considered in these calculations). As noted earlier in this chapter, sentences can run consecutively or concurrently; sometimes the judge's intentions are not clearly stated on the **warrants of committal** (the documents authorizing a prisoner's incarceration), and correctional officers must verify the sentence. The officers calculating sentences must also consider any days that an inmate did not serve due to an escape or failure to return from a **temporary release** from custody (e.g., when an inmate is sent to the community to work, study, or visit with family). Calculating an inmate's sentence can be further complicated if a person is serving a youth custody sentence and then is sentenced in an adult court for an offence committed after his or her eighteenth birthday. This would result in the custodial sentence being converted to an adult sentence, and the individual would be transferred from a youth facility to an adult correctional centre or penitentiary.

Provincial inmates are eligible for **earned remission**, which is an early release based on their good behaviour. In Ontario, "sentenced offenders can be credited with 15 days earned remission for each month served," although they can lose remission for negative behaviour within the correctional facility, including "violating any institutional rules, regulations, or conditions" (Ontario Ministry of Community Safety and Correctional Services, 2018, para. 2 and 5). There is some variation between the provinces in the manner that earned remission is calculated. According to British Columbia's *Correction Act* (BC Laws, 2017), remission is calculated based on the inmate's conduct; poor performance can result in 0 to 7 days earned remission per month served, fair performance can result in 8 to 14 days, and good performance enables the inmate to earn one day of remission for every two days served in custody.

Given the tasks of accurately interpreting the judge's intentions for an individual's sentence, calculating the exact release date, and factoring in earned remission and days away from custody, it is natural that mistakes will occur. Dale (2015) reports that in Ontario provincial correctional institutions, "98 prisoners were freed prematurely between 2009 and 2013, mostly because of clerical errors. Four of these prisoners committed new offences while they should have been behind bars." This problem is not isolated to Ontario, and these mistakes are expected given that there were almost 80,000 admissions to provincial or territorial custody in 2017/2018 (Malakieh, 2019). Not all errors work in the inmate's favour, however, and some inmates have also been held *past* their warrant expiry date due to calculation mistakes.

warrants of committal
Documents that authorize an individual's incarceration.

temporary release
A type of release granted from a correctional facility so that inmates can participate in employment, education, treatment, or family visits.

earned remission
A type of early release from a provincial correctional centre that has been earned by the inmate through good behaviour.

Mikael Karlsson/Alamy Stock Photo

Shortly after an individual is admitted to a provincial correctional centre, officers conduct a sentence calculation to verify their warrant expiry date. While officers make every effort to ensure that these calculations are correct, clerical errors can occur and prisoners are sometimes discharged early or kept past their actual release dates.

INDIVIDUALIZED JUSTICE: PRE-SENTENCE REPORTS

In order to make the best sentencing decisions, judges often request that probation officers conduct pre-sentence investigations about the person awaiting sentencing, their circumstances (including the success of prior criminal justice system interventions), and their role in the offence. This information is compiled in a pre-sentence report (PSR), which is authorized by section 721 of the *Criminal Code*. The chief justice of the Nova Scotia Court of Appeal commented in the *R v Bartkow* (1978) decision that the purpose of the report was "to supply a picture of the accused as a person in society—his background, family, education, employment record, his physical and mental health, his associates and social activities, and his potentialities and motivations."

Although the format and content of a PSR may differ somewhat among provinces, section 721(3) of the *Criminal Code* specifies that these reports should contain the following information:

a. "the offender's age, maturity, character, behaviour, attitude and willingness to make amends";
b. the individual's criminal history (as a youth and an adult); and
c. "the history of any alternative measures used to deal with the offender, and the offender's response to those measures."

In addition, the probation officer preparing the report is required to investigate specific issues of interest to the judge, including the person's suitability for community-based treatment such as electronic monitoring or participation in a residential treatment program for substance abuse. Some provinces allow the probation officer to include information about risk assessments and

pre-sentence report (PSR) A report ordered by judges prior to sentencing to provide a comprehensive overview of the individual's strengths and weaknesses, and whether prior justice system interventions were successful.

Judges order pre-sentence reports to increase their understanding of the offenders and their roles in the offences, which in turn helps judges make better sentencing decisions. After the individual is sentenced, the pre-sentence report is also used by correctional and probation officers to develop their rehabilitative plans.

to make formal recommendations about sentencing (Bonta, Bourgon, Jesseman, & Yessine, 2005). All together, these reports provide judges with a comprehensive overview of the individual, their strengths and weaknesses, and the success or failure of their prior criminal justice interventions.

Probation officers ordered to write a PSR will interview the individual and will sometimes speak with their close relatives, such as a parent for a young person, or a spouse. Their employers are sometimes asked about their functioning on the job. The probation officers will also speak to people working in health, education, or social service agencies that are involved with the individual, especially if they have mental health or other problems. In addition, an offender's co-accused might also be interviewed in order for the probation officer to better understand their respective roles in the crime. The police officers who carried out the investigation or arrested the offender are sometimes interviewed to obtain additional insight into the offence and the individuals involved. As noted earlier, victims are also given the opportunity to make a statement about the impacts the offence had on their lives. These reports require a substantial amount of time to complete, and the length of time increases in cases involving multiple victims or serious violence.

Judges typically give officers about a month to prepare a PSR. That time is required to track down the information and interview the subject, victims, police officers, and service providers involved with the offender. Bonta, Bourgon, Jesseman, and Yessine (2005, p. 21) found that the average PSR in Canada took about 14.2 hours to complete and the documents averaged about 11 pages. Because of the time needed to conduct these investigations and prepare the reports, some judges will order them only if they are deliberating whether a community-based or custodial sentence is the most appropriate sanction. Officers preparing these reports are expected to ensure that the documents are accurate and comprehensive as they often form the foundation of an offender's case plan—for community-based supervision or for treatment in custody (see Chapter 9). A PSR may also be used for release planning, to

make parole decisions, and to conduct research. These investigations result in documents that may be used by different officials for many years.

Additional reports about the subject's mental health functioning are sometimes requested by the judge, including psychological or psychiatric reports. Psychological reports are commonly ordered for sexual offenders to give the judge insight into their risks to public safety and likelihood of rehabilitation. Psychiatric reports, by contrast, are often carried out in psychiatric facilities or forensic units (mental health units in correctional facilities) and can take a month or longer to complete.

Although PSRs help judges make sentencing decisions based on the strengths and weaknesses of the individual, these investigations can be controversial. PSRs have been criticized because probation officials may develop their recommendations based on their knowledge of a judge's sentencing expectations and practices. Bonta et al. (2005, p. ii) found that judges accepted the recommendations for community-based sentences in most cases (71 per cent), and a similar US study revealed that judges accepted a slightly higher proportion (73 per cent) of probation officer recommendations (Norman & Wadman, 2000, p. 48).

Some scholars are critical of PSRs as they believe that probation officers may unconsciously favour offenders who have middle-class backgrounds, beliefs, and values. Some reports written by probation officers can be poorly researched or report incorrect or biased information about the individual or the circumstances surrounding an offence. In the case of *R v Junkert*, the Ontario Court of Appeal found that:

> The pre-sentence report painted a very negative picture of the accused, including failing to set out his medical issues and failed to refer to a report from the accused's counselor stating that the accused was genuinely remorseful. Defence counsel cross-examined the probation officer who prepared the report and exposed the factual flaws in the report.

Canadian researchers have also raised the issue of whether probation officers receive enough

Race, Class, and Gender

The Challenges of Indigenous Sentencing

In Chapter 6, we looked at the Supreme Court of Canada (SCC) decision in the *R v Gladue* case, which was a response to the overrepresentation of Indigenous peoples in youth and criminal justice systems. Jamie Tanis Gladue, a 19-year-old Indigenous woman who killed her common-law spouse, was sentenced to a three-year prison term after being convicted of manslaughter. The SCC found that while the three-year sentence was appropriate for the seriousness of the offence, the sentencing judge should have specifically considered the background factors that may have led Gladue to commit the offence. The SCC made the following summary in the case of *R v Gladue* (1999):

> In sentencing an aboriginal offender, the judge must consider: (a) the unique systemic or background factors which may have played a part in bringing the particular aboriginal offender before the courts; and (b) the types of sentencing procedures and sanctions which may be appropriate in the circumstances for the offender because of his or her particular aboriginal heritage or connection. In order to undertake these considerations, the sentencing judge will require information pertaining to the accused. Judges may take judicial notice of the broad systemic and background factors affecting aboriginal people, and of the priority given in aboriginal cultures to a restorative approach to sentencing.

This decision was incorporated into section 718 of the *Criminal Code*, and it directs judges to recognize how the histories and circumstances of Indigenous offenders may influence their involvement in crime. One intention of the SCC was to keep these people in the community unless there were no alternatives to incarceration. Amoud (2014, p. 14), a defence attorney in the Northwest Territories, reminds us that the purpose of *Gladue* is not "to provide a 'discount' on sentences for Aboriginal offenders. . . . When discussing *Gladue*, I have had to explain to my clients that the more serious the offence or the offender's criminal background, the less likely the offender will get much of a different sentence from someone who is not Aboriginal."

In a national study conducted for the Department of Justice Canada, April and Orsi (2013, p. 1) found that 19 specialized courts for Indigenous people exist throughout the country. The study also found that *Gladue* training and awareness activities were being provided for justice system officials, bail and parole decision-making decisions were being informed by *Gladue*, and community justice programs existed in most jurisdictions (April & Orsi, 2013). Despite those positive steps, however, Cuthand (2018) argues that efforts taken to reduce the overrepresentation of

info@aptn.ca • May 15, June 7, 25, July 5

Clint Sinclair (pictured here) did not have the benefit of a *Gladue* report at his 2016 sentencing for drug trafficking; he pursued a *Gladue* report for his own case, but in Manitoba these reports are appended to pre-sentence reports rather than being their own separate, comprehensive reports. The majority of provinces and territories in Canada do not have an established *Gladue* writing units even though the Supreme Court found risk assessments in pre-sentence reports to be culturally biased.

Continued

Indigenous people in the justice system, such as preparing *Gladue* reports, have fallen short of the Supreme Court's expectations because they have not been widely implemented throughout the country (see also Milward & Parkes, 2011).

Courts across Canada have developed initiatives to ensure that the distinctive circumstances of Indigenous defendants are considered. A cornerstone in crafting a just and fair sentence is for the judge to be aware of the offender's circumstances. Ordering a *Gladue* report is one step that judges can take to ensure that an Indigenous person's circumstances are considered at sentencing. The University of Saskatchewan (2018, para. 4) notes that *Gladue* reports "can contain recommendations to a court on an appropriate sentence and provide details about the impacts of settler colonialism on an Indigenous person's background, such as residential school history, physical or sexual abuse, interactions with the child welfare system, addictions, and other health issues" (see also Legal Services Society of British Columbia, 2018).

Decades after the 1999 *Gladue* decision, there is criticism that only a small proportion of Indigenous offenders ever receive a *Gladue* report. In 2017, for example, there were 131 *Gladue* reports written for the entire province of British Columbia (Karstens-Smith, 2018). Given there were about 15,000 people found guilty in BC courts in 2016/2017 and at least one-third of them were of

Indigenous ancestry (see Malakieh, 2018, Tables 4 and 5), these reports are written for less than one per cent of Indigenous offenders—and that count does not include youth. In some provinces, such as Manitoba, probation officers will add a *Gladue* section to a regular pre-sentence report. These reports, however, might fall short when it comes to fully accounting for how the individual's Indigenous background impacted their involvement in crime (Milward & Parkes, 2011). Some provinces, such as Alberta, have increased the number of *Gladue* reports being written. Parsons (2018) found a substantial increase between 2013 and 2018; those totals are shown in Figure 8.7. Alberta was able to increase the number of *Gladue* reports by contracting with individuals who are specially trained to write them (Parsons, 2018).

Some agencies specialize in the preparation of *Gladue* reports, including the Aboriginal Legal Services of Toronto (ALST). ALST staff members will prepare a *Gladue* report for people in Ontario communities who have been convicted of an offence and are in jeopardy of a custodial sentence of 90 days or longer. In addition to preparing *Gladue* reports, ALST case workers also develop plans to meet the offenders' rehabilitative needs, including community-based alternatives to incarceration.

Roach (2019) observes that *Gladue* has failed to reduce the overrepresentation of Indigenous peoples in Canada's correctional centres and

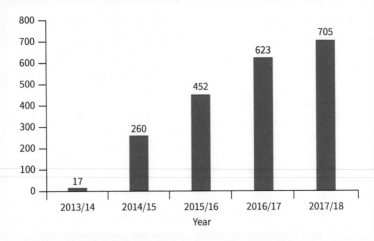

FIGURE 8.7 **Gladue Reports Written in Alberta, 2013/2014 to 2017/2018**
Parsons (2018)

prisons. Despite having been authorized for over two decades, only a small proportion of these reports are ordered by judges to help inform sentencing, and few provincial or territorial governments have made an effort to (a) train probation officers to write these reports; (b) contract with agencies—such as the ALST in Toronto— to carry out these investigations and prepare these reports; or (c) hire caseworkers to prepare *Gladue* reports, as is the practice in Alberta. But even if a greater number of these reports were written, we question whether there would be much of a difference in the outcomes of Indigenous peoples before the courts. For instance, if there are no realistic community-based alternatives to incarceration, the number of Indigenous peoples admitted to custody is unlikely to drop. Governments must expand the capacity of health, educational, and social service resources to support these people. This is a difficult and costly

proposition, and Amoud (2014) observes that community-based services that might help Indigenous offenders are not readily available in many rural and remote locations, where these peoples are disproportionately located.

The response to the *Gladue* decision shows that reforms to justice system operations are often slow to occur, and are sometimes thwarted by local, provincial, and federal governments. This reluctance to make reforms is sometimes based on economic factors ("it is too expensive") or because these changes threaten to disrupt long-standing social arrangements, such as the relationships between Indigenous and non-Indigenous peoples. Moreover, criminal justice reforms can sometimes be threatening to the individuals working within the system if their agencies will lose resources, or if their personnel are required to change their priorities or practices.

training to properly conduct their assessments (Bonta et al., 2005; Storey, Watt, & Hart, 2015). However, since there is so little research on officers and the preparation of these reports, we do not know whether these claims are accurate. Another controversial factor is that reports in some provinces can include hearsay information that the probation officer does not have to verify (e.g., about an individual's alcohol use or gang involvement). These issues are worthy of research, as pre-sentence reports may have a significant impact on an individual's freedom and may influence decisions made by correctional officials after sentencing. Hannah-Moffat and Maurutto (2010) are also critical of including formal risk assessments in PSRs as this practice may contribute to higher incarceration rates of people from some marginalized groups. Most risk assessments, for example, consider individuals to be at higher risk of reoffending if they have arrests at early ages, lack a formal education, or have a long history of prior arrests and convictions.

SUMMARY

Although sentencing an individual looks like a relatively straightforward process when shown on television, it is a very important undertaking as we all have an interest in ensuring that sentences are fair, unbiased, and just, and that they increase our safety. Sentencing in Canada is guided by several principles, but the foremost is proportionality, which says that the punishment must be related to the seriousness of the crime. In order to better understand the offender's strengths and weaknesses, judges often order a PSR. Despite criticisms of these reports, they are a useful tool that guides sentencing, and they are used by probation and correctional officials to develop rehabilitative plans after the sentence is imposed. With respect to Indigenous peoples, there is a growing interest in ensuring that they have access to *Gladue* reports, which are PSRs that highlight the systemic issues that might have contributed to their involvement in crime.

MYTH OR REALITY

Is Plea Bargaining Really a Pact with the Devil?

Over 90 per cent of criminal cases end after a plea has been negotiated between the Crown and the defence attorneys (Verdun-Jones, 2016). These arrangements usually involve the defendant entering a plea of guilty in return for less severe punishments, such as the reduction of a charge to a lesser offence, a withdrawal or stay of other charges, an agreement not to proceed on a charge, a promise not to charge other people, a reduction in the number of charges to one all-inclusive charge, or a recommendation from the prosecutor on the severity of a sentence (Burke Scott, 2018). Pleas of guilt are negotiated before a sentencing hearing happens, and the Crown and defence attorney enter a joint submission to the judge. Although judges are not obliged to accept those submissions, it is rare that they do not (Verdun-Jones, 2016).

Our reliance on plea bargaining is a relatively new practice, and up until the 1960s most serious cases went to trial and defendants pleaded guilty to most minor offences. Writing about plea bargaining in the US, Rakoff (2014) observes that in many other countries the practice "was viewed as a kind of 'devil's pact' that allowed guilty defendants to avoid the full force of the law." Yet plea bargains can also benefit prosecutors when the defendant has been charged with an offence that carries a mandatory minimum sentence. Prosecutors are further advantaged since the Supreme Court, in the *R v Nixon* (2011) case, agreed that Crown prosecutors can break their plea agreements, although that rarely occurs.

While plea bargaining is widely criticized, the courts, prosecution units, and legal aid systems would collapse if every defendant wanted his or her case argued in court. Piccinato (2004, p. 14) describes the pros and cons of plea bargaining; they are summarized in Table 8.4. Plea bargaining has benefits for the justice system: police officers and prosecutors save time as there is no need to collect, organize, and present evidence to a jury. The defence counsel does not need to prepare and present a case. Moreover, judges do not need to preside over a trial, and the courts can be reserved for other cases. But victims have criticized plea bargains because they have very little input into the decisions that prosecutors make. Charges, for example, are routinely stayed by prosecutors, which can make some victims feel betrayed by the justice system (Moore, 2015).

TABLE 8.4 **Advantages and Criticisms of Plea Bargaining**

Advantages	Criticisms
• Contributes to the efficiency of the justice system • Reduces costs and workloads • Provides certainty for all parties • Reduces inconvenience on witnesses • Reduces the stress of being a witness • Allows prosecutors to get a conviction on weak cases	• Leads to manipulation of the judicial system • Encourages abuses of power by prosecutors and judges • Creates a situation in which the defence counsel may put his or her interests over those of the client • Results in offenders receiving lenient sentences • Increases the risk of wrongful convictions

Adapted from Piccinato (2004)

One limitation in our knowledge of sentencing is that our predictions about the offender's potential for rehabilitation or dangerousness lack accuracy. As a result, we often give people a number of chances to reform, realizing that making a significant change in one's life is a challenge for anybody (think back to your success in keeping your New Year's resolutions), and there will be some failures. The hazard of sentencing, of course, is that the courtroom work group will make mistakes, and some individuals who receive a second chance will go on to commit serious offences. On the other hand, keeping individuals incarcerated for longer than necessary does not make us any safer—which is a criticism of "tough on crime" punishments.

Achieving the goals of public safety and holding wrongdoers accountable is a difficult undertaking, and one tension is how we balance the pursuit of individualized justice against the goal of treating offenders who commit the same types of crime in a similar manner. Additional considerations must be made when sentencing Indigenous people; judges must consider their distinctive circumstances. More than 20 years after the *Gladue* decision, however, there is widespread agreement that efforts to produce these reports have fallen short because they have not been widely implemented, nor have they been supported by an increase in community-based alternatives to incarceration. As a result, they have not reduced the overrepresentation of Indigenous inmates in provincial, territorial, or federal corrections. Such findings reinforce a theme that underlies the entire study of the criminal justice system: changes occur slowly and sometimes the interventions that we have introduced to reduce problems might not have the desired (or any) effect.

Another theme addressed in this chapter is the variation in the way that justice is carried out throughout the nation. Some provinces are more punitive and incarcerate a higher number of individuals per 100,000 residents. Prior research has shown that incarceration is not directly related to levels of crime, suggesting that other political, economic, and legal factors influence the use of punishment (Neil & Carmichael, 2015; Ruddell & Jones, 2017). While almost everybody agrees that we need to be able to incapacitate people who represent a risk to public safety, there is less agreement on how such individuals should be imprisoned.

Career SNAPSHOT

Probation Officer

Like other careers in the justice system, probation officers can work in a variety of roles. One important duty of probation officers is preparing pre-sentence reports, and this role might be of interest to students who want to gain experience in carrying out investigations. Pre-sentence reports are prepared for the court and are read by the individual being sentenced, counsel, and Crown prosecutor, so they require careful attention to detail and excellent writing skills.

Probation officers also work with individuals accused of offences. Some officers monitor judicial interim releases or oversee alternative measures programs for first-time and non-violent offenders. Probation officers can also supervise probationers in a variety of caseloads. Officers working in small offices are likely to be generalists who take care of every type of offender, while those working in larger offices may be more likely to supervise specialized caseloads or work in specialized roles such as being assigned to a mental health court. While most probation officers start off working in generalist caseloads, most can expect to be assigned to specialized roles after they have gained several years of experience.

Profile

Name: Elizabeth Engel
Job title: Probation Officer, Regina Adult Community Corrections
Employed in current job since: 2013
Present location: Regina, Saskatchewan
Education: Bachelor in Human Justice, Minor in Sociology, University of Regina

Background

Upon entering university, I had few ideas about what type of career I wanted to pursue. I enrolled in a general arts degree program, but I soon realized that I was not interested in any typical subject as a major, so I transferred into the human justice program and became energized with the thought of being able to help people facing adversity. I am currently a probation officer with the Saskatchewan Ministry of Corrections in Regina, and I have come to realize that this was my career goal even though I was not fully aware of what I was working toward during my time at the University of Regina.

Continued

It was not until after I completed my two practicum (internship) placements that I decided to pursue a career in community corrections.

Work Experience

I began my career at the Ranch Ehrlo Society in Pilot Butte, Saskatchewan, working with at-risk youth during a practicum placement as a student. Prior to my convocation, I also completed an advanced practicum placement at the Crown Prosecutor's Office in Regina. In that role, I was able to gain exposure to all of the aspects of the justice system, including court procedures, community-based partnerships, corrections and policing agencies, and offender services, and I learned how they operate together. This experience fuelled my motivation to become a probation officer. I am very dedicated to promoting public safety by strengthening the offenders' ability to contribute to and live positively in their communities.

My experiences at both of my practicum placements helped me to learn about the diversity of human behaviour and to identify and understand factors associated with those at risk. My front-line role working with offenders has given me the experience to develop the skills necessary to assess human behaviour and risk while implementing intervention strategies to encourage offenders to be successful in their communities.

In my work as a probation officer, I value the positive impact I have had in the lives of probationers by helping them work toward their rehabilitation and address their risk areas with interventions I have recommended. This has had a positive impact on public safety. Although I am in the first years of my career, I have been required to testify in court to explain a risk assessment that I administered, and I have also received positive recognition and accolades from a judge for a pre-sentence report that I prepared. In my work, I have supervised dangerous, violent, and difficult people who have worked toward their rehabilitation and success by managing their high-risk behaviours; this of course, reduces recidivism, which is the most rewarding part of my job.

Advice to Students

Students who are interested in a career in community corrections should never ignore their instincts or capabilities. You should try to experience and learn from all of the opportunities given to you—good or bad. In addition, you should ensure that your self-care is a priority as well as supporting your team, and you have to remember that public safety is in your hands. Students interested in working with offenders should become engaged in their communities and should volunteer as often as possible, as these experiences demonstrate humility and kindness. My final piece of advice is to never be afraid to absorb all experiences, to be confident, and to listen to yourself.

REVIEW QUESTIONS

1. What are the main types of community and custodial sentences that a judge can impose?
2. Define the principles of proportionality and totality and explain why these factors are important in the administration of justice.
3. Describe the differences between aggravating and mitigating factors and explain how they are related to individualized justice.
4. What are the components of a pre-sentence report?
5. Why are sentences in some provinces or territories more severe than in others, even if they have similar rates of crime?

DISCUSSION QUESTIONS

1. Should decisions about the use of imprisonment be driven by public opinion, or should we leave these decisions to experts?
2. Ideally, we would like to treat everybody who commits a crime in the same manner: Why is this not practical?

3. Some people believe that "getting tough" on offenders when crime rates are dropping is not good public policy. What is your opinion on "getting tough" on offenders?

4. When imposing a prison sentence on an offender, should the cost of that prisoner's care also be publicized?

5. How can our justice system best respond to career criminals?

INTERNET SITE

The victim impact statements, pre-sentence reports, and psychological reports for Justin Bourque—the offender who killed three RCMP members in 2014—can be found on the Canadian Broadcasting Corporation website. These materials provide readers with a better understanding of the components of these reports.
www.cbc.ca/news/canada/new—brunswick/-justin-bourque-evidence-posted-with-discretion-at-cbc-1.2865791

CASES CITED

R v Bartkow (1978), 24 NSR (2d) 518
R v Gladue, [1999] 1 SCR 688
R v Johnson, 2012 ONCA 339
R v Junkert, 2010 ONCA 549
R v Lavallee, [1990] 1 SCR 852

R v Lloyd, 2016 SCC 13, [2016] 1 SCR 130
R v Nixon, 2011 SCC 34
R v Nur, 2015 SCC 15, [2015] 1 SCR 773
R v O'Keefe, 2018 NLCA 11

▲ Probationers perform community service work beside a highway. What benefits do you think this scenario has for those serving their community sentence, and for those in the community? What are some objections that community members might have? What about objections of the offenders? (Photo credit: Mikael Karlsson/Alamy Stock Photo)

9 Provincial Corrections: Probation and Short-term Incarceration

LEARNING OUTLINE

After reading this chapter, you will be able to

- Describe the key issues shaping probation in Canada
- Identify the best practices in community supervision
- Describe the evolution of provincial and territorial correctional systems
- Explain how the characteristics of inmates influence their conduct while incarcerated
- Describe the steps officials have taken to increase correctional safety and security

A High-Risk Probationer Murders Three Ontario Women

On December 6, 2017, 60-year-old Basil Borutski was sentenced to serve almost 70 years in prison before he can apply for parole for killing three women in Renfrew County, Ontario, in a September 2015 crime spree. Borutski had been involved with the justice system since the 1970s and numerous individuals had made complaints to the police about his threatening and violent behaviours. He was also well-known to the workers from domestic violence shelters where his former partners had sought help (McQuigge, 2015).

Borutski was on probation when the killings occurred. Mayor and Culbert (2016) observe that the "system failed women" and the family, friends, and neighbours of the victims "question why the police, probation officers and courts failed to protect these women." According to Sibley (2015), "Borutski was well known to police in the area," and a year before the murders "he was found guilty . . . on a variety of charges, including assault, choking, auto theft, mischief under $5,000, operating a motor vehicle while disqualified and breach of probation. There was also a firearms-related offence." At his 2014 sentencing on those crimes, the Crown prosecutor said that:

> It's just simply violation after violation of orders . . . and all they required him to do . . .

is simply keep the peace and be of good behaviour, and he can't manage that." (as cited in Nease, 2017, para. 8)

Mayor and Culbert (2016) point out that Borutski served only five months of his 17-month custody sentence and refused to sign his probation order when released. He disregarded the conditions of his new probation orders by failing to attend anger-management classes and he continued to drive, despite having surrendered his driver's licence to the court.

Some probationers do not abide by the conditions of their probation orders and go on to commit serious and violent crimes. One of the challenges in a legal system where an individual is presumed innocent until proven guilty is that while the police and probation officials are aware of potentially violent individuals within the community they cannot act based on a person's potential for violence, but only after an actual offence occurs. While judges can order that high-risk probationers be monitored electronically (so their whereabouts are known to probation officials), taking this step will not prevent them from acting violently. Additionally, few violations of court orders result in harsh punishments. Maxwell (2017, p. 20) reports that the median custody sentence for a breach of probation offence in 2014/2015 was 15 days.

Critical Questions

1. How should the justice system respond to an individual who commits criminal offences throughout their entire adult life?
2. What strategies should we use to protect people who have been in abusive relationships with those who continue to threaten them?
3. About 100,000 offenders are sentenced to probation every year and almost 25,000 each year are convicted of violating the conditions of their probation (Miladinovic, 2019). Based on those numbers, would you say probation is a successful approach to punishing offenders? Justify your answer.

INTRODUCTION

When considering the punishment of wrongdoers, most of our attention is focused on custody populations, even though they only house a fraction of all sentenced offenders (Malakieh, 2019). For the most part the public supports community-based sentencing; a survey conducted by the federal Department of Justice (2018, p. 1) revealed that:

- Most Canadians (73 per cent) supported community-based sentences for non-violent crimes.
- Over one-half of respondents (55 per cent) thought that too many Canadians were incarcerated.
- About three-quarters believed that restorative justice interventions, community services, and responding to an offender's unmet needs (e.g., substance abuse treatment or job training) would reduce crime.
- Almost two-thirds (63 per cent) thought community-based interventions would increase public safety.

Supporters of the due process perspective point out that most probationers successfully finish their community-based sentences without reoffending.

Yet, there are also millions of Canadians who believe that community-based sentences do not hold offenders accountable (Mandel, 2017). They point out that individuals such as Basil Borutski, who had a history of committing serious and violent crimes, must be supervised more closely. Ultimately, we rely on the judgment of provincial and territorial correctional officials to ensure our safety by closely monitoring these probationers. One of the challenges for provincial corrections departments, however, is that the demands on their officers is high and some probationers receive inadequate supervision (Global News, 2017).

There are several arguments for supervising offenders in the community. Probationary and conditional sentences allow sentenced offenders to remain in school, maintain their employment, and

care for their families. Imposing harsher punishments, such as incarcerating them, might further disadvantage or discourage individuals and push them further into criminality. Moreover, we can supervise probationers at a fraction of the cost of incarcerating them. Despite those advantages, there is also a place for the short-term incarceration of some offenders. Inmates in provincial or territorial facilities are composed of two groups: remands and those serving sentences of less than two years. Although few inmates in correctional centres serve more than a few weeks, some present significant challenges for the staff when they display very disruptive or aggressive behaviour. This chapter focuses on the delivery of these correctional services—probation and short-term incarceration—by provincial and territorial authorities.

In the pages that follow, a more complete description of probation and corrections is presented. The first section gives an overview of probation, describing the evolution of probation in Canada and identifying the factors that shape the practice of probation. That section is followed by an overview of provincial and territorial corrections, the characteristics of these facilities and the inmates living in them, and a discussion about the challenges the correctional staff confront. These descriptions set the stage for our discussion of federal imprisonment and parole in the next chapter.

AN OVERVIEW OF PROBATION IN CANADA

On any given day in 2017/2018, there were about 25,000 provincial or territorial correctional centre inmates and another 95,000 offenders who were serving some form of community sentence (Malakieh, 2019). These numbers show the importance of probation and conditional sentences to Canada's criminal justice system. An offender may be sentenced to a probationary or conditional sentence or may serve a period of probation after serving a custody sentence. The one common factor to all these community-based sentences is that the offender lives in the community under the supervision of a probation officer. Each probationer in Canada is required to meet three standard conditions on their probation orders: (a) keeping the peace and being of good behaviour (which may include a ban on communicating with witnesses, co-accused, or victims), (b) reporting to the court when required, and (c) notifying the court or probation officer of any significant changes, such as getting a new job or residence. In addition to these standard conditions, there is a range of additional restrictions that can be placed on the individual, including prohibiting alcohol or drug use, abiding by a curfew, attending counselling, making restitution, and completing community service hours.

There are various levels of intensity when it comes to supervising probationers, and some low-risk offenders might never meet with their probation officer after an initial appointment whereas high-risk sexual offenders may be required to meet with them several times a week. Probation officers also conduct home visits and meet with some probationers at their workplaces. These supervision practices are rooted in social work. Similar to social work, a term commonly used by probation officers is caseload, which they use to refer to the number of probationers under

their supervision. Also similar to social work is the practice of developing case plans with an officer's higher-risk probationers, which act as the roadmaps for their rehabilitation. These high-risk probationers, including some chronic domestic violence offenders, may have very extensive case plans requiring them to participate in treatment. These case plans are often based on an assessment of the probationer's strengths and unmet needs as well as the factors that contributed to their involvement in crime, such as substance abuse or anger management problems. Case plans have traditionally focused on issues such as substance abuse, education, and employment. Some Canadian researchers, however, have been critical that such plans have failed to challenge the values and beliefs that led to the offender's involvement in crime (Bonta, Rugge, Scott, Bourgon, & Yessine, 2008).

Figure 9.1 shows the use of probation and provincial incarceration from 1979 to 2017. These rates peaked in the mid-1990s and while the rate of probationers per 100,000 residents has been dropping, the provincial incarceration rate has been relatively stable over time, even after crime rates decreased. Most probationary sentences are imposed for non-violent crimes and common

standard conditions All Canadians on probation are required to keep the peace and be of good behaviour, report to the court or probation officer when required, and report any significant changes to the probation officer or court.

caseload The number of individuals under the supervision of a probation or parole officer.

case plan The "roadmap" for an individual's rehabilitation that is developed by the offender and the caseworker.

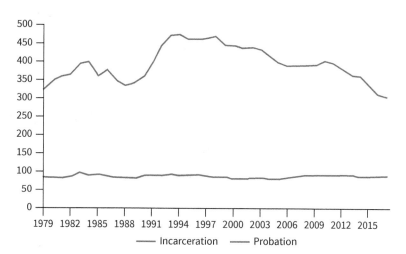

FIGURE 9.1 Provincial and Territorial Incarceration and Probation Rates per 100,000 Population: Canada, 1979–2017

Statistics Canada (2018a)

assaults, although individuals sentenced to custody on serious charges sometimes are required to serve a probationary sentence once released from the correctional centre. While judges can impose up to a three-year probationary sentence, the average probation term was 468 days in 2016/2017 (Statistics Canada, 2019c).

Every province and territory operates a community corrections division; the goals of these organizations are to supervise offenders in the community. Calverley and Beattie (2005, pp. 7–10) identified these programs, summarized as follows:

- administer adult alternative measures programs
- supervise offenders serving probationary sentences
- supervise individuals serving conditional sentences
- deliver rehabilitative programs
- supervise individuals on provincial parole (in Ontario and Quebec) or temporary absences from custody longer than 72 hours
- oversee fine option programs
- carry out pretrial supervision in some provinces
- administer community service work programs
- prepare pre-sentence investigations for the courts

provincial parole
Provincial parole boards are operated in Ontario and Quebec for prisoners in provincial correctional centres, while individuals serving less than two years in all the remaining provinces and territories can apply to the Parole Board of Canada for early releases.

Probation Caseloads

Probation officers are assigned a caseload of offenders who are serving a community-based sentence. In rural areas and small cities, they often supervise generalist caseloads involving every type of low- and high-risk probationer. One of the shortcomings of these generalist caseloads is that probationers with distinctive crime histories or specific needs—such as people with mental health problems or chronic domestic violence offenders—account for only a small percentage of any generalized caseload. As a result, the officers do not have the time to develop specialized knowledge or skills to excel at managing these different types of cases. Depending on the nature

of their offences, untreated sexual offenders, for example, pose distinct risks to the public, and reducing those risks requires an understanding of their offence histories (including their preferred victims), the circumstances that led to their sexual offences, and the best practices in their supervision. In urban areas, by contrast, caseloads tend to be specialized.

Average caseload sizes typically range from 50 to 60 probationers per officer. The Office of the Auditor General Manitoba (2014, p. 271) reports the average caseload size was 53 probationers, while Ontario probation officers supervised about 64 probationers (Reevely, 2014), and BC officers supervised an average of 59 cases (Hansard, 2018). We must be careful about understanding service delivery based on averages as they can mask some very diverse caseloads. Probation officers supervising high-risk sexual offenders, for example, might only have 25 individuals on their caseload, while another officer might supervise 200 low-risk cases. The British Columbia Justice and Public Safety Council (2018, p. 24) contends that the complexity of cases officers must now manage has been increasing and officers are now supervising a greater proportion of high-risk probationers on their caseloads, as well as offenders convicted of sexual and domestic violence offences.

Focusing on High-Risk Probationers

Probation supervision approaches vary throughout the nation and depend somewhat on the nature of the caseload. There is agreement in the correctional literature that scarce treatment resources and officer supervision time should be prioritized for the offenders who pose the highest risks. This approach is based on research showing that low-risk probationers require very little supervision (Bonta & Andrews, 2017). Some low-risk probationers, for example, might be required to report to their officer by phone once a month. High-risk probationers are a comparatively smaller group, but have more unmet treatment needs. Many of those treatment needs are related to unresolved addictions issues, mental

Race, Class, and Gender

Fines and Fairness: Should the Rich Pay More?

Almost 64,000 adults in criminal court cases in 2016/2017 were fined as part of their punishment; the average amount was almost $1,000 (Statistics Canada 2019b). From 2013 to 2018, courts were also required to impose an additional victim surcharge for anybody convicted of a crime (McDonald, Northcott, & Raguparan, 2014). These surcharges were used to fund victims' services throughout the country. While funding victims' services using money collected from offenders is in theory a good idea, some soon recognized that this practice discriminates against the poor, and the amounts were sometimes very high if an individual was involved in numerous offences. It is no secret that the poor are disadvantaged when it comes to paying fines, and many are incarcerated in provincial correctional centres because they cannot not pay their fines and surcharges. Seymour (2014) describes the case of a homeless 26-year-old in Ottawa who was convicted of nine offences stemming from a single incident where he stole a bottle of rye from a liquor store "and then kicked a loss prevention officer and police officer, confronted a snow plow operator and broke a shelter window, and lashed out at police after being stopped wandering down the middle of a busy street." The minimum surcharge for these offences was $900, which is beyond the reach of a man with a $250 monthly income. Fines had potentially turned correctional centres into modern-day debtor's prisons.

In December 2018, the Supreme Court agreed with civil libertarians and advocates for the poor that mandatory victim surcharges were a cruel and unusual punishment (Hassan, 2019).

To reduce the incarceration of people who couldn't pay their fines, most provincial and territorial governments—with the exception of British Columbia, Ontario, and Newfoundland and Labrador—introduced **fine option programs**, where individuals can work off their fine in a community setting being credited at the minimum wage rather than sending money directly to the court to pay their debt (Nunavut Justice, 2018). One critical question we should ask is why those three provinces do not offer fine option programs. Moreover, the legislation authorizing fine option programs varies across the nation and some provinces do not allow individuals to use fine option programs for traffic tickets.

fine option programs Enable people to pay their court-ordered fines using their labour (typically by working in jobs related to community service).

Although speeding is not a criminal offence, Schierenbeck (2018) observes that in Argentina and Finland the fines that speeders pay are linked to their annual income; this approach was also introduced in the United Kingdom in 2017 (Murray, 2017). As a result, the rich pay higher fines than speeders who have lower incomes, thus helping to deter the rich from speeding just as much as those with lower incomes. Canadian researcher McKenna (2018) reports that a wealthy Swedish businessman was fined more than $1.3 million Canadian for travelling 290 km/hour in Switzerland.

It is important to consider how we deter crime, and whether those deterrents have the same impact on everyone who is a potential offender.

health problems, negative peer group associations (such as being involved in a gang), poor employment histories, and attitudes and beliefs that are supportive of crime. In order to reduce their risks, they require more attention from probation officials.

As a probationer's risk level increases, the frequency and intensity of supervision also rises, which is the theory behind intensive supervision probation (ISP) programs. Although ISP was introduced in the 1980s, research shows that its effectiveness is mixed (Hyatt & Barnes, 2017). For example, many

intensive supervision probation (ISP) Places higher levels of supervision on high-risk probationers, and probation officers typically meet more frequently with them.

Dmitry Pichugin/Shutterstock

In a growing number of countries, traffic fines are not the same for every violator and are based on the individual's income. As a result, the president of your college or university—who is very well-paid—would pay a much higher fine than an unemployed student, even though both of them were travelling at the same speed. Are fines based on one's income more fair than the current system? Why or why not?

electronic monitoring (EM) Requires probationers or parolees living in the community to wear a device that communicates their whereabouts to a facility that tracks their movements.

home confinement A sanction that requires an individual on community supervision to remain at home; this is usually coupled with electronic monitoring.

Officials can increase the supervision of probationers using electronic monitoring (EM)—an approach introduced in the 1980s. Probationers in these programs are required to wear a monitor attached to their ankles that alerts correctional officials if they are more than a short distance from their home's landline phone (e.g., 30 metres). Many of these probationers are sentenced to home confinement, where they must remain at home unless arrangements to leave their residence are made with their probation officer. Newer versions of EM use global positioning systems (GPS) to continuously track the probationer's whereabouts, and some of these monitors can test for alcohol consumption.

Wallace-Capretta and Roberts (2013, p. 56) report that EM is used:

- as a condition of judicial interim release/bail;
- to monitor offenders serving intermittent sentences of custody;
- to monitor offenders serving a conditional sentence of imprisonment at home;
- as a condition of probation in high-risk cases;
- to monitor adult prisoners leaving a correctional institution on a Temporary Absence Program; and
- to assist in the supervision of offenders released on parole.

of these high-intensity supervision programs result in higher rates of breaches of probation because the probationers are more closely monitored (and so more breaches of probation are caught), but that might be a positive outcome if their involvement in more serious offences is reduced. A Manitoba study of ISP with high-risk probationers carried out by Weinrath, Doerksen, and Watts (2015) reveals that:

Tight supervision results in higher technical violations, failure rates are higher than desirable, and subjects can end up under state supervision for extended periods. Not all findings are negative, however, as deterrence and treatment elements appear to result in less serious offending. (p. 279)

Some potentially dangerous probationers, however, can fall through the cracks in the system and receive very little supervision. A report by Global News (2017) found that some high-risk sexual offenders serving more than a year on probation had never received a home visit by a probation officer.

Research carried out by the highly regarded Washington State Institute for Public Policy (2018) reveals that EM is a cost-effective crime-reduction practice. While many probationers are good candidates for EM, it is seldom used (Wallace-Capretta & Roberts, 2013), although the Canada Border Services Agency has started to use EM as an alternative to detaining individuals in custody (Blanchfield, 2018). One shortcoming of EM, however, is that while we know the individual's whereabouts, we don't know what they're doing—they could still be engaging in crime. Moreover, some scholars contend that being placed on EM has a psychological impact on these individuals, and

Gacek (2016) found that offenders on EM express feelings akin to being imprisoned even though they are living in the community.

Violations of Probation

Figure 9.2 shows just a few of the characteristics of probationers in 2016/2017. Most notably, about one-third of them (31,337 probationers) appeared in court after being charged with a breach of probation offence, which is one of the most common crimes heard in adult courts (Malakieh, 2019). Of those individuals, about 25,000 were found guilty (about 2 per cent were acquitted, and the charges were stayed in about 20 per cent of such cases). While some of those found guilty of violating their probation were sentenced prior to 2016/2017, a rough estimate is that about one in four probationers was unsuccessful in 2016/2017. That estimate is close to the results published in Johnson's (2006) examination of breach of probation offences in five provinces and the results of a Saskatchewan study carried out by Gossner, Simon, Rector, and Ruddell (2016).

As noted earlier, all probationers are required to abide by three standard probation conditions: (a) keeping the peace and being of good behaviour; (b) reporting to the court when required, and; (c) notifying the court or probation officer of any significant changes. Judges also impose additional conditions that respond to the probationer's

Although electronic monitoring (EM) enables correctional officials to monitor the whereabouts of people being supervised in the community, these devices are rarely used. Malakieh (2018, p. 16) reports there are about 10,000 offenders under some form of community supervision (including bail) in Saskatchewan, although the province only has 125 EM devices, which works out to about one in 80 individuals being monitored.

specific needs or offence. People convicted of domestic violence, for example, might be required to attend specialized treatment or an anger-management course. Johnson (2006, p. 8) identifies the most commonly imposed probationary conditions:

> Attend counselling
> Abstain from drugs or alcohol
> Restricted contact with certain people
> Community service work
> Driving prohibition
> Restitution/compensation order
> Attend work or school
> Reside in a specific place/house arrest
> Curfew
> Area restriction

Judges are also free to impose additional conditions related to a probationer's specific circumstances. For example, offenders convicted of viewing child pornography may be restricted from using a computer or other device with

Total Individuals Placed on Probation in 2016/17	• 99,902
Probation Sentence Length	• Less than 6 months: 10% • Six months to 1 year: 52% • One year or longer: 37%
Charged with Breach of Probation Offences	• About 1/3 (31,337)
Total Guilty: Breach of Probation Cases	• About 1/4 (24,507)

FIGURE 9.2 Probation Statistics, Canada, 2016/2017

Based on Malakieh, 2019; Statistics Canada (2019a; 2019c)

internet access. Moreover, judges can also restrict probationers convicted of violent crimes or firearms offences from possessing firearms or ammunition.

A common condition of probation is a community service order, which requires a probationer to perform unpaid community service work—most often by working for non-profit organizations such as libraries or hospitals or by performing tasks that benefit the community, such as picking up trash alongside a roadway. In many provinces the probation agencies fund non-profit organizations to operate these programs so probationers can complete their community service work. Administering these programs can be a challenge, as some probationers are not very motivated to carry out the work and their participation must constantly be monitored. Another commonly imposed condition of probation is that the offender make restitution to the victim(s) of their crimes.

This brings us to the question of what happens when an offender violates the conditions of their probation. Like other front-line personnel in the justice system, probation officers have a lot of discretion and if they discover that a probationer has breached the conditions of their probation—Americans and some Canadians call this a technical violation—they can choose to take no action, counsel the probationer, or refer the case to a prosecutor, who may take the case to court. Some of these outcomes are related to the seriousness of a breach. Failing to advise one's probation officer of a minor change in their circumstances is unlikely to be referred to a prosecutor, but a sex offender who refuses to attend their court-ordered treatment would be referred.

breach of probation
A violation of an offender's condition of probation, such as using drugs or alcohol when it is forbidden, or violating a curfew.

Figure 9.3 shows that about one in four probationary sentences results in a conviction for a breach of probation, which becomes a new offence. For probationers found guilty of these breach of probation offences in 2016/2017, over one-half (57 per cent) were sentenced to custody, probation was extended for about one-fifth (21 per cent), and 17 per cent were fined. The remaining

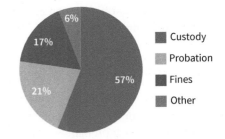

FIGURE 9.3 Outcomes for Individuals Convicted of Breach of Probation Offences, 2016/2017
Statistics Canada (2019a)

six per cent, classified as "other" in Figure 9.3, were placed on a conditional sentence, required to do community service or make restitution, or may have received an absolute or conditional discharge. Is a failure rate of about one in four bad news? We know that only about half of US probationers successfully complete their community sentences, but one of the problems with the US statistics is that probation agencies lose track of about one-fifth of their probationers (Kaeble, 2018). Despite that limitation, we can safely say that the probation failure rate in Canada is generally lower than in the United States.

The reasons that one in four probationers are convicted of a breach of probation offence are complex. A common issue identified in the previous eight chapters is that our society does not provide enough economic and social supports to help offenders succeed, especially if they have chronic problems with mental health or addictions. As a result, it is no surprise to workers in the justice system when they reoffend. Some probationers are required to abide by a dozen or more conditions on their probation orders, but there is growing awareness that imposing that many conditions increases their likelihood of failure. Another emerging challenge is that offenders not represented by a lawyer in court will often agree to almost any condition in order to secure their release from custody. Once they are released, however, those conditions can become overwhelming, and it is more likely they will be breached (Damon, 2014). Some also argue that homeless probationers are set up to fail as they cannot abide by curfews, and life on the street

A COMPARATIVE VIEW

Offender Rehabilitation versus Surveillance in Canada and the United States

Miller, Copeland, and Sullivan (2014) identify the differences between community corrections organizations that place a priority on offender rehabilitation and agencies that prioritize law enforcement functions such as the surveillance, monitoring, and control of probationers. There will always be a tension between these two approaches, and it is difficult to balance them when dealing with probationers with histories of violence or managing offenders with lengthy criminal histories. Canadian probation officers, however, have stayed much closer to their roots in social work than their US counterparts. Although supervising and monitoring probationers are important aspects of an officer's job, there may be an over-reliance on control in some US jurisdictions. A further barrier to finishing one's probation is that many US agencies charge probationers monthly user fees for their supervision; Human Rights Watch (2018) argues this practice sets these probationers up to fail.

One important difference between the two nations is that while Canadian probation officers are employees of provincial or territorial governments, most US officers are employed by local (municipal) or county governments. As a result, there are thousands of probation offices throughout America and there is incredible diversity in agency leadership, officer training, policies, procedures, and funding. Agencies that receive adequate funding and hire professional and well-trained staff members may deliver programs that have lower rates of probationer recidivism (Still, 2016).

Unlike their Canadian counterparts, it is common for US probation officers to engage in formal partnerships with the police and patrol with them (Kim & Matz, 2018). In that enforcement role, American probation officers routinely carry sidearms and many also wear bullet-resistant vests. The ultimate goal of some US probation agencies is the monitoring and surveillance of offenders and is summarized by the saying "tail 'em, nail 'em, and jail 'em" (Western & Schiraldi, 2017). Given that sentiment, we expect that some offenders are likely afraid of their probation officers—which makes it difficult to form meaningful helping relationships.

ZUMA Press Inc/Alamy Stock Photo

Many US jurisdictions authorize probation officers to carry sidearms, and these officers will sometimes patrol with the police. Some critics have suggested that these officers have lost their rehabilitation orientation in favour of surveillance and control. Do you think Canada should adopt the "tough on crime" approach of the United States? Why or why not?

will result in frequent interactions with the police, which might result in further charges. A former probationer says:

When I was on probation, there was factors of homelessness, addiction, family life circumstances, the violence that comes on the street. . . . You're not thinking about going into an office when you haven't showered for three days, have no place to live and checking in to make sure you don't go back to jail. (CBC News, 2015, para. 9)

There is very little research about the acts that result in new criminal charges for probationers or their outcomes after their convictions. There is, however, a growing interest in identifying the factors that lead to successful probation outcomes; these are described in the following section.

INCREASING PROBATIONER SUCCESS

Research has consistently demonstrated the effectiveness of correctional interventions based on the risk-need-responsivity (RNR) approach. Effective supervision starts with an assessment of the probationer's risk and needs, and the probation officer and their client work together to develop plans to address those issues. Table 9.1 highlights the three components of this approach. A key factor that makes RNR different from other correctional interventions is the recognition of an inmate's self-determination: that offenders should have a say in decisions affecting their lives. Under this approach, probation staff recognize that offenders have their own goals, wants, and needs, and that the "mission of the correctional agency is rehabilitation (not punishment) through respectful, ethical, humane, psychologically informed treatment" (Bonta, Bourgeon, & Rugge, 2018, p. 184).

There are, however, several barriers to a probationer's rehabilitation. Young, Farrell, and Taxman (2013, p. 1071) observe that probation staff must accurately assess the offender's risks and needs and

that the interventions based on those assessments must be available and implemented correctly. Staff members, for example, must receive training that enables them to deliver a high-quality intervention that is faithful to the rehabilitative model. In other words, if the probationer is supposed to receive 10 hours of counselling by a trained psychologist, agency leaders should not try to reduce the treatment to six hours or substitute another type of counsellor such as a nurse. When agencies reduce the intensity of the intervention or attempt to save money by using less-qualified staff, the results are often less effective than expected.

Officer Skills Matter in Reducing Recidivism

In addition to delivering rehabilitative services that are responsive to a probationer's risk and needs, there is a growing body of research that highlights the importance of probation officer skills in reducing recidivism. Raynor, Ugwudike, and Vanstone (2014) found that highly skilled officers had caseloads with lower rates of recidivism. Those findings lend support to research done by Canadian researchers who developed the Strategic Training Initiative in Community Supervision (STICS), which is intended to improve worker skills and knowledge so that they can effectively target a probationer's needs and reduce their recidivism (Bonta, Bourgeon, & Rugge, 2018; Doob, Hunter, Rachamalla, Sprott, & Webster, 2017).

The attitude that the probation officers have toward rehabilitation and the relationships they have with their clients is also important. Steiner, Travis, Makarios, and Brickley (2011) report that some officers can express punitive or rehabilitative values, and these values influence their approach to offender supervision. Miller's (2015, p. 19) national-level study of US probation officers found that some "seemed far more actively engaged in supervision than others . . . [and their approach depends on the officer's] personal values and characteristics." Researchers have found that officers who have better relationships with the probationers they supervise have lower recidivism rates (Chamberlain, Gricius, Wallace, Borjas, &

Strategic Training Initiative in Community Supervision (STICS) An approach to the community supervision of probationers that is based on the notion that probation officers who have stronger relationships with their clients and challenge their pro-criminal or antisocial beliefs have lower rates of recidivism on their caseloads.

TABLE 9.1 Risk-Need-Responsivity Model

Risk	Match the level of intervention to the risk level of the cases, working with moderate- and high-risk offenders (and not intervening with low-risk offenders).
Need	Treat the unmet needs associated with criminal thinking and behaviour, such as substance abuse or negative attitudes toward the law or conventional lifestyles.
Responsivity	Adapt correctional treatment to account for the individual's strengths, motivations, preferences, personality, age, gender, and ethnicity.

You Don't Need Theory to Understand How the Justice System Operates

In the previous chapters, the terms theory and theories have been avoided, as the focus of this book is developing a better understanding how Canada's criminal justice system works in practice. Many people say that theories aren't very relevant in the real world and that they don't really apply when it comes to crime and criminals. Yet, a set of theories underlie all the interventions of the criminal justice system from our crime prevention efforts to offender rehabilitation. And while most of us can't provide a scientific name to our opinions about crime and offenders, our ideas are founded on theories that were first proposed centuries ago. In fact, most of the philosophies of punishment described in Chapter 2 are related to different criminological theories; the next paragraphs briefly describe some of those theories and how different practices of the justice system are based on them.

When it comes to theories of crime, perhaps the most asked question is: *Why did the offender commit the crime*? Once we answer that question, we can develop strategies to reduce the offender's chances of engaging in future offences. Many of us think that offenders commit crimes because they think they will "get away with it" and won't be punished for their actions. As a result, many crime control policies are based on deterrence, which is based on the belief that if the police do a better job of catching offenders and judges swiftly impose harsh punishments the offender will learn their lesson and will refrain from crime. Do you believe that deterrence works? Obviously, this is a very simple explanation of a complex subject—entire books have been written on deterrence (see Nagin, Cullen, & Lero Jonson, 2016).

Many theories that explain why people commit crimes are based on the notion that there is something wrong with an individual that leads them to criminal behaviour. All critical criminologists, however, believe that our economic system and class structure (where 87 Canadian families have more assets than the 12 million lowest earning Canadians—see Macdonald, 2018) create the conditions that contribute to crime. They contend that social problems such as unemployment, poverty, inequality, racism, and the marginalization of different social groups push people into committing crimes. Moreover, they also argue that our police, courts, and correctional systems are designed to maintain those unequal relationships. Critical criminologists observe that the poor are harshly punished for their involvement in relatively minor street crimes, while the rich owners of corporations are seldom held accountable for crimes such as making their employees work in dangerous or unsafe conditions, or dumping toxic wastes into our lakes and rivers. As a result, a critical criminologist would say that by reducing poverty and inequality we would increase the quality of life for the poor and middle classes and reduce crime. These ideas about reducing crime by making economic and social changes are based on conflict theory.

Another important theoretical question is: *How do we reform offenders*? *Should we even try*? How we answer these questions informs what our interventions and rehabilitation programs look like. The risk-need-responsivity approach involves challenging an individual's criminogenic attitudes and values—what we call the offender's criminal thinking. An individual's antisocial values and beliefs can be decreased, and research shows that doing so reduces the risk of recidivism (Bonta & Andrews, 2017). But this is just one example of correctional rehabilitation, and many Canadians believe that we shouldn't try to reform offenders at all, that we should instead simply "lock them up and throw away the key." That belief is founded on a theory called incapacitation, and people who believe in that approach say that the best way to prevent someone from reoffending is to imprison them. This belief informs changes to policy such as longer prison sentences and stricter conditions for release.

The reality is that understanding different theories about human behaviour, crime, and justice is important because the operations of Canada's criminal justice system are based on different ideas about offender motivation and the nature of crime. These ideas also influence how we approach the issue of crime control, and whether we focus on "fixing" the offender or "fixing" society. By understanding the underlying theory, we can better understand the motivations of the policy, and can better assess whether it will be effective.

Ware, 2017). Punitive and less supportive officers, by contrast, may contribute to higher levels of anxiety in female probationers, for example, which in turn increases their recidivism (Morash, Kashy, Smith, & Cobbina, 2016).

In addition to a probation officer's clinical skills and attitude toward rehabilitation, research also shows that diligent workers have lower rates of recidivism. A Saskatchewan study examining the outcomes of high-risk probationers found that officers who were more conscientious (e.g., their assessments were more likely to be completed on time, their case plans were more comprehensive, and they made more referrals to community agencies) also had fewer probationers that reoffended (Gossner et al., 2016). This research suggests that probation departments can improve their success rates by:

- using interventions that have been proven to be effective with probationers;
- focusing officer time and resources on high-risk offenders;
- confronting attitudes and values that support criminal behaviour;
- hiring competent and skilled probation officers; and
- ensuring that their case work is comprehensive and up-to-date.

It is important to recognize, however, that despite the best efforts of probation officers, some probationers will fail, and a very small percentage of them will go on to commit serious and violent offences.

PROVINCIAL AND TERRITORIAL CORRECTIONS

There were 177 provincial and territorial correctional facilities in Canada in 2009, and they held almost 24,000 inmates (Calverley, 2010). There is a great deal of diversity in those operations. For example, size varies considerably. Some

correctional facilities in remote or rural locations are small, such as the 15-bed minimum-security Kugluktuk Ilavut Centre in Nunavut. The Edmonton Remand Centre, by contrast, is the largest provincially operated facility in Canada and holds almost 2,000 inmates. There are also provincial or territorial correctional facilities that hold only sentenced offenders or that offer specialized treatment programs, such as the Clarenville Correctional Centre, a women's facility in Newfoundland and Labrador that developed a horse therapy program (CBC News, 2018a). It is important to note that there are less than three dozen women-only correctional centres in the country. The low number of these facilities creates a hardship for some inmates as there might be only one women's facility in some provinces and it might be located far away from offenders' homes, making it difficult for them to get family visits. Multi-purpose facilities, by contrast, hold both sentenced offenders and remanded inmates, and may also house males and females, although coed facilities are rare.

Like the consolidation of police services across Canada discussed in Chapter 4, dozens of smaller and older provincial and territorial correctional centres have closed. Calverley (2010, p. 22) notes that the number of facilities dropped from 225 in 2000/2001 to 177 in 2008/2009, and consolidation has continued since. Many facilities with fewer than 50 beds close because it is difficult to deliver cost-effective correctional programs in very small institutions. Correctional centres have become the transfer point for the entire justice system, as most arrestees and people convicted of crimes pass through these places. This was not always the case: A century ago these facilities had a more local orientation and most were small, underfunded, and run by correctional personnel who had very little expertise in managing inmates. The following section briefly describes how provincial and territorial corrections have been evolving over time to operate in a more professional manner.

The Evolution of Provincial and Territorial Corrections

In the early colonization of the lands that would become Canada, there was not much need for incarceration as populations were sparse and informal social control was an effective method of reducing crime. As immigration increased and towns became cities, more formal approaches to law enforcement were required, including the need to secure some arrestees until their court dates. Places to temporarily hold arrestees went by several names, including gaols, detention centres, and police lock-ups (called police cells today). Some of these operations were makeshift structures, meaning that they were originally intended for some other use but were adapted to hold inmates. Many local jails were attached to the courthouse or other town buildings.

Like other examples of Canada's adult and youth justice systems, most correctional practices were imported by the British and French colonists who favoured sanctions that were familiar to them. In Europe, the practice of temporarily holding people accused of crimes behind bars dates back over 1,000 years. During that era, men, women, and children were often incarcerated together. Like today's correctional populations most of the people accused of crimes and held in detention were poor, had substance abuse problems, and were in poor mental and physical health. Unlike today, however, the living conditions for inmates were so grim that few received enough food or medical care and the facilities were poorly heated during the winter. As a result, many inmates died of "jail fever" (an outdated term for typhus—a disease transmitted by lice) and other illnesses.

Because incarceration was not used as a long-term punishment during the 1700s and 1800s most wrongdoers who were convicted of minor crimes were fined, beaten, or whipped (Ekstedt & Griffiths, 1988, pp. 20–21). Fyson (2006, p. 259) reports that in Montreal between 1765 and 1799, 61 per cent of offenders were fined, 23 per cent were

released on their recognizance, 8 per cent were incarcerated, and 7 per cent were whipped. Fyson and Fenchel (2015) observe that most of these inmates were held on minor charges, and less than 10 per cent of all Quebec City or Montreal jail inmates were violent offenders in the mid- to late-1800s.

By the time of Confederation in 1867, several different arrangements to manage offenders and populations deemed "problematic" (such as the poor or people with mental health problems) were being established throughout the nation. Locally operated detention facilities were first

Chamille White/Shutterstock

Punishment in the early days of the colony that would become Canada was swift, severe, and sometimes humiliating. Some wrongdoers were placed in pillories, and townspeople would throw their household waste at them, while others were whipped; serious offenders were sometimes pelted with rocks.

gaols The historic term for jails.

police lock-ups A historic term used to describe police cells, which are places where arrestees are temporarily held until their first court appearance (e.g., overnight).

workhouses
Places developed in the 1800s where the poor and people with mental illnesses were given basic necessities (e.g., beds, meals, and clothes) in return for work.

established in the more populated eastern provinces, and similar facilities were established in the west as populations grew in the Prairies and British Columbia. In addition, workhouses were established to manage "vagrants, beggars, prostitutes and fortune tellers, runaways, gamblers, stubborn children and servants, drunkards, and orphans" (Kroll, as cited in Ekstedt & Griffiths, 1988, p. 21). Moreover, there was a growing number of psychiatric hospitals being built throughout the country in the late 1800s and early 1900s to hold people who displayed disruptive behaviours and would otherwise have been placed in jails. The population of psychiatric facilities increased until the 1970s, when newly developed drugs became widely used to manage patients'

behaviour, and many were released back into their communities.

As Canada became more populated, makeshift jails were replaced with structures specifically designed and built as correctional facilities. There was also a move away from smaller locally-operated facilities toward larger provincially-funded correctional centres throughout the 1960s and 1970s. As noted above, there are now fewer than 200 facilities operated by provincial and territorial governments, and most of them were designed and built to promote safety and security, which is an important consideration as correctional centre inmates can act more unpredictably than long-term prisoners in federal facilities.

This small jail was established in 1912 in St Claude, Manitoba, and it was used until the 1930s. Few small towns required a large facility, and this structure contained only two wooden cells.

Provincial and Territorial Corrections Today

Figure 9.4 shows there are about one-quarter million admissions to provincial and territorial correctional facilities in Canada every year, although that number is somewhat deceptive as one person could be admitted more than once in a year. Almost 65,000 individuals were sentenced to terms of incarceration of less than two years in 2016/2017, and that number has increased somewhat from the previous years (Malakieh, 2018). The one constant factor in these places is the constant flow of inmates in and out of these facilities, what some have called the revolving door of corrections (Woo, 2018).

Most people remanded to custody are held for relatively short periods of time. In 2017/2018, half of males (50 per cent) and 59 per cent of females were released within one week, and three-quarters (75 per cent) served one month or less, and only about 5 per cent served more than six months (see Figure 9.5). Again, those are national averages and some adults facing serious charges, such as homicide, can serve years in a provincial facility as their cases work their way through the justice system.

Additionally, the length of stay on remand tends to be higher in northern Canada as there are fewer court dates in some rural locations (see Chapter 7). With respect to inmates sentenced to provincial or territorial custody, the sentences are also very short, and 60 per cent serve less than one month (Malakieh, 2019).

Provincial and territorial correctional centres have a short-term orientation toward inmate care, and this reduces their participation in rehabilitative programs. If the average sentence is one month, there is not much time to assess the inmate's rehabilitative needs and to place them in meaningful programs, even if these inmates wanted to participate in these programs. Providing few amenities other than a bed and meals is often called warehousing.

Inmates are eligible to work toward an early release through their good behaviour, and this earned remission (which was introduced in Chapter 8) further reduces the number of days they will serve in custody. As a result, many correctional centre activities are based on keeping inmates constructively occupied in recreational or work programs such as institutional cleaning, building maintenance, doing laundry, and

warehousing When inmates receive only their basic needs and few or no rehabilitative opportunities.

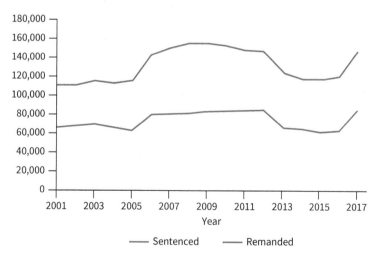

FIGURE 9.4 **Annual Admissions to Provincial and Territorial Corrections, 2000–2018**

Statistics Canada (2019d)

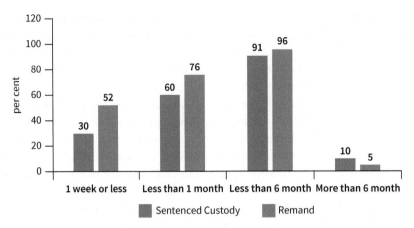

FIGURE 9.5 Time Served in Provincial/Territorial Custody, 2017/2018

Adapted from Statistics Canada (2019d)

preparing meals. Provincial inmates serving longer sentences may participate in literacy courses, addictions education, employment or vocational training, or life skills courses. Nova Scotia Corrections (2013), for example, offers the programs listed in Figure 9.6.

Many of these programs are delivered internally, although some sexual offenders are escorted into the community to receive their treatment in mental health agencies. Last, some low-risk inmates are also released into the community to participate in work programs or education during the day and return to the correctional centre in the evenings.

CHARACTERISTICS OF PROVINCIAL CORRECTIONAL CENTRE INMATES

The characteristics of the inmate population play a significant role in shaping the behaviours and incidents occurring within correctional facilities. Historically, most correctional centre inmates were held on relatively minor offences such as impaired driving, breach of probation, common assaults, or property offences such as break, enter and theft. Those individuals were often repeat offenders (some officers call them "frequent flyers"); a relatively small group of them can account for a

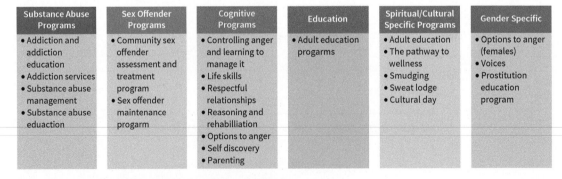

FIGURE 9.6 Nova Scotia Corrections Program Options, 2013
These programs were offered by the provincial corrections department of Nova Scotia. In what ways would these services affect offender rehabilitation outcomes?

Adapted from Nova Scotia Corrections (2013)

significant number of correctional centre admissions, and place significant demands on the entire justice system (Woo, 2018). Many frequent flyers have serious substance abuse or mental health problems. Although people who repeatedly commit minor offences still represent a significant proportion of the correctional centre population, there have been some long-term changes in the characteristics of provincial inmates. There has been, for instance, an increase in the number of people accused of committing serious or violent crimes, as well as a growing number of gang-involved inmates residing within provincial correctional centres. These changes have resulted in increased misconduct (such as rule violations, including importing contraband into these facilities) and violence in provincial correctional centres in some provinces (CBC, 2018b).

Table 9.2 shows the offence-related and demographic characteristics of provincial and territorial inmates. Of the approximately 25,000 inmates held on any given day, more than one-half (61 per cent) are awaiting court dates on remand, and these inmates are typically placed in high-security units. Most inmates are males (86 per cent), and Indigenous people are overrepresented in provincial correctional populations (28 per cent, while they account for only 5 per cent of the national population). Almost four-fifths of these inmates are 25 years old or older.

Of the hundreds of thousands of people admitted to correctional centres every year, a growing number of them have special needs. Over two-thirds of arrestees are under the influence of drugs or alcohol when they come into contact with the police. Kouyoumdjian, Calzavara, Kiefer, Main,

contraband
Any item that is forbidden in a correctional facility, such as cellular phones, illicit drugs, home-made liquor, or weapons.

TABLE 9.2 Inmate Population Characteristics: Provincial and Territorial Custody, 2017/2018

Total average daily population	24,657
Legal status and time served	
• Sentenced custody	39%
• Time served (sentenced inmates): One month or less	60%
• Remanded to custody	61%
• Time served (remanded inmates): One month or less	75%
Demographic characteristics	
• Male inmates (admissions)	85%
• Indigenous inmates (identity known)	28%
• Age (Admission): 18–24 years	21%
• Age (Admission): 25–34 years	38%
• Age (Admission): 35 and older	40%
Deaths in custody – 2006/2007 to 2015/2016	
• Ave. homicides per year	< 1.0
• Ave. suicides per year	8.9
• Ave. deaths from natural causes/accidents per year	32.0
Incarceration costs per inmate	
• All provinces and territories (annual cost)	$84,915
• All provinces and territories (average daily cost)	$233

Adapted from Malakieh (2019) and Public Safety Canada (2018)

Chris Scott/CTV Ottawa

One issue unique to women's corrections is the responsibility to provide care to pregnant inmates and new mothers. There is sometimes a reluctance in providing appropriate health care for inmates; this was illustrated when an Alberta inmate waited for over a month before an ultrasound confirmed her fetus had died, and she still had to wait several days after that test before she was taken to a hospital to have the tissue removed. These challenges are not unique to Alberta; the Ottawa-Carleton Detention Centre was sued by an inmate who gave birth on the floor of her segregation cell (Wakefield, 2018).

and Bondy (2014) surveyed Ontario inmates and found that more than one-half (56 per cent) had used opioids (medications that reduce pain, such as morphine, OxyContin, or codeine), cocaine, crack, or methamphetamine in the previous year. Long-term substance abusers may go through withdrawal during their first weeks of incarceration, which can affect behaviour.

Like jail populations 200 years ago, a disproportionate number of correctional centre inmates today are poor and members of marginalized populations. These inmates often suffer from physical health-related problems at a higher rate than the general population, including from communicable diseases such as HIV, AIDS, or hepatitis (Kouyoumdjian, Schuler, Matheson, & Hwang, 2016). Correctional centre staff must respond to those health-related problems. Between 2006/2007 and 2015/2016, 288 inmates died of natural causes or accidents (Public Safety Canada, 2018, p. 70). One barrier to studying deaths in custody is that information about these incidents is not collected and reported in the same manner across the country,

making it difficult to fully understand the scope of the problem (Winterdyk & Antonowicz, 2016).

An individual's admission to a correctional facility can be a very stressful event and this can worsen existing mental health problems. Many inmates are suffering from depression, anxiety, and borderline personality disorders, while fewer have very serious mental illnesses such as schizophrenia. Brown, Hirdes, and Fries (2015) estimate that 41.1 per cent of Ontario correctional centre inmates have at least one symptom of a mental health problem, and women and Indigenous people have even higher rates of mental health issues. Archambault, Joubert, and Brown (2013) report that female correctional centre inmates were more likely to receive mental health care than their male counterparts, although some individuals do not get the care they require, and lack of care may increase incidents of self-harm and suicide.

On average, women inmates have a greater set of unmet needs; they require greater access to mental and physical health services compared with male inmates, and therefore need additional supports (Zinger, 2017). The stress of being arrested and the uncertainty of forthcoming court appearances can also increase the need for psychological services, and such stressful feelings may intensify in mothers separated from their children. Paynter (2018) observes, for example, that most adult female inmates in Canada are mothers. Some new mothers are able to care for their infants in mother-child programs operating in some correctional centres. For example, a unit at the Alouette Correctional Centre for Women in Maple Ridge, British Columbia, has been open since 2004, although the number of participants in this program has been very small (Givetash, 2016).

INSTITUTIONAL SAFETY AND SECURITY

Although most people are not very sympathetic toward prisoners, ensuring they live in safe and secure correctional environments is important for everybody's long-term safety. Almost all inmates return to the community, and they become our neighbours and the people we encounter in our daily lives. As a result, it is in our best interests that people held in correctional institutions are not returned to the community more damaged than when they were admitted. This damage can take several forms. Being physically or sexually assaulted while incarcerated, for example, can have lifelong physical and mental health consequences. Even inmates who witness another person being assaulted can develop **post-traumatic stress disorder** (PTSD). Many inmates already have histories of being victimized or have experienced other trauma before their admissions to a correctional facility, and being victimized or witnessing these acts places them at higher risk of developing psychological problems (Cabeldue, Blackburn, & Mullings, 2019).

When it comes to violence in correctional centres, common assaults and verbal harassment occur often and few of these acts are detected or punished. Although serious violent crimes also occur, less than one inmate per year is murdered in all the provincial facilities put together (Public Safety Canada, 2018). There are several possible reasons for correctional centre violence, including the characteristics of the inmates (e.g., the number of inmates accused or convicted of violent crimes), although researchers have also attributed a recent uptick in violence to the increased number of gang-involved inmates (CBC, 2018a). Given these increases, correctional officials have taken several steps to increase the safety of the staff, visitors, and inmates. Some of these steps have included making significant changes to the physical design of correctional facilities, and this has changed the nature of inmate supervision. In the end, however, it is the daily activities of the correctional officers who work toward ensuring a safe and secure environment. The following sections describe how provincial and territorial correctional officials are working toward increasing institutional safety.

Facility Design and Safety

The physical layout of a correctional centre shapes how much supervision the inmates receive. Given that inmates greatly outnumber the staff, correctional officials have developed several strategies

Gina Chung/CTV Windsor

Prior to the 1970s, most correctional facilities were designed using a linear design, where rows of cells made it difficult for correctional officers to supervise inmates and the numerous blind spots increased inmate misconduct and reduced safety. This picture was taken of the former Windsor Jail, opened in 1925 and closed in 2014 with the opening of the South West Detention Centre.

over the past century to ensure the safety of workers as well as to protect inmates and reduce facility damage. For example, until the 1970s correctional facilities were constructed using the "big house" design, which featured long hallways that contained cells in a linear layout first introduced in the 1830s. In larger correctional facilities these rows of cells were stacked on top of each other. With this design, the correctional officers make periodic rounds along these hallways and to see what any inmate is doing the officer has to look into their cell. One limitation of this approach is that the officer's ability to know what is going on is limited by blind spots caused by the design.

Facilities constructed using the linear design were not very safe because of the large number of blind spots, and COs could only observe these areas when making their rounds. Since the 1970s most newly constructed correctional facilities have been built using the new generation design (also called the podular design), where the inmates' cells are constructed on the exterior walls of the living unit. These cells overlook a central

"big house" prisons
A style of high-security prisons that emerged in the 1800s and featured large stone buildings surrounded by high stone fences.

new generation design A correctional facility where the cells are arranged on the perimeter of the living unit and the prisoners eat and recreate in a common area (also called a podular design).

living unit
Refers to where inmates live within a facility, usually featuring cells that surround an area used for dining, education, and recreation.

strip-searches
Searches carried out by staff members to detect contraband by requiring inmates to remove their clothing (inmates may be strip-searched after visiting with their family members, for example).

courtyard or common area, which is used for recreation, classes, and dining. The new generation design reduces blind spots and enables COs to view the entire unit from their post, which deters misconduct due to the closer supervision.

The size of these living units varies somewhat by the populations being supervised. Units in youth custody facilities, for instance, are often designed to hold fewer than 25 residents, whereas a minimum-security unit for adults might hold 100 or more inmates. Some of these modern facilities resemble college dorms and the Hamilton-Wentworth Detention Centre looks more like an office complex than a correctional facility. The security of modern correctional facilities is also embedded in their design and construction. Iron bars that were once used to contain riots or disturbances have been replaced by windows constructed of thick polycarbonate see-through

materials that are resistant to breakage. Instead of moveable tables and chairs that could be thrown or used as weapons, these fixtures are now bolted to the floor. All the steps that correctional leaders take to embed security into a facility's physical design, including the perimeter fencing, are called *static security*.

In addition to changes in the physical design of correctional facilities, technology is playing a larger role today in ensuring correctional safety and security. Closed-circuit television (CCTV) cameras on living units can reduce inmate and staff misconduct (Jackson et al., 2015). In some cases, these cameras are so sensitive they can alert staff to rapid or unusual movements such as when an assault occurs. In addition, many facilities place sensors in their external fences to ensure that unauthorized people are not entering or leaving the facility. Some technological tools such

CC BY-ND 2.0 Alberta Justice and Solicitor General

The Edmonton Remand Centre uses a new generation design where the inmates' rooms are arranged around a central courtyard that is used for dining, recreation, and classes. This design promotes safety for both inmates and correctional staff.

as walk-through metal detectors (used to reduce the flow of weapons into or within a facility) and cell phone detectors are already commonly encountered. Metal detectors are being replaced, in some correctional facilities, by more sophisticated backscatter x-ray systems that reduce the need for strip-searches (where an inmate is required to disrobe in order to search for contraband). Replacing strip searches with x-ray technology is a positive step as most inmates consider strip-searches humiliating and they can be traumatizing to victims of sexual violence.

Technology is a two-way street, however, and inmates and their associates living in the community can also use the newest equipment to continue their criminal enterprises. Cellular phones have always been banned in correctional facilities given the concern that inmates possessing these devices will use them to make unauthorized calls (e.g., to a co-accused) or to thwart justice, such as arranging for witnesses to be threatened. Furthermore, drones—also referred to as unmanned aerial vehicles—have been used to drop drugs and other contraband into the yards of Canadian correctional facilities (Judd, 2018). As a result, some facilities are experimenting with devices that "jam" the signals transmitted to a drone (Collins, 2018). A growing number of correctional facilities are also using low-tech solutions, such as draping nets over the walls in some courtyards to decrease the success of dropping contraband into the facilities.

Dynamic Security

In addition to changing the physical design of correctional facilities, a new approach to supervising inmates has also been introduced, called direct supervision. Direct supervision is based on COs having more frequent interactions with inmates, which is a departure from earlier models of supervision where COs rarely left their posts to talk with prisoners. This regular interaction between inmates and officers is also called dynamic security, which Beijersbergen, Dirkzwager, van der Laan, and Nieuwbeerta (2016, p. 844) say is "based on positive interactions and constructive relationships between staff and prisoners, with mutual respect and trust." Wener (2012, p. 52) explains that the main reason for introducing the direct supervision model was to create a new way for COs to interact with inmates in small living units by promoting a normalized rather than an institutional environment. One of the goals of more frequent contact between officers and inmates is to help the inmates develop their problem-solving skills and thus reduce misconduct and recidivism. Developing these dynamic security skills can be a challenge, as the method requires a CO to have effective interpersonal skills and training to implement this approach.

Assessment and Classification

One of the foundations for ensuring the safety and security of correctional facilities is offender classification. Classification is an assessment of an inmate's risk by the correctional staff members in order to place the inmate in a facility (and/or living unit or cell) that best matches the risks they pose. There are some differences in the sophistication of these assessments. Arrestees held overnight in a police cell who are appearing in court the next day will receive an informal assessment where the admitting officers consider their apparent risks of suicide or self-harm, as well as their health status, including whether they are intoxicated, injured, or have a communicable disease. They also assess the arrestee's risk of escape or harming others (e.g., if the individual has been charged with violent crime or has a history of acting violently within correctional institutions). These assessments are often based on a simple checklist. If inmates are perceived to be at high risk of self-harm or aggressive behaviour, they will be placed in a cell or living unit that best matches their perceived risks. These informal assessments are called subjective classification and they are at least partially based on the gut feelings, or intuition, of the admitting officers.

Inmates admitted to a provincial correctional centre, or who are spending more than a few hours in custody, often receive a more formal assessment

drones Unmanned aerial vehicles that have been used to drop contraband into correctional facilities.

direct supervision A method of inmate supervision where officers directly interact with inmates.

dynamic security The regular interaction between prisoners and correctional officers that promotes problem-solving, information sharing, and rapport building.

offender classification The process by which an individual's risks and needs are assessed in order to assign the inmate to the most appropriate living unit.

subjective classification Informal assessments of inmates based on the judgment or gut feelings of the correctional supervisor or admitting officer.

called an objective classification. Factors considered in these assessments include the inmate's criminal history and their current functioning, including their withdrawal from alcohol and drugs and mental health status. The admitting officers also assess the seriousness of the inmate's current offence, their prior adjustment to custody (e.g., if the individual was involved in an escape attempt in a prior incarceration), and whether they are gang-involved. These objective classification instruments are based on scores, and higher scores usually lead to placement in higher security units. Inmates may also be separated from other arrestees who were involved in the same offence (co-accused).

Classification is also used to assess an individual's dynamic needs to determine the most appropriate rehabilitative placement, although those assessments are usually carried out for sentenced offenders. The Correctional Service of Canada, for example, has a very extensive admissions process, and a federal prisoner could be assessed over a period of weeks or months. These assessments

are primarily done at the federal level and so are described in Chapter 10.

Violence, Escapes, and Major Incidents

The goal of introducing new prison designs and new forms of inmate supervision was to reduce misconduct, suicide, and violence. Although murders in provincial and territorial corrections are very rare, there is growing concern about the numbers of inmate-on-inmate and inmate-on-staff assaults in provincial facilities. Few provinces report about incidents of inmate misconduct or violence, although British Columbia released statistics regarding the overall number of incidents in their correctional centres, and then classified those incidents into contraband, inmate-on-inmate, and inmate-on-staff assaults (Godfrey, 2018a, 2018b).

Table 9.3 shows the number of these acts per 100 inmates in BC facilities, and these results reveal that some types of institutions have higher rates

TABLE 9.3 **Incidents per 100 Inmates, British Columbia Correctional Centres, 2017**

Facility	Inmate Rule Violations	Contraband Incidents	Inmate-on-Inmate Assaults	Inmate-on-Staff Assaults
Alouette Correctional Centre for Women	117	30	18	4
Ford Mountain Correctional Centre	76	31	4	0
Fraser Regional Correctional Centre	161	40	14	2
Kamloops Regional Correctional Centre	193	33	35	4
Nanaimo Correctional Centre	196	69	7	0
North Fraser Pretrial Centre	225	41	38	8
Okanagan Correctional Centre	261	67	39	3
Prince George Regional Correctional Centre	233	51	39	6
Surrey Pretrial Services Centre	206	32	28	5
Vancouver Island Regional Correctional Centre	191	35	37	4

Adapted from Godfrey (2018a; 2018b)

of misconduct. For example, remand facilities—called pretrial facilities in the table—tend to be higher-risk environments for both staff and inmates; the two pretrial institutions had an average of 272 total incidents per 100 inmates, compared with an average of 255 for the other eight facilities. Many of the inmates have only been in custody for a short time, some may be going through withdrawal from alcohol and drugs, and almost all of them are anxious about their futures. Many also have mental health problems, and once admitted into custody, those with mental health issues are at higher risk of acting violently than other inmates. Other factors that could influence the number of misconduct incidents are levels of staff experience, overcrowding, the presence of activities that enable inmates to constructively use their leisure time, understaffing, and the staff and inmate cultures of these institutions.

Inmate Advocacy

COs can also contribute to violence. Ontario's ombudsman (2018) reveals that 74 complaints about the excessive use of force by correctional staff members were reported in 2017/2018. The excessive use of force had been identified as a problem in the Ombudsman Ontario (2013) report, which highlighted how a negative culture existed that covered up this misconduct. Like the discussion of use of force in policing, we must remember that anybody in custody can claim they were subjected to excessive force. In order to reduce the number of these claims, all planned use of force, such as cell-extractions (where an inmate is forcibly removed from their cell) are now videotaped, and these records provide more objective evidence of the intervention. CCTV cameras are also present in the common areas of most correctional facilities, and they record the interactions among inmates and between inmates and staff.

The presence of a provincial ombudsman enables correctional centre inmates to raise concerns about their treatment to investigators from independent government bodies. This oversight of provincial and territorial corrections is important as inmates are often out of sight and out of mind. One of the things that the public tends to forget is that inmates have very little ability to challenge decisions that can have a significant effect on their lives, and issues that are relatively minor for the public can be very important to an inmate's daily life because of their powerlessness. Every province has an ombudsman or similar advocate, and the Quebec Ombudsman also provides services to Nunavut, closely monitoring the conditions in Nunavut detention and correctional centres (Quebec Ombudsman, 2018).

Despite the best efforts of correctional staff, major incidents such as escapes occur. Most escapes from custody are relatively low-profile incidents where minimum-security inmates simply walk away from a facility, as few of them have security fences. Although escapes from medium- and maximum-security institutions are rare, in June 2014 three remanded inmates from a Quebec detention centre escaped by boarding a helicopter that landed in the exercise yard; they were not apprehended for two weeks (Shingler, 2014). Given the large number of people who pass through provincial correctional facilities each year, there are bound to be some dramatic escapes. The following are just five examples:

- Two Quebec prisoners escaped from jail in a hijacked helicopter in 2013 but were apprehended the same day: one of the inmates was sentenced to a 16-year sentence for his role in the escape and subsequent criminal offences (Feith, 2016).
- Four inmates escaped from a Red Deer facility after they were placed in a less secure holding area due to facility construction. Three were apprehended within a day and the last was at large for less than three weeks (Ramsay, 2018).
- Two sentenced inmates escaped from a Newfoundland correctional facility in 2010 by breaking through a wooden window

ombudsman An appointed official who investigates complaints made against organizations operated by provincial or territorial governments.

covering and then burrowing under a fence. Both were apprehended within two days (Canadian Press, 2010).

- A British Columbia correctional officer aided Omid Tahvili's 2007 escape in return for $50,000. The officer was sentenced to 39 months in prison but Tahvili has never been apprehended (CBC, 2008).
- Over a four-month period six inmates from the Regina Provincial Correctional Centre broke through the facility's interior and exterior walls using pieces of metal they found within the institution; all six escapees were recaptured within a month. During that time, 87 different correctional officers working on this unit failed to detect the damage to the facility (CBC, 2009).

Other less dramatic escapes can occur when low-risk inmates are being transported to various medical appointments or hospitals; these escorts are often done by a single correctional officer, and the inmate may not be in restraints such as handcuffs. Although escapes from medium- and maximum-security facilities are rare, they often speak to the creativity of those in custody and to what can happen when correctional staff members become complacent or corrupted.

CORRECTIONAL OFFICERS

Correctional officers play a key role in establishing the foundation of security in correctional facilities. Compared with police work, many of the duties of a CO may seem routine and boring, but they are nonetheless important. The following lists job tasks of a CO as identified by Statistics Canada (2018b):

- Observe conduct and behaviour of offenders and detainees to prevent disturbances and escapes
- Supervise offenders during work assignments, meals, and recreational periods

- Patrol assigned area and report any problems to supervisor
- Conduct security checks and scanning of visitors, inmates and their cells, working areas, and recreational activity areas
- Observe behaviour of offenders and prepare reports
- Escort detainees in transit and during temporary leaves
- Prepare admission, program, release, transfer, and other reports
- May supervise and coordinate work of other correctional service officers

These tasks are critical in reducing the flow of contraband into correctional facilities, limiting the number of weapons in circulation, and reducing misconduct by helping inmates solve problems without engaging in violence. Furthermore, ensuring that the physical security of the facility is maintained during perimeter patrols and carrying out cell searches reduces misconduct such as inmates making illicit alcohol from fruit and yeast (called "moose milk" in some northern facilities and "brew" elsewhere).

There is some variety in CO career paths, and many officers develop specialized skills throughout their careers (see the "A Closer Look" box). Some provincial officers are responsible for conducting assessments after an individual's admission. Others are partnered with dogs trained to detect contraband such as drugs or cellular phones. COs also play an important role in conducting investigations within facilities. These COs go by several different names, including security intelligence officers (SIOs), and they are often tasked with gang suppression activities. Not only is intelligence about these groups collected, but SIOs are also responsible for validating gang membership (proving that inmates are, in fact, affiliated with a gang). In order to reduce violence within Ontario's correctional facilities, the province hired 26 of these intelligence officers in 2018 to "seize contraband smuggled into jails, monitor gang members and work proactively with inmates to help curb violence" (CBC, 2018b).

A Closer Look

Correctional Training

In the 1970s and 1980s, many COs learned on the job and received very little training prior to working their first shifts with inmates. Much has changed since that time, and most provinces now require some form of pre-employment learning prior to academy training. The province of Ontario, for example, gives their cadets a reading package that provides information about the Ministry of Community Safety and Correctional Services and how the criminal justice system operates. Other provinces make attendance at training dependent on the individual having a current first aid/CPR certificate and driver's licence.

Whereas police cadets receive about 20 to 24 weeks of in-class academy training prior to becoming an officer, correctional officer cadets receive from six weeks in British Columbia to 10 weeks in Saskatchewan. Some provinces also expect them to apply the skills and knowledge from their classroom learning in a correctional centre prior to their graduation, which adds additional time to their training. In terms of training content, the Ontario Ministry of Community Safety and Corrections (2019) requires their cadets to master five basic themes in their eight weeks of in-class training:

- **Correctional System Orientation**: Includes developing interpersonal skills in order to increase effectiveness working with inmates and staff. Cadets receive an introduction to effective correctional practices, including how to ensure the safety and security of facilities.
- **Effective Communication**: Focuses on developing listening and communication skills so cadets can work effectively with diverse populations. Cadets are also trained in how to write accident, incident, injury, or search reports, and make appropriate logbook entries.
- **Inmate Management and Intervention Techniques**: Includes learning how to interact with

and manage inmates in a professional manner. Cadets are exposed to different scenarios they might confront in their work and learn how to deal with these situations, including using force.

- **Inmate Programs and Services**: Involves building the cadet's skills in using correctional interventions to create an environment that helps inmates to develop the attitudinal and behavioural changes that reduces their risk of recidivism.
- **Workplace Safety and Security**: Develops recruits' awareness of the environmental factors, including the potential exposure to infectious diseases that pose health risks to the inmates and staff.

These training topics are common across the nation, although some provinces will prioritize different themes, and recruits in one province, for example, might receive more training in physical intervention such as restraint training, than in provinces that might place a greater priority on reducing recidivism. In addition to their academy training, once an officer starts working, they will serve a probationary period of up to one year; during that time these new officers will typically receive mentoring and support from senior officers.

In addition to their initial academy training, every province requires that their officers receive ongoing training to ensure their perishable skills, such as first aid/CPR, are up-to-date. Ongoing training might also include an introduction into new ways of managing offenders and issues related to workplace safety, including responding to emerging technologies or new threats. One emerging threat, for example, is the increasing danger of exposure to fentanyl in correctional facilities (Grant, 2017).

SUMMARY

Two distinct correctional systems have evolved in Canada. The first are the ten provincial and three territorial correctional systems that hold about 25,000 remanded and short-term inmates on any given day and supervise another 95,000 offenders in the community. The second is the federal system that supervises about 23,000 offenders serving sentences of two years and longer, and about one-third of them are supervised in the community on a conditional release (Malakieh, 2019). There are distinct differences in these systems as there is considerably more variation in the operations of the provincial systems, which are overseen by 13 governments that have different priorities and operational goals. (By contrast, the supervision for all 23,000 federal offenders falls under the management of one agency, the Correctional Service of Canada. As a result, there tends to be more consistency in the priorities of the federal system. This will be discussed in Chapter 10.)

Although probation services receive very little media attention—unless a probationer commits a high-profile offence—they play a key role in the administration of justice in Canada. Probation has been called the workhorse of the criminal justice system, as there are over twice as many offenders serving a probationary sentence than remanded or sentenced inmates behind bars. Researchers are finding that we can increase the success of probationers by hiring skilled probation officers who develop case plans and intervention strategies that target the offender's antisocial and criminal thinking (Bonta et al., 2018; Doob et al., 2017). These efforts, however, must also be supported by strong health, education, and social service programs in the community to support rehabilitative efforts. The public generally supports community-based sentencing and wants probationers to be employed or going to school, and maintaining strong relationships with their families and neighbours so they have a greater stake in society, both of which reduce their risks of recidivism.

Provincial correctional centres are a core part of Canada's criminal justice system as most arrestees held for more than a day or two are taken to these places. These facilities have been described as the transfer point for the police, mental health agencies and federal prisons, as most arrestees pass through their doors. A review of statistics shows that few correctional centre inmates serve more than 30 days before their release. Those short terms of incarceration, however, make it unlikely that they will participate in any meaningful rehabilitative efforts.

Working at these provincial facilities can be challenging for the staff members, as the arrestees admitted into these places are often suffering from mental health and substance abuse problems and they are forced to manage the uncertainty of their futures as they await their next court appearances. These factors can lead to disruptive, aggressive, unpredictable, and suicidal behaviours, and those risks are intensified as the constant flow of inmates in and out of these places makes it difficult to predict an inmate's behaviour. As a result, provincial correctional officers are often exposed to violence and other highly stressful situations, and Canadian researchers found that this stress is intensified when facilities are understaffed and overcrowded (Ricciardelli, Power, & Simas Medeiros, 2018). In addition to the risks of being assaulted, exposure to these situations also contributes to high levels of post-traumatic stress disorder in correctional personnel (Carleton et al., 2018).

Career SNAPSHOT

Correctional Officer

The federal prison system employed almost 18,000 employees in 2016/2017, and over three-quarters of them worked in institutions; of those, most were correctional officers (Public Safety Canada, 2018, p. 23). Correctional officers (COs) working with the Correctional Service of Canada are employed in a variety of roles, including dog handling and security or intelligence. These professionals can work with male or female offenders, and they might work in institutions that hold primarily Indigenous inmates or prisoners with mental health problems. Although COs are employed in different roles and institutions throughout their careers, their work can be very stressful. Hours of tedious work can transition to a crisis in a heartbeat when officers are faced with an offender's misconduct, a riot, a hostage-taking situation, or prisoner self-harm or suicide. Furthermore, as correctional facilities operate around the clock and throughout the week, the unusual working hours can impact an officer's family relationships. As a result, COs are at some risk of developing PTSD in their careers (Carleton et al., 2018).

Like other human service professionals, COs must possess excellent interpersonal skills and have the confidence to confront prisoners who have had difficult lives and may feel that they have little to lose. In order to carry out their duties, officers work in teams and develop a supportive culture. A sense of humour also goes a long way in making correctional work more manageable.

Profile

Name: Jennifer Wolfreys
Job title: Correctional Officer II and Acting Parole Officer
Employed in current job since: 1998
Present location: Bath Institution, Ontario
Education: BA, Athabasca University; Certificate (Correctional Worker), St Lawrence College

Background

I started my career in corrections working in a halfway house for women, as well as tutoring offenders at Millhaven Institution. I decided to work as a correctional officer in order to get a full-time job, with the intention of becoming a parole officer. I am currently working at Bath Institution, a federal facility in Ontario.

Work Experience

I have been a CO since 1998 and in that time I have had several opportunities to work in parole officer and correctional manager roles. I love my work and feel extremely confident in my position as a supervisory correctional officer. About half of my job is security-related and the other half is casework with a designated caseload. The work requires strong writing and interpersonal skills, as well as the ability to work on a team. I really enjoy these aspects of my work, and I get a lot of satisfaction completing the extensive and varied requirements of my job. Most of the work with the inmates involves providing "dynamic security," which entails both observing and talking with inmates to ensure that everything is okay within the unit and the institution.

The beginning of my career was sometimes challenging, because I worked at Kingston Penitentiary, which held dangerous inmates. There were some older staff who were uncomfortable working with younger, university-educated women COs in a correctional environment. However, I respected and learned from many of them about how to deal with inmates and manage the living units. I'll never forget some good advice I received early on in my career: watch, listen, be yourself—a woman. I tried to display courage even when I was scared, and I did my best to show respect to staff and offenders alike. In this business, it is important to both command respect from, and show respect to, offenders, so my aim was to be "firm, fair, and consistent" in my duties.

I've worked at Bath Institution since 2002 and it's well-suited to my personality. I generally enjoy working and interacting with offenders, but it is important to be clear about professional boundaries, especially as a woman.

What I find most rewarding about my work is the ability to treat people with dignity. Many offenders I work with have led difficult lives; some may be old, sick, or dying at the institution. Treating people with dignity and respect does not dismiss their past or the crimes that they have committed, but I don't believe it is my job to judge them further. Many offenders are very remorseful and work hard to rehabilitate themselves, to fulfil their correctional plan, and to repay their debt to society.

The biggest surprise or challenge related to my work is my hesitancy to discuss my job in social environments, as it is often misunderstood. COs are not simply "guards;" we are the front-line face of corrections, along with nurses, psychologists, and case workers. It can be very demanding and complex work that requires dedication and commitment to the job and to the overarching goal of improving public safety.

Advice to Students

I would recommend taking courses in criminology, (abnormal) psychology, and counselling in order to better understand criminal mindsets and how to interact with people including offenders. It's really important to understand yourself and to be confident as a CO. Be mindful of, and take responsibility for, your actions, words, and conduct—and strive to uphold a good reputation with your colleagues and offenders alike.

REVIEW QUESTIONS

1. Describe the steps that correctional officials have taken to increase safety and security.
2. Provide examples of dynamic and static security.
3. Describe strategies that are intended to increase the effectiveness of probation supervision in reducing recidivism.
4. Describe how provincial corrections systems have evolved since the early 1900s.
5. Explain why specialized probation caseloads might be preferable to generalized caseloads.

DISCUSSION QUESTIONS

1. Do the lack of fine option programs in British Columbia, Newfoundland, and Ontario make provincial correctional centres into "debtors' prisons" for those unable to pay their fines? Why or why not?
2. Do you support the use of traffic fines that are based on the individual's income, like the practice in the United Kingdom, rather than a fixed amount, which is used in Canada, where every person pays the same amount for committing the same violation, regardless of income?
3. Provide reasons why the behaviours of inmates in provincial corrections may be volatile and unpredictable.
4. Is the best strategy for supervising probationers based on rehabilitation or surveillance and monitoring?
5. US probation officers in most states are authorized to carry firearms on duty. How would issuing Canadian probation officers firearms change their relationships with probationers?

▲ Melissa Ann Shepard, also known as the Internet Black Widow, was convicted of poisoning her intimate partners in addition to committing forgery, fraud, and stealing from people over 65 years of age. As part of the conditions of her March 2016 release following the end of her sentence, she was required to report any new romantic relationships to police and was barred from accessing the internet. In April 2016, at age 81, she was arrested (as seen in this photo) for using a Dartmouth, Nova Scotia library to access the internet, but those charges were dropped. What kinds of considerations must the Parole Board of Canada consider when placing restrictions on those being released? (Photo credit: THE CANADIAN PRESS/Andrew Vaughan)

10 Federal Corrections

LEARNING OUTLINE

After reading this chapter, you will be able to

- Describe how our ideas about offender rehabilitation have changed over time
- Explain the importance of inmate classification for corrections
- Explain why the profile of federal inmates influences institutional conduct
- Describe the different forms of prison releases to the community for CSC prisoners
- Describe some of the barriers to community re-entry for ex-prisoners

A Federal Prisoner Commits Suicide After Falling Through the Cracks in the System

In August 2010, 24-year-old Edward 'Eddie' Snowshoe, an inmate who was originally from the Northwest Territories, committed suicide in the Edmonton Institution, a maximum-security Correctional Service of Canada (CSC) facility. Snowshoe, who was serving a five-year sentence for shooting a cab driver in an armed robbery, had a difficult time adjusting to prison life. After sentencing, he was sent to the Stony Mountain Institution near Winnipeg, which is a medium-security facility, but in March 2010, "he was put in segregation—with no access to the general population—after brandishing a knife made from a juice box" (CBC, 2014, para. 9) for 134 days and was then transferred to the Edmonton Institution. After arriving in Edmonton, Snowshoe was directly placed in segregation where he remained for the 28 days until his death: altogether he served more than five months (162 days) in segregation before taking his life.

Newspaper accounts reveal that Snowshoe's mental health was failing during his stay in segregation. White (2014, para. 3) describes how he was "withdrawn and lethargic, he refused to speak with psychologists, take his allotted hour of daily recreation time, or attend monthly meetings where he could argue for a transfer." While imprisoned at Stony Mountain, he had tried to commit suicide three times between 2007 and 2009 and had engaged in one act of self-harm (Report to the Minister of Justice and Attorney General, 2014).

The judge who reviewed the circumstances of Eddie Snowshoe's death says he fell through the cracks in the system. His prior suicide attempts were well-documented, but the Edmonton staff members did not review the reports and were unaware that he had spent more than four months in segregation prior to coming to their facility. Once Snowshoe arrived at the Edmonton Institution, he submitted a written request to be moved from segregation to the general population, but the paperwork didn't turn up until after his death (Report to the Minister of Justice and Attorney General, 2014). When asked if he needed help, Snowshoe would tell the staff members that he was okay, but the judge observed that "just asking someone if they need help doesn't cut it when there is a clear history of psychological need" (Report to the Minister of Justice and Attorney General, 2014, p. 4). Although the CSC has psychologists, nurses, and case managers to help inmates with mental health problems, the staff failed to follow up on concerns raised when Snowshoe was first admitted.

Long-term placements in segregation have been very controversial. In 2018, the British Columbia Court of Appeal found that the CSC segregation policy was unconstitutional. A year later the Court required the federal prison system to take steps to reduce the time prisoners spend in segregation, allow them to get help from advocates, and let them spend more time out of their cells (Harris, 2019). In March 2019 the Ontario Court of Appeal ruled that placement in solitary confinement for more than 15 days was a cruel and unusual punishment (White, 2019), forcing correctional facilities to change their practices. All these changes were too late for Snowshoe. His mother said, "If a dog owner had a dog locked up for that long, that owner would be charged for animal cruelty" (as cited by the CBC, 2014, para. 3).

Critical Questions

1. Does Eddie Snowshoe's original misconduct (making a knife from a juice box) warrant 134 days in segregation prior to his move to another prison? Why or why not?

2. Why is it important to examine and investigate cases where people die in police custody or in a correctional facility?
3. Can you think of some of the possible impacts of a prisoner who dies by suicide on their family, the other inmates within the facility, as well as the correctional personnel who respond to these incidents?

INTRODUCTION

The Correctional Service of Canada (CSC) supervises about 23,000 offenders and almost two-thirds of them are in institutions while the rest live in their communities. While the average stay in a provincial correctional centre is about one month, as discussed in Chapter 9, all federal prisoners are sentenced to two years or longer and half of them are sentenced to five years or longer (Public Safety Canada, 2018). Helping inmates survive these lengthy prison terms can be difficult, especially when we consider the deprivations they experience, including limited contact with family and friends, restrictions on obtaining desirable goods and services—such as accessing the internet or having a home-cooked meal—and living with the constant threat of violence, the forced celibacy, and the lack of self-determination, as most of an inmate's daily activities are directed by correctional personnel (see Sykes, 1958/2007). Although the conditions of confinement in federal prisons can be harsh, including sharing cells that were originally designed for one person, longer sentences also provide an opportunity for inmates to work toward their rehabilitation, and the success of ex-prisoners on parole shows the CSC can safely reintegrate convicted offenders into society.

For most of us, our exposure to prison life is what we see in movies or in TV programs such as *Orange is the New Black*. One limitation of basing our knowledge on entertainment programs is their depiction of the worst aspects of prison life, such as inmates assaulting other prisoners or other acts of prison misconduct, which are violations of the prison's rules. Although correctional facilities can be violent places, few fictional accounts of life behind bars accurately portray the boredom, despair, and loneliness that inmates experience, as well as the bleak living conditions. These issues are present in Canadian federal prisons even though we spend more money per incarcerated individual than most other nations.

While the priorities of federal and provincial correctional systems differ somewhat, there are some common goals in the operations of any correctional facility, including the priority to provide a safe and secure environment. This can be challenging, because most federal inmates have long-term problems with addictions, mental and physical health disorders, history of unemployment, a lack of stability in their lives, and unhealthy family relationships. Prisoners can overcome these obstacles, and Canadian researchers have been on the forefront of developing correctional interventions that reduce prison misconduct and recidivism (Bonta & Andrews, 2017). Most of these efforts have focused on the notion that prison programs can respond to the unmet psychological needs of inmates and thereby reduce the risks they pose.

Bonta and Andrews' (2017) work on identifying offender risks, needs, and responsivity (discussed in Chapter 9) and developing treatment interventions to address those factors has been adopted by correctional services around the globe, because their approach improves outcomes for prisoners. Despite the barriers to the safe transition of prisoners into the community, staff working within Canada's federal prison system have demonstrated success in reducing recidivism (Public Safety Canada, 2018). Reforming prisoners, however, is only one goal of the prison system. Federal correctional officials must also manage prisoners who will never return to the community and will die in prison.

prison misconduct A violation of the rules of a correctional facility; often classified as major misconduct, such as assault, or minor misconduct, such as being in an unauthorized area or possessing contraband (e.g., drugs or a cell phone).

The path to developing successful correctional interventions has not been smooth, and in the following sections we take a closer look at the types of interventions introduced to ensure the of safety of prisoners in federal facilities and the steps taken to increase their successful release into the community. Our examination of federal corrections starts with the establishment of the first Canadian penitentiaries in the 1800s, as the location, design, and philosophy of these facilities shaped the delivery of federal corrections for over a century.

THE ESTABLISHMENT OF CANADIAN PENITENTIARIES

Penitentiaries holding offenders for lengthy terms of imprisonment have been used for less than two centuries. As noted in Chapter 3, prior to the 1800s offenders in the British Empire involved in serious crimes were usually physically punished, transported to penal colonies, or executed. As our attitudes toward the value of human life changed and our optimism for reforming criminals increased, the penitentiary with its emphasis on rehabilitation was introduced. Eastern State Penitentiary (ESP), which was founded in 1829 in Pennsylvania, is considered the world's first penitentiary. ESP is a large castle-like structure surrounded by nine-metre-high stone walls, and was the most expensive structure in America when it was built. Inside the walls, the prison was designed like a wheel with a central hub and seven long hallways resembling spokes radiating from that point: the inmate cells were located along these hallways.

ESP was based on the silent system, where inmates were kept in solitary confinement for their entire sentence and were forbidden to talk with other prisoners or staff. To further increase their isolation, the prisoner's heads were covered when they were escorted within the facility so they could not interact with others. Prisoners were expected to reform themselves by reflecting on their crimes. Each was given a Bible, although since almost all adults in the early 1800s were illiterate, one questions how many prisoners read these books. Not

silent system
An early approach to rehabilitation where prisoners were held in solitary confinement and were forbidden to talk to other prisoners or guards outside their cells.

"big house" prisons
A style of high-security prisons that emerged in the 1800s and featured large stone buildings surrounded by high stone fences.

surprisingly, the long periods of isolation and harsh conditions of confinement resulted in a high proportion of prisoners developing mental health problems, much like the experience of Eddie Snowshoe 150 years later (see the Case Study box at the start of the chapter).

Large prisons like ESP, with their castle-like design and imposing stone walls, made a powerful statement about the state's ability to punish wrongdoers. These prisons quickly became popular attractions. ESP was a destination for scholars, philosophers, and politicians from around the globe, and it served as a prototype for prisons in other nations, including Canada. Many prisons constructed throughout the 1800s were based on the ESP model—they are called "big house" prisons today given their fortress-like construction and high stone fences (see Chapter 9).

Prior to Confederation in 1867, the administration of corrections was a provincial responsibility. The first prison was the Kingston Penitentiary, which was originally called the Provincial Penitentiary of the Province of Upper Canada; it was modeled on the ESP design and used the silent system. The facility admitted its first prisoners in 1835 even though it was still under construction (Schwartz, 2016). During the 1800s conditions of confinement were grim, rules were strict, and punishments were severe for breaking rules. Enforcing the rules under the leadership of the facility's first warden, Henry Smith, resulted in prisoner abuse, and revelations of their mistreatment led to an 1849 commission of inquiry. The inquiry revealed evidence of extreme brutality and cruelty, including a prisoner suffering from mental illnesses receiving 720 lashes (Townson, 1960). Townson (1960) also describes how child prisoners, some under ten years of age, were flogged for smiling, winking, or laughing, which were prohibited acts. The inquiry also heard evidence that some prisoners were starved, and women prisoners sexually abused (McCoy, 2012).

Despite this early setback, a series of social changes, including population growth and higher crime rates, led to the gradual expansion of Canada's prison system. With the passage of the

Penitentiary Act in 1868, the three original provincial prisons—located in Kingston, Saint John, and Halifax—became a federal responsibility. Over the next few decades federal prisons were constructed in Saint-Vincent-de-Paul (Quebec), Stony Mountain (Manitoba), New Westminster (British Columbia), Dorchester (New Brunswick), and Prince Albert (Saskatchewan) (Correctional Service of Canada, 2014b). Most of these facilities were in rural areas, and until the mid-1900s these prisons were considered closed systems, which means they had minimal contact with the outside world and were almost self-sufficient: the prisoners grew crops and raised animals for food, and built the furniture and fixtures needed for the institutions. In addition, the power for the prison was often generated on site. The self-sufficient nature of these prisons reduced interactions with outsiders and lowered operating costs, but the downside to this isolation was that activities occurring within these places lacked external scrutiny or oversight, which led to unprofessional conduct, including prisoner abuse.

Correctional Service Canada

The motto of the Correctional Service of Canada is *Futura Recipere,* which means "to grasp the future"—a statement encouraging offenders to look forward.

While the focus of the federal correctional system was on reforming prisoners through hard work, several innovations were occurring over time. The Parole Board of Canada (2018a) describes how parole—where prisoners are released to the community prior to the end of their sentence—was introduced in 1899. Prisoners applying for parole were investigated by officials from the Ministry of Justice to evaluate their likelihood of a successful community re-entry. As no agency existed to supervise ex-prisoners in the community, they reported to the police and were required to abide by conditions such as obeying the law and (in some cases) refraining from alcohol. The Parole Board of Canada (2018a) notes that while there were few formal guidelines for ex-prisoners, parole could be revoked if an ex-prisoner committed a crime or violated the conditions of their release.

Throughout its history, the federal prison system has weathered a series of crises and reforms, and despite innovations such as introducing parole, inquiries into the operations of the entire penal system were carried out in 1913 and again in 1920. Furthermore, a Royal Commission was conducted by Justice Joseph Archambault after a series of prison riots occurred in the 1930s. The *Report of the Royal Commission to Investigate the Penal System of Canada*, released in 1938, suggested a series of changes be made to the federal prison system. Archambault recommended that prisoners receive better access to education and recreation, and he advocated for the separation of people with mental illnesses from the general prison population, for prisoners to serve their time in facilities close to their homes and families, and for the reduced use of corporal punishment (Kidman, 1938, pp. 112–113). Although much has changed in terms of our ideas about corrections, the foremost goals for a prison system identified by the Archambault Commission seem as difficult to achieve today as they were almost a century ago. These goals are:

- the protection of society
- the safe custody of inmates

closed system
A type of prison administration where there is little interaction with the community.

Kingston's Prison for Women (P4W), shown here, was based on the big house design that made it difficult to closely supervise the inmates and contributed to increased misconduct. As a result, P4W was described in one report as "unfit for bears" (Perkel, 2018, para. 2). As this was the only women's facility in Canada for many decades, families were often unable to visit their loved ones because they lived too far away. Closed in 2000, P4W has since been purchased by developers who hope to convert the former prison into condominiums or a student residence.

- strict but humane discipline
- reformation and rehabilitation of prisoners (Kidman, 1938, p. 114)

Since the 1930s, the federal prison population continued to grow along with the national population and increasing crime rates. Offender rehabilitation became a priority of the prison system and applications for parole became more formalized. Prisons slowly moved away from their closed-system orientation and were more open to community input and external scrutiny. There was also growing recognition of the special needs of Indigenous and women inmates. One important legislative change was the introduction of the *Corrections and Conditional Release Act* (1992), which specifies the minimum conditions of confinement for federal prisoners and their pathways to community release—including the overriding principle of the protection of society. One of the ongoing challenges faced by CSC personnel, however, is supervising some very difficult-to-manage prisoners.

CSC PRISONER CHARACTERISTICS

The CSC supervises about 23,000 federal offenders, and almost two-thirds of them live in prisons (Malakieh, 2019). In order to respond to the diverse needs of the institutional population, the CSC, headquartered in Ottawa, operates 43 institutions in the Atlantic, Ontario, Quebec, Prairie, and Pacific regions. Those institutions include four Indigenous healing lodges and five psychiatric treatment facilities. The remaining CSC facilities are a mix of minimum-, medium-, and high-security institutions, and some facilities have more than one security rating (called multi-level institutions). The CSC also has a high-security special handling unit in the Quebec region to manage the most dangerous offenders in a super-maximum-security setting.

Table 10.1 shows the demographic characteristics of the CSC population. When it comes to punishment, about half of federal prisoners serve sentences of five years or longer—although almost all of them are released prior to the expiry of their sentence on either parole or a statutory release. Almost one-quarter (23.4 per cent) of CSC prisoners are serving life sentences or have been designated as dangerous offenders (Public Safety Canada, 2018), and they will likely remain under correctional supervision—whether living in an institution or in the community—for the rest of their lives. On March 31, 2108, about 5 per cent of the in-custody population, or about 700 inmates, were women (Office of the Correctional Investigator, 2018).

Table 10.1 also shows that most federal prisoners have at least one violent offence in their current sentence (69 per cent) and the remaining inmates are convicted of drug (18 per cent) and all other offences (13 per cent). Housing so many

TABLE 10.1 Correctional Service of Canada Population Characteristics, 2017/2018

Total Population	23,172
Custody	61%
Community supervision (parole, statutory release, and long-term supervision orders)	39%
Male offenders (in institutions)	95%
Female offenders (in institutions)	5%
White offenders	58.8%
Indigenous offenders	22.7%
Black offenders	7.8%
Median age at admission	34 years
Sentence Characteristics	
Less than 3 years	24.6%
Less than 5 years	50.2%
Lifers/dangerous offenders	23.4%
Minimum-security risk	21.7%
Medium-security risk	63.4%
Maximum-security risk	14.9%
Offence Characteristics	
Violent offenders	69%
Drug offenders	18%
All other offenders	13%
Institutional Problems	
Homicides (avg. per year, 2006/2007 to 2015/2016)	2
Suicides (avg. per year, 2006/2007 to 2015/2016)	9
Escapes (avg. per year, 2007/2008 to 2016/2017)	20
Admissions to segregation (2016/2017)	6,788
Imprisonment Costs	
Average per inmate (all security levels)	$120,571 ($330 per day)

Adapted from Malakieh (2019), Correctional Service of Canada (2018), and Public Safety Canada (2018)

individuals who have engaged in violent crimes may contribute to higher numbers of prison homicides than in other countries (see "Comparative View" box). Although homicide and suicide rates are higher in Canadian prisons, major incidents are rare, and the last major riot occurred in 2017, when an inmate was killed in the Prince Albert penitentiary. Prior to that incident, the last major disturbance in a federal prison happened in 2008, so these events are unusual. Escapes are also rare: eight inmates escaped from federal prisons in 2016/2017, seven of which were from minimum-security institutions. Escapes from minimum-security facilities are not surprising as most lack perimeter fences, so inmates can simply walk away. Because minimum-security institutions cannot prevent a determined prisoner from escaping, fewer than one-quarter (22 per cent) of inmates are placed in these facilities and almost two-thirds (63 per cent) are placed in medium-security facilities (Public Safety Canada, 2018).

Special Needs Prison Populations

Table 10.1 also shows the demographic characteristics of the CSC population. Within these groups are at least eight special-needs populations, and many of these prisoners require additional resources and supports.

Indigenous Offenders

Almost one-quarter of the CSC population are of Indigenous ancestry, and that population has been growing (Office of the Correctional Investigator, 2018). As discussed in Chapter 3, Indigenous peoples have unique circumstances within Canada that require specific and culturally sensitive interventions. Since the 1990s the prison system has become more responsive in meeting the distinctive needs of Indigenous people, including incorporating Indigenous traditions and cultural beliefs into correctional programs. In order to be more responsive to these offenders, four healing lodges were established between 1995 and 2004, and the CSC funds another five healing lodges operated by community-based organizations (Correctional Service of Canada, 2019a). The delivery of these programs is supported by the participation of elders and other Indigenous community groups and members. The need for these interventions is higher among women offenders, as slightly over one-third (37 per cent) of the in-custody women's population are Indigenous offenders (Public Safety Canada, 2018).

Mothers and Pregnant Inmates

One ongoing challenge for the federal correctional system is providing appropriate care for pregnant inmates and new birth parents. Although the number of pregnant inmates in provincial corrections is higher, pregnant women admitted to federal prison present several ongoing challenges given their lengthy sentences. The CSC has offered a mother-child program since the 1990s that enables children to stay with their mothers until they are five years old, and on a part-time basis after that. The mother-child program is intended to promote a positive and healthy relationship although there are only about a dozen women participating in these programs. The low number reflects the relatively small number of pregnant women admitted to federal custody, as well as screening programs that might reject some women from participating due to their behaviours while in custody (e.g., misconduct) or criminal histories. Writing about her experience as a pregnant inmate and mother, Deschene (2017) says that prison officials were unsympathetic toward her situation and after giving birth she only saw her child about once per month.

Radicalized Inmates

Prisons can be places where non-violent prisoners are radicalized to violence. The Royal Canadian Mounted Police (2016, p. 6) defines radicalization to violence as "a process by which individuals are introduced to an overtly ideological message and belief system that encourages movement from moderate, mainstream beliefs toward extreme views." Prisons may be ideal recruiting grounds for racist or other radical groups as inmates are often discouraged, depressed, and isolated from positive influences in their lives, which makes them easily influenced and vulnerable to extremist ideas. In response to this challenge, the CSC has developed programs and interventions to challenge radical beliefs (Stys, McEachran, & Axford, 2016).

Aging Prisoners

Public Safety Canada (2018, p. 46) reports that the average age of admission for CSC prisoners has been increasing since the mid-2000s. The CSC is currently supervising over 700 prisoners 65 years and older in prisons and another 1,000 in the community (Public Safety Canada, 2018, p. 48). This population of senior citizens will continue to grow given that one-quarter of all prisoners are lifers or dangerous offenders, and they will be under CSC supervision until their deaths. Older inmates pose some challenges for prison systems, as they have greater health care needs than their younger counterparts due to chronic health conditions and the need for end-of-life care. These prisoners are also vulnerable to being victimized, and the Office of the Correctional Investigator (2019) is critical that many of them are being warehoused, with their basic needs addressed but receiving few rehabilitative interventions.

Prisoners with Mental Health Problems

The description of inmates in provincial and territorial correctional centres revealed that most had addictions and mental health problems. Table 10.2 shows the prevalence of mental health disorders (at the national level) among males admitted to the CSC.

A follow-up study was carried out for women offenders admitted to CSC facilities; 79 per cent of them were found to be suffering from at least one disorder, and with the exception of gambling, for every other category the prevalence rates were higher than the men (Brown et al., 2018). Inmates with mental health problems may be more likely to be involved in assaults (as victims as well as perpetrators), use-of-force incidents, as well as self-harming and suicidal

TABLE 10.2 Prevalence of Mental Health Disorders in Men Admitted to Canadian Federal Corrections Facilities, 2015

Disorder	Percentage
Mood disorders	17
Psychotic	3
Alcohol/substance abuse	50
Anxiety disorders	30
Eating disorders	1
Pathological gambling	6
Borderline personality disorder	16
Antisocial personality disorder	44

Note: These percentages will add up to more than 100 per cent as some individuals meet the criteria for more than one category.
Beaudette, Power, and Stewart (2015)

behaviours. In response to these risks, the CSC operates five regional treatment centres, and has trained counsellors to respond to prisoners with mental health problems. Those efforts, however, have been evaluated as insufficient to meet their needs (Office of the Correctional Investigator, 2018).

Prisoners Suffering from Fetal Alcohol Spectrum Disorder (FASD)

One group of prisoners not counted in CSC studies of mental health populations are people suffering from fetal alcohol spectrum disorder (FASD), the effects of the maternal use of alcohol when they were still in the womb. While FASD is not considered a mental health disorder, individuals suffering from FASD often have numerous behavioural challenges and can find it difficult to link their actions to consequences, which increases their likelihood of involvement in the justice system and can lead to violations of prison rules and routines. Canadian research finds that children with FASD are overrepresented in provincial care, such as foster placements (between 3 and 11 per cent) and between 11 and 23 per cent of youth and 10 and 18 per cent of adults involved in the justice system are thought to have this disorder (Flannigan, Unsworth, & Harding, 2018). Admitting a higher proportion of people suffering from FASD into a prison system strains the operations of these facilities, given this population's learning difficulties and problems living in structured environments with strict rules.

Gang Members

The CSC says that about one in ten federal inmates is gang-involved, although the real number may be much higher as few prisoners willingly acknowledge their gang affiliations (Harris, 2018a). All together, there are an estimated 65 different gangs operating in Canadian prisons. Some offenders admitted to prison are already gang-affiliated while others join gangs after their admission, believing they will be safer if affiliated with a gang.

A Closer Look

Assessing Risks and Needs

In Chapter 9 the issue of inmate classification was briefly described as it related to the admission of arrestees serving short terms of incarceration, such as an overnight detention in police cells. Classification takes on more importance for inmates sentenced to lengthy prison terms, and the process used by the CSC is both comprehensive and complex, and guided by the *Corrections and Conditional Release Act*. Like provincial correctional centres, the federal prison system also assesses the risks a prisoner poses in order to place them in the most appropriate living unit. Unlike the provincial centres, the federal system also uses the classification to assign inmates to various correctional programs.

In order to carry out a comprehensive classification, the CSC admits new prisoners to a reception centre after their sentencing and conducts an offender intake assessment. The stay in the reception centre can last several months, and during that time institutional parole officers conduct several assessments. One of the most important is the custody rating scale, an instrument that helps predict a prisoner's adjustment to custody, risk of escape, and danger to the public. In addition to assessing risks, the CSC also evaluates the inmate's dynamic needs in order to establish priorities for correctional programming. Assessing these dynamic needs is a complex undertaking as each factor might be composed of several dozen specific questions about the offender's functioning. Stewart et al. (2017) describe the seven dynamic needs; these are summarized in Table 10.3.

Higher scores on these indicators reflect greater unmet needs, as well as higher risks and a greater likelihood of recidivism. But these indicators are called dynamic because they can be changed. Offenders can, for example, increase their employability, stabilize their family relationships, learn to manage their anger, and develop more conventional attitudes toward work and the law, and these changes can lower their likelihood of involvement in prison misconduct or recidivism. The CSC assessed

reception centre A prison unit that receives prisoners from the courts and holds them until their assessment and classification is complete.

offender intake assessment Assessing an individual's future risk of criminal behaviour based on their criminal history and their needs (e.g., whether they require help with employment or substance abuse).

institutional parole officers Officers employed by the CSC who work with inmates to develop case plans that enable prisoners to make a safe transition to the community.

A former gang member describes his entry into a prison gang:

> I was in and out of jail. Then you start going to adult jail for longer sentences. Now you're with killers and rapists. Before you know it, you begin to fit in, in order to survive. You take on that . . . gangster mentality. That disregard for everything that's right. (Global News, 2018)

In addition to contributing to higher levels of violence, gangs are also involved in the underground prison economy (e.g., the sale of drugs and other contraband), undermine rehabilitative programming, and contribute to recidivism once these gang-involved inmates return to the community (Winterdyk & Ruddell, 2010). As a result, the CSC invests considerable time, energy, and resources into gang-suppression efforts.

Women Offenders

On March 31, 2018, there were 1,397 women under the supervision of the CSC; 676 were imprisoned, and the remaining 721 were living in the community (Office of the Correctional Investigator, 2018, p. 83). Although accounting for about 5 per cent of the entire Canadian prison population, most women prisoners have special needs for physical and mental health care;

the outcomes of almost 18,000 individuals released from federal prisons and found that three of these factors had the greatest impact on increased recidivism: unresolved substance abuse problems, poor self-control (relating to the personal/emotional factor), and antisocial attitudes (Stewart et al., 2017, p. 88).

custody rating scale An instrument that predicts a prisoner's risk of misconduct, adjustment to prison life, and potential for escape.

dynamic needs Factors that can be changed by offenders, such as their education level or employability.

TABLE 10.3 Dynamic Needs

Employment and education	The offender lacks stable employment, lacks an employment history, has limited job-related skills, or lacks a high school education.
Family and marital	The individual has strained or unhealthy relationships with parents, siblings, and/or intimate partners.
Associates	The offender associates mostly with substance abusers and has mostly criminal friends, peers (e.g., gang members), and/or family members, and receives little pro-social supports from their intimate partner.
Substance abuse	The person abuses alcohol/drugs and started using substances at an early age; substance abuse interferes with their job and health.
Community functioning	The offender has unstable accommodation, poor social supports, and does not participate in any organized activities.
Personal/emotional	The individual has poor self-control and may be impulsive, aggressive, inflexible, hostile, and/or manipulative, and may engage in thrill-seeking.
Attitude	The offender has a negative attitude toward the justice system or employment and displays non-conforming attitudes toward society, lacks direction, or values a substance-abusing lifestyle.

Stewart et al. (2017)

133 were serving life or indeterminate sentences in 2017/2018 (Correctional Service of Canada, 2019e). Many have suffered trauma in the form of physical, psychological, or sexual abuse and this victimization, combined with marginalization, relationship problems, and substance abuse contributes to their involvement in crime (Wright & Cullen, 2012). The Brown et al. (2018) study found, for instance, that 79 per cent of women admitted to CSC facilities had at least one psychological disorder. Given these findings there is a growing acknowledgement that gender-responsive correctional programs and interventions are required for these women. In order to accommodate this population, the CSC has a branch that focuses on the delivery of services to women offenders.

Larger populations of special-needs inmates within a prison system increase the costs of imprisonment. The average annual cost to house one federal prisoner in 2016/2017 was $120,571 (Malakieh, 2019). That amount increases along with the security level, and placement in maximum security has the highest costs. Figure 10.1 shows the average daily cost of housing male and female federal prisoners in 2014/2015. The average cost of housing a female inmate is almost double that of a male prisoner, as most women are held in very small facilities that are costly to operate. In addition, as discussed above, women prisoners typically have more extensive physical and mental health needs, and responding to these needs increases the costs of their care.

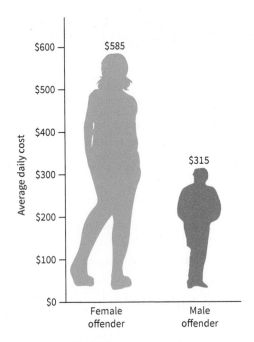

FIGURE 10.1 Average Daily Cost of a Federal Prisoner, 2014/2015

Adapted from Public Safety Canada (2018)

CHALLENGES OF MANAGING LONG-TERM PRISONERS

Delivering Meaningful Correctional Interventions

One of the historical challenges for prison personnel was keeping inmates constructively occupied. In the past, correctional treatments were often based on (a) educational programs, (b) drug and alcohol treatment, and (c) employment and vocational training. With respect to employment training, for example, correctional officials tried to keep prisoners busy working within the prison, preparing meals, cleaning, doing the prison's laundry, and maintaining the facilities. These efforts were also intended to help prisoners develop a set of job-related skills they could use once returned to the community. While these efforts are admirable, they did little to increase the prisoner's knowledge or skills that would land them a well-paying job after their release.

In 1992, the CSC established CORCAN, which is the agency overseeing federal prison industries.

CORCAN employs prisoners in five industries that are intended to build marketable skills they can use once returned to the community:

- Manufacturing: includes the production of office furniture, lockers, and shelving, as well as vehicle repair
- Textiles: includes the production of offender clothing, government uniforms, bedding, and towels
- Construction: includes house framing and repairs, and installing and maintaining plumbing and electrical systems
- Services: includes the production of office supplies, signs, and clothing, as well as working in printing, vehicle-related areas, and industrial laundries
- Agriculture: such as crop production or raising dairy cows and goats (Correctional Service of Canada, 2018b)

The Correctional Service of Canada (2019d, p. 1) says that on an given day there are almost 1,100 offenders working in CORCAN operations, and in 2017/2018, almost 600 offenders were working toward apprenticeships in the trades (such as carpentry, plumbing, welding, and painting). Although exposure to these industries helps to develop a prisoner's employment-related skills, their work experiences do not address other unmet psychological needs such as negative attitudes toward conventional lifestyles or poor self-control, which are factors associated with recidivism (James, 2018; Stewart et al., 2017).

In order to help prisoners address their attitudes, values, and beliefs, the CSC (2014a) developed five types of treatment programs: (a) general crime prevention programs that focus on goal setting and problem solving; (b) violence prevention programs (e.g., managing anger, risk, and emotions); (c) sex offender programs that teach participants how to manage their behaviour and understand how their actions harm victims; (d) substance abuse programs that help inmates understand how alcohol and drug use leads to crime; and (e) integrated interventions that enable participants to develop skills to overcome everyday challenges and stress. Some of these correctional programs can take a prisoner more than a year to complete. The high-intensity violence prevention program, for example, requires 83 group sessions and four individual sessions each lasting two hours (Correctional Service of Canada, 2014a).

The number and intensity of these sessions is needed to confront an individual's criminogenic thinking, but an offender's illness, placement in segregation, or transfer to another facility can interfere with participation in these programs—which could then derail their eligibility for transfer to lower levels of security and delay their potential release. Despite this limitation, the long-term benefits of correctional treatments based on the risk, needs, and responsivity model (introduced in Chapter 9) are significant. Bonta and Andrews (2017) report that prison-based interventions using this approach reduce recidivism by about 17 per cent, and that finding is consistent across males and females and in adult and youth populations. Although 17 per cent might not seem like a lot, if we consider the cost savings in investigating and prosecuting crimes and then punishing offenders, and the reduction in pain and misery experienced by crime victims—that reduction represents a substantial savings to society.

In order for them to be effective, intensive correctional programs must be delivered in a consistent manner by skilled facilitators. Barnowski (2004, p. 3) found that a program for residents in a youth facility delivered by competent staff members *decreased* 18-month recidivism by over one-third, whereas a program delivered by staff who were not competent *increased* recidivism by almost one-fifth (see also Makarios, Lovins, Latessa, & Smith, 2016, pp. 349–50, and Latessa, 2018). Competent personnel refers to skilled staff members who have professional training such as psychologists, and who deliver the rehabilitative programs in the manner in which they were designed. So, what benefits can we gain when we implement

TABLE 10.4 Benefits in Reduced Crime for Each Dollar Spent in Correctional Programming

Program Name	Benefit
Correctional education (post-secondary education)	$19.77
Employment counselling and job training	$9.86
Vocational education	$11.98
Correctional industries	$12.80
Treatment for sex offenders	$1.30

Washington State Institute for Public Policy (2018)

correctional programs with qualified and motivated personnel? Cost benefit analyses carried out by the Washington State Institute for Public Policy (2018), and shown in Table 10.4, reveal the benefits (in reduced crime) from each dollar spent on the five types of correctional programs. All together, research is showing us that correctional rehabilitation is a good investment in crime reduction.

Violence Reduction in Federal Prisons

Canadian prison officials report mixed success in reducing correctional violence. Between 2006/2007 and 2015/2016, there were 21 homicides in prisons (Public Safety Canada, 2018, p. 6) and thousands of acts of serious misconduct including assaults. Figure 10.2 shows that as the number of inmates in solitary confinement decreased by almost two-thirds (62.1 per cent), the number of physical assaults on inmates rose by 90 per cent. Figure 10.2 suggests there is a relationship between these two factors—the decreased use of segregation might have led to more violence—but other factors could also be responsible, such as an increase in gang violence or perhaps an increase in inmates' likelihood to report their victimization to correctional officers. As a result, we cannot say with certainty that these two factors are related. Some inmate assaults can be expected given that over two-thirds of Canada's prison population has at least one conviction

segregation Placement of an inmate in a locked high-security cell within a correctional facility (e.g., administrative segregation), usually in response to their misconduct.

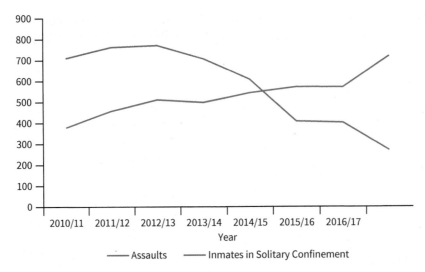

FIGURE 10.2 **The Relationship Between Solitary Confinement and Inmate Assaults, 2010 to 2017**
White (2017)

for violence. Yet, Figure 10.2 also suggests that how prison staff manage prisoners impacts institutional safety. Can you think of factors other than placing prisoners in segregation that might increase or decrease prison violence?

One of the frustrations of working with prisoners who might be a decade or longer away from their release is that staff members have few options other than placing disruptive inmates in segregation—which is like a "prison within a prison." Inmates in segregation might only receive a few hours each day outside their cells, which generally consist of a cement-walled room with a metal bunk that is bolted to the floor and a stainless-steel toilet.

Given the overcrowded, bleak, and sometimes noisy conditions in many facilities, it is not surprising that most inmates will break the institutional rules at some point. Placement in administrative segregation, however, is reserved for prisoners who have engaged in assaults, threatened others, or breached security. In 2015/2016, almost half of all CSC inmates were admitted to segregation at least once; almost three-quarters of male prisoners were returned to the general population within 30 days, while only 6 per cent of women inmates served more than 30 days (Public Safety Canada, 2018, p. 67).

As the Eddie Snowshoe case illustrates, there are concerns about the adverse effects of using segregation to manage an offender's behaviour. Long-term confinement in segregation can increase mental health problems such as anxiety and depression (Haney, 2018). Prisoners in segregation sometimes engage in self-harm behaviours such as slashing themselves with sharp objects or hitting their heads against the wall. These incidents tend to happen more often in segregation, treatment centres, and maximum security facilities—places the Office of the Correctional Investigator (2013) has called austere. The Office of the Correctional Investigator statistics show that there are about three self-injuries per day or over 1,100 incidents per year in all the CSC facilities (Zinger, 2017, p. 11). Women tend to be overrepresented in these acts of self-harm, and a relatively small number of inmates who slash are generally responsible for a large proportion of these incidents; these prisoners may be at a higher risk of dying by suicide.

Prisoner Advocacy

In Chapter 9, the role of provincial ombudsmen in advocating for correctional centre inmates was briefly described. Several federal and community-based organizations also advocate on behalf of federal prisoners. The Correctional Investigator of

slashing
When a prisoner engages in self-harming behaviour by cutting their skin using metal or plastic objects.

A COMPARATIVE VIEW

Prison Murders

Canadian prisoners are at higher risk of being murdered in custody than their American counterparts. Table 10.5 shows that between 2005 and 2014 the prison murder rate was Canada per 100,000 inmates was over three times as high as the US rate. Given that Canadian facilities tend to be smaller and we spend twice as much on corrections per inmate than do US facilities, an important question to ask is why the murder rate is higher in Canadian prisons.

There are two possible reasons the murder rate in Canada is higher. First, the proportion of violent offenders is much higher in Canada (69 per cent in Canada and 54 per cent in the US – see Carson, 2018, p. 1). A second possible reason is the relatively high prison-gang population in Canadian facilities. Harris (2018a) reports how the CSC gang population has been increasing, and their activities have been associated with increased correctional violence as rival groups compete for control of the underground prison economy (e.g., the distribution of drugs or cellular phones). Gang activities can also increase racial tension and undermine correctional programming as they tend to form on racial and ethnic lines (Winterdyk & Ruddell, 2010).

TABLE 10.5 **Prison Murders in Canada and the United States per 100,000 Prisoners, 2005–2014**

Year	US Prison Murder Rate	Canadian Prison Murder Rate
2005	4	24
2006	4	24
2007	4	16
2008	3	15
2009	4	8
2010	5	38
2011	5	22
2012	7	7
2013	7	14
2014	7	6.5
Average murder rate	5.0	17.4

Adapted from Noonan (2016), Public Safety Canada (2017a, 2018), and Office of the Correctional Investigator (2017)

Canada, for example, is an ombudsman who acts on complaints raised by federal prisoners. Funded by the federal government, the Correctional Investigator is independent of the CSC and can make recommendations for system-wide changes. In addition to issues raised by inmates, the Office of the Correctional Investigator (OCI) also investigates serious incidents including murders or suicides, and also reviews the use of force by correctional officers. A count of inmate complaints and grievances found that between 2014/2015 and 2016/2017, there were 79,771 grievances. The top five concerns were (Correctional Service of Canada, 2018a, p. 30):

- Staff performance, such as inappropriate use of force or staff misconduct
- Correspondence and access to telephone communications

Race, Class, and Gender

Do White-Collar Criminals Receive Privileged Prison Treatment?

In 2011, mandatory sentences were introduced in the *Criminal Code* for offenders committing fraud and financial crimes resulting in more than one million dollars in losses. Despite this attempt to get tough, Brown (2018) questions whether there is a political willingness to investigate and prosecute white-collar criminals in Canada. Many Canadians believe these individuals are not punished severely enough, and results of a national survey show the public wants the federal government to get tougher on them (Angus Reid Global, 2014). Many Canadians, for example, have expressed disapproval over the federal government's handling of the SNC-Lavalin affair, where Attorney General Jody Wilson-Raybould refused to enter into a deferred-prosecution agreement with the company, which was facing fraud and corruption charges,

and was subsequently removed from her cabinet position (Coletto & Anderson, 2019).

When white-collar criminals are sentenced to prison, they are typically placed in minimum-security facilities. Although victims of financial crimes are often outraged that white-collar offenders are not punished more severely, few pose a risk to correctional operations or the public as they are typically first-time, non-violent offenders with no histories of escaping custody. Placing these low-risk inmates in higher-security living units might be popular with the public, but it would also raise correctional costs and would not increase prison safety. In fact, mixing low- and high-risk prisoners together might increase the recidivism rates in the lower-risk inmates (Bonta & Andrews, 2017).

- Amenities, food, and diet, including insufficient or low-quality meals
- Personal effects, such as lost items
- Non-urgent health services, such as arranging an appointment with a specialist

Of these complaints, over 8,000 of them were submitted by just 14 inmates in 2017; a federal government auditor found that many of them were trivial matters and that these prisoners were sometimes submitting multiple grievances for a single issue (Harris, 2018b). Although grievances are an important mechanism for offenders to address issues in a constructive manner, the time and resources needed to manage these trivial complaints likely reduces the time officials can spend on more legitimate issues.

Most inmate concerns relate to their powerlessness. Prisoners do not, for instance, have choices about which doctor they will see, whether they are assigned to a damaged or overcrowded cell, or their access to a phone to call home. Moreover, there has been widespread criticism of the meals federal

inmates receive; many complain that the quality is poor and portion sizes are too small (Zinger, 2017). While people living outside prisons have little sympathy for these inmates, meeting their basic needs reduces tensions within a facility.

Strong advocacy for prisoners carried out by the Correctional Investigator has resulted in positive changes throughout the entire CSC. Various community-based organizations, including the John Howard Society and the Elizabeth Fry Society, have also advocated for prison reforms. Correctional officers have also lent their support to improve the living conditions of prisoners. The Union of Canadian Correctional Officers (2015) released a report that was critical of the practice of double bunking—where two inmates are placed in a cell originally intended for one person—due to prison overcrowding. The union argues that this practice leads to unsafe conditions for prisoners and staff. This example illustrates the shared interests of prisoners and COs, as more tolerable living conditions benefit both parties.

MYTH OR REALITY

Parole Is "Soft" on Prisoners

Parole plays an important role in the safe transition of federal prisoners into the community. The Parole Board of Canada (2018b) publishes a list of myths or mistaken assumptions related to parole. The following list—which is summarized from their work—presents five facts about parole:

1. **Parole does NOT reduce the sentence imposed by the courts.** An individual must serve their entire sentence and granting day or full parole allows federal prisoners to transition to the community under the supervision of a parole officer. Parole can be revoked if the parolee does not abide by the conditions of their release, as the protection of society is the overriding consideration in any release decision.

2. **Parole is NOT automatically granted.** Prisoners must be eligible to apply for parole (typically after serving one-third of their sentence) and they must convince the parole board that the risk they pose to the community can be managed. When reviewing an application for parole, the Board considers three factors:
   (a) the individual's criminal history
   (b) the applicant's behaviour within the institution and whether they benefited from the programs (e.g., education or work programs)
   (c) the applicant's release plan

3. **Parole is NOT the same as statutory release.** Statutory release is an automatic release that is mandated by law and is granted to most prisoners in the last third of their sentence. While their cases are not reviewed by the Parole Board of Canada (PBC), they are supervised by CSC parole officers while in the community. Because the transition to the community for parolees is generally better planned and structured (and approved by the PBC), their rates of recidivism are lower than inmates who are statutorily released.

4. **Parole and probation are NOT the same.** Probationary sentences are imposed by judges, and probationers are supervised by officers employed by provincial or territorial governments. Parolees, by contrast, are serving custodial sentences of at least two years, and their re-entry into the community is supervised by parole officers employed by the CSC.

5. **Individuals on parole or statutory release are NOT free to live their lives as they please.** Ex-prisoners supervised in the community must abide by a strict set of conditions including keeping the peace, being of good behaviour, obeying the law, and reporting to a CSC parole officer or the police as required. In addition to those standard conditions, the individual's place of residence is often specified, and they must remain in the country. Additional conditions of release might include having no contact with their victim(s), abstaining from alcohol and drugs, or avoid associating with criminals.

The overriding goal of the PBC is that public safety should not be compromised by a prisoner's release to the community. In order to achieve that goal, the PBC relies on decision-making that focuses only on public safety and not on other considerations such as whether prisons are crowded. This approach to the community re-entry of federal prisoners has been successful, as demonstrated by a Public Safety Canada (2018) report showing that 99 per cent of day parole and 97 per cent of full parole placements were completed without any further crimes from the time the prisoner was released until their sentence ended.

AN OVERVIEW OF FEDERAL PAROLE

Prison officials have no control over the numbers or types of offenders who are admitted into their facilities, nor the length of their sentences, as those decisions are made by judges. Soon after an offender's admission to prison, the correctional staff work with them to develop plans to return them to the community. This is not an easy proposition given the large number of unmet needs that most prisoners have, including problems with mental health and addictions, as well as their antisocial attitudes that make it difficult for them to pursue conventional lifestyles. Despite those challenges, the CSC has been successful in reintegrating prisoners into the community on parole, although offenders released on a statutory release (a mandatory release for offenders who have served two-thirds of their sentence) are less successful. This section focuses on the transition of federal prisoners from a penitentiary to the community.

As noted above, federal inmates are assessed soon after their prison admissions and almost two-thirds are classified as medium-security offenders. These individuals can earn their way to a minimum-security facility by avoiding prison misconduct and following their rehabilitative plans. If they continue working on their correctional plans, most inmates will make the transition from a minimum-security facility to day parole and ultimately full parole. Public Safety Canada (2018, p. 74) reports that as of March 31, 2017, almost 9,000 federal ex-prisoners were being supervised in the community. Another 840 offenders with long-term supervision orders (LTSOs) are also supervised by CSC parole officers. LTSOs are imposed by judges to increase the period of an ex-prisoner's community supervision past the expiry of their formal sentences (Public Safety Canada, 2018, p. 109). These orders are made when the judge believes the offender poses a substantial risk to reoffend, but that their risks can be managed in their communities; almost two-thirds of offenders with LTSOs were sex offenders in 2017/2018 (Public Safety Canada, 2018).

In the sections that follow, we look at the pathways to three different forms of community supervision: day parole, full parole, and statutory release. All these releases are governed by the *Corrections and Conditional Releases Act*, which specifies how much of a prisoner's sentence must be served prior to parole eligibility. Although parole eligibility can come early in an individual's sentence, there are no guarantees that the Parole Board of Canada (PBC) will approve an application for parole. Moreover, once released from prison, ex-prisoners must abide by the conditions of their release or they can be returned to prison.

A Short History of Parole in Canada

For over a century, the federal prison system has been developing strategies to increase the likelihood of an offender's safe transition to the community. The practice of parole was introduced by Alexander Maconochie, a British naval officer who believed the way that convicts were treated worked against their rehabilitation. Maconochie was involved in the supervision of prisoners who had been transported from England to the penal colonies of Van Diemen's Land and Norfolk Island, off the coast of Australia. This warden, who had been held as a prisoner of war for several years prior to his correctional work, was critical that conditions in the colony discouraged prisoners from working toward their reform. He developed the idea of marks of commendation, which rewarded an offender's positive behaviour and allowed them to earn more freedoms and better living conditions within the colony. Continued positive behaviour earned the convicts a ticket of leave, which was a form of conditional release, and some were able to return to England. This early form of parole was introduced in Ireland and was based on a system of gradual release from prison to the community.

The idea that prisoners could earn their freedom by demonstrating positive behaviour became popular, and in 1899 the Canadian Parliament authorized early releases from prison with the passage of *An Act to Provide for the Conditional Liberation of Convicts*, known as the *Ticket of Leave Act*. Conditional releases were intended for young and first-time prisoners who had committed minor offences. Inmates had to apply for parole, and prison officials conducted investigations to determine their suitability for release. As there were no staff members supervising these ex-prisoners in the community, they reported to the police each month. Later, officials from the Salvation Army—such as Walter Archibald, who was appointed the first Dominion

long-term supervision orders (LTSOs) Orders that can be imposed by a judge to increase the period of an offender's community supervision past the end of their formal sentence.

ticket of leave A release established in penal colonies for prisoners who had demonstrated positive changes and were considered rehabilitated.

Portrait of Captain Alexander Maconochie RN KH by EV Rippingille, 1836

Alexander Maconochie promoted the idea of tickets of leave to encourage residents of penal colonies to work toward their reform. Maconochie had himself been a prisoner of war, and he used his insight about prison conditions to motivate convicts.

Parole Officer in 1905—played a role in supervising these ex-prisoners (Ruddell, 2017). Although the prison system's experiment with these conditional releases started tentatively, the Parole Board of Canada (2018a) observes that most ex-prisoners granted conditional releases were successful and this led to the expansion of these releases.

Conditional and Community Releases

Parolees are federal prisoners who have been released prior to their warrant expiry date after their cases have been reviewed by the PBC. Given the longer prison terms that federal inmates serve—and the fact that over two-thirds have been convicted of violent offences—the public is generally more concerned about the safe transition of federal prisoners into the community than they are about provincial inmates. The community re-entry of parolees is carefully managed in a gradual process in order to decrease recidivism.

Federal prisoners start earning their parole by working their way down the security classification system. About two-thirds of prisoners start in medium-security facilities or units and then are transferred to minimum-security facilities—the CSC calls this downward movement cascading. Inmates earn a lower security classification by participating in rehabilitative programs and avoiding misconduct.

The transition from a minimum-security living unit to the community usually starts with day parole (the planned movement of a federal inmate from prison to a supervised setting such as a halfway house or CSC-operated community correctional centre), and this move must be approved by the PBC. Prisoners must apply for day parole, and 75 per cent of these applications are approved (Parole Board of Canada, 2018b). Representatives from the PBC review the prisoner's progress in custody and consider their plans for a successful return to the community. Individuals who are successful in day parole may apply for full parole, and if full parole is granted, most return home. Alternatively, most offenders who have served two-thirds of their sentences are released on a statutory release. Because individuals on statutory release did not have to demonstrate their progress to the PBC to secure an early release, they are generally less successful in their return to the community (this is discussed in greater detail later in this chapter).

Goals of Parole

The overriding purpose of parole is to ensure the safe transition of CSC prisoners to the community. In order to help ex-prisoners achieve that goal, parole officers work in 15 community correctional centres and 92 offices throughout the nation (Correctional Service of Canada, 2019c). One factor differentiating provincial and federal caseloads is the number of offenders an officer supervises. Whereas provincial probation officers average about 60 cases, CSC parole officers supervise fewer offenders, thus allowing them to spend more time with each parolee and ensure they are following their correctional plan. The duties that

cascading
A term used by the Correctional Service of Canada to refer to a prisoner's movement to lower levels of supervision, such as from medium- to minimum-security facilities.

full parole
A less restrictive form of parole granted by the Parole Board of Canada to federal prisoners who have been successful in day parole.

statutory release A form of supervised release that is automatically granted after federal prisoners with determinate sentences of three years or longer have served two-thirds of their sentences (does not apply to dangerous offenders or lifers serving indeterminate sentences).

Commissioner's Directives Guidelines established by the Commissioner of the CSC for the operations of the correctional system and the treatment of prisoners and parolees.

CSC parole officers carry out are guided by policy statements called **Commissioner's Directives** that are related to specific sections of the *Corrections and Conditional Release Act*. Commissioner's Directive 715-1, for example, provides the guidelines for community supervision and defines a parole officer's work activities, including the following:

- maintain and update the correctional plan in consultation with the offender
- assist and support the offender to actively participate in meeting the objectives of their correctional plan
- monitor the offender's behaviour, release conditions, and compliance with court-ordered obligations
- obtain all relevant information from community-based residential facilities (CBRF) as identified in the contract requirements
- develop and implement interventions which address and respond to the offender's risk and needs
- document all relevant information about the offender's circumstances, within established timeframes and parameters (Correctional Service of Canada, 2019b).

Monitoring a parolee's conduct in the community is a core requirement of the parole officer's job and is a key part of the case management process. Successful case management is based on developing plans *with* the prisoner when they are in custody—rather than developing plans *for* them—and then supporting them in their efforts toward making positive rehabilitative changes. As noted in the previous chapter, the effectiveness of these interventions increases when the parole officer is highly skilled, and when their work is done according to the timelines and case management requirements established by the agency.

The Commissioner's Directive on community supervision, for example, provides guidelines on how often parolees are seen by parole officers (Correctional Service of Canada, 2019b). Those guidelines are based on the risks the individual poses, and the highest-risk offenders require more frequent face-to-face meetings. Individuals on a statutory release may be required to meet with their parole officer a minimum of eight times per month, which is considered intensive supervision. As their risks decrease, the frequency of contacts also drops. A parolee who has been living in the community for several years and is assessed as low-risk might receive only one face-to-face contact every three months. These guidelines for supervision are dynamic, which means that officers can provide more supervision and support if they feel that parolees are engaging in behaviours that increase their risks of recidivism, such as quitting their job, breaking up with an intimate partner, moving frequently, abusing drugs or alcohol, or associating with other offenders, such as gang members.

Community Supervision of Parolees

Most federal prisoners make their first entries into the community on temporary releases from custody accompanied by staff members. An escorted temporary absence can occur at any time during a prisoner's sentence, often for medical or rehabilitative purposes such as attending counselling or seeing a medical specialist. Depending on the circumstances, some prisoners are escorted to attend family functions or funerals. Levels of security vary on these escorts. Medium- or high-security inmates are typically escorted in handcuffs and/or shackles by one or two correctional officers depending on the nature of the escort and the presence of other security arrangements, such as access to a prisoner transport vehicle (e.g., a van with iron mesh barriers between the passenger and driver compartments and covering the windows in order to prevent escapes).

Most prisoners are eligible for temporary unescorted absences after serving one-sixth of their sentence if their sentence is three years or more, or after six months for sentences of two to three years (Parole Board of Canada, 2019a). Lifers must wait considerably longer before earning an unescorted absence; for example, if they

Material reprinted with the express permission of: Chatham Daily News, a division of Postmedia Network Inc.

A Correctional Service of Canada prisoner was escorted by two correctional officers to his grandmother's funeral. How might allowing for temporary absences to events such as a funeral help a future parolee improve his or her chances at a successful return to public life?

were convicted of first-degree murder, they have to wait 22 years to be eligible, and there are no guarantees their applications will be approved. These unescorted absences might involve a family visit and some are related to employment, treatment, or education. Successfully completing these absences builds trust and the prisoner can use this in their presentations to the parole board when requesting day parole. The timelines for conditional releases are shown in Figure 10.3, using the example of a prisoner serving a six-year sentence.

Being granted day parole enables prisoners to live in the community in halfway houses (which the CSC calls community correctional centres) that provide only minimum supervision, and most residents will work, attend classes, or participate in treatment during the day and report back to the centre in the evenings. The CSC operates 15 community correctional centres in larger cities and contracts with agencies such as the Salvation Army to house day parolees in community residential facilities. The CSC (2019c) also places some ex-prisoners in hostels, private homes, and supervised apartments.

Full parole may be granted by the PBC if the individual has demonstrated success on day parole. Even though many prisoners become eligible for full parole, the PBC only approves 37 per cent of applications. A larger percentage of prisoners are released after serving two-thirds of their sentence; this is called a statutory release. As these releases

halfway houses Facilities where inmates reside during their transition from a correctional centre or prison to the community. The CSC calls their facilities community correctional centres.

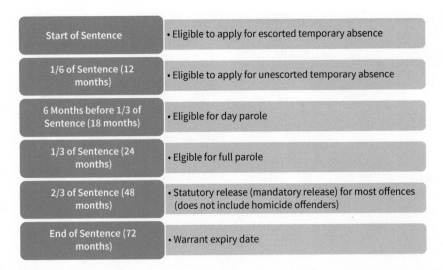

FIGURE 10.3 **Timeline for Conditional Release: Prisoner Serving a Six-year Federal Sentence**
Parole Board of Canada (2019a)

occur automatically once the inmate has served two-thirds of his or her sentence, the PBC is not involved in the decision to release them. CSC officials, however, can deny a statutory release if they believe that the prisoner is at risk of committing a violent crime or a serious drug offence.

Figure 10.4 shows the average percentage that federal prisoners served of their sentences prior to receiving their first day parole in 2016/2017. Public Safety Canada (2018, p. 90) reports that an average prisoner serves 37 per cent of their sentence prior to being granted their first day parole and 46 per cent

of their sentence before being granted full parole. But there were differences within those averages, and the time to first release on day parole for Indigenous prisoners (40.8 per cent) was longer than the time served for non-Indigenous inmates (36.2 per cent) (Public Safety Canada, 2018, p. 92). When it comes to gender, women inmates were in custody for a shorter period of their sentence (33.6 per cent) prior to their release on day parole compared with male prisoners (37.5 per cent). In order to increase the success of Indigenous offenders in their applications for parole, a growing number of applicants

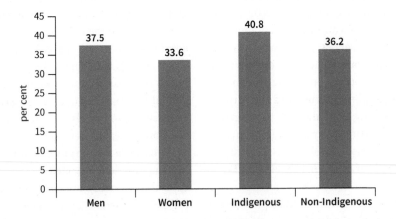

FIGURE 10.4 **Proportion of Federal Prison Sentence Served Before Being Released on Day Parole, 2016/2017**
Adapted from Public Safety Canada (2018)

are supported by Indigenous cultural advisers, "who ensure that conditional release hearings are sensitive to Indigenous cultural values and traditions" (Public Safety Canada, 2018, p. 87).

Parole Success

Public Safety Canada (2018, p. 94) considers day parole successful "if it was completed without a return to prison for a breach of conditions or for a new offence." Table 10.6 shows the success rates of ex-prisoners sentenced to determinate prison sentences (not including dangerous offenders or lifers) released on day parole, full parole, and statutory release. The findings show that individuals who earn their parole are more successful than prisoners who obtain a statutory release.

Twenty-nine of the 3,499 day parolees in 2016/2017 (less than 1 per cent) were readmitted to prison with a new offence, and three of them were readmitted for committing a violent crime: in other words less than 1 in 1,000 of day parolees was convicted of committing a violent crime. The total number of successful completions for full parole was somewhat less than for day parole, although that is expected as offenders on full parole serve more time in the community (day parole might last only a few months, whereas an individual might serve years on full parole). In 2016/2017, 937 prisoners were granted full parole and three of them were returned to prison after their involvement in a violent crime (a rate of 3.2 per 1,000 parolees). Of the 5,575 inmates granted a statutory release, by contrast, 323 were returned to prison with new non-violent offences and 47 of them had

committed violent crimes, which works out to 8.4 per 1,000 offenders (Public Safety Canada, 2018, p. 98).

Reforming High-Risk Sexual Offenders: Circles of Support and Accountability (COSAs)

The public has little sympathy for sexual offenders given their histories of violence, although our assumptions are often the result of inaccurate or distorted media portrayals and stereotypes rather than the actual risks they pose (Harper, 2018). These ex-prisoners are routinely returned to the community and research shows that recidivism rates for some classifications of these offenders are very low (Duwe, 2018). The risks that sex offenders pose have been studied extensively, and research shows that most of them are willing to participate in treatment; those efforts can be very effective in reducing recidivism (Kim, Benekos, & Merlo, 2016). Canadian researchers have found that the success of sex offenders returning to the community increases when they are receiving the proper supports, resources, and supervision (Wilson & McWhinnie, 2016). We also increase their risk of reoffending when we isolate and shun them, or when we prevent them from participating in activities that keep them constructively occupied, such as work and engaging in positive social relationships. One way to reduce the risk of recidivism is for offenders to participate in Circles of Support and Accountability (COSAs), which is a community-based intervention where volunteers provide support to high-risk sex offenders released from prison.

COSA started with one high-risk sex offender, named Charlie Taylor, who returned to an Ontario community in 1994 after serving his entire prison sentence, so he was not supervised by a parole officer. According to Wilson, McWhinnie, Picheca, Prinzo, and Cortoni (2007), Taylor was well-known to the police and his release attracted widespread media attention, as nobody wanted him "on the streets." A CSC psychologist approached Harry Nigh, who was the pastor of a Mennonite church (which Taylor had previously

Circles of Support and Accountability (COSAs) Groups of volunteers who support the transition of high-risk sexual offenders from prison to the community.

TABLE 10.6 Success Rates of Federal Prisoners Conditionally Released, 2016/2017

Category	Success Rate (%)	Violent Conviction Rate After Release (Per 1,000 Offenders)
Day parole	93	0.9
Full parole	90	3.2
Statutory release	67	8.4

Adapted from Public Safety Canada (2018)

attended), and encouraged him to help in Taylor's return to the community. Nigh put a group of volunteers together in what they called a "circle" to provide guidance and support for this ex-prisoner. The volunteers met frequently with Taylor and provided encouragement and advice, and Wilson (2018) observes that the group reduced Taylor's isolation from the rest of the world with their friendship. This approach was successful as it responded to Taylor's unmet needs. When Charlie Taylor died in 2006, he had been crime-free since his release from prison 12 years earlier.

There are about 20 COSA sites throughout Canada providing services to about 200 high-risk sexual offenders, which is a fraction of all sex offenders living in the community. Because of the difficulty in recruiting volunteers, the program prioritizes recently released high-risk ex-prisoners who have few community supports. Each circle is comprised of the ex-prisoner (called a core member) and three to five volunteers who commit to a long-term relationship with that individual; it is not unusual for these groups to exist for years. The circle volunteers are, in turn, supported by the COSA organization, and this support often includes an "outer circle" where trained professionals mentor and provide training to the volunteers.

The COSA approach is based on restorative justice principles that emphasize reintegration. According to the Church Council on Justice and Corrections (2011), circles have a life cycle with three phases:

1. In the initial phase, the core member (the ex-prisoner) establishes trust with the volunteers and receives support from them. Meetings of the circle might occur several times a week—often at coffee shops and other informal settings. During this phase, the volunteers may help the core member find a residence and employment, and take the core member to appointments. In addition to providing support, the core member's living circumstances are stabilized, and their feelings of social isolation, powerlessness, and hopelessness

are reduced—which in turn lowers their risks of reoffending.

2. The second phase of a circle builds on trust built between the core member and volunteers. The volunteers might address the attitudes and behaviours of the core member that place the individual at higher risk of recidivism, such as feelings of hostility toward women, associations with negative peers (such as other sex offenders), or risky or impulsive behaviours such as substance use. During this phase, the core member builds on their problem-solving skills, and the circle members meet less frequently.

3. After the core member is fully reintegrated into the community, the need for support decreases and the circles eventually close, although volunteers remain available to help the core member if their circumstances change. In some cases, the relationship has changed from that of volunteer to friend.

Neither the volunteers nor the local COSA organizations are associated with the police or parole authorities, although volunteers are required to inform the police if the core member has talked about committing a crime. A Canada-wide evaluation of the approach found that COSA reduces sex offender recidivism (Chouinard & Riddick,

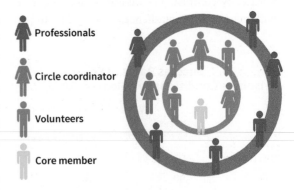

Professionals

Circle coordinator

Volunteers

Core member

FIGURE 10.5 Circles of Support and Accountability

Adapted from Wilson and McWhinnie (2013)

2015). This approach is gaining in popularity and has been adopted throughout Europe, the United Kingdom, and the United States (Wilson, 2018). Yet, despite research showing that COSA is a successful method of reducing recidivism and its worldwide adoption, Canadian governments have been reluctant to fund the agencies providing COSA services, although Doran (2018) points out the federal government provided $7.48 million in 2017 to fund COSA as a crime prevention strategy.

BARRIERS TO COMMUNITY RE-ENTRY

There are many barriers to an ex-prisoner's successful return into the community, and some of them, such as high unemployment rates or a lack of safe and affordable housing, are out of their control. Historically, one of the most significant barriers to a successful community re-entry was the lack of resources to establish a residence and cover basic needs. Instead, ex-prisoners were often released directly onto the streets with a bus ticket and a cheque for the money they had saved in their inmate accounts. These individuals often had uncertain plans about where they were going to live and work once released. Given that many ex-prisoners had no formal plan on how to succeed once released, or had few resources to support their community re-entry, it is not surprising that many committed new crimes and were soon returned to custody.

Although correctional plans are more comprehensive today, and ex-prisoners can receive social assistance, there are still barriers to their success. Most ex-prisoners must overcome poor educational and employment histories, maintain their sobriety, and deal with family and friends who have criminogenic attitudes and values. They must also avoid their former associates who may still be involved in crime and substance abuse. The availability of halfway houses and social programs to support the gradual re-entry of inmates has reduced some of these barriers to reintegration. Yet, as Figure 10.6 shows, most ex-prisoners have at least six issues to overcome. While the Office of the Correctional Investigator (2017) created this list based on information from women parolees, the barriers for men are similar.

In addition to confronting issues such as poverty, a lack of a stable work history, or the inability to obtain safe and affordable housing, ex-prisoners must also contend with government policies some call collateral consequences. Collateral consequences are intended to increase public safety by restricting someone with a criminal record from obtaining a security clearance, government contract, or various licences and permits (Adams, Chen, & Chapman, 2017). A common example is a driving licence suspension for people convicted of impaired driving. Although that sanction is not very controversial, individuals requiring a driver's licence for their jobs can be fired when they lose their licences. Another non-controversial consequence is restricting sexual offenders from working with children in paid or voluntary roles.

collateral consequences Government policies that are developed to deter potential offenders and include job restrictions on people with specific types of criminal histories.

FIGURE 10.6 **Barriers to Community Re-entry: Women Parolees**

Office of the Correctional Investigator (2017)

A Closer Look

Record Suspensions

Public Safety Canada (2017b) estimates that about 10 per cent of Canadians, or about 3.6 million people, have criminal records. One way individuals can reduce the stigma of a criminal conviction is through a record suspension, formerly known as a pardon. A person with a criminal record can apply for a record suspension after ensuring that all of the conditions of their conviction have been completed—such as paying fines and meeting the conditions of their probation order—as well as waiting five years after a summary conviction or ten years after an indictable offence. This program is administered by the PBC. Applicants for suspensions must pay a fee ($631 in 2019) and submit a package of information to the PBC. people convicted of cannabis possession, however, do not have to pay any fees,

and the government has promised those suspensions will be quickly approved (Bell, 2019). While the PBC approves most applicants after conducting a brief investigation, there is no guarantee that applications will be approved, and some offenders—such as people who were convicted of sexual offences involving children—are ineligible for record suspensions. According to the PBC (2019b, pp. 6–15), the top five categories of offences for which suspensions were granted in 2017/2018 were:

- Driving with more than 80 mgs of alcohol in 100 ml of blood
- Driving while ability impaired
- Assault
- Breach of *Narcotics Control Act*
- Theft under $5,000

Some collateral consequences can have a profound impact on a person's life. For example, permanent Canadian residents convicted of crimes such as impaired driving may be deported

In this photo, a parole officer visits a parolee at work to ensure that he is following the rules and settling in. One of the most important factors for a successful re-entry is getting a job. What factors might get in the way of a parolee obtaining employment?

(Keung, 2018). In May 2016, an Ontario appeal court reduced an individual's six-month jail sentence by one day so he would not be deported upon his release from custody. The individual was a permanent resident and had legally resided in the country since 1989, but his six-month sentence for assault and breach of probation could have led to his deportation (Canadian Press, 2016).

There are also informal barriers to community re-entry of prisoners that are related to the types of offences that led to their incarceration. Crimes committed against one's family and friends, for instance, often lead to social rejection, and some ex-prisoners (especially people with mental illnesses) have "burned their bridges" with their friends and family. The stigma resulting from the media's publication of an individual's criminal behaviour also makes it difficult to re-enter society, especially in small towns and rural areas where there is little anonymity. Strained relationships also increase social isolation, making it difficult for ex-prisoners to establish a support network, find work, or constructively use their time, which in turn increases their risks of reoffending.

The number of record suspensions for these offences is not surprising given these are the same types of crimes most commonly encountered in adult courts (Miladinovic, 2019).

The criminal convictions of successful applicants are set aside, which means they are removed from the information reported by the Canadian Police Information Centre (CPIC). An individual's previous convictions can be used at sentencing if they are convicted of a subsequent offence, although re-convictions of individuals granted suspensions are rare. According to the PBC (2019c, p. 139) by April 1, 2018, over half a million pardons/record suspensions had been ordered since their introduction in 1970, and 95 per cent were successful (5 per cent had been revoked).

One of the most important benefits of being granted a record suspension is that a person who has been convicted of a criminal offence can state on a job application that they do not have a criminal record (employers can only ask whether the individual has a criminal record for which a pardon has *not* been granted). The John Howard Society of Ontario (2018) estimates that having a criminal record can reduce one's chance of getting a job by half, and this estimate increases for people living in poverty and members of visible minority or Indigenous populations. Survey results show that the public supports granting record suspensions as they enable individuals to move forward with their lives, act as a reward for good behaviour, remove the stigma of a criminal conviction, and give people a second chance (Ekos Research Associates, 2017).

One of the most important factors for an ex-prisoner's successful return to the community is getting a job. Obtaining a good job, however, is a challenge given that many ex-prisoners lack long-term work histories or positive references. As a result, most employers are leery of hiring ex-prisoners, especially during tough economic times when many people without criminal records are also competing for scarce jobs (Decker, Ortiz, Spohn, & Hedberg, 2015). Ex-prisoners lucky enough to find work often end up in undesirable jobs (Bumiller, 2015). One step the federal government has taken to reduce the stigma of a criminal record is to offer record suspensions (formerly known as pardons), which enable a person to declare on job applications that they do not have a criminal record (see the "A Closer Look" box for details).

SUMMARY

In 1938, the Royal Commission's investigation into riots in Canadian prisons established a number of goals for the system, including the protection of society, the humane treatment and safe custody of inmates, and the rehabilitation of these prisoners (Kidman, 1938). Even though more than 80 years have passed since the Commission's report, these goals are still difficult to achieve. A review of this chapter, however, shows that CSC officials and their personnel, have made significant progress in making facilities safer, as well as more humane and rehabilitative, places. These reforms have taken place over decades and have involved some trial and error, but the current success rate of ex-prisoners returning to the community on parole demonstrates the effectiveness of the CSC and PBC approach to increasing public safety.

One of the things we often forget about corrections is that those running the prison systems have no control over who is sentenced to serve a prison term, or how long they will be imprisoned. As a result, new prisoners are admitted to facilities with a variety of risks, unmet needs, and distinctive criminal histories, whether or not the facilities have the resources necessary to meet those needs. Long-term correctional officers have observed that the profile of prisoners has changed over time; they must now manage a growing population of gang members, prisoners with histories of violent crime, and special-needs inmates, such as those with substance abuse and mental health problems, sex offenders, and elderly and Indigenous peoples.

The CSC's success is founded on providing a safe and secure environment. A second challenge for CSC personnel is to help these inmates prepare for their eventual return to the community. About half of federal prisoners are sentenced to serve five years or longer in prison. During that time, the correctional staff do their best to provide the supports needed for a prisoner to both survive their prison sentence and have opportunities to address their unmet needs so they can live crime-free lives upon release. This is not an easy undertaking and rates of suicide and self-harm in the CSC are high compared with US prisons.

Despite those challenges, a very small proportion of ex-prisoners on federal day and full parole are ever returned to prison, although prisoners receiving a statutory or mandatory release after serving two-thirds of their sentences are less successful than parolees (Public Safety Canada, 2018). We know that some parolees will commit crimes after their release from prison, but their community-based supervision is still desirable for several reasons. In addition to saving taxpayer dollars on incarceration, community-based supervision can help offenders work toward their rehabilitation by continuing their education, working, and supporting and rebuilding relationships with their families. Research shows that most ex-prisoners will not return to prison, and that finding should guide the correctional services that are delivered (Rhodes et al., 2016).

Career SNAPSHOT

Community Parole Officer

About 8 per cent of Correctional Service of Canada staff members work in the community, and many of them are parole officers supervising ex-prisoners on conditional releases or parole (Public Safety Canada, 2018, p. 23). One of the strengths of working for the federal government is that an employee can apply for opportunities throughout the country, which creates more opportunities for promotion or change. While CSC employees have good career mobility, the pathway to a career as a parole officer generally entails gaining experience with offenders in correctional settings. Most parole officers were first employed as correctional officers in federal institutions, although some have experience working as provincial probation officers or youth workers.

Throughout their careers, parole officers are expected to build relationships with the police, court officials, organizations and individuals delivering rehabilitative programs (such as psychologists), and staff from non-governmental agencies who provide services to parolees. In order to be successful as a parole officer, one has to have excellent interpersonal skills, self-confidence, and the ability to manage heavy workloads and work independently. Tara Tomasi shares her experiences as a community parole officer working in British Columbia.

Profile

Name: Tara Tomasi
Job Title: Community Parole Officer, Correctional Service of Canada
Employed In Current Job Since: 1999
Present Location: Abbotsford Parole Office
Education: Diploma and BA (Criminal Justice), University of the Fraser Valley

Background

As far back as I can remember, my life plan involved working in the criminal justice field. As a teenager, I planned to pursue my post-secondary education in a field that would allow me to work in law, policing, or corrections. As I progressed through my education, I developed a strong interest in Canada's correctional system and began exploring employment opportunities within it. Although my long-term goal was to work as a parole officer, I first wanted the opportunity to work as a correctional officer. Therefore, upon completing my Bachelor of Arts degree in the spring of 1999, I wrote the Correctional Service of Canada's entry examination. Shortly thereafter, I completed the Correctional Officer Physical Abilities Test, and I began working as an officer in August 1999. In 2003, I started work as an institutional parole officer, and in 2009, I transitioned to the community as a community parole officer.

Work Experience

One of the most rewarding aspects of being a community parole officer is the opportunity to develop ties between the parole office and community partners. After all, working as a parole officer cannot be done in isolation. An integral part of my work is to contribute to public safety while assisting and encouraging paroled offenders to become law-abiding, productive members of society, which is a role defined by the CSC's mission statement. Working closely with community-based partners such as police agencies, non-profit organizations, and social services promotes a holistic approach that I believe increases an offender's chances for success in the community. Personal examples of developing ties between partners include providing orientation sessions to local police recruits and attending various meetings involving social service agencies.

One of the biggest challenges facing a community parole officer is the balance between contributing to public safety and safely managing an offender's risk to reoffend. Many offenders who are on parole have committed serious and sometimes violent offences, and their risk to reoffend can be increased by substance abuse, a lack of employment and community support, and an inability to find affordable housing. Therefore, one of our primary responsibilities is to identify and determine what level of risk can be safely managed in the community. Risk assessment is done by community parole officers on a continual basis, and it includes consultations with one's supervisor and other officials at the Parole Board of Canada. Although sometimes a challenge, safely supervising offenders in the community while encouraging and assisting them to be law-abiding citizens is highly rewarding. It's a satisfying feeling to know you've made a difference in the community around you!

Advice to Students

Having strong communication skills, both written and verbal, is vital to having a successful career as a community parole officer. Our work involves liaising with many different community partners and writing reports for a variety of audiences, including federal institutions, the Parole Board of Canada, and the Supreme Court of Canada. In addition to communication, important skills a parole officer should possess are the ability to work well with others, to assess human behaviour, and to make analytical, concise decisions. Annual mandatory training (referred to as parole officer continuous development) helps strengthen these skills.

As an employee of CSC, a parole officer's role is that of public servant. Strong values, ethics, and integrity are characteristics of a successful parole officer, and accountability and behavioural expectations are also very high. Therefore, students interested in pursuing a career as a parole officer must lead law-abiding, pro-social lives free from inappropriate and/or illegal behaviour (this also applies to social media). As a community parole officer, assisting and encouraging offenders to safely reintegrate, and the responsibility of contributing to public safety, are honours and privileges not to be taken lightly. One fact is certain: there is never a dull moment!

REVIEW QUESTIONS

1. What are the main differences in the operations of provincial correctional facilities and federal prisons?
2. What steps can inmates take to make complaints about their living conditions or their treatment?
3. How do the characteristics of inmates influence behaviours within correctional facilities?
4. What are the two different forms of parole and how do they differ from statutory release?
5. Provide reasons why the Circles of Support and Accountability (COSA) approach has been effective in reducing sex offender recidivism.

DISCUSSION QUESTIONS

1. Prison administrators are criticized when inmates are idle, yet they are also criticized when prisoners produce goods that compete against private manufacturers, such as office furniture. Under these circumstances, what is the best option to keep prisoners occupied?

2. Describe the main differences between provincial probation and federal parole.

3. Explain the impact of a five-year prison sentence on a mother, a gang member, a middle-aged wage earner, and an elderly offender. Should these impacts be taken into account when sentencing?

4. Prison murders occur at a higher rate in Canada compared with US prisons, despite the fact that Canadians spend more than twice as much to keep offenders imprisoned. Provide some reasons for this difference.

5. Provide some reasons why women's correctional facilities in Canada are more expensive to operate than male institutions.

INTERNET SITES

The Correctional Investigator of Canada acts as an ombudsman for federal prisoners. Although the main function of the correctional investigator is to investigate and resolve complaints, the correctional investigator also prepares reports on issues related to offender treatment and rehabilitation.
www.oci-bec.gc.ca/index-eng.aspx

Beyond the Fence: Take a virtual tour of a Canadian penitentiary. This website lets you view a Canadian prison's inner workings.
http://www.csc-scc.gc.ca/csc-virtual-tour/index-eng.shtml

▲ On 8 July 2019, there were only 26 youth held in custody facilities in all of Atlantic Canada (Davie, 2019). Prior to the introduction of the *Youth Criminal Justice Act* in 2003, the number of youth behind bars was much higher; in 2001/2002, the four provinces incarcerated 364 youth (Statistics Canada, 2019a). Why did youth incarceration drop by more than 90 per cent? A change in legislation in 2003 made it more difficult to place non-violent youth in custody, and youth crime rates have been decreasing. The drop in youth incarceration has happened throughout the nation, although in many provinces the unused correctional beds have been filled by adults. (Photo credit: Emma Davie/CBC)

11 Youth Justice in Canada

LEARNING OUTLINE

After reading this chapter, you will be able to

- Describe current trends in youth crime
- Identify the differences between the *Juvenile Delinquents Act*, the *Young Offenders Act*, and the *Youth Criminal Justice Act*
- Provide some reasons why sentences for youth are mitigated
- Describe the differences between open and secure custody
- Identify the pathways to girls' involvement in crime

Youth Involved in Homicide

Brett Wiese, a University of Calgary student, was stabbed to death in 2013 after a group of young people who had been kicked out of a house party "returned with a 'posse'" to carry out a "revenge-motivated group attack" (Martin, 2015, para. 2). Wiese was stabbed seven times, another partygoer was severely wounded, and several others were assaulted. Jazlyn Radke, who was 17 years old at the time, was found guilty of second-degree murder, two counts of assault, and one count of aggravated assault for her role in the offences: she stabbed Brett Wiese once in the back after her co-accused, Mitchell Harkes, had already stabbed him six times. While Harkes had inflicted serious wounds, Radke's knife severed Weise's aorta (the largest artery in the body), which led to his death. According to the Canadian Broadcasting Corporation (2015), Radke had been kicked out of the party but she "refused to go and was screaming, swearing and swinging at partygoers before vowing to return."

Although the murder occurred in January 2013, and Radke was convicted in April 2014, the sentencing did not occur until May 2015. Radke was sentenced to life imprisonment. The judge ruled that Radke can stay in a youth custody facility until she turns 21 years of age, and then she will be transferred to a Correctional Service of Canada prison. Because she was under 18 years of age at the time of the offence, Radke will have to serve at least seven years before she can apply for parole. As with any other Canadian sentenced to life imprisonment, she will be under correctional supervision for the rest of her life.

Mitchell Harkes—who was 19 years old when the murder occurred—was also sentenced to life imprisonment. Like other case studies starting these chapters, the Harkes matter has taken years to work its way through the court system, and in 2017 the Alberta Court of Appeal decided his second-degree murder conviction should be overturned as the judge made

an error instructing the jury. Mitchell Harkes's case was retried in 2019, and he was again found guilty; he then filed another appeal (Grant, 2019b). Weise's parents, who sat through more than 80 days in court in the previous six years, expressed their frustration with the court process, calling it "never ending and gruelling" (Grant, 2019a).

Five years after the Weise murder, Mitchell's father, 65-year-old Keith Harkes, was sentenced to six years in prison for trying to kill his ex-wife and her boyfriend with a shotgun in a December 2017 incident (Martin, 2018). Keith Harkes had been convicted of assault with a weapon in 2009 and was banned from possessing firearms, although he used a gun in the 2017 attack. Do the separate convictions of a father and son for violent crimes a few years apart suggest that violence was seen as an acceptable way of solving problems in this family?

Mitchell Harkes, the 19-year-old who was sentenced to life imprisonment along with Jazlyn Radke, is shown here being arrested. The public is generally understanding of youth who commit minor crimes but is less forgiving of youth who commit violent offences. Although sentences for youth are often mitigated due to factors such as lack of maturity, youth convicted of murder will be under the supervision of the Correctional Service of Canada for the remainder of their lives.

Critical Questions

1. Why do we hold such punitive feelings toward young people who commit serious and violent crimes?
2. Does the gender of an individual convicted of homicide change your perceptions about the amount or type of punishment they should receive? Why or why not?
3. Jazlyn Radke will be eligible to apply for parole in 2022: what factors should the parole board consider when she applies?

INTRODUCTION

It is not uncommon for youth to engage in minor criminal offences such as shoplifting, theft, trespassing, drug use, or mischief. In addition, there are a variety of actions that are considered lawful for adults but are violations of provincial regulations for youth, such as drinking alcohol, gambling, running away from home, skipping classes, or possessing cannabis products. Young people caught engaging in these acts are rarely arrested, and the police will typically caution them or take them home to face their parents. With respect to minor criminal offences, many officers are reluctant to go through with an arrest because of the lifelong consequences an arrest or conviction can have on an individual, including for minor offences. Even supporters of "tough on crime" punishments are often sympathetic toward young people who have committed minor offences. As a result, justice system officials have developed alternative measures programs to divert young people who have been involved in minor crimes from the formal justice system.

Our positive or sympathetic feelings toward youth are challenged by young people who have repeatedly appeared before the courts and continue to reoffend. But support for juvenile rehabilitation is generally fairly high, even in cases of violent or repeat offenders. Mays and Ruddell (2019, pp. 265–6) found that over three-quarters of respondents in 12 US polls conducted between 1998 and 2017 supported placing youthful offenders in rehabilitative programs—and Americans tend to be more punitive than Canadians. Yet many Canadians also believe that young people who have committed violent offences should be treated similarly to adults by "locking them up and throwing away the key." This raises the question of whether youth should be treated the same as adults in the justice system.

In the past, Canadian juvenile delinquents (an outdated term for young people who committed a criminal act or a status offence—which is an act that is unlawful for a youth but legal for an adult, such as drinking alcohol) were treated much like adults. By the 1850s there was growing awareness that children and youth are different than adults in terms of their development. Youth were acknowledged as being less mature and more impulsive, having poorer decision-making skills, and lacking sophistication compared to adults. As a result, the sentences that youth received for committing crimes were often mitigated due to their immaturity. Bernard and Kurlychek (2010) say that children less than seven years of age were seldom held criminally responsible because they lacked the maturity to differentiate between right and wrong. Criminal sentences for youngsters aged eight to 14 were also mitigated in many jurisdictions. Older adolescents, however, were often treated the same as adults. Pfeifer and Leighton-Brown (2007) report how three British Columbia brothers and one of their friends were hanged on January 31, 1881, for their involvement in a murder, even though three of them were under 18 years of age at the time of the offence.

In the pages that follow, a short discussion of youth crime in Canada is presented, as examining the volume and seriousness of youth crime is a first step in understanding and then solving the

delinquents
An outdated term for young people who committed criminal acts.

status offence
Under the *Juvenile Delinquents Act*, this term refers to actions that were not considered crimes for adults but were unlawful for youth, such as drinking alcohol.

Daxus/iStockphoto

Rates of crime committed by youthful offenders have been decreasing since the mid-1990s, and homicides committed by youth are at their lowest level since the 1980s. Although those statistics suggest that current strategies to control youth crime are successful, some people are still pessimistic about youth involved in crime.

problem. This discussion is followed by a description of the evolution of the youth justice system in Canada since 1908. An overview of Canada's youth laws is provided, and boxed features pay special attention to topics such as adolescent brain development, Indigenous youth in the justice system, and pathways to crime for young women.

YOUTH CRIME IN CANADA

In developing responses to crime, there are several questions that need to be considered. How much crime do young people commit? How serious are these offences? What are the characteristics of these youthful offenders? Table 11.1 shows that the

number of youth court cases in Canada has been declining for over two decades. There were about 29,000 youth court cases in 2016/2017, which is part of a long-term decrease of about two-thirds since 1991/1992 (Miladinovic, 2019). Of those individuals, slightly more than half of them (54 per cent) are actually found guilty; over 40 per cent of these cases are withdrawn or stayed (Statistics Canada, 2019d). What is remarkable about this decrease is that the size of the youth population (aged 12 to 17 years) increased during that time. While fewer youth are involved in crime, there might be other explanations for this decrease in court appearances, including the fact that alternative measures programs, such as diversion, have reduced the number of youth appearing before the courts.

The types of offences for which youth are appearing in court can shed light on the seriousness of youth crime. The "top 10" most common offences committed by youth and reported to the police are presented in Figure 11.1. According to Allen (2018), the most common offence is theft, which is followed by level 1 (common) assault, mischief, administration of justice offences—such as failure to appear in court or breaching the conditions of a probation order—and drug possession: together, these five categories of offences account for about 60 per cent of all youth crimes reported to the police. This finding supports the observation that most youth offences are relatively minor. Of those youth accused of crime, more half have their cases stayed, dropped, or diverted from the formal court processes. When assessing the seriousness of

TABLE 11.1   Youth Crime Trends, Canada

Number of Cases Before Youth Courts, 1992 to 2017	69% Decrease	⬇
Crime Severity Index, Youth, 1998 to 2017	60% Decrease	⬇
Youth Accused of Homicide, 1974 to 2017	36% Decrease	⬇

Adapted from Allen (2018); Statistics Canada (2019a; 2019b); Beattie, David, and Roy (2018)

youth crime, we can also consider the youth Crime Severity Index, which is also shown in Table 11.1. The volume and severity of youth crime (overall) and violent youth crime have been decreasing since 1998 (Allen, 2018). Although Table 11.1 and Figure 11.1 show all youth crimes, the public is also very concerned about youth involved in homicides and other serious assaults. The number of youth aged 12 to 17 years old accused of murder (also presented in Table 11.1) has dropped by 60 per cent since 1974. When discussing youth homicides, it is important to note that one-year totals can fluctuate somewhat; between 2016 and 2017, for example, the number of youth accused of homicide doubled (Beattie, David, & Roy, 2018). To account for this in Table 11.1, the average of 1974–1976 was compared with the average of 2015–2017.

One aspect of crime that differs between juveniles and adults is the group nature of adolescent involvement in crime (Allen & Superle, 2016). Carrington, Brennan, Matarazzo, and Radulescu (2013, p. 3) examined Canadian crime statistics and found that offences involving more than one individual were over twice as common for youth (44 per cent) as for adults (19 per cent). Because violent youth offending tends to be a group offence, that pattern influences the number of youth

This photograph shows a youth courtroom in Toronto. Although there has been a decline in the number of youth court cases over the past two decades, some of the youth appearing before the courts have unstable lifestyles that make it difficult for judges to return them to the community.

accused of homicide. Allen and Superle (2016, p. 12) note that "from 2005 to 2014, 60 per cent of youth accused in homicides were co-offenders compared to 35 per cent of adults." As individuals age, they are less likely to be involved in crimes

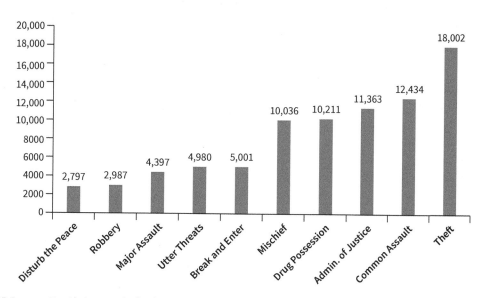

FIGURE 11.1 Youth Accused of Crimes Reported to the Police: Ten Most Common Offences, 2017

Adapted from Allen (2018)

involving more than one person. It is rare to have more than two people involved in a crime and most adult group offences are related to drugs or property crimes (Carrington et al., 2013).

Some of the youth crime occurring in groups is gang related. Although a bit dated, a study by Public Safety Canada (2007, p. 2) surveyed data collected by police organizations and estimated that there were 434 gangs in the country and about 7,000 youth involved in them. Dunbar (2017) explains that one of the challenges of estimating the true number of gangs in the country is that their activities are often hidden. We do know, however, that gangs tend to form along racial or ethnic lines. Public Safety Canada (2007, p. 2) reports that "the largest proportion of youth gang members are African Canadian (25 per cent) followed by First Nations (21 per cent) and Caucasian (18 per cent)." Those proportions vary across the country: African-Canadian gangs are more likely to be encountered in Ontario, Indigenous gangs are more prevalent in the Prairies, and Asian or Indo-Canadian gangs are active in British Columbia.

Youth gangs are engaged in the drug and sex trades and other criminal activities. As the money involved in these criminal enterprises increases, there is often a growth in gun-related violence as well. David (2017, p. 7) reports that the number of youth accused of gang-related homicides decreased in 2016, which was "contrary to the average for the previous 10 years, where youth accused of homicide were on average two times more likely to be involved in a gang-related incident compared to adults." Beattie, David, and Roy (2018, p. 15) report that youth were responsible for about one in 10 homicides in 2017, and were just as likely to be involved in a gang-related homicide as adults.

Although most gang activities are carried out by males, a small number of young women are involved in gangs. Researchers have estimated that up to one-third of all gang members are female, and suggests those populations are increasing (Dunbar, 2017, p. 17). As so little research has been done examining women in Canadian gangs, most of our knowledge is based on reports from officials who work with them, such as police officers and youth workers. Dunbar (2017, p. 17) says that some women are playing important roles in gangs including dealing drugs, recruiting new members, and collecting debts. In their study of the gang problem in Surrey, BC, Ference and Company Consulting (2018, p. 8) found that "because females are less likely to be targeted by law enforcement, they are being used by gang members to carry guns and drugs, and to provide their names for houses, cars, credit cards, and cell phones. Females are also becoming more involved in drug trafficking, recruiting, and committing gang violence." Like their male counterparts, females from marginalized populations may be more likely to join gangs as few of them have access to legitimate ways of generating wealth or increasing their status in a short period of time.

One question that is difficult to answer is why youth join gangs. While some turn to gangs due to parental neglect or because they lack positive supports in their lives, others grow up in gang-involved families. Furthermore, youth living on the street are at a relatively high risk of joining a gang (Marshall, DeBeck, Simo, Kerr, & Wood, 2015). Gang lifestyles often feature a "live for the moment" mindset. Tom Walker, a Toronto social worker and gang expert, observes that "a lot of the kids I work with, they think they're going to be dead before they're 18, 19. They're not looking at the future, they're looking at living today" (as cited in Steele, 2015). Having interviewed 175 male and female gang members in Alberta correctional centres, Chalas and Grekul (2017) say that young people are drawn to gangs to get respect, money, protection (safety from others), and to fit in. Those results are similar to the Ference and Company (2018, pp. 17–18) report that identifies three reasons why young people join gangs: (a) they want status and money, (b) they do not fear legal consequences, and (c) they become financially indebted to the gang and must carry out activities for the gang in order to pay their debts.

Although youth in gangs represent a relatively small proportion of all youth involved in crime, they are responsible for a disproportionately high amount of crime. Writing about gun and gang violence, Public Safety Canada (2018b, p. 1) observes that "gun crime often involves young offenders and young adults. Across Canada, youth and young adults are charged with firearm-related violent crime at a higher rate than adults." While the police are generally aware of gang activities, gangs themselves are difficult to eradicate. In some cases, youth gangs are associated with adult gangs or criminal organizations that have existed for generations (Schneider, 2018). Witnesses are often fearful of being victimized by gang members, and it is difficult for the police to obtain information about some gang-related crimes. Adult gang members have also attempted to intimidate Canadian police officers (Gomez del Prado, 2011), and members of the Hells Angels Motorcycle Club were involved in the murder of two Quebec correctional officers in 1997 (Cherry, 2018).

In order to increase the punishments for gang members and organized crime offenders involved in crime, the government enacted legislation in 1997 and strengthened it in 2001. Moreover, the federal government has been funding anti-gang-violence programs throughout Canada and has pledged to provide $327 million to the provinces to counter gang violence (Meissner, 2019). As with other crime-related issues described throughout this book, it is desirable to develop strategies to prevent at-risk youth from joining gangs in the first place, and gang resistance programs are emerging throughout the nation. Some of these efforts are funded by the federal government's Youth Gang Prevention Fund (Public Safety Canada, 2018a).

Even though some youth are involved in gangs, we have much to feel optimistic when it comes to youth crime. The youth Crime Severity Index and the violent Crime Severity Index have been decreasing for decades, and the number of youth court cases has also dropped. When youth do appear before the courts, over half of the cases involve relatively minor non-violent offences. When it comes to serious crimes, there has been a downward trend in homicide rates since 2009, and the youth murder rate per 100,000 youth in 2017 was less than it was in 1983. Yet every year tens of thousands of youth appear in youth courts, and a common question is, why does youth crime occur? In this chapter's "A Closer Look" box, the issue of adolescent brain development is addressed as one explanation for the involvement of youth in crime.

Figure 11.2 shows the number of Canadians accused of crimes in 2017 per 100,000 residents in the population by gender and age group. The results indicate that involvement in crime increases during early adolescence, peaks during the teenage years and early adulthood, and then

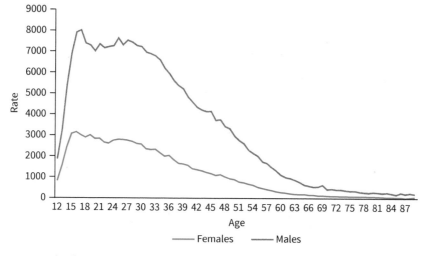

FIGURE 11.2 **Rate of Offending, by Gender and Age of Accused, Canada, 2017**
Savage (2019)

A Closer Look

Adolescent Brain Development and Crime

Anybody who has spent time with teenagers knows that they are generally less mature than adults and are more likely to engage in impulsive and unpredictable behaviours. Some teenagers have problems controlling their anger and engage in temper tantrums or other displays of low self-control. They may be negatively influenced by peers, test authority, engage in risky behaviours such as alcohol or drug use, and have a "live for the moment" orientation rather than planning for the future. Taken together, these traits result in some youth making very poor decisions, and this has been the case for thousands of years. Although we know that peer pressure pushes young people toward involvement in crime, there might also be a biological basis for such behaviour, including attraction to highly emotional situations, which can lead to violence (Scott, Duell, & Steinberg, 2018). For instance, a fear of rejection "may draw a teen to engage in behaviors, including illegal activity, even when they know better" (Cohen & Casey, 2014, p. 64).

As you will recall from Chapter 6, age is an excuse defence for involvement in crime, and immaturity is the core notion that led to the development of a separate youth justice system. The issue of immaturity raises the question of whether we should give similar punishments to youth and adults convicted of the same type of offence, given that youth have less ability to control their behaviours. It is sometimes difficult for us to remember that children are not miniature adults and should not be treated as such by the justice system. Bala (2003) notes that youth do not always have insight into their behaviours, and he observes the following:

Youths who are apprehended and asked why they committed a crime most commonly respond: "I don't know." Because of their lack of judgment and foresight, youths tend to be poor criminals as well, and, at least in comparison to adults, are relatively easy to apprehend. Often youths who commit horrible murders will boast of their deeds to their friends, or even take their friends to see the body of the victim, making their arrest inevitable. This is not to argue that adolescent offenders should not be morally or legally accountable for their criminal acts, but only that their accountability should, in general, be more limited than is the case for adults. (p. 3)

Although the differences between adult and youth behaviour have long been recognized, in the past there was little scientific evidence to tell us why these differences existed. We know today that there is a biological basis for immaturity. Medical research shows that the parts of the brain that are responsible for impulse control, judgment, future planning, and other factors about being legally responsible are not fully formed until we are in our twenties (Scott et al., 2018). Furthermore, brain development does not finish until individuals have passed their teenage years. Given those facts, we can explain some adolescent behaviour as a function of biological development. The recognition that people under 20 years of age might not be fully responsible for their actions due to their developmental stage has resulted in some US states considering whether the upper end of juvenile court responsibility should be higher than 18 years of age (Cauffman, Fine, Mahler, & Simmons, 2018).

age–crime curve Involvement in crime increases during early adolescence, peaks during the teenage years and early adulthood, and then decreases throughout adulthood (some social scientists call this "aging out" of crime).

decreases as individuals get older: social scientists call this an age–crime curve. Savage (2019, p. 6) notes that male involvement in crime is almost four times greater than female involvement. Figure 11.2 shows that rates of offending per 100,000 Canadians peaks at 16 years old for females and 17 years old for males. There are also gender differences in the types of crimes young males and females commit; in 2017,

males were almost three times more likely to be accused of committing a violent or drug-related crime and twice as likely to be accused of carrying out a property offence (Savage, 2019, pp. 16–17). Those gender differences are shown in Figure 11.3 based on the population aged 12 to 17 years. Given their involvement in crime, males are more likely to be incarcerated than females (Malakieh, 2019).

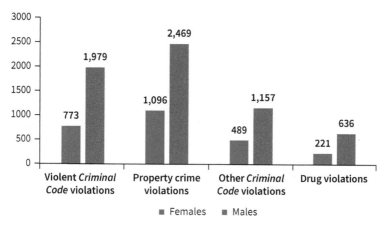

FIGURE 11.3 Rate of Youth Offending, by Violation Type and Gender of Accused, Canada, 2017
Savage (2019)

Although some youth populations across the globe may have a somewhat different involvement in crime, the statistics in Figures 11.2 and 11.3 have remained fairly consistent throughout history (Bernard & Kurlychek, 2010). As a result, we need to acknowledge two facts about youth crime: (a) most serious offences are committed by young males, and (b) most people will age out of crime and delinquency—meaning that people will generally engage in fewer offences as they get older. The trouble is that some people will continue to engage in criminal activities well into adulthood, and it is very difficult to predict who will become part of that group. These observations have implications for the justice system because wherever the population of young males is high, crime rates will also be elevated, and a small percentage of this group will continue to commit offences throughout their entire lives.

THE EVOLUTION OF YOUTH JUSTICE IN CANADA

For the past 200 years, there has been a growing interest in responding to the unmet needs of youth in order to reduce their involvement in crime. Prior to the 1800s, there was less need for a separate youth justice system, as serious crimes and delinquency committed by youth were rare. Most people lived on farms or in small settlements, and informal social control was often effective in controlling behaviour. In addition, youth living in the countryside typically worked from morning to night on family farms or small businesses, and they were often married by 16 or 17 years of age and became parents soon after, leaving very little time or opportunity to engage in crime.

During the late 1800s and early 1900s, living conditions were harsh and large numbers of young people were neglected, orphaned, or abandoned by their families. Tens of thousands of orphaned youth arrived in Canada from Europe. Many of them were placed with families as indentured servants, where they would work for several years and then be granted their freedom. However, not all youth were able to constructively occupy their time. The Department of Justice (2004) describes juvenile crime by the late 1860s as follows:

Much of the crime was minor in nature; it was manifested in urban more than in rural areas; and boys committed crime in larger numbers than girls. ... In any large community young boys and girls were to be found loitering around the streets, idle, neglected and undisciplined. Many children suffered from a lack of proper diet, malnutrition, unsanitary living conditions, drunken and dissolute parents and inadequate or no medical care. Parental neglect also contributed to such personal and social problems as truancy, lack of interest in schooling, mental and emotional difficulties, and crime. (p. 4)

indentured servants Workers who were bound by a contract to work without pay for a given period of time; this included abandoned or orphaned children who immigrated to Canada and were placed with families for several years until they could "work off" the costs of their travel to Canada.

Houston (1972, p. 259) notes that while the problem of youth delinquency was growing in cities, most offences committed by youth were relatively minor, including vagrancy, disorderly conduct, and intoxication.

Because there was no national-level legislation to confront youth crime prior to 1908, each province developed a strategy to manage delinquency. As there was no separate juvenile justice system, delinquents were brought before adult criminal courts. Police also rounded up children who had not committed a crime but were begging on the streets, were not attending school, or were otherwise out of their parents' control. Some youth lacked proper supervision because they were neglected or orphaned. These delinquent youth, status offenders, or other at-risk youth were sometimes placed together in reformatories. For instance, the prison on Île aux Noix, Quebec, was described as:

> A Reformatory Prison for Juvenile Criminals, where they would be free from the corrupting influences derived from their association with hardened criminals, and where by a proper system of discipline, education, moral and religious instruction, they might be weaned from the evil habits which time could have hardly yet hardened their youthful minds to. (Ryerson & Hodgins, 1859, p. 2)

The idea of developing a separate justice system for youth was becoming increasingly popular in Canada and led to the development of national-level legislation in 1908.

The *Juvenile Delinquents Act*, 1908 to 1984

The first truly national-level youth strategy in Canada was the *Juvenile Delinquents Act* (JDA), which was introduced in 1908. The JDA reflected the social service interests of reformers who advocated for a separate youth justice system. Section 38 of the JDA prioritized the treatment and rehabilitation

of young people by stating that "as far as practicable every juvenile delinquent shall be treated not as a criminal, but as a misdirected and misguided child, and one needing aid, encouragement, help and assistance." The focus of the legislation was on responding to the needs of youth involved in crime rather than focusing on the offence(s) they committed. As a result, the overall philosophy of the legislation was to act "in the best interests of the child" (Smandych & Corrado, 2018).

Despite the best intentions of the youth justice reformers, there were many shortcomings of the JDA. Leon (1977) observes that this legislation attempted to manage child welfare—where the court responded to the problems of abused, neglected, and dependent children—and the criminal and risky behaviours of youth, which included failing to attend school, drinking alcohol, or being incorrigible or unmanageable (which were considered status offences). One of the limitations of this approach was that some abused or neglected youth were treated no differently than youth who had committed serious crimes. Youth could be removed from their homes and placed into custody for needing help or because they were engaging in status offending, and the conditions in some of the facilities were grim: mortality rates were high, conditions were austere, and children were sometimes victimized by the staff. In addition, ideas about correctional rehabilitation were not very well developed, and the rehabilitative activities in these institutions were often limited to education and keeping youth busy by putting them to work.

The new juvenile justice system had to confront a small number of youth who had committed violent offences, such as serious assaults and homicide. Some of these youth were sent to training schools (another term for reformatories), but they could not be held past their twenty-first birthday. One problem was that older youth, for instance a 17-year-old, could be placed in a training school for only four years prior to release—and some people felt that sentence was too short for killing someone. In response to that challenge, youth over 14 years of age who

training schools Secure placements that were similar to today's secure custody facilities (also called reformatories, reform schools, or industrial schools).

committed serious offences could be transferred to adult courts. If they were found guilty, they were given adult sentences, including the death penalty.

An alternative problem was that some youth accused of non-criminal acts, such as being out of parental control, could be placed in a training school or reformatory for an indefinite term: youth would be released on their twenty-first birthday or after convincing the facility staff they had made rehabilitative progress. In both Canada and the United States, many young women were placed in youth correctional facilities for experimenting with their sexuality—their parents and the juvenile court judges were more concerned about unwanted pregnancies than the stigma of being placed in a training school.

There were also differences on the upper age limit of the court's jurisdiction between the provinces. Prior to 1984, an individual became an adult at 18 years of age in Manitoba and Quebec, at 17 years in Newfoundland and British Columbia, and at 16 years in the remaining provinces (Bala & Lilles, 1984). In other words, a 16-year-old shoplifter in Nova Scotia was considered an adult, but a 17-year-old committing the same offence in Quebec was considered a juvenile and would not have an adult criminal record if convicted. The Department of Justice (2004) notes that youth awaiting court dates were to be kept apart from adults, and the "proceedings were also to be private and neither the names of the accused nor their parents could be published." Given the fact that the JDA dealt with abused, neglected, and dependent children, the JDA did not have a lower age limit, and as a result, preteens could be placed in custody.

Another shortcoming of the JDA was that many youth did not have access to a lawyer to ensure that their rights were protected—even though their liberty was at stake—and "judges often did not follow the rules of evidence or procedure applicable to trials in adult court" (Bala & Lilles, 1984, p. 73). Karpoff and Vaughan (1962, iii) found that over 95 per cent of youth appeared before juvenile courts without a lawyer. Policy-makers

In addition to provincial authorities, a number of charitable organizations historically provided services to delinquent youth in Canada. In 1911, five sisters of the Soeurs du Bon-Pasteur order established the first of a series of homes for delinquent and neglected girls in Winnipeg. Woloschuk (2006) notes that in the 1910s, delinquent girls spent an average of 16 months in one of the programs, which was intended to build their academic skills and prepare them for employment. The programs were based on "the idea that girls' morality could be 'preserved' through religious training and discipline" (Woloschuk, 2006). The photo above shows two girls participating in the fencing program at the Marymound reformatory in Winnipeg.

were not very concerned about the rights of these young people as they were "being helped and not punished," although tens of thousands were incarcerated. A large number of youth were labelled as delinquent between 1927 and 1969, and about 10 per cent of them were placed in training schools or in detention (Statistics Canada, 2014).

The Young Offenders Act, 1984 to 2003

By the 1960s, there was growing agreement that the JDA did a poor job of responding to either child welfare or criminal behaviour. That problem was corrected with the introduction of the *Young Offenders Act (YOA)* in 1984, which only dealt with youth accused of committing crimes. Bala and Lilles (1984, p. 73) observe that "the YOA marks a shift from the welfare approach of the JDA to one recognizing accountability of young people for their offences and

A COMPARATIVE VIEW

Minimum Ages of Criminal Responsibility

One of the most controversial questions about youth justice is when a young person should become criminally responsible for their actions, or in other words, when should he or she be subject to criminal punishments? Going back hundreds of years, youngsters less than seven years of age were not subject to punishments, but the age has gradually been increasing over time. Today, Canadians younger than 12 years of age cannot be held criminally responsible for their actions, and for the most part, that age limit works for most youth. The trouble with this lower age limit, however, is that every year or two there is a case of a 10- or 11-year-old involved in a horrible crime, and the justice system is seen as powerless to respond to those acts. In 2013, for example, a 10-year-old Saskatchewan youngster who was in foster care killed a 6-year-old. Because of his age he could not be charged under the *Youth Criminal Justice Act*. In a similar case, Leamon (2016, para. 2) describes a 10-year-old Winnipeg youth who already had 22 encounters with the police and was suspected to have been involved in "arson, car theft, drug possession, robbery, break-and-enter, uttering threats, assault, and most recently and perhaps most disturbingly, a near-fatal stabbing."

Youth under 12 years of age who are well-known to the police because of their involvement in crimes are typically referred to the child welfare system, which can intervene by providing supports and treatment. Yet, some youth engage in crime because they know they cannot be punished. Nicholas Bala, Canada's foremost expert on the issue of youth justice, describes an 11-year-old who sexually assaulted a 13-year-old girl and told the police that "you got me. So what are you going to do?" (Bala, 2013, para. 9). Bala (2013) argues that the minimum age for criminal responsibility should be lowered to 10 years for these rare cases. The problem, however, is that lowering the age might result in a greater number of youth with relatively minor offences coming into contact with the youth justice system.

One of the strengths of cross-national research is that we can compare what happens in Canada with the laws and practices in other countries. The Child Rights International Network (2018) reports on the minimum age of criminal responsibility for youth for over 100 countries; Figure 11.4 presents the information from ten developed nations. The nations shown range from 10 to 15 years—a very large difference when it comes to the developmental status of a young person.

The First Youth Justice Systems

Although the movement to develop formal responses to delinquency was occurring in all English-speaking common-law nations, the first juvenile court was founded in Chicago in 1899. The establishment of a separate youth justice system was popular with policy-makers, and by 1908 a separate youth justice

accepting the need for society to be protected from illegal behaviour." In addition, youth had due process protections guaranteed under section 11, and giving them access to lawyers was important given their immaturity and vulnerability to punishments. The 1982 enactment of the *Canadian Charter of Rights and Freedoms* also made it necessary to ensure equality rights—such as standardizing the upper age limit of being criminally responsible. The *YOA* also had a lower age limit. Youth had to be 12 years old in order to be charged with an offence, although the rare cases of serious or persistent offenders under that age were often referred to other social service agencies by the police.

It was not long, however, before some of the limitations of the *YOA* became apparent. One controversial aspect of the *YOA* was the maximum sentence length of three years in custody, and the only way to manage very serious cases, such as older youth convicted of murder, was to transfer them to adult courts. There was also criticism that the *YOA* led to the overuse of

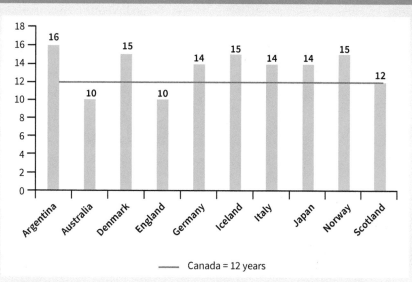

— Canada = 12 years

FIGURE 11.4 **The Minimum Age of Criminal Responsibility in Ten Developed Nations**
Child Rights International Network (2018)

system was introduced in Canada. Leon (1977, p. 72) called this juvenile justice system "a product of a diverse social reform movement dedicated to 'saving' or 'rescuing' children from what were perceived to be undesirable and harmful aspects of life."

US juvenile courts attempted to blend the powers of criminal courts with those of a social service agency that could respond to the needs of abused, neglected, dependent, and delinquent youth. Many of the young people appearing before these courts were from poor families, and they were often socially and educationally disadvantaged. Given those

challenging conditions, these youth were thought to require support and assistance rather than punishment. In fact, the US juvenile court was founded on the principle of *parens patriae* (a concept from Britain that recognizes a government's legal authority over citizens who are not able to protect themselves because of their dependency or immaturity) that enabled the courts to act *in loco parentis*—in other words, to take the place of the parents if they were not doing a proper job. Youths needed protection, sometimes from others and sometimes from themselves (Leon, 1977).

incarceration, and one reason for placing youth behind bars was a lack of community-based alternatives to custody. In some respects, the *YOA* was a victim of bad timing because it was introduced when rates of violent youth crime were increasing throughout North America, and the number of Canadian youth accused of homicide peaked in 1994/1995.

In 1908 and 1984, Canada introduced two national-level responses to reduce youth crime. Although both the *JDA* and the *YOA* had their

strengths, the biggest challenge was to develop one model that could respond to the bulk of youth crime, which consists of relatively minor offences, and also provide a just and fair response to the rare events of serious and violent crime. In addition, the system had to manage difficult cases where individuals continued to commit offences even though they had received treatment and support from the youth justice system. The legislative response to manage those two distinct groups was the *Youth Criminal Justice Act* (YCJA).

the canadian press/Frank Gunn

Sentences for youth could be very harsh when transferred to adult courts. In 1959, 14-year-old Steven Truscott was sentenced to death for the murder of a female classmate. His sentence was commuted to life imprisonment, and he was eventually paroled from prison in 1969. Truscott had always maintained his innocence, and in 2007 he was acquitted of the murder. A year later he was awarded $6.5 million in compensation from the province of Ontario.

The *Youth Criminal Justice Act*, 2003 to Present

The YCJA is the legislation that determines how youth aged 12 to 17 years will be treated by the justice system after they commit a crime. The YCJA was introduced on April 1, 2003, to respond to a number of shortcomings of the YOA, including "the overuse of the courts and incarceration in less serious cases, disparity and unfairness in sentencing, a lack of effective reintegration of young people released from custody, and the need to better take into account the interests of victims" (Department of Justice, 2013, p. 1). Kuehn and Corrado (2011) observe that the YCJA is a three-tiered system that involves the following components:

- First, minimal or no interventions for minor offences (diversion); youth who commit minor (even multiple) offences, or are first-time offenders, are generally to be dealt with outside the formal court system in the community (e.g., extrajudicial measures and extrajudicial sanctions).
- Second, youth courts imposing "intermediate" sanctions (e.g., probation and short-term custody and supervision sentences) for offenders who are neither first-time offenders nor serious and violent offenders.
- Third, the possibility of adult sentences for serious and violent offenders. These sentences are restricted to cases where a youth sentence would not be of sufficient length to hold the youth accountable. (p. 223)

The declaration of principles is outlined in section 3 of the YCJA, and they are summarized as follows:

(a) the protection of the public;
(b) the use of a separate justice system for youth that is based on diminished blameworthiness;
(c) the use of fair and proportionate sanctions; and
(d) the acknowledgement of due process protections for youth.

These principles shed light on the priorities of the reformers responsible for introducing this legislation. The tension between rehabilitation and punishment is also evident in these principles. For example, the YCJA highlights the importance of holding youth accountable for their actions, but it also addresses the importance of their rehabilitation. While these two concepts are not inconsistent with each other, achieving both outcomes for a single youth is easier said than done.

The YCJA was amended in 2012 to make punishments more severe for youth involved in serious crimes. These amendments emphasized the protection of society and removed some of the barriers to placing youth accused of violent offences in detention or custody. Furthermore, publication bans on naming youth can be lifted in certain circumstances, including cases of youth involved in violent offences such as homicide. Although lifting these bans is rare, in July 2018 the Toronto police received approval from a judge to publicize the name and distribute photographs of a 16-year-old allegedly involved in a double murder (CBC, 2018). The *YCJA* also requires prosecutors to seek adult sentences for youth aged 14 and older who are involved in homicide, attempted murder, or aggravated sexual assault, although the youth court judge decides whether an adult sentence is appropriate.

The 2012 amendments to the *YCJA* are the latest steps that increase the likelihood that harsh punishments can be imposed on serious or violent youthful offenders. For example, although the *YOA* was introduced in 1984, amendments were made in 1986, 1992, and 1995 to make it easier to transfer youth to adult courts, extend the length of custody sentences, and increase punishments of youth convicted of first- and second-degree murder (Department of Justice, 2004). Table 11.2 shows the key differences between the three federal

TABLE 11.2 **Comparison of the Federal Laws in Canada's Youth Justice System**

	Juvenile Delinquents Act	*Young Offenders Act*	*Youth Criminal Justice Act*
Introduced	1908	1984	2003
Lower age limit	None	12 years	12 years
Upper age limit	16, 17, or 18 years (depending on the province)	17 years	17 years
Focus	Child welfare and youth crime	Youth crime	Youth crime
Offences	Federal offences (e.g., *Criminal Code* offences) as well as provincial and municipal offences	Federal offences	Federal offences
Alternative measures/diversion	No formal mention in the act (although often done informally)	Identified in the act	Prioritized in the act
Right to counsel	No	Yes	Yes
Right to trial	No	Yes—trials only for youth charged with murder	Yes—jury trials for youth charged with murder or for youth who could receive an adult sentence
Victim participation	None	Yes—minimal (e.g., victims can make a victim impact statement)	Yes—victims have greater participation in the process and are more informed
Transfers to adult court allowed	Yes	Yes	No—courts may impose an adult sentence if the youth committed a serious and violent offence and is over 14 years of age
Maximum sentence in youth court	Until the youth turned 21 years of age	3 years custody	10 years for first-degree murder (maximum 6 years in custody, followed by community supervision)
Maximum sentence in adult court	Death penalty until 1976; life imprisonment	Life imprisonment	Life imprisonment
Sentences	Indeterminate	Determinate	Determinate
Courtrooms	Closed to public	Open to public	Open to public
Names publicized	No	No	Yes—for some violent offenders

youth justice acts. It is noteworthy that under the *YOA*, youth benefited from having more due process protections, including being represented by counsel, receiving determinate sentences (sentences that have a release date), and having access to trials. These benefits were, however, offset by the possibility of receiving very harsh sentences. Ruddell and Gileno (2013) found that 35 individuals under the age of 18 years were admitted to Correctional Service of Canada penitentiaries between 1984 and 2005. They also estimated that the total number of youth sent to prison was actually higher because their data did not count people who committed offences at 16 or 17 years of age but were admitted to prison after they turned 18 years of age—which is a very real possibility given the lengthy case processing times for homicide offences. This was shown in the Jazlyn Radke case study at the beginning of this chapter.

CASE FLOW OF A YOUNG OFFENDER THROUGH THE JUSTICE SYSTEM

A youth's involvement in the justice system starts when the police believe that he or she has broken the law—and at that point, an officer can proceed informally (e.g., by taking no action or by issuing a warning), refer the youth to a program, or charge them with an offence. Figure 11.5 traces the steps that might happen if the police suspected that a youth had committed a crime. The likelihood of being charged increases with the seriousness of the offence, the willingness of the victim(s) to participate in the investigation, and to some extent the demeanour of the suspect (e.g., is the individual cooperative and respectful, or confrontational and aggressive?). In other words, less serious offences carried out by polite youth may be less likely to result in a court appearance. Figure 11.6 shows the steps that might happen if a youth were *charged* with a crime.

Crown prosecutors screen the cases of youth who are charged, and they can caution them, refer them to an extrajudicial sanction program (discussed in the next section), or schedule a court date. At this point, the Crown can proceed in an adult or a youth court, but referrals to adult courts are rare unless the youth is accused of a serious offence—and those referrals can be appealed by the youth. The process is similar to what occurs in adult courts (see Chapter 7), as judges may order a pre-sentence report for those found guilty. Once the judge has reviewed these documents, the youth will be sentenced. Unlike pre-sentence reports prepared for adults, a youth's report requires interviews with family members that specifically investigate the maturity, character, and attitude of the youth, as well as the youth's willingness to make amends. One difference between the *YOA* and the *YCJA* is the requirement for probation officers preparing these reports to consider alternatives to custody so that sentences are the least restrictive and are proportionate to the seriousness of the offence. Probation officials must also consider the special circumstances of Indigenous youth. Given those requirements, these investigations and reports can take a long time to complete, and judges typically give the probation staff about a month to prepare one.

Youth may be detained in custody until their court dates, but this is considered a last resort due to the impact that detention can have on them, such as interrupting their schooling and family life. Moreover, there is evidence to suggest that mixing low- and high-risk youth might push low-risk youth further toward crime (Bonta & Andrews, 2017). According to section 29(2) of the *YCJA*, youth should not be detained unless they have been charged with a serious offence, have shown a pattern of reoffending (or have outstanding charges), pose a risk of failing to appear in court, or pose a risk to public safety. If the youth do not have a safe or stable home, they can live with a responsible adult who is able to take care of them in a judicial interim release.

Malakieh (2019) reports that on any given day in 2017/2018 there were about 800 youth in custody—although that total does not include

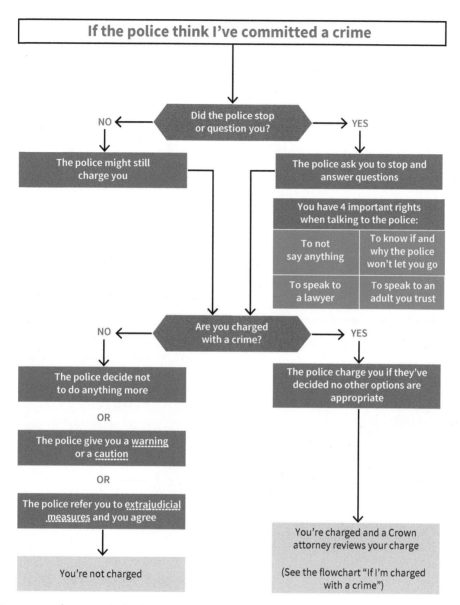

FIGURE 11.5 Youth Accused of Crime Flowchart

Reprinted from cleo's Youth Criminal Law website at youth.cleo.on.ca

Quebec and Yukon—and about 60 per cent were being held on pretrial detention (remand). Generally, these periods of detention are short, and over three-quarters of them last less than one month (Malakieh, 2019). Longer periods of detention are usually associated with more serious offences, as these cases take longer to complete. Alam (2015) reports that while the median charge-processing time (the time between the first and last appearance) in youth courts was about 120 days, serious cases took much longer to work their way through the system, and the median case processing time was 611 days for homicide offences. Statistics Canada (2019c) reports that charge-processing time has been increasing, and rose from 114 to 134 days (17.5 per cent) from 2014 to 2017.

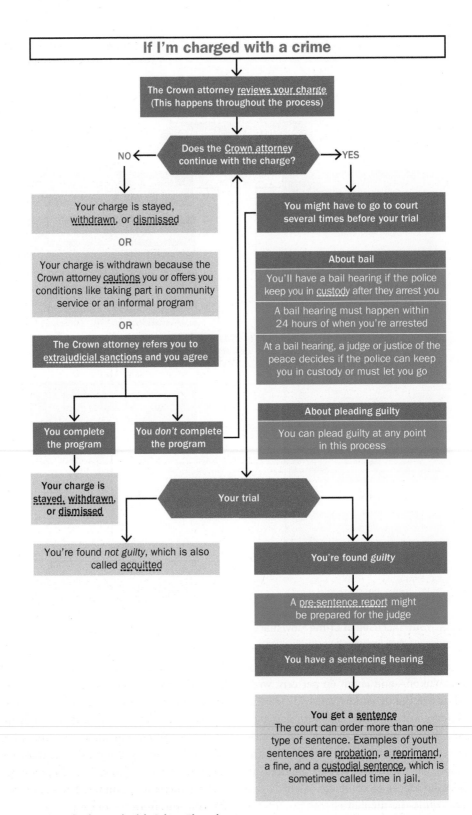

FIGURE 11.6 Youth Charged with Crime Flowchart

Reprinted from cleo's Youth Criminal Law website at youth.cleo.on.ca

YOUTH CRIMINAL JUSTICE ACT SANCTIONS

Extrajudicial Sanctions

One of the most significant differences between the *YOA* and the *YCJA* to confront criminal behaviour is the *YCJA*'s emphasis on using extrajudicial measures. The *YOA* allowed for alternative measures, which Bala and Lilles (1984, p. 2) define as "measures other than judicial proceedings under this act used to deal with a young person alleged to have committed an offence." Provinces were not, however, required to implement alternative measures programs and after the *YOA* was introduced, there was a decrease in the use of informal alternatives to the youth court and the use of custody increased (Carrington & Schulenberg, 2004, p. 220). In contrast with the *YOA*, the *YCJA* requires the police to consider extrajudicial measures before a youth is charged. Extrajudicial measures are intended to hold youth accountable but avoid court appearances, which could label or otherwise stigmatize them.

The Department of Justice (2015, p. 1) identifies the following six extrajudicial measures:

1. **Taking no further action:** The police officer takes no response to a complaint or incident.
2. **Police warning:** The officer informally warns the youth that his or her continued wrongdoing will result in more formal interventions.
3. **Police caution:** The officer takes a more formal approach and may write a letter to the youth (or to their parents), or the officer may ask to meet at the police station to discuss the youth's behaviour.
4. **Referral:** Youth are sometimes referred to community-based treatment that might be related to their offending. For example, if a youth has an alcohol problem that leads to involvement in theft, a referral for an alcohol assessment may be appropriate.
5. **Crown caution:** As noted in Figure 11.6, the Crown prosecutor might decide to caution the youth after the case has been transferred to the prosecution unit.
6. **Extrajudicial sanction:** These sanctions are the most formal and involve participation in programs established by the provinces, which may involve some restorative justice approaches such as volunteer work, community service work, or making some form of compensation to the victim(s).

Participation in more formal extrajudicial measures programs is restricted to those who accept responsibility for the offence, and the youth's parents must be aware of their child's participation. As with other community-based programs, some youth will fail to fulfill the expectations of the extrajudicial measures programs and that can lead to a court appearance. There is also a possibility that more formal sanctions such as imposing a probationary sentence will occur.

Community-Based Sanctions

Probation is the most common sentence handed down by youth courts, imposed in 57 per cent of cases (Miladinovic, 2019). Similar to adult probation (discussed in Chapter 9), youth probation permits the individual to live in the community while abiding by a number of conditions including keeping the peace and reporting to the youth court or probation office when required. Most judges also impose additional probationary conditions such as restrictions on residency (the youth's residence must be approved by a community youth worker), refraining from possessing or consuming drugs or alcohol, or a curfew. Community supervision is a fairly broad category that can include sanctions such as deferred custody and supervision, intensive support and supervision programs, fine option programs, restitution orders, compensation, and community service and personal service (Perreault, 2014). These sanctions are typically very similar to those imposed on adults, and there are few meaningful differences in fine option programs, restitution orders, or bail supervision

personal service order
Requires a youthful offender to compensate the crime victims through work supervised by a youth probation officer.

bail supervision
Allows a youth accused of a crime to remain in the community even though there may be a lack of specialized mental health or child welfare services that he or she requires.

intensive support and supervision
Enhanced supervision that is provided to youth who are considered to be at high risk or to have high needs.

deferred custody
Provides youth with an opportunity to serve their custodial sentence in the community, but if they do not abide by the conditions of their release, judges can order the youth to serve the remainder of their sentence in custody.

community youth workers
Individuals whose job is to prepare pre-sentence reports for the court, monitor youth on bail supervision, and supervise youth on probation.

for youth or adults; these activities for both age groups are often run from a single office. Restitution, for example, occurs when a youth reimburses the victim(s) for economic damage, such as when a homeowner's door is broken during a residential break and enter. A personal service order, by contrast, involves the offender compensating the victim(s) by completing labour under the supervision of a community youth worker.

Bail supervision differs from other types of community supervision as the individual has only been accused of a crime and remains in the community prior to their court date. The *YCJA* is clear that a youth cannot be detained because of a lack of community-based child welfare or mental health services. In order to manage those complicated cases, judges are imposing a large number of conditions on the youth involved, such as curfews and specifying where they will live. One challenge of that approach, however, is that some youth are required to abide by so many conditions they are almost set up to fail. Sprott and Manson (2017) found that Ontario youth on bail supervision had an average of about seven conditions and that girls were more often required to participate in a treatment program than males. Given those results, these researchers questioned whether girls were being treated fairly by the justice system.

The Department of Justice (2013, p. 12) describes several community-based sanctions to address youth crime. An intensive support and supervision order is similar to intensive supervision probation for adults and "provides closer monitoring and more support than a probation order" (Department of Justice, 2013, p. 12). Deferred custody is a sentencing option that is similar to a conditional sentence for adults and "allows a young person who would otherwise be sentenced to custody to serve the sentence in the community under conditions. If the conditions are violated, the young person can be sent to custody" (Department of Justice, 2013, p. 12). In some respects these deferred custody orders represent a "last chance" for the youth to avoid custody, and they cannot exceed six months, nor can they be used

for youth accused of serious violent crimes. Deferred custody orders are seldom used (in less than five per cent of all youth court cases), and a study of Quebec youth shows that success rates are relatively low (Dufour, Villeneuve, & Lafortune, 2018).

Last, there is the community portion of a custodial sentence, which is very similar to parole for adults. Most youth will serve two-thirds of a custody sentence within a facility and the remaining one-third in the community. Given the split between custody and community, the most time that a youth can serve in custody is two years for most regular crimes, but three years for acts for which an adult could receive a term of life imprisonment. For serious violent offences such as attempted murder, manslaughter, and aggravated sexual assault, the court orders the amount of time to be served in custody and in the community.

Most community youth workers (youth probation officers) supervise caseloads that are somewhat smaller than the caseloads of officers who work with adults. The issue of caseload specialization addressed in Chapter 9 is also evident in some urban areas, where officers might have smaller caseloads that include youth with special needs (e.g., mental health problems) or specific types of offenders such as those convicted of sexual offences. Kuehn and Corrado (2011) report that the complexity of youth probation work increased after the *YCJA* was introduced. Moreover, there is often a lack of resources to support community-based sentences. As a result, a key role in a community youth worker's job is to collaborate with workers in other systems to access health, educational, social, and psychological services (Umamaheswar, 2012).

The youth justice system attempts to reduce labelling or stigmatizing youth appearing in courts by banning the media from reporting their names (one exception is for those convicted of homicide). Unlike in the *JDA* era, however, youth courts are open to the public and a youth's friends, classmates, and victims can witness what happens in court. Those individuals can talk to others about the offence and the accused youth—so what happens to them is seldom a secret.

Involvement in the youth justice system will also result in a youth record, and while the file is active (e.g., the youth is on probation), the record is considered open and is accessible to the police. These records can be closed once a youth has fulfilled all of the conditions of his or her sentence and waited a period of three years for a summary conviction or five years for an indictable offence. If youths are convicted as adults, their record will stay open for the remainder of their life (unless they obtain a record suspension; see Chapter 10 for more details).

Open Custody

Each province and territory operates custody facilities to house sentenced and remanded youth (those awaiting court appearances). Facilities go by two names: open and secure custody. Open custody facilities are often small operations with fewer than 15 beds and they offer limited security (e.g., there are no fences or hardened confinement cells, and the exterior doors of the building might be locked only at night). These facilities offer a bridge between the community and more restrictive custody placements, and many are located in neighbourhoods beside conventional homes. They closely resemble group homes, and some group homes may have beds designated for youth serving an open custody sentence. Open custody facilities can be directly operated by the provincial or territorial governments although provinces also fund non-profit agencies, such as the John Howard Society or the Salvation Army, or they fund Indigenous communities to provide these custody services.

Most youth placed in open custody facilities go to school or are employed during the day and then return to the facility in the evenings. Some youth also participate in treatment or rehabilitative activities while serving their sentences and they may be escorted to their appointments by facility staff members. Some larger facilities deliver their own programs, and they might address common problems such as anger management or substance abuse. Youth are also expected to complete chores within the facility and are frequently assigned to

Youth custody facilities tend to be much smaller than adult facilities and open custody operations seldom have much security—there are no fences and few locked doors. The Youth Centre in Victoria was a provincially operated open custody facility that was shut down in 2016, and the empty space was used as a temporary homeless shelter when relocating tent city residents in BC. Many small open custody facilities are located in residential neighbourhoods, which is not always popular with neighbours worried about their property values. Lower numbers of incarcerated youth have resulted in the closure of a number of youth facilities throughout the country.

kitchen or cleanup duties. Unlike adult facilities, few youth custody facilities—either open or secure custody—require the residents to wear "uniforms," and most youth wear their street clothes.

Some provinces also place youth in private homes that have been designated as open custody facilities. These operations go by different names across Canada (e.g., community custody homes in Newfoundland and Labrador, and open custody homes in Saskatchewan). These open custody settings offer a home-like environment for the young person, and, ideally, the resident is treated as a family member who benefits from consistent parenting by a positive role model. These community homes are sometimes located in the countryside and they can enable rural youth to live close to their families as larger provincially operated facilities may be hundreds of kilometres from their homes.

Secure Custody

Secure custody facilities offer a higher level of security than open custody facilities. They are intended to prevent escapes and provide a safe environment for residents who present a greater risk to public safety, such as youth who have escaped from open custody, those with serious charges, and repeat offenders. Youth who are remanded to custody are typically placed in secure custody facilities to ensure they appear in court. As these youth often require more extensive education, recreational activities, and rehabilitative programming, these facilities will typically have classrooms and gyms, and some facilities also offer employment-oriented programs operated out of workshops and commercial kitchens.

Secure custody institutions often have more in common with adult correctional facilities than group homes or open custody facilities and they tend to be large buildings, or a series of structures surrounded with high wire fences to deter potential escapes. Residents are placed in living units that typically hold between 10 and 20 youth. Most youth facilities are constructed using the new generation design, similar to the adult correctional facilities described in Chapters 9 and 10. These units typically have open spaces for education, recreation, and dining, with individual bedrooms arranged around the perimeter of the living units. Although juvenile placements are intended to be more home-like than adult prisons, a tour of a secure custody facility would reveal that many of the fixtures and furniture are intended to prevent tampering: toilets are made of stainless steel, and beds, dining room tables, and chairs are often bolted to the floor to prevent them from being used as weapons. Whereas most open custody facilities have unlocked doors during the day, secure custody operations are closed to the public and the doors between different units are locked to prevent a disturbance on one living unit from spreading throughout the entire facility.

Another factor differentiating adult and youth operations is that the ratio of staff members to residents is higher in a youth facility. A single correctional officer might supervise a living unit of 40 to 50 adult inmates whereas a youth facility staff member might supervise

only 10 residents. The greater need for staff is a result of the increased volatility and unpredictability of youth. Leone, Lockwood, and Gagnon (2017) describe how one of the key goals of staff in youth corrections is to prevent further harm, although that task is difficult given that many youth are admitted to facilities with mental health disorders, alcohol and drug dependency, learning difficulties, and/or extensive histories of involvement in crime. Another reason for a higher number of staff-to-facility residents is the expectation that staff will keep the residents constructively occupied, and this

Richard Ross Photography

Youth placed in secure custody facilities often feel depressed given the lack of freedom due to high levels of security and the prison-like environment. Some youth experience stressful interactions with other youth (many of whom are serious and violent offenders), and some live far away from family members, making it difficult to have visits. Despite the best efforts of the staff members, these facilities can be dangerous places for some youth.

might include participating in recreational and treatment-oriented activities.

A review of youth court statistics reveals that the number of youth placed in open and secure custody facilities has dropped dramatically since the introduction of the *YCJA*. Indigenous youth, however, continue to be overrepresented in youth correctional populations. In 2017/2018, for example, Indigenous youth represented almost half (48 per cent) of all admissions to custody facilities and 39 per cent of all admissions to community corrections (Malakieh, 2019). The disparity between Indigenous and non-Indigenous people was greater when it came to girls, and 60 per cent of all admissions to open and secure custody were Indigenous girls (Malakieh, 2019). The focus of these court statistics is on Indigenous youth, and we have very little understanding of whether other racial disparities exist, such as an overrepresentation of African-Canadian youth in Ontario mirroring the pattern of adult incarceration in that province (Office of the Correctional Investigator, 2014).

There is no single reason for the overrepresentation of Indigenous youth in the justice system. Most scholars suggest that key factors include a greater involvement in crime, bias on the part of justice system officials, and the marginalization of Indigenous peoples, which makes it difficult to escape the cycle of crime and violence. The Truth and Reconciliation Commission of Canada (2015, p. 1) also reminds us of the long-term impact of colonial practices that attempted to "eliminate Aboriginal governments; ignore Aboriginal rights; terminate the Treaties; and,

MYTH OR REALITY

Indigenous Youth: Factors in Criminality

Some scholars believe that Indigenous youth are disproportionately involved in the justice system because of over-policing or bias in the system (Comack, 2012). Yet other factors might also be responsible. Are Indigenous youth, for example, more likely to participate in activities that get them incarcerated? Are their behaviours and motivations similar to non-Indigenous youth? In order to better understand the factors contributing to the incarceration of Indigenous youth, Corrado, Kuehn, and Margaritescu (2014) examined the criminal histories and characteristics of 404 youths incarcerated in a British Columbia youth facility between 2005 and 2009. These researchers found that there were more similarities than differences between Indigenous and non-Indigenous youth, and they observed the following:

> Caucasian incarcerated young offenders came from adverse family situations, including experienced physical and sexual abuse, criminal activity, and substance abuse histories. However, incarcerated Aboriginal young offenders had statistically significant and . . . higher

inter-generational family adversity. (Corrado, Kuehn, & Margaritescu, 2014, p. 52)

Corrado et al. (2014, p. 56) suggest that targeting problems such as "poverty, chronic ill health, mental illness, intrafamily abuse, and intimate community violence" are steps that could be taken to respond to the problem of overrepresentation of incarcerated Indigenous youth. Cesaroni, Grol, and Fredericks (2019) interviewed Indigenous youth who had been involved with the justice system and they expressed their frustrations with having no voice and being left out of decisions that were made about them. This lack of self-determination was inconsistent with traditional cultural practices in Indigenous communities where youth were involved in decisions about their lives. These youth also say that being able to participate in practices that incorporated Indigenous history, tradition, culture, and ceremony played a role in their recoveries (Cesaroni et al., 2019, p. 123). Incorporating these approaches is consistent with many of the recommendations made by the Truth and Reconciliation Commission of Canada (2015).

Race, Class, and Gender

Pathways to Female Youth Crime

Some of the early interventions that were developed for girls in the justice system were ineffective in responding to their distinctive needs because the programs failed to acknowledge that girls and women become involved in crime in different ways than males. We know that girls and women have far less involvement in crime, but we now understand that females who commit crime often have different pathways to it. Being aware of these gender differences is important because the interventions that young women require can be different from those that work for young men. We always have to remember that "one size does not fit all" when we try to help someone, as everyone's needs are so different.

As shown in the age–crime curve, women have a lower involvement in crime than do men. The subject of how and why young women become involved in crime has received considerable recent attention. Feminist scholars link involvement in crime to early trauma such as caregiver abuse, witnessing violence, long-term mental health problems (including post-traumatic stress disorder), intimate-partner violence, substance abuse, the inability to access community resources, and poverty (see DeHart, Lynch, Belknap, Dass-Brailsford, & Green, 2014; Jones, Brown, Wanamaker, & Greiner, 2014). Researchers have developed a number of different models to explain how girls become involved in crime. Boppre, Salisbury, and Parker (2018, pp. 7–10) summarized this research and found that four factors contributed to different pathways to crime for females than for males. It is important to acknowledge that many young women experience abuse, have unhealthy relationships, abuse drugs and alcohol, or suffer from low self-esteem and other psychological impairments, and never engage in any criminal activity, but these factors do seem to push some young women toward crime:

- Childhood abuse: Women tend to have more extensive histories of abuse than men, and attempts to escape that abuse such as running away from an abusive home or engaging in substance abuse to self-medicate can lead to contact with the justice system. Selling drugs or working in the sex trade to survive on the streets also increases the likelihood of contact with the system. Abuse can also lead to mental health problems including PTSD, depression, and other problems related to anxiety.
- Substance abuse: Victimized women "often use and abuse substances (drugs and alcohol) as a means to self-medicate, or cope

through a process of assimilation, cause Aboriginal peoples to cease to exist as distinct legal, social, cultural, religious, and racial entities in Canada." Many of the challenges that Indigenous people face today are linked to the practice of forcing Indigenous children into residential schools, which disrupted their family and community relationships. Aguiar and Halseth (2015, p. 5) observe that "residential schools eroded and undermined all aspects of well-being for Aboriginal peoples through disruption of the structure, cohesion and quality of family life; loss of cultural identity; diminished parenting skills; and low self-esteem and self-concept problems" for those who directly experienced those schools as well as their descendants.

YOUTH INTERVENTIONS

There is much to be optimistic about when we consider that youth crime rates have decreased and there are about half as many young Canadians behind bars today than there were in 2000. Although we will always have to confront youth crime, youth justice systems today are more responsive to young people who are in conflict with the law, and our interventions are more advanced than they were prior to the introduction of the with, negative life experiences such as abuse or trauma," and "this process becomes a damaging cycle: women are victimized, seek out illicit substances in order to self-medicate and manage their resulting emotional or mental health problems, participate in criminal acts in order to obtain more drugs or property they can sell or trade for drugs." (Boppre, Salisbury, & Parker, 2018, pp. 8–9)

- Unhealthy intimate relationships: Harmful or exploitative relationships can expose a female to criminal behaviour, illicit drugs, and criminal organizations, such as gangs. In addition, intimate partners can be abusive and girls or women suffering from low self-esteem may be vulnerable to staying in these destructive relationships This risk increases if these women are isolated from positive supports, such as family and non-criminal friends.
- Lack of self-efficacy: A lack of personal confidence may keep some girls and women in unhealthy lifestyles or relationships. Boppre et al. highlight how some women are disadvantaged compared to men with respect to their employment, economic status, and education, and these factors can both limit their opportunities and increase feelings of powerlessness. These factors can push women into committing

property crimes, such as theft and fraud, to meet their basic needs. Girls who are parents and are also dealing with the effects of abuse and poverty may also feel they have fewer choices.

These four factors can also be interrelated, and they also could be shaped by biological influences such as the early onset of puberty, or other risk factors, such as family criminality or instability, exposure to violence, and attachment to and engagement with social institutions such as places of worship or schools (Zahn, Hawkins, Chiancone, & Whitworth, 2008).

It is important to note that there is no single set of circumstances that leads to a youth's involvement in crime; other researchers have developed pathways models that include other factors, such as the use of violence (DeHart, 2018) and involvement in subcultures, such as drug-trafficking and criminal networks (Brennan, 2015). Regardless of which model one prefers, a common finding in the pathways research is that girls' involvement in crime often starts in the teen years and is different from what happens with males. Given those findings, we are unlikely to find a single intervention that will work with both males and females, and all different types of individuals within those groups (Mays & Ruddell, 2019).

YCJA in 2003. These evidence-based interventions were developed using an understanding of the factors contributing to adolescent crime. In addition, researchers today are better able to identify the interventions that provide the best bang for taxpayer dollars. In the prior chapters a number of evidence-based practices were identified that have been demonstrated to reduce recidivism.

Cost-benefit analyses are increasingly being used to estimate the costs of justice system interventions, such as different types of treatment, and to compare those costs to the benefits in reduced crime. There is a growing interest in applying cost-benefit analyses to adult and youth justice

interventions, and studies consistently show that some programs are very effective at reducing youth crime. The Washington State Institute for Public Policy (2018a), for example, has identified a number of treatment interventions that are proven to reduce youth recidivism, and a short list of the most successful interventions is shown in Table 11.3. These results are based on cost-benefit analyses and reflect the savings for each dollar invested in these programs.

There are a number of common themes in interventions proven to successfully reduce youth recidivism, and the programs providing the highest returns are based on interventions delivered by

cost-benefit analyses An approach to estimating the costs of justice-system interventions, such as different types of treatment, and comparing those costs to the benefits in reduced crime.

TABLE 11.3 Crime Reduction Benefits for $1 Invested in Youth Justice Programs

Program	Total Benefits
Dialectical behaviour therapy	$28
Cognitive behavioural therapy	$38
Education and employment training	$42
Coordination of services	$24
Functional family therapy	$12
Parenting program	$9

Washington Institute for Public Police (2018a)

skilled therapists. The intervention that provides the best return per dollar of investment for youth programs is dialectical behaviour therapy. This has been described as a treatment for young people with complex mental health problems and is based on enhancing a youth's skills in dealing with difficult situations, motivating them to change their behaviours, and ensuring that they practice these skills in a custody environment (Washington State Institute for Public Policy, 2018b, para. 2).

One issue that is gaining more attention in the youth justice field is providing trauma-informed care. Researchers are finding that a large percentage of the young men and women in the justice system have been exposed to traumatic events such as being victimized or witnessing a violent attack, and that experiencing these acts can have long-term negative effects on their mental health. Loughran and Reid (2018, p. 5) say that individuals can be traumatized after exposure to a single event, such as experiencing or witnessing gang-related violence, a serious accident, an assault, or the sudden death of a loved one. Their experiences with trauma can also be due to long-term exposure to negative events such as ongoing physical and sexual abuse or domestic violence. Witnessing traumatic events can reduce an individual's self-confidence and feelings of safety or well-being, inhibit their ability to form attachments to others, and lead to anxiety, depression, and PTSD.

Loughran and Reid (2018, p. 6) observe that exposure to trauma can lead to "disturbed sleep, difficulty paying attention and concentrating, anger and irritability, withdrawal, repeated and intrusive thoughts, and extreme distress—when confronted by anything that reminds them of their traumatic experiences (i.e., triggers)." Oudshoorn (2015) says that many Canadian justice officials do not have the awareness or skills to manage these cases and youth involved in the system are sometimes re-traumatized by the actions of these officials, such as such as requiring everybody admitted to a facility to undergo a strip search for contraband; such a practice might be routine for facility youth workers but can be very upsetting to some youth.

In order to provide trauma-informed services, youth justice systems must acknowledge the impacts of trauma on their clients, and all staff must be aware of how the trauma experienced by individuals can affect their behaviours years after their exposure. Agencies providing care to youth must be careful to ensure that their policies do not re-traumatize their clients, and practices such as physically restraining an out-of-control youth, for instance, can trigger unpleasant memories for survivors of sexual abuse. Trauma-informed services are also culturally competent, which means they "reduce/avoid disparities related to race/ethnicity, gender, sexual orientation, developmental level and socio-economic status" (Branson, Baetz, Horwitz, & Hoagwood, 2017, p. 641).

Similar to working with adult prisoners, some youth residents in open or secure custody can make substantial improvements in their attitudes and beliefs. One of the challenges common to both justice systems (adult and youth), however, is that when these residents return to their home communities, they are often subjected to the same temptations that existed prior to their arrests, including substance abuse, crime-involved peers and family members, and poverty and chaotic family living conditions. Moreover, many of them may find it difficult to return to school or find a job due to the stigma of having been incarcerated. As a result, despite the positive steps they have made in treatment while in custody, many of them start to engage in the same behaviours that resulted in their involvement in crime in the first place.

trauma-informed care An approach to delivering interventions that acknowledges the impacts of trauma on individuals and the importance of providing services in a safe, healing, and empowering manner.

Given the difficulties that many youth have in their return to the community, there is an increasing emphasis on designing programs that involve probation staff and other professionals—such as teachers and counsellors—who support the youth, along with other role models, such as family members. The process of supporting an individual's return to the community was once called aftercare, but the term wraparound services is now being used to reflect the involvement of these professionals and family members in the youth's case plan. According to the Office of Juvenile Justice and Delinquency Prevention (2014, p. 1), the wraparound process "is a youth-guided, family-driven team planning process that provides coordinated and individualized community-based services for youth and their families to help them achieve positive outcomes." While the names of aftercare or wraparound services will differ across the country, a key goal of these programs is to provide a range of supports to youth to reduce their recidivism.

SUMMARY

The crime trends discussed in this chapter show that the number of youth appearing before the courts has decreased and that most are accused of non-violent offences. Even the biggest supporters of the crime control model express some positive feelings toward youthful offenders and support policies that divert individuals who have been engaging in minor crimes from the formal justice system. Most of us made mistakes growing up, and saddling a youth with a criminal record for a minor offence creates more problems than it solves, especially when that record sets up long-term barriers to employment and other opportunities. Some youth, however, are not able to take advantage of the leniency that is extended to them, and they continue engaging in crime. Others commit serious and violent offences. These are the youth that challenge the public's patience and create the most significant challenges for the justice system and lawmakers. Although the public believes that these youth "should know better," the latest brain research shows that there is a biological basis to youth immaturity, impulsiveness, and a "live for the moment" orientation that can lead to tragedies.

Canada has experimented with three different approaches to youth justice, beginning with the *JDA* introduced in 1908. This approach was based almost entirely on the notion of rehabilitating at-risk youth, although most Canadians would agree that the *JDA* fell short in protecting the rights of children or actually providing them with the services they needed to make positive changes. The introduction of the *YOA* in 1984 extended due process protections to youth, but also led to the overuse of custody, and its three-year maximum sentence failed to inspire public confidence (although youth accused of serious offences could be transferred to adult courts). In some respects, the *YOA* was a victim of bad timing, as youth crime rates increased throughout North America during the mid-1980s and persisted for a decade; then declined prior to the introduction of the *YCJA* in 2003. Court and custody statistics show that the number of youth appearing before the courts has decreased, and that the use of custody has dropped by almost two-thirds with no increase in youth violence.

Although we have made some headway since the *YCJA* was introduced in 2003 in terms of reducing the number of youth who are behind bars, there are still some challenges to overcome. Indigenous youth, for example, remain overrepresented in custody populations (Smandych & Corrado, 2018). In addition, the programs developed for youth, especially for girls, do not always take into account their distinctive needs and pathways to crime. Regardless of the type of youth justice legislation that is introduced, one common failing is that we seldom have enough health, educational, and social service resources to support the efforts of the youth justice system. These limitations are multiplied in some rural areas, where access to medical, educational, and social services is further limited.

Although the costs of providing comprehensive youth services can be significant, there are

wraparound services An approach to developing an individualized, community-based case plan for a young offender by involving a team of their family and community professionals.

substantial long-term benefits once we consider the costs when we fail to respond to the risks and needs of at-risk youth. The direct costs of crime include funding policing, the courts, and corrections, and they can quickly add up. An attempted murder that results in a ten-year federal prison sentence, for example, will cost Canadians over $1.2 million to incarcerate the offender, and it may take $1 million to provide hospital care for the victim. The indirect costs of crime are harder to determine, but they include the impacts on the lives and opportunities of victims and their families. In 2009, Cohen and Piquero (p. 25) estimated the "value of saving a 14-year-old high risk juvenile from a life of crime to range from $2.6 to $5.3 million," and that amount would now be $3 to $6.2 million once we account for inflation.

Career SNAPSHOT

Facility Youth Worker

Many students express interest in working with troubled youth, and there are many career opportunities in the community and in facilities. Facility youth workers—also known as youth correctional officers—are employed in open and secure custody facilities throughout the country, and they work in a variety of positions. One of the most important roles that facility youth workers play is to supervise youth and ensure that they abide by facility rules. This can be challenging because placement in custody may be the first time that these youth are away from home and they may be experiencing difficult circumstances such as withdrawal from substance abuse. Furthermore, many youth awaiting their court appearances are facing considerable uncertainty. Taken together, these various factors can contribute to youth acting out and displaying aggressive behaviour. One way that youth facilities attempt to reduce challenging behaviour is to keep the youth constructively occupied through a variety of educational, recreational, and rehabilitative programs.

Profile

Name: Catherine Wimmer
Job title: Correctional Service Worker II, Calgary Young Offender Centre
Employed in current job since: 1992
Present location: Calgary, Alberta
Education: BA (Advanced), University of Saskatchewan

Background

I had a brush with the law in my youth, and at that point I realized that I needed to fill my routine with positive activities. I worked hard in high school, excelled in sports, and relied on a number of my teachers for guidance. It was around this time in my life when I realized that I wanted to work with youth. I was accepted into the education program at the University of Regina with the goal of becoming a guidance counsellor. After completing my first year of university, I decided to transfer to the University of Saskatchewan in order to be closer to family and friends. Since the education program was full, I applied and was accepted into the Bachelor of Arts program. After four years, I completed a Bachelor of Arts advanced degree with a major in psychology and a minor in sociology.

Work Experience

After finishing my degree in 1992, I applied for a job at the North Battleford Youth Centre, which was a secure custody facility. I obtained a casual (part-time) position as a facility youth worker, and I eventually became a permanent employee. After nine years of working in that position, I relocated to Alberta and got a job as a youth worker position at the Calgary Young Offender Centre, where I continue to be employed.

One of the biggest challenges facing youth involved in the justice system is recidivism. Government agencies along with community organizations and outreach programs work to provide treatment and rehabilitation of youth while they are in custody, in the community, and in transition. We work very hard to provide a stable and safe environment for the youth in our care, but unfortunately most of them are released into unstable homes or shelters with few community resources to support them. As a result, a number of our youth return to custody to have their basic needs met. For youth workers, this is very disheartening and frustrating, because we work extremely hard to involve families and communities in the process, participate in case conferences to address the youth's specific unmet needs, and develop release plans to address those shortcomings. But how can we expect youth to be successful if their home environments are unstable or if they do not have a home to return to?

The most rewarding experiences of working with youth are the success stories; knowing that you are a part of someone's success can be very fulfilling. As a youth worker, you are a guardian, a counsellor, a disciplinarian, and a role model—the list goes on—but knowing that a youth may rely on you makes all of your hard work worthwhile. Even if it was just one youth that I personally helped to succeed, it would make all of the negative aspects of my job appear minimal. As a youth worker, you can make a big difference in someone's life!

Throughout my career in corrections, I have witnessed events ranging from minor assaults to serious violent offences and riots. I have been assaulted by offenders, and I have assisted in de-escalating suicidal youth and other volatile situations. We draw on our professionalism, extensive training, and dedication, and we work as a team to protect each other, the youth, and the public. The youth workers that I work with consider our group to be a "correctional family," and the team atmosphere in correctional facilities is really one of the best.

Advice to Students

In order to become an effective youth worker, you must be willing to adapt to all different types of people and work styles, and most importantly, you must be open to receiving criticism and feedback. Additionally, you must have strong communication skills—both written and verbal—and you must be able to bounce back from your mistakes. In the criminal justice field, and specifically in corrections, you will be exposed to many different challenges. In order to overcome these challenges, you must have strong values, ethics, and morals.

In regards to education, I would recommend taking criminology, psychology, and sociology courses. I would also recommend volunteering to work with at-risk youth. This will give you the foundation you need to become an effective youth worker.

REVIEW QUESTIONS

1. Describe how the volume and seriousness of youth crime has changed over the past two decades.
2. What are the main differences between the *Juvenile Delinquents Act*, the *Young Offenders Act*, and the *Youth Criminal Justice Act*?
3. Provide some reasons why youth are not held as accountable for their involvement in crime as are adults.
4. Describe how the *YCJA* provides a graduated approach to respond to a range of minor to serious crimes committed by youthful offenders.
5. Describe the different pathways to girls' involvement in crime.

DISCUSSION QUESTIONS

1. List some reasons why a youth under 18 years of age involved in a homicide should, or should not, receive a life sentence.
2. Would you support a youth justice policy that does not formally punish first-time non-violent offenders? How does a "doing nothing" practice contrast with extrajudicial measures?
3. Research shows that the parts of the brain responsible for reasoning and maturity do not fully develop until a person is in their twenties. Given that fact, should the *YCJA* be changed to increase the maximum age limit from 17 to 19 years of age?
4. Researchers have found that saving one high-risk youth from a life of crime saves taxpayers millions of dollars over the life of the individual. What are some of the costs to taxpayers, victims, and society for an individual who continues to commit crime?
5. Rural offenders typically have limited access to rehabilitative services that respond to their unmet needs. Given that fact, should rural offenders receive less severe punishments?

INTERNET SITES

The US Office of Juvenile Justice and Delinquency Prevention has been supporting the study of girls' delinquency. They report on the efforts of the Girls Study Group, which is a group of prominent researchers who identify the distinctive pathways to crime and the most promising strategies to respond to the unmet needs of these young women.
https://www.ncjrs.gov/pdffiles1/ojjdp/223434.pdf

Statistics Canada provides a detailed flowchart of youth court statistics in Canada for 2013/2014. The chart summarizes the total number of cases broken down by the different decisions and sentences.
http://www.statcan.gc.ca/pub/85-002-x/2015001/article/14224/c-g/c-g10-eng.htm

▲ Michel Cadotte, centre, is shown here walking to the courtroom with court staff to hear final arguments in his case. In 2019, Cadotte was found guilty of manslaughter for killing his wife, Lizotte, who had late-stage Alzheimer's, in 2017. His actions took place after Canada legalized medically-assisted dying in 2016, which he sought but his wife did not qualify for. Should there be a law on "compassionate homicide"? How do the circumstances of this homicide differ from the Robert Latimer case presented in Chapter 7? (Photo credit: THE CANADIAN PRESS/Ryan Remiorz)

Looking Forward: Criminal Justice in the Twenty-First Century

LEARNING OUTLINE

After reading this chapter, you will be able to

- Describe the elements of a PESTEL analysis
- Identify the political factors that may shape the future of the Canadian justice system
- Describe how our reliance on technology makes us increasingly vulnerable to victimization
- Explain how social and cultural changes will impact the operations of the justice system
- Identify the different challenges confronting the future of urban and rural justice systems

Self-Driving Vehicles and the Justice System

Self-driving vehicles (also called autonomous vehicles) that require no driving on the part of the occupants are predicted to be widely introduced by 2025 and become the norm a decade later. Self-driving vehicles have already travelled millions of kilometres. While most of these trips were uneventful, there have been hundreds of crashes, and while most only resulted in minor damages, a growing number of people have been injured in such collisions (California Department of Motor Vehicles, 2019), and several individuals have been killed. Although there is a long way to go before the use of self-driving cars is widespread, the technology used in many cars and trucks is becoming increasingly sophisticated—a growing number of vehicles have sensors to warn drivers of hazardous situations, and some automatically brake in emergency situations. Other vehicles, including some Cadillac, Mercedes, and Tesla models, have semi-autonomous driving options enabling the vehicle to drive on the highway without human assistance, while other manufacturers offer cars that can parallel park without drivers having to touch the steering wheel: smart machines are replacing human drivers.

Autonomous vehicles will have significant implications for justice and social systems. For example, could passengers who drank too much alcohol be convicted of impaired driving if they had no control over the vehicle? Furthermore, if autonomous vehicles followed all of the traffic rules, there would be few reasons for police traffic stops—freeing the police for other duties. It is also projected that the number of crashes would be reduced by a significant proportion as over 90 per cent of collisions today are the result of driver error (National Highway Traffic Safety Administration, 2018). Police pursuits would not occur if officers could override the computer of a self-driving car and instruct it to pull over in a safe location, or even instruct the car to drive the occupants to the nearest police station!

There may also be a dark side to the introduction of driverless vehicles. Black (2018) warns us that these vehicles could be used by terrorists as weapons that would replace suicide bombers. Perhaps the most profound impact of this new technology could be on employment, as hundreds of thousands of drivers of taxis, shuttle services, delivery trucks, and trucks may no longer be needed. A Government of Canada study, however, also points out that technological innovation often results in new jobs being created (Cutean, 2018).

The Economist (2018) predicts that the number of vehicles on the road could drop by up to half if

JasonDoiy/iStockphoto

In the future, self-driving cars may have a significant impact on reducing deaths from traffic collisions as well as reducing the need for traffic enforcement. It has been estimated that self-driving cars will reduce collisions by 80–90 per cent. In the meantime, Volvo is planning on installing sensors and in-car cameras allowing the vehicles to slow down, stop, or even notify company representatives if they detect impaired or inattentive drivers; if there is no response to a representative's call, the system "can instruct the car to park itself and notify emergency responders" (Cole, 2019, para. 4).

privately owned vehicles were replaced by self-driving taxis. In addition, reducing collisions by 80–90 per cent could mean that fewer workers would be needed to repair or insure vehicles. Last, it has also been speculated that roadside motels would become obsolete as there would be no need to stop overnight on cross-country trips; the cars would keep driving while the passengers slept. Altogether, this one innovation might have a significant impact on justice systems, employment, and our everyday lives.

Critical Questions

1. Elon Musk, the chief executive officer of Tesla Motors, said that self-driving cars will be so safe that "they may outlaw driven cars because they're too dangerous" (Bell, 2015). Uber and other transportation companies have advocated for banning privately owned vehicles in central cities in the future (Scribner, 2018). Are these realistic predictions? Why or why not?

2. Insurance companies might charge much higher rates for human drivers as they pose greater risks than self-driving vehicles. Can you think of other examples where financial penalties or rewards are used to change our behaviours?

3. While technology has reduced the need for human employment, how will that trend affect existing social problems, including crime?

INTRODUCTION

This book started with an overview of the Donald Marshall Jr. case, an example of bias that resulted in a miscarriage of justice. In the chapters that followed, we explored the operations of the justice system, various challenges in understanding crime and responding to those acts, and some promising solutions to these complex issues. Why are these topics important? The World Justice Project (2019, p. 28) observes that "an effective criminal justice system is a key aspect of the rule of law as it constitutes the conventional mechanism to redress grievances and bring action against individuals for offenses against society." A key objective of this book was to provide readers with a basic knowledge of justice systems and to build a foundation for future studies. The previous 11 chapters have highlighted the operations of Canada's criminal justice system.

We learned that most of our ideas about crime and justice come from the entertainment media, and throughout this book it was pointed out that many of these messages are misleading or wrong (McKnight, 2016). In addition, news accounts about the operations of the justice system can be condensed into short articles, internet posts, and television reports that simplify very complex issues. As you take more classes in criminology and criminal justice, you will discover that this book has also simplified many issues. A university graduate can attend three years of law school and have a year of experience articling (which is like an internship for lawyers) and still not be prepared to argue a criminal case in court—so a single chapter on the court system, such as Chapter 7, can provide readers with only a basic overview of the key issues. In other words, even after you read through this book, there is still much to learn about justice systems.

In this chapter, we take a closer look at the changes that are likely to occur in the Canadian justice system over the next decade. These types of exercises of predicting future trends are routinely done by agency leaders as they do not want their organizations to be blindsided by unforeseen events. All of us have a stake in the future operations of justice systems as we will be directly or indirectly affected by changing police practices, court reforms, and the effectiveness of correctional systems. In addition, some readers may be interested in working in the justice system, and reviewing future trends may help them make better choices about potential careers.

THE CANADIAN JUSTICE SYSTEM: WHERE ARE WE TODAY?

Positive Changes

In reading the previous chapters, one is reminded of how far we have progressed in a relatively short period of time. Several chapters included short descriptions of historical practices carried out by the police, the courts, and correctional employees. These accounts revealed that justice systems 100 years ago were staffed by personnel with little training, and there were few written policies or procedures for workers to follow. Because there were no national- or provincial-level standards, the policing in Dartmouth, Nova Scotia, might not have resembled what occurred in The Pas, Manitoba. By contrast, if a driver on a cross-country trip is stopped today by the police in British Columbia for speeding, the driver's interactions with the officer will be quite similar to those of a driver stopped in Quebec for the same violation.

In addition to the lack of formal standards, suspects were sometimes assaulted by police officers to obtain confessions (during a process of questioning known as the third degree), and some suspects were beaten instead of being arrested—the process of forcing a suspected offender to submit to an unauthorized form of punishment is called street justice. Police officers were hired for their physical size and ability to intimidate others rather than for their interpersonal skills or ability to solve problems. While police misconduct still occurs, officers today are held more accountable; the public is less tolerant of wrongdoing, and especially when it comes to the use of excessive force. Even though Canadian officers are about one-fourth as likely to kill a suspect than are American officers, there has been increased scrutiny of these acts, and the Green Party does not believe that Canadian police officers should carry firearms (CTV News Montreal, 2018).

There have been other positive changes in courts and corrections. The likelihood of a wrongful conviction was higher in the past than it is today as there were fewer safeguards for suspects. In addition, legal aid funded by provincial governments for poor defendants was introduced in 1967 in Ontario and in the remaining provinces by the mid-1970s, although, as pointed out in earlier chapters, these programs are underfunded and any full-time minimum wage earner would be ineligible for their help. With respect to corrections, punishments such as whipping were carried out in prisons until 1968 for inmates who broke institutional rules (Correctional Service of Canada, 2015). Furthermore, the death penalty fell out of favour in the 1950s; the last Canadian executions occurred in 1962 and the punishment was abolished in 1976. The "good old days" were not so pleasant for those accused or convicted of crimes.

Despite the progress that we have made toward fair and just outcomes for victims and offenders, the past 11 chapters also revealed that we still need to overcome challenges in the operations of justice systems. As in other professions, mistakes can be made at all points of the justice system, from arresting innocent suspects to releasing inmates from correctional facilities prior to their warrant expiry dates because someone made a mistake calculating their sentences. In addition to making mistakes, some justice system personnel engage in misconduct: police and correctional officials obtain evidence illegally, fail to abide by the policies of their agencies, or engage in crimes and cover-ups. Because these officials work with very little direct supervision and with marginalized people who have very little power, their offences have often gone unreported.

The activities of court officials, by contrast, are more transparent as their work in courtrooms is conducted in full public view. Despite this transparency, prosecutors also engage in misconduct, although suspects are unlikely to have their charges stayed in these incidents (see *R v Babos*, 2014). Judges are also accused of misconduct, and in 2017/2018, the Canadian Judicial Council (2018) opened 359 complaints about the conduct of judges presiding in federal courts or superior courts in the provinces such as Queen's Bench courts. Although that number seems high, most

third degree
A long and intense interrogation, which in extreme cases has involved threats of violence or the unlawful use of force, to obtain a confession from a suspect.

street justice
Occurs when a suspected offender is forced to submit to an unauthorized punishment by a police officer, such as doing push-ups in return for not getting a speeding ticket.

of the complaints referred to relatively minor incidents, such as judges thought to have acted in a disrespectful, inappropriate, or condescending manner. Since 1971, the Canadian Judicial Council has recommended removing fewer than ten judges from office (Canadian Press, 2017).

Judges today, however, may be held to a higher standard due to the publicity that can occur after their mistakes or actions become publicized in the press and on social media. In a 2014 trial, Robin Camp, an Alberta provincial court judge, asked the survivor of a sexual assault questions such as, "Why couldn't you just keep your knees together?" and "Why didn't you just sink your bottom down into the basin so he couldn't penetrate you?" (cited in Southey, 2015). In March 2017, the Canadian Judicial Council recommended he be removed from the bench, and Camp resigned his position. One fact about this case is clear: when the misconduct of officials in the justice system becomes viral on social media, the public's outrage can result in swift action.

Given the difficult nature of the jobs and the range of personnel working within justice systems, mistakes and misconduct will always occur. We hold the employees of our justice systems to a higher standard than workers in other professions—and most of the time they meet our

A Calgary police officer talks to cannabis users at a rally outside government offices following marijuana legalization in 2018. The Calgary Police Service banned officers involved in front-line policing from using recreational marijuana, even while off-duty (Smith, 2018). Other police services are grappling with the issue and the Toronto Police Service and the RCMP have developed policies where officers must refrain from using marijuana for 28 days prior to working. The Vancouver Police, by contrast, do not have rules related to off-duty marijuana use, as long as officers show up fit for duty for their assigned shifts. While these off-duty drug use policies are being challenged by the officers' unions, these decisions show that the expectations of workers in the justice system can be very high, including regulating their off-duty behaviours.

A Closer Look

Using PESTEL to Scan the Environment

Leaders in every criminal justice agency try to predict the future to reduce the uncertainty confronting their organizations, especially when it comes to forces external to the agency. Corporate leaders have used PESTEL analysis to monitor the external environment for possible threats and opportunities. This "big picture" approach has also been used by researchers to help predict how external factors will impact the operations of justice organizations (see van den Born et al., 2013). Writing about the police in Canada, Griffiths, Pollard, and Stamatakis (2015, p. 177) observe that "Environmental scans are studies designed to identify community, legislative, policy, and other forces in the community ... that will result in demands on the police." Figure 12.1 shows the factors considered in a PESTEL analysis, which are summarized as follows.

PESTEL analysis
A method of scanning the environment that considers political, economic, social, technological, environmental, and legal factors.

FIGURE 12.1   PESTEL Analysis

- **Political.** This factor considers the political climate in a nation (both liberal and conservative positions) and the fact that politicians will introduce crime control policies based on either the due process or crime control perspectives. Csanady (2015) notes that between 2006 and 2015, the Conservative government "tabled 68 bills that directly amend the Criminal Code," and of those, 30 became law. All of these legislative changes affected the activities of justice systems personnel as well as the lives of crime victims and offenders. Demonstrating the dynamic nature of justice systems, the Liberal government, elected in 2015, pledged to reform the criminal justice system, but Spratt (2019) says their promises have fallen short.

- **Economic.** Between 1948 and 2011, there were 11 economic recessions (or about one every

expectations. We sometimes forget, however, that these personnel are often overworked and required to interact with very difficult people in dangerous and uncertain situations. The police, for example, have no information about the intent of someone they encounter on the street—will the individual warmly greet the officers or try to kill them? Although it is easy to criticize the actions of police or correctional officers, they are often forced to act with limited information in a matter of seconds, and they do not have the luxury of taking weeks

to debate "what should have been done" from the comfort of a soft chair in a quiet office.

The scrutiny of justice system personnel by internal and external watchdogs, advocacy organizations, ombudsmen, and the media has increased. And this oversight has resulted in some positive outcomes. When it comes to officials working in the justice system, for example, the police are better trained, more diverse, and have higher professional standards today than in the 1980s. In addition, accused people in court have access to lawyers who

4.5 years). These economic downturns affect both the amount of crime (in some recessions crime increased, while in others it decreased) and the system's ability to respond to it, especially when funding is cut to the operations of the justice system, and the police, courts, and corrections are asked to do more with less.

- **Social.** This factor includes demographic and cultural changes. In terms of demographic changes, aging populations are usually associated with less crime whereas rapid population growth is associated with more crime. Crime rates are also linked to the number of 15- to 25-year-old males in the population, as shown in the age–crime curve in Chapter 11, and the higher their numbers, the more crime we can expect. Cultural changes include a reduction in trust and confidence in the police, courts, and correctional systems, which may in turn reduce citizen cooperation with the police and courts. Not all social or cultural changes are negative. In the 1970s, for example, impaired driving had a greater social acceptance whereas drunk drivers are shunned today. These changes in our attitudes were shaped by the public education efforts of advocacy organizations, such as Mothers Against Drunk Driving.
- **Technological.** Technology has had a significant impact on the operations of the justice system in terms of offenders (who have used the internet to develop new ways of committing crimes – see the Police Executive Research Forum, 2018) and

justice systems officials (such as police officers who have access to automated licence-plate readers that can detect stolen or uninsured vehicles). Police organizations are also using social media in investigations as well as to communicate with the public through Facebook and Twitter.
- **Environmental.** Concern over environmental protection is playing a greater role in government regulations, and there are more officials tasked with these duties. Environmental factors also include climate change and this could have a long-term impact on conditions in Canada, such as opening the North to more ocean traffic, which would require an increase in policing as well as search and rescue operations.
- **Legal.** Supreme Court decisions play a significant role in the operations of the justice system, and the rulings of the Supreme Court can place administrative burdens on agencies that can cost millions of dollars, and have far-reaching impacts on the entire justice system. Appellate court decisions impact the activities of police, court, and correctional personnel, such as the legality of the police accessing information on the cell phones of suspects they arrest or the decision to strike down Canada's prostitution laws. In the *R v Jordan* decision, for example, the Supreme Court established strict limits to the time that courts can take before a case is resolved, and this has resulted in hundreds of cases being stayed by prosecutors.

work for agencies funded by provincial governments to protect their rights (Michael, 2018). If convicted and sentenced, probationers or provincial or federal inmates are more likely today to participate in evidence-based rehabilitative programs that have a greater likelihood of helping them overcome the attitudes and behaviours that contributed to their involvement in crime.

Crime victims, who in the past were often ignored by the justice system, are now treated with more respect, and the *Canadian Victims Bill of*

Rights extended their rights in 2015. Victim services operations exist across the country to inform these victims of their rights and to ensure that they get the medical and psychological help they need to overcome the impact of their experiences (Department of Justice, 2018). Not only do individuals have the right to make victim impact statements prior to an offender's sentencing, but correctional systems must inform victims when a prisoner is being returned to the community. Victims of family violence also have better access to resources such

Doug Menuez/Photodisc/Thinkstock

There have been a number of false claims that individuals in Saskatoon, Winnipeg, and Thunder Bay were detained by the police and then dropped off on the outskirts of town, often in cold weather. These so-called "starlight tours" did happen in the 1990s and resulted in the deaths of several Indigenous Saskatchewan men, but since the whereabouts of all police patrol vehicles are tracked by GPS, these recent claims were proven to be false.

as residential centres and counselling to help them rebuild their lives (Beattie & Hutchins, 2015). Yet, despite this renewed emphasis on victims' rights, the Office of the Federal Ombudsman for Victims of Crime (2018, p. 10) reported they received 399 complaints in 2016/2017.

Developing a More Effective Justice System

While the previous section paints a somewhat optimistic picture, there are still shortcomings with the operations of the justice system; that can be expected given that there are over 250,000 police officers, court workers, and correctional officials working throughout the nation (Charron, Nemr, & Vaillancourt, 2009). Some of these workers are poorly suited for their jobs, and this leads to mistakes and misconduct. Every year, police officers are convicted of wrongdoing, lawyers are disbarred for misconduct, and correctional officials are charged with engaging in illegal acts. Many

of these acts would have been covered up 20 or 30 years ago, but officials working in the justice system today are less tolerant of misconduct and less willing to "look the other way." While the increased expectations are a significant step in the right direction, any criminal behaviours or acts of misconduct are now widely reported on television and social media. The irony is that this increased scrutiny and reporting of these cases may actually contribute to our lack of faith in these officials.

The evolution of the Canadian justice system has not been quick or painless, as individuals in organizations are often resistant to reform, and when changes do happen, they are often very minor, and occur slowly. Moreover, most changes are driven by external factors: Supreme Court decisions, economic crises, changes in legislation, or media publicity that shames justice system officials into taking action.

Politicians have also played a key role in defining the boundaries of crime. The former Harper government, for example, attempted to make punishments for offenders more severe—although many of these efforts were struck down by the Supreme Court. Moreover, many of our current practices are being scrutinized, and Harris (2018) observes how the Trudeau government has proposed that changes are required to modernize the justice system and speed up the court system. Yet, while some changes may look relatively easy to make, the reality is quite different. The legalization of marijuana, for example, took almost two years longer than originally proposed, and it will be years before the full impact of this change in laws is fully understood, especially when it comes to managing drivers under the influence of this drug and how marijuana use will be managed in the workplace. One reason to move slowly when considering changes to the *Criminal Code* is that reforms might result in unanticipated impacts that could reduce public safety or increase injustice.

One key difference between Canada and the United States is that the justice system in Canada is far less political. Many American politicians have based their election campaigns on "tough on crime" activities and policies; this has had a destructive impact on the US justice system, and "politics driven by fear of crime had direct, destructive social costs" (Chettiar & Ofer, 2018, para. 3). Some scholars have been critical of conservative governments' attempts to politicize the Canadian justice system (Tonry, 2013) and make it more like the US system (Webster & Doob, 2015).

EXTERNAL FORCES SHAPING CANADIAN CRIMINAL JUSTICE IN THE TWENTY-FIRST CENTURY

In the pages that follow, a PESTEL analysis is used to identify the broader external trends that will shape the future of Canada's justice system. Understanding these external forces enables agencies and individuals to plan for the future—especially in terms of the type of work each of us will be doing throughout our careers. Of course, one of the hazards of attempting to predict the future is that many of our best guesses will be incorrect as forecasting involves some guesswork. While some larger agencies produce comprehensive reports identifying different potential threats and opportunities as part of their short- and long-term planning (e.g., Hamilton Police Service, 2018), the efforts of smaller organizations are often less formal. The problem is that there are sometimes unforeseen events that upset our best plans. The further we look into the future, the more difficult it becomes to make accurate predictions. For example, few predicted the effects of the economic recession that started in 2008, which persisted longer than most policy-makers anticipated. This downturn had a significant impact on all criminal justice agencies, as well as the health, education, and social service agencies that support the activities of the justice system.

When reading through these sections, try to think about how these factors will affect your life and your career choices, especially for those considering working in adult or youth justice systems.

After being elected as Premier of Ontario in 2018, Doug Ford (left) appointed Ron Taverner—a family friend who had served with the Toronto Police Service for 51 years—as Commissioner of the Ontario Provincial Police (OPP). This appointment was widely criticized, as Taverner did not meet the minimum standards for the position, and an OPP executive officer critical of the appointment was fired. While a report carried out by Ontario's Integrity Commissioner found no criminal wrongdoing, the hiring process was called "flawed" (Gray & Stone, 2019). How does this example influence our ideas of relationships between politicians and the police?

Political Changes

Because of their visibility and expense, the operations of the justice system are of interest to politicians. Municipal, provincial, and federal politicians play a role in setting the crime control agenda. Legislators establish priorities based on factors such as: (a) public and stakeholder input into policies and practices; (b) practices from other jurisdictions (which may or may not be based on evidence, cost-benefit analyses, or other forms of research); and (c) gaining public support in order to win elections. The extent of political influence varies, and while municipal politicians are primarily interested in local crime problems, federal politicians often express a greater interest in national-level issues such as environmental protection, organized crime, and terrorism.

One of the issues addressed earlier in this book was the extent to which politicians attempt to interfere with the officials in the justice system. In February 2019 there were allegations of inappropriate political influence after staff members from Prime Minister Justin Trudeau's office (PMO) attempted to pressure Jody Wilson-Raybould, the Minister of Justice and Attorney General of Canada, to overturn a decision made by the Director of Public Prosecutions to prosecute SNC-Lavalin for corporate crimes. PMO staffers wanted Wilson-Raybould to enter into a deferred prosecution agreement, which would enable SNC-Lavalin to avoid prosecution and avoid sanctions, including a 10-year ban on applying for government contracts. This scandal resulted in two cabinet members and a number of prominent officials resigning (Connolly, 2019).

Most municipal government politicians use budgets to influence the operations of the police, and provincial and territorial leaders play a greater role in corrections and to a lesser extent the courts. For example, adding more officers to a police service, whether they are needed or not, is generally considered to be good politics as it allows governments to show support for police, support for public safety, and opposition to "villains" (Robertson, 2012, p. 358). Alternatively, increasing funding for correctional rehabilitation may lead to lower recidivism rates, although these budget increases will rarely attract much public support. So while it is difficult to predict future trends in this respect, it is likely that more funding will be directed to highly visible elements of the justice system such as the police, although research shows that other interventions may produce a better return on taxpayer dollars (Washington State Institute for Public Policy, 2018).

The comparative analyses presented throughout this book reveal that the Canadian justice system is less punitive than the US justice system. In order to make our methods of punishing offenders similar to those of our southern neighbours, the former Conservative government introduced dozens of "tough on crime" policies between 2006 and 2015 (Csanady, 2015). These policies were popular with the Canadian public, but many of them were rejected by appellate courts who ruled they were cruel and unusual punishments, making them unconstitutional. Although the previous federal government implemented a "tough on crime" agenda, it is unlikely that we will mimic what has happened in the United States. The US incarceration rate in 2017 was 669 for every 100,000 residents (Bronson & Carson, 2019; Zeng, 2019), whereas in Canada the incarceration rate was 131 for every 100,000 residents (Malakieh, 2019, p.3).

So what does the future hold? One thing that we have to remember is that politics and crime control are tied together. Canadians, for the most part, have resisted the worst of US-style "tough on crime" policies, what Roberts, Stalans, Indermaur, and Hough (2003) call penal populism (see Chapter 3). Instead, justice system policies in Canada have been shaped by bureaucrats with expert knowledge rather than by politicians. It is likely this trend will continue, and when governments attempt to rule by penal populism, the courts will reject it.

Economic Factors

The 2008 recession forced Canadians to acknowledge the growing costs of the justice system, and many municipalities continue to have trouble paying for these services. Given the fact that crime rates have been decreasing since the mid-1990s, many local, provincial, and federal politicians argue that the costs of policing, courts, and correctional services should also drop. But the costs of the criminal justice system continue to rise. Figure 12.2 shows that between 2001 and 2017 policing costs increased by 82 per cent and the daily cost to incarcerate an inmate grew by 60 per cent, while at the same time the Crime Severity Index (CSI) decreased by 30 per cent.

Many politicians, researchers, and public policy analysts believed that the economic crisis that started in 2008 was an opportunity to change the

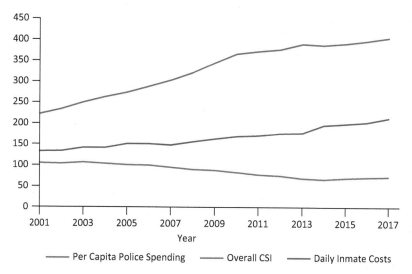

FIGURE 12.2 **Per Capita Police Costs, Daily Inmate Costs, and Overall Crime Severity Index, 2001–2017**
Adapted from Allen (2018), Conor (2018), and Statistics Canada (2018b)

way that justice systems operated (Toews, 2013). As shown in Figure 12.2, the costs continue to increase while crime is dropping. Why are the costs of our justice system so high? Salaries represent the biggest cost of operating justice systems and usually account for about 85 per cent of an agency's entire budget. Wages for public safety workers have been increasing, and a review of the "sunshine list" (a list of people earning more than $100,000 per year) shows that almost two-thirds of the personnel employed by the Toronto Police Service were on that list in 2018 (Province of Ontario, 2019). Although that is good news for those intending on working for a police service, many smaller and rural municipalities are having trouble paying those costs (Baxter, 2018).

So, how expensive is it to operate the justice system? Figure 12.3 presents an estimate of the costs in Alberta's justice system from arrest to incarceration. This sheds light on how expensive justice system interventions can be, even for relatively minor crimes. These amounts will differ from province to province, but this gives a good estimate for each action in the justice system.

As economic downturns typically occur about once every five years, we can all expect to experience several of them throughout our careers. For

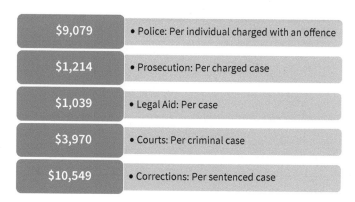

FIGURE 12.3 **Unit Costs in the Alberta Justice System**
Note: Unit costs are based on 2010–2011 values but have been adjusted for inflation to provide estimates for 2018.
Adapted from Institute of Health Economics (2014)

recessions lasting more than a year, there are a number of common outcomes such as cuts to public services (Gascon & Foglesong, 2010). The police in some places may no longer respond to reports of minor property offences, rehabilitative programs in corrections may be cut, and probation officers may carry out fewer home visits and might supervise larger caseloads. Moreover, public services such as afterschool programs, libraries, health care services, and public transportation are often cut.

There are three main outcomes of cutting these services. First, being expected to carry out one's job with fewer resources can reduce staff morale. Second, cutting services may reduce the public's trust and confidence. Third, reducing funding to non-justice agencies might also contribute to increased crime. If we cut the budgets for playgrounds, recreation centres, and libraries, for example, where will kids go and what will they do when they are not in school? One finding important in understanding the relationship between crime and economic downturns is that each recession is different. Researchers examining the downturn in the Alberta economy in 2014/2015 could not find a clear relationship between the recession and overall increases in crime, although some offences, such as domestic violence, did rise (Fotheringham, 2016).

Social Changes

PESTEL analyses consider two broad social influences: cultural factors and the demographic characteristics of a population (see the "Race, Class, and Gender" box in this chapter on Canada's changing demographic profile). Cultural factors can take a number of different forms, including our perceptions toward crime and the justice system. Figure 12.4 shows the results from Angus Reid Institute polls carried out between 2012 and 2018, which reveal that Canadians had more confidence in their police and courts in 2018 than they did in 2012. Those results, however, are based on national averages, while there are differences between the provincial results: confidence in the police and courts, for example, is the lowest in Atlantic Canada, and Ontarians have the greatest confidence in the police in the nation (Angus Reid Institute, 2018).

Laws also reflect our changing social interests. A series of highly publicized accusations of sexual harassment and assault were made against high-profile male entertainers, politicians,

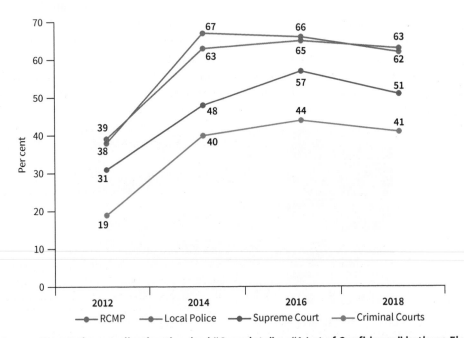

FIGURE 12.4 Respondents Indicating they had "Complete" or "A Lot of Confidence" in these Elements of Canada's Justice System

Angus Reid Institute (2018)

public officials, and sporting figures starting in October 2017. This came to be known as the "Me Too" movement, and the widespread volume of sexually inappropriate behaviour has been extensively publicized by the media. We will not, however, have a full understanding of the impact of this movement on the justice system in terms of the number of sexual assaults reported to the police and whether prosecutors will charge more people with these crimes. We know that only a small proportion of sexual assaults are ever reported, and some believe that a greater number of survivors will report their victimization. Yet, research carried out by the Canadian Centre for Justice Statistics shows that even when individuals report their victimization, the police and prosecutors will not necessarily determine that a crime actually occurred. Greenland and Cotter (2017) found, for instance, that almost one-quarter of indecent or harassing communications (23 per cent) and 14 per cent of sexual assaults were considered unfounded, which means the police investigation determined the offence did not occur, nor was it attempted (Rotenberg, 2019, p. 31). Changes in our awareness and interests, and the influences of social movements such as "Me Too," may also result in changes to the long-term practices of the police, courts, and corrections.

Many readers of this book are interested in crime and justice, but our interests might be different from other Canadians. When it comes to the concerns of the general public, polls can inform us about the top concerns. A review of national surveys since 2010 reveals that Canadians are primarily concerned about their economic well-being as well as climate change, health, education, and social services, but less so about crime. Armstrong (2019) reported on the top 12 concerns of Canadians, which are summarized in Table 12.1; only three per cent of us felt that crime was the most important problem facing the nation. Armstrong's results were very similar to those reported by Anderson and Coletto (2017), who found that only 4 per cent of Canadians listed crime or law and order as their top concern.

Throughout this book, we've looked at the influence of politicians and the media on our ideas of crime and justice. Most of our understanding of

TABLE 12.1 Top Concerns of Canadians

Category	Top Concerns (%)
Cost of living	32
Climate change	19
Health (my health/family member health)	10
Immigration	8
International relations/trade	7
Social inequality	6
My job/finding a job	5
Crime, public safety	3
Truth in media	3
None of these issues	3
Terrorism	2
Racism	1

Adapted from Armstrong (2019)

the justice system and our treatment of offenders comes from these sources, and most of the cases focused on in the media are rare violent crimes or offences that are somehow exceptional: often these

Black Lives Matter Toronto protesting the death of Abdirahman Abdi, who was killed by an Ottawa police officer in 2016. Between 2014 and 2016, Canadians witnessed the protests after the police-involved deaths of unarmed Black suspects in the United States. These events contributed to a reduced trust and confidence in America's justice system, and Canadians considered these protests to be the top US news story of 2014 (Logan, 2014). It is unknown, however, whether these acts influence how Canadians think about our justice system.

Race, Class, and Gender

Canada's Changing Demographic Profile

One of the most significant challenges that will affect the future of Canada's justice system is the changing population and the accompanying cultural and social changes. Statistics Canada (2017b) reports that more than one in five Canadians was born in another nation, and a growing number of them are visible minority residents. When we add the population of Indigenous peoples, who account for about 5 per cent of the national population, almost one in four Canadians is a member of a visible minority group or is of Indigenous ancestry. An increasingly diverse population can create some challenges for the operations of justice systems, as trust in the police can vary between ethnic groups, and people who have more trust and confidence in the police are more likely to cooperate with them.

Cotter (2015, p. 7) analyzed the results of the 2014 General Social Survey, and he found that immigrants who came to Canada after 2000 had the *highest* confidence in the police and justice system compared with non-immigrants and immigrants who came to Canada prior to 2000. Some new Canadians, however, came from countries where the justice systems were corrupt or were used by political officials to repress and control the people (World Justice Project, 2019). Given these experiences, individuals from such nations might distrust the police and court personnel, especially if they believe their ethnic group has been over-policed (Owusu-Bempah & Wortley, 2014). As a result, they may be reluctant to help the police in investigations, to testify in court, or to fully cooperate with probation or correctional staff members. Justice system personnel

might also find it difficult to provide services for members of some ethnocultural groups as they may lack employees with the necessary language skills and understanding of cultural values and traditions.

Prior research has generally shown that Indigenous Canadians and members of visible minority groups express less trust and confidence in the justice system than White respondents when asked in surveys. Figure 12.5 shows the results from an Angus Reid Institute (2018) poll of Canadians about their confidence in the justice system. Visible minority respondents expressed having lower confidence in the RCMP, their local police, and the courts than respondents who were not a member of a visible minority group. Cotter (2015) did find, however, that visible minorities and immigrants who came to Canada after 2000 had more confidence in public institutions than immigrants who had been in the country longer.

In the previous chapters, the difficult relationships between Indigenous people and the justice system were described. Indigenous peoples are overrepresented in every aspect of the justice system from arrests to placement in corrections. Malakieh (2019, p. 20) reports that in 2017/2018, Indigenous peoples accounted for over a quarter of admissions to provincial and territorial corrections or federal prisons (30 and 29 per cent, respectively). This pattern is similar for youth corrections: Indigenous youth represented 48 per cent of admissions to corrections while accounting for 8 per cent of the youth population (Malakieh, 2019, p. 26).

In addition to being overrepresented in correctional populations, Indigenous peoples are

cases involve celebrity offenders (or victims), multiple victims, or vulnerable victims (McKnight, 2016). It is likely that our preoccupation with exceptional cases will continue, although most of the work of justice system personnel is in response to relatively minor offences. The top five offences before criminal courts in 2016/2017 were impaired driving, theft, failure to comply with a

court order, common assault, and breach of probation; together these crimes accounted for nearly half (47 per cent) of all cases (Miladinovic, 2019, p. 6). Perhaps the most significant changes will occur in the composition of our population as it becomes more diverse, as highlighted in this chapter's "Race, Class, and Gender" box on Canada's changing demographic profile.

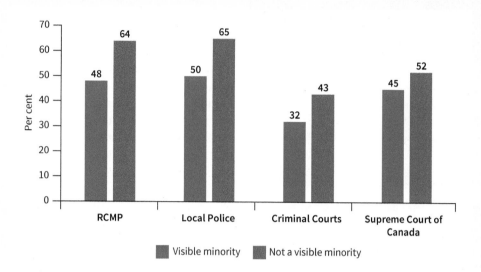

FIGURE 12.5 Respondents Indicting They Had "Complete" or "A Lot of Confidence" in Canada's Justice System: Visible Minorities and Not Visible Minorities, 2018

Angus Reid Institute (2018)

also overrepresented as individuals charged with involvement in crime and as victims. Using results from the 2014 victimization survey, Perreault (2015) reports that Indigenous peoples are twice as likely to be victims of break and enter and sexual assault offences than are non-Indigenous peoples. Indigenous peoples are also six times more likely than non-Indigenous Canadians to be murdered. In 2017, for instance, while representing 5 per cent of the population, Indigenous peoples made up almost one-quarter (24 per cent) of all homicide victims. Indigenous people were also 12 times more likely than non-Indigenous people to be accused of homicide in 2017 (Beattie, David, & Roy, 2018).

One statistic that has potential implications for the justice system is that the youthful Indigenous population is high. Statistics Canada (2017a, p. 15) reports that almost one-third (29 per cent) of them are 14 years of age or younger, whereas the non-Indigenous population of the same age accounts for about 16 per cent of that population. Regardless of ethnocultural status, the proportion of young males in a population is usually a good predictor of involvement in crime (Bernard & Kurlychek, 2010). Given the high number of young males in the Indigenous population, there is a higher at-risk population. As a result, unless something is done to better support these youth, they may continue to be, or even become further, overrepresented in the justice system.

Technology

Technology has changed the way that crimes are carried out today, and it will continue to pose a challenge for justice system personnel for the foreseeable future. The Police Executive Research Forum (2018) observes that criminals are becoming increasingly involved in cybercrimes as

the rewards are high and the risks of an arrest or prosecution are very low. For example, thieves steal from residents of other nations using internet scams and frauds. Apprehending these offenders is complicated because Canadian police officers have no authority to investigate crimes occurring in other countries, and they must get the help of the police in other nations. This can

Carol Todd/Amanda Todd Legacy/www.amandatoddlegacy.org

Amanda Todd, a 15-year-old from British Columbia, killed herself in October 2012 after being tormented by a Dutch man named Aydin Coban, who was over 30 years old at the time. Coban allegedly threatened to release indecent pictures of Todd; court documents revealed that he cyberbullied dozens of other young girls and gay men (Global News, 2017). In 2017, Coban was sentenced to over 10 years in prison in the Netherlands, and the Dutch government has ruled that he can be extradited to face five charges in a Canadian court for his role in Amanda Todd's death (Lazatin, 2018).

be further complicated by language barriers and by the fact police officers in other nations may have little time to pursue such crimes. As a result, Canadians victimized by foreigners may have little hope the offenders will be prosecuted for their crimes.

Technology enables offenders to victimize large numbers of individuals. It was difficult for offenders in the past to steal from more than one person at a time. Corporate criminals, by contrast, work together to increase prices on goods or services (which is called price-fixing) so that thousands of us are victimized by paying higher costs. Because consumers pay only slightly higher prices for an item, we are usually unaware of our victimization. For example, tens of thousands of Canadians who bought computers, MP3 players, DVD players, or printers between 1999 and 2002 were victims of price-fixing and were eligible for a $20 refund (Tencer, 2015). We looked at another example in Chapter 2, where Canada's Competition Bureau found the nation's largest bakeries had plotted to keep the price of bread artificially

high, which may have cost each Canadian family over $800.

Because we are so dependent on the internet for our work, communications, banking, purchases, and recreation, we are increasingly vulnerable to being victimized and losing our privacy due to internet attacks. Whereas in the past, computer- and internet-based crimes were carried out by individuals, Goodman (2015, p. 25) observes that "nation-states, neighborhood thugs, transnational organized crime groups, foreign intelligence services, hacktivists, military personnel, cyber warriors, state-sponsored proxy fighters, script kiddies, garden-variety hackers, phreakers, carders, crackers, disgruntled insiders, and industrial spies" are all engaged in cybercrimes today. Holt (2018) explains that there are two types of hackers—those motivated by financial gain and those driven by ideology, such as terrorists. Figure 12.6 shows some of the key findings from a review of the cybercrime literature in Canada. Cybercrimes are the crimes of the future, and Brenda Lucki, the Commissioner of the RCMP, says that her organization is not able to keep pace with the increased volume of internet-based crimes (Tunney, 2018).

Although most discussion about the future of technology and crime has described internet-based offences, other forms of technology are also changing the options available to offenders. A growing number of firearms, for example, are illegally smuggled into Canada across the US border, and these guns are being used in crimes: City News (2018) reports that Canada Border Security Agency officials from the Toronto area seized 112 illegal guns coming across the US border in 2017, which was up from the two guns they seized in 2016. The availability of inexpensive 3D printers, however, may make it unnecessary to smuggle guns into the country as individuals will be able to build the parts required to make a gun using software available online. All together, it costs less than $2,000 to buy the printer and the software needed to make a gun, and an individual with modest manufacturing skills could build an unlimited number of untraceable guns in this way. Elliot (2018) reports that making a firearm in

CYBERCRIME

SOME KEY FINDINGS

BUSINESSES SPENT $14 BILLION ON
CYBER SECURITY IN 2017

OVER ONE IN FIVE

BUSINESSES ARE IMPACTED BY A CYBERCRIME ATTACK
ONE ATTACK CAN BANKRUPT A SMALL BUSINESS

ONLY 1 IN 10 CYBER
SECURITY INCIDENTS
ARE REPORTED TO
POLICE

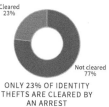

Cleared
23%

Not cleared
77%

ONLY 23% OF IDENTITY
THEFTS ARE CLEARED BY
AN ARREST

58%

INCREASE IN CYBERCRIME
BETWEEN 2014 AND 2016

ONE IN FIVE
FACEBOOK ACCOUNTS
IN CANADA ARE
HACKED

$11.8 M

LOST BY MACEWAN
UNIVERSITY IN AN INTERNET SCAM

FIGURE 12.6 Cybercrime in Canada
Based on data from Greenland and Cotter (2018); Statistics Canada (2018a)

Canada is a criminal offence unless one has the proper business licence. While the firearms built using this technology are not very sophisticated, Hafner (2018, para. 23) observes that their quality will undoubtedly improve, but "until then, those firing the potentially faulty guns may face the greatest danger" as these guns sometimes explode.

As unmanned aerial vehicles (UAVs), which are also called drones, become cheaper, their use by offenders and the police will also increase. Some of these small aircraft can carry a 10-kilogram payload and smugglers have used them to fly illegal drugs from Mexico to the United States (Mikelionis, 2018). Offenders using these aircraft have also dropped drugs and contraband such as cellular phones into Canadian correctional facilities (Judd, 2018), and in December 2015, a handgun was dropped into a Quebec detention centre by a UAV (Ling, 2015). Law enforcement leaders are also concerned that terrorists could crash UAVs loaded with explosives into passenger planes. Perhaps the most common misuse

Everybody's personal information is vulnerable to cyberattack. In October 2018, the Facebook accounts of over 50 million users were hacked, and the individuals responsible could have accessed all of the online activities of these users, including the content of private messages. Those private messages could be released online, which would be a significant attack on a user's privacy (O'Sullivan, 2018).

of drones occurs when they are used to violate our privacy by filming us in our homes or on the beach without our awareness. Canadians have complained about camera-equipped UAVs hovering outside the windows of their homes (Gawdin, 2018).

Although drug smugglers were among the first groups to take advantage of UAV technology, Canadian police services have also used drones fitted with heat-sensing cameras for search and rescue operations. Drones can be fitted with cameras, firearms, microphones, and licence-plate readers, and they can be used in situations that would expose officers to high risk by providing a "bird's-eye view" of an active crime scene. Because UAVs are so much cheaper to operate than planes or helicopters, and they can fly above lands that are impassable by vehicles, they have also been used to patrol the Canada–US borders. Both offenders and law enforcement personnel will likely increase their reliance on UAV technology over the next 10 years, and The Crime Report (2018) predicts that in the future every police patrol car will have its own drone.

In some respects, technological innovation has moved faster than our legal system's ability to develop guidelines for its appropriate use. In terms of policing, for example, Chen (2014) identifies a number of tools used to carry out large-scale surveillance on the public, including:

- Facial recognition software enables officers to compare a photograph of someone they encounter with a database of arrestees or people in public spaces viewed on cameras.
- Automated licence-plate readers can scan hundreds of licence plates per hour and alert officers to stolen and uninsured vehicles or people of interest; these readers can be mounted on patrol vehicles or on street lights, signs, or buildings, and they can also be used to track our movements.
- Enhanced streetlights can record video images, gunshots, or conversations and transmit them using wireless technology.
- Stingray technology allows users to "mimic cellphone towers in order to trick nearby cellphones into connecting. Once they are connected, the Stingray user can collect information transmitted by the phone,

including its location, data transmissions, texts, emails and voice conversations" (Canadian Broadcasting Corporation, 2016).
- Software applications can predict where crimes will occur and some programs can carry out data mining (where the relationships between thousands of different variables, including information about individuals, are examined).

Although most people support the police using technology to reduce crime, there are concerns about how much data the police are collecting and how they use that information. Writing about "big data" in policing, Mark (2018) describes how police are accessing an ever-increasing amount of data about the public and are using that information to monitor and predict our activities. Most people do not fully understand the implications of the government collecting so much information about our attitudes (such as our Facebook "likes") and online activities.

Technology also introduces new products, and these products may influence the operations of the justice system. Fentanyl, for example, is a powerful prescription drug used to treat chronic pain, and since 2013 the abuse of this drug has led to thousands of deaths across Canada. Figure 12.7 shows how the number of monthly deaths from illicit drugs in British Columbia has changed between 2008 and 2019. To put that number into perspective, in 2018, for every murder in the province there were 17 fatal illicit drug overdoses (89 and 1,535 deaths respectively). Not only has fentanyl increased deaths, but the Red Deer RCMP attribute addiction to this drug to an increase in property crime (Barrett, 2018), and fentanyl-related deaths are increasing as the drug moves toward eastern Canada. These changes are similar to the introduction and movement of crack cocaine throughout the US in the 1980s.

One question that we might ask is whether the increased use of fentanyl is a problem for the criminal justice system, or should it be treated as a medical or public health problem? Brennan and Mazowita (2019) looked at the people

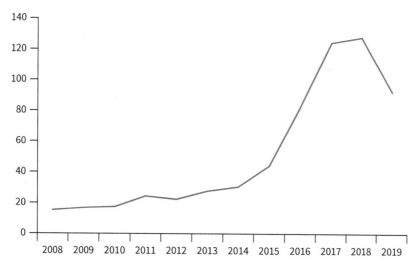

FIGURE 12.7 Monthly Deaths from Illicit Drugs, British Columbia, 1 January 2008, to 31 May 2019
British Columbia Coroners Service (2019)

who died from illicit drug overdoses in British Columbia between 2011 and 2016. They found that two-thirds of them had not been arrested in the two years prior to their deaths, and more than 80 per cent of those who *had* come into contact with the police had been arrested for non-violent offences; the most common offence was shoplifting. Do these findings change your ideas about these people and whether using illicit drugs should be treated as a crime or a health problem?

Environmental Factors

Environmental forces may also shape the future operations of justice systems. Although there is some debate over how much of climate change is caused by human activities or whether it is part of long-term global cycles, there is agreement that our climate is changing and becoming more volatile, with an increasing number of severe conditions such as extreme hot or cold weather, storms, and flooding. Some areas are experiencing droughts that have persisted for years. Extreme weather has also led to environmental disasters, and responding to avalanches, forest fires, and tornados is a routine part of policing the countryside. These disasters can be very destructive and costly, such as the 2013 flooding

in southern Alberta, the wildfires that destroyed parts of Fort McMurray, Alberta, in 2016, or the British Columbia wildfires that persisted through the summer of 2018. Other environmental disasters are less obvious, but they can still have devastating effects; the heat wave that struck eastern Canada in 2018 contributed to the deaths of over 90 Quebec residents (Woods, 2018). Public Safety Canada (2018) has a database of natural and manmade disasters that can be accessed at https://www.publicsafety.gc.ca/cnt/rsrcs/cndn-dsstr-dtbs/index-en.aspx.

There is a growing interest in protecting the environment. Scholars have defined green criminology as "the study of those harms against humanity, against the environment and against animals other than humans . . . committed both by powerful institutions (for example, governments, transnational corporations, military apparatuses, scientific laboratories) and also by ordinary people" (Beirne & South, 2012, p. 23). There are a number of crimes committed against the environment, including:

- abuse and exploitation of ecological systems (including animal life)
- corporate disregard for damage to land, air, and water quality

green criminology A branch of criminology that focuses on environmental crimes and harms to the environment.

- profiting from trades and practices that destroy lives and leave a legacy of damage for subsequent generations
- military actions in war that adversely affect the environment and animals
- illicit markets in nuclear materials
- legal monopolization of natural resources (e.g., privatization of water, patenting of natural products) leading to divisions between the resource-rich and the resource-poor (Beirne & South, 2012, p. 23)

We are increasingly concerned about the long-term impact of crimes committed against the environment, especially when these acts harm endangered species. McCune et al. (2017, p. 1) polled Canadians and found 89 per cent were "strongly committed to species conservation." Those results are similar to polls of Canadians carried out by Environics Research Group (2015) and Ipsos Reid (2012) that found an overwhelming majority of their respondents (93 and 97 per cent respectively) considered protecting endangered animals as important.

Most law enforcement responses to environmental crimes are carried out by conservation and fisheries officers employed by federal and provincial governments. Although the public is generally supportive of their efforts to reduce environmental crimes, governments have been reluctant to pay for

this enforcement. Figure 12.8 shows the number of conservation officers per 100,000 residents in 2016 and in that year there was approximately one conservation officer for every 14 police officers.

Environmental forces will play a less significant role in shaping the future operations of justice systems than technology, political factors, or the law. Yet, for a growing number of Canadians the protection of the environment is a key priority, and about $1.5 billion has been pledged by the federal government every year to counter climate change (Government of Canada, 2018). What will be the outcomes of that interest over the next decade? It is likely that federal, provincial, and territorial governments will enact new laws to deter and punish environmental criminals. This may, in turn, create more opportunities for personnel in front-line enforcement roles such as conservation officers, and an increasing number of environmental offences may be processed by the courts. In addition, if the extremes in climate continue, there will be an increased demand for officials trained in disaster management and emergency response.

Legal Changes

Supporters of the due process perspective believe that strengthening protections for people accused of committing crimes reduces errors and increases the legitimacy of the justice system, which in turn makes all of us more willing to abide by the

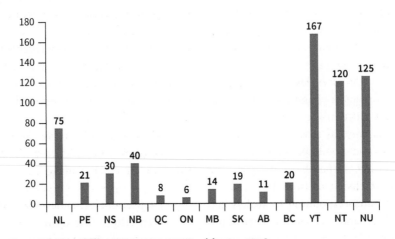

FIGURE 12.8 Conservation Officers per 100,000 Residents, 2016

Statistics Canada (2019)

law (Tyler, 2006). In any given year, the Supreme Court of Canada rules on about two dozen issues related to the criminal law. In several important cases, the Supreme Court has limited police and prosecutorial powers by restricting the admissibility of confessions made in "Mr. Big" investigations (where suspects are asked by police officers pretending to be organized crime offenders to disclose information about crimes), as in the case of *R v Hart* (2014). The Supreme Court also permitted medically-assisted deaths (*Carter v Canada*, 2015), restricted the ability of police to access histories of an individual's text messages (*R v Marakah*, 2017), recognized that the police are obliged to inform detained suspects of their right to counsel and to respect the suspect's ability to exercise that right (*R v Taylor*, 2014), and clarified the position that people on bail had the presumption of innocence (*R v Antic*, 2017). Perhaps the most controversial Supreme Court rulings since 2010 have been the limits they have placed on case processing time in the *R v Jordan* (2016) case.

Predicting the outcomes of future Supreme Court decisions is a difficult task, as the justices only consider a small number of cases each year. Between 2007 and 2017, the Supreme Court heard an average of 56 cases per year, and of those judgments, fewer than two dozen were criminal matters (Supreme Court of Canada, 2018). About 390,000 adult and youth cases were heard in criminal courts in 2016/2017 (Miladinovic, 2019, p. 3), and if 20 cases are heard in the Supreme Court, this means that only one in about 20,000 criminal cases is heard before that Court, making these matters very rare events.

Supreme Court decisions can have a significant impact on all aspects of the justice system. Requiring prosecutors to make a complete disclosure of their evidence to defence counsel, for example, has required countless hours of police and prosecutors' time (see *R v Stinchcombe*, 1991). The *R v Jordan* (2016) decision, by contrast, has led to Crown prosecutors staying hundreds of charges, many of them for serious crimes, as it took too long to bring these matters to court. The Jordan decision has been called a ticking time bomb

that "has woken the criminal justice system up from its 25-year slumber to address trial delay" (Lundrigan, 2018, p. 146). We have to remember, however, that while some of the Court's decisions can be costly to agencies, they increase the due process protections for all defendants.

Few of us spend much time thinking about the Crown's burden to provide disclosure, but there are negative consequences when Crown attorneys fail to get that information to the defence counsel in a timely manner. Perrin, Audas, and Peloquin-Ladany (2016) observed the following:

In Sherbrooke, Quebec, in October 2015, murder and conspiracy charges against five members of that city's chapter of the Hells Angels were stayed. The men were released from custody because of a lengthy delay in the Crown's disclosure to the Defence. Thirty-one Hells Angels members and associates who were caught in the same police investigation similarly had drug charges against them stayed, also because of unreasonable delay (p. 2).

The impacts of these outcomes are widespread, including how the family members of a murder victim would feel about the justice system knowing the accused were returned to the street without a trial. In addition to our ideas about the justice system, these acts also influence public safety as these accused people are now "back on the streets" without being punished or rehabilitated. Last, if you were one of the police officers who gathered evidence to pursue the homicide and drug charges on these 36 suspects, would you think your efforts were wasted, and how would that affect your morale?

Some Supreme Court decisions may reduce the due process protections of suspects. In 2015, the Supreme Court held that British Columbia's immediate roadside prohibition (IRP) legislation was constitutional (see *Goodwin v British Columbia (Superintendent of Motor Vehicles)*). The IRP program targets drunk drivers and allows police officers to issue licence suspensions of up to

"Mr Big" investigations Investigations carried out by undercover police officers posing as criminals to obtain confessions from suspects about their involvement in serious crimes.

A COMPARATIVE VIEW

The Future of Urban and Rural Justice Systems

Few urban residents spend much time thinking about what happens in the countryside because they typically have fewer connections to rural Canada than they would have in the past. Perreault (2019), for instance, reports that less than 20 per cent of Canadians, or about six million people, live in rural areas. We tend to think of the countryside as being relatively peaceful with a slow pace of life, but in Chapter 2 we saw that rural crime rates in some places can be very high. Some offences, for example, are distinctively rural, and certain crimes committed against wildlife or the environment seldom occur in cities.

There are significant differences in rural crime rates across the country, and although crime is rare in some places, some northern communities have very high crime rates (Allen & Perreault, 2015). Overall, Perreault (2019) reports that both the total and violent crime rates are higher in rural Canada, and especially in the Prairies. Some offences are more likely to be overrepresented in rural Canada, including impaired driving (Perreault, 2013) and all forms of family violence (Burczycka, 2018; Conroy, 2018; Savage, 2018). Rates of victimization are also high in the countryside; Perreault and Simpson (2016, p. 3) report that "more than one-quarter of residents of the territories (28 per cent) reported being the victim of at least one crime in 2014." The issue of rural crime

was widely reported by the media in the Prairie provinces between 2016 and 2018, and became a controversial political issue (Macpherson, 2019).

The countryside can be a dangerous place. More than half of fatal collisions occur on rural roads (Transport Canada, 2019) and most forest fires, floods, tornados, and avalanches occur in rural areas. In addition, the quality of life of rural residents is decreased when environmental crimes such as the illegal dumping of toxic waste occur. Our perceptions about the quiet pace of life in rural Canada are sometimes mistaken.

Table 12.2 presents the possible future of urban and rural justice systems in Canada using a PESTEL analysis. For the most part, the conditions in all of Canada will be relatively similar, and the differences between urban and rural issues are often subtle. Many of the key differences are related to the decreasing rural population and how that will impact other factors. For instance, a declining rural economy with fewer job opportunities drives some young rural residents to move to cities for work. This has a number of implications for rural justice systems, and as the rural population ages it should result in reduced crime. Rural crime rates have, however, been increasing, and some scholars blame this on city people who travel to the countryside to carry out property crimes (Ruddell, 2017).

Rural crime victims may find it harder to access supportive services such as domestic violence shelters, and a fear of being the topic of gossip prevents some rural victims from seeking help.

TABLE 12.2 Forecasting the Future of Urban and Rural Justice Systems

Issue	Urban	Rural
Political	• Increase in politically liberal views, and less support for the justice system • Less support for "tough on crime" policies • Most justice system research is funded for issues related to cities	• Increase in politically conservative views, and greater support for the justice system • Greater support for "tough on crime" policies • Little research is carried out on rural justice systems • Rural crime becomes an increasingly controversial political issue
Economic	• Policing costs remain stable as agencies hire more non-sworn uniformed officers to carry out "non-core" police duties • Big city police departments will operate more efficiently and costs will remain stable • Fewer manufacturing jobs exist, increasing unemployment (and possibly crime) • Increased use of private security	• Per capita rural policing costs increase as populations drop • Businesses close due to decreasing populations, and the potential for crime increases due to higher unemployment • Fewer government services (health, education, and social services) are provided due to decreasing populations • Fewer opportunities to access offender rehabilitation programs (e.g., substance abuse treatment)
Social/ demographic	• Urban populations increase with higher levels of immigration • Urban populations become more diverse • Increased use of opioids and overdose deaths • Indigenous populations increase in urban areas	• Populations drop as young people move to the cities for employment, which results in closures of businesses and reductions in government services • Rural non-Indigenous population ages • Indigenous youth populations increase • Increased use of opioids and overdose deaths • Increased numbers of urban residents and Indigenous peoples protesting environmental issues in the countryside (e.g., pipelines) • Greater reliance on volunteers for fire and emergency services, but fewer young people in the population makes it difficult to replace existing volunteers • Little change in population diversity
Technological	• Closed-circuit television becomes more prevalent in cities to deter crime and to identify and apprehend offenders • Increasing use of semi-autonomous vehicles in cities and decreased private ownership of vehicles • Expansion in police surveillance • Greater use of social media to publicize crime-related issues	• Introduction of self-driving farm equipment and the expansion of corporate, rather than family farms, reduces rural employment • Increased use of unmanned aerial vehicles for search and rescue • Rural critical infrastructure (such as hydro, nuclear plants, or water treatment plants) are vulnerable to internet (e.g., hacking) or terrorist attacks • Reduced prisoner transportation due to a greater use of video-based court appearances • Greater use of social media to publicize rural crime issues • Increased use of privately owned surveillance technology to monitor rural property

Continued

Issue	Urban	Rural
Environmental	• Environmental protection becomes more popular with urban residents	• Environmental crimes such as the illegal dumping of toxic waste reduces the quality of rural life • More government personnel will be working in environmental protection roles • Climate change may increase the number of extreme weather events
Legal	• More lawsuits and litigation launched for damages caused by personnel working within justice systems • More specialized courts (e.g., mental health, domestic, *Gladue*, or drug courts) are introduced	• Increased interest in restorative justice and non-traditional interventions for Indigenous people • Number of lawyers providing services in rural Canada decreases • Greater restrictions on firearms ownership and use has a greater impact on rural peoples • Police staff fewer detachments and deploy "fly-in, fly-out" officers rather than permanent staffing

90 days if the driver refuses to provide a breath sample or if they receive a "fail" on a roadside breathalyzer. In addition to the licence restrictions, there are numerous costs to the driver, including having his or her vehicle towed and impounded in a storage facility and being required to pay higher licensing fees. All together, a person guilty of these infractions could lose their driving privileges, lose the use of their vehicle, and pay thousands of dollars in costs. But, as these enforcement practices are not *Criminal Code* matters, the provinces have the jurisdiction to enact these laws much like any other non-criminal driving regulation. So, how does that affect drivers? Between September 1, 2010, when the program was implemented, and May 31, 2019, almost 225,000 BC drivers received these roadside prohibitions, varying from 24 hours to 90 days (RoadSafetyBC, 2019).

Robichaud (2014) contends that the rights of people accused of crimes were also eroded by a series of Supreme Court decisions, including allowing the police to search the contents of an arrestee's cell phone without a warrant (*R v Fearon*, 2014), failing to place limits on experts who are testifying about matters outside their expertise (*R v Sekhon*, 2014), allowing searches of dwellings without a warrant when officers believe that their safety is in jeopardy (*R v MacDonald*, 2014), and considering threats of violence (and not requiring actual acts of violence) when judges are deliberating whether to designate an individual as a dangerous offender (*R v Steele*, 2014).

So how will appellate court decisions influence justice systems in the future? In their decisions, appellate court judges interpret the law amidst changing factors including the influence of technology, the outcomes of research (looking at things like adolescent brain development), and changing police practices, and some of their decisions have been controversial. As a result, neither the supporters of the due process or crime control perspectives will be entirely satisfied with the Court's decisions.

MYTH OR REALITY

Will Future Justice Policies Be Driven By Revolutionary Change?

There are different views on how the criminal and youth justice systems should be transformed to ensure just and fair outcomes for victims and offenders. Some scholars advocate for change that is revolutionary. Prominent Canadian criminologists Anthony Doob and Cheryl Webster (2015) suggest that in the past, the justice system was based on four broad principles: (a) acknowledging the importance of social conditions such as poverty, unemployment, and the marginalization of social groups; (b) the fact that harsh punishments do not reduce crime; (c) that the development of criminal justice policies should be informed by expert knowledge; and (d) that changes in the law should address real problems (rather than being based on political reasons). All of these ideas have been presented throughout this book, and regardless of whether one is a supporter of the due process or crime control perspective, most of us would generally agree with two or three of these principles.

Doob and Webster (2015) argue that "rather than making piecemeal changes [the next government should] review large areas of the criminal justice system, instituting changes that reflect broad integrated knowledge of current problems." Consistent with that recommendation, the Trudeau government has proposed making major reforms to the justice system, but they seem to have fallen short of expectations (Spratt, 2019). One question that some are asking is whether the government's incremental or piecemeal changes will be enough to satisfy people who believe the justice system is fundamentally flawed and oppressive. Activists and critical scholars throughout Canada and the United States are advocating for radical change, including the abolishment of the police (Meares, 2017; Vitale, 2017)—or at least disarming them (Wright, 2018). In terms of corrections, Brock University students held a Prison Abolition Symposium in 2017 (Brock University, 2017) while Boccio, Chan, and Sicora (2017) advocate for the use of restorative justice in their vision of a world without prisons. The legalization of marijuana has led some advocates from the Liberal and New Democratic parties to propose the legalization of all illicit drugs. Moreover, Parkes (2018) and others argue that mandatory minimum sentences be abolished, including the parole eligibility dates for first- and second-degree murder.

Many younger Canadians are unhappy waiting for social and economic changes to happen, and instead of reforming the system based on piecemeal changes they argue for a radical social transformation to share society's wealth; they claim this would reduce many social problems, including crime. To achieve that goal some have become involved in social movements that resulted in clashes with the police, such as the protests against the G20 (Beare, Des Rosiers, & Deshman, 2014), the Idle No More (Barker, 2015), Black Lives Matter, and Occupy Toronto (Woods, 2012) movements, and it is likely that Indigenous protests will be associated with any pipeline developments in the future. There is growing recognition that social changes are moving faster today due to the influences of social media and technology, as well as increased population diversity and the rising activism of members of marginalized social groups. Those issues, combined with a significant economic downturn, could result in growth of new political parties and sweeping social changes.

Is revolutionary change possible? Throughout this book, there are many examples of the justice system making slow and steady progress. Many Canadians support this approach because there is generally considerable resistance to major legal or social reforms. Even when the need to make changes has been identified, the personnel working within the justice system tend to be fairly conservative and are resistant to reform (Duxbury, Bennell, Halinski, & Murphy, 2017). In fact, most justice system reforms have been driven by external factors such as scandals or shortcomings that have resulted in media attention, Royal Commissions, inquiries, lawsuits, and court judgments.

While there is considerable interest in rapid and revolutionary change, it is doubtful that such changes will occur in the justice system, and it is likely that reforms will continue to happen slowly. While these evolutionary changes can be frustrating to those who want to ensure just and fair outcomes to everybody involved in the justice system, it may be preferable to making rapid changes that result in unanticipated or unforeseen outcomes that actually reduce public safety or increase bias or injustice.

SUMMARY

Although the leaders of every police service, court, and corrections system attempt to predict the external and internal factors that might influence their agency's operations, it is difficult to make accurate forecasts a decade or more into the future. One of the barriers for criminal justice personnel to engage in these exercises is that they are so busy in their day-to-day activities they have little time to devote to scanning the external environment for potential threats or opportunities. So, why should they bother? Some changes are predictable and forecasting makes sense. A municipal police department with 100 officers, for example, recently constructed a new police headquarters. As the population of the community was projected to double in the next 25 years, the agency's leaders designed the facility so that it could be expanded in size at a lower cost. As a result, the planners today reduced a financial burden on tomorrow's taxpayers.

We tend to think of the future in a linear manner, meaning that we think that our experiences next year will be much the same as they were this year. The problem with that approach to forecasting is that it fails to consider unforeseen events, like the 9/11 attacks. In addition, few of us would have predicted the impact of new forms of drugs—such as fentanyl—on overdose deaths and increasing crime, or the influence of the internet on criminal activities. Moreover, preventing terrorist acts continues to divert the time and resources of the police away from traditional crime control activities; Freeze (2017) notes that the RCMP shelved hundreds of organized crime cases so they could focus on fighting terrorism. Last, another unforeseen social force was the great recession of 2008 and the economic recovery that took much longer than most of us predicted.

The impact of policies such as getting tough on crime has some predictable outcomes. Increasing the severity of punishments for offenders will expand the size of correctional populations, which can be an expensive proposition for cash-strapped governments. A more diverse and foreign-born population will also create changes in the operations of justice systems as agency leaders try to employ a workforce representative of this changing population. These findings reinforce the important role that political factors play in the operations of justice systems. Despite the fact that politics and justice are closely related in Canada, the political influence is minor compared with the operations of the US justice system, where local sheriffs, prosecutors, and judges are elected officials who often advocate for severe punishments so voters do not think they are weak (Pfaff, 2017).

In some respects, the "getting tough on offenders" approach in Canada may prove to be a fad, although one that lasted for almost a decade during the Harper era, which only ended in 2015. Criminal justice reforms are sometimes based on ideas that have a "common sense" appeal, but these practices are often ineffective or actually push some individuals toward crime. Most fads are short-lived as they are introduced with enthusiasm but then disappear after their value is called into question (Denver, Best, & Haas, 2008). Examples of criminal justice fads include boot camps—a US correctional approach featuring a physically demanding, short-term military-style program that was intended to improve self-esteem but has failed to reduce recidivism. Another fad was the popularity of "scared straight" programs, where youngsters on probation for engaging in minor crimes were taken to prisons where they were confronted by inmates who told them they were headed to prison if they did not change their attitudes and behaviours.

Because we are more careful when introducing criminal justice programs today, it is likely that research on the operations of justice systems will play a greater influence on agency operations in the future. Research that compares the costs and benefits of different policing, court, and correctional practices attempts to identify the best impact for each taxpayer dollar invested in crime reduction. Evidence-based practices, where police, court, and correctional interventions must be demonstrated by research to be effective, will become the norm in the future. As a result, it is likely that academics and researchers will play a larger role in studying the justice system and providing suggestions to agency leaders. The potential impacts from these partnerships are important as jurisdictions using their resources more carefully may be rewarded with lower crime rates. Cost-benefit analyses have demonstrated that introducing policing, court, and correctional programming that has been demonstrated to reduce crime is a cost-effective investment in public safety (Washington State Institute for Public Policy, 2018).

In this chapter, and throughout this book, the operations of the justice system were presented, and readers were exposed to a number of ways of defining, analyzing, and interpreting crime and our responses to the acts we define as crimes. A key theme of the book is that political, economic, social, technological, environmental, and legal factors shape the ways we define a crime and how

the justice system should respond to these acts. However, there is seldom agreement on crime-reduction strategies, and most people have different ideas about what the priorities of the justice system should be. Regardless of our differences in opinion, we will always have to confront the challenges caused by crime and work toward building a justice system that respects victims, provides due process protections to people accused and convicted of crimes, and protects all of us in a fair and unbiased manner. While this is an optimistic goal, it is hoped that the readers of this text—many of whom might be considering working within the justice system—will develop the mindset to prepare for these challenges.

Career SNAPSHOT

Conservation Officers

Conservation officers (COs) are employed by federal, provincial, and/or territorial governments, and a number of municipal governments such as Ottawa's National Capital Commission employ COs to patrol urban parks and wilderness areas. The enforcement-related powers of these officials varies greatly, and some uniformed officials are employed in federal, provincial, or territorial parks where their main role is to provide information to visitors, as well as to participate in conservation and public education efforts. A smaller percentage of COs work in enforcement roles, such as park wardens in Canada's national parks, and they carry firearms. Several thousand COs working for provincial and territorial governments also have peace officer status and are authorized to enforce the *Criminal Code of Canada* as well as other federal and provincial/territorial acts related to environmental protection.

Although educational requirements for CO jobs vary across the country, most officers are graduates of resource management programs. After they are hired, all COs in the western provinces and the territories attend the Western Conservation Law Enforcement Academy (which is currently in Saskatchewan), and provincial officers in the Maritimes attend the conservation enforcement program at Holland College in Prince Edward Island. Ontario and Quebec have their own training programs, and officers hired by Fisheries or Parks Canada receive training at federal facilities such as the

Coast Guard College in Sydney, Nova Scotia, and the Royal Canadian Mounted Police depot in Regina, Saskatchewan.

Profile

Name: David Bakica
Job title: District Conservation Officer, Environment Yukon
Employed in current job since: 1989
Present location: Whitehorse, Yukon
Education: Renewable Resource Management Diploma, Lethbridge Community College

Background

I grew up in Whitehorse and always wanted a job working in the outdoors and with wildlife. After graduating from high school I attended the two-year Renewable Resource Management program at Lethbridge Community College (LCC). I worked during the summers while in college for Yukon Department of Environment as a Fish and Wildlife Technician. Once I graduated from LCC, I was hired as a seasonal conservation officer in the Watson Lake District. I worked for three six-month contracts over two years. While on these seasonal contracts, I was sent for an additional five weeks of conservation officer training at the Leslie Frost Natural Resource Centre in Ontario. Near the end of my third six-month contract, I competed for an open position and became the district conservation officer in the Ross River District.

Continued

Work Experience

Like most COs, I started my career working in part-time summer positions after high school and was hired as a full-time officer after completing my post-secondary education and working in seasonal positions for several years. My job assignments have varied depending on where I was posted and on my role. Most of my duties are related to enforcing the *Wildlife Act, the Fisheries Act,* and the *Environment Act.* Although the public believes that most of our work is related to enforcing hunting and fishing legislation, we have a diverse range of job duties that varies from day to day. COs are responsible for enforcing all environmental legislation, and that includes regulating wilderness tourism operations and game farms and investigating violations of natural resource laws, such as illegally dumping waste materials and importing non-native species, which can threaten the environment. Some of my job is also related to human–wildlife conflicts where large animals such as elk disrupt farming operations. I have also responded to many calls to manage bears, which can cause problems for people living in the countryside or for tourists, and I recently flew by helicopter to British Columbia to help federal parks officials with a problem bear on the Chilkoot Trail that was putting hikers at risk.

The public does not always understand how much of a conservation officer's job is related to office work; only about half of my job involves being on patrol. Some of my office work involves collecting information related to investigations; I have been involved in major ones related to poaching as well as the illegal dumping of environmental waste. While I have a lot of flexibility in my job, there is also a large volume of work that must be done. Some of that work is seasonal, of course; COs are very busy during the summer, in the fishing and hunting seasons. But while the winters are supposed to be quiet, we can be busy when wolves cause problems for farmers.

Advice to Students

Students who want to be a CO must have good communication and people skills, and most officers have extensive backgrounds in the outdoors and are fishers and hunters. In addition, the job can be physically demanding and being fit is important. COs often work alone in remote areas, so they must also develop effective problem-solving skills in working with the public—some of whom are offenders.

One of the most important things that a person who wants a CO career can do is to get as much conservation-related experience as possible, and show the full-time staff their enthusiasm for the job and determination to be a full-time CO. Students can also learn more about the job by doing a ride-along with a conservation officer. Potential COs can also get experience working in voluntary and paid jobs. In Yukon, Deputy Conservation Officers are unpaid volunteers who patrol alongside conservation officers. Most COs start their careers working in summer-job placements in the outdoors, such as parks. Often these jobs are in remote locations far away from cities, and once hired most new full-time COs are posted in those remote locations; they are able to move to larger communities as they gain time on the job and experience. While the pathway to full-time conservation officer employment may take a while, it is a very rewarding career to those who love the outdoors, and there is rarely a dull moment in our jobs.

REVIEW QUESTIONS

1. Why would agency leaders engage in a PESTEL analysis?
2. Provide reasons why some politicians support a "tough on crime" agenda.
3. Discuss how our reliance on technology makes us increasingly vulnerable to victimization.
4. How might the changing demographic characteristics of the Canadian population influence the future operations of police, court, and correctional organizations?
5. How would advocates of Packer's crime control and due process approaches explain recent Supreme Court decisions?

DISCUSSION QUESTIONS

1. Why are people living in rural areas (and representing about 20 per cent of all Canadians) disadvantaged when it comes to their interactions with the justice system? How can we overcome these challenges?
2. Which of the PESTEL factors is the most important in shaping the future of the Canadian justice system? Why?
3. Given the changes projected for justice systems in the future, how can you best prepare for a career in this field?
4. Describe how governments and corporations attempt to influence your risky or crime-related behaviours without involving the criminal justice system.
5. How would you explain to a person from a developing nation about the importance of the rule of law in Canada?

INTERNET SITE

As our reliance on technology—and especially on the internet—increases, individuals, corporations, and governments are vulnerable to potentially devastating attacks. Goodman (2015) explores the threats of technology to our safety and well-being in his book *Future Crimes*, and the accompanying website contains a number of relevant videos and written materials. **http://www.futurecrimesbook.com/**

CASES CITED

Carter v Canada (Attorney General), 2015 SCC 5, [2015] 1 SCR 331

Goodwin v British Columbia (Superintendent of Motor Vehicles), 2015 SCC 46, [2015] 3 SCR 250

R v Antic, 2017 SCC 27, [2017] 1 SCR 509

R v Babos, 2014 SCC 16, [2014] 1 SCR 309

R v Fearon, 2014 SCC 77, [2014] 3 SCR 621

R v Hart, 2014 SCC 52, [2014] 2 SCR 544

R v MacDonald, 2014 SCC 3, [2014] 1 SCR 37

R v Marakah, 2017 SCC 59, [2017] 2 SCR 608

R v Sekhon, 2014 SCC 15, [2014] 1 SCR 272

R v Steele, 2014 SCC 61, [2014] 3 SCR 138

R v Stinchcombe, [1991] 3 SCR 326

R v Taylor, 2014 SCC 50, [2014] 2 SCR 495

Glossary

absolute discharge The least severe sanction that can be imposed, resulting in a finding of guilt but with no conviction registered.

actus reus The criminal action or conduct of a person committing an offence.

administration of justice offences Offences that occur because an individual disobeys a pretrial condition or an imposed sentence, such as failing to attend court or failing to comply with a probation order. Also known as *system-generated offences*.

adultery When a married person has a sexual relationship with a person to whom they are not married.

age defence A defence that considers immaturity and recognizes that youth under 12 years of age cannot be held criminally responsible; sanctions might also be mitigated for young defendants.

age-crime curve Involvement in crime increases during early adolescence, peaks during the teenage years and early adulthood, and then decreases throughout adulthood (some social scientists call this "aging out" of crime).

aggravating factors Facts related to the offence that might lead to a more severe sentence, including if the offence involved a particularly vulnerable victim, such as a child, or if the crime was related to bias, prejudice, or hate.

alibis Witnesses or other forms of evidence that show that the defendant could not have committed the offence.

alternative measures programs Programs that divert individuals involved in minor crimes, such as property offences, from the formal justice system and usually require the individual to participate in community service work, make restitution to victims, attend counselling, or make an apology to victims.

antisocial behaviour Conduct that can be disruptive and reduce our quality of life, but might not be considered a criminal act.

assault A crime of violence that can range from a relatively minor act (level 1, also called common assaults) to a serious crime resulting in severe bodily harm (level 3).

assembly-line justice An approach to justice where a priority is placed on quickly processing minor matters in criminal courts with the assumption that most defendants are guilty.

automatism An involuntary act where an individual is in a state of impaired consciousness and lacks the intent to commit a crime.

aviation units Officers who use fixed-wing aircraft and helicopters for traffic enforcement (including vehicle pursuits), transporting prisoners, and providing information to officers on the ground.

bail supervision Allows a youth accused of a crime to remain in the community even though there may be a lack of specialized mental health or child welfare services that he or she requires.

battered woman syndrome A defence that has been used by some victims of domestic violence who argued they had no way of escaping their victimization and no had other choice but to attack their abuser.

"big house" prisons A style of high-security prisons that emerged in the 1800s and featured large stone buildings surrounded by high stone fences.

blaming the victim Occurs when the victim is held responsible for being harmed (instead of or in addition to holding the offender responsible).

breach of probation A violation of an offender's condition of probation, such as using drugs or alcohol when it is forbidden, or violating a curfew.

break and enter When an individual breaks into a residence or business, usually with the intent to steal items.

Canadian Centre for Justice Statistics (CCJS) An organization operated by Statistics Canada that produces reports on crime, offenders, victims, and the operations of the justice system.

Canadian Charter of Rights and Freedoms The part of the Constitution that defines the rights and freedoms of Canadians, including those accused of committing crimes.

Canadian Police Information Centre (CPIC) A database that can be accessed by law enforcement personnel that reports the criminal histories of Canadians.

canine (K9) officers Officers who are partnered with dogs to engage in patrol activities, detect drugs or explosives, and track suspects or escaped prisoners.

carding A controversial police practice where information is collected about people who are stopped at random and questioned.

cascading A term used by the Correctional Service of Canada to refer to a prisoner's movement to lower levels of supervision, such as from medium- to minimum-security facilities.

case plan The "roadmap" for an individual's rehabilitation that is developed by the offender and the caseworker.

case processing time The time between an individual's arrest and when the case is resolved, such as when a sentence is imposed or the case is stayed. Also called charge-processing time.

caseload The number of individuals under the supervision of a probation or parole officer.

chain of command The lines of authority in a police organization, which are clearly defined and range from a constable (on the bottom of the pyramid) to the chief or commissioner (at the top).

chivalry The lenient treatment of girls and women by employees within justice systems.

circle sentencing A justice practice intended for Indigenous offenders, where sanctions for criminal conduct are developed by members of a circle, including a judge, the offender, victims (and their supporters), the police, and other community members. In some jurisdictions these practices are called healing or peacemaking circles.

Circles of Support and Accountability (COSA) Groups of volunteers who support the transition of high-risk sexual offenders from prison to the community.

civilianization The employment of civilian personnel in police organizations.

closed system A type of prison administration where there is little interaction with the community.

collateral consequences Government policies that are developed to deter potential offenders and include job restrictions on people with specific types of criminal histories.

Commissioner's Directives Guidelines established by the Commissioner of the csc for the operations of the correctional system and the treatment of prisoners and parolees.

common law An approach to law that is based on tradition, where judges follow decisions or precedents made by other courts.

community service work A condition of a probation order that requires an offender to participate in unpaid work programs that benefit the community, such as working at a library or a community centre.

community youth workers Individuals whose job is to prepare pre-sentence reports for the court, monitor youth on bail supervision, and supervise youth on probation.

community-oriented policing An approach to policing that relies on community involvement to take a proactive approach to reducing antisocial behaviour and crime.

concurrent sentence Multiple sentences that are served at the same time (e.g., a person sentenced to two 11-month sentences to be served concurrently would be released after 11 months).

conditional discharge Requires the individual to comply with a number of conditions, and after they fulfill those conditions, the discharge becomes absolute.

conditional sentences Custodial sentences of up to two years that are served in the community. Individuals who do not meet the conditions of their release can be returned to court and ordered to serve the remainder of their sentence in a correctional centre.

conducted energy devices Less-lethal devices, such as tasers, that send an electrical charge that temporarily incapacitates an individual.

consecutive sentence Multiple sentences that are served one after the other (e.g., a person sentenced to two 11-month sentences to be served consecutively would be released after 22 months).

consent A defence that is almost always used by defendants accused of assault, where they contend that the victim was a willing party in the offence, such as when a hockey player injures another player.

contraband Any item that is forbidden in a correctional facility, such as cellular phones, illicit drugs, home-made liquor, or weapons.

contract policing A form of policing where a police service, such as the RCMP or OPP, provides policing to a municipality under a contract.

correctional centres Facilities that hold inmates sentenced to terms of incarceration of two years or less.

cost-benefit analyses An approach to estimating the costs of justice-system interventions, such as different types of treatment, and comparing those costs to the benefits in reduced crime.

court clerks Responsible for ensuring that a court's paperwork and records are maintained, creating the court's docket, and sometimes administering oaths to witnesses.

courtroom work group Composed of the judges, Crown prosecutors, defence counsel, and court clerks from a local court.

crime control model An approach to justice that is based on the philosophy that it is more important to protect society than the rights of any individual.

crime of omission An act where the accused has failed to take some action, such as a school social worker failing to report child abuse to child welfare authorities.

Crime Severity Index (CSI) A measure of the volume and seriousness of crime based on all *Criminal Code* and federal statute offences reported to the police.

crimes against humanity Violent acts and persecution of a civilian population that are committed as part of a systematic attack.

Criminal Code of Canada A federal statute that lists the criminal offences and punishments defined by Parliament, as well as justice system procedures.

criminal negligence An act that shows reckless disregard for the lives or safety of other people.

critical criminologists Scholars who argue that justice systems are designed to maintain class relationships.

cronyism Occurs when friends of people in authority are appointed to jobs without regard to their qualifications.

CSI effect Unrealistic expectations about the use of scientific evidence in criminal investigations that are based on inaccurate information portrayed on television.

custody rating scale An instrument that attempts to predict a prisoner's risk of misconduct, adjustment to prison life, and potential for escape.

dangerous offenders Individuals who the court has deemed to be a threat to the life, safety, or physical or mental well-being of the public.

dark figure of crime The difference between the amount of crime that occurs and the amount of crime that is reported to the police.

day parole A type of release for federal prisoners who live in a community-based facility and usually work, attend school, or participate in treatment during the day.

deferred custody Provides youth with an opportunity to serve their custodial sentence in the community, but if they do not abide by the conditions of their release, judges can order the youth to serve the remainder of their sentence in custody.

delinquents An outdated term for young people who have committed criminal acts.

detention centres Facilities where individuals are held awaiting their court dates or serving short periods of incarceration (called provincial correctional centres in some provinces).

determinate sentence Sentences that have a warrant expiry date on which the inmate will be released from a correctional centre or federal prison.

deterrence The use of punishment to impede or discourage wrongful behaviour.

direct supervision A method of inmate supervision where officers directly interact with inmates.

discretion Refers to when judgment is used to determine which of several options to pursue; in the case of policing, this includes whether to take no action, provide a warning, make a formal caution, issue a ticket, or arrest a suspect.

docket The list of cases scheduled for court for the day.

drones Unmanned aerial vehicles that have been used to drop contraband into correctional facilities.

dual offences Offences that can be prosecuted as either summary offences or indictable offences.

due process model An approach to justice that is based on the philosophy that the justice system needs to protect the rights of a defendant.

duress A defence where the accused people claim that their actions were not voluntary but that they acted in response to being threatened by another person.

dynamic needs Factors that can be changed by offenders, such as their education level or employability.

dynamic security The regular interaction between prisoners and correctional officers that promotes problem-solving, information sharing, and rapport building.

earned remission A type of early release from a provincial correctional centre that has been earned by the inmate through good behaviour.

electronic monitoring (EM) Requires probationers or parolees living in the community to wear a device that communicates their whereabouts to a facility that tracks their movements.

evidence-based practices Strategies that research has demonstrated to be effective and have positive impacts.

evil woman hypothesis Women who commit violent offences may be treated more harshly by the justice system.

excuse defences Based on the argument that one's criminal conduct can be excused because the accused could not form the intent to commit a crime.

executive protection Protection provided by police officers to the Prime Minister, the Governor General of Canada, provincial premiers, mayors of large cities, and visiting dignitaries.

extrajudicial sanctions Alternative measures programs for youth.

extralegal factors Conditions that affect sentencing but are not related to the offender or offence, such as the location of a sentencing court.

failure to comply Violating the conditions of a probation order is a criminal offence that can result in additional charges and further punishments.

field training officers Experienced police officers who train and mentor new police officers during their first months on the job.

fine option programs Enable people to pay their court-ordered fines using their labour (typically by working in jobs related to community service).

First Nations A term used to describe the Indigenous people of Canada, not including the Inuit or Métis; the term can also refer to the lands set aside for Indigenous peoples.

First Nations Policing Program A federal government policing strategy that gives Indigenous communities the choice between operating their own police services or contracting with other police organizations to police their communities.

first responders Professionals who respond to emergencies, such as police officers, paramedics, and firefighters (both paid and volunteer).

first-degree murder A planned and deliberate act that results in death.

front-line officers Officers who occupy front-line policing positions (e.g., up to the rank of sergeant) and do not have executive authority.

full parole A less restrictive form of parole granted by the Parole Board of Canada to federal prisoners who have been successful in day parole.

fundamental justice A principle of Canadian justice that states that people who acted reasonably may not be punished unless there is proof that they did something wrong.

gaols The historic term for jails.

General Social Survey (GSS) An annual survey of Canadians that is conducted by Statistics Canada about a range of social trends, with each annual survey addressing one theme in depth.

genocide The systematic killing of a population, such as an ethnic, racial, religious, or national group.

going rate The average sanction or punishment for a criminal offence in a local court, which can vary between different courts.

graduated sanctions Punishments that start with the least restrictive response and then become more severe if the individual continues to reoffend.

green criminology A branch of criminology that focuses on environmental crimes and harms to the environment.

habeas corpus The right of a person who is being detained to challenge the legality of his or her detention before a court.

halfway houses Facilities where inmates reside during their transition from a correctional centre or prison to the community. The CSC calls their facilities community correctional centres.

hate crimes Offences intended to intimidate or harm a person or the group to which they belong based on race, ethnicity, gender, sexual orientation, national origin, disability, or other similar factors.

home confinement A sanction that requires an individual on community supervision to remain at home; this is usually coupled with electronic monitoring.

homicide When someone causes the death of another person.

hot spots Areas where a high volume of crimes occur (e.g., near rowdy bars).

identity theft When an individual obtains another person's information in order to commit offences such as fraud or forgery.

incapacitation A crime-reduction strategy based on the idea that removing offenders from society reduces reoffending.

indentured servants Workers who were bound by a contract to work without pay for a given period of time; this included abandoned or orphaned children who immigrated to Canada and were placed with families for several years until they could "work off" the costs of their travel to Canada.

indeterminate sentences Sentences imposed on dangerous and life-sentenced offenders who do not have a formal release date and remain under correctional supervision for the rest of their lives, whether in an institution or in a community.

indictable offences Serious offences, such as homicide, where the defendants must appear in court and cases are heard before federally appointed judges.

Indigenous courtworkers Provide services to Indigenous people accused of an offence and to their family members, including advocating on the accused's behalf, providing information about the accused's rights and what to expect in court, and offering translation services.

individualized justice Enables judges to consider aggravating and mitigating factors as well as the individual's strengths and limitations when imposing a sentence; it is the opposite of mandatory sentences.

inferior courts Provincial and territorial courts that have limited jurisdiction and deal with less serious adult and youth criminal matters, as well as civil, family, traffic, and municipal bylaw cases.

informal social control When people conform to the law and other social norms because of the actions and opinions of other individuals, such as praise or disapproval.

institutional parole officers Officers employed by the CSC who work with inmates to develop case plans that enable prisoners to make a safe transition to the community.

intensive supervision probation (ISP) Places higher levels of supervision on high-risk probationers, and probation officers typically meet more frequently with them.

intensive support and supervision Enhanced supervision that is provided to youth who are considered to be at high risk or to have high needs.

intent The criminal intention (guilty mind) in *mens rea*.

intermittent sentence Sentences of 90 days or less that are served in segments of time rather than all at once; can be imposed on inmates who would be unduly harmed by full-time incarceration, such as losing their job or interrupting their studies.

intimate partners Current and former spouses, dating partners, or other intimate relationships.

iron law of imprisonment The concept that most prisoners will return to the community, so it is in the public's best interest to help those individuals succeed in their re-entry.

jails Facilities where individuals are held awaiting their court appearances (called provincial correctional centres in most provinces, but jails in Ontario).

judicial interim release A form of pretrial release where defendants can be released on their promise to appear in court or by providing bail.

jurisdiction The range of a government's or court's authority (e.g., provinces have jurisdiction over non-criminal traffic matters).

jury nullification Occurs when a jury refuses to convict an individual who is obviously guilty, as the jury believes that the conviction and punishment are worse than the crime that was committed.

jury rolls The lists from which a jury is drawn; in Ontario, lists of potential jurors are compiled using the most recent voters' lists and the band lists from First Nations.

just deserts An expression used to suggest that a punishment reflects the seriousness of an offender's crimes ("they got what they deserved").

justice by geography The differences in case outcomes that are a result of where a court is located (e.g., some rural courts may be more punitive than urban courts).

justice of the peace A person who is appointed to carry out minor judicial functions such as authorizing searches, reviewing the legality of a suspect's detention, and determining whether there are sufficient grounds for a criminal case to proceed to court.

justification defences Used when the accused admits to committing an offence but the act was justified under the circumstances.

less-than-lethal weapons Alternatives to firearms that are intended to temporarily incapacitate or confuse an individual.

lifestyle exposure model of victimization The idea that certain activities, careers, places of living, and lifestyles place individuals at higher risk of victimization.

lip service When more time is spent talking about something than actually implementing the approach.

living unit Refers to where inmates live within a facility, usually featuring cells that surround an area used for dining, education, and recreation.

long-term supervision orders (LTSOs) Orders that can be imposed by a judge to increase the period of an offender's community supervision past the end of their formal sentence.

malum in se An act that is universally considered by the public as being evil or harmful to society, such as homicide.

malum prohibitum An act that is defined as illegal or wrong by a government, but is not considered wrong in itself, such as speeding on a highway.

marine units Officers who are deployed in boats to patrol waterfront areas and harbours, including conducting search and rescue activities, promoting water safety, and engaging in crime prevention.

mass imprisonment The overuse of imprisonment as a crime control strategy.

mens rea The state of mind of a person committing a criminal act.

mental disorder defence An excuse defence based on the argument that people suffering from serious mental disorders are incapable of forming *mens rea* to be held fully accountable.

mission creep Occurs when organizations take on more duties than were originally envisioned by the founders of those agencies.

mistake defence A defence where accused people claim they were unaware of the law and therefore unaware that they'd committed a crime, or that they were aware of the law but honestly believed they were not breaking it.

mitigating factors Facts related to the individual that might encourage a judge to impose a less severe sentence, such as if the individual is a youth, a young adult, or a first-time offender.

motor vehicle theft The theft or attempted theft of a land-based motorized vehicle.

"Mr Big" investigations Investigations carried out by undercover police officers posing as criminals to obtain confessions from suspects about their involvement in serious crimes.

National Flagging System A system that tracks people who have been convicted of serious violent crimes to ensure that their prior criminal histories are considered by prosecutors if they reoffend.

necessity A type of defence claiming that an illegal act was committed in order to prevent a more serious harm, such as speeding to get to a hospital for emergency treatment.

negligence An act that shows disregard for the well-being of others.

neighbourhood watch Programs that encourage community members to work together to report suspicious people or unusual activities to the police.

nepotism Preferential hiring carried out by people in powerful positions of their family members or friends.

new generation design A correctional facility where the cells are arranged on the perimeter of the living unit and the prisoners eat and recreate in a common area (also called a podular design).

non-violent Crime Severity Index A measure that considers all crimes that are not included in the violent CSI category.

norms Standards of acceptable behaviour that are based on tradition, customs, and values.

North-West Mounted Police (NWMP) A police force established in 1873 in response to lawlessness in the North-West Territories (in what is now Alberta and Saskatchewan) and to reinforce Canadian sovereignty in that region. The organization became the Royal North-West Mounted Police in 1904 and the Royal Canadian Mounted Police in 1920.

objective classification A formal method of prisoner classification that uses risk assessment instruments.

occupational crimes Offences that are committed by individuals for their own benefit in the course of their employment.

offender classification The process by which an individual's risks and needs are assessed in order to assign the inmate to the most appropriate living unit.

offender intake assessment Assessing an individual's future risk of criminal behaviour based on their criminal history and their needs (e.g., whether they require help with employment or substance abuse).

officer-involved shootings Occur when police officers discharge their firearm, including accidental and intentional discharges.

ombudsman An appointed official who investigates complaints made against organizations operated by provincial or territorial governments.

open court principle Gives the media the freedom to publicize court proceedings, although some information, such as the identity of a child victim of sexual abuse, may be subject to a publication ban.

open custody facilities Low-security youth custody facilities that are generally small and are sometimes located in residential neighbourhoods.

order maintenance Involves managing minor offences, antisocial behaviour, and other conduct that disturbs the public, such as loud parties.

organizational crimes Offences committed by employees of legitimate businesses that are intended to increase profits or otherwise benefit the organization.

over-policed Refers to when members of a social group or neighbourhood are treated suspiciously, watched, stopped, searched, questioned, or otherwise negatively paid attention to by the police by virtue of being members of that group.

paralegals Licensed paralegals have some legal training and perform legal work for law firms and lawyers.

paramilitary organizations Services organized along military lines, which have a chain of command where lines of authority are clearly defined by the organization.

parole A form of conditional release from a federal correctional facility to the community, where the ex-prisoner is supervised by a parole officer.

paternalism The unfair treatment of girls and young women based on the rationale that their treatment was in their best interests.

patrol zone A defined area within a community that officers are assigned to patrol.

personal service order Requires a youthful offender to compensate the crime victims through work supervised by a youth probation officer.

PESTEL analysis A method of scanning the environment that considers political, economic, social, technological, environmental, and legal factors.

plea agreement An agreement arranged by a defendant's counsel and a prosecutor that usually involves the accused pleading guilty in return for a less serious punishment.

police lock-ups A historic term used to describe police cells, which are places where arrestees are temporarily held until their first court appearance (e.g., overnight).

police militarization Occurs when police services use military equipment, tactics, and training as regular methods to police civilians.

police strength The ratio of police to civilians; the Canadian average is about two officers for every 1,000 residents.

police subculture A set of informal rules and expectations that shape police attitudes, values, and behaviours.

political interference The inappropriate use of political authority to influence police operations.

precedent The practice of judges basing decisions about current cases on the outcomes of prior judgments.

pre-sentence report (PSR) A report ordered by judges prior to sentencing to provide a comprehensive overview of the individual's strengths and weaknesses, and whether prior justice system interventions were successful.

price-fixing When business owners engage in a conspiracy to reduce competition or to keep prices of a product or service artificially high.

prison misconduct A violation of the rules of a correctional facility; often classified as major misconduct, such as assault, or minor misconduct, such as being in an unauthorized area or possessing contraband (e.g., drugs or a cell phone).

private law Legal matters that relate to the relationships between individuals or businesses that involve contracts.

private policing Involves the social control efforts of individuals who are not government employees, but instead are hired to provide security or policing services.

probation officers Provincial officials who prepare reports for the courts about sentencing options for individuals convicted of crimes and monitor their activities if serving community-based sentences.

procedural law Focuses on the rules that determine the enforcement of rights or due process.

professional model of policing A model that emphasizes a "top down" style of police management with an emphasis on random patrols and rapid response, where citizens play a passive role in crime control.

proportionality The principle that the sentence imposed on offenders is proportionate to the seriousness of their offence and their degree of responsibility.

prosecutorial discretion Refers to the prosecutor's authority to decide whether to proceed with a case, withdraw a charge, enter into a plea agreement with defence counsel, or prosecute an offence as a summary or indictable offence.

provincial parole Provincial parole boards are operated in Ontario and Quebec for prisoners in provincial correctional centres, while individuals serving less than two years in all the remaining provinces and territories can apply to the Parole Board of Canada for early releases.

provincial prosecutors Officials (including police officers in some courts) who prosecute minor criminal cases (e.g., summary matters), traffic cases, and infractions of local bylaws.

provocation A defence based on an accused claiming that he or she was provoked into committing a crime, although this defence can only be used to argue that an act of murder be reduced to manslaughter.

public law A type of law addressing matters that affect society, such as responding to a person who commits a criminal act.

public order policing The use of police during mass demonstrations (such as protests) to maintain the balance between the rights and interests of government, society, and individuals.

publication bans Made by courts in order to protect the identity of some victims or specific information about cases.

random preventative patrol A patrol method thought to reduce crime by providing a visible police presence in the community.

reception centre A prison unit that receives prisoners from the courts and holds them until their assessment and classification is complete.

recidivism Occurs when a person who has been previously convicted of an offence reoffends by committing another crime.

reckless behaviours Occur when people act in a manner that they know is dangerous or risky.

rehabilitation The process of helping offenders develop the skills, knowledge, and attitudes they require in order to reduce their likelihood of recidivism.

representativeness A concept related to the composition of juries and whether they reflect the demographic characteristics of a community.

restitution When an individual makes a payment to the victim for the losses that were experienced by the victim, such as property damage or loss.

restorative justice An alternative approach to conventional practices of justice that focuses on interventions intended to repair the harm that was experienced by the victim and the community when the offence occurred.

retribution A crime control philosophy that involves taking revenge on the offender often through harsh punishments, as expressed by the biblical principle of "an eye for an eye, a tooth for a tooth."

ride-along When members of the public accompany a police officer on patrol to learn about policing.

robbery An act of theft that also involves violence or the threat of violence.

Royal Irish Constabulary (RIC) A police force that emphasized mounted patrols and was a model for early Canadian police services.

Royal Newfoundland Constabulary Established in 1729, this police force claims to be Canada's oldest police service and still provides services throughout Newfoundland and Labrador.

Royal North-West Mounted Police (RNWMP) The policing authority of the Canadian North from 1904 to 1919; it became the RCMP in 1920.

rule of law The principle that the law is supreme over any individual or body of government.

school resource officers Officers placed on a part- or full-time basis in schools to provide security, teach classes, act as positive role models, and build positive relationships with students.

second-degree murder A deliberate but unplanned act that results in death.

secure custody facilities High-security youth custody facilities that are usually large and often look similar to adult correctional centres. Also known as *closed custody facilities*.

segregation Placement of an inmate in a locked high-security cell within a correctional facility (e.g., administrative segregation), usually in response to their misconduct.

selective incapacitation A concept based on the notion that incapacitating the highest-risk offenders will reduce crime (e.g., "three strikes" policies in the United States are based on this idea).

self-defence A defence arguing that the harm that was inflicted on another person was carried out to ensure the defendant's safety or the safety of others.

self-determination Occurs when Indigenous communities are able to exert more control over their economic, social, and cultural development, including taking ownership over policing.

self-report surveys A type of survey where respondents answer questions about their attitudes, beliefs, or experiences, including being an offender or crime victim.

sequencing The treatment of people involved in the justice system follows a set pattern that is dictated by law and policy.

sexting Transmitting sexually explicit images online or via text message.

sexual assault An assault of a sexual nature, including assaults committed by individuals of the same sex or assaults committed against one's spouse.

sheriffs In many provinces, sheriffs provide court security and transport prisoners from the court to correctional facilities.

silent system An early approach to rehabilitation where prisoners were held in solitary confinement and were forbidden to talk to other prisoners or guards outside their cells.

slashing When a prisoner engages in self-harming behaviour by cutting their skin using metal or plastic objects.

sovereignty A nation's claim on its territory.

special handling units High-security units within a maximum-security penitentiary where the movement of prisoners is very controlled.

special prosecutors Experienced lawyers who are appointed by a province or territory to investigate offences where government prosecutors might be perceived as biased, such as the investigation of an alleged case of prosecutorial misconduct.

special weapons and tactics (SWAT) teams or **emergency response teams** A group of officers who receive specialized training and have access to military-style weapons to confront armed and/or dangerous suspects.

specialized courts Courts that specialize in working with distinctive groups of offenders, including people with mental illnesses or individuals convicted of specific offences such as domestic violence. Also called *problem-solving courts* or *therapeutic courts.*

stand-alone police services Police services that are typically small and are not part of a larger police organization.

standard conditions All Canadians on probation are required to keep the peace and be of good behaviour, report to the court or probation officer when required, and report any significant changes to the probation officer or court.

stand your ground laws Laws that give some US residents the right to use force to protect their lives and property in a way that would be considered excessive and illegal in Canada. Also known as the castle doctrine.

stare decisis A legal principle whereby courts are bound by their prior decisions and the decisions of higher courts.

status offence Under the *Juvenile Delinquents Act,* this term refers to actions that were not considered crimes for adults but were unlawful for youth, such as drinking alcohol.

statutory release A form of supervised release that is automatically granted after federal prisoners with determinate sentences of three years or longer have served two-thirds of their sentences (does not apply to dangerous offenders or lifers serving indeterminate sentences).

Strategic Training Initiative in Community Supervision (STICS) An approach to the community supervision of probationers that is based on the notion that probation officers who have stronger relationships with their clients and challenge their pro-criminal or antisocial beliefs have lower rates of recidivism on their caseloads.

street checks A practice where individuals engaged in suspicious activities are questioned by the police.

street crimes Violent, property, and public order offences that are contrasted against crimes of the powerful (such as white-collar crimes).

street justice Occurs when a suspected offender is forced to submit to an unauthorized punishment by a police officer, such as doing push-ups in return for not getting a speeding ticket.

strip-searches Searches carried out by staff members to detect contraband by requiring inmates to remove their clothing (inmates may be strip-searched after visiting with their family members, for example).

subjective classification Informal assessments of inmates based on the judgment or gut feelings of the correctional supervisor or psychologist.

substantive law Consists of the written rules that define crimes and punishments, and the rights and obligations of citizens and criminal justice personnel.

suicide by cop Occurs when individuals deliberately provoke the police into shooting them, such as by pointing an unloaded firearm at an officer.

summary offences Crimes that carry a less serious punishment in which judges can impose a jail sentence of up to six months and/or a maximum fine of $5,000.

Supreme Court of Canada The highest court in Canada; it only hears cases that are being appealed out of a lower court.

surety A responsible person, such as an employer or family member, who ensures that the accused will appear in court.

sworn officers Police officers with the legal authority to arrest and use force (as opposed to peace officers, who have less legal authority).

temporary release A type of release granted from a correctional facility so that inmates can participate in employment, education, treatment, or family visits.

theft Taking another person's possessions without his or her consent.

third degree A long and intense interrogation, which in extreme cases has involved threats of violence or the unlawful use of force, to obtain a confession from a suspect.

ticket of leave A release established in penal colonies for prisoners who had demonstrated positive changes and were considered rehabilitated.

totality A sentencing principle that considers the overall length of a sentence and requires that a single global sentence be imposed to avoid an unjustly long sentence.

training schools Secure placements that were similar to today's secure custody facilities (also called reformatories, reform schools, or industrial schools).

trauma-informed care An approach to delivering interventions that acknowledges the impacts of trauma on individuals and the importance of providing services in a safe, healing, and empowering manner.

truth in sentencing Limits the amount of a sentence that can be granted as "time served" when an individual has been remanded prior to sentencing.

undercover roles Officers carry out investigations in a covert manner that can involve immersing themselves into criminal worlds.

unlawful act An act that is not authorized or justified by law.

vicarious traumatization Occurs when an individual is subjected to disturbing content, such as counsellors listening to stories of their clients' victimization or jurors at a murder trial viewing crime-scene photographs.

victimless crimes Acts that are legally defined as crimes even though there is no direct victim (e.g., illegal gambling).

victimology The study of crime victims and their interactions with the justice system.

vigilante justice The unlawful practice of a person or group of people who take the law into their own hands without legal authority to do so.

violent Crime Severity Index A measure of the volume and seriousness of all violent offences that includes homicide, all three levels of assault, robbery, sexual assault, uttering threats, forcible confinement/kidnapping, attempted murder, and criminal harassment.

warehousing When inmates receive only their basic needs and few or no rehabilitative opportunities.

warrant expiry date An inmate's release date from custody.

warrants of committal Documents that authorize an individual's incarceration.

white-collar crimes Non-violent crimes that are committed for monetary gain and include acts of corruption.

white-collar offenders People who engage in financially motivated, non-violent crimes.

wilful blindness Occurs when an accused is aware that a crime was likely being committed but chose to ignore the facts.

workhouses Places developed in the 1800s where the poor and people with mental illnesses were given basic necessities (e.g., beds, meals, and clothes) in return for work.

wraparound services An approach to developing an individualized, community-based case plan for a young offender by involving a team of their family and other community professionals.

youth Crime Severity Index A measure of the volume and seriousness of all crimes committed by youth between 12 and 17 years of age.

youth justice conference A group of community members, sometimes including a judge, who come together to develop a sanction for a young person who has committed an offence.

References

Chapter 1

Allen, M. (2014). *Victim services in Canada, 2011/2012*. Ottawa, ON: Canadian Centre for Justice Statistics.

Allen, M. (2017). *Mandatory minimum penalties: An analysis of criminal justice system outcomes for selected offences*. Ottawa, ON: Canadian Centre for Justice Statistics.

Anderson, B., & Coletto, D. (2016). Canadians' moral compass set differently from that of our neighbours to the south. *Abacus Data*. Retrieved from http://abacusdata.ca/canadians-moral-compass-set-differently-from-that-of-our-neighbours-to-the-south/

Angus Reid Global. (2013). *Three-in-five Canadians would bring back death penalty*. Vancouver, BC: Author.

Angus Reid Global. (2014). *Canadian confidence in police, courts sees significant rebound over 2012 sentiment*. Retrieved from http://angusreidglobal.com/wp-content/uploads/2014/05/ARG-Canadian-Perceptions-Police-Crime-2014.pdf

Angus Reid Institute. (2018). *Confidence in the justice system: Visible minorities have less faith in courts than other Canadians*. Retrieved from http://angusreid.org/justice-system-confidence/

Armstrong, J. (2018). Once wrongfully convicted, Marshall faces new woes. *The Globe and Mail*. Retrieved from https://www.theglobeandmail.com/news/national/once-wrongly-convicted-marshall-faces-new-woes/article18152123/

Balko, R. (2013). *Rise of the warrior cop: The militarization of America's police forces*. New York: Public Affairs Books.

Beattie, S., David, J. D., & Roy, J. (2018). *Homicide in Canada, 2017*. Ottawa, ON: Canadian Centre for Justice Statistics.

Bowal, P., & Brierton, T. D. (2018). Stinchcombe: Crown disclosure of criminal evidence. *LawNow*. Retrieved from https://www.lawnow.org/stinchcombe-and-crown-disclosure-of-criminal-evidence-2/

Boyce, J. (2016). *Victimization of Aboriginal people in Canada, 2014*. Ottawa, ON: Canadian Centre for Justice Statistics.

Boyce, J., Rotenberg, C., & Karam, M. (2015). *Mental health and contact with police in Canada, 2012*. Ottawa, ON: Canadian Centre for Justice Statistics.

British Columbia Courts. (2018a). *Annual report 2017*. Supreme Court of British Columbia. Victoria, BC: Author.

British Columbia Courts. (2018b). *Annual report 2016/2017*. Victoria, BC: Author.

Britto, S., Ruddell, R., & Jones, N. A. (2019). Constructing retributive sentiments: Offence characteristics and crime causation on Canadian police procedurals. Presented at the Digitizing Justice conference: Winnipeg, MB.

Campbell, K. M., & Denov, M. (2016). Wrongful convictions in Canada: Causes, consequences, and responses. In J. V. Roberts & M G. Grossman (Eds.), *Criminal justice in Canada: A reader* (5th ed.) (pp. 225–242). Toronto, ON: Nelson.

Canadian Press. (2018, March 29). Liberals look to "abolish peremptory challenges" with Bill C-75 following Colten Boushie acquittal. *Calgary Herald*. Retrieved from http://calgaryherald.com/news/national/liberals-look-to-abolish-peremptory-challenges-with-bill-c-75-following-colten-boushie-acquittal/wcm/1c67b614-e33f-46cf-8dbb-66d6217d3030

Carstairs, C. (2000). "Hop heads" and "hypes": Drug use, regulation and resistance in Canada, 1920–1961. Ph.D. dissertation, University of Toronto.

Cole, G. F., Smith, C. E., & DeJong, C. (2018). *Criminal justice in America*. Scarborough, ON: Nelson Education.

Conor, P. (2018). *Police resources in Canada, 2017*. Ottawa, ON: Canadian Centre for Justice Statistics.

Correctional Service Canada. (2016). *Correctional Service Canada healing lodges*. Retrieved from http://www.csc-scc.gc.ca/aboriginal/002003-2000-eng.shtml

Cotter, A. (2015). *Spotlight on Canadians: Results from the General Social Survey: Public confidence in Canadian institutions*. Ottawa, ON: Statistics Canada.

Coughlan, S., Yogis, J. A., & Cotter, C. (2013). *Canadian law dictionary* (7th ed.). Hauppauge, NY: Barron's.

Cryderman, K. (2018, February 23). Bias played role in Indigenous victim's jailing: report. *The Globe and Mail*. Retrieved from https://www.theglobeandmail.com/news/alberta/alberta-report-condemns-treatment-of-indigenous-sexual-assault-victim/article38088903/

CTV News. (2018). A look at each province's rules for marijuana legislation. Retrieved from https://www.ctvnews.ca/canada/a-look-at-each-province-s-rules-for-marijuana-legalization-1.3894944

Cuciz, S. (2018). Child sexual exploitation in Canada: Survivors reveal terrifying reality. *Global News*. Retrieved from https://globalnews.ca/news/4047182/child-sexual-exploitation-in-canada-survivors-reveal-terrifying-reality/

Deadly statistics, unanswered questions and missing Aboriginal women [Editorial]. (2014, May 4). *The Globe and Mail*. Retrieved from http://www.theglobeandmail.com/globe-debate/editorials/deadly-statistics-unanswered-questions-and-missing-aboriginal-women/article18407550/

Department of Justice. (2005). *Canada's court system*. Retrieved from http://publications.gc.ca/collections/collection_2012/jus/J2-128-2005-eng.pdf

Department of Justice. (2015a). *Canada's court system*. Retrieved from http://www.justice.gc.ca/eng/csj-sjc/ccs-ajc/pdf/courten.pdf

Department of Justice. (2015b). *Canada's system of justice*. Retrieved from http://www.justice.gc.ca/eng/csj-sjc/just/img/courten.pdf

Department of Justice. (2018a). *Applications for ministerial review – Miscarriages of justice*. Ottawa, ON: Author.

Department of Justice. (2018b). *What we heard: Transforming Canada's criminal justice system*. Ottawa, ON: Author.

Department of Justice. (2019). *Legal aid in Canada, 2017/18*. Ottawa, ON: Author.

Dubinski, K. (2019, June 13). Selling sex is 'a social blight,' Crown argues in prostitution charter challenge. CBC News. Retrieved from https://www.cbc.ca/news/canada/london/sex-trade-charter-challenge-london-ontario-fantasy-world-escorts-1.5172469

Fallon, K. (2018, June 13). Confessions of a true-crime re-enactor: Inside TV's hottest, most morbid genre. *Daily Beast*. Retrieved from https://www.thedailybeast.com/confessions-of-a-true-crime-re-enactor-inside-tvs-hottest-most-morbid-genre

Government of British Columbia. (2017). *Police resources in British Columbia, 2016.* Victoria, B.C.: Ministry of Public Safety and Solicitor General.

Government of British Columbia. (2018). BC's criminal justice system. Retrieved from http://www2.gov.bc.ca/gov/content/justice/criminal-justice/bcs-criminal-justice-system

Government of Canada. (2015). *Canadian Victims Bill of Rights.* Retrieved from http://laws-lois.justice.gc.ca/PDF/C-23.7.pdf

Government of Canada. (2018). Cannabis regulations: SOR/2018-144. Retrieved from http://www.gazette.gc.ca/rp-pr/p2/2018/2018-07-11/html/sor-dors144-eng.html

Innocence Canada (2019). *Current cases.* Retrieved from: https://www.innocencecanada.com/current-cases/

Ipsos. (2017). Consumption of marijuana likely to increase in Canada with many saying they'll light up after legislation. Retrieved from https://www.ipsos.com/sites/default/files/ct/news/documents/2017-09/consumption-of-marijuana-increase-PR-2017-9-16v1.pdf

Ivison, J. (2018, January 18). Liberal foot-dragging on prostitution law may lead to Charter challenge. *National Post.* Retrieved from http://nationalpost.com/opinion/john-ivison-liberal-foot-dragging-on-prostitution-law-may-lead-to-charter-challenge

Kerbel, M. R. (2018). *If it bleeds, it leads: An anatomy of television news.* New York: Routledge.

Kiedrowski, J., Ruddell, R., & Petrunik, M. (2019). Police civilianization in Canada: A mixed methods investigation. *Policing and Society: An International Journal of Research and Policy, 9*(2), 204–222. doi: 10.1080/10439463.2017.1281925

Kirkey, S. (2018, June 15). 14 years for selling pot to youth? Lawyers say punishments under Liberal pot bill ludicrous. *National Post.* Retrieved from http://nationalpost.com/news/canada/14-years-for-selling-pot-to-youth-lawyers-say-punishments-under-liberal-pot-bill-ludicrous

Malakieh, J. (2019). *Adult and youth correctional statistics in Canada, 2017/2018.* Ottawa, ON: Canadian Centre for Justice Statistics.

Mays, G. L., & Ruddell, R. (2019). *Making sense of criminal justice: Policies and practices* (3rd ed.). New York: Oxford University Press.

Miladinovic, Z. (2019). *Adult criminal and youth court statistics in Canada, 2016/2017.* Ottawa, ON: Canadian Centre for Justice Statistics.

Montgomery, R., & Griffiths, C. T. (2015). *The use of private security services for policing.* Ottawa, ON: Public Safety Canada.

National Inquiry into Missing and Murdered Indigenous Women and Girls. (2019). *Reclaiming power and place.* Vancouver, BC: Author.

Ontario Ministry of the Attorney General. (2015). How should compensation be determined. Retrieved from https://www.attorneygeneral.jus.gov.on.ca/english/about/pubs/truscott/section9.php

Ontario Ministry of Community Safety and Correctional Services. (2018). Correctional services: Facilities - jails. Retrieved from https://www.mcscs.jus.gov.on.ca/english/Corrections/Facilitieslocationsandvisitinghours/Jails.html

Packer, H. (1968). *The limits of the criminal sanction.* Stanford, CA: Stanford University Press.

Perreault, S. (2015). *Criminal victimization in Canada, 2014.* Ottawa, ON: Statistics Canada, Minister of Industry. Retrieved from http://www.statcan.gc.ca/pub/85-002-x/2015001/article/14241-eng.pdf

Petrovsky, P. (2018, October 19). Milton woman charged with witchcraft. *InHalton.* Retrieved from https://www.inhalton.com/milton-woman-charged-with-witchcraft

Police Executive Research Forum. (2018). *The changing nature of crime and criminal investigations.* Washington, DC: Author.

Public Safety Canada. (2018). *Corrections and conditional release statistical overview, 2017.* Ottawa, ON: Author.

Roberts, J. V. (2016). Criminal justice in Canada: An overview. In J. V. Roberts & M. G. Grossman (Eds.), *Criminal justice in Canada: A reader* (5th ed.) (pp. 2–15). Toronto, ON: Nelson.

Robertson, N. (2012). Policing: Fundamental principles in a Canadian context. *Canadian Public Administration, 55*(3), 343–363.

Royal Canadian Mounted Police. (2014). *Missing and murdered Aboriginal women: A national operational overview.* Ottawa, ON: Author.

Royal Commission on the Donald Marshall, Jr., prosecution. (1989). Digest of findings and recommendations. Sydney, NS: Province of Nova Scotia.

Schwartz, Z. (2018, March 1). Canadian universities are failing students on sexual assault. *Maclean's* Retrieved from https://www.macleans.ca/education/university/canadian-universities-are-failing-students-on-sexual-assault/

Smith, J. (2014, June 11). Don't be fooled by the pro-prostitution lobby. *Winnipeg Free Press.* Retrieved from http://www.winnipegfreepress.com/opinion/analysis/dont-be-fooled-by-the-pro-prostitution-lobby-262654711.html

Statistics Canada. (2018a). *Incident based crime statistics, by detailed violations, police services in British Columbia* [Table 35-10-0184-01]. Retrieved from https://www150.statcan.gc.ca/t1/tbl1/en/tv.action?pid=3510018401

Statistics Canada. (2018b). *Labour statistics consistent with the System of National Accounts (SNA), by job category and industry* [Table 36-10-0489-01]. Retrieved from https://www150.statcan.gc.ca/t1/tbl1/en/tv.action?pid=3610048901

Surette, R. (2015). *Media, crime, and criminal justice: Images, realities, and policies* (5th ed.). Stamford, CT: Cengage learning.

Tyler, T. R., & Trinkner, R. (2017). *Why children follow rules: legal socialization and the development of legitimacy.* New York: Oxford University Press.

Volokh, A. (1997). Guilty men. *University of Pennsylvania Law Review, 146*(2), 173–216.

Waller, I. (2014). *Smarter crime control: A guide to a safer future for citizens, communities, and politicians.* Lanham, MD: Rowman & Littlefield.

Washington State Institute for Public Policy. (2018). *Benefit-cost results.* Retrieved from http://www.wsipp.wa.gov/BenefitCost

Wemmers, J. M. (2017). *Victimology: A Canadian perspective.* Toronto, ON: University of Toronto Press.

Chapter 2

Alberta MP Rural Crime Task Force. (2018). Toward a *safer* Alberta. Addressing rural crime. Retrieved from http://johnbarlowmp.ca/wp-content/uploads/2018/11/Toward-a-Safer-Alberta-AB-Rural-Crime-Task-Force-Report-FINAL.pdf

Allen, M. (2018). *Police-reported crime statistics in Canada, 2017.* Ottawa, ON: Canadian Centre for Justice Statistics.

Allen, M., & McCarthy, K. (2018). *Victims of police-reported violent crime in Canada: National, provincial and territorial fact sheets, 2016.* Ottawa, ON: Canadian Centre for Justice Statistics.

Allen, M., & Perreault, S. (2015). *Police-reported crime in Canada's provincial north and territories, 2013.* Ottawa, ON: Canadian Centre for Justice Statistics.

Association of Workers' Compensation Boards of Canada. (2018). *National work injury, disease and fatality statistics.* Retrieved from http://awcbc.org/wp-content/uploads/2018/03/National-Work-Injury-Disease-and-Fatality-Statistics-Publication-2015-2017.pdf

Beattie, S., David, J. D., & Roy, J. (2018). *Homicide in Canada, 2017.* Ottawa, ON: Canadian Centre for Justice Statistics.

Bittle, S. (2016). Criminal (in)justice: Responding to corporate crime in the workplace. In J. V. Roberts & M. G. Grossman (Eds.), *Criminal justice in Canada: A reader* (5th ed.) (pp. 324–337). Toronto, ON: Nelson.

Bolan, K. (2018, Jan. 15). Lack of "criminal" designation for Hells Angels in B.C. allows biker gang to flourish. *Vancouver Sun.* Retrieved from http://vancouversun.com/news/crime/will-a-b-c-court-finally-declare-the-hells-angels-a-criminal-organization

Burczycka, M., & Conroy, S. (2018). *Family violence in Canada: A statistical profile, 2016.* Ottawa, ON: Canadian Centre for Justice Statistics.

Burns, I. (2018, January 9). Low fine collection by securities regulators not due to lax enforcement, observers say. *The Lawyer's Daily.* Retrieved from https://www.thelawyersdaily.ca/articles/5615/low-fine-collection-by-securities-regulators-not-due-to-lax-enforcement-observers-say

Campigotto, J. (2019, February 11). A shocking portrait of sexual abuse in sports and some good advice for parents. *CBC Sports.* Retrieved from https://www.cbc.ca/sports/the-buzzer/the-buzzer-sexual-abuse-in-sports-1.5014821

Canadian Anti-Fraud Centre. (2018). *CAFC summary report: May 2018.* Data obtained from the Canadian Anti-Fraud Centre.

Canadian Broadcasting Corporation. (2011, October 1). Winnipeg crime prompts Air Canada hotel move. *CBC News.* Retrieved from http://www.cbc.ca/news/canada/manitoba/story/2011/10/01/air-canada-winnipeg-security.html

Canadian Broadcasting Corporation. (2017, December 6). Volkswagen executive gets 7 years in prison for emissions scandal. *CBC News.* Retrieved from https://www.cbc.ca/news/business/oliver-schmidt-sentencing-1.4436312

Canadian Centre for Child Protection. (2018). *Child sexual abuse by K-12 school personnel in Canada.* Winnipeg, MB: Author.

Canadian Press. (2017, November 10). Police in Newfoundland pulled over a driver who owed $158K in fines. *National Post.* Retrieved from http://nationalpost.com/news/canada/n-l-driver-with-158k-in-unpaid-fines-allegedly-caught-driving-with-no-licence

Castillo-Manzano, J. I., Castro-Nuno, M., & Fageda, X. (2015). Are traffic violators criminals? Searching for answers in the experiences of European Countries. *Transport Policy, 38*(1), 86–94.

Connolly, A. (2019, May 29). SNC-Lavalin will stand trial on criminal corruption charges, Quebec judge rules. *Global News.* Retrieved from https://globalnews.ca/news/5329173/snc-lavalin-criminal-trial/

Conroy, S., & Cotter, A. (2017). *Self-reported sexual assault in Canada, 2014.* Ottawa, ON: Canadian Centre for Justice Statistics.

Corbella, L. (2018, February 28). As rural crime soars, residents go to desperate measures to protect their property. *Calgary Herald.* Retrieved from http://calgaryherald.com/news/local-news/corbella-crime-epidemic-leaves-rural-families-frightened-in-their-homes

Cotter, A., & Beaupre, P. (2014). *Police-reported sexual offences against children and youth in Canada, 2012.* Ottawa, ON: Canadian Centre for Justice Statistics.

Coughlan, S., Yogis, J. A., & Cotter, C. (2013). *Canadian law dictionary* (7th ed.). Hauppauge, NY: Barron's.

Criminal Intelligence Service Canada. (2014). *Backgrounder on organized crime.* Retrieved from http://www.cisc.gc.ca/media/2014/2014-08-22-eng.htm

CTV News. (2017, June 15). Canadians at risk as counterfeit goods sneak through customs. Retrieved from https://www.ctvnews.ca/canada/canadians-at-risk-as-counterfeit-goods-sneak-through-customs-1.3460549

Dangerfield, K. (2018). Food fraud: 6 of the most commonly faked products and how to avoid them. *Global News.* Retrieved from https://globalnews.ca/news/4014182/food-fraud-avoiding-fake-product/

David, J. D. (2017). *Homicide in Canada, 2016.* Ottawa, ON: Canadian Centre for Justice Statistics.

DeAngelo, G. (2018, June 27). *CTSS empirical analysis.* Presentation at the combined traffic services Saskatchewan meeting, Regina, SK.

DeAngelo, G., & Hansen, B. (2014). Life and death in the fast lane: Police enforcement and traffic fatalities. *American Economic Journal: Economic Policy, 6*(2), 231–257.

Dentons Canada LLP. (2018, March 16). Canada's 2018 budget heralds introduction of deferred prosecution agreements for corporate wrongdoing. Retrieved from https://www.dentons.com/en/insights/alerts/2018/march/16/canadas-2018-budget-heralds-introduction-of-deferred-prosecution-agreements-for-corporate-wrongdoing

Department of Infrastructure and Regional Development. (2017). *Road trauma Australia 2016 statistical summary.* Canberra, Australia: Author.

Easton, S., Furness, H., & Brantingham, P. (2014). *The cost of crime in Canada.* Vancouver, BC: Fraser Institute. Retrieved from https://www.fraserinstitute.org/sites/default/files/cost-of-crime-in-canada.pdf

Feith, J., & Quan, D. (2018, March 1). Quebec mother who killed newborn ordered to take pregnancy tests every six months. *National Post.* Retrieved from http://nationalpost.com/news/canada/quebecer-who-pleaded-guilty-to-infanticide-must-get-pregnancy-tests-twice-a-year

Fitzgerald, R. T., & Carrington, P. J. (2011). Disproportionate minority contact in Canada: Police and visible minority youth. *Canadian Journal of Criminology and Criminal Justice, 53*(4), 449–486.

Fleiter, J., Watson, A., Watson, B., & Siskind, V. (2015). *Criminal histories of crash and non-crash involved Queensland speeding offenders: Evidence supporting the idea that we drive as we live.* 2015 Australasian Road Safety Conference, Gold Coast, Queensland.

Francisco, J. & Chenier, C. (2007). *A comparison of large urban, small urban and rural crime rates, 2005.* Ottawa, ON: Canadian Centre for Justice Statistics.

Freeze, C. (2017, September 17). RCMP shelved hundreds of organized-crime cases after terror attacks. *The Globe and Mail.* Retrieved from https://www.theglobeandmail.com/news/national/mounties-put-hundreds-of-files-on-hold-in-shift-toward-anti-terrorism/article36285597/

Gardner, G. (2018, January 19). Judge rejects GM ignition switch deal for car owners. *USA Today.* Retrieved from https://www.usatoday.com/story/money/cars/2018/01/19/judge-rejects-gm-ignition-switch-deal-car-owners/1047873001/

Goodman, M. (2015). *Future crimes.* Toronto, ON: Doubleday.

Government of Canada. (2018). *Detailed tables for the Canadian student tobacco, alcohol and drugs survey 2016-17.* Retrieved from https://www.canada.ca/en/health-canada/services/canadian-student-tobacco-alcohol-drugs-survey/2016-2017-supplementary-tables.html#t19

Hamilton, C. (2018, February 14). Frustrated and helpless: Rural residents say Stanley trial highlights crime, police response time concerns. *CBC News.* Retrieved from https://www.cbc.ca/news/canada/saskatoon/stanley-verdict-again-raising-concerns-over-rural-crime-1.4535146

Hamp-Gonsalves, D. (2019). *Halifax crime statistics.* Unpublished data obtained from the researcher.

Hayman, S. (2011). Older people in Canada: Their victimization and fear of crime. *Canadian Journal on Aging, 30*(3), 423–436.

Hodgkinson, T., Andresen, M. A., & Farrell, G. (2016). The decline and locational shift of automotive theft: A local level analysis. *Journal of Criminal Justice, 44*(1), 49–57.

Hoekstra, G. (2018, January 15). Hundreds of millions of penalties issued by B.C. Securities Commission going unpaid. *Vancouver Sun.* Retrieved from http://vancouversun.com/business/local-business/hundreds-of-millions-of-penalties-issued-by-b-c-securities-commission-going-unpaid

Holfeld, B., & Leadbeater, B. J. (2015). The nature and frequency of cyber bullying behaviors and victimization experiences in young Canadian children. *Canadian Journal of School Psychology, 30*(2), 116–135.

Hu, Y., Huang, S. Y., Hanner, R., Levin, J., & Lu, X. (2018). Study of fish products in Metro Vancouver using DNA barcoding reveals fraudulent labeling. *Food Control.* doi: 10.1016/j.foodcont.2018.06.023

Identity Theft Resource Center. (2017). *Identity theft: The aftermath 2017.* Retrieved from https://www.ftc.gov/system/files/documents/public_comments/2017/10/00004-141444.pdf

Insurance Bureau of Canada. (2019). *Top 10 stolen vehicles.* Retrieved from http://www.ibc.ca/on/auto/theft/top-ten-stolen-cars?p=National

Kauzlarich, D., & Rothe, D. L. (2014). Crimes of the powerful. In G. Bruinsma & D. Weisburd (Eds.), *Encyclopedia of criminology and criminal justice* (pp. 778–786). New York: Springer.

Kay, B. (2014, January 30). With Calgary court ruling on mom who dumped her babies, it's open season on unwanted infants. *National Post.* Retrieved from https://nationalpost.com/opinion/barbara-kay-with-calgary-court-ruling-on-mom-who-dumped-her-babies-its-open-season-on-unwanted-infants

Keighley, K. (2017). *Police-reported crime statistics in Canada, 2016.* Ottawa, ON: Canadian Centre for Justice Statistics.

Kramer, K. (2006). *Unwilling mothers, unwanted babies.* Vancouver, BC: University of British Columbia Press.

Layson, G. (2018, April 19). VW's $290M settlement with owners of 3-litre diesels gets court OK. *Automotive News Canada.* Retrieved from http://canada.autonews.com/article/20180419/CANADA/180419713/vw's-$290m-settlement-with-owners-of-3-litre-diesels-gets-court-ok

Linning, S. J., Andresen, M. A., Ghaseminejad, A. H., & Brantingham, P. J. (2017). Crime seasonality across multiple jurisdictions in British Columbia, Canada. *Canadian Journal of Criminology and Criminal Justice, 59*(2), 251–280.

Macnab, A. (2018, May 22). Protection against the state: Top 10 criminal law boutiques. *Canadian Lawyer.* Retrieved from https://www.canadianlawyermag.com/author/aidan-macnab/protection-against-the-state-top-10-criminal-law-boutiques-15722/

Markusoff, J. (2018, January 11). Loblaws' price-fixing may have cost you at least $400. *Maclean's.* Retrieved from https://www.macleans.ca/economy/economicanalysis/14-years-of-loblaws-bread-price-fixing-may-have-cost-you-at-least-400/

Maxwell, A. (2017). *Adult criminal court statistics in Canada, 2015/2016.* Ottawa, ON: Canadian Centre for Justice Statistics.

Mays, G. L., & Ruddell, R. (2019). *Making sense of criminal justice: Policies and practices* (3rd ed.). New York: Oxford University Press.

Miladinovic, Z. (2019). *Adult criminal and youth court statistics in Canada, 2016/2017.* Ottawa, ON: Canadian Centre for Justice Statistics.

Mothers Against Drunk Driving. (2018). *Alcohol and/or drugs among crash victims dying within 12 months of a crash on a public road, by jurisdiction: Canada, 2014.* Retrieved from https://madd.ca/pages/wp-content/uploads/2018/05/Alcohol-and-or-Drugs-Among-Crash-Victims-Dying-Within-12-Months2c-by-Jurisdiction-Canada2c-2014_April-202c-2018.pdf

Moulton, E. (2013). Myth and reality: Interpreting the dynamics of crime trends: Lies, damn lies and (criminal) statistics. *Police Practice and Research: An International Journal, 14*(3), 219–227.

Munch, C., & Silver, W. (2017). *Measuring organized crime in Canada: Results of a pilot project.* Ottawa, ON: Canadian Centre for Justice Statistics.

National Inquiry into Missing and Murdered Indigenous Women and Girls. (2019). *Reclaiming power and place.* Vancouver, BC: Author.

Newark, S. (2013). *Police-reported crime statistics in Canada: Still more questions than answers.* Ottawa, Ontario: Macdonald-Laurier Institute.

Ogrodnik, L. (2010). *Child and youth victims of police-reported crime, 2008.* Ottawa, ON: Canadian Center for Justice Statistics.

Perreault, S. (2015). *Criminal victimization in Canada, 2014.* Ottawa, ON: Statistics Canada, Minister of Industry. Retrieved from http://www.statcan.gc.ca/pub/85-002-x/2015001/article/14241-eng.pdf

Perreault, S. (2017). *Impaired driving in Canada, 2015.* Ottawa, ON: Canadian Centre for Justice Statistics.

Perreault. S. (2019). *Police-reported crime in rural and urban areas in the Canadian provinces, 2017.* Ottawa, ON: Canadian Centre for Justice Statistics.

Pierson, P. B., & Bucy, B. P. (2018). Trade fraud: The wild, new frontier of white collar crime. *Oregon Review of International Law, 19*(1), 1–91.

Police Executive Research Forum. (2018). *The changing nature of crime and criminal investigations.* Washington, DC: Author.

Pontell, H. N., Black, W. K., & Geis, G. (2014). Too big to fail, too powerful to jail? On the absence of criminal prosecutions after the 2008 financial meltdown. *Crime, Law, and Social Change, 61*(1), 1–13.

Price Waterhouse Coopers. (2018). *PWC's 2018 global economic crime survey, Canadian supplement.* Toronto, ON: Author.

Reiman, J., & Leighton, P. (2017). *The rich get richer and the poor get prison.* New York: Pearson.

Riddell, J., Pepler, D., & Craig, W. (2018). Cyberbullying in Canada. In A. C. Baldry, C. Blaya, & D. P. Farrington (Eds.) *International perspectives on cyberbullying* (pp. 39–64). London: Palgrave Macmillan.

Road Safety Education. (2015, July). Can we really make a difference? *RSE Newsletter*, 26. Retrieved from http://www.rse.org.au/wp-content/uploads/2015/08/Newsletter-2015-2.pdf

Robertson, G., & Cardoso, T. (2018, March 28). Ontario beefs up securities enforcement in budget, gives OSC new tools. *The Globe and Mail*. Retrieved from https://www.theglobeandmail.com/canada/article-ontario-beefs-up-securities-enforcement-in-budget-gives-osc-new-tools/

Schmidt, C. (2018, January 19). Operation cold start coaches hundreds of drivers about auto theft prevention. *CTV News*. Retrieved from https://calgary.ctvnews.ca/operation-cold-start-coaches-hundreds-of-drivers-about-auto-theft-prevention-1.3767083

Schneider, S. (2018). *Canadian organized crime*. Toronto, ON: Canadian Scholars Press.

Scott, H. (2015). Victims of crime. In N. Boyd (Ed.), *Understanding crime in Canada* (pp. 97–114). Toronto, ON: Emond Montgomery.

South Kesteven District Council. (2019). *What is anti-social behaviour?* Retrieved from http://www.southkesteven.gov.uk/index.aspx?articleid=8355

Statistics Canada. (2018a). *Crowdsourced cannabis prices, February, 2018*. Retrieved from https://www150.statcan.gc.ca/n1/daily-quotidien/180309/dq180309e-eng.htm

Statistics Canada. (2018b). *Evaluation of the Canadian Centre for Justice Statistics program (2011/2012 to 2015/2016)*. Ottawa, ON: Author.

Statistics Canada. (2018c). *Incident-based crime statistics, by detailed violations* [Table 35-10-0177-01]. Retrieved from https://www150.statcan.gc.ca/t1/tbl1/en/tv.action?pid=3510017701

Statistics Canada. (2019). *StatsCannabis data availability: Crowdsourced cannabis prices, fourth quarter 2018*. Ottawa, ON: Author.

Stow, N., & Akbar, J. (2018, December 19). London murder rate 2018 – how many murders have there been so far and which city has the world's highest murder rate? *The Sun*. Retrieved from https://www.thesun.co.uk/news/5963434/london-murder-rate-2018-city-highest-rate/

Transport Canada. (2019). *Canadian motor vehicle traffic collision statistics, 2017*. Ottawa, ON: Author.

Tremblay, P., & Sauvetre, N. (2014). "Jockeys and joyriders" revisited: Young offenders' involvement in motor vehicle thefts in the province of Quebec. *Canadian Journal of Criminology and Criminal Justice, 56*(2), 167–183.

Wallace, M., Turner, J., Matarazzo, A., & Babyak, C. (2009). *Measuring crime in Canada: Introducing the crime severity index and improvements to the uniform crime reporting survey*. Ottawa, ON: Canadian Centre for Justice Statistics.

Waller, I. (2014). *Smarter crime control: A guide to a safer future for citizens, communities, and politicians*. Lanham, MD: Rowman & Littlefield.

Will, S., Handelman, S., & Brotherton, D.C. (2013). *How they got away with it: White collar criminals and the financial meltdown*. New York: Columbia University Press.

Willett, T. C. (1964/2001). *Criminal on the road: A study of serious motoring offences and those who commit them*. London: Routledge.

Women's Legal Education and Action Fund. (2014). *R. v. LB. (Ontario Court of Appeal) Judgment March 2, 2011*. Retrieved from http://www.leaf.ca/cases/r-v-l-b-ontario-court-of-appeal/

World Health Organization. (2015). *Global status report on road safety, 2015*. Geneva, Switzerland: Author.

Chapter 3

Adam, B. A. (2014, January 2). Sentencing circles fall out of favour. *StarPhoenix* (Saskatoon), p. A1.

Alberta Civil Liberties Research Centre. (2015). What does access to justice mean for the homeless? Retrieved from http://www.aclrc.com/homelessness-and-access-to-justice/

Anderson, D. A. (2002). The deterrence hypothesis and picking pockets at the pickpocket's hanging. *American Law and Economics Review, 4*(2), 295–313.

Association of Workers' Compensation Boards of Canada. (2018). *National work injury, disease and fatality statistics*. Toronto, ON: Author.

Bala, N. (1997). *Young offenders law*. Concord, ON: Irwin Law.

Bala, N., & Carrington, P. J. (2016). The changing nature of youth justice: Assessing the impact of the *Youth Criminal Justice Act*. In J. V. Roberts & M. G. Grossman (Eds.), *Criminal justice in Canada: A reader* (5th ed.) (pp. 265–277). Toronto, ON: Nelson.

Beare, M. E., & Des Rosiers, N. (2015). Introduction. In M. E. Beare, N. Des Rosiers, & A. C. Deshman (Eds.), *Putting the state on trial: The policing of protest during the G20 summit* (pp. 3–22), Vancouver, BC: UBC Press.

Beattie, S., David, J. D., & Roy, J. (2018). *Homicide in Canada, 2017*. Ottawa, ON: Canadian Centre for Justice Statistics.

Bellemare, A. (2018, March 2). Stacks of tickets are "psychological weight" on marginalized itinerants, advocates say. *CBC News*. Retrieved from https://www.cbc.ca/news/canada/montreal/homeless-overticketed-montreal-police-1.4556351

Bittle, S. (2012). *Still dying for a living: Corporate criminal liability after the Westray mine disaster*. Vancouver, BC: UBC Press.

Blais, T. (2015, December 22). Crown appealing sentence for Edmonton man who killed Geo Mounsef. *Edmonton Sun*. Retrieved from http://www.edmontonsun.com/2015/12/22/crown-appealing-sentence-for-edmonton-man-who-killed-geo-mounsef

Boyce, J. (2016). *Victimization of Aboriginal people in Canada, 2014*. Ottawa, ON: Canadian Centre for Justice Statistics.

Bradbury, T. (2017). Man agrees to exile. *The Northern Pen*. Retrieved from https://www.northernpen.ca/news/local/man-agrees-to-exile-25530/

Braithwaite, J. (2018). Minimally sufficient deterrence. *Crime and Justice, 47*(1), 69–118.

Britto, S. (2015, October 22). *Justice in prime time: Media and crime related public perceptions*. Presented at the University of Regina, Saskatchewan.

Brzozowski, J., Taylor-Butts, A., & Johnson, S. (2006). *Victimization and offending among the Aboriginal population in Canada*. Ottawa, ON: Canadian Centre for Justice Statistics.

Bureau of Justice Statistics. (2018). Imprisonment rate of sentenced prisoners under the jurisdiction of state or federal correctional authorities per 100,000 US residents. Retrieved from http://www.bjs.gov/index.cfm?ty=nps

Bureau of Justice Statistics. (2019). *Corrections statistical analysis tool (CSAT) – prisoners*. Retrieved from https://www.bjs.gov/index.cfm?ty=nps

Canadian Broadcasting Corporation. (2012, May 8). Westray remembered: Explosion killed 26 NS coal miners in 1992. *CBC News*. Retrieved from http://www.cbc.ca/news/canada/nova-scotia/westray-remembered-explosion-killed-26-n-s-coal-miners-in-1992-1.1240122

Canadian Broadcasting Corporation. (2015, January 24). Geo Mounsef's mother condemns assault of accused drunk driver Richard Suter. *CBC News*. Retrieved from http://www.cbc.ca/news/canada/edmonton/geo-mounsef-s-mother-condemns-assault-of-accused-drunk-driver-richard-suter-1.2930734

Canadian Broadcasting Corporation. (2016, March 2). Homeless man's $110K in fines sign of "systemic" issue with police, advocate says. *CBC News*. Retrieved from http://www.cbc.ca/news/canada/montreal/montreal-homeless-man-100k-fines-1.3473707

Canadian Council of Academies. (2019). *The expert panel on policing in Indigenous communities*. Ottawa, ON: Author.

Canadian Press. (2014, May 21). "Gentle" Quebec man who slapped teen daughter to death after she failed to finish chores gets 60 days in jail. *National Post*. Retrieved from https://nationalpost.com/news/canada/quebec-man-who-slapped-his-13-year-old-daughter-so-hard-she-died-sentenced-to-60-days-in-jail

Canadian Resource Centre for Victims of Crime. (2011). *Restorative justice in Canada: What victims should know*. Ottawa, ON: Author.

Cesaroni, C., Grol, C., & Fredericks, K. (2018). Overrepresentation of Indigenous youth in Canada's criminal justice system: Perspectives of Indigenous young people. *Australian and New Zealand Journal of Criminology, 52*(1), 111–128.

Cesaroni, C., & Pelvin, H. (2016). Young people doing time: Consequences of custody for young offenders. In J. V. Roberts & M. G. Grossman (Eds.), *Criminal justice in Canada: A reader* (5th ed.) (pp. 278–292). Toronto, ON: Nelson.

Cole, S. A., & Dioso-Villa, R. (2011). Should judges worry about the "CSI effect"? *Court Review, 47*(1), 20–31.

Collins, M. E., & Loughran, T. A. (2017). Rational choice theory, heuristics, and biases. In W. Bernasco, J. van Gelder, & H. Elffers (Eds.) *The Oxford handbook of offender decision making* (pp. 10–23), New York: Oxford University Press.

Corrado, R. R., Kuehn, S., & Margaritescu, I. (2014). Policy issues regarding the overrepresentation of incarcerated Aboriginal young offenders in a Canadian context. *Youth Justice, 14*(1), 40–62.

Correctional Service of Canada. (2014a). *Corrections in Canada: A historical timeline*. Retrieved from http://www.csc-scc.gc.ca/about-us/006-2000-eng.shtml

Correctional Service of Canada. (2014b). *History of penitentiaries in Canada*. Retrieved from http://www.csc-scc.gc.ca/about-us/006-1006-eng.shtml

Courtemanche, Z. T. (2015). The *Restorative Justice Act*: An enhancement to justice in Manitoba? *Manitoba Law Journal, 38*(2), 1–16.

Death Penalty Information Center. (2019, March 12). *Facts about the Death Penalty*. Washington, DC: Author. Retrieved from http://www.deathpenaltyinfo.org/documents/FactSheet.pdf

Department of Justice. (2015). *Youth justice: Conference and committees*. Retrieved from http://www.justice.gc.ca/eng/cj-jp/yj-jj/tools-outils/sheets-feuillets/pdf/commi-comit.pdf

Desjarlais, B. (2001, Sept. 20). *Criminal code: Private members' business*. 37th Parliament, 1st session. Hansard, 82.

Douai, A., & Perry, B. (2018). A different lens? How ethnic minority media cover crime. *Canadian Journal of Criminology and Criminal Justice, 60*(1), 96–21.

Fagan, L. (2017, August 23). Indigenous peoples courts: How they can help offenders. *CBC News*. Retrieved from https://www.cbc.ca/news/canada/ottawa/how-indigenous-peoples-court-help-offenders-1.4258203

Federal Bureau of Investigation. (2018). *Crime in the United States, 2017*. Washington, DC: Author.

First Nations Information Governance Centre. (2018). *The First Nations regional health survey*. Retrieved from http://fnigc.ca/sites/default/files/docs/fnigc_rhs_phase_3_national_report_vol_1_en_final_sm_1.pdf

Gamson, W. A., Croteau, D., Hoynes, W., & Sasson, T. (1992). Media images and the social construction of reality. *Annual Review of Sociology, 18*, 373–93.

Gartner, R. (2011). Sex, gender and crime. In M. Tonry (Ed.), *Oxford handbook of crime and criminal justice* (pp. 348–384). New York: Oxford University Press.

Greenwood, P.W., & Abrahamse, A. (1982). *Selective incapacitation*. Santa Monica, CA: RAND Corporation.

Huey, L. (2010). "I've seen this on CSI": Criminal investigators' perceptions about the management of public expectations in the field. *Crime, Media, Culture: An International Journal, 6*(1), 49–68.

Huey, L. (2015). Understanding critical criminology. In N. Boyd (Ed.), *Understanding crime in Canada: An introduction to criminology* (pp. 193–212). Toronto, ON: Emond Montgomery Publications.

Johnson, J. (2016, June 17). Man who kidnapped, tortured Richard Suter to be sentenced in August. *CBC News*. Retrieved from https://www.cbc.ca/news/canada/edmonton/man-who-kidnapped-tortured-richard-suter-to-be-sentenced-in-august-1.3641571

Jones, N. A., Ruddell, R., & Winterdyk, J. (2017). Crime, political economy, and punishment: A cross-national analysis. *Bucharest University Annual Review, 16*(1), 20–34.

Kappeler, V. E., & Potter, G. W. (2018). *The mythology of crime and criminal justice* (5th ed). Long Grove, IL: Waveland Press.

Kelly, J. B., & Puddister, K. (2017). Criminal justice policy during the Harper era: Private member's bills, penal populism, and the *Criminal Code* of Canada. *Canadian Journal of Law and Society, 32*(3), 391–415.

Kennedy, J. L. D., Tuliao, A. P., Flower, K. N., Tibbs, J. J., & McChargue, D. E. (2018). Long-term effectiveness of a brief restorative justice intervention. *International Journal of Offender Therapy and Comparative Criminology, 63*(1), 3–17. doi: 10.1177/0306624X18779202

Lightstone, M. (2018, March 1). Restorative justice works well, but not in all cases: Ontario judge. *Halifax Today*. Retrieved from https://www.halifaxtoday.ca/local-news/restorative-justice-works-well-but-not-in-all-cases-ontario-judge-851534

Lilly, J. R., Cullen, F. T., & Ball, R. A. (2019). *Criminological theory: Context and consequences*. Thousand Oaks, CA: Sage.

Lithopoulos, S. (2013, October 16). *First nations policing policy/program (FNPP) update*. Presented at the University of Regina, Saskatchewan.

Lithopoulos, S., & Ruddell, R. (2016). Criminal justice and Aboriginal Canadians. In J. V. Roberts & M. G. Grossman (Eds.), *Criminal justice in Canada: A reader* (5th ed.) (pp. 186–198). Toronto, ON: Nelson.

MacDonald, M. (2017, May 9). Families mark the 25th anniversary of the Westray mine disaster. *Maclean's*. Retrieved from https://www.macleans.ca/news/canada/families-mark-the-25th-anniversary-of-the-westray-mine-disaster/

Macdonald, N. (2018, March 21). *Are prisons Canada's new residential schools?* University of Regina Stapleford lecture.

McDonald, S. (2010). "Explain please!" Working with victims and restitution. *Victims of Crime Research Digest, 3*, 9–14.

Malakieh, J. (2019). *Adult and youth correctional statistics in Canada, 2017/2018*. Ottawa, ON: Canadian Centre for Justice Statistics.

Maxwell, A. (2017). *Adult criminal court statistics in Canada, 2014/2015*. Ottawa, ON: Canadian Centre for Justice Statistics.

Maurutto, P., & Hannah-Moffat, K. (2016). Aboriginal knowledges in specialized courts: Emerging practices in Gladue courts. *Canadian Journal of Law and Society, 31*(3), 451–471.

Mays, G. L., & Ruddell, R. (2019). *Making sense of criminal justice: Policies and practices* (3rd ed.). New York: Oxford University Press.

Meng, Y. (2018). Profiling minorities: police stop and search procedures in Toronto, Canada. *Human Geographies, 11*(1), 5–23.

Miedema, A. (2015, April 8). *Criminal liability for OHS violations: A review of 10 years of Bill C-45 cases*. Webinar presented through Bongarde.

Miladinovic, Z. (2016). *Youth court statistics, 2014/2015*. Ottawa, ON: Canadian Centre for Justice Statistics.

Miladinovic, Z. (2019). *Adult criminal and youth court statistics in Canada, 2016/2017*. Ottawa, ON: Canadian Centre for Justice Statistics.

Montreal Gazette. (2019, March 11). Crown to appeal Quebec mosque gunman Alexandre Bissonnette's sentence. *Montreal Gazette*. Retrieved from https://montrealgazette.com/news/local-news/crown-to-appeal-quebec-mosque-gunman-alexandre-bissonnettes-sentence

Nagin, D. S. (2013). Deterrence in the twenty-first century. *Crime and Justice, 42*(1), 199–263.

Nova Scotia Public Prosecution Service. (2013). *National flagging system for high risk, violent offenders*. Halifax, NS: Author.

Packer, H. (1968). *The limits of the criminal sanction*. Stanford, CA: Stanford University Press.

Parrott, S., & Titcomb Parrott, C. (2015). US television's "mean world" for white women: The portrayal of gender and race on fictional crime dramas. *Sex Roles, 73*(1), 70–82.

Perreault, S. (2014). *Admissions to adult correctional services in Canada, 2011/2012*. Ottawa, ON: Canadian Centre for Justice Statistics.

Perreault, S. (2015). *Criminal victimization in Canada, 2014*. Ottawa, ON: Statistics Canada, Minister of Industry.

Peterson, J., Sommers, I., Baskin, D., & Johnson, D. (2010). *The role and impact of forensic evidence in the criminal justice process*. Los Angeles: California State University, Los Angeles.

Polischuk, H. (2015, November 12). Regina man approaching 100 break and enters sentenced to 32 months in latest court appearance. *Leader Post*. Retrieved from http://www.leaderpost.com/news/Regina+approaching+break+enters+sentenced+months+latest+court+appearance/11489643/story.html

Province of Nova Scotia. (1997). *The Westray story: A predictable path to disaster: Report of the Westray mine public inquiry, Justice K. Peter Richard, Commissioner*. Halifax, NS: Author.

Public Safety Canada. (2017). *Corrections and conditional release statistical overview, 2016*. Ottawa, ON: Author.

Public Safety Canada. (2018). *Corrections and conditional release statistical overview, 2017*. Ottawa, ON: Author.

Reale, K., Beauregard, E., & Martineau, M. (2017). Is investigative awareness a distinctive feature of sexual sadism? *Journal of Interpersonal Violence*. Published online ahead of print. doi: 10.1177/0886260517698824

Reiman, J., & Leighton, P. (2017). *The rich get richer and the poor get prison*. New York: Pearson.

Revell, P. (2018, June 9). Southern Alberta man up to 97 charges after another 25 added. *Medicine Hat News*. Retrieved from https://medicinehatnews.com/news/local-news/2018/06/09/southern-alberta-man-up-to-97-charges-after-another-25-added/

Rhodes, B. (2015, September 8). Nova Scotia criminals failing to make restitution in most cases. *CBC News*. Retrieved from https://www.cbc.ca/news/canada/nova-scotia/nova-scotia-criminals-failing-to-make-restitution-in-most-cases-1.3216482

Roberts, J. V. (2016). Criminal justice in Canada: An overview. In J. V. Roberts and M. G. Grossman (Eds.), *Criminal justice in Canada: A reader* (5th ed.) (pp. 2–15). Toronto, ON: Nelson.

Rocque, M., Posick, C., Haen Marshall, I., & Piquero, A. R. (2015). A comparative, cross-national criminal career analysis. *European Journal of Criminology, 12*(4), 400–419.

Romain, D. M., & Freiburger, T. L. (2016). Chivalry revisited: Gender, race/ethnicity, and offense type on domestic violence charge reduction. *Feminist Criminology, 11*(2), 191–222.

Royal Canadian Mounted Police. (2015). *Missing and murdered Aboriginal women: 2015 update to the national operational review*. Ottawa, ON: Author.

Royal Canadian Mounted Police. (2017a). *Forensic science and identification services key performance indicators*. Retrieved from http://www.rcmp-grc.gc.ca/en/forensic-science-and-identification-services-key-performance-indicators

Royal Canadian Mounted Police. (2017b). *The national DNA data bank of Canada*. Ottawa, ON: Author.

Royal Commission on Aboriginal Peoples. (1996). *Bridging the cultural divide: A report on Aboriginal peoples and criminal justice in Canada*. Ottawa, ON: Supply and Services Canada.

Rugge, T., & Cormier, R. (2013). Restorative justice in cases of serious crime: An evaluation. In E. Elliott & R. M Gordon (Eds.). *New directions in restorative justice* (pp. 266–277). New York: Willan.

Saskatchewan Ministry of Justice. (2018). *Sentencing circles*. Personal communication.

Savage, L. (2019). *Female offenders in Canada, 2017*. Ottawa, ON: Canadian Centre for Justice Statistics.

Savignac, J., & Dunbar, L. (2015). *Guide for selecting an effective crime prevention program*. Ottawa, ON: Public Safety Canada.

Serani, D. (2008). If it bleeds, it leads: The clinical implications of fear-based programming in news media. *Psychoanalysis & Psychotherapy, 24*(4), 240–250.

Smith, L. (2018, April 4). *Prolific offender takes the bait*. RCMP, Kelowna detachment Press Release. Retrieved from http://bc.rcmp-grc.gc.ca/ViewPage.action?siteNodeId=2087&languageId=1&contentId=54935

Standing Senate Committee on Human Rights Evidence. (2018). Testimony of Renee Acoby. *Senate of Canada*. Retrieved from https://sencanada.ca/en/Content/Sen/Committee/421/RIDR/54206-e

Statistics Canada. (2018). *Census profile, 2016 (Canada)*. Retrieved from https://www.statcan.gc.ca/eng/start

Statistics Canada. (2019a). *Average counts of adults in provincial and territorial corrections programs* [Table 35-10-0154-01]. Retrieved from https://www150.statcan.gc.ca/t1/tbl1/en/tv.action?pid=3510015401

Statistics Canada. (2019b). *Average counts of young persons in provincial and territorial correctional services* [Table 35-10-0003-01]. Retrieved from https://www150.statcan.gc.ca/t1/tbl1/en/tv.action?pid=3510000301

Statistics Canada. (2019c). *Youth admissions to correctional services, by Aboriginal identity and sex* [Table 35-10-0007-01]. Retrieved from https://www150.statcan.gc.ca/t1/tbl1/en/tv.action?pid=3510000701

Tonry, M. H. (2013). "Nothing" works: Sentencing "reform" in Canada and the United States. *Canadian Journal of Criminology and Criminal Justice, 55*(4), 465–480.

Truth and Reconciliation Commission of Canada. (2015). *Honouring the truth, reconciling for the future.* Ottawa, ON: Author.

von Hirsch, A. (1994). Proportionality in the philosophy of punishment. *Crime and Justice, 16*, 55–98.

Walmsley, R. (2016). *World prison population list* (11th ed.). London: Institute for Criminal Policy Research.

Wane, N. (2013). African Canadian women and the criminal justice system. In N. Wane, J. Jagire, & Z. Murad (Eds.), *Ruptures: Anti-colonial & anti-racist feminist theorizing* (pp. 107–125). Rotterdam: Sense Publishers.

Washington State Institute for Public Policy. (2018). *Benefit-cost results.* Retrieved from http://www.wsipp.wa.gov/BenefitCost

Wolfgang, M. & Tracy, P. E. (1982). *The 1945 and 1958 birth cohorts: A comparison of the prevalence, incidence, and severity of delinquent behavior.* University of Philadelphia, PA: Center for Studies in Criminology and Criminal Law.

Yarr, K. (2018, March 12). "Naive approach" or "having an impact"? Why P.E.I. jails drunk drivers. *CBC News.* Retrieved from https://www.cbc.ca/news/canada/prince-edward-island/pei-incarcerating-drunk-drivers-1.4572392

Zehr, H. (2014). *The little book of restorative justice.* New York: Good Books.

Chapter 4

Allen, M. (2014). *Victim services in Canada, 2011/2012.* Ottawa, ON: Canadian Centre for Justice Statistics.

Allen, M. (2018). *Police-reported crime statistics in Canada, 2017.* Ottawa, ON: Canadian Centre for Justice Statistics.

Anastakis, D. (2015). *Death in the peaceable kingdom: Canadian history since 1867 through murder, execution, assassination, and suicide.* Toronto, ON: University of Toronto Press.

Anderson, M. (2011). *In thrall to political change: Police and gendarmerie in France.* Oxford, UK: Oxford University Press.

Auditor General of Canada. (2014). *First nations policing program, Public Safety Canada.* Ottawa, ON: Author.

Barghout, C. (2018, February 23). Tina Fontaine met social workers, police and health care workers—but no one kept her safe. *CBC News.* Retrieved from https://www.cbc.ca/news/canada/manitoba/tina-fontaine-system-failed-1.4548314

Barnsley, P. (2002). Aboriginal policing underfunded from the start. *Windspeaker, 20*(5), n.p.

Baxter, M. (2018, February 2). Small towns can't afford independent policing, but don't know where to turn. *TVO.* Retrieved from https://tvo.org/article/current-affairs/small-towns-cant-afford-independent-policing-but-dont-know-where-to-turn

Beattie, S., David, J. D., & Roy, J. (2018). *Homicide in Canada, 2017.* Ottawa, ON: Canadian Centre for Justice Statistics.

Bradford, B., & Tiratelli, M. (2019). *Does stop and search reduce crime?* London: Centre for Crime and Justice Studies.

Broadbeck, T. (2018, February 22). Tina Fontaine murder case never had a chance. *Winnipeg Sun.* Retrieved from https://winnipegsun.com/opinion/columnists/tina-fontaine-murder-case-never-had-a-chance

Brunton-Smith, I., & Bullock, K. (2018). Patterns and drivers of co-production in neighbourhood watch in England and Wales: From neo-liberalism to new localism. *British Journal of Criminology, 59*(1), 85–106. doi:10.1093/bjc/azy012

Canadian Council of Academies. (2019). *The expert panel on policing in Indigenous communities.* Ottawa, ON: Author.

Canadian Press. (2018, January 31). Cause of Tina Fontaine's death could not be determined, forensic pathologist testifies. *The Globe and Mail.* Retrieved from https://www.theglobeandmail.com/news/national/cause-of-tina-fontaines-death-could-not-be-determined-forensic-pathologist-testifies/article37810077/

Carmichael, J. T., & Kent, S. L. (2015a). The use of lethal force by Canadian police officers: Assessing the influence of female police officers and minority threat explanations on police shootings across large cities. *American Journal of Criminal Justice, 40*(4), 703–721.

Carmichael, J. T., & Kent, S. L. (2015b). Structural determinants of municipal police force size in large cities across Canada: Assessing the applicability of ethnic threat theories in the Canadian context. *International Criminal Justice Review, 25*(3), 263–280.

City of Toronto. (2018). Budget.

Clairmont, D. (2013). Canada: Aboriginal. In M. K. Nalla & G. R. Newman (Eds.), *Community policing in Indigenous communities* (pp. 83–89). Boca Raton, FL: CRC Press.

Comack, E. (2012). *Racialized policing: Aboriginal people's encounters with the police.* Winnipeg, MB: Fernwood.

Conor, P. (2018). *Police resources in Canada, 2017.* Ottawa, ON: Canadian Centre for Justice Statistics.

Conor, P., Robson, J., & Marcellus, S. (2019). *Police resources in Canada, 2018.* Ottawa, ON: Canadian Centre for Justice Statistics.

Corsianos, M. (2009). *Policing and gendered justice: Examining the possibilities.* Toronto, ON: University of Toronto Press.

Dawson, M., & Hotton, T. (2014). Police charging practices for incidents of intimate partner violence in Canada. *Journal of Research in Crime and Delinquency, 51*(5), 655–683.

DeAngelo, G. (2018). *Combined traffic services Saskatchewan (CTSS): Preliminary quantitative results of Phase I.* Regina, SK: Collaborative Centre for Justice & Safety.

de Finney, S. (2017). Indigenous girls' resilience in settler states: Honouring body and land sovereignty. *Agenda, 31*(2), 10–21.

de Lint, W. (2004). *Public order policing in Canada: An analysis of operations in recent high stakes events.* Retrieved from http://www.archives.gov.on.ca/en/e_records/ipperwash/policy_part/research/pdf/deLint.pdf

Dhillon, S. (2018, June 15). Vancouver police department's use of carding disproportionately targets Indigenous people. *The Globe and Mail.* Retrieved from https://www.theglobeandmail.com/canada/british-columbia/article-vancouver-police-departments-use-of-carding-disproportionately/

Dobrin, A. (2006). Professional and community oriented policing: The Mayberry model. *Journal of Criminal Justice and Popular Culture, 13*(1), 19–28.

Dolski, M. (2013). Firefighters describe "colossal task" of battling "unprecedented" fire that engulfed downtown Lac-Megantic. *National Post*. Retrieved from http://news.nationalpost.com/2013/07/14/firefighters-describe-colossal-task-of-battling-unprecedented-fire-that-engulfed-downtown-lac-megantic/

Doolittle, R. (2017, February 3). Why police dismiss 1 in 5 sexual assault claims as baseless. *The Globe and Mail*. Retrieved from https://www.theglobeandmail.com/news/investigations/unfounded-sexual-assault-canada-main/article33891309/

Doucette, C. (2018, September 29). Killing carding: The deadly toll of putting street checks on ice. *Toronto Sun*. Retrieved from https://torontosun.com/news/local-news/killing-carding-the-deadly-toll-of-putting-street-checks-on-ice

Eurostat. (2019). *Personnel in the criminal justice system by sex – number and rate for the relevant sex group*. Retrieved from https://ec.europa.eu/eurostat/web/products-datasets/product?code=crim_just_job

Fair Change Community Legal Clinic. (2018, May 28). Evidence filed in Charter challenge of Safe Streets Act alleges infringements on Ontario's most vulnerable people [Press release]. Retrieved from https://static1.squarespace.com/static/5574f20ce4b0156262b571ed/t/5b15d02baa4a99890c4208bf/1528156207645/Fair+Change+Press+Release+-+May+28+2018+%281%29.pdf

Fanning, S. (2012). Forging a frontier: Social capital and Canada's Mounted Police, 1867–1914. *American Review of Canadian Studies, 42*(4), 515–529.

Finegan, S. (2013). Watching the watchers: The growing privatization of criminal law enforcement and the need for limits on neighborhood watch associations. *University of Massachusetts Law Review, 8*(1), 88–134.

Gillis, A. R. (1989). Crime and state surveillance in nineteenth-century France. *American Journal of Sociology, 95*(2), 307–341.

Griffiths, C. T., Montgomery, R., & Murphy, J. J. (2018). *City of Edmonton street checks policy and practice review*. Retrieved from https://edmontonpolicecommission.com/wp-content/uploads/2019/02/EPS-Street-Check-Study-Executive-Summary-June-26.pdf

Hayes, M., & Gray, J. (2018, June 28). Toronto area chief faults new Ontario restrictions on carding for rise in violent crime. *The Globe and Mail*. Retrieved from https://www.theglobeandmail.com/canada/article-toronto-area-police-chief-faults-new-ontario-restrictions-on-carding/

Heyer, G. den. (2018, March 12). Book review [Review of the book *The end of policing*, by A. Vitale.] *Policing: A Journal of Policy and Practice*. Retrieved from https://academic.oup.com/policing/advance-article/doi/10.1093/police/pay019/4930783

International Association of Chiefs of Police. (2014). *The death of community policing*. Alexandria, VA: Author.

Jones, N. A., Ruddell, R., Nestor, R., Quinn, K., & Phillips, B. (2014). *First Nations policing: A review of the literature*. Regina, SK: Collaborative Centre for Justice and Safety.

Kang, J. H. (2015). Participation in the community social control, the neighborhood watch groups: Individual- and neighborhood-related factors. *Crime & Delinquency, 61*(1), 188–212.

Kiedrowski, J., Jones, N. A., & Ruddell, R. (2017). "Set up to fail?" An analysis of self-administered Indigenous police services in Canada. *Police Practice and Research: An International Journal, 18*(6), 584–598.

Leighton, B. N. (2016). Community policing in Canada: The broad blue line. In J. V. Roberts & M. G. Grossman (Eds.), *Criminal justice in Canada: A reader* (5th ed.) (pp. 128–141). Toronto, ON: Nelson.

Lithopoulos, S. (2013, October 16). *First nations policing policy/program (FNPP) update*. Presented at the University of Regina, Saskatchewan.

Lithopoulos, S. (2014). *Municipal police amalgamation*. Unpublished paper (contains data from Statistics Canada, CANSIM tables 254-004 and 254-006).

Loader, I. (2016). In search of civic policing: Recasting the "Peelian" principles. *Criminal Law and Philosophy, 10*(3), 427–440.

McClearn, M., Freeze, C., & Dhillon, S. (2018, March 7). The RCMP's thin red line: Is contract policing unsustainable? *The Globe and Mail*. Retrieved from https://www.theglobeandmail.com/news/investigations/rcmp-contract-policing-investigation/article38085153/

McGahan, P., & Thomson, A. (2003). Valley policing: The pre-modern era. In A. Thomson, D. Clairmont, & L. Clairmont (Eds.), *Policing the valley: Small town and rural policing in Nova Scotia* (pp. 17–41). Halifax, NS: Dalhousie University Atlantic Institute of Criminology.

Macdonald, W. A. (2017, December 21). The rule of law still matters. *The Globe and Mail*. Retrieved from https://www.theglobeandmail.com/opinion/the-rule-of-law-still-matters/article37403020/

Maguire, S., & Dyke, L., (2012). *Survey results: CACP professionalism in policing research project*. Ottawa, ON: Canadian Association of Chiefs of Police.

Manitoba Advocate for Children and Youth. (2019). *A place where it feels like home: The story of Tina Fontaine*. Winnipeg, MB: Author.

Marchand, G. (2017, November 3). Online neighbourhood watch groups helpful, but must tread carefully. *CTV News*. Retrieved from https://winnipeg.ctvnews.ca/online-neighbourhood-watch-groups-helpful-but-must-tread-carefully-police-1.3663406

Marquis, G. (2016). *The vigilant eye: Policing Canada from 1867 to 9/11*. Winnipeg, MB: Fernwood Publishing.

Mathieu, E. (2018, May 29). Plight of panhandlers only made worse by fines, legal clinic says. *Toronto Star*. Retrieved from https://www.thestar.com/news/gta/2018/05/28/plight-of-panhandlers-only-made-worse-by-fines-legal-clinic-says.html

May, K. (2018, January 31). "There was pressure to solve this:" International attention affected how police investigated Fontaine murder, court told. *Winnipeg Free Press*. Retrieved from https://www.winnipegfreepress.com/local/tina-fontaines-cause-of-death-unknown-pathologist-471973853.html

Meares, T. L. (2017). Policing: A public good gone bad. *Boston Review*. Retrieved from https://bostonreview.net/law-justice/tracey-l-meares-policing-public-good-gone-bad

Meng, Y. (2017). Profiling minorities: Police stop and search practices in Toronto, Canada. *Human Geographies, 11*(1), 5–23.

Mohamed, B., & Walters, R. (2017, June 30). Opinion: Police carding is nothing but racial profiling. *Edmonton Journal*. Retrieved from https://edmontonjournal.com/opinion/columnists/opinion-carding-black-or-indigenous-people-is-nothing-but-racial-profiling

Molnar, A., Whelan, C., & Boyle, P. J. (2019). Securing the Brisbane 2014 G20 in the wake of the Toronto G20: "Failure-inspired" learning in public order policing. *British Journal of Criminology, 59*(1), 107–125.

Mugford, R. (2018). *First Nations police services.* Unpublished data. Ottawa, ON: Public Safety Canada.

National Academies of Science. (2018). *Proactive policing: Effects on crime and communities.* Washington DC: National Academies Press.

Ngo, H. V., Neote, K., Cala, C., Antonio, M., & Hickey, J. (2018). The experience of ethno-cultural members with racial profiling. *Journal of Ethnic & Cultural Diversity in Social Work, 27*(3), 253–270.

Nicholson, K. (2018, February 22). "I am not a saint": What Raymond Cormier revealed to CBC about the case against him in Tina Fontaine's death. *CBC News.* Retrieved from https://www.cbc.ca/news/canada/manitoba/raymond-cormier-conversation-with-cbc-1.4546319

Nilson, C. (2018). *Community safety and well-being.* Saskatoon, SK: Community Safety Knowledge Alliance.

O'Grady, B., Gaetz, S., & Buccieri, K. (2013). Tickets . . . and more tickets: A case study of the enforcement of the Ontario Safe Streets Act. *Canadian Public Policy, 39*(4), 541–558.

Ottawa Police Service. (2018). *Annual report, 2017.* Ottawa, ON: Author.

Page, J. (2018, July 4). 5 years after Lac-Megantic tragedy, residents still waiting to feel safe. *CBC News.* Retrieved from https://www.cbc.ca/news/canada/montreal/lac-megantic-five-years-rail-safety-questions-remain-1.4733803

Police Association of Ontario. (2014). A history of the PAO, 1933-1997. Retrieved from https://www.pao.ca/public/index.php?ref=history

Press, J., & Blatchford, A. (2015). New Lac-Megantic charges laid by federal government. *Canadian Press.* Retrieved from http://www.huffingtonpost.ca/2015/06/22/federal-government-lays-n_n_7637418.html

Robertson, N. (2012). Policing: Fundamental principles in a Canadian context. *Canadian Public Administration, 55*(3), 343–363.

Royal Canadian Mounted Police. (2018). *RCMP "F" division calls for service, 2012 to 2017.* Unpublished data obtained from the RCMP.

Royal Newfoundland Constabulary. (2018). *Corporate plan: 2018-2021.* St. John's, NL: Author.

Ruddell, R. (2017). *Policing rural Canada: Police, partners, and public safety.* Whitby, ON: de Sitter Publications.

Ruddell, R., & Jones, N. A. (2018, February 9). Policing the "middle of nowhere": Officer working strategies in isolated communities. *Policing: A Journal of Policy and Practice.* Published online ahead of print at https://academic.oup.com/policing/advance-article/doi/10.1093/police/pay007/4850523

Ruddell, R., Lithopoulos, S., & Jones, N.A. (2015). Crime, costs, and well-being: Policing Canadian Aboriginal Communities. *Policing: An International Journal of Police Strategies & Management.*

Ruddell, R., & Thomas, M. O. (2009). Does politics matter: Cross-national correlates of police strength. *Policing: An International Journal of Police Strategies & Management, 32*(4), 654–674.

Ruddell, R. & Thomas, M. O. (2015). Determinants of police strength in Canadian cities: Assessing the impact of minority threat. *Canadian Journal of Criminology and Criminal Justice, 57*(2), 215–252.

Schulenberg, J. (2014). Systematic social observation of police decision-making: The process, logistics, and challenges in a Canadian context. *Quality & Quantity, 48*(1), 297–315.

Shaw, D. (2019, March 4). Ten charts on the rise of knife crime in England and Wales. *BBC.* Retrieved from https://www.bbc.com/news/uk-42749089

Sheptycki, J. (2017). Contemporary reflections on the history of Canadian policing [Review of the book *The vigilant eye: Policing Canada from 1867 to 9/11,* by G. Marquis]. *Police Practice and Research, 18*(6), 624–629.

Smith, K. (2018, January 1). We were wrong about stop-and-frisk. *National Review.* Retrieved from https://www.nationalreview.com/2018/01/new-york-city-stop-and-frisk-crime-decline-conservatives-wrong/

South Kesteven District Council. (2019). *What is anti-social behaviour?* Retrieved from http://www.southkesteven.gov.uk/index.aspx?articleid=8355

Tanovich, D. M. (2006). *The colour of justice: Policing race in Canada.* Toronto: Irwin Law.

Thomson, A. (2003). The transformation of valley policing. In A. Thomson, D. Clairmont, & L. Clairmont (Eds.), *Policing the valley: Small town and rural policing in Nova Scotia* (pp. 42–71). Halifax, NS: Dalhousie University Atlantic Institute of Criminology.

Thomson, A., & Clairmont, D. (2013). Canada: The Annapolis Valley. In M. K. Nalla & G. R. Newman (Eds.), *Community policing in Indigenous communities* (pp. 91–98). Boca Raton, FL: CRC Press.

Tulloch, M. H. (2018). *Report of the independent street checks review.* Toronto, ON: Queen's Printer for Ontario.

van Steden, R., Miltenburg, E., & Boutellier, H. (2014). 101 things to do: Unravelling and interpreting community policing. *Policing, 8*(2), 144–153.

Waller, I. (2014). *Smarter crime control: A guide to a safer future for citizens, communities, and politicians.* Lanham, MD: Rowman & Littlefield.

Warnica, R. (2015, April 29). Toronto police chief won't abolish controversial practice of carding: "There will be an increase in crime." *National Post.* Retrieved from http://news.nationalpost.com/toronto/torontos-new-police-chief-wont-abolish-controversial-practice-of-carding-there-will-be-an-increase-in-crime

White, E. (2018, April 25). Espanola town council votes to disband local police force and hire OPP. *CBC News.* Retrieved from https://www.cbc.ca/news/canada/sudbury/espanola-police-opp-1.4634334

Chapter 5

Alberton, A. M., & Gorey, K. M. (2018). Contact is a stronger predictor of attitudes toward police than race: a state-of-the-art review. *Policing: An International Journal of Police Strategies & Management, 41*(1), 2–23.

Allen, G., & Jackson, L. (2018). *Police service strength.* London: UK Parliament, House of Commons Library.

Association of Workers' Compensation Boards of Canada. (2019). *National work injury/disease statistics program.* Toronto, ON: Author.

Australian Federal Police. (2018). *AFP staff statistics.* Retrieved from https://www.afp.gov.au/news-media/facts-and-stats/afp-staff-statistics

Bayley, D. H., & Nixon, C. (2010). *The changing environment for policing, 1985–2008.* Cambridge, MA: Harvard Kennedy School.

Beattie, S., David, J. D., & Roy, J. (2018). *Homicide in Canada, 2017.* Ottawa, ON: Canadian Centre for Justice Statistics.

Berman, P. (2018, June 18). Nova Scotia's police watchdog 'spread too thin.' *CBC News.* Retrieved from https://www.cbc.ca/news/canada/nova-scotia/nova-scotia-police-watchdog-spread-thin-need-more-investigators-1.4711366

Bikos, L. J. (2016). "I took the blue pill": The effect of the hegemonic masculine police culture on Canadian policewomen's identities. MA Research Paper 7, University of Western Ontario.

Boivin, R., & Obartel, P. (2017). Visitor inflows and police use of force in a Canadian city. *Canadian Journal of Criminology and Criminal Justice, 59*(3), 373–396.

Braga, A., A., Sousa, W. H., Coldren, J. R., & Rodriguez, D. (2018). The effects of body-worn cameras on police activity and police-citizen encounters: A randomized controlled trial. *Journal of Criminal Law and Criminology, 108*(3), 511–538.

Bud, T. K. (2016). The risk and risks of police body-worn cameras in Canada. *Surveillance & Society, 14*(1), 117–123

Bueckert, K. (2019, January 4). Nine police suicides prompt review from Ontario's chief coroner. *CBC News.* Retrieved from https://www.cbc.ca/news/canada/kitchener-waterloo/ontario-police-officer-suicides-chief-coroner-expert-panel-1.4966154

Campeau, H. (2015). Making sense of police oversight. *British Journal of Criminology, 55*(4), 669–687.

Canadian Broadcasting Corporation. (2017, September 29). RCMP failed to provide equipment, training in Moncton shootings, judge says. *CBC News.* Retrieved from https://www.cbc.ca/news/canada/new-brunswick/rcmp-labour-code-trial-moncton-shooting-1.4312673

Canadian Broadcasting Corporation. (2018a, April 24). Officer praised after taking down Toronto van attack suspect without gunfire. *CBC News.* Retrieved from https://www.cbc.ca/news/canada/toronto/officer-praised-taking-van-attack-suspect-custody-peaceful-1.4632661

Canadian Broadcasting Corporation. (2018b, June 14). Lisa Dudley murder inquest recommends better follow-up in cases of potentially 'grievous' injuries. *CBC News.* Retrieved from https://www.cbc.ca/news/canada/british-columbia/lisa-dudley-murder-inquest-1.4707271

Canadian Broadcasting Corporation. (2019, February 19). Attorney General announces major changes to Ontario's police oversight system. *CBC News.* Retrieved from https://www.cbc.ca/news/canada/toronto/ontario-attorney-general-news-conference-1.5024326

Canadian Civil Liberties Association. (2016, April 19). Stingrays: It's time for transparency. Retrieved from https://ccla.org/stingrays-its-time-for-transparency/

Canadian Police and Peace Officer's Memorial. (2018). *Honour roll.* Retrieved from https://www.thememorial.ca/memorial/index/honourroll

Cao, L. (2011). Visible minorities and confidence in the police. *Canadian Journal of Criminology and Criminal Justice, 53*(1), 1–26.

Cao, L. (2014). Aboriginal people and confidence in the police. *Canadian Journal of Criminology and Criminal Justice, 56*(5), 499–525.

Carleton, R. N., Afifi, T. O., Turner, S., Taillieu, T., Duranceau, S., LeBouthillier, D. M., … Asmundson, G. J. G. (2018a). Mental health disorder symptoms among public safety personnel in Canada. *The Canadian Journal of Psychiatry, 63*(1), 54–64.

Carleton, R. N., Afifi, T. O., Turner, S., Taillieu, T., LeBouthillier, D. M., Duranceau, S., … Asmundson, G. J. G. (2018b). Suicidal ideation, plans, and attempts among public safety personnel in Canada. *Canadian Psychology, 59*(3), 220–231. doi: 10.1037/cap0000136

Chrismas, R. (2013). *Canadian policing in the 21st century.* Montreal: McGill-Queen's University Press.

Civilian Review and Complaints Commission for the RCMP. (2018). *Annual report 2017-2018.* Ottawa, ON: Author.

Clark, M., Davidson, R., Hanrahan, V., & Taylor, N. (2017). Public trust in policing: A global search for the genetic code to inform policy and practice in Canada. *Journal of Community Safety & Well-Being, 2*(3), 101–111.

Conor, P. (2018). *Police resources in Canada, 2017.* Ottawa, ON: Canadian Centre for Justice Statistics.

Conor, P., Robson, J., Marcellus, S. (2019). *Police resources in Canada, 2018.* Ottawa, ON: Canadian Centre for Justice Statistics.

Cordner, G. (2017). Police culture: Individual and organizational differences in police officer perspectives. *Policing: An International Journal of Police Strategies & Management, 40*(1), 11–25.

Cordner, G. W. (2019). *Police administration.* New York: Routledge.

Cordner, G., & Cordner, A. M. (2011). Stuck on a plateau? Obstacles to recruitment, selection, and retention of women police. *Police Quarterly, 14*(3), 207–226.

Corsianos, M. (2009). *Policing and gendered justice: Examining the possibilities.* Toronto, ON: University of Toronto Press.

Cotter, A. (2015). *Spotlight on Canadians: Results from the General Social Survey: Public confidence in Canadian institutions.* Ottawa, ON: Statistics Canada.

Criminal Intelligence Service Canada. (2014). *Backgrounder on organized crime.* Retrieved from http://www.cisc.gc.ca/media/2014/2014-08-22-eng.htm

CTV News Vancouver. (2017, February 10). 10-year sentence for the last man convicted in Dudley, McKay murders. Retrieved from https://bc.ctvnews.ca/10-year-sentence-for-last-man-convicted-in-dudley-mckay-murders-1.3280104

Davis, S. (2018, January 10). Hundreds of police misconduct cases dealt with in secret. *CityNews.* Retrieved from https://toronto.citynews.ca/2018/01/10/hundreds-police-misconduct-cases-dealt-secret/

DeAngelo, G. (2018). *Combined traffic services Saskatchewan (CTSS): Preliminary quantitative results of phase I.* Regina, SK: Collaborative Centre for Justice & Safety.

Dion, A. (2017, September 29). RCMP found guilty of negligence in Moncton shootings. *Ottawa Life Magazine.* Retrieved from https://www.ottawalife.com/article/rcmp-found-guilty-of-negligence-in-moncton-shootings

Duxbury, L., & Bennell, C. (2018). *Assigning value to Peel Regional Police's school resource officer program.* Ottawa, ON: Carleton University.

Duxbury, L., Bennell, C., Halinski, M., & Murphy, S. (2018). Change or be changed: Diagnosing the readiness to change in the Canadian policing sector. *The Police Journal: Theory, Practice and Principles, 91*(4), 316–338. doi: 10.1177/0032258X17740317

Duxbury, L., & Higgins, C. (2012). *Caring for and about those who serve: Work-life conflict and employee well-being within Canada's police departments.* Ottawa, ON: Sprott School of Business.

Fasman, J. (2018). More data and surveillance are transforming justice systems. *The Economist.* Retrieved from https://www.economist.com/technology-quarterly/2018-05-02/justice

Federal Bureau of Investigation. (2017). *Crime in the United States, 2016.* Washington, DC: Author.

Ferdik, F., Rojek, J., & Alpert, G. P. (2013). Civilian oversight in the United States and Canada: An overview. *Police Practice and Research, 14*(2), 104–116.

Germano, D. (2018, July 13). Ontario court doesn't have jurisdiction to hear proposed class-action lawsuit against Waterloo police. Retrieved from https://globalnews.ca/news/4331634/ontario-superior-court-class-action-lawsuit-waterloo-police/

Hall, C., Votova, K., & Wood, D. (2013). *Prospective analysis of police use of force in four Canadian cities: Nature of events and their outcomes.* Ottawa, ON: Defence Research and Development Canada.

Hall, R. G. (2002). *A brief discussion of police culture and how it affects police responses to internal investigations and civilian oversight.* Ottawa, ON: Canadian Association for Civilian Oversight of Law Enforcement.

Hayes, M. (2017, November 13). Police seize illicit drugs in four-year investigation as opioid crisis grows in Canada. *The Globe and Mail.* Retrieved from https://www.theglobeandmail.com/news/national/rcmp-announce-major-drug-bust-with-links-to-organized-crime-in-canada-us/article36893016/

Hogan, J., Bennell, C., & Taylor, A. (2011). The challenges of moving into middle management: Responses from police officers. *Journal of Police and Criminal Psychology, 26*(2), 100–111.

Houlihan, R., & Seglins, D. (2018a, January 31). RCMP harassment claims could hit 4,000 in wake of #MeToo, lawyers say. *CBC News.* Retrieved from https://www.cbc.ca/news/investigates/rcmp-harassment-claims-could-hit-4-000-in-wake-of-metoo-lawyers-say-1.4510891

Houlihan, R., & Seglins, D. (2018b, June 25). RCMP faces $1.1B lawsuit over bullying, harassment claims dating back decades. *CBC News.* Retrieved from https://www.cbc.ca/news/canada/rcmp-bullying-harassment-claims-lawsuit-1.4720126

Huey, L., Cyr, K., & Ricciardelli, R. (2016). Austerity policing's imperative. *International Journal of Police Science & Management, 18*(2), 133–139.

Iacobucci, F. (2014). *Police encounters with people in crisis.* Toronto, ON: Toronto Police Service.

Insight West. (2016). *Nurses and farmers seen as Canada's most respected professions.* Retrieved from https://insightswest.com/news/nurses-and-farmers-seen-as-canadas-most-respected-professions/

Insight West. (2017). *Nurses, doctors and scientists are Canada's most respected professionals.* Retrieved from https://insightswest.com/news/nurses-doctors-and-scientists-are-canadas-most-respected-professionals/

Ipsos Reid. (2012). Life-savers, medical professionals top the list of most trusted professionals. Retrieved from http://www.ipsos.com/en-ca/news-polls/life-savers-medical-professionals-top-list-most-trusted-professionals

Jain, H. C. (1987). Recruitment of racial minorities in Canadian police forces. *Industrial Relations, 42*(4), 790–805.

Jain, H. C., Singh, P., & Agocs, C. (2000). Recruitment, selection and promotion of visible-minority and aboriginal police officers in selected Canadian police services. *Canadian Public Administration, 42*(3), 46–74.

Karp, A. (2018). *Estimating global civilian-held firearms numbers.* Geneva, Switzerland: Small Arms Survey.

Khenti, A. (2014). The Canadian war on drugs: Structural violence and unequal treatment of Black Canadians. *International Journal of Drug Policy, 25*(2), 190–195.

Kiedrowski, J., Ruddell, R., & Petrunik, M. (2017). Police civilianization in Canada: A mixed methods investigation. *Policing and Society: An International Journal of Research and Policy, 9*(2), 204–222. doi: 10.1080/10439463.2017.1281925

Langan, D., Sanders, C.B., & Gouweloos, J. (2018). Policing women's bodies: Pregnancy, embodiment, and gender relations in Canadian police work. *Feminist Criminology.* Published online ahead of print. doi:10.1177/1557085118763083

Lord, V. (2014). Police responses in officer-involved violent deaths: Comparison of suicide by cop and non-suicide by cop incidents. *Police Quarterly, 17*(1), 79–100.

Lott, J. R. (2017). *Concealed carry permit holders across the United States: 2017.* Crime Prevention Research Center. Retrieved from https://papers.ssrn.com/sol3/papers.cfm?abstract_id=3004915

Lum, C., & Nagin, D. (2017). Reinventing American policing. *Crime and Justice, 46*(1), 339–393.

McGuckin, A. (2018, April 26). Winnipeg police service working to recruit next round of cadets. *Global News.* Retrieved from https://globalnews.ca/news/4169682/winnipeg-police-service-working-to-recruit-next-round-of-cadets/

Marcoux, J., & Nicholson, K. (2018). *Deadly force: Fatal encounters with police in Canada: 2000-2017. CBC News.* Retrieved from https://newsinteractives.cbc.ca/longform-custom/deadly-force

Mays, G. L., & Ruddell, R. (2019). *Making sense of criminal justice: Policies and Practices* (3rd ed.). New York: Oxford University Press.

Meares, T. L. (2017, August 1). Policing: A public good gone bad. *Boston Review.* Retrieved from https://bostonreview.net/law-justice/tracey-l-meares-policing-public-good-gone-bad

Millie, A. (2013). The policing task and the expansion (and contraction) of British policing. *Criminology & Criminal Justice, 13*(2), 143–160.

Mills, K. (2019, June 24). "I feel free" says mother of BC murder victim after daughter's belongings returned. *Maple Ridge-Pitt Meadows News.* Retrieved from https://www.mapleridgenews.com/news/i-feel-free-says-mother-of-bc-murder-victim-after-daughters-belongings-returned/

Mohandie, K., Meloy, J. R., & Collins, P. I. (2009). Suicide by cop among officer-involved shooting cases. *Journal of Forensic Science, 54*(2), 456–462.

Montgomery, R., & Griffiths, C. T. (2015). *The use of private security services for policing.* Ottawa, ON: Public Safety Canada.

Murphy, C., & McKenna, C. (2007). *Rethinking police governance, culture and management.* Halifax, NS: Dalhousie University.

Nasser, S. (2017, November 22). Canada's largest school board votes to end armed police presence in schools. *CBC News.* Retrieved from https://www.cbc.ca/news/canada/toronto/school-resource-officers-toronto-board-police-1.4415064

National Post. (2014, October 23). Masked gunman killed after Canadian solider, Cpl. Nathan Cirillo, fatally shot at National War Memorial. *National Post.* Retrieved from https://nationalpost.com/news/canada/soldier-shot-outside-of-parliament-at-national-war-memorial-active-shooter-believed-to-be-on-the-loose

Office of the Independent Police Review Director. (2018). *Annual report 2017–2018.* Toronto, ON: Author.

Oriola, T. B., Rollwagen, H., Neverson, N., & Adeyanju, C. T. (2016). *Public support for conducted energy weapons: Evidence from the 2014 Alberta survey, 58*(4), 530–564.

Police Association of Ontario. (2018, March 8). *Ontario's police associations: Bill 175 disappoints police with changes that do not reflect the reality of policing in Ontario.* Press Release: Author.

Police Executive Research Forum. (2018). *The changing nature of crime and criminal investigations.* Washington, DC: Author.

Police Sector Council. (2013). *A guide to competency-based management in police services.* Ottawa, ON: Author.

Police Sector Council. (2018). *Constable competency profile.* Ottawa, ON: Author.

Prenzler, T., Mihinjac, M., & Porter, L. E. (2013). Reconciling stakeholder interests in police complaints and discipline systems. *Police Practice and Research, 14*(2), 155–168.

Public Safety Canada. (2012, January 25). *Economics of policing.* Presentation delivered to the ministers responsible for justice and public safety. Charlottetown, PEI.

Reiner, R. (2010). *The politics of the police* (4th ed.). New York, NY: Oxford University Press.

Reuters. (2019). Factbox: U.S. communities rethinking taser use after deaths. Retrieved from https://www.reuters.com/article/us-usa-taser-deaths-factbox/factbox-u-s-communities-rethinking-taser-use-after-deaths-idUSKCN1PToZN

Robertson, N. (2012). Policing: Fundamental principles in a Canadian context. *Canadian Public Administration, 55*(3), 343–363.

Royal Canadian Mounted Police. (2018a). Canadians' views of RCMP policing services 2017-2018. Retrieved from http://www.rcmp-grc.gc.ca/en/canadians-views-rcmp-policing-services-2016

Royal Canadian Mounted Police. (2018b). *Commissioner's mandate letter.* Retrieved from http://www.rcmp-grc.gc.ca/about-ausujet/mand-eng.htm

Roziere, B., & Walby, K. (2018). The expansion and normalization of police militarization in Canada. *Critical Criminology, 26*(1), 29–48.

Ruddell, R., & Eaton, J. (2015). *Reviewer's report on the proposed honours B.A. program in policing at Wilfrid Laurier University.* Unpublished report.

Saskatchewan Police Commission. (2018). *Annual report for 2017–18.* Regina, SK: Author.

Sawa, T., Ivany, K., & Kelley, M. (2019, March 10). *Officer down. The Fifth Estate.* Retrieved from https://newsinteractives.cbc.ca/longform/ontario-provincial-police-suicide

Schafer, J. A. & Varano, S. P. (2017). Change in police organizations: Perceptions, experiences, and the failure to launch. *Journal of Contemporary Criminal Justice, 33*(4), 392–410.

Schneider, S. (2018). *Canadian organized crime.* Toronto, ON: Canadian Scholars Press.

Special Investigations Unit. (2018). *Annual Report, 2017.* Toronto, ON: Author.

Sprott, J. B., & Doob, A. N. (2014). Confidence in the police: Variation across groups classified as visible minorities. *Canadian Journal of Criminology and Criminal Justice, 56*(3), 367–379.

Statistics Canada. (2018a). *Aboriginal peoples highlight tables, 2016 census.* Retrieved from https://www12.statcan.gc.ca/census-recensement/2016/dp-pd/hlt-fst/abo-aut/index-eng.cfm

Statistics Canada. (2018b). *Homicide victims and persons accused of homicide by age group and sex* [Table 35-10-0070-01]. Retrieved from https://www12.statcan.gc.ca/t1/tbl1/en/tv.action?pid=3510007001

Statistics Canada. (2018c). *Immigration and ethnocultural diversity highlight tables, 2016.* Retrieved from https://www12.statcan.gc.ca/census-recensement/2016/dp-pd/hlt-fst/imm/index-eng.cfm

Statistics Canada. (2018d). *Incident-based crime statistics, by detailed violations, Canada, provinces, territories and census metropolitan areas* [(Table 35-10-0177-01)]. Retrieved from https://www150.statcan.gc.ca/t1/tbl1/en/tv.action?pid=3510017701

Statistics Canada. (2018e). *Labour statistics consistent with the system of national accounts by job category and industry* [Table 36-10-0489-01]. Retrieved from https://www12.statcan.gc.ca/t1/tbl1/en/tv.action?pid=3610048901

Stone, L. (2017, June 30). RCMP's Bob Paulson sounds alarm on organized crime in exit interview. *The Globe and Mail.* Retrieved from https://beta.theglobeandmail.com/news/politics/rcmps-bob-paulson-sounds-alarm-on-organized-crime-in-exit-interview/article35507580/

Tonry, M. (2017). From policing to parole: Reconfiguring American criminal justice. *Crime and Justice, 46*(1), 1–25.

Toronto Police Service. (2016). Aboriginal Peacekeeping Unit. Retrieved from http://www.torontopolice.on.ca/community/aboriginal.php

Transport Canada. (2019). *Canadian motor vehicle traffic collision statistics, 2017.* Retrieved from https://www.tc.gc.ca/eng/motorvehiclesafety/canadian-motor-vehicle-traffic-collision-statistics-2017.html

Tutton, M. (2017, July 10). Single Atlantic police watchdog proposed, though questions raised on mandate. *The Globe and Mail.* Retrieved from https://www.theglobeandmail.com/news/national/single-atlantic-police-watchdog-proposed-though-questions-raised-on-mandate/article35648698/

Tyler, T. R. (2006). *Why people obey the law.* Princeton, NJ: Princeton University Press.

Underwood, C. (2018, November 21). Calgary's 1st female police chief says same problems plague force 23 years later. *CBC News.* Retrieved from https://www.cbc.ca/news/canada/calgary/christine-silverberg-calgary-police-1.4914068

Valiante, G. (2019, February 10). "Not ready for prime time": Montreal rejects body cameras for police officers. *The National Post.* Retrieved from https://nationalpost.com/pmn/news-pmn/canada-news-pmn/not-ready-for-prime-time-montreal-rejects-body-cameras-for-police-officers

Waby, M. (2016). Scenes from the life of a police officer. In J. V. Roberts & M. G. Grossman (Eds.), *Criminal justice in Canada: A reader* (5th ed.) (pp. 41–50). Toronto, ON: Nelson.

Washington Post. (2018). *Fatal force* [2017 database of police shootings]. Retrieved from https://www.washingtonpost.com/graphics/national/police-shootings-2017/

Wilson, J. Q. (1968). *Varieties of police behavior: The management of law and order in eight communities.* Cambridge, MA: Harvard University Press.

Winnipeg Police Service. (2019). *Salary level.* Retrieved from https://www.winnipeg.ca/police/policerecruiting/officer/benefits.aspx

Wittmann, N. (2018). *Independent review of use of force in the Calgary police service.* Retrieved from http://www.calgary.ca/cps/Pages/Use-of-Force-Review.aspx

Woodward, J. (2016, September 6). Guilty plea in 2008 murders of Dudley, McKay in Mission. *CTV News Vancouver.* Retrieved from https://bc.ctvnews.ca/guilty-plea-in-2008-murders-of-dudley-mckay-in-mission-1.3060196

Zhao, J., & Hassell, K. D. (2005). Policing styles and organizational priorities: Retesting Wilson's theory of local political culture. *Police Quarterly, 8*(4), 411–430.

Chapter 6

Allen, M. (2018). *Police-reported crime statistics in Canada, 2017.* Ottawa, ON: Canadian Centre for Justice Statistics.

Armstrong, A. (2019). *Police-reported hate crime in Canada.* Ottawa, ON: Canadian Centre for Justice Statistics.

Azpiri, J., & Daya, R. (2018, January 16). RCMP spent almost $1 million in overtime on undercover anti-terrorism operation. *Global News.* Retrieved from https://globalnews.ca/news/3969463/rcmp-spent-1m-on-victoria-terror-plot-investigation-including-90k-on-nuttall-and-korody/

Baehre, R. (1981). Pauper emigration to Upper Canada in the 1830s. *Histoire sociale/Social History, 14*(28), 339–367.

Boudreau, D. (2016). *How big are Jian Ghomeshi's legal bills going to be?* Retrieved from http://www.danielleboudreau.ca/recent-work/2016/2/9/how-big-are-jian-ghomeshis-legal-bills-going-to-be

Boyce, J., Rotenberg, C., & Karam, M. (2015). *Mental health and contact with the police in Canada, 2012.* Ottawa, ON: Canadian Centre for Justice Statistics.

Breay, C., & Harrison, J. (2015). *Magna Carta: Law, liberty, legacy.* London: British Library.

Bresge, A., & Tutton, M. (2016). Charges in "sexting" ring a quandary for Nova Scotia town, and for experts. *The Globe and Mail.* Retrieved from http://www.theglobeandmail.com/news/national/charges-in-sexting-ring-a-quandary-for-nova-scotia-town-and-for-experts/article31400376/

Bruineman, M. (2018). The right price. *Canadian Lawyer Magazine,* April, 20–25. Retrieved from https://www.canadianlawyermag.com/staticcontent/AttachedDocs/CL_Apr_18_LegalFees Survey.pdf

Burczycka, M. (2018). *Violent victimization of Canadians with mental health-related disabilities, 2014.* Ottawa, ON: Canadian Centre for Justice Statistics.

Campbell, H. (2018, March 6). Killers with dementia: Canada's overlooked criminal defendants. *The Lawyer's Daily.* Retrieved from https://www.thelawyersdaily.ca/articles/6010/killers-with-dementia-canada-s-overlooked-criminal-defendants

Canadian Bar Association. (2015, July 14). *Legal aid in Canada: The costs of inadequate legal aid services.* Retrieved from http://www.cba.org/Sections/Legal-Aid-Liaison/Resources/Resources/Legal-Aid-in-Canada

Canadian Broadcasting Corporation. (2012, May 22). Greyhound killer believed man he beheaded was an alien. *CBC News.* Retrieved from https://www.cbc.ca/news/canada/manitoba/greyhound-killer-believed-man-he-beheaded-was-an-alien-1.1131575

Canadian Broadcasting Corporation. (2015, May 26). John Nuttall, Amanda Korody, accused BC terrorists, were manipulated by undercover cops: Defence lawyer. *The Canadian Press.* Retrieved from http://www.cbc.ca/news/canada/british-columbia/john-nuttall-amanda-korody-accused-b-c-terrorists-were-manipulated-by-undercover-cops-defence-lawyer-1.3088771

Canadian Broadcasting Corporation. (2017, December 17). Beverley McLachlin on her controversies, activism, supreme court legacy. *CBC News.* Retrieved from https://www.cbc.ca/news/thenational/beverley-mclachlin-supreme-court-chief-justice-interview-1.4446434

Canadian Broadcasting Corporation. (2018, March 23). More Canadians are acting as their own lawyer because they don't have a choice. *CBC Radio.* Retrieved from https://www.cbc.ca/radio/thesundayedition/the-sunday-edition-march-25-2018-1.4589621/more-canadians-are-acting-as-their-own-lawyer-because-they-don-t-have-a-choice-1.4589633

Canadian Broadcasting Corporation. (2018, January 29). One year later: Anniversary of mosque attack marked by events, vigils across Canada. *CBC News.* Retrieved from https://www.cbc.ca/news/canada/montreal/quebec-city-mosque-shooting-anniversary-events-1.4507943

Canadian Judicial Council. (2006). *Statement of principles on self-represented litigants and accused persons.* Ottawa, ON: Author.

Canadian Press. (2018, December 19). B.C. Appeal Court upholds stay in terror case over alleged bomb plot. Retrieved from https://www.ctvnews.ca/canada/b-c-appeal-court-upholds-stay-in-terror-case-over-alleged-bomb-plot-1.4223861

Chaster, S. (2018). Cruel, unusual, and constitutionally infirm: Mandatory minimum sentences in Canada. *Appeal, 23*(1), 89–119.

Cotter, A. (2015). *Spotlight on Canadians: Results from the General Social Survey: Public confidence in Canadian institutions.* Ottawa, ON: Statistics Canada.

Cotton, D., & Coleman, T. (2010). Canadian police agencies and their interactions with persons with a mental illness: a systems approach. *Police Practice and Research: An International Journal, 11*(4), 301–314.

Coughlan, S., Yogis, J. A., & Cotter, C. (2013). *Canadian law dictionary* (7th ed.). Hauppauge, NY: Barron's.

Death Penalty Information Center. (2019, March 12). *Facts about the death penalty.* Washington, DC: Author. Retrieved from http://www.deathpenaltyinfo.org/documents/FactSheet.pdf

Defence Group. (2018). *What is an alibi?* Retrieved from http://www.defencegroup.ca/blog/court-process/what-is-an-alibi/

Department of Justice. (2019). *Legal aid in Canada, 2017-18.* Ottawa, ON: Author.

Duhaime's Law Dictionary. (2018). Battered woman syndrome definition. Retrieved from http://www.duhaime.org/LegalDictionary/B/BatteredWomanSyndrome.aspx

Dunn, T. (2017, December 13). Laura Babcock's dad asked that he not be questioned by daughter's accused killer, but judge allowed it. *CBC News.* Retrieved from https://www.cbc.ca/news/canada/toronto/babcock-witnesses-millard-self-represent-1.4442636

Dupuis, M. D. (2015). *Legal aid in Canada, 2013/2014.* Ottawa, ON: Canadian Centre for Justice Statistics.

Edwards, P. (2017, October 31). Second man charged in Vaughan café explosion. *Toronto Star.* Retrieved from https://www.

thestar.com/news/gta/2017/10/31/second-man-charged-in-vaughan-caf-explosion.html

Ellwood Evidence Inc. (2014). How the Canadian legal system differs from American. Retrieved from http://ellwoodevidence.com/articles/2014/3/14/how-the-canadian-legal-system-differs-from-american

Forsey, E. A. (1980/2012). *How Canadians govern themselves* (8th ed.). Ottawa, ON: Library of Parliament.

Friesen, E. S. (2012). *We live and move and have our being.* Victoria, BC: Friesen Press.

Government of Canada. (2017). *Guide to the Canadian Charter of Rights and Freedoms.* Retrieved from https://www.canada.ca/en/canadian-heritage/services/how-rights-protected/guide-canadian-charter-rights-freedoms.html

Hann, R. G., Nuffield, J., Meredith, C., & Svoboda, M. (2002). *Court site study of adult unrepresented accused in the provincial criminal courts, part I: Overview report.* Legal Aid Research Series. Department of Justice Canada. Retrieved from http://www.justice.gc.ca/eng/rp-pr/csj-sjc/ccs-ajc/rr03_la2-rr03_aj2/rr03_la2.pdf

Harris, K. (2019, February 27). Wilson-Raybould says she faced pressure, "veiled threats" on SNC-Lavalin; Scheer calls on PM to resign. *CBC News.* Retrieved from https://www.cbc.ca/news/politics/wilson-raybould-testifies-justice-committee-1.5035219

Herault, C. (2019, July 18). Largest mafia bust in Ontario history: 15 arrests, $35 million worth of homes seized. *CTV News.* Retrieved from https://toronto.ctvnews.ca/largest-mafia-bust-in-ontario-history-15-arrests-35-million-worth-of-homes-seized-1.4513261

Innocence Project. (2019). *Eyewitness misidentification.* Retrieved from https://www.innocenceproject.org/causes/eyewitness-misidentification/

McCann, K. (2013). *Policing and the mentally ill: A review of issues related to mental health apprehensions by police in British Columbia.* Vancouver, BC: International Centre for Criminal Law Reform and Criminal Justice Policy

McLachlin, B. (2013, May 27). *Administrative tribunals and the courts: An evolutionary relationship.* Sixth annual conference of the Council of Canadian Administrative Tribunals, Toronto, Ontario. Retrieved from http://www.scc-csc.ca/judges-juges/spe-dis/bm-2013-05-27-eng.aspx

Miladinovic, Z. & Lukassen, J. (2014). *Verdicts of not criminally responsible on account of mental disorder in adult criminal courts, 2005/2006–2011/2012.* Ottawa, ON: Canadian Centre for Justice Statistics.

Mok, T. (2013). Saskatchewan woman who was fleeing for her life acquitted of "necessary" drunk driving in "unusual" case. *National Post.* Retrieved from http://news.nationalpost.com/2013/10/14/saskatchewan-woman-who-was-fleeing-for-her-life-acquitted-of-necessary-drunk-driving-in-unusual-case/

Myrah, J. (2012). Criminal law: Final outline. Retrieved from http://uviclss.ca/outlines/Myrah%20-%20LAW%20102%20-%20Final.pdf

National Self-Represented Litigants Project. (2015, June 23). *Incarcerating self-represented litigants for overzealous advocacy.* Retrieved from https://representingyourselfcanada.com/incarcerating-self-represented-litigants-for-overzealous-advocacy/

Nowlin, C. (2018). Canada's provocation reform and the need to revisit culpability in "loss of control" cases. *Canadian Criminal Law Review, 23*(1), 43–75.

Office of the Correctional Investigator. (2017). *Annual report, 2016-2017.* Ottawa, ON: Author.

Packer, H. (1968). *The limits of the criminal sanction.* Stanford, CA: Stanford University Press.

Palmer, A. (2019). *Mental health care in extended care facilities.* Personal communication.

Pernanen, K., Cousineau, M., Brochu, S., & Sun, F. (2002). *Proportions of crimes associated with alcohol and other drugs in Canada.* Ottawa, ON: Canadian Centre on Substance Abuse.

Perreault, S. (2015). *Criminal victimization in Canada, 2014.* Ottawa, ON: Statistics Canada, Minister of Industry. Retrieved from http://www.statcan.gc.ca/pub/85-002-x/2015001/article/14241-eng.pdf

Perry, B. (2011). *Diversity, crime, and justice in Canada.* Don Mills, ON: Oxford University Press.

Pfaff, J. (2017). *Locked in: The true causes of mass incarceration and how to achieve real reform.* New York: Basic Books.

Plucknett, T. F. T. (2010). *A concise history of the common law* (5th ed.). Clark, NJ: Lawbook Exchange.

Provincial Court of British Columbia. (2018a). *Do Canadian judges use gavels?* Retrieved from http://www.provincialcourt.bc.ca/enews/enews-08-05-2018

Provincial Court of British Columbia. (2018b). *Provincial court of BC annual report 2016/2017.* Vancouver, BC: Author.

Ruby, C., & Enenajor, A. (2017, November 22). Self-represented defendants in murder cases. *The Lawyer's Daily.* Retrieved from https://www.thelawyersdaily.ca/articles/5235/self-represented-defendants-in-murder-cases-clayton-ruby-and-annamaria-enenajor

Sentis. (2015). *Legal services society: 2015 public opinion poll.* Vancouver, BC: Author.

Sheehy, E., Stubbs, J., & Tolmie, J. (2017). When self-defence fails. *University of New South Wales Law Research Series.* Retrieved from https://papers.ssrn.com/sol3/papers.cfm?abstract_id=3047141

Stewart, H. (2012). *Fundamental justice: Section 7 of the Canadian Charter of Rights and Freedoms.* Toronto, ON: Irwin Law.

Tyler, T. R. (2006). *Why people obey the law.* Princeton, NJ: Princeton University Press.

Walker, S. (2015). *Sense and nonsense about crime and drugs* (8th ed.). Belmont, CA: Thomson Wadsworth.

Warren, J. (2018, January 28). Betting on the Super Bowl in Canada shouldn't be illegal. *Toronto Sun.* Retrieved from https://torontosun.com/opinion/columnists/warren-betting-on-the-super-bowl-in-canada-shouldnt-be-illegal

Zakreski, D. (2018, June 29). Need a legal aid lawyer in Saskatoon? Get ready to phone a Regina call centre. *CBC News.* Retrieved from https://www.cbc.ca/news/canada/saskatoon/need-a-legal-aid-lawyer-in-saskatoon-get-ready-to-phone-a-regina-call-centre-1.4729417

Chapter 7

Addario, F. (2015, February 16). Role of defence counsel poorly understood. *Toronto Star.* Retrieved from http://www.thestar.com/opinion/commentary/2015/02/16/role-of-defence-counsel-poorly-understood.html

Alberta Justice and Solicitor General. (2013). *Best practices for investigating and prosecuting sexual assault.* Edmonton, AB: Author.

Alberta Justice and Solicitor General. (2018). *Defence counsel roles and responsibilities.* Edmonton, AB: Author.

Angus Reid Institute. (2018). *Confidence in the justice system: Visible minorities have less faith in courts than other*

Canadians. Retrieved from http://angusreid.org/wp-content/uploads/2018/02/2018.02.20_justice-system.pdf

Baxter, J., & Yoon, A. (2014). No lawyer for a hundred miles: Mapping the new geography of access to justice in Canada. *Osgoode Hall Law Journal, 52*(1), 9–57.

Bellin, J. (2015). Justice for the 1 percent: A corrupt governor stays free, those who should have never been jailed die there. *Popular media*. Retrieved from http://scholarship.law.wm.edu/popular_media/390/

Bernard, R. (2018, March 13). Anonymous and the new ace of hacktivisim: What to look out for in 2018. *Digital Shadows* blog. Retrieved from https://www.digitalshadows.com/blog-and-research/anonymous-and-the-new-face-of-hacktivism-what-to-look-out-for-in-2018/

British Columbia Ministry of Justice. (2016). *Role of crown counsel*. Retrieved from https://www2.gov.bc.ca/assets/gov/law-crime-and-justice/criminal-justice/prosecution-service/information-sheets/infosheet_role-crowncounsel.pdf

British Columbia Ministry of Justice. (2018). *Court registry services*. Retrieved from https://www2.gov.bc.ca/gov/content/justice/courthouse-services/courthouse-roles/court-registry-services

British Columbia Prosecution Service. (2017). *Bail (conditional release)*. Retrieved from https://www2.gov.bc.ca/assets/gov/law-crime-and-justice/criminal-justice/prosecution-service/information-sheets/infosheet_bail_conditional_release. pdf

Campbell, K. M., & Denov, M. (2016). Wrongful convictions in Canada: Causes, consequences, and responses. In J. V. Roberts & M G. Grossman (Eds.), *Criminal justice in Canada: A reader* (5th ed.) (pp. 225–242). Toronto, ON: Nelson.

Canadian Bar Association. (2013). *The future of legal services in Canada: Trends and issues*. Ottawa, ON: Author.

Canadian Broadcasting Corporation. (2010a, August 31). Choosing judges in Canada. *CBC News*. Retrieved from http://www.cbc.ca/news/canada/choosing-judges-in-canada-1.866668

Canadian Broadcasting Corporation. (2010b, December 6). "Compassionate homicide": The law and Robert Latimer. *CBC News*. Retrieved from http://www.cbc.ca/news/canada/compassionate-homicide-the-law-and-robert-latimer-1.972561

Canadian Broadcasting Corporation. (2018, April 12). "I have a right to be named": Child pornography survivor fails to lift publication ban. *CBC Radio*. Retrieved from https://www.cbc.ca/radio/thecurrent/the-current-for-april-11-2018-1.4613272/i-have-a-right-to-be-named-child-pornography-survivor-fails-to-lift-publication-ban-1.4613443

Canadian Civil Liberties Association. (2014). *Set up to fail: Bail and the revolving door of pre-trial detention*. Toronto, ON: Author.

Canadian Press. (2016, April 21). Mike Duffy leaves an Ottawa court a free man. *The Guardian* (Charlottetown). Retrieved from http://www.theguardian.pe.ca/News/Local/Mike-Duffy-leaves-an-Ottawa-court-a-free-man-101518/

Canadian Press. (2018, April 6). N.S. justice minister says province is still fine-tuning cyberbullying law. *Global News*. Retrieved from https://globalnews.ca/news/4128343/n-s-cyberbullying-law/

Canales, D., Campbell, M. A., & McTague, J. (2017). *Problem solving court evaluation: Survey results addendum*. St. John, NB: Centre for Criminal Justice Studies.

Carling, A. (2018, May 23). Pleading guilty when innocent: A truth for too many Indigenous people. *The Globe and Mail*. Retrieved from https://www.theglobeandmail.com/opinion/article-pleading-guilty-when-innocent-a-truth-for-too-many-indigenous-people/

Casper, J., & Brereton, D. (1984). Evaluating criminal justice reforms. *Law & Society Review, 18*(1), 121–144.

Cole, D. P. (2016). A day in the life of a judge. In J. V. Roberts & M G. Grossman (Eds.), *Criminal justice in Canada: A reader* (5th ed.) (pp. 75–90). Toronto, ON: Nelson.

Cotter, A. (2015). *Spotlight on Canadians: Results from the General Social Survey: Public confidence in Canadian institutions*. Ottawa, ON: Statistics Canada.

Davis, K. M., Peterson-Badali, M., Weagant, B., & Skilling, T. A. (2015). A process evaluation of Toronto's first youth mental health court. *Canadian Journal of Criminology and Criminal Justice, 57*(2), 159–187.

DePalma, A. (1997). Father's killing of Canadian girl: Mercy or murder? *New York Times*. Retrieved from http://www.nytimes.com/1997/12/01/world/father-s-killing-of-canadian-girl-mercy-or-murder.html

Department of Justice. (2016). *How does Canada's court system work?* Retrieved from http://www.justice.gc.ca/eng/csj-sjc/ccs-ajc/01.html

Department of Justice. (2017). *Indigenous courtwork program*. Retrieved from http://www.justice.gc.ca/eng/fund-fina/gov-gouv/acp-apc/index.html

Department of Justice and Public Safety, Newfoundland and Labrador. (2007). *Guide book of policies and procedures for the conduct of criminal prosecutions in Newfoundland and Labrador*. St John's, NL: Author.

Doob, A. N. (2014, January). *Research on public confidence in the criminal justice system: A compendium of research findings from Criminological Highlights*. Ottawa, ON: Sixth Annual Reinventing Criminal Justice Symposium.

Fennario, T. (2015, March 18). Imported justice: A look inside Quebec's travelling court in Nunavik. *APTN National News*. Retrieved from http://aptn.ca/news/2015/03/18/imported-justice-a-look-inside-quebecs-travelling-court-in-nunavik/

Ferrazzi, P., & Krupa, T. (2016). "Symptoms of something all around us": Mental health, Inuit culture, and criminal justice in Arctic communities in Nunavut, Canada. *Social Science & Medicine, 165* (September), 159–167.

Fine, S. (2017, April 13). New advisory committees could- change the face of Canada's judiciary. *The Globe and Mail*. Retrieved from https://www.theglobeandmail.com/news/national/new-advisory-committees-could-change-the-face-of-canadas-judiciary/article33699039/

Fraser, K. (2018, January 2). Ivan Henry files response to lawsuit alleging he sexually assaulted 5 women. *Vancouver Sun*. Retrieved from https://vancouversun.com/news/local-news/henry-files-response-to-lawsuit-alleging-he-sexually-assaulted-5-women

Grech, D. C. (2017). Culture before law? Comparing bail decision-making in England and Canada. Ph.D. dissertation, University of Leeds.

Griffiths, C. T., Murphy, J. J., & Tatz, M. (2015). *Improving police efficiency: Challenges and opportunities*. Ottawa, ON: Public Safety Canada.

Hannah-Moffat, K., & Maurutto, P. (2012). Shifting and targeted forms of penal governance: Bail, punishment and specialized courts. *Theoretical Criminology, 16*(2), 201–219.

Ipsos Reid. (1999). Three quarters (73%) of Canadians believe Robert Latimer ended his daughter's life out of compassion. Retrieved from https://www.ipsos.com/en-ca/

three-quarters-73-canadians-believe-robert-latimer-ended-his-daughters-life-out-compassion

Irish, D. (2017, April 28). Opioid court celebrates 'incredible progress' of 1st female graduate. *CBC News*. Retrieved from https://www.cbc.ca/news/canada/nova-scotia/special-opioid-court-danielle-macpherson-follow-1.4089789

Lutze, F. E. (2014). *Professional lives of community corrections officers*. Thousand Oaks, CA: Sage.

McKnight, P. (2016). The funhouse mirror: Media misrepresentations of crime and justice. In J. V. Roberts & M. G. Grossman (Eds.), *Criminal justice in Canada: A reader* (5th ed.) (pp. 28–38). Toronto, ON: Nelson.

MacPherson, A. (2017, October 31). "What I did was right": Robert Latimer steadfast 24 years after daughter's death. *StarPhoenix* (Saskatoon). Retrieved from https://thestarphoenix.com/news/local-news/robert-latimer-mclachlin

Malakieh, J. (2019). *Adult and youth correctional statistics in Canada, 2017/2018*. Ottawa, ON: Canadian Centre for Justice Statistics.

Manitoba Justice. (2018). *The criminal case: Step-by-step*. Retrieved from https://www.gov.mb.ca/justice/prosecutions/stepbystep.html

Medwick, H., & Chudley, A. E. (2018). A global research collaboration on fetal alcohol spectrum disorder. *Biochemistry and Cell Biology, 96*(2), vii–viii.

Michalski, J. H. (2017). Mental health issues and the Canadian criminal justice system. *Contemporary Justice Review, 20*(1), 2–25.

Miladinovic, Z. (2019). *Adult criminal and youth court statistics in Canada, 2016/2017*. Ottawa, ON: Canadian Centre for Justice Statistics.

Moch, J. (2018, July 9). Open court principle: ABCA agrees with less than full disclosure in some cases. *ABlawg*. Retrieved from http://ablawg.ca/wp-content/uploads/2018/07/Blog_JM_APTN_July2018.pdf

Mulgrew, I. (2016, Nov. 21). Provincial stubbornness rewarded in Ivan Henry case. *Vancouver Sun*. Retrieved from https://vancouversun.com/opinion/columnists/ian-mulgrew-provincial-stubbornness-rewarded-in-ivan-henry-case

Murchison, M. J. (2013). *Law, morality and social discourse: Jury nullification in a Canadian context* (Research Paper No. 21). Belfast, Ireland: Queen's University Belfast Law.

National Institute of Justice, United States. (2017, August 23). Drug courts (number and types of drug courts). Retrieved from http://www.nij.gov/topics/courts/drug-courts/Pages/welcome.aspx

Office of the Commissioner for Federal Judicial Affairs Canada. (2019). *Number of federally appointed judges as of March 1, 2019*. Retrieved from http://www.fja.gc.ca/appointments-nominations/judges-juges-eng.aspx

Omand, G. (2015, August 3). Rehtaeh Parsons' father says Anonymous hackers needed for "broken" justice system. *Toronto Star*. Retrieved from http://www.thestar.com/news/canada/2015/08/03/rehtaeh-parsons-father-says-anonymous-hackers-needed-for-broken-justice-system.html

Ontario Ministry of the Attorney General. (2015). The criminal appeal process in Ontario. Retrieved from http://www.attorneygeneral.jus.gov.on.ca/english/about/pubs/criminal_appeal.php

Pfaff, J. (2017). *Locked in: The true causes of mass incarceration and how to achieve real reform*. New York: Basic Books.

Postmedia News. (2017, January 14). Small-town justice: In rural Saskatchewan, a curling rink doubles as a courtroom. *National Post*. Retrieved from https://nationalpost.com/news/canada/small-town-justice-in-rural-saskatchewan-a-curling-rink-doubles-as-a-courtroom

Previl, S. (2019, June 23). Jurors with PTSD advocate for greater mental health support during, after trials. *Global News*. Retrieved from https://globalnews.ca/news/5363654/jury-duty-ptsd-mental-health-support-canada/

Quirouette, M., Hannah-Moffat, K., & Maurutto, P. (2016). "A precarious place": Housing and clients of specialized courts. *British Journal of Criminology, 56*(1), 370–388.

Renaud, G. (2016). The decision to detain or release: The nuts and bolts of bail. In J. V. Roberts & M. G. Grossman (Eds.), *Criminal Justice in Canada: A reader* (5th ed.) (pp. 157–167). Toronto, ON: Nelson.

Roach, K. (2017). Reforming and resisting criminal law: Criminal justice and the tragically hip. *Manitoba Law Journal, 40*(3), 1–51.

Roach, K. (2018, February 28). The urgent need to reform jury selection after the Gerald Stanley and Colten Boushie case. *University of Toronto Faculty of Law Faculty Blog*. Retrieved from https://www.law.utoronto.ca/blog/faculty/urgent-need-reform-jury-selection-after-gerald-stanley-and-colten-boushie-case

Roberts, J. V. (2016). Criminal justice in Canada: An overview. In J. V. Roberts and M. G. Grossman (Eds.), *Criminal justice in Canada: A reader* (5th ed.) (pp. 2–15). Toronto, ON: Nelson.

Saskatchewan Provincial Court Judges Association. (2011). *Submission to the Saskatchewan Provincial Court Association*. Regina, SK: Author.

Scassa, T. (2018, May 1). Ontario court rules that open courts principle trumps privacy; finds part of Ontario's access to information law unconstitutional. *Teresa Scassa blog*. Retrieved from http://www.teresascassa.ca/index.php?option=com_k2&view=item&id=275:ontario-court-rules-that-open-courts-principle-trumps-privacy-finds-part-of-ontarios-access-to-information-law-unconstitutional

Senate of Canada. (2019). *Perspectives* – February 19-21, 2019. Retrieved from https://sencanada.ca/en/sencaplus/opinion/perspectives-february-19-21-2019/

Somers, J. M., Rezansoff, S. N., & Moniruzzaman, A. (2014). Comparative analysis of recidivism outcomes following drug treatment court in Vancouver, Canada. *International Journal of Offender Therapy and Comparative Criminology, 58*(6), 655–671.

Strong, S. M., Rantala, R. R., Kyckelhahn, T. (2016). *Census of problem-solving courts, 2012*. Washington, DC: Bureau of Justice Statistics.

Supreme Court of Canada. (2018). *Applications for leave submitted*. Retrieved from https://www.scc-csc.ca/case-dossier/stat/cat2-eng.aspx#cat2a

Sylvestre, M., Damon, W., Blomley, N., & Bellot, C. (2015). Spatial tactics in criminal courts and the politics of legal technicalities. *Antipode, 47*(5), 1346–1366.

Verdun-Jones, S. N. (2016). Plea bargaining. In J. V. Roberts & M G. Grossman (Eds.), *Criminal justice in Canada: A reader* (5th ed.) (pp. 168–184). Toronto, ON: Nelson.

Washington State Institute for Public Policy. (2018). *Benefit-cost results*. Olympia, WA: Author.

World Justice Project. (2019). *World justice project rule of law index 2019*. Washington, DC: Author.

Chapter 8

Allen, M. (2017). *Mandatory minimum penalties: An analysis of criminal justice system outcomes for selected offences.* Ottawa, ON: Canadian Centre for Justice Statistics.

Allen, M. (2018). *Police-reported crime statistics in Canada, 2017.* Ottawa, ON: Canadian Centre for Justice Statistics.

Amoud, T. C. (2014, Summer). From east to north: A perspective on the application of *Gladue* in the Northwest Territories. *Arctic Obiter*, 13–15.

April, S., & Orsi, M. M. (2013). *Gladue practices in the provinces and territories.* Ottawa, ON: Department of Justice Canada.

BC Laws. (2017). *Correction Act Regulation:* Division 4 – Performance appraisal and earned remission. Retrieved from http://www.bclaws.ca/Recon/document/ID/freeside/10_58_2005#division_d2e3311

Beattie, S., David, J. D., & Roy, J. (2018). *Homicide in Canada, 2017.* Ottawa: ON: Canadian Centre for Justice Statistics.

Berglund, N. (2017). Norway may stop sending prisoners to the Netherlands. *News in English.no.* Retrieved from http://www.newsinenglish.no/2017/12/24/norway-may-stop-sending-prisoners-to-the-netherlands/

Bonta, J., Bourgon, G., Jesseman, R., & Yessine, A. K. (2005). *Presentence reports in Canada.* Ottawa, ON: Public Safety and Emergency Preparedness Canada.

Bowal, P., Callbeck, S., & Lines, B. (2014, September 5). Absolute and conditional discharges in Canadian criminal law. *LawNow.* Retrieved from http://www.lawnow.org/absolute-conditional-discharges-canadian-criminal-law/

Boyce, J. (2015). *Police-reported crime statistics in Canada, 2014.* Ottawa, ON: Canadian Centre for Justice Statistics.

Burczycka, M. (2018). *Police-reported intimate partner violence in Canada, 2017.* Ottawa, ON: Canadian Centre for Justice Statistics.

Burczycka, M., & Conroy, S. (2017). *Family violence in Canada: A statistical profile, 2015.* Ottawa, ON: Canadian Centre for Justice Statistics.

Burczycka, M., & Munch, C. (2015). *Trends in offences against the administration of justice.* Ottawa, ON: Canadian Centre for Justice Statistics.

Burgess, S. (2018, January 22). Family of Cornwall crash victim denied chance to face man responsible. *CBC News.* Retrieved from https://www.cbc.ca/news/canada/ottawa/cornwall-careless-driving-victim-impact-1.4494602

Burke Scott, Z. L. (2018). An inconvenient bargain: The ethical implications of plea bargaining in Canada. *Saskatchewan Law Review, 81*(1), 53–85.

Canadian Bar Association, British Columbia Branch. (2015). *Conditional sentences, probation and discharges.* Retrieved from http://cbabc.org/For-the-Public/Dial-A-Law/Scripts/Criminal-Law/203

Canadian Centre for Justice Statistics. (2016). *Family violence in Canada: A statistical profile, 2014.* Ottawa, ON: Author.

Caylor, L., & Beaulne, G. G. (2014). *A defence of mandatory minimum sentences.* Ottawa, ON: MacDonald-Laurier Institute.

Cole, D. P. (2016). A day in the life of a judge. In J. V. Roberts & M G. Grossman (Eds.), *Criminal justice in Canada: A reader* (5th ed.) (pp. 75–90). Toronto, ON: Nelson.

Conroy, S. (2018). *Police-reported family violence against children and youth.* Ottawa, ON: Canadian Centre for Justice Statistics.

Cotter, A. (2014). *Homicide in Canada, 2013.* Ottawa, ON: Canadian Centre for Criminal Justice Statistics.

Coughlan, S., Yogis, J. A., & Cotter, C. (2013). *Canadian law dictionary* (7th ed.). Hauppauge, NY: Barron's.

Cuthand, D. (2018, August 11). Cuthand: Gladue reports need to be implemented in Saskatchewan. *StarPhoenix (Saskatoon).* Retrieved from https://thestarphoenix.com/opinion/columnists/cuthand-gladue-reports-need-to-be-implemented-in-saskatchewan

Dale, D. (2015, January 2). Serious offenders among dozens mistakenly released from Ontario jails. *Toronto Star.* Retrieved from http://www.thestar.com/news/canada/2015/01/02/serious_offenders_among_dozensmistakenly_released_from_ontario_jails.html

Death Penalty Information Center. (2019, March 12). Facts about the death penalty. Retrieved from https://deathpenaltyinfo.org/documents/FactSheet.pdf

Doob, A. N., Webster, C. M., & Gartner, R. (2014). *Issues related to harsh sentences and mandatory minimum sentences: General deterrence and incapacitation.* Toronto, ON: Centre for Criminology & Sociological Studies, University of Toronto.

Doucette, K. (2018, June 21). How weekend-only jail sentences can cause security risks, overcrowding. *CBC News.* Retrieved from https://www.cbc.ca/news/canada/nova-scotia/weekend-only-jail-sentence-can-cause-security-risks-overcrowding-1.4715648

Drelsinger, B. (2018, July 19). I toured prisons around the world—and the system that seems the most relaxed is also one that works. *Business Insider.* Retrieved from https://www.businessinsider.com/norways-prisons-are-better-than-the-american-prisons-2018-6

Egan, K. (2018a, January 31). Fatal crash court case "an insult to my family." *Ottawa Citizen,* p. 1.

Egan, K. (2018b, April 4). Egan: Sorry was a hard word – life without mom a harder sentence. *Ottawa Citizen.* Retrieved from https://ottawacitizen.com/news/local-news/egan-sorry-was-a-hard-word-life-without-mom-a-harder-sentence

Faris, N. (2019, February 8). Why McArthur, Bissonnette and Millard got wildly different sentences for killing multiple people. *National Post.* Retrieved from https://nationalpost.com/news/canada/why-mcarthur-bissonnette-and-millard-got-wildly-different-sentences-for-killing-multiple-people

Feld, B., & Schaefer, S. (2010). The right to counsel in juvenile court: Law reform to deliver legal services and reduce justice by geography. *Criminology & Public Policy, 9*(2), 327–336.

Fine, S. (2018, March 6). Mandatory-minimum sentencing rules unravelling into patchwork. *The Globe and Mail.* Retrieved from https://www.theglobeandmail.com/news/national/mandatory-minimum-sentencing-rules-unravelling-into-patchwork/article38205652/

Guyot, B. (2018, August 23). Majority of provinces, territories lack "indispensable" Gladue writing programs. *Aboriginal Peoples Television Network.* Retrieved from https://aptnnews.ca/2018/08/23/majority-of-provinces-territories-lack-indispensable-gladue-report-writing-programs

Hannah-Moffat, K., & Maurutto, P. (2010). Re-contextualizing pre-sentence reports, risk and race. *Punishment & Society, 12*(3), 262–286.

Johnson, C. (2019, March 15). Seriously ill federal prisoners freed as compassionate release law takes effect. *National Public Radio.* Retrieved from https://www.npr.org/2019/03/15/703784886/seriously-ill-federal-prisoners-freed-as-compassionate-release-law-takes-effect

Kaeble, D., & Cowhig, M. (2018). *Correctional populations in the United States, 2016*. Washington, DC: Bureau of Justice Statistics.

Karstens-Smith, G. (2018, May 13). Nearly 20 years after the Gladue decision, lawyers say national standards lacking. *The Globe and Mail*. Retrieved from https://www.theglobeandmail.com/canada/article-nearly-20-years-after-the-gladue-decision-lawyers-say-national/

Kelly, J. B., & Puddister, K. (2017). Criminal justice policy during the Harper era: Private member's bills, penal populism, and the *Criminal Code* of Canada. *Canadian Journal of Law and Society*, *32*(3), 391–415.

Kornhauser, R. (2015). Economic individualism and punitive attitudes: A cross-national analysis. *Punishment & Society*, *17*(1), 27–53.

Legal Aid Ontario. (2019). Circumstances LAO may consider before making a decision. Retrieved from http://www.legalaid.on.ca/en/getting/eligibility_circumstances.asp

Legal Services Society of British Columbia. (2018). Gladue report guide. Retrieved from https://api.lss.bc.ca/resources/pdfs/pubs/Gladue-Report-Guide-eng.pdf.

Lincoln County Law Association. (2015). Adult probation conditions. Retrieved from http://thelcla.ca/wp-content/uploads/2016/05/ADULT-PROBATION-ORDER-CONDITIONS-Nov-2015.pdf

MacLean, J., Verrelli, N., & Chambers, L. (2016). Battered women under duress: The Supreme Court of Canada's abandonment of context and purpose in *R v Ryan*. *Canadian Journal of Women and the Law*, *29*(1), 60–82.

Malakieh, J. (2019). *Adult and youth correctional statistics in Canada, 2017/2018*. Ottawa, ON: Canadian Centre for Justice Statistics.

Manson, A. (2013). Some thoughts on multiple sentences and the totality principle: Can we get it right? *Canadian Journal of Criminology and Criminal Justice*, *55*(4), 481–494.

Maxwell, A. (2017). *Adult criminal court statistics in Canada, 2014/2015*. Ottawa, ON: Canadian Centre for Justice Statistics.

Menart, R. (2018). California sentencing institute now shows 2016 trends. Center on Juvenile and Criminal Justice. Retrieved from http://www.cjcj.org/news/12040

Miladinovic, Z. (2019). *Adult criminal and youth court statistics in Canada, 2016/2017*. Ottawa, ON: Canadian Centre for Justice Statistics.

Milward, D., & Parkes, D. (2011). *Gladue*: Beyond myth and towards implementation in Manitoba. *Manitoba Law Journal*, *35*(1), 84–110.

Mohsin, S. (2014, September 18). To solve prison crowding, Norway goes Dutch. *Bloomberg Businessweek*. Retrieved from http://www.businessweek.com/articles/2014-09-18/norway-exports-inmates-to-netherlands-to-solve-prison-crowding

Moore, H. (2015, January 21). Manitoba woman in hiding feels "betrayed" by plea bargain for gun-stashing ex. CBC *News*. Retrieved from http://www.cbc.ca/news/canada/manitoba/manitoba-woman-in-hiding-feels-betrayed-by-plea-bargain-for-gun-stashing-ex-1.2920183

Neil, R., & Carmichael, J. T. (2015). The use of incarceration in Canada: A test of political and social threat explanations on the variation in prison admissions across Canadian provinces, 2001–2010. *Sociological Inquiry*, *85*(2), 309–332.

Norman, M. D., & Wadman, R. C. (2000). Probation department sentencing recommendations in two Utah counties. *Federal Probation*, *64*(2), 47–51.

Ontario Ministry of Community Safety and Correctional Services. (2018). Correctional services: Earned remission. Retrieved from http://www.mcscs.jus.gov.on.ca/english/corr_serv/earned_rem/earned_rem.html

Palacios, M., & Lammam, C. (2018). *Taxes versus the necessities of life: The Canadian consumer tax index, 2018 edition*. Vancouver, BC: The Fraser Institute.

Parsons, P. (2018, October 5). That's the wound: Reports detailing offenders' Indigenous backgrounds are surging in Alberta's courts. *Edmonton Journal*. Retrieved from https://edmontonjournal.com/news/insight/albertas-gladue-report-writers-speak-out-about-their-unique-role-in-the-justice-system

Penal Reform International. (2018). *Life imprisonment: A policy briefing*. Retrieved from https://www.penalreform.org/wp-content/uploads/2018/04/PRI_Life-Imprisonment-Briefing.pdf

Perkel, C. (2015, July 15). "Cultural gap" not a reason for lighter sentence for Iranian immigrant guilty of raping wife, beating children: court. *National Post*. Retrieved from http://news.nationalpost.com/news/canada/cultural-gap-not-a-reason-for-lighter-sentence-for-iranian-immigrant-guilt-of-raping-wife-beating-children-court

Pew Charitable Trusts (2018). *35 states reform criminal justice policies through justice reinvestment*. Washington, DC: Author.

Piccinato, M. P. (2004). *Plea bargaining*. Ottawa, ON: Department of Justice Canada.

Porter, L., & Calverley, D. (2011). *Trends in the use of remand in Canada*. Ottawa, ON: Canadian Centre for Justice Statistics.

Provincial Court of British Columbia. (2018). *Annual report 2016/2017*. Victoria, BC: Author.

Public Safety Canada. (2018). *Corrections and conditional release statistical overview, 2017*. Ottawa, ON: Author.

Rakoff, J. S. (2014, November 20). Why innocent people plead guilty. *The New York Review of Books*. Retrieved from http://www.nybooks.com/articles/archives/2014/nov/20/why-innocent-people-plead-guilty/

Reckdenwald, A., & Parker, K. F. (2011). Understanding the change in male and female intimate partner homicide over time: A policy- and theory-relevant investigation. *Feminist Criminology*, *7*(3), 167–195.

Roach, K. (2019). *Plan B for implementing Gladue: The need to apply background factors to the punitive sentencing purposes*. Retrieved from https://papers.ssrn.com/sol3/papers.cfm?abstract_id=3367159

Roberts, J. V., Stalans, L. J., Indermaur, D., & Hough, M. (2003). *Penal populism and public opinion: Lessons from five countries*. New York: Oxford University Press.

Ruddell, R., & Jones, N. A. (2017). Cross-national imprisonment. In K. R. Kerley, H. Copes, S. Li, J. Lane, & S. Sharpe (Eds.), *The encyclopedia of corrections* (pp. 169–176). New York: Wiley Blackwell.

Savage, L. (2018). *Police-reported family violence against seniors in Canada, 2017*. Ottawa, ON: Canadian Centre for Justice Statistics.

Sheehy, E. (2014). *Defending battered women on trial: Lessons from transcripts*. Vancouver, BC: UBC Press.

Sheehy, E. (2018). Expert evidence on coercive control in support of self-defence: The trial of Teresa Craig. *Criminology & Criminal Justice*, *18*(1), 100–114.

Sheehy, E., Stubbs, J., & Tolmie, J. (2012). Battered women charged with homicide in Australia, Canada and New Zealand: How do they fare? *Australian & New Zealand Journal of Criminology*, 45(3), 383–399.

Sprott, J. B., & Doob, A. N. (1998). Understanding provincial variation in incarceration rates. *Canadian Journal of Criminology*, 40(3), 305–322.

Statistics Canada. (2019a). *Adult criminal courts, guilty cases by type of sentence* [Table 35-10-0030-01]. Retrieved from https://www150.statcan.gc.ca/t1/tbl1/en/tv.action?pid=3510003001

Statistics Canada. (2019b). *Adult criminal courts, guilty cases by mean and median length of custody* [Table 35-10-0033-01]. Retrieved from https://www150.statcan.gc.ca/t1/tbl1/en/tv.action?pid=3510003301

Statistics Canada. (2019c). *Adult criminal courts, number of cases and charges by type of decision.* [Table 35-10-0027-01]. Retrieved from https://www150.statcan.gc.ca/t1/tbl1/en/tv.action?pid=3510002701

Storey, J. E., Watt, K. A, & Hart, S. D. (2015). An examination of violence risk communication in practice using a structured professional judgment framework. *Behavioral Sciences & the Law*, 33(1), 39–55.

University of Saskatchewan. (2018, May 15). U of S *Gladue* rights research database first of its kind in Canada. Retrieved from https://news.usask.ca/articles/colleges/2018/u-of-s-gladue-rights-research-database-first-of-its-kind-in-canada.php

Verdun-Jones, S. N. (2016). Plea bargaining. In J. V. Roberts & M G. Grossman (Eds.), *Criminal justice in Canada: A reader* (5th ed.) (pp. 168–184). Toronto, ON: Nelson.

Wilson, R. (2012, June 16). So you want to be a judge? *National Magazine*. Retrieved from http://www.nationalmagazine.ca/Articles/January-February/So-you-want-to-be-a-judge.aspx

Chapter 9

Archambault, K., Joubert, D., & Brown, G. (2013). Gender, psychiatric symptomatology, problem behaviors and mental health treatment in a Canadian provincial correctional population: Disentangling the associations between care and institutional control. *International Journal of Forensic Mental Health*, 12(1), 93–106.

Beijersbergen, K. A., Dirkzwager, A. J. E., van der Laan, P. H., & Nieuwbeerta, P. (2016). A social building? Prison architecture and staff-prisoner relationships. *Crime & Delinquency*, 62(7), 843–874.

Blanchfield, M. (2018, July 24). Canada to use voice recognition, monitoring technology to keep migrants out of detention. *Global News*. Retrieved from https://globalnews.ca/news/4350419/canada-migrant-detention-policy/

Bonta, J., & Andrews, D. A. (2017). *The psychology of criminal conduct* (6th ed.). New York: Routledge.

Bonta, J., Bourgon, G., & Rugge, T. (2018). From evidence-informed to evidence-based: the strategic training initiative in community supervision. In P. Ugwudike, P. Raynor, & J. Annison (Eds.), *Evidence-based skills in criminal justice: International research on supporting rehabilitation and desistance* (pp. 169–192). Bristol, UK: Policy Press.

Bonta, J., Rugge, T., Scott, T. L., Bourgon, G., & Yessine, A. K. (2008). Exploring the black box of community supervision. *Journal of Offender Rehabilitation*, 47(3), 248–270.

British Columbia Justice and Public Safety Council. (2018). *Strategic plan for the justice and public safety sector 2018-21*. Victoria, BC: Author.

Brown, G. P., Hirdes, J. P., & Fries, B. E. (2015). Measuring the prevalence of current, severe symptoms of mental health problems in a Canadian correctional population: Implications for delivery of mental health services for inmates. *International Journal of Offender Therapy and Comparative Criminology*, 59(1), 27–50.

Cabeldue, M., Blackburn, A., & Mullings, J. L. (2019). Mental health among incarcerated women: An examination of factors impacting depression and PTSD symptomology. *Women & Criminal Justice*, 29(1), pp. 52–72.

Calverley, D. (2010). *Adult correctional services in Canada, 2008/2009*. Ottawa, ON: Canadian Centre for Justice Statistics.

Calverley, D., & Beattie, K. (2005). *Community corrections in Canada, 2004*. Ottawa, ON: Canadian Centre for Justice Statistics.

Canadian Broadcasting Corporation. (2008, August 8). Prison guard gets 3 years for aiding escape. *CBC News*. Retrieved from https://www.cbc.ca/news/canada/british-columbia/prison-guard-gets-3-years-for-aiding-escape-1.750285

Canadian Broadcasting Corporation. (2009, March 12). Brazen escape from Regina jail shouldn't have happened: report. *CBC News*. Retrieved from https://www.cbc.ca/news/canada/saskatchewan/brazen-escape-from-regina-jail-shouldn-t-have-happened-report-1.824611

Canadian Broadcasting Corporation. (2015, Oct. 15). Probation system set up for failure, former inmates say. *CBC News*. Retrieved from https://www.cbc.ca/news/canada/saskatoon/probation-system-set-up-for-failure-former-inmates-say-1.3273523

Canadian Broadcasting Corporation. (2018a, June 13). Horse therapy program expanding to women's prison. *CBC News*. Retrieved from https://www.cbc.ca/news/canada/newfoundland-labrador/spirit-horse-program-womens-prison-clarenville-1.4704406

Canadian Broadcasting Corporation. (2018b, May 3). Special advisor to probe 'disturbing' rise in jail violence. *CBC News*. Retrieved from https://www.cbc.ca/news/canada/ottawa/lalonde-corrections-officers-segregation-review-1.4646400

Canadian Press. (2010, September 9). Two N.L. inmates captured by police after escape. *CTV News*. Retrieved from https://www.ctvnews.ca/two-n-l-inmates-captured-by-police-after-escape-1.550981

Carleton, R. N., Afifi, T. O., Turner, S., Taillieu, T., Duranceau, S., LeBouthillier, D., M., ... Asmundson, G. J. G. (2018). Mental disorder symptoms among public safety personnel in Canada. *The Canadian Journal of Psychiatry*, 63(1), 54–-64.

Chamberlain, A. W., Gricius, M., Wallace, D. M., Borjas, D., & Ware, V. M. (2017). Parolee-parole officer rapport: Does it impact recidivism? *International Journal of Offender Therapy and Comparative Criminology*, 62(11), 3581–3602.

Collins, J. (2018, July 26). Prisons aim to jam phones, detect drones carrying contraband. *Associated Press*. Retrieved from https://apnews.com/4283e6e823e040fcbf968f12189ffe10

Damon, W. (2014). Failure to comply: How administration of justice offences are growing BC's prison population. *The Tyee*. Retrieved from https://thetyee.ca/News/2014/04/05/Failure-to-Comply/

Department of Justice. (2018). Community-based sentencing. *Research at a Glance*. Retrieved from http://www.justice.gc.ca/eng/rp-pr/jr/rg-rco/2018/mar07.pdf

Doob, A., Hunter, A., Rachamalla, T., Sprott, J., & Webster, C. (2017). *Corrections in Ontario: Directions for reform*. Toronto, ON: Ministry of Community Safety and Correctional Services.

Ekstedt, J. W., & Griffiths, C. T. (1988). *Corrections in Canada: Policy and practice* (2nd ed.). Toronto, ON: Butterworths Canada.

Feith, J. (2016, January 11). Two men plead guilty to hijacking helicopter in 2013 prison escape. *Montreal Gazette.* Retrieved from https://montrealgazette.com/news/two-men-plead-guilty-to-hijacking-helicopter-in-2013-prison-escape

Fyson, D. (2006). *Magistrates, police, and people: Everyday criminal justice in Quebec and Lower Canada, 1764–1837.* Toronto, ON: University of Toronto Press.

Fyson, D., & Fenchel, F. (2015). Prison registers, their possibilities and their pitfalls: the case of local prisons in nineteenth-century Quebec. *The History of the Family, 20*(2), 163–188.

Gacek, J. (2016). Doing time differently: Imaginative mobilities to/from inmates' inner/outer spaces. In J. Turner & K. Peters (Eds.), *Carceral mobilities: Interrogating movement in Incarceration* (pp. 73–84). London: Routledge.

Givetash, L. (2016, July 17). Jail program gives moms a new start, helps babies develop, advocates say. *CTV News.* Retrieved from https://www.ctvnews.ca/canada/jail-program-gives-moms-a-new-start-helps-babies-develop-advocates-say-1.2990230

Global News. (2017, May 9). Who's watching? Ontario's probation system "a joke," say offenders. Retrieved from https://globalnews.ca/news/3429225/ontarios-probation-system-a-joke-say-offenders/

Godfrey, D. (2018a, April 13). More violence at B.C.'s newest jail than nearly any other. *Salmon Arm Observer.* Retrieved from https://www.saobserver.net/news/more-violence-at-b-c-s-newest-jail-than-nearly-any-other/

Godfrey, D. (2018b, April 24). Isolation likely factor in drugs, rule-breaking at Okanagan jail. *Salmon Arm Observer.* Retrieved from https://www.saobserver.net/news/isolation-likely-factor-in-drugs-rule-breaking-at-okanagan-jail/

Gossner, D., Simon, T., Rector, B., & Ruddell, R. (2016). Case planning and recidivism of high risk and violent adult probationers. *Journal of Community Safety and Well-Being, 1*(1) 32–43.

Grant, M. (2017, Aug. 8), "A huge problem": Correctional officers in Alberta hospitalized after exposure to fentanyl during searches. *CBC News.* Retrieved from https://www.cbc.ca/news/canada/calgary/prison-guards-alberta-overdosing-fentanyl-searches-narcan-1.4235919

Hansard. (2018, March 5). *Official report of debates.* Retrieved from https://www.leg.bc.ca/content/Hansard/41st3rd/20180305pm-Hansard-n94.html

Hassan, S. (2019). Nixing victim surcharges a good move. *Law Times.* Retrieved from https://www.lawtimesnews.com/article/nixing-victim-surcharges-a-good-move-16993/

Human Rights Watch. (2018). *"Set up to fail": The impact of offender-funded private probation on the poor.* New York: Author.

Hyatt, J. M., & Barnes, G. C. (2017). An experimental evaluation of the impact of intensive supervision on the recidivism of high-risk probationers. *Crime & Delinquency, 63*(1), 3–38.

Jackson, B. A., Russo, J., Hollywood, J. S., Woods, D., Silberglitt, R., Drake, G. B., Shaffer, J. S., Zaydman, M., & Chow, B. G. (2015). *Fostering innovation in community and institutional corrections.* San Diego, CA: RAND Corporation.

Johnson, S. (2006). *Outcomes of probation and conditional sentence supervision: An analysis of Newfoundland and Labrador, Nova Scotia, New Brunswick, Saskatchewan and Alberta, 2003/2004 to 2004/2005.* Ottawa, ON: Statistics Canada.

Judd, A. (2018, January 12). Someone used a drone to drop $26,500 of drugs, tobacco over a B.C. prison wall. *Global News.* Retrieved from https://globalnews.ca/news/3961889/drone-drugs-b-c-prison-wall/

Kaeble, D. (2018). *Probation and parole in the United States, 2016.* Washington, DC: Bureau of Justice Statistics.

Kim, B., & Matz, A. (2018). The reality of partnership: formal collaborations between law enforcement and community corrections agencies in Pennsylvania. *Policing and Society: An International Journal of Research and Policy, 28*(8), 947–967.

Kouyoumdjian, F. G., Calzavara, L. M., Kiefer, L., Main, C., & Bondy, S. J. (2014). Drug use prior to incarceration and associated socio-behavioural factors among males in a provincial correctional facility in Ontario, Canada. *Canadian Journal of Public Health, 105*(3), 198–202.

Kouyoumdjian, F., Schuler, A., Matheson, F I., & Hwang, S. W. (2016). Health status of prisoners in Canada. *Canadian Family Physician, 62*(3), 215–222.

Macdonald, D. (2018). *Born to win: Wealth concentration in Canada since 1999.* Ottawa, ON: Canadian Centre for Policy Alternatives.

McDonald, S., Northcott, M., & Raguparen, M. (2014). *The federal victim surcharge in Saskatchewan.* Ottawa, ON: Department of Justice, Canada.

McKenna, J. (2018). In Finland, speeding tickets are linked to your income. *World Economic Forum.* Retrieved from https://www.weforum.org/agenda/2018/06/in-finland-speeding-tickets-are-linked-to-your-income/

McQuigge, M. (2015, September 24). Suspect in Ottawa Valley homicides was known to women's shelters. *Toronto Star.* Retrieved from https://www.thestar.com/news/canada/2015/09/24/suspect-in-ottawa-valley-homicides-was-known-to-womens-shelters.html

Malakieh, J. (2018). *Adult and youth correctional statistics in Canada, 2016/2017.* Ottawa, ON: Canadian Centre for Justice Statistics.

Malakieh, J. (2019). *Adult and youth correctional statistics in Canada, 2017/2018.* Ottawa, ON: Canadian Centre for Justice Statistics.

Mandel, M. (2017). Ontario's probation system is a joke. *Toronto Sun.* Retrieved from https://torontosun.com/2017/05/20/ontarios-probation-system-is-a-joke/wcm/c0927464-b592-47a0-ab7c-4c7ce4c00746

Maxwell, A. (2017). *Adult criminal court statistics in Canada, 2014/2015.* Ottawa, ON: Canadian Centre for Justice Statistics.

Mayor, L., & Culbert, A. (2016, January 15). Basil Borutski, charged with 3 Wilno, Ont. murders, blames police harassment. *CBC News.* Retrieved from http://www.cbc.ca/news/canada/borutski-wilno-murders-fifth-estate-1.3404238

Miladinovic, Z. (2019). *Adult criminal and youth court statistics in Canada, 2016/2017.* Ottawa, ON: Canadian Centre for Justice Statistics.

Miller, J. (2015). Contemporary modes of probation officer supervision: The triumph of the "synthetic" officer? *Justice Quarterly, 32*(2), 314–336.

Miller, J., Copeland, K., & Sullivan, M. L. (2014). How probation officers leverage "third parties" in offender supervision. *Journal of Offender Rehabilitation, 53*(8), 641–657.

Morash, M., Kashy, D. A., Smith, S. W., & Cobbina, J. E. (2016). The connection of probation/parole officer actions to women offenders' recidivism. *Criminal Justice and Behavior, 43*(4), 506–524.

Murray, A. (2017, April 21). Speeding fines rise to 175pc of weekly wages from Monday. *The Telegraph.* Retrieved from https://www.telegraph.co.uk/money/consumer-affairs/speeding-fines-rise-175pc-weekly-wages-monday/

Nagin, D. S., Cullen, F. T., & Lero Jonson, C. (2016). *Deterrence, choice, and crime*. London: Routledge.

Nease, K. (2017, December 6). Basil Borutski will die in prison for "vicious, cold-blooded" murder of 3 women. *CBC News*. Retrieved from https://www.cbc.ca/news/canada/ottawa/basil-borutski-sentencing-life-prison-1.4435066

Nova Scotia Corrections. (2013). *Offender programs*. Retrieved from https://novascotia.ca/just/Corrections/offender_programs.asp

Nunavut Justice. (2018). *Fine option program*. Retrieved from https://www.justice.gov.nt.ca/en/fine-option-program/

Office of the Auditor General, Manitoba. (2014). *Annual report to the legislature*. Winnipeg, MB: Author.

Ombudsman Ontario. (2013). *The code: Investigation into the Ministry of Community Safety and Correctional Service in response to allegations of excessive use of force against inmates*. Toronto, ON: Author.

Ombudsman Ontario. (2018). *2017-2018 Annual report*. Toronto, ON: Author.

Ontario Ministry of the Solicitor General. (2019). *Becoming a correctional services officer*. Retrieved from https://www.mcscs.jus.gov.on.ca/english/corr_serv/careers_in_corr/become_corr_off/COTraining/cs_cotraining.html

Paynter, M. J. (2018). Policy and legal protection for breastfeeding and incarcerated women in Canada. *Journal of Human Lactation*, 34(2), 276–281.

Public Safety Canada. (2018). *Corrections and conditional release statistical overview, 2017*. Ottawa, ON: Author.

Quebec Ombudsman. (2018). *Assessment of follow-up to the recommendations from the special report by the Quebec Ombudsman: Detention conditions, administration of justice and crime prevention in Nunavut, 2016*. Retrieved from https://protecteurducitoyen.qc.ca/sites/default/files/pdf/rapports_speciaux/assessment-follow-up-special-report-detention-condition-nunavik.pdf

Ramsay, C. (2018, June 29). Last of 4 inmates who escaped Red Deer remand centre arrested in Rocky Mountain House. *Global News*. Retrieved from https://globalnews.ca/news/4305948/red-deer-escaped-inmates-arrested/

Raynor, P., Ugwudike, P., & Vanstone, M. (2014). The impact of skills in probation work: A reconviction study. *Criminology & Criminal Justice*, 14(2), 235–249.

Reevely, D. (2014, December 12). Ontario's probation system in shambles, auditor reports. *Ottawa Citizen*. Retrieved from http://ottawacitizen.com/news/national/reevely-ontarios-probation-system-in-shambles-auditor-reports

Ricciardelli, R., Power, N., & Simas Medeiros, D. (2019). Correctional officers in Canada: Interpreting workplace violence. *Criminal Justice Review*, 43(4), 458–476.

Schierenbeck, A. (2018, March 15). A billionaire and a nurse shouldn't pay the same fine for speeding. *New York Times*. Retrieved from https://www.nytimes.com/2018/03/15/opinion/flat-fines-wealthy-poor.html

Seymour, A. (2014, July 31). Prominent Ottawa judge strikes down mandatory victim surcharge. *Ottawa Citizen*. Retrieved from http://ottawacitizen.com/news/local-news/prominent-ottawa-judge-strikes-down-mandatory-victim-surcharge

Shingler, B. (2014, June 8). Helicopter escape from Quebec jail has police hunting for three inmates. *National Post*. Retrieved from http://news.nationalpost.com/2014/06/08/helicopter-escape-from-quebec-jail-has-police-hunting-for-three-inmates/

Sibley, R. (2015, Sept. 24). Third woman identified in Wilno area slayings; suspect to appear in court. *Ottawa Citizen*. Retrieved from http://ottawacitizen.com/news/local-news/manhunt-for-in-wilno-following-shooting-death

Statistics Canada. (2018a). *Average counts of adults in provincial and territorial correctional programs* [Table 35-10-0154-01]. Retrieved from https://www150.statcan.gc.ca/t1/tbl1/en/tv.action?pid=3510015401

Statistics Canada. (2018b). *National occupation classification. Correctional service officers*. Retrieved from http://www23.statcan.gc.ca/imdb/p3VD.pl?Function=getVD&TVD=314243&CVD=314247&CPV=4422&CST=01012016&CLV=4&MLV=4

Statistics Canada. (2019a). *Adult admissions to correctional services* [Table 35-10-0014-01]. Retrieved from https://www150.statcan.gc.ca/t1/tbl1/en/tv.action?pid=3510001401

Statistics Canada. (2019b). *Adult criminal courts, guilty cases by mean and median amount of fine* [Table 35-10-0037-01]. Retrieved from https://www150.statcan.gc.ca/t1/tbl1/en/tv.action?pid=3510003701

Statistics Canada. (2019c). *Adult criminal courts, guilty cases by mean and median length of probation* [Table 35-10-00350-01]. Retrieved from https://www150.statcan.gc.ca/t1/tbl1/en/tv.action?pid=3510003501

Statistics Canada. (2019d) *Adult sentenced custody admissions to correctional services by sex and sentence length ordered* [Table 35-10-0018-01]. Retrieved from https://www150.statcan.gc.ca/t1/tbl1/en/tv.action?pid=3510001801

Steiner, B., Travis, L. F., Makarios, M. D., & Brickley, T. (2011). The influence of parole officers' attitudes on supervision practices. *Justice Quarterly*, 28(6), 903–927.

Still, W. S. (2016). A practitioner's perspective on realignment: A giant win in San Francisco. *The ANNALS of the American Academy of Political and Social Science*, 664(1), 221–235.

Wakefield, J. (2018, March 26). Former Alberta inmate carried stillborn baby for weeks after seeking help from staff. *Edmonton Journal*. Retrieved from https://edmontonjournal.com/news/local-news/former-alberta-inmate-carried-stillborn-baby-for-weeks-after-seeking-help-from-staff

Wallace-Capretta, S., & Roberts, J. V. (2013). The evolution of electronic monitoring in Canada: From corrections to sentencing and beyond. In M. Nellis, K. Beyens, & D. Kaminski (Eds.), *Electronically monitored punishment: International and critical perspectives* (pp. 44–62). New York: Routledge.

Washington State Institute for Public Policy. (2018). *Benefit-cost results, adult criminal justice*. Olympia, WA: Author.

Weinrath, M., Doerksen, M., & Watts, J. (2015). The impact of an intensive supervision program on high-risk offenders: Manitoba's COHROU program. *Canadian Journal of Criminology and Criminal Justice*, 57(2), 253–288.

Wener, R. E. (2012). *The environmental psychology of prisons and jails: Creating humane spaces in secure settings*. New York: Cambridge University Press.

Western, B., & Schiraldi, V. (2017). Want to shrink our prisons? Fix probation and parole. *The Crime Report*. Retrieved from https://thecrimereport.org/2017/07/20/want-to-end-mass-incarceration-fix-probation-and-parole/

Winterdyk, J. A., & Antonowicz, D. (2016). Deaths in custody. In J. V. Roberts & M. G. Grossman (Eds.), *Criminal justice in Canada: A reader* (5th ed.) (pp. 364–375). Toronto, ON: Nelson.

Woo, A. (2018, May 16). Vancouver subset struggling to escape corrections system's 'revolving door' study says. *The Globe and Mail*. Retrieved from https://www.theglobeandmail.com/news/british-columbia/vancouver-subset-struggling-to-escape-corrections-systems-revolving-door-study-says/article28046243/

Young, D. W., Farrell, J. L., & Taxman, F. S. (2013). Impacts of juvenile probation training models on youth recidivism. *Justice Quarterly*, 30(6), 1068–1089

Zinger, I. (2017). *Annual report: Office of the correctional investigator*. Ottawa, ON: Office of the Correctional Investigator.

Chapter 10

Adams, E. B., Chen, E. Y., & Chapman, R. (2017). Erasing the mark of a criminal past: Ex-offenders' expectations and experiences with record clearance. *Punishment & Society*, 19(1), 23–52.

Angus Reid Global. (2014). Six-in-ten Canadians support legalizing marijuana, but say it's not a top justice priority. Retrieved from http://angusreid.org/wp-content/uploads/2014/12/ARG-Marijuana-Opinions2.pdf

Barnowski, R. (2004). *Outcome evaluation of Washington State's research-based programs for juvenile offenders*. Olympia, WA: Washington State Institute for Public Policy.

Beaudette, J. N., Power, J., & Stewart, L. A. (2015). *National prevalence of mental disorders among incoming federally-sentenced men offenders*. Correctional Service of Canada Research at a Glance. Retrieved from https://www.csc-scc.gc.ca/005/008/092/005008-0357-eng.pdf

Bell, D. (2019, Mar. 4). "Smallest of steps": Cannabis legal expert says pardon changes not enough. *CBC News*. Retrieved from https://www.cbc.ca/news/canada/calgary/cannabis-legal-expert-pardon-changes-bill-c-93-jack-lloyd-1.5042476

Bonta, J., & Andrews, D. A. (2017). *The psychology of criminal conduct* (6th ed.). New York: Routledge.

Brown, G., Barker, J., McMillan, K., Norman, R., Derkzen, D., & Stewart, L. (2018). *National prevalence of mental disorders among federally sentenced women offenders: In custody sample*. Ottawa, ON: Correctional Service of Canada.

Brown, J. (2018, August 20). Enforcement lacking in anti-money-laundering efforts. *Canadian Lawyer*. Retrieved from https://www.canadianlawyermag.com/author/jennifer-brown/enforcement-lacking-in-anti-money-laundering-efforts-16110/

Bumiller, K. (2015). Bad jobs and good workers: The hiring of ex-prisoners in a segmented economy. *Theoretical Criminology*, 19(3), 336–354.

Canadian Broadcasting Corporation. (2014, July 11). Edward Snowshoe spent 162 days in segregation before suicide. *CBC News*. Retrieved from https://www.cbc.ca/news/canada/north/edward-snowshoe-spent-162-days-in-segregation-before-suicide-1.2703542

Canadian Press. (2016, May 24). Appeal court cuts man's assault sentence by a day to avoid risking his permanent resident status. *National Post*. Retrieved from http://news.nationalpost.com/news/canada/appeal-court-cuts-mans-assault-sentence-by-a-day-to-avoid-risking-his-permanent-resident-status

Carson, E. A. (2018). *Prisoners in 2016*. Washington, DC: Bureau of Justice Statistics.

Chouinard, J. A., & Riddick, C. (2015). *An evaluation of the circles of support and accountability demonstration project*. Ottawa, ON: Author.

Church Council on Justice and Corrections. (2011). *Circles of Support and Accountability: CoSA in Canada, 2011 gathering report*. Ottawa, ON: Author.

Coletto, D., & Anderson, B. (2019). Has the SNC-Lavalin/Wilson-Raybould controversy impacted public opinion? *Abacus Data*. Retrieved from https://abacusdata.ca/has-the-snc-lavalin-wilson-raybould-controversy-impacted-public-opinion/

Correctional Service of Canada. (2014a). *Correctional programs*. Retrieved from https://www.csc-scc.gc.ca/correctional-process/002001-2001-eng.shtml

Correctional Service of Canada. (2014b). *History of penitentiaries in Canada*. Retrieved from http://www.csc-scc.gc.ca/about-us/006-1006-eng.shtml

Correctional Service of Canada. (2018a). *Audit of offender redress*. Ottawa, ON: Author.

Correctional Service of Canada. (2018b). *CORCAN advisory board*. Retrieved from https://www.csc-scc.gc.ca/corcan/002005-0007-en.shtml

Correctional Service of Canada. (2019a). *Aboriginal healing lodges*. Retrieved from https://www.csc-scc.gc.ca/aboriginal/002003-2000-en.shtml

Correctional Service of Canada. (2019b). *Commissioner's Directive 715-1 community supervision*. Retrieved from https://www.csc-scc.gc.ca/politiques-et-lois/715-1-cd-en.shtml

Correctional Service of Canada. (2019c). *Community corrections*. Retrieved from https://www.csc-scc.gc.ca/publications/005007-3008-en.shtml

Correctional Service of Canada. (2019d). *CORCAN. Employment and employability*. Retrieved from https://www.csc-scc.gc.ca/publications/092/005007-3016-en.pdf

Correctional Service of Canada. (2019e). *Women offenders* Retrieved from s://www.csc-scc.gc.ca/publications/092/005007-3012-en.pdf

Decker, S. H., Ortiz, N., Spohn, C., & Hedberg, E. (2015). Criminal stigma, race, and ethnicity: The consequences of imprisonment for employment. *Journal of Criminal Justice*, 43(2), 108–121.

Deschene, S. (2017). Fraser Valley Institution for Women. *Journal of Prisoners on Prisons*, 26(1&2), 40–42.

Doran, L. (2018). Finding common ground on a journey from pain to hope: CoSA as restorative justice. Honours thesis, Saint Mary's University (Halifax).

Duwe, G. (2018). Can circles of support and accountability (CoSA) significantly reduce sexual recidivism? Results from a randomized controlled trial in Minnesota. *Journal of Experimental Criminology*, 14(4), 463–484.

Ekos Research Associates Inc. (2017). *Public consultation on the records suspension program*. Ottawa, ON: Public Safety and Emergency Preparedness.

Flannigan, K., Unsworth, K., & Harding, K. (2018). FASD prevalence in special populations. *Canada FASD Research Network*. Retrieved from https://canfasd.ca/wp-content/uploads/sites/35/2018/08/Prevalence-2-Issue-Paper-FINAL.pdf

Global News. (2018, July 6). Analysis: A gang member's perspective on Canada's gang violence. Retrieved from https://globalnews.ca/news/4313201/analysis-gang-member-perspective-canada-gun-violence/

Gossner, D., Simon, T., Rector, B., & Ruddell, R. (2016). Case planning and recidivism of high risk and violent adult probationers. *Journal of Community Safety and Well-Being*, 1(2), 32-43.

Haney, C. (2018). The psychological effects of solitary confinement: A systematic critique. *Crime & Justice*, 47(1), 365–416.

Harper, C. A. (2018). The role of the media in shaping responses to sexual offending. In H. Elliott, K. Hocken, R. Lievesley, N. Blagden, B. Winder, & P. Banyard (Eds.), *Sexual crime and circles of support and accountability* (pp. 127–150). London: Palgrave Macmillan.

Harris, K. (2018a, March 25). Diverse mix of gangs a growing security challenge for federal prisons. *CBC News*. Retrieved from https://www.cbc.ca/news/politics/prison-gangs-diverse-csc-1.4590649

Harris, K. (2018b, July 2). A handful of prison inmates floods grievance system, filing more than 8,000 complaints. *CBC News*. Retrieved from https://www.cbc.ca/news/politics/prisoner-complaints-csc-grievances-1.4721039

Harris. K. (2019, January 7). Court orders new rules for holding prisoners in solitary confinement. *CBC News*. Retrieved from https://www.cbc.ca/news/politics/court-ruling-solitary-confinement-goodale-1.4968577

James, N. (2018). *Risk and needs assessment in the federal prison system*. Washington, DC: Congressional Research Service.

John Howard Society of Ontario. (2018). *The invisible burden: Police records and the barriers to employment in Toronto*. Toronto, ON: Author.

Keung, N. (2018, June 11). Tougher impaired driving penalty "a double whammy" for immigrants. *Toronto Star*. Retrieved from https://www.thestar.com/news/gta/2018/06/08/tougher-impaired-driving-penalty-a-double-whammy-for-immigrants.html

Kidman, J. (1938). Prison reform in Canada: The report of Royal Commission on Penal System. *Howard Journal of Criminal Justice*, 5(2), 112–115.

Kim, B., Benekos, P. J., & Merlo, A. V. (2016). Sex offender recidivism revisited: Review of recent meta-analyses on the effects of sex offender treatment. *Trauma, Violence, & Abuse*. 17(1), 105–117.

Latessa, E. J. (2018). Does treatment quality matter? Of course it does, and there is growing evidence to support it. *Criminology & Public Policy*, 17(1), 181–187.

McCoy, T. (2012). *Hard time: reforming the penitentiary in nineteenth-century Canada*. Edmonton, AB: Athabasca Press.

Makarios, M., Lovins, L., Latessa, E., & Smith, P. (2016). Staff quality and treatment effectiveness: An examination of the relationship between staff factors and the effectiveness of correctional programs. *Justice Quarterly*, 33(2), 348–367.

Malakieh, J. (2018). *Adult and youth correctional statistics in Canada, 2016/2017*. Ottawa, ON: Canadian Centre for Justice Statistics.

Malakieh, J. (2019). *Adult and youth correctional statistics in Canada, 2017/2018*. Ottawa, ON: Canadian Centre for Justice Statistics.

Miladinovic, Z. (2019). *Adult criminal and youth court statistics in Canada, 2016/2017*. Ottawa, ON: Canadian Centre for Justice Statistics.

Noonan, M. E. (2016). *Mortality in local jails and state prisons, 2002–2014—Statistical tables*. Washington, DC: Bureau of Justice Statistics.

Office of the Correctional Investigator. (2013). *Summary of issues and challenges in the management of prison self-injury*. Retrieved from https://www.oci-bec.gc.ca/cnt/comm/presentations/presentationsAR-RA1112Info-eng.aspx

Office of the Correctional Investigator. (2017). *Annual report, 2016–2017*. Ottawa, ON: Author.

Office of the Correctional Investigator. (2018). *Annual report, 2017–2018*. Ottawa, ON: Author.

Office of the Correctional Investigator. (2019). *Aging and dying in prison: An investigation into the experiences of older individuals in federal custody*. Ottawa, ON: Author.

Parole Board of Canada. (2018a). History of parole in Canada. Retrieved from https://www.canada.ca/en/parole-board/corporate/history-of-parole-in-canada.html

Parole Board of Canada. (2018b). *Parole decision-making: Myths and realities*. Retrieved from https://www.canada.ca/en/parole-board/corporate/publications-and-forms/parole-decision-making-myths-and-realities.html

Parole Board of Canada. (2019a). *Timeline for conditional release*. Retrieved from https://www.canada.ca/content/dam/canada/parole-board/migration/001/093/timeline-eng.PDF

Parole Board of Canada. (2019b). *2017-2018 report to parliament, record suspension program*. Ottawa, ON: Author.

Parole Board of Canada. (2019c). *Performance monitoring report, 2017-2018*. Ottawa, ON: Author.

Perkel, C. (2018). Women want memorial at notorious former Kingston prison. *CTV News*. Retrieved from https://www.ctvnews.ca/canada/women-want-memorial-at-notorious-former-kingston-prison-1.4047489

Public Safety Canada. (2017a). *Corrections and conditional release statistical overview, 2016*. Ottawa, ON: Author.

Public Safety Canada. (2017b, October 10). *Results released from the criminal records act and record suspension user consultations*. News Release. Retrieved from https://www.canada.ca/en/public-safety-canada/news/2017/10/results_releasedfromthecriminalrecordsactandrecordsuspensionuser.html

Public Safety Canada. (2018). *Corrections and conditional release statistical overview, 2017*. Ottawa, ON: Author.

Report to the Minister of Justice and Attorney General. (2014). *Public fatality inquiry*. Retrieved from https://open.alberta.ca/dataset/d8bedb35-398a-4e24-befa-bef1d49531de/resource/2736fe62-60e2-4179-b919-eb4febbb93ed/download/2014-fatality-report-snowshoe.pdf

Rhodes, W., Gaes, G., Luallen, J., Kling, R., Rich, T., & Shively, M. (2016). Following incarceration, most offenders never return to prison. *Crime & Delinquency*, 62(8), 1003–1025.

Royal Canadian Mounted Police. (2016). *Terrorism and violent extremism awareness guide*. Ottawa, ON: Author.

Ruddell, R. (2017). Pioneers in corrections. In J. Winterdyk (Ed.), *Pioneers in Canadian criminology* (pp. 267–286). Oakville, ON: Rock's Mills Press.

Schwartz, S. (2016). The professional life of a federal parole officer. In J. V. Roberts & M. G. Grossman (Eds.), *Criminal justice in Canada: A Reader* (5th ed.) (pp. 105–116). Toronto, ON: Nelson.

Stewart, L. A., Wardrop, K., Wilton, G., Thompson, J., Dzekzen, D., & Motiuk, L. (2017). Reliability and validity of the dynamic factors identification and analysis—revised. Ottawa, ON: Correctional Service of Canada.

Stys, Y., McEachran, R., & Axford, M. (2016). *Ways forward: Applying lessons learned in the management of radicalized offenders to Canadian federal corrections.* Ottawa, ON: Correctional Service of Canada.

Sykes, G. M. (1958/2007) *The society of captives: A study of a maximum security prison.* Princeton, NJ: Princeton University Press.

Townson, D. (1960, September 24). Kingston's sadistic warden Smith. *Maclean's.* Retrieved from http://archive.macleans.ca/article/1960/9/24/kingstons-sadistic-warden-smith

Union of Canadian Correctional Officers. (2015). *A critical review of the practice of double bunking within corrections.* Montreal, QC: Author.

Washington State Institute for Public Policy. (2018). *Benefit-cost results.* Retrieved from http://www.wsipp.wa.gov/BenefitCost?topicId=2

White, P. (2014, December 5). Confined: The death of Eddie Snowshoe. *The Globe and Mail.* Retrieved from https://www.theglobeandmail.com/news/national/confined-the-death-of-eddie-snowshoe/article21815548/

White, P. (2017, September 28). Prisons more dangerous for inmates as use of solitary confinement drops: Ombudsman. *The Globe and Mail.* Retrieved from https://www.theglobeandmail.com/news/national/inmates-released-from-solitary-confinement-must-be-monitored-ombudsman/article36417079/

White, P. (2019, April 10). Landmark ruling in Ontario caps solitary confinement at 15 days. *The Globe and Mail.* Retrieved from https://www.theglobeandmail.com/canada/article-solitary-confinement-for-more-than-15-days-constitutes-cruel-and/

Wilson, C. (2018). The history of the development of circles of support and accountability. In H. Elliott, K. Hocken, R. Lievesley, N. Blagden, B. Winder, & P. Banyard (Eds.). *Sexual crime and circles of support and accountability* (pp. 1–23). London: Palgrave Macmillan.

Wilson, R. J., & McWhinnie, A. J. (2013). Putting the "community" back in community risk management of persons who have sexually abused. *International Journal of Behavioural Consultation and Therapy, 8*(3-4), 72–79.

Wilson, R. J., & McWhinnie, A. J. (2016). Circles of support & accountability: The role of the community in effective sexual offender risk management. In A. Phenix & H. M. Hoberman (Eds.), *Sexual offending* (pp. 745–754). New York: Springer.

Wilson, R. J., McWhinnie, A., Picheca, J. E., Prinzo, M., & Cortoni, F. (2007). Circles of support and accountability: Engaging community volunteers in the management of high-risk sexual offenders. *The Howard Journal, 46*(1), 1–15.

Winterdyk, J. A., & Ruddell, R. (2010). Managing prison gangs: Results from a survey of US prison systems. *Journal of Criminal Justice, 38*(4), 730–736.

Wright, J. P., & Cullen, F. T. (2012). The future of biosocial criminology: Beyond scholars' professional ideology. *Journal of Contemporary Criminal Justice, 28*(3), 237–253.

Zinger, I. (2017). *Annual report: Office of the correctional investigator.* Ottawa, ON: Office of the Correctional Investigator.

Chapter 11

Aguiar, W., Halseth, R. (2015). *Aboriginal peoples and historical trauma.* Prince George, BC: National Collaborating Centre for Aboriginal Health.

Alam, S. (2015). *Youth court statistics in Canada, 2013/2014.* Ottawa, ON: Canadian Centre for Justice Statistics.

Allen, M. (2018). *Police-reported crime statistics in Canada, 2017.* Ottawa, ON: Canadian Centre for Justice Statistics.

Allen, M., & Superle, T. (2016). *Youth crime in Canada, 2014.* Ottawa, ON: Canadian Centre for Justice Statistics.

Bala, N. (2003). *Youth criminal justice law.* Concord, ON: Irwin Law.

Bala, N. (2013, September 5). When a child kills in Canada, there's no sense of justice. *The Globe and Mail.* Retrieved from https://www.theglobeandmail.com/opinion/when-a-child-kills-in-canada-theres-no-sense-of-justice/article14119129/

Bala, N., & Lilles, H. (1984). *The Young Offenders Act annotated.* Don Mills, ON: Richard De Boo Publishers.

Beattie, S., David, J. D., & Roy, J. (2018). *Homicide in Canada, 2017.* Ottawa, ON: Canadian Centre for Justice Statistics.

Bernard, T., & Kurlychek, M. (2010). *The cycle of juvenile justice* (2nd ed.). New York: Oxford University Press.

Bonta, J., & Andrews, D. A. (2017). *The psychology of criminal conduct* (6th ed.). New York: Routledge.

Boppre, B., Salisbury, E. J., & Parker, J. (2018). *Pathways to crime: Criminal Behavior, Criminological Theory, Women, Crime, and Justice.* Retrieved from http://criminology.oxfordre.com/abstract/10.1093/acrefore/9780190264079.001.0001/acrefore-9780190264079-e-99

Branson, C. E., Baetz, C. L., Horwitz, S. M., & Hoagwood, K. E. (2017). Trauma-informed juvenile justice systems: A systematic review of definitions and core components. *Psychological Trauma: Theory, Research, Practice, and Policy, 9*(6), 635–646.

Brennan, T. (2015). *A women's typology of pathways to serious crime with custody and treatment implications.* Retrieved from http://go.volarisgroup.com/rs/volarisgroup/images/Women-Typology-Descriptions-Gender-Responsive-4-15.pdf

Canadian Broadcasting Corporation. (2015, January 13). Brett Wiese's friends share emotional impact statements at murder trial. *CBC News.* Retrieved from http://www.cbc.ca/news/canada/calgary/brett-wiese-s-friends-share-emotional-impact-statements-at-murder-trial-1.2899195

Canadian Broadcasting Corporation. (2018, July 12). Police identify 16-year-old suspect wanted for brazen Queen and Peter double homicide. *CBC News.* Retrieved from https://www.cbc.ca/news/canada/toronto/keyshawn-jones-wanted-1.4744955

Carrington, P. J., Brennan, S., Matarazzo, A., & Radulescu, M. (2013). *Co-offending in Canada, 2011.* Ottawa, ON: Canadian Centre for Justice Statistics.

Carrington, P. J., & Schulenberg, J. L. (2004). Introduction: The Youth Criminal Justice Act—A new era in Canadian juvenile justice? *Canadian Journal of Criminology and Criminal Justice, 46*(3), 219–224.

Cauffman, E., Fine, A., Mahler, A., & Simmons, C. (2018). How developmental science influences juvenile justice reform. *UC Irvine Law Review, 8*(1), 21–40.

Cesaroni, C., Grol, C., & Fredericks, K. (2019). Overrepresentation of Indigenous youth in Canada's criminal justice system: Perspectives of Indigenous young people. *Australian & New Zealand Journal of Criminology, 52*(1), 111–128.

Chalas, D. M., & Grekul, J. (2017). I've had enough: Exploring gang life from the perspective of (Ex) members in Alberta. *The Prison Journal, 97*(3), 364–386.

Cherry, P. (2018, October 17). Man who killed prison guards for Hells Angels gets closer to parole. *Montreal Gazette.* Retrieved from https://montrealgazette.com/news/local-news/

man-who-killed-prison-guards-for-hells-angels-goes-before-parole-board

Child Rights International Network. (2018). Minimum ages of criminal responsibility around the world. Retrieved from https://archive.crin.org/en/home/what-we-do/policy/minimum-ages.html

Cohen, A. O., & Casey, B. J. (2014). Rewiring juvenile justice: The intersection of developmental neuroscience and legal policy. *Trends in Cognitive Sciences*, 18(2), 63–65.

Cohen, M. A., & Piquero, A. R. (2009). New evidence on the monetary value of saving a high risk youth. *Journal of Quantitative Criminology*, 25(1), 25–49.

Comack, E. (2012). *Racialized policing: Aboriginal people's encounters with the police*. Winnipeg, MB: Fernwood Publishing.

Community Legal Education Ontario. (2015). Steps in a youth case. Retrieved from http://youth.cleo.on.ca/en/steps-youth-case/if-charged/

Corrado, R. R., Kuehn, S., & Margaritescu, I. (2014). Policy issues regarding the overrepresentation of incarcerated Aboriginal young offenders in a Canadian context. *Youth Justice*, 14(1), 40–62.

David, J., (2017). *Homicide in Canada, 2016*. Ottawa, ON: Canadian Centre for Justice Statistics.

Davie, E. (2019, July 16). Atlantic Canada has an enviable problem: its youth jails are emptying out. *CBC News*. Retrieved from https://www.cbc.ca/news/canada/nova-scotia/youth-jails-vacant-atlantic-canada-1.5207035

DeHart, D., Lynch, S., Belknap, J., Dass-Brailsford, P., & Green, B. (2014). Life history models of female offending: The roles of serious mental illness and trauma in women's pathways to jail. *Psychology of Women Quarterly*, 38(1), 138–151.

DeHart, D. (2018). Women's pathways to crime: A heuristic typology of offenders. *Criminal Justice and Behavior*, 45(10), 1461–1482.

Department of Justice. (2004). *The evolution of juvenile justice in Canada*. Ottawa, ON: Author.

Department of Justice. (2013). *The Youth Criminal Justice Act: Summary and background*. Ottawa, ON: Author.

Department of Justice. (2015). *Extrajudicial measures*. Ottawa, ON: Author.

Dufour, I., Villeneuve, M., & Lafortune, D. (2018). Does the "last chance" sentence work? Ten years of failures and successes under a juvenile intermediate sanction in Canada. *Punishment & Society*, 20(5), 539–561.

Dunbar, L. (2017). *Youth gangs in Canada: A review of current topics and issues*. Ottawa, ON: Public Safety Canada.

Ference and Company Consulting. (2018). *Mayor's task force on gang violence prevention. Findings and action steps*. Vancouver, BC: Author.

Gomez del Prado, G. (2011). Outlaw motorcycle gangs' attempted intimidation of Quebec's police forces. *Police Practice and Research*, 12(1), 66–80.

Grant, M. (2019a, June 27). "It's taking a toll and we're tired," murder victim's family says after Calgary killer sentenced again. *CBC News*. Retrieved from https://www.cbc.ca/news/canada/calgary/mitchell-harkes-brett-wiese-murder-sentence-1.5192423

Grant, M. (2019b, July 25). Killer who stabbed student over hurt feelings at party appeals his sentence again. *CBC News*. Retrieved from https://www.cbc.ca/news/canada/calgary/mitchell-harkes-brett-wiese-murder-appeal-1.5224818

Houston, S. E. (1972). Victorian origins of juvenile delinquency: A Canadian experience. *History of Education Quarterly*, 12(3), 254–280.

Jones, N. J., Brown, S. L., Wanamaker, K. A., & Greiner, L. E. (2014). A quantitative exploration of gendered pathways to crime in a sample of male and female juvenile offenders. *Feminist Criminology*, 9(2), 113–136.

Karpoff, J. C., & Vaughan, J. S. (1962). Legal aid for juveniles in Canada. Master's thesis, School of Social Work, University of British Columbia.

Kuehn, S., & Corrado, R. R. (2011). Youth probation officers' interpretation and implementation of the Youth Criminal Justice Act: A case study of youth justice in Canada. *International Journal of Comparative and Applied Criminal Justice*, 35(3), 221–241.

Leamon, S. E. (2016). Criminal offenders under 12 should not walk free in Canada. *Huffington Post*. Leon, J. S. (1977). The development of Canadian juvenile justice: A background for reform. *Osgood Hall Law Journal*, 15(1), 71–106.

Leone, P. E., Lockwood, S., & Gagnon, J. C. (2017). Creating and sustaining safe environments in juvenile corrections. In P. Sturmey (Ed.), *The Wiley handbook of violence and aggression*. Retrieved from https://onlinelibrary.wiley.com/doi/abs/10.1002/9781119057574.whbva115

Loughran, T. A., & Reid, J. (2018). *A longitudinal investigation of trauma exposure, retraumatization, and post-traumatic stress of justice-involved adolescents*. Washington, DC: Office of Justice Programs.

Malakieh, J. (2019). *Adult and youth correctional statistics in Canada, 2017/2018*. Ottawa, ON: Canadian Centre for Justice Statistics.

Marshall, B. D. L., DeBeck, K., Simo, A., Kerr, T., & Wood, E. (2015). Gang involvement among street-involved youth in a Canadian setting: A gender-based analysis. *Public Health*, 129(1), 74–77.

Martin, K. (2015, May 19). Woman, 19, gets life for group murder. *Toronto Sun*. Retrieved from https://torontosun.com/2015/05/19/woman-19-gets-life-for-group-revenge-murder/wcm/7c0264f2-1885-4122-9690-61d7f145c0e9

Martin, K. (2018, August 21). Plan to kill ex-wife and her boyfriend failed because man botched firing of shotgun: court. *Calgary Sun*. Retrieved from https://calgarysun.com/news/crime/plan-to-kill-ex-wife-and-her-boyfriend-failed-because-man-botched-firing-of-shotgun-court

Mays, G. L., & Ruddell, R. (2019). *Making sense of criminal justice: Policies and practices* (3rd ed.). New York: Oxford University Press.

Meissner, D. (2019, March 4). Federal government targets B.C. guns and gang violence with $5.3 M fund. *The Globe and Mail*. Retrieved from https://www.theglobeandmail.com/canada/article-federal-government-targets-bc-guns-and-gang-violence-with-53-m-2/

Miladinovic, Z. (2016). *Youth court statistics in Canada, 2014/2015*. Ottawa, ON: Canadian Centre for Justice Statistics.

Miladinovic, Z. (2019). *Adult and youth court statistics in Canada, 2016/2017*. Ottawa, ON: Canadian Centre for Justice Statistics.

Office of Juvenile Justice and Delinquency Prevention. (2014). *Wraparound process*. Retrieved from https://www.ojjdp.gov/mpg/litreviews/Wraparound_Process.pdf

Office of the Correctional Investigator. (2014). *A case study of diversity in corrections: The Black inmate experience in federal penitentiaries*. Ottawa, ON: Author.

Oudshoorn, J. (2015). *Trauma-informed youth justice in Canada*. Toronto, ON: Canadian Scholars Press.

Perreault, S. (2014). *Admissions to youth correctional services in Canada, 2011/2012*. Ottawa, ON: Canadian Centre for Justice Statistics.

Pfeifer, J., & Leyton-Brown, K. (2007). *Death by rope: Volume One, 1867 to 1923*. Regina, SK: Centax Books.

Public Safety Canada. (2007). *Youth gangs in Canada: What do we know?* Ottawa, ON: Author.

Public Safety Canada. (2018a). Crime prevention funding programs: Youth gang prevention fund. Retrieved from https://www.publicsafety.gc.ca/cnt/cntrng-crm/crm-prvntn/fndng-prgrms/index-en.aspx

Public Safety Canada. (2018b). *Criminal gun and gang violence in Canada*. Ottawa, ON: Author.

Ruddell, R., & Gileno, J. (2013). Lifers admitted as juveniles in the Canadian prison population. *Youth Justice, 13*(3), 234–248.

Ryerson, E., & Hodgins, J. G. (Eds.). (1859). The reformatory prisons and kindred institutions for Upper and Lower Canada. *Journal of Education for Upper Canada, 12*(1), 1–2.

Savage, L. (2019). *Female offenders in Canada, 2017*. Ottawa, ON: Canadian Centre for Justice Statistics.

Schneider, S. (2018). *Canadian organized crime*. Toronto, ON: Canadian Scholar's Press.

Scott, E. S., Duell, N., & Steinberg, L. (2018). Brain development, social context and justice policy. *Washington University Journal of Law and Policy, 57*, 13–74.

Smandych, R. C., & Corrado, R. R. (2018). "Too bad, so sad": Observations on key outstanding policy challenges of twenty years of youth justice reform in Canada, 1995–2015. *Manitoba Law Review, 41*(3), 191–240.

Sprott, J. B., & Manson, A. (2017). YCJA bail conditions: "Treating" girls and boys differently. *Canadian Criminal Law Review, 22*(1), 77–94.

Statistics Canada. (2014). *Juveniles adjudged delinquent, Canada, 1927 to 1973*. Retrieved from http://www.statcan.gc.ca/pub/11-516-x/sectionz/4147446-eng.htm#4

Statistics Canada. (2019a). *Average counts of young persons in provincial and territorial correctional services* [Table 35-10-0003-01]. Retrieved from https://www150.statcan.gc.ca/t1/tbl1/en/cv.action?pid=3510000301

Statistics Canada. (2019b). *Crime severity index and weighted clearance rates, Canada, provinces, territories and census metropolitan areas* [Table 35-10-0026-01]. Retrieved from https://www150.statcan.gc.ca/t1/tbl1/en/tv.action?pid=3510002601

Statistics Canada. (2019c). *Youth courts, cases by median elapsed time in days* [Table 35-10-0040-01]. Retrieved from https://www150.statcan.gc.ca/t1/tbl1/en/tv.action?pid=3510004001

Statistics Canada. (2019d). *Youth courts, number of cases and charges by type of decision* [Table 35-10-0038-01]. Retrieved from https://www150.statcan.gc.ca/t1/tbl1/en/tv.action?pid=3510003801

Steele, A. (2015, February 27). Deal with youth trauma to deal with gang problems, says social worker. *CBC News*. Retrieved from http://www.cbc.ca/news/canada/ottawa/deal-with-youth-trauma-to-deal-with-gang-problems-says-social-worker-1.2976479

Truth and Reconciliation Commission of Canada. (2015). *Honouring the truth, reconciling for the future*. Winnipeg, MB: Author.

Umamaheswar, J. (2012). Bringing hope and change: A study of youth probation officers in Toronto. *International Journal of Offender Therapy and Comparative Criminology, 57*(9), 1158–1182.

Washington State Institute for Public Policy. (2018a). *Benefit-cost results*. Retrieved from http://www.wsipp.wa.gov/BenefitCost

Washington State Institute for Public Policy. (2018b). *Dialectical behavior therapy (DBT) for youth in the juvenile justice system*. Retrieved from http://www.wsipp.wa.gov/BenefitCost/Program/264

Woloschuk, T. (2006, February). A promise of redemption: The Soeurs du Bon Pasteur and delinquent girls in Winnipeg, 1911–1948. *Manitoba History, 51*. Retrieved from http://www.mhs.mb.ca/docs/mb_history/51/marymound.shtml

Zahn, M., Hawkins, S. R., Chiancone, J., & Whitworth, A. (2008). *The girls study group: Charting the way to delinquency prevention for girls*. Washington, DC: Office of Juvenile Justice and Delinquency Prevention.

Chapter 12

Allen, M. (2014). *Victim services in Canada, 2011/2012*. Ottawa, ON: Canadian Centre for Justice Statistics.

Allen, M., & Perreault, S. (2015). *Police-reported crime in Canada's provincial north and territories, 2013*. Ottawa, ON: Canadian Centre for Justice Statistics.

Anderson, B., & Coletto, D. (2017). What keeps us awake: Top national issues. Abacus Data. Retrieved from http://abacusdata.ca/wp-content/uploads/2016/11/Abacus-Release-National-4-Nov-2017.pdf

Angus Reid Institute. (2018). *Confidence in the justice system: Visible minorities have less faith in courts than other Canadians*. Vancouver, BC: Author.

Armstrong, P. (2019, July 2). Despite a strong economy, cost of living still top of mind for Canadians. *CBC News*. Retrieved from https://www.cbc.ca/news/business/anxiety-cost-of-living-canada-economic-data-1.5192401

Barker, A. J. (2015). "A direct act of resurgence, a direct act of sovereignty": Reflections on Idle No More, Indigenous activism, and Canadian settler colonialism. *Globalizations, 12*(1), 43–65.

Barrett, J. (2018, March 29). Red Deer weathers "perfect storm" of recession, crime and addiction to find its way forward. *CBC News*. Retrieved from https://www.cbc.ca/news/canada/calgary/red-deer-perfect-storm-recession-crime-addiction-1.4598301

Baxter, M. (2018, February 2). Small towns can't afford independent policing, but don't know where to turn. *TVO*. Retrieved from https://tvo.org/article/current-affairs/small-towns-cant-afford-independent-policing-but-dont-know-where-to-turn

Beare, M. E., Des Rosiers, N., & Deshman, A. C. (Eds.). (2014). *Putting the State on Trial: The Policing of Protest during the G20 Summit*. Vancouver: UBC Press.

Beattie, S., David, J. D., & Roy, J. (2018). *Homicide in Canada, 2017*. Ottawa, ON: Canadian Centre for Justice Statistics.

Beattie, S., & Hutchins, H. (2015). *Shelters for abused women in Canada, 2014*. Ottawa, ON: Canadian Centre for Justice Statistics.

Beirne, P., & South, N. (2012). Greening criminology. In S. D. Fassbinder, A. J. Nocella, & R. Kahn (Eds.), *Greening the academy: Ecopedagogy through the liberal arts* (pp. 23–32). Rotterdam, Netherlands: Sense Publishing.

Bell, K. (2015, March 17). Elon Musk: In the future, human-driven cars may be illegal. *Mashable*. Retrieved from https://mashable.com/2015/03/17/elon-musk-nvidia/

Bernard, T., & Kurlychek, M. (2010). *The cycle of juvenile justice* (2nd ed.). New York: Oxford University Press.

Black, J. (2018). Autonomous vehicles: Terrorist threat or security opportunity? RAND Corporation. Retrieved from https://www.rand.org/blog/2018/01/autonomous-vehicles-terrorist-threat-or-security-opportunity.html

Boccio, R., Chan, J., & Sicora, R. (2017). A world without prisons: Bringing restorative justice to The Leap. *The Leap*. Retrieved from https://theleap.org/portfolio-items/a-world-without-prisons-bringing-restorative-justice-to-the-leap/

Brennan, S., & Mazowita, B. (2019). *Prior contact with the criminal justice system among people who fatally overdosed on illicit drugs in Surrey and in British Columbia, 2011 to 2016*. Ottawa, ON: Canadian Centre for Justice Statistics.

British Columbia Coroners Service. (2019). *Illicit drug toxicity deaths in BC, January 1, 2009 – May 31, 2019*. Retrieved from https://www2.gov.bc.ca/assets/gov/birth-adoption-death-marriage-and-divorce/deaths/coroners-service/statistical/illicit-drug.pdf

Brock University. (2017). *Prison abolition symposium*. Retrieved from https://brocku.ca/prison-abolition/

Bronson, J., & Carson, E. A. (2019). *Prisoners in 2017*. Washington, DC: Bureau of Justice Statistics.

Burczycka, M. (2018). *Police-reported intimate partner violence in Canada, 2017*. Ottawa, ON: Canadian Centre for Justice Statistics.

California Department of Motor Vehicles. (2019, March 19). *Report of traffic collision involving an autonomous vehicle*. Retrieved from https://www.dmv.ca.gov/portal/dmv/detail/vr/autonomous/autonomousveh_ol316+

Canadian Broadcasting Corporation. (2016). Stingray surveillance device questions prompt federal privacy complaint. *CBC News*. Retrieved from http://www.cbc.ca/news/technology/stingray-open-media-1.3533417

Canadian Judicial Council. (2018). *Canadian Judicial Council annual report, 2017/2018*. Ottawa, ON: Author.

Canadian Press. (2017, March 9). A look at previous Canadian Judicial Council conduct cases. *CTV News*. Retrieved from https://www.ctvnews.ca/canada/a-look-at-previous-canadian-judicial-council-conduct-cases-1.3318423

Charron, M., Nemr, R., & Vaillancourt, R. (2009). *Aging of justice personnel*. Ottawa, ON: Canadian Centre for Justice Statistics.

Chen, K. (2014, May 6). 7 mass surveillance tools your local police might be using. *Reveal* (The Center for Investigative Reporting). Retrieved from https://www.revealnews.org/article/7-mass-surveillance-tools-your-local-police-might-be-using/

Chettiar, I. M., & Ofer, U. (2018, January 16). The "tough on crime" wave is finally cresting. Brennan Center for Justice. Retrieved from https://www.brennancenter.org/blog/tough-crime-wave-finally-cresting

City News. (2018 July 4). Influx of smuggled guns make it easy to get one in Toronto: crime specialist. Retrieved from https://toronto.citynews.ca/2018/07/04/guns-toronto-border/

Cole, A. (2019, March 21). Volvo's in-car cameras will spot, slow or stop drunk or distracted drivers. *KPIC*. Retrieved from https://kpic.com/news/auto-matters/volvos-in-car-cameras-will-spot-slow-or-stop-drunk-or-distracted-drivers

Connolly, A. (2019, March 22). Jody Wilson-Raybould to offer more details on her testimony in SNC-Lavalin scandal. *Global News*. Retrieved from https://globalnews.ca/news/5084553/jody-wilson-raybould-more-testimony-snc-lavalin-scandal/

Conor, P. (2018). *Police resources in Canada, 2017*. Ottawa, ON: Canadian Centre for Justice Statistics.

Conroy, S. (2018). *Police-reported family violence against children and youth in Canada, 2017*. Ottawa, ON: Canadian Centre for Justice Statistics.

Correctional Service of Canada. (2015). *Abolition of corporal punishment, 1972*. Retrieved from http://www.csc-scc.gc.ca/text/pblct/rht-drt/05-eng.shtml

Cotter, A. (2015). *Spotlight on Canadians: Results from the General Social Survey: Public confidence in Canadian institutions*. Ottawa, ON: Statistics Canada.

The Crime Report. (2018, September 7) *Prediction: Every police patrol car will have a drone*. Retrieved from https://thecrimereport.org/2018/09/07/prediction-every-police-patrol-car-will-have-a-drone/

Csanady, A. (2015, March 6). NP explainer: Tough-on-crime and the Tories, a brief history by the numbers. *National Post*. Retrieved from http://news.nationalpost.com/2015/03/06/np-explainer-tough-on-crime-and-the-tories-a-brief-history-by-the-numbers-video/

CTV News Montreal. (2018, April 23). Firearm-free police? Green Party calls for patrollers to give up guns. Retrieved from https://montreal.ctvnews.ca/firearm-free-police-green-party-calls-for-patrollers-to-give-up-guns-1.3898112

Cutean, A. (2018). *Autonomous vehicles and the future of work in Canada*. Ottawa, ON: Information and Communications Technology Council.

Denver, M., Best, J., & Haas, K. C. (2008). Methods of execution as institutional fads. *Punishment & Society, 10*(3), 227–252.

Department of Justice. (2018). *Victims' roles and rights in the criminal justice system*. Retrieved from http://www.justice.gc.ca/eng/cj-jp/victims-victimes/rights-droits/

Doob, A.N., & Webster, C.M. (2015). The Harper revolution in criminal justice policy … and what comes next. *Policy Options*. Retrieved from http://policyoptions.irpp.org/magazines/is-it-the-best-of-times-or-the-worst/doob-webster/

Duxbury, L., Bennell, C., Halinski, M., & Murphy, S. (2017). Change or be changed: Diagnosing the readiness to change in the Canadian police sector. *Police Journal: Theory, Practice and Principles, 91*(4), 316–338.

The Economist. (2018). Why driverless cars will mostly be shared, not owned. Retrieved from https://www.economist.com/the-economist-explains/2018/03/05/why-driverless-cars-will-mostly-be-shared-not-owned

Elliot, J. K. (2018, August 1). Ready or not: U.S. unleashing 3D-printed 'ghost guns' for the entire internet. *Global News*. Retrieved from https://globalnews.ca/news/4356869/3d-printed-gun-liberator-plans-online/

Environics Research Group (2015). *Canadian attitudes toward animal issues – June 2015*. Toronto, ON: Author.

Fotheringham, S. (2016). *Social impacts of an economic downturn: Considerations for the city of Calgary*. Calgary, AB: University of Calgary.

Freeze, C. (2017, September 17). RCMP shelved hundreds of organized-crime cases after terror attacks. *The Globe and Mail*. Retrieved from https://www.theglobeandmail.

com/news/national/mounties-put-hundreds-of-files-on-hold-in-shift-toward-anti-terrorism/article36285597/

Gascon, G., & Foglesong, T. (2010). *Making policing more affordable: Managing costs and measuring value in policing.* Washington, DC: U.S. Department of Justice.

Gawdin, S. (2018, July 27). Chilliwack residents complain about drones spying on backyards. *The Chilliwack Progress.* Retrieved from https://www.theprogress.com/news/chilliwack-residents-complain-about-drones-spying-on-backyards/

Global News. (2017, March 16). Amanda Todd's accused cyberbully sentenced to 11 years in Dutch prison. Retrieved from https://globalnews.ca/news/3313729/amanda-todd-cyberbullying-aydin-coban-sentenced/

Goodman, M. (2015). *Future crimes.* Toronto, ON: Doubleday.

Government of Canada. (2018). *Departmental plan 2018 to 2019 report.* Ottawa, ON: Environment Change and Climate Change Canada.

Gray, J., & Stone, L. (2019, March 20). Ford did not break rules in hiring Taverner, integrity commissioner rules, but calls process "flawed." *The Globe and Mail.* Retrieved from https://www.theglobeandmail.com/canada/article-ford-did-not-break-rules-in-hiring-taverner-integrity-commissioner/

Greenland, J., & Cotter, A. (2018). *Unfounded criminal incidents in Canada, 2017.* Ottawa, ON: Canadian Centre for Justice Statistics.

Griffiths, C. T., Pollard, N., & Stamatakis, T. (2015). Assessing the effectiveness and efficiency of a police service: the analytics of operational reviews. *Police Practice and Research: An International Journal, 16*(2), 175–187.

Hafner, J. (2018, August 1). What is a 3D printed gun, and how is it legal? Your questions, answered. *USA Today.* Retrieved from https://www.usatoday.com/story/tech/nation-now/2018/08/01/3-d-guns-how-3-d-printed-gun-parts-made-and-how-theyre-legal/879349002/

Hamilton Police Service. (2018). *Business plan.* Retrieved from https://hamiltonpolice.on.ca/about/business-plan

Harris, K. (2018). Liberals propose major criminal justice changes to unclog Canada's courts. *CBC News.* Retrieved from https://www.cbc.ca/news/politics/liberal-crime-justice-reform-1.4598480

Holt, T. (2018, October 15). *Why hacker shack.* Dr. Gordon Wicijowski Law Foundation of Saskatchewan Lecture, University of Regina.

Institute of Health Economics. (2014). *Criminal justice and forensic psychiatry costs in Alberta.* Edmonton, AB: Author.

Ipsos Reid. (2012). Three in five (62%) Canadians say the federal government is doing too little to protect species at risk. Retrieved from https://www.ipsos.com/en-ca/three-five-62-canadians-say-federal-government-doing-too-little-protect-species-risk

Judd, A. (2018, January 12). Someone used a drone to drop $26,500 of drugs, tobacco over a B.C. prison wall. *Global News.* Retrieved from https://globalnews.ca/news/3961889/drone-drugs-b-c-prison-wall/

Lazatin, E. (2018, October 22). Appeal case to be begin in Netherlands for Amanda Todd's alleged tormentor. *Global News.* Retrieved from https://globalnews.ca/news/4581300/amanda-todd-dutch-accused-criminal-appeal/

Ling, J. (2015, December 14). Someone used a drone to deliver a handgun into a notorious Canadian prison. *Vice News.* Retrieved from https://www.vice.com/en_us/article/gy9wnj/someone-used-a-drone-to-deliver-a-handgun-into-a-notorious-canadian-prison

Logan, N. (2014, December 29). Canadians say Michael Brown, Eric Garner protests top U.S. news story: poll. *Global News.* Retrieved from https://globalnews.ca/news/1747176/canadians-say-michael-brown-eric-garner-protests-top-u-s-story-poll/

Lundrigan, K. (2018). *R v Jordan*: A ticking time bomb. *Manitoba Law Journal, 41*(4), 113–147.

McCune, J. L., Carlsson, A. M., Colla, S., Davy, C., Favaro, B., Ford, A. T., … Martins, E. G. (2017). Assessing public commitment to endangered species protection: A Canadian case study. *FACETS, 2*, 178–194.

McKnight, P. (2016). The funhouse mirror: Media misrepresentations of crime and justice. In J. V. Roberts & M. G. Grossman (Eds.), *Criminal justice in Canada: A reader* (5th ed.) (pp. 28–38). Toronto, ON: Nelson.

Macpherson, A. (2019, March 11). Carbon tax, rural crime top of mind for SARM residents. *StarPhoenix* (Saskatoon). Retrieved from https://thestarphoenix.com/news/local-news/carbon-tax-rural-crime-top-of-mind-for-sarm-delegates

Malakieh, J. (2019). *Adult and youth correctional statistics in Canada, 2017/2018.* Ottawa, ON: Canadian Centre for Justice Statistics.

Mark, A. (2018). Big data policing: Exploring some strengths and concerns. *Canadian Society of Evidence-Based Policing.* Retrieved from http://www.can-sebp.net/single-post/2018/03/17/Big-Data-Policing-%E2%80%93-exploring-some-strengths-and-concerns

Meares. T. (2017, August 1). Policing: A public good gone bad. *Boston Review.* Retrieved from https://bostonreview.net/law-justice/tracey-l-meares-policing-public-good-gone-bad

Michael, D. (2018). *Understanding legal aid Ontario.* Retrieved from http://mycriminaldefence.ca/legal-aid.html

Mikelionis, L. (2018, January 3). Drug cartels using drones to smuggle drugs at border. *Fox News.* Retrieved from https://www.foxnews.com/us/drug-cartels-using-drones-to-smuggle-drugs-at-border

Miladinovic, Z. (2019). *Adult and youth court statistics in Canada, 2016/2017.* Ottawa, ON: Canadian Centre for Justice Statistics.

National Highway Traffic Safety Administration. (2018). *Critical reasons for crashes investigated in the national motor vehicle crash causation survey.* Washington, DC: Author.

Office of the Federal Ombudsman for Victims of Crime. (2018). *Annual report, 2016-2017.* Ottawa, ON: Author.

O'Sullivan, D. (2018, October 4). Facebook just had its worst hack ever – and it could get worse. *CNN Business.* Retrieved from https://www.cnn.com/2018/10/04/tech/facebook-hack-explainer/index.html

Owusu-Bempah, A., & Wortley, S. (2014). Race, crime, and criminal justice in Canada. In S. M. Bucerius & M. Tonry (Eds.), *The Oxford handbook of ethnicity, crime, and immigration* (pp. 281–320). Toronto, ON: Oxford University Press.

Parkes, D. (2018, September 25). Mandatory minimum sentences for murder should be abolished. *The Globe and Mail.* Retrieved from https://www.theglobeandmail.com/opinion/article-mandatory-minimum-sentences-for-murder-should-be-abolished/

Perreault, S. (2013). *Impaired driving in Canada, 2011*. Ottawa, ON: Canadian Centre for Justice Statistics.

Perreault, S. (2015). *Criminal victimization in Canada, 2014*. Ottawa, ON: Statistics Canada, Minister of Industry. Retrieved from http://www.statcan.gc.ca/pub/85-002-x/2015001/article/14241-eng.pdf

Perreault, S. (2019). *Police-reported crime in rural and urban areas in the Canadian provinces, 2017*. Ottawa, ON: Canadian Centre for Justice Statistics.

Perreault, S., & Simpson, L. (2016). *Criminal victimization in the territories, 2014*. Ottawa, ON: Canadian Centre for Justice Statistics.

Perrin, B., Audas, R., & Peloquin-Ladany, S. (2016). *Canada's justice deficit: The case for a justice system report card*. Ottawa, ON: Macdonald-Laurier Institute.

Pfaff, J. (2017). *Locked in: the true causes of mass incarceration and how to achieve real reform*. New York: Basic Books.

Police Executive Research Forum. (2018). *The changing nature of crime and criminal investigations*. Washington, DC: Author.

Province of Ontario. (2019). *Public sector salary disclosure*. Retrieved from https://www.ontario.ca/page/public-sector-salary-disclosure

Public Safety Canada. (2018). *The Canadian disaster database*. Retrieved from: https://www.publicsafety.gc.ca/cnt/rsrcs/cndn-dsstr-dtbs/index-en.aspx

RoadSafetyBC. (2019). *Administrative alcohol and drug related driving prohibitions (May 31, 2019)*. Retrieved from https://www2.gov.bc.ca/assets/gov/driving-and-transportation/driving/publications/drinking-driving-report-May-2019.pdf

Roberts, J. V., Stalans, L. J., Indermaur, D., & Hough, M. (2003). *Penal populism and public opinion: Lessons from five countries*. New York: Oxford University Press.

Robertson, N. (2012). Policing: Fundamental principles in a Canadian context. *Canadian Public Administration, 55*(3), 343–363.

Rotenberg, C. (2019). *Police-reported violent crimes against young women and girls in Canada's provincial north and territories*. Ottawa, ON: Canadian Centre for Justice Statistics.

Ruddell, R. (2017). *Policing rural Canada*. Whitby, ON: deSitter Publications.

Savage, L. (2018). *Police-reported family violence against seniors in Canada, 2017*. Ottawa, ON: Canadian Centre for Justice Statistics.

Scribner, M. (2018, February 1). Uber wants to make it illegal to operate your own self-driving car in cities. *Competitive Enterprise Institute*. Retrieved from https://cei.org/blog/uber-wants-make-it-illegal-operate-your-own-self-driving-car-cities

Smith, M. (2018, September 26). Calgary police to ban recreational cannabis use for officers–even off-duty. *Toronto Star*. Retrieved from https://www.thestar.com/news/cannabis/2018/09/26/calgary-police-to-ban-recreational-cannabis-use-for-officers-even-off-duty.html

Southey, T. (2015, November 13). Justice Robin Camp: Canada's toughest sensitivity training student. *The Globe and Mail*. Retrieved from http://www.theglobeandmail.com/globe-debate/justice-robin-camp-the-toughest-sensitivity-training-student-possible/article27250702/

Spratt, M. (2019, January 28). Don't expect new justice minister to deliver on progressive criminal justice reform. *Canadian Lawyer*. Retrieved from https://www.canadianlawyermag.com/author/michael-spratt/dont-expect-new-justice-minister-to-deliver-on-progressive-criminal-justice-reform-16772/

Statistics Canada. (2017a). *Aboriginal peoples in Canada: Key results from the 2016 census*. Ottawa, ON: Author.

Statistics Canada. (2017b). *Immigration and ethnocultural diversity: Key results from the 2016 census*. Ottawa, ON: Author.

Statistics Canada. (2018a). *Impact of cybercrime on Canadian businesses, 2017*. Ottawa, ON: Author.

Statistics Canada. (2018b). *Operating expenditures for adult correctional services* [Table 35-10-0013-01]. Retrieved from https://www150.statcan.gc.ca/t1/tbl1/en/tv.action?pid=3510001301

Statistics Canada. (2019). *Data tables (National occupational classification). 2016 Census*. Retrieved from https://www12.statcan.gc.ca/census-recensement/index-eng.cfm

Supreme Court of Canada. (2018). *Applications for leave submitted*. Retrieved from https://www.scc-csc.ca/case-dossier/stat/cat2-eng.aspx#cat2a

Tencer, D. (2015, February 27). Bought electronics in Canada from '99 to '02? You have $20 (or more) coming. *Huffington Post Canada*. Retrieved from http://www.huffingtonpost.ca/2015/02/26/dram-price-fixing-reimbursement_n_6764070.html

Toews, V. (2013, January 16). *Speech for the Honourable Vic Toews, Minister of Public Safety, at the Summit on the Economics of Policing*. Retrieved from https://www.publicsafety.gc.ca/cnt/nws/spchs/2013/20130116-en.aspx

Tonry, M. H. (2013). "Nothing" works: Sentencing "reform" in Canada and the United States. *Canadian Journal of Criminology and Criminal Justice, 55*(4), 465–480.

Toronto Star Editorial Board. (2018, August 13). Solutions to gun crime don't boil down to Ford's "good guys and bad guys" rhetoric. *Toronto Star*. Retrieved from https://www.thestar.com/opinion/editorials/2018/08/13/solutions-to-gun-crime-dont-boil-down-to-fords-good-guys-and-bad-guys-rhetoric.html

Transport Canada. (2019). *Canadian motor vehicle traffic collision statistics, 2017*. Ottawa, ON: Author.

Tunney, C. (2018, September 24). RCMP's ability to police digital realm "rapidly declining," commissioner warned. *CBC News*. Retrieved from https://www.cbc.ca/news/politics/lucki-briefing-binde-cybercrime-1.4831340

Tyler, T. R. (2006). *Why people obey the law*. Princeton, NJ: Princeton University Press.

van den Born, A. (2013). Policing opportunities and threats in Europe. *Journal of Organizational Change, 26*(5), 811–829.

Vitale, A. S. (2017). *The end of policing*. New York: Verso Books.

Washington State Institute for Public Policy. (2018). *Benefit-cost results, adult criminal justice*. Olympia, WA: Author.

Webster, C. M., & Doob, A. N. (2015). US punitiveness "Canadian style"? Cultural values and Canadian punishment policy. *Punishment & Society, 17*(3), 299–321.

Woods, A. (2018). More than 90 deaths now linked to heat wave in Quebec. *Toronto Star*. Retrieved from https://www.thestar.com/

news/canada/2018/07/18/89-deaths-now-linked-to-heat-wave-in-quebec.html

Woods, M. (2012). Occupy Wall Street protests spreading to Canada. *Toronto Star*. Retrieved from https://www.thestar.com/news/gta/2011/10/02/occupy_wall_street_protests_spreading_to_canada.html

World Justice Project. (2019). *Rule of law index, 2018-2019*. New York: Author.

Wright, A. (2018, October 5). Police forces across the country should give up their weapons. The *Globe and Mail*. Retrieved from https://www.theglobeandmail.com/opinion/article-police-forces-across-the-country-should-give-up-their-weapons/

Zeng, Z. (2019). *Jail inmates in 2017*. Washington, DC: Bureau of Justice Statistics.

Index

Note: Page numbers in **bold** indicate definitions, and those in *italics* indicate figures or captions.